...ning hours:

...5 – 21.00

TH!
NE
B/
F

Un...

6

WITHDRAWN

7

To Simon, Grant, and Hannah

Understanding Emotions

Keith Oatley
Center for Applied Cognitive Science
Ontario Institute for Studies in Education
and Department of Psychology, University of Toronto

and

Jennifer M. Jenkins
Institute for Child Study
and Department of Psychology, University of Toronto

First published 1996
Reprinted 1996

Blackwell Publishers Inc.
238 Main Street
Cambridge, Massachusetts 02142, USA

Blackwell Publishers Ltd
108 Cowley Road
Oxford OX4 1JF, UK

Library of Congress Cataloging in Publication Data
Oatley, Keith.
Understanding emotions / Keith Oatley and Jennifer M. Jenkins.
Cambridge, MA : Blackwell Publishers, 1996.
p.   cm.
BF531.019   1996   152.4   20
ISBN 1–55786–494–2 (hbk: alk. paper) — ISBN 1–55786–495–0 (pbk: alk. paper)
Includes bibliographical references and index.
Emotions.   Jenkins, Jennifer M.   95031515

British Library Cataloguing in Publication Data
A CIP catalogue record for this book is available from the British Library

Commissioning Editor: Alison Mudditt
Desk Editor: Hazel Coleman
Production Controller: Lisa Eaton
Text Designer: Lisa Eaton

Typeset in 10.5/12.5 Garamond
by Photoprint, Torquay
Printed and bound in Great Britain by Alden Press, Oxford

This book is printed on acid-free paper

Short Contents

Contents

Figures

Tables

Foreword

One of the most difficult tasks for experts in any area is communicating in an exciting, probing, and questioning way, the knowledge they have learned and struggled with in order to succeed in their profession. Passion is required – a drive that signals a love of the topic, the marvelous ideas the topic carries with it, and how these ideas can be used to enrich and extend self knowledge. This quality is often the first dimension to be compromised in writing a book that is suitable for use as a text.,

What compelled me to write this foreword is that the passion and excitement of learning about emotions is conveyed throughout the Oatley and Jenkins volume. Miraculously, scientific accuracy does not suffer because of this passion. The book reads like a novel that cannot be put down – I kept coming back to it, rereading it because of its driving storytelling quality. Further, the unanswered questions in the area of emotion are presented, so I found myself debating with Oatley and Jenkins while I was reading. I often disagreed with some of what they said, but I was also forced to go back into my library and seek out the studies and references they cite – to determine whether I really disagreed with them or whether, clever as they are, they had taught me something new along the way. My feeling is that most of the time, I learned new ways of thinking about emotional understanding that I certainly had not acquired before reading the book.

Finally, Oatley and Jenkins use the most up-to-date literature on emotional understanding and integrate it with the most historically significant studies in the area of emotion. Combining the new with the old makes this book unusual because most textbooks are either so antiquated that you are forced into a twenty-year deep sleep by the end of the first chapter, or you get the sense that nothing from the past has been relevant or worthwhile.

Oatley and Jenkins have managed to combine the best of the past with the excitement of the present, point the way to the future, and detailing the nagging questions that still remain for anyone trying to understand emotions. Enjoy the reading, and maybe by the end you can come up with the next chapters to continue the saga.

Nancy L. Stein
Professor of Psychology
University of Chicago

Preface

The strange thing about life is that though the nature of it must have been apparent to everyone for hundreds of years, no one has left any adequate account of it. The streets of London have their map; but our passions are uncharted.

Virginia Woolf, *Jacob's Room, p. 90*

According to written and oral traditions people have been interested in emotions since the earliest times. In most societies emotions are at the center of ordinary understandings of psychology – called folk psychology. It seems strange, then, that within research in psychology emotions have been relatively neglected. That situation has changed. There has been a recent burst of research and clinical interest; within the next few years emotions are likely to take their proper place in our understandings of social science.

Science depends on entering the tradition of what has gone before. Each of us is able to see further by standing on the shoulders of giants, as Robert Burton, the seventeenth-century author of *Anatomy of Melancholy*, said. Our job as writers is to present some of what can be seen from this position, as well as some of the more everyday research on emotions, and to evaluate theories and evidence. You can then evaluate what we say in relation to what else you know, and take part in the debate which is the social process of science, the means by which understanding is increased.

This book is intended for anyone with an interest in emotions, to show how far conceptualization and research have progressed towards understanding. The book, and we would claim the whole topic, extends across psychology, psychiatry, biology, anthropology, sociology, literature, and philosophy. We believe that at last order is emerging; from a complex field some outlines are becoming clear.

Trying to write an introduction to human emotions without a point of view would make not only for dullness but for incomprehensibility. The quantity of publications in the field makes it impossible to be exhaustive, so we have chosen studies and ideas that we believe are representative, hoping to convey a sufficient image for you to think productively. So, as well as an overall story, there is a story line for each chapter. Where there are controversies we discuss them. But we have also tried hard to produce something coherent. Ours is not the only point of view; but we think that by seeing that there is a coherent perspective in this area, you the reader will be able to agree, or to disagree, or to modify it. Knowing that any piece of evidence is not conclusive on its own, but that each can provide a step towards exploring an idea, or tending to make some theory more or less plausible, we hope that an integrated picture can form for you, the reader, applicable to your own interests.

We have done our best to be fair-minded in our treatment of evidence, but we do not believe it possible to be unbiased because we must select what is interesting and worth presenting. So we will be explicit about our biases. Our interest is in conceptualizing emotions in cognitive and developmental terms, in understanding their role in mediating everyday social interaction, and in seeing what goes wrong in the states known as emotional disorders. We see emotions as based on biological processes, and elaborated by culture. Like the skilled action needed when you write your signature, an emotion has a biological basis of components and constraints. It also has a history of individual development. It is only fully understandable within a cultural and interpersonal context.

We write about emotions in the Western tradition – not to imply universality of Euro-American assumptions but because we and most of our readers are members of that tradition. Our belief is that by characterizing a tradition, and by identifying with it, the ideas and findings that have substance within it can be seen for what they are. We can form understandings based in that tradition, and then understand better other culturally distinctive ways of thinking.

As well as a general introduction to the area, the book is designed for use as a textbook for a course on emotions for third- or fourth-year undergraduates, and in some circumstances for second-year undergraduates or for master's level students. But it is a textbook of a particular kind. Most textbooks in psychology nowadays are compendiums of many things to be remembered and a few to be conceptualized. By contrast, I. A. Richards (1925) said that a book is "a machine to think with" (p. 1). We have written our book in that way – we have not concentrated on providing things to recall; instead we have tried to aid thinking. Our conclusions make up our narrative thread. But by offering you sufficient detail of the evidence from which we draw our conclusions we hope to make it possible for you too to draw your conclusions.

The 12 chapters can be covered at the rate of one a week for courses lasting one semester, or each can be divided into two for full-year courses. Throughout, we keep in mind both the issue of prompting an understanding of emotions and practical applications in clinical psychology and psychiatry, health care, education, and organizational psychology. We envisage that most instructors using the book will wish to supplement it with reprints or other readings that they themselves provide. At the end of each chapter we offer some suggestions for further reading; also mentioned in the text as we cover each topic, though not necessarily discussed in detail, are references to up-to-date reviews and books.

We have tested our ideas and coverage by attending to the currents of publications in the field which now has its own journals, its international society for research, its review volumes, its handbooks. Also, we have asked colleagues in North America and Europe to advise us on the balance, representativeness, content, and accuracy, of our presentation.

Acknowledgments

The following friends and colleagues each read a draft of the whole book, and gave us very helpful comments on everything from wordings to our whole approach, and how we might achieve it. We are tremendously grateful to them: Aaron Ben Ze'ev, University of Haifa; Margaret S. Clark, Carnegie Mellon University; Gerry Cupchik, University of Toronto; Alison Fleming, University of Toronto; Laurette Larocque, Ontario Institute for Studies in Education; Nancy Link, Private Practice; Bernie Schiff, University of Toronto; Nancy Stein, University of Chicago.

These friends and colleagues read some substantial part of the book, and furthermore have helped us very much by their comments, clarifications, and discussion: Fabia Franco, University of Padua; Nico Fridja, University of Amsterdam; Joan Grusec, University of Toronto; Paul Harris, Oxford University; George Mandler, University of California, San Diego; Tara Moroz, University of Toronto; Jim Russell, University of British Columbia.

We wrote also to the following asking if they would read a chapter or part of a chapter. Each kindly gave us helpful suggestions, which have been carefully considered and incorporated: Gregory Burton, Seton Hall University, New Jersey; Linda Camras, De Paul University, Chicago; Antonio Damasio, University of Iowa; Nancy Dess, Occidental College, California; Ralph Hupka, California State University at Long Beach; Norman Kinney, Southeast Missouri State University; Craig Kinsley, University of Richmond, Virginia; Cheryl Olson, Allegeny College, Pennsylvania; Mark Plonsky, University of Wisconsin at Stevens Point; Gary Severence, Franciscan University, Ohio; Theo Sonderegger, University of Nebraska; Leland Swenson, Loyola Marymount University, California; Jack Thomson, Center College, Kentucky; Glenn Weisfeld, Wayne State University, Michigan; Frank Wicker, University of Texas at Austin.

As well as the above we have, during the writing of the book, also had discussions with the following people who have helped us clarify issues we were grappling with: Janet Wilde Astington, Jim Averill, George Brown, Robbie Case, Sue Goldberg, Marc Lewis, Michael Lewis, Jerry Parrott, Debra Pepler, Tom Scheff, Phil Shaver, Franco Vaccarino.

To the graduate student members of Keith Oatley's research group and seminar – Laurette Larocque, Ilaria Grazzani, Alison Kerr, Hiroko Yokota, Seema Nundy, Janet Sinclair, Tim Smith, John Thompson – and to the members of the graduate course on Attachment and Other Aspects of Emotional Development taught by Jenny Jenkins, Joan Grusec, and Sue Goldberg – Kirsten Blokland, Tara Burke, Bruce Morton, Alan Polak, Tanya Martini, Norma Mammone, Doreen Prasse, Ruwa Sabbagh, Alex Shendelman, Tracy Soloman – we are grateful for discussion, and for their research

Acknowledgments

input to the matters we discuss here. Warm thanks go to the undergraduate students of University of Toronto who took the Psychology Course 394S based on a draft of the book in the spring of 1994. They paid polite attention throughout, and did well in the exams and term papers. The following each kindly agreed to write a critique of a chapter, say where it worked and did not work, and make suggestions for improvement: Cristina Atrance, Linda Attoe, Sherry Ann Bartram, Christopher Bassel, Margit Bishop, Sarah Bogue, Joel Brody, Alana Butler, Janet Crocker, Shira Dollar-Camar, Jennifer Downie, Joanne Dunford, Jill Farr, Rachel Greenbaum, Nicolette Grenier, Sarah Hales, Anna Hamer, Susan Harris, Lanhee Hong, Karyn Hood, Tina Ishaik, Carmen Jerome-Parkes, Izabella Juchniewicz, Ruchi Kashyap, Megumi Kawasaki, Gita Lakhanpal, Angela Lam, Rebecca Lee, Laura Lin, Bernice Liuson, Marci Longo, Ann Low, Tanuja Persaud, Pamela Pettifer, Susan Pickles, James Prochazka, Adam Radomsky, Ranaissah Samah, Dale Summers, Monique Traubici, Brian Vincent, Lanette Ward, Pui Man Wong, Stephen Yach, Romina Zachariadis. We are very grateful to them; their suggestions have been welcome and helpful. Laurette Larocque and Tim Smith acted as teaching assistants on this course, and also helped in many ways with their comments.

The help, the encouragement, the knowledgable pointing out of errors, the generous suggestions for improvement, of those who have given us comments have made this a much better book than we would have been able to manage on our own. The errors and inappropriate omissions that remain, through our ignorance or willfulness, are our own, and we apologize for them.

For bibliographic and other assistance we thank Maria Medved and we thank Laurette Larocque and Jane King, who did the indexes. Susan Milmoe commissioned the book; for most of its progress Alison Mudditt, senior commissioning editor at Blackwells, gave wonderful encouragement and support, and saw it through. Jan Leahy worked on the book in Cambridge, MA, Elsa Peterson did much of the picture research. Hazel Coleman was desk editor, and Jenny Roberts the copy-editor. We are grateful to all of these for their skill and kindness.

To our agents, Sara Menguc, who looks after nonfiction, and to Celia Catchpole and Murray Pollinger, as always we are grateful for their expertise and support.

The authors and publishers gratefully acknowledge the copyright holders for permission to reproduce copyright material. Permissions and sources for individual figures are given in the List of Figures. Every effort has been made to trace copyright holders, but if any have been inadvertently overlooked the publishers will be glad to rectify the omission in reprints of the book.

CHAPTER *1*

Approaches to Understanding

(a)

(b)

(c)

Figure 1.0 Three photographs from Charles Darwin's founding book of 1872, *The Expression of the Emotions in Man and Animals*: (a) Plate I No. 6; (b) Plate III No. 4; (c) Plate III No. 3.

Contents

Introduction

In this chapter we introduce some of the lines of thinking that have been developed to understand emotions. Each line is a coherent approach, and we associate it with one or two people who founded the line, or changed its direction. Each is still represented in a current mode of thought. Typically, at its center is an insight into what emotions are, or a discovery about them.

If you were just to start reading in the scientific literature on the subject, you might conclude after a little while that emotions were merely scattered aspects of human mental life and behavior, with nothing but the name "emotion" in common. We believe emotions are well-defined phenomena. What we do in this chapter is to introduce some approaches to research and thinking, to set some ideas going. Here the question is not: "Who is right and who is wrong?" These approaches are complementary, and the question is how the diverse themes that they represent might fit together.

Founding a psychology of emotions

In an area where not everything is obvious, the insights of the people we introduce here remain fresh, and the discoveries are still being built upon. Some of these people – Darwin, James, and Freud – laid foundations for psychology, psychiatry, and biology as a whole, as well as for the understanding of emotions. This first group of people can be thought of as establishing the understanding of emotions in the tradition of biological and social sciences.

Charles Darwin: the biological approach

> *Our descent, then, is the origin of our evil passions!! –*
> *The Devil under form of baboon is our grandfather*
> > *Charles Darwin, cited in Gruber & Barrett, 1974, p. 123*

Charles Darwin, the central figure in modern biology, was also one of the founders of psychology. In 1872 he published the most important book on emotions yet written – *The Expression of the Emotions in Man and Animals* (1872). Earlier, in *The Origin of Species* (1859) Darwin had described how living things are adapted to their environments. Knowing this you might imagine that Darwin would have proposed that emotions had functions in our survival. Indeed many psychologists and biologists assume, with or without reading his book on emotions, that this is what he said in it. But he did not. His argument was both closer to common sense, and more subtle than anything that we might commonsensically believe.

In *The Origin of Species* Darwin had mentioned human beings only in passing and in vague terms, although there is a short paragraph in the final section saying: "In the distant future I see open fields for more important researches.

Psychology will be based on a new foundation, that of the necessary acquirement of each mental power and capacity by gradation. Light will be thrown on the origin of man and his history" (Darwin, 1859, p. 458). Darwin began his own observations on emotions in 1838. His interest was not, as it has become in our day, interest in emotions as such; it was an interest in emotional expressions as possible evidence for the evolution of the human species, the continuity of human behavior with that of other animals, and the physical bases of mind. He proceeded on a broad front, observing emotional expressions in animals, as well as in both adult and infant humans. He was interested in both the normal and the abnormal, and enlisted the help of the director of a large mental asylum in the North of England to make observations of patients there. He developed new methods too, realizing the importance of cross-cultural study: he was one of the first to use questionnaires. He sent a set of printed questions to missionaries and others who could observe people in other cultures, asking them to observe particular expressions. He received 36 replies.

Darwin also studied paintings and became interested in photography; *The Expression of the Emotions* was one of the first books in which photographs (such as those at the head of this chapter) were used to make scientific points to the reader. Darwin worked with a photographer and collected pictures of children and adults expressing emotions naturally, and in enacted poses. The innovative aspect of Darwin's work here was to use photography to show human faces in terms of emotional expressions and not in terms of physiognomy – the popular but questionable idea that you can read people's personality in their faces.

The book had two components. One was a set of Darwin's observations and findings based upon the many methods he had adopted or developed. From these he formed a taxonomy, giving names to principal emotional expressions (see table 1.1).

The second component of Darwin's book on expressions was his set of theoretical conclusions. He concluded that emotional expressions are patterns of action that occur even "though they may not . . . be of the least use" (p. 28). Darwin's main idea about expressions of emotion was that they derive from habits which in our evolutionary or individual past had once been useful. These are based on reflex-like mechanisms. Some actions occur whether they are useful or not, and are triggered involuntarily in circumstances analogous to those that had triggered the original habits. His book is full of examples of such actions: of tears that do not function to lubricate the eyes, of laughter that seems not to assist the performance of any task, and so on. Had he been writing today Darwin would surely have described people smiling and gesturing as they speak on the telephone.

For Darwin, emotional expressions showed the continuity of adult human behavioral mechanisms with those of lower animals and with those of infancy. Because these expressions occur in adults "though they may not . . . be of the least use," they had for Darwin a significance in evolutionary thinking rather like that of the fossils that allow us to trace the evolutionary ancestry of species.

Table 1.1 Emotional expressions discussed by Darwin (1872), the motor apparatus used, and the type of emotion which was expressed. This table outlines part of Darwin's taxonomy of emotional expressions and the emotions to which they relate

Expression	Motor apparatus	Emotion example
Blushing	Blood vessels	Shame, modesty
Body contact	Somatic muscles	Affection
Clenching fists	Somatic muscles	Anger
Crying	Tear ducts	Sadness
Frowning	Facial muscles	Anger, frustration
Laughing	Breathing apparatus	Pleasure
Perspiration	Sweat glands	Pain
Hair standing on end	Dermal apparatus	Fear, anger
Screaming	Vocal apparatus	Pain
Shrugging	Somatic muscles	Resignation
Sneering	Facial muscles	Contempt
Trembling	Somatic muscles	Fear, anxiety

Source: Oatley (1992)

More precisely, he thought emotional expressions were like vestigial parts of our bodies. In our digestive system for instance is a small, functionless organ, the appendix. Darwin pointed out that it is evidence that we are descended from prehuman ancestors in whom this organ had a use. Emotional expressions have the same quality: Darwin argued that sneering, an expression in which we partially uncover the teeth on one side, is a behavioral vestige of snarling, and of preparing to bite. This preparation was functional in some distant ancestor, but is so no longer. Though we sometimes make mordant remarks, adult human beings do not now use the teeth for attack.

Darwin traced other expressions to infancy: crying, he argued, is the vestige of screaming in infancy, though in adulthood it is partly inhibited. He carefully

(a)

(b)

Figure 1.1 Two of Charles Darwin's photographs, sneering and crying: (a) Plate IV No. 1; (b) Plate 1 No. 1.

described screaming in young babies, and gave an argument for the function of closing the eyes and the secretion of tears to help protect them when this occurred. When adults cry they still secrete tears, but the tears no longer have any protective function. One of Darwin's most interesting suggestions is that patterns of adult affection, of taking those whom we love in our arms, are based on patterns of parents hugging young infants.

Darwin's insight, then, is that our emotions have a primitive quality. They are links to our past, both to the past of our species and to our own individual history. They are not fully under voluntary control. Although they seem to aid communication between people, they also indicate our animal and infant origins.

Though Darwin's purpose was to show continuities between humans and other animals, his message can be read in another way: perhaps as adult humans we should be able to rise above our bestial and infantile origins! This is the message of the quotation from Darwin at the head of this section, asserting that evil derives from animal passions. This aspect has been taken up eagerly in our culture. Emotions are often seen as childish, as destructive, as enemies of rationality. And to give a firmer scientific basis Berkowitz (1993) has conducted many experiments to show that anger is based on a mechanism with aspects that are irrational and destructive in modern societies. This kind of thinking was not new in the Victorian age. The Stoics, discussed below, had for centuries distrusted emotions because of their disturbing influence on life and rationality. Darwin added the observations of biological science to this distrust. But with his idea of human evolution from previous forms, he also provided one of the most important bases for understanding emotions that we have, an idea we take up in chapter 3.

William James: the bodily approach

> . . . *bodily changes follow directly the perception of the exciting fact . . . and feeling of the same changes as they occur, IS the emotion.*
>
> *James, 1890, p. 449*

The quotation at the head of this section is from William James's (1890) famous textbook *The Principles of Psychology*. It reasserts James's theory of emotions, first published in 1884. He argued that the common sense idea that when we feel an emotion it impels us to a certain kind of activity – that if we were to meet a bear in the woods we would feel frightened and run – is quite wrong. According to James, we perceive the object of fear, a bear, "the exciting fact" as he put it, then the emotion is the perception of changes of our body as we react to that fact. An emotion of fear is the feeling of trembling, running, and so forth, the feeling of our bodily responses to what we perceive.

For a while James's theory, reactions to it, and extensions of it, were almost the whole of the psychology of emotions in America. In this tradition almost every psychology textbook duly noted that the Danish psychologist Carl Lange

(1885) had independently proposed a similar idea to James's, and the theory became known as the James–Lange theory of emotions.

What James stressed was the way in which emotions move us, and how some of them – the coarse emotions as he called them – move us bodily. We may tremble or perspire, our heart may thump in our chest, our breathing may be taken over by an involuntary force as we weep or laugh helplessly. Emotions are not pale or insubstantial. A part of the sensory system is aimed, as it were, at our insides. The vital point of James's theory is captured in this saying, which he wrote in italics: *"If we fancy some strong emotion and then try to abstract from our consciousness of it all the feelings of its bodily symptoms, we find we have nothing left behind"* (James, 1890, p. 451). The enthusiasm with which James's theory was received indicates that generations of psychologists have also found this an important insight. Its importance is twofold.

First, James stressed the embodiment of emotions, including the idea that bodily symptoms can contribute to their felt intensity. It is not uncommon now in thriller movies for the sound track to include the sound of a heartbeat to give us, at the edge of our consciousness, the sense that this might be our own heart beating. The intensification of emotions in this way has been demonstrated experimentally (Valins, 1966). The main focus of bodily feelings, according to this theory, is the set of changes made by the autonomic nervous system, that part of the nervous system that concerns inner organs including

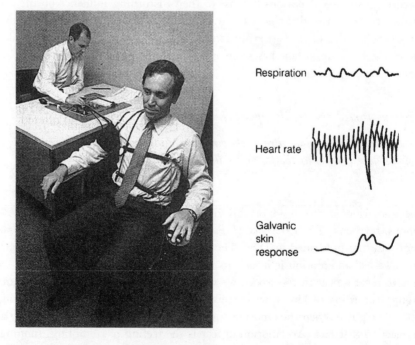

Figure 1.2 This illustration shows a subject from whom recordings of physiological measures of emotions, such as respiration, heart rate, and Galvanic Skin Response (GSR, or skin conductance, a measure of minute changes in sweating), are being taken.

the heart, the blood vessels, the stomach, the sweat glands. James also allowed that changes from movements of muscles and joints contributed to felt bodily changes.

Attending to bodily feelings is for many people an important step in the process of reducing stress, and managing anxiety. Darwin suffered from severe anxiety attacks: in his case they induced nausea and vomiting. He attributed them, probably wrongly, to a hereditary poor constitution and he worried terribly that he would die and leave his children destitute (Bowlby, 1991). Many people have experienced bodily anxiety symptoms perhaps in particular situations. They are not rare: you might ask yourself what your own version is.

James was right: what he called the coarse emotions are associated with bodily disturbances, and often the disturbances (as with Darwin's fits of nausea) can be so strong that they themselves cause fear. We can take James's theory as a reminder that we are not disembodied spirits. By shaking our bodies our emotions show us that something important is happening.

Second, James proposed that emotions give "color and warmth" to experience. Without these effects of emotion, he said, everything would be pale. This idea that emotion gives color to experience has continued in psychological understandings of emotion, for instance in the idea that these colors can be pleasant or unpleasant and that emotions with their own feeling states can be things to seek or avoid.

Sigmund Freud: the psychotherapeutic approach

"I came away from the window at once, and leant up against the wall and couldn't get my breath . . ." (description given by Katharina, subject of one of Freud's early case histories).

Freud & Breuer, 1895

Sigmund Freud did not propose a theory of emotions as such. In fact he proposed three theories about the effects of emotionally significant issues: his theory of emotional traumas, which we will discuss here; his theory of inner conflicts (Freud, 1915–16); and his theory of repetition compulsion (Freud, 1920). Each time he modified his previous theory because it did not work as well as he had thought.

Freud's first theory of emotional effects was that certain events, usually of a sexual kind, can be so damaging that they leave psychological scars that can affect the rest of our lives. His principal exposition was in a series of short cases: here is one, the case of Katharina (Freud & Breuer, 1895, pp. 190–201). Freud was walking in the Eastern Alps in the early 1890s trying, as he said, to get medicine and the neuroses completely out of his mind. He said he had just about succeeded when, at an inn at a mountain summit, a voice interrupted his contemplation of the scenery asking: "Are you a doctor, Sir?" Freud had given himself away in the visitors' book. The voice belonged to a "rather sulky-looking girl of perhaps eighteen who had served [Freud's] meal" (p. 190). Her name was Katharina, and she was a niece of the proprietor. She said her nerves were bad, and she had consulted a doctor but was still not well.

So Freud was back with the neuroses – the technical name he gave to the problems popularly known as "nerves." Katharina described how she suffered from attacks in which she thought she would suffocate. There was a buzzing and a hammering that seemed about to burst her head, giddiness so that she almost collapsed, and a crushing of the chest so that she could not get her breath.

Freud asked her if she felt frightened. She said she did: normally, she said, she was brave and went anywhere, but in these attacks she felt she was about to die and on these days did not dare go out.

This would now be called a panic attack (American Psychiatric Association, 1994). Such attacks often occur in anxiety disorders – which are usually chronic disabling states in which a person may lose all confidence and feel unable to take part in social life. In terms of emotions, these attacks are episodes of fear with violent bodily perturbations of the kind that William James described. Panic attacks often occur without any sense of what the fear is about, and sometimes as with Katharina, making the sufferer think that the perturbations will themselves cause death. In her attacks Katherina said: "I always see an awful face that looks at me in a dreadful way, so that I am frightened" (p. 192). Katharina could not say whose face this was.

Freud was clear that the attack was one of fear, also called anxiety. His aim in therapy was to discover how the attacks had started, and what – or whom – the feared object was. He said that the top of a mountain did not seem quite the right place to try hypnosis, so he questioned Katharina. The attacks, she said, started some two years previously. Freud thought he would try a lucky guess, since he had often found that young women experienced horror when confronted for the first time with the world of sexuality. "If you don't know," he said, "I'll tell you how *I* think you got your attack . . . you must have seen or heard something that very much embarrassed you" (p. 192). "Heavens, yes!" she replied. "That was when I caught my uncle with the girl, with Franziska, my cousin" (p. 193).

Freud questioned her further: she had peeped through a window in a passage, into a room to see her uncle lying on top of Franziska. She said: "I came away from the window at once, and leant up against the wall and couldn't get my breath – just what happens to me since. Everything went blank, my eyelids were forced together and there was a hammering and buzzing in my head" (p. 193).

Katharina maintained that she did not understand the significance of the scene at the time. The face she saw during her attacks was not that of Franziska. It was a man's face. Her uncle's? She did not know. She had not seen it that clearly, and why, she asked, "should he have been making such a dreadful face just then?" (p. 194). Freud agreed, but continued to question. Three days later Katharina said she had felt giddy again, and then suffered from nausea and vomiting for three days. Freud suggested that this sickness meant she had felt disgusted when she had looked into the room. "Yes, I'm sure I felt disgusted," she said reflectively, "but disgusted at what?" (p. 195).

Neither Freud nor Katharina could make it out, but he asked her to continue her story. She said that she had at last reported the incident to her aunt, who had come to suspect that she was concealing some secret. There followed disagreeable scenes between the uncle and aunt in the course of which things were heard that it would have been better not to hear. In the end her aunt had moved out with Katharina to take over the present inn, leaving the uncle with Franziska who was by then pregnant. But, Freud says, instead of continuing with the story of this distressing separation, Katharina now broke off to relate an incident from two years before these events. She had gone with her uncle on an expedition, and in the inn where they stayed he had got into bed with her. She said she "woke up suddenly, 'feeling his body' in the bed."

She had remonstrated: "What are you up to uncle? Why don't you stay in your own bed?" He tried to pacify her: "Go on you silly girl, keep still. You don't know how nice it is." – "I don't like your 'nice' things" (p. 195). She went to stand by the door, ready to escape to the passage until he gave up. Freud says that from her description and from questioning her, she had not recognized the nature of this incident. On other occasions too, when her uncle was drunk, she had had to defend herself from him. It was then she had begun to feel the pressure on her eyes and chest, but with nothing like the strength of her current attacks.

Then she mentioned other memories: one was when the whole family had slept in a hayloft. She had awoken to a noise and thought she noticed her uncle who had been lying between her and Franziska was turning away, but she did not know what was happening. Then there was another occasion at night when her uncle seemed to be trying to go into Franziska's room. She had just noticed both of these incidents at the time, but without thinking anything of them.

Freud describes how, as she finished this account, "She was like someone transformed. The sulky unhappy face had grown lively, her eyes were bright, she was lightened and exalted" (p. 197).

Freud says the meaning of the case had become clear: she had carried the two sets of experiences, of her uncle's attempts to interfere with her, and the obscure goings on between her uncle and Franziska. But she did not understand any of them. Then she saw her uncle on top of Franziska. At that moment she began to understand – but at the same time, says Freud, her mind fended off the implications. After three days' incubation, her symptoms set in with vomiting, an indication of her disgust, which was not from what she had seen through the passageway window but from the realization of what had been going on two years earlier when she had "felt her uncle's body."

Freud gave Katharina his conclusions: "You thought," said Freud, "now he is doing with her what he wanted to do with me, that night and those other times." "It may well be," she replied, "that that was what I was disgusted at, and that that was what I thought" (p. 197).

Freud felt bold enough now to ask what part of her uncle's body had touched her. She smiled in an embarrassed way, as though she had been found out, but gave no answer. She did say that the face that had persecuted her during her attacks was now recognizable as her uncle's. But it did not come from any of these scenes but from the time of her uncle and aunt's divorce. He would be contorted in rage, making threats to her, saying it was all her fault.

Freud never saw Katharina again – but hoped she benefited from their conversation. In a footnote added in 1924, however, he wrote: "I venture after the lapse of so many years to lift the veil of discretion and reveal the fact that Katharina was not the niece of the landlady, but her daughter. The girl fell ill, therefore, as a result of sexual attempts on the part of her own father" (p. 210). This revelation makes the case history suddenly more shocking but also more compelling.

Freud showed that emotions are not always simple. Often they are felt obscurely, or with effects that we do not understand. Some emotions and their meanings become clear only by expressing them, or in talking about them to another person, or in reflecting upon them.

Figure 1.3 The group photograph of the conference which accompanied the ceremony of Freud's honorary degree at Clark University in 1909. This was the occasion of Freud's first substantial public recognition. The members of the conference do not quite make up a roll-call of famous American psychologists of the time, but they come close. In the front row of the photo is Freud fourth from the right, and Jung third from the right, William James is third from the left, Edward Titchener is second from the left and Stanley Hall, founder of developmental psychology, who organized the honorary degree and the conference, is fifth from the right. In the second row, third from the left is James Cattell.

Already in the case of Katharina, from 100 years ago, there are many of the elements of psychoanalytic therapy as it has developed since: the telling of one's life story which is found to have gaps, the filling of these gaps by "interpretations" or suggestions of the therapist, and the insights of the person receiving the therapy as she or he realizes something that had been unknown or unconscious, as when Katharina said: "Heavens, yes! That was when I caught my uncle with the girl, with Franziska" (p. 193).

Other elements of Katharina's case are common to all forms of psychotherapy. They include a focus on emotions as among the main problems to be dealt with. Such emotions, when they become deeply troubling or disabling, are called symptoms. Symptoms maintain their emotional bases, although they are often more intense, and more long-lasting than ordinary emotions. They are abnormal partly in that the sufferers experience them as inappropriate, disabling, sometimes incomprehensible. Psychotherapy is often directed to loosening their grip by understanding them, or by regulating them, or by making them more bearable.

For understanding emotions, Freud's work started the idea that, deliberately or involuntarily, the mind seems to guard against unpleasant emotions. Freud called such processes mechanisms of defense, and his daughter Anna Freud developed the idea (1937). More generally, researchers who have extended the work of Freud on dealing with emotionally stressful events talk in terms of coping with the event, and of coping with the emotions it produces (Lazarus, 1991).

Philosophical and literary background

Darwin, James, and Freud were by no means the first in the Western tradition to think about emotions. Reflections on emotions can be found in some of the oldest written documents to survive. Some writing has affected modern thinking profoundly. In this section we consider the approaches of four writers who represent important currents in thinking about emotions.

Aristotle: the conceptual approach

> *. . . there is nothing either good or bad but thinking makes it so.*
> *Shakespeare, HAMLET, II, 2, 1. 249–250*

Aristotle, who lived from 384 to 322 BCE (Before the Common Era), laid some of the foundations of the European and American psychology of emotions. His most fundamental insight was that emotions are connected with action, and that they derive from what we believe. One reason Aristotle's approach is important is that in other approaches emotions are seen as simply happening to us (as implied by Darwin and James). Such arguments can imply that emotions are merely biological events like sneezing with no meaning, or that they are the opposite of thinking. So what did Aristotle mean when he argued that emotions depend on what we believe?

Aristotle's main discussion of emotions is in his book on *Rhetoric*, where he had practical concerns: how does one make persuasive arguments, especially when speaking about practical decisions? In many cases what one should believe and what one should do are not certain. One must therefore try to approach the truth by making an argument which is persuasive. Three general principles apply, says Aristotle. First, a hearer is more likely to believe a good person than a bad one. Second, people are persuaded when what is said stirs their emotions. Third, people are persuaded by arguments that approach a truth, or an apparent truth, about the matter in hand.

On the topic of emotions Aristotle makes it clear that he is not interested in emotions to arouse prejudice, pity, anger, and so forth, to sway people irrationally. He conceives rhetoric as a search for truth, by speaking and discussion. He says about speaking in a law court: "It is not right to pervert the judge by moving him to anger or envy or pity — one might as well warp a carpenter's rule before using it" (1984, 1354a, 1.24). His concern with emotions is that speaking is a personal matter. When speaking to persuade, you must know something about the people to whom you speak, about their values, and about the effects that speaking may have on them. When "people are feeling friendly and placable they think one sort of thing; when they are feeling angry or hostile, they think either something totally different, or the same thing with different intensity" (1377b, 1.29). "The emotions," Aristotle continues, "are all those feelings that so change [people] as to affect their judgments, and are also attended by pain or pleasure. Such are anger, pity, fear and the like, with their opposites" (1378a, 1.20).

Aristotle goes on to define and discuss different emotions, starting with anger: "Anger may be defined as an impulse, accompanied by pain, to a conspicuous revenge for a conspicuous slight directed without justification towards what concerns oneself or towards what concerns one's friends" (1378b, 1.32).

Anger is defined in the cognitive terms of the knowledge a person has, and the way in which this knowledge is used. Aristotle talks of analysis — breaking something down into its parts. This is what his cognitive definitions aim at. He makes the properties of each part clear. What is meant by being slighted, for instance, is that someone has treated you with contempt, or thwarted your wishes, or caused you shame.

In this ancient discussion we see elements that continue to concern psychologists today. First, emotions are cognitively based: they can be analyzed into parts based on what we know and believe. Second, emotions are typically pleasant or unpleasant — anger is usually unpleasant. This distinction continues today, in thinking about emotions as primarily positive or negative. Third, emotions involve an urge to action. In anger the urge is towards revenge, towards getting even. Fourth, Aristotle indicates that emotions have effects which are themselves cognitive – they are based on our evaluations of events, and they can affect further judgments we might make.

Aristotle's postulate, the one echoed by Shakespeare's Hamlet in the quotation at the head of this section, is that we experience events as good or bad according to our evaluations of them. Think of it like this: it is a warm summer evening and you are lightly dressed, waiting in line at the theater. You feel a touch on your arm. If the touch were made by a person you have just fallen in love with, you might find it highly pleasurable, even erotic. If the touch were made by a different kind of friend, perhaps guiding you to stand out of the way to let someone pass, you might not feel any emotion at all but notice what was happening and move over. If the touch were from a person you had never met, you might feel intruded upon, angry, repelled. Exactly the same pattern of stimulation on the skin can mean quite different things according to how you evaluate it.

The second book in which Aristotle discussed emotions is the *Poetics*, which is about narrative writing. Aristotle was fascinated by drama, and the book is mainly concerned with tragedy in the theater. It is thought to be the first half of a larger book. The lost part dealt with comedy.

Drama, said Aristotle, is about human action. History is about particulars, about actions that have happened. But drama is universal. It is about what can happen when human beings act. With the fading of ideas that fate rules human lives, the great discovery of Greek dramatists was that even when well-intentioned, human actions can miscarry. They have effects that are unforeseen. We are human, not gods. We simply do not know enough to predict the consequences of everything we do. Nonetheless, and this is the root of human tragedy, we remain responsible for our actions.

Aristotle noticed two important effects of tragic drama. First, people are moved emotionally. As the principal character grapples with consequences that were unforeseen and uninvited, we see the somber spectacle of a person who is good being tortured by circumstances to which he or she has contributed. This person starts to act in ways that contradict his or her own beliefs and standards. We are moved to pity for this person – and to fear for ourselves, because in the universal appeal of these plays we know that the principal character is also ourself.

Second we can experience what Aristotle called *katharsis* of our emotions. This term is widely mistranslated as having a medical or spiritual meaning – of purgation or purification. The idea arose that by using the term Aristotle meant that there was something inappropriate about emotions. Certainly Aristotle's teacher Plato had thought that emotions are like drugs, that they pervert reason. According to this view, one might go to the theater and get rid of troublesome emotions, as with a laxative. The English word "catharsis" has very much this sense. Or, according to a more spiritualized view, one could have one's base emotions purified. In either case one could emerge from the theater freed from emotions, and then be able to think and act rationally.

But, as Nussbaum (1986) argues, for Aristotle *katharsis* meant neither purgation nor purification. It meant clarification – clearing away obstacles – and it included the cognitive meaning of understanding clearly, without obstacles. Aristotle meant *katharsis* as clarification, to say that: "The function of the theater is to accomplish through pity and fear, a clarification (or illumination) of experiences of the pitiable and fearful kind" (Nussbaum, 1986, p. 391). So, by seeing universal predicaments of human action at the theater we may come to experience emotions of pity and fear, and understand consciously for ourselves their relation to the consequences of human action in a world that can be known only imperfectly.

So here, in the Western history of ideas, are beginnings of explicit thinking about emotions and their effects. This is the cognitive approach. It was taken up in the third century BCE by the Stoics who wished to find a philosophical cure for the soul by right thinking, based on evaluations that would control or moderate emotions. Their influence, which we mention from time to time in this book, has continued ever since. According to many psychologists the cognitive approach is still the most fruitful approach for understanding

Figure 1.4 The theater in classical times was an important institution. If you visit ruins of cities in the ancient Greek world you find in each one that the largest building was a theater with a seating capacity not much less than the population of the city. Rather than being constructed to create a private image, as the cinema and television now do, theaters were constructed to portray action in the context of one's fellow citizens who were there in one's full view.

emotions. Not only do emotions result from cognitive evaluations, but we catch a glimpse of how, in the universal human pursuit of listening to and watching human stories, our own emotions are stirred. In reflection, we can come to understand why they are stirred.

René Descartes and Baruch Spinoza: the philosophical approach

The Passions of the Soul

book title of Descartes

Of human bondage

Chapter heading in Spinoza's Ethics

Descartes and Spinoza both wrote in the seventeenth century. Both lived in Holland which had just blossomed from having been an obscure Spanish colony on the North Sea to a center of commercial and intellectual life, perhaps at that time one of the few places in Europe where bold thinkers could work and publish without persecution. Both philosophers were concerned to give an account that would illuminate the nature of human beings, and give clues to understanding the emotions.

Descartes

René Descartes is generally regarded as the founder of modern philosophy. He can equally be regarded as making possible the modern scientific view of the world. In many of the things he wrote he started by saying that we had to throw away all previous writings on the subject and start afresh. He was, in fact, enormously well educated and well read, clearly influenced by writers who had preceded him – and we might be excused for thinking that his opening paragraphs were designed to get his readers' attention. They do.

Here is the opening of *The Passions of the Soul* (1649): "There is nothing in which the defective nature of the sciences which we have received from the ancients appears more clearly than in what they have written on the passions" (p. 331).

So anyone with an interest in the subject can scarcely wait to read what the real answer is. Descartes's book lays out the basis for modern neurophysiology. In it he describes the body as a kind of machine, correctly distinguishes sensory and motor nerves, indicates how memory might operate, and discusses how reflexes work. But principally the book is about emotions. It has three main parts. In the first he discusses emotions in relation to their neurophysiological bases. In the second he gives an account of six fundamental emotions – wonder, desire, joy, love, hatred, and sadness – and discusses their bodily aspects. In the third he shows how the six fundamental emotions combine to produce the many different individual emotions to which we are subject: disdain, pride, hope, fear, jealousy, remorse, envy, and so on.

Descartes's account of the nature of emotions is that they occur in the thinking aspect of ourselves – which he called the soul. At the same time they are closely connected to our bodies, for example, to our heart beating rapidly, to blushing, or to tears. "Passion" here means something that happens to us; its opposite is action which is something that we ourselves cause. So, among the passions are perceptions that arise from aspects of the outside world that happen upon our sense organs and also events within the body such as hunger and pain. But unlike perceptual and bodily passions, emotions happen to our souls, to our thinking parts. Descartes's fertile idea triggers the thought that just as perceptions tell us about what is important in the outside world, just as hunger and pain tell us about important events in the body, emotions tell us what is important in our souls – as we might now say, in our real selves.

Descartes describes how emotions cannot be entirely controlled by thinking, but they can be regulated by thoughts, especially thoughts which are true. So, he says:

> . . . in order to excite courage in oneself and remove fear, it is not sufficient to have the will to do so, but we must also apply ourselves to consider the reasons, the objects or examples which persuade us that the peril is not great; that there is always more security in defense than flight; that . . . we could expect nothing but regret and shame for having fled, and so on. (Descartes, 1649, p. 352)

Although he does not acknowledge Aristotle, it is clear from this kind of account that Descartes accepts Aristotle's idea that emotions, though they happen to us, depend on how we evaluate events. Their intensity and effects on us are affected by how we think about these events and their implications.

Perhaps most of all Descartes's account of emotions is remarkable for combining an account of the mechanism of emotions with the idea of function. Here is what he says:

> . . . the utility of all the passions consists alone in their fortifying and perpetuating in the soul thoughts which it is good it should preserve, and which without that might easily be effaced from it. And again, all the harm which they can cause consists in the fact that they fortify and conserve those thoughts more than necessary, or that they fortify and conserve others on which it is not good to dwell. (ibid, p. 364)

We might reflect on how, when we love someone our love perpetuates and extends our thoughts of this person, and when we are overanxious or depressed we dwell on issues we cannot affect. Descartes's idea, then, is that we are provided by our biological makeup with emotions that are functional, but which can sometimes be dysfunctional.

Spinoza

Like Descartes, born a generation before him, and like his contemporary Leibnitz, Baruch Spinoza is considered one of the great rationalist philosophers – philosophers who believed that how human beings think can reflect the way the universe works, so that true understanding can arise purely from rational thought.

In his most important work, *Ethics* (1675), Spinoza sets forth a vision of the universe as a great interconnected system, and a large part of the book is about emotions. The universe is an expression of the mind of God. It is everything that is — actuated according to what physicists now call laws. So everything that happens is due to the causal properties of the universe: human beings are not separate from each other or from the world. Each individual is more like a tiny wrinkle in a huge piece of cloth. The proper function of our conscious minds, therefore, both in general and in the events of everyday life, is to understand our connectedness to the universe and its laws.

We can accept what happens, the proper attitude, since everything, including what happens to us personally, is the expression of the mind of God in this great system. Spinoza's argument is that God, being perfect, cannot be incomplete. Therefore God and the world, including human beings, are one. When we understand and accept this, we have what Spinoza calls active emotions, based on love for what is. But we can have passive emotions, passions, such as bitterness, resentment, and envy, which are based on confused ideas, rejecting and rebelling against what is, wanting the world to be different.

The chapter in Spinoza's *Ethics* in which he discusses these passions and our "human infirmity in moderating and checking these emotions," is entitled "Of human bondage," for as he says: "When a man is prey to his emotions, he is not his own master, but lies at the mercy of fortune" (p. 187). People are conscious of their desires, but generally ignorant of the causes of their desires. So they mistakenly think these desires are prime movers, getting angry and frustrated if the desires are not met. In reality what happens is an expression of the all-encompassing mind of God, which is perfect. We can, on the one hand, try to understand this perfection, or on the other hand we can think about the imperfection that results from our unsatisfied desires.

Spinoza is in direct line of descent from Aristotle: his theory of emotions is thoroughly cognitive. Emotions are based on evaluations, modes of thinking. When we see the world as it is, we have true beliefs, and from them flow the active emotions of love for others and the world, based on acceptance. By contrast the passions, according to Spinoza, are confused ideas based on false beliefs, rejecting the world as it is.

Spinoza was a kind of intellectual mystic: his view of the world is related to that of people in Jewish, Christian, Islamic, and Buddhist mystical traditions. This may be a kind of view that you share, or it may not. One of the interesting aspects of Spinoza's writing, however, is the great respect it commands even among those who have no mystical leanings, even among atheists.

Seeing emotions, or passions, as the real source of trouble for us humans has not been unusual, either in Western or Eastern traditions. What Spinoza proposed, apparently for the first time, in Europe, is that to understand our emotions and their origins is to be liberated from bondage. As we pointed out in the section on Freud, psychotherapy in the West is focused on understanding emotion. But the revolutionary idea of accepting and understanding our emotions, as a step towards being liberated from their compulsive effects, was Spinoza's.

Like Descartes, Spinoza gives a long list of various emotions, with an explanatory paragraph on each one. In these he was not above giving us hints, some with an ironic tone, about how we should view our emotions:

> Definition 7. *Hatred* is pain, accompanied by the idea of an external cause. (p. 176)

> Definition 23. *Envy* is hatred, in so far as it induces a man to be pained by another's good fortune, and to rejoice in another's evil fortune. (p. 178)

So when Spinoza says hatred includes "the idea" of an external cause, he intends us to question this idea. He argues that understanding our emotions can be all-important, even though aspects of this understanding can be paradoxical. He acknowledges the difficulties at the end of the *Ethics*, when he says:

> If the way that I have pointed out as leading to this result [wisdom in being conscious of self, of God, and of things] seems exceedingly hard, it may nevertheless be discovered . . . How would it be possible, if salvation were ready to our hand, and could without labor be found, that it would by almost all men be neglected? (Spinoza 1675, pp. 270–271)

George Eliot: the literary approach

> *No life would have been possible to Dorothea which was not filled with emotion . . .*
>
> George Eliot, Middlemarch, p. 894

George Eliot (pen-name of Mary Ann Evans) thought Darwin's *The Origin of Species* "not impressive from want of luminous and orderly presentation" (Burrow, 1968, p. 12). She was concentrating on a different kind of natural history, wondering how to develop a social science founded like biology on accurate observation, but which also moved people emotionally.

In 1856 she had written an essay for a magazine of which she was an editor, the *Westminster Review*. The essay was entitled "The natural history of German life" (Pinney, 1963). In it she reviewed two books by von Riehl, a pioneer anthropologist, describing the life of German peasants. Her essay was a kind of manifesto for her own novels. It includes the following:

> The greatest benefit we owe to the artist, whether painter, poet or novelist, is the extension of our sympathies. Appeals founded on generalizations and statistics require a sympathy ready-made, a moral sentiment already in activity; but a picture of human life such as a great artist can give, surprises even the trivial and the selfish into that attention to what is apart from themselves, which may be called the raw material of moral sentiment . . . Art is the nearest thing to life; it is a mode of

amplifying experience and extending our contact with our fellow-men beyond the bounds of our personal lot. (George Eliot, 1856, reprinted in Pinney, 1963, p. 270)

On September 23, 1856, George Eliot the novelist was born: she began writing "The sad fortunes of the Rev. Amos Barton," now collected with two other stories in *Scenes from Clerical Life*. When in the years 1871 to 1872 she published *Middlemarch* it was clear that she had achieved the aim she had sketched in her essay on von Riehl. Virginia Woolf called *Middlemarch* a "magnificent book which with all its imperfections is one of the few English novels written for grown-up people" (Woolf, 1919).

Middlemarch is a novel about emotions, and it centers on two young people, Dorothea Brooke and Tertius Lydgate. The ardent Dorothea longs to do some good in her life, and to gain an entrance to the male world of learning, and partly with this in mind she marries the middle-aged scholar, Edward Casaubon, who is working on a compendious study, "The Key to All Mythologies." George Eliot's description of this relationship, as each partner projects onto the other hopes and expectations that the other cannot fulfill, is

Figure 1.5 William Holman Hunt's "The Hireling Shepherd." George Eliot wrote of this painting in "The natural history of German life": "How little the real characteristics of the working classes are known to those who are outside them, how little their natural history has been studied . . . Even one of our greatest painters of the pre-eminently realistic school, while, in his picture "The Hireling Shepherd," he gave us a landscape of marvelous truthfulness, placed a pair of peasants in the foreground who were not much more real than the idyllic swans of our chimney ornaments."

one of the most moving portraits of an unhappy marriage in literature. Tertius Lydgate is a doctor engaged in medical researches, building up his practice, and appointed as director of the town's new fever hospital about to be built. He attracts the attention of Rosamund Vincy, the town beauty, and these two fall in love and marry.

Each character in *Middlemarch* has aspirations. Each puts plans into effect, but each is affected by the accidents of life, by the unforeseeable. There is no grand plan, no agency behind the scenes pulling strings. George Eliot's question is this: if our plans only partly succeed, if we are unable to foresee the outcomes of all our actions, if there is no fate guiding us towards an inevitable destiny, if we live in a time when by no means everyone believes in divine guidance, or if they interpret such guidance in very different ways, how should we find our way in life?

Her answer is that our emotions can act as a sort of compass, and they are also the principal means by which each affects others. In the book she draws many contrasts, for instance between Dorothea who is full of unsatisfied yearnings but is responsive to the emotional currents of her own and others' lives, and Casaubon who barely recognizes his emotions at all. About a third of the way through the book, Casaubon has a heart attack in suppressed anger following an argument with Dorothea. Lydgate attends and counsels Dorothea to avoid all occasions that might agitate her husband.

Some days later Lydgate makes another call and Casaubon asks him to be candid about his condition. Lydgate says that although prediction is difficult, he is at risk. Casaubon perceives that he might die, and becomes sunk in bitterness. When Lydgate leaves, Dorothea goes into the garden with an impulse to go at once to her husband.

> But she hesitated, fearing to offend him by obtruding herself; for her ardour, continually repulsed, served with her intense memory to heighten her dread, as thwarted energy subsides into a shudder, and she wandered slowly round the nearer clumps of trees until she saw him advancing. Then she went towards him, and might have represented a heaven-sent angel coming with a promise that the short hours remaining should yet be filled with that faithful love which clings the closer to a comprehended grief. His glance in reply to hers was so chill that she felt her timidity increased; yet turned and passed her hand through his arm.
>
> Mr Casaubon kept his hands behind him, and allowed her pliant arm to cling with difficulty against his rigid arm.
>
> There was something horrible to Dorothea in the sensation which this unresponsive hardness inflicted on her. That is a strong word, but not too strong; it is in these acts called trivialities that the seeds of joy are for ever wasted. (Eliot, 1871–1872, p. 462)

In this short passage we see many of the elements of George Eliot's writing: She shows how emotions arise and are communicated between one person and another, and she gives a commentary indicating the kinds of effects they have – a commentary to which some literary critics have objected. Perhaps most important, here, more or less for the first time in the English novel, there begins the portrait of experience from inside the person's own consciousness – ". . . she hesitated, fearing to offend him by obtruding herself; for her ardour, continually repulsed, served with her intense memory to heighten her dread." As D. H. Lawrence later put it: "It was really George Eliot who started it all . . . it was she who started putting all the action inside" (Purkis, 1985, p. 104).

Later George Eliot wrote in a letter: ". . . my writing is simply a set of experiments in life – an endeavour to see what our thought and emotion may be capable of – what stores of motive, actual or hinted as possible, give promise of a better after which we can strive" (Haight, 1985, p. 466).

Brief biography: George Eliot

George Eliot was one of the greatest English novelists. She was born Mary Ann Evans in 1819, on a farm near Coventry. Her father, Robert Evans, was a carpenter and farm manager, and her mother, Christiana Pearson, was from a yeoman family. Mary Ann learned French and German from pious teachers, and was influenced by Evangelical Christianity. At 16 she was withdrawn from school due to her mother's ill health, but by her thirties she had also learned Italian, Latin, and Greek, and had translated theological and philosophical books as well as keeping house for her father, who died when she was 30. She moved to London, calling herself Marian Evans, and became assistant editor of the *Westminster Review*. She must have been one of the few women of her time to support herself financially in such a way. She became a close friend of the philosopher and psychologist Herbert Spencer. Later she lived with George Henry Lewes until he died in 1878. Lewes was a literary critic and biologist, whose work won the esteem of Charles Darwin. Lewes was separated: his wife had left him to live with another man. Divorce was unobtainable since Lewes had tolerated the affair, so he and Marian Evans were unable to marry – a scandal to polite society. Theirs is one of the great emotional and intellectual relationships of the history of letters. They traveled, read together, commented on each other's work, discussed everything, worked on joint projects. For instance, Lewes was in the forefront of popularizing Spinoza, and Marian set to work translating Spinoza's *Ethics*. In the end no publisher would take the book. It was Lewes who encouraged her to start writing fiction. *The Mill on the Floss* (Eliot, 1860) established her reputation, and brought financial security. Lewes was delighted at her success, even when it outstripped his own. (Biographical information from Haight, 1968).

In *Middlemarch* George Eliot explores some fundamental facts about emotions – including the fact that we understand our own emotions quite differently from those of other people. Perhaps most importantly, we the readers experience emotions as we identify with and sympathize with the characters – as Aristotle had described in the *Poetics*. Not only are we given portraits of ordinary life, as one might expect from a natural history, not only are these from inside as well as outside in ways that we could not expect of biology, but we ourselves are moved emotionally in ways that do indeed succeed in "extending our sympathies," which do succeed in "amplifying experience and extending our contact with our fellow-men beyond the bounds of our personal lot."

George Eliot knew well enough what it would be to write philosophy or natural history, or sociology, or psychology, in a conventional way. She had read such subjects more avidly than almost anyone else in her time, in four modern and two ancient languages. She traveled widely, and lived at the center of intellectual debate in one of the world's liveliest cities during a period when thought had scarcely been more active, when revolutions were occurring in science, in technology, in social institutions. She had discussed social science with leading thinkers. But she perceived that to write about emotions something more than conventional scientific and philosophical articles was needed. She wrote so that people could experience emotions and their relation to aspirations. In her hands the novel allowed a kind of exploration of emotions and their effects which is simply not possible by means of generalizations, of statistics, or of diagrams.

The writing that George Eliot pioneered allows us, as Aristotle proposed in his theory of *katharsis*, to understand emotions as we experience them in reading. This kind of understanding has an important place beside more analytical methods.

The gathering momentum of modern research

During the twentieth century, the study of emotions has moved forward into many channels – biological, social, developmental, applied. Until recently the flow of research has been uneven and fitful, with little sense of the interrelation among its various channels. In the next section we present some of the founders of twentieth-century psychology, physiology, and social science. With each one there began a particular kind of research on emotions that became and remains influential.

John Harlow and Walter Hess: brain science

> *Most often the cat in its defense/attack reaction turns against the nearest person participating in the experiment.*
>
> Hess & Brügger, 1943, p. 184

From Darwin's day the hypothesis of a physical basis of mind progressed, until now few psychologists deny that mental processes depend on the neural and chemical actions of the brain. As part of this understanding it has emerged that particular parts of the brain are associated with emotions, in different ways.

Some of the observations that have pointed to the brain as the seat of emotions derive from accidental brain damage: for instance there was the case of Phineas Gage, a likeable foreman working on the construction of the Rutland and Burlington Railroad in Vermont, written up by a country doctor called John Harlow. On September 13, 1848, the constructors were about to blast a rock. The rock was drilled and the hole filled with gunpowder. Gage himself rammed the powder down with an iron rod, three and a half feet long, an inch and a quarter in diameter, weighing 13 pounds. This tamping iron must have struck up a spark, for there was an explosion. The iron entered Gage's skull just beneath the left eyebrow, exited from a hole in the top of his head, and landed 50 feet away. He bled terribly. His men took him on an ox cart to a local hotel, where Harlow attended him. Though he suffered an infection of his wound, Gage recovered.

Harlow wrote, in a phrase that prefigured Darwin's theory of emotions, that the "balance, so to speak, between his intellectual faculties and his animal propensities seems to have been destroyed" (Harlow, 1868, p. 277). In place of Phineas Gage there was another, whom his friends said was "no longer Gage." Instead of being amiable and efficient, he was impatient, irreverent, and easily moved to anger. He was "capricious and vacillating, devising many plans of future operation, which are no sooner arranged than they are abandoned" (p. 277). His employers who had regarded him as their "most efficient and capable foreman" could not give him his job again. He drifted around the United States, exhibiting himself at fairgrounds, and taking with him the iron bar that had caused his injury.

Harlow did not learn of Gage's death in San Francisco, where he had gone to live with his mother, until five years after it occurred. So Harlow was unable to examine the brain. But he prevailed upon Gage's family to have the body exhumed. The skull, and the iron bar which had been placed in the coffin with Gage, were sent back East. In his paper, read to the Massachusetts Medical Society on June 3, 1868, Harlow says that Gage's mother and friends "waiving the claims of personal and private affection . . . have cheerfully placed this skull (which I now show you) in my hands, for the benefit of science" (p. 278).

There are two main methods of physiological psychology: one can study the effects of lesions, damage to the brain that occurs accidentally as it did in the case of Phineas Gage or that can be made deliberately in experiments on animals, and one can study the effects of stimulating the brain, either electrically or by means of chemicals. Perhaps the most striking discoveries — corresponding as they do with what we know from the naturalistic observations pioneered by Darwin — have been from stimulation. Well-coordinated patterns of response, propensities characteristic of emotions, can be induced experimentally by applying electrical stimulation to specific areas of the brain. The

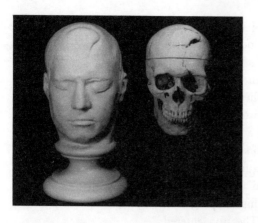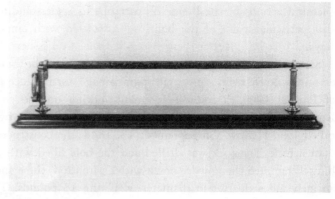

Figure 1.6 (a) Phineas Gage's skull showing the exit hole made by the iron bar that caused his injury in 1848, and (b) the iron bar itself, now in the Museum of Harvard Medical School.

pioneer was the Swiss physiologist, Walter Hess, working in his laboratory in Zurich.

During the 1920s Hess conceived an imaginative, novel, and technically demanding program of research (Hess, 1950). He implanted electrodes into the hypothalamic region of the brains of cats. When each cat had recovered from its operation, electrical stimulation could be applied to the brain via these electrodes, as the animal moved freely around. To do these experiments Hess had to aim the electrodes into a region deep in the brain and attach them to the skull so the cat would tolerate them for long periods. He had to develop the electrodes, insulated wires one-hundredth of an inch in diameter, so that they would not damage the brain. Also he had to develop electrical stimulation to excite the brain tissue in these deep sites, since the stimulation that had traditionally been used in physiology was not suitable. Then, after the experiments were finished, the sites of stimulation had to be verified by marking thin slices of the brain for examination under the microscope to find where the stimulating tips of the electrodes had been. Maps of the brain had to be prepared to help aim the electrodes and identify these sites. All this took time, but in the end Hess's experiments on freely moving animals were convincing.

Besides the many findings concerning the working of the autonomic nervous system, Hess's striking result for understanding emotions was this. When electrodes had been implanted into one part of the hypothalamus, stimulation produced a characteristic response: the heart speeded up, the cat became alert and aroused, and if the stimulation were continued it would become angry, even ferociously attacking objects in its environment. "Most often the cat in its defense/attack reaction turns against the nearest person participating in the experiment" (Hess & Brügger, 1943, p. 184). Hess called the reaction an "affective defense reaction," and suggested that one region of the hypothalamus was specialized to organize responses of fighting or fleeing. From another region of the hypothalamus further forward, stimulation slowed the heart and induced calmness and drowsiness.

What is striking about these results is that an initially meaningless train of electrical pulses is applied. The organization of part of the brain produces from it a well-coordinated, recognizable, emotional response characteristic of the species. It evidently depends on a motor program embodied in the brain. The program is not stereotyped, however: the angry attack is made in a skillful and directed way.

Now, after more than a century of analyses of effects of accidents to the brain in humans, and more than 50 years of experiments on the brains of animals, the following picture is widely agreed. Some areas of the brain such as the hypothalamus and the closely associated limbic system are said to be lower, in that they were prominent in animals that emerged earlier in the course of vertebrate evolution. These regions are associated with emotions. Ordinarily in mammals they are thought to be under the control of parts of the brain that are higher, and more recently evolved, such as the cerebral cortex which has reached its most extensive development in the human species. So, if the higher centers are damaged, as occurred with the frontal region of the unfortunate Phineas Gage, this control of the lower centers may no longer occur. Their activity may be exhibited in emotional behavior, uncontrolled and unsocialized.

The view was put succinctly by the Victorian neurologist John Hughlings-Jackson.

> The higher nervous arrangements evolved out of the lower, keep down those lower, just as a government evolved out of a nation controls and directs that nation. If this be the process of evolution then the reverse process of dissolution is not only a "taking off" of the higher, but is at the very same time "letting go" of the lower. If the governing body of this nation were destroyed suddenly we should have two causes for lamentation (1) the loss of the services of eminent men; and (2) the anarchy of the now uncontrolled people. (Taylor, 1959)

Jackson was an acute observer, and his schema was a compelling one. He proposed, for instance, that the unpredictable emotional behavior of drunkenness was a result of just such a "letting go" as he had postulated, as the higher centers are inactivated by alcohol. So we have an explanation of how a drunken person can at one moment be immersed in amiable sentimentality, and at the next caught up in a violent fight.

An engaging theme was abroad, proposed by Darwin's younger contemporary Haeckel (Sulloway, 1979). The slogan was "ontogeny recapitulates phylogeny." What this means is that development of each individual, starting with the embryo, goes through again the stages of evolution from the single cell onwards. Though biologists no longer think this is quite the way to look at embryological development, a version of the idea has become practically an orthodoxy in physiological explanations of behavior. The very lowest parts of the nervous system, such as the spinal cord and medulla, are concerned with simple reflexes — reflexes are characteristic of the evolutionarily oldest vertebrates. The behavior of human infants too is thought at first to be largely a set of reflexes. Layers in the middle of the brain were added next in evolution and they come next to mature in the brain of the developing individual. They include the hypothalamus and the limbic system. These are concerned with emotions, such as becoming angry, and with delivering the organized patterns of action such as those of attack described by Hess. Such patterns are characteristic of lower mammals, and of young children, not yet socialized. Finally there has evolved the cortex — the topmost layer. In human adulthood this region, devoted as it is thought to higher mental processes, takes control over the reflex and emotional centers below it.

In 1949 Hess was awarded a Nobel Prize for Medicine and Physiology "for the discovery of the functional organization of the diencephalon for the coordination of internal organs." It is an odd quirk of history that he shared the prize with Egas Moniz who had developed the operation of prefrontal leucotomy for the relief of certain psychoses. In this operation the surgeon caused effects similar to those that the iron tamping rod had performed accidentally on poor Phineas Gage. For a while, before the advent of modern drugs in psychiatry, prefrontal leucotomy was popular as a means of calming certain emotionally agitated psychiatric patients. Between 1936 and 1955 it has been estimated that 40,000 to 50,000 people were given this operation (Freeman, 1971). You may think it odd that the effect of calming, which the surgeons intended in such operations, was the opposite of the effect that the injury had on Phineas Gage. Probably the common element was an emotional blunting, a distancing of the self from emotional consequences. By the 1960s prefrontal leucotomy fell into disuse, indeed into disgrace (Valenstein, 1973). Large-scale destructive operations (though not more localized removals of brain tissue) have now been abandoned. Though the human brain withstands damage quite remarkably, it is too complex to be benefited by destruction of substantial parts of it.

Magda Arnold and Sylvan Tomkins: new psychological theories

> *. . . emotions involve a double reference, both to the object and to the self experiencing the object.*
>
> *Magda Arnold and J. Gasson, 1954*

> *It is my intention to reopen issues which have long remained in disrepute in American psychology.*
>
> *Sylvan Tomkins, 1962*

In the second half of the twentieth century, faintly at first, voices were heard expressing concerns that emotions had been neglected in the academy. Among the voices were those of Magda Arnold and Sylvan Tomkins; in 1954 both published something significant. Arnold (with J. Gasson, 1954) proposed that emotions are based on appraising events, and Tomkins proposed an idea that gave priority to research on emotional expressions of the face.

"Appraisal" in modern research on emotions is the idea that any emotion is based on evaluating an event. If we know what appraisals (or evaluations) are made we can predict the emotion; and if we know what the emotion is we can describe the appraisals. Frijda has written: "Appraisal is the central issue in emotion theory" (1993b, p. 225). Many would agree.

Here is the idea: Arnold and Gasson proposed that an emotion relates self to object. Unlike perception, which is about how we know what is out there, or personality, which is about what each of us is like in ourselves, emotions are essentially relational. Arnold and Gasson put it like this: "An emotion . . . is a felt tendency toward an object judged suitable, or away from an object judged unsuitable, reinforced by specific bodily changes according to the type of emotion" (1954, p. 294). Though appraisal is not far removed from Aristotle's idea of evaluation the idea of relational appraisals gave rise to a whole new way of thinking.

Arnold and Gasson say more about their idea. The felt tendency is the attraction to, or repulsion from, some object. The judgment (conscious or unconscious) is that the object is suitable or unsuitable to the self, so that the emotion becomes positive or negative accordingly. Then come further distinctions, depending on whether the object is present or not, and whether there are difficulties in acting. If there is no difficulty in attaining or avoiding an object, then the person simply tends towards or away from it, and they call such emotions "impulsive"; if there are difficulties then Arnold and Gasson call these "emotions of contention." On the basis of such distinctions they propose a table of positive and negative emotions, each defined according to its characteristic appraisals. So if an object is judged suitable and if it is present, then the impulse emotion is love; if an object is judged unsuitable and is not present, then the contending emotion is fear. The idea was taken up by Lazarus (1966) in a formulation of the transactions of people with their environments which has had wide theoretical and practical application to the idea of stress and illness, and more recently many experimenters have looked to see exactly what appraisals are made in what circumstance, and how they map onto emotions.

Like Magda Arnold, Sylvan Tomkins saw emotions as central to human life. His hypotheses, founded on the idea of feedback (from control theory) and the functions of emotions and of consciousness, were first proposed at a meeting of the International Congress of Psychology in 1954. The theory began to emerge in full in 1962, and a book of his selected works has been published (1995).

Tomkins's writing is discursive, thought-provoking, pushing into new territory – and difficult to summarize. But several of his concepts have attained wide currency. The main one is his idea that affect is the primary motivational system – the central concept of this idea is that emotions are amplifiers. It had been thought in psychology that the problem of motivation was solved by the idea of drives, such as hunger, thirst, and sex. Not so, argued Tomkins: "This is a radical error. The intensity, the urgency, the imperiousness, the 'umph' of drives is an illusion. The illusion is created by the misidentification of the drive 'signal' with its 'amplifier.' Its amplifier is its affective response" (Tomkins, 1970, p. 101). Tomkins's image was of a number of motivational systems, each capable of fulfilling a certain function (eating, breathing, sex), each potentially capable of competing with the others and taking over the whole person. What is it that gives the priority? It is emotion. It does so by amplifying one particular drive signal, just as loudness of sound on an audio system is amplified by turning up a control which adjusts its volume.

Here are two of Tomkins's illustrations. First: when, for any reason, there is some sudden obstruction to breathing, as when drowning or choking, it is not the shortness of oxygen that is obvious, it is a panicky fear that amplifies the drive signal making us struggle to breathe again. Those pilots in World War II who refused to wear oxygen masks also suffered lack of oxygen, but slowly. The effect was not unpleasant; it was pleasant. The signal was not amplified, and some of these pilots died with smiles on their lips. Second: when we are sexually excited, it is not the sexual organs that become emotionally excited, though distinct changes take place in them. It is the person who is excited, moving towards the other person and to fulfillment. What the bodily changes do is to amplify the sexual drive, making it urgent, and taking priority over other matters.

Tomkins went on to argue that the face and its expressions are the primary amplifiers of emotions in humans. The physiological changes of blood flow and muscle movements snowball to direct attention to some particular need or goal. So it has come about that the face has become a focus of research on emotions: two of those whose work has this focus, Paul Ekman and Carroll Izard, both trace the inspiration of their research to Tomkins.

Arnold, with her idea of appraisal, can be seen as focusing largely on inputs, on the perceptual side. Tomkins, with his idea of bodily feedback and priorities among drives focused on outputs, on the motor side. What they had in common was a concept of emotion as central to normal functioning, which made possible a new era of research.

Alice Isen and Gordon Bower: experimenting on effects of emotions

> *The warm glow of success*
>
> *From the title of a paper by Alice Isen, 1970*

Experimental psychology has been the dominant movement in psychological research for most of this century. Emotions did not entirely escape attention. Among the earliest experiments were Pavlov's (1927) studies of conditioning in animals. Though often described in other terms, these really concern emotions – we discuss Pavlov's method and its implications in chapter 5.

On humans too, there has been a variety of approaches to experimentation, some of them used to test hypotheses about bodily changes of emotion as predicted by James's theory discussed earlier in the chapter (Ruckmick, 1936).

What has happened more recently is that there has been an upsurge of a newer kind of human experimental work, not just on emotions themselves but on their effects. One of the pioneers here is Alice Isen. In an early experiment (1970) she gave a test of perceptual-motor skills. Some people, randomly selected, were told that they had succeeded in this test. As a result they were mildly happy. Isen looked at the effects of this emotion. As compared with other subjects who had taken the same perceptual motor test but who were not told they had succeeded, they were more likely to help a stranger (an associate of the experimenter) who dropped her books.

Perhaps the most striking of Isen's experiments, however, came not on social responses such as helping people – but on what might be thought of as cognitive effects. Isen et al. (1978) induced a mildly happy mood in people in a shopping mall by giving them a free gift. In an apparently unrelated consumer survey these people said their cars and television sets performed better and had required fewer repairs than those of control subjects who had received no gift. Isen has gone on to show that happiness has rather widespread effects on cognitive organization (Isen et al., 1978). It can make people more creative in problem solving, and induce them to give more unusual associations to words. A summary of results of Isen and her colleagues is presented in table 1.2.

Table 1.2 Examples of effects found by Isen and her associates in which happiness was induced. In each study comparisons were made with effects of neutral and/or negative moods. Except for the children in the developmental studies described in Isen (1990) the subjects were adults, typically university students

Study	Method of induction	Effect of induction
Isen, 1970	Told of skill success	Larger donation to charity, and help stranger
Isen & Levin, 1972	Given cookies	More helpful, less annoying in library
Isen et al., 1978	Free gift	Better recall of positive memories Report fewer problems with consumer goods
Isen et al., 1985	Positive word association and two other methods	More unusual word associations
Carnevale & Isen, 1986	Cartoons and gift	Integrative bargaining, less contentiousness
Isen & Geva, 1987	Bag of candy	More cautious about loss when risk is high, less cautious about loss when risk is low
Isen et al., 1987	Comedy film or candy	Better creative problem solving
Kraiger, Billings, & Isen, 1989	Watching TV bloopers	More satisfaction in performing task
Isen, 1990	"Stickers" for children	More advanced developmental levels
Isen et al., 1991	Told of anagram success	Faster clinical diagnosis, extra interest in patients

In the late 1970s Gordon Bower also began to study effects of mood on remembering and other kinds of cognitive performance. In an article that became very well known (Bower, 1981) he reported a large number of experiments on effects of inducing happiness and sadness. Bower used hypnosis in some of his studies, but other forms of induction are also widely used, and seem to have equivalent effects: some are mentioned in table 1.2, others involve having people read 60 happy or sad statements about themselves (Velten, 1968), yet others involve having subjects listen to happy and sad pieces of music (Niedenthal & Setterlund, 1994).

In one study, Bower asked his subjects to recall incidents of any kind from their childhood before age 15, hopping around in their memory for 10 minutes or so and saying a sentence or two about each incident. The next day, in a neutral mood, the subjects were asked to consider each incident, and categorize it as pleasant, unpleasant, or neutral. On the day after the categorization, a happy or sad mood was induced in each subject. Subjects with induced happiness had a large tendency to remember incidents they had categorized as happy, but they remembered only a few of the incidents they had categorized as sad. Subjects whose mood was sad had a slightly greater tendency to remember sad incidents as compared to happy ones, see figure 1.7.

The usual explanation of such results is mood-congruent recall: in Isen et al.'s (1978) experiment with the consumer survey more positive experiences came to mind relating to cars, television sets, and so forth when in a happy mood, and in Bower's experiment too more happy childhood memories came to mind when the subjects were happy.

Here are effects from two more of Bower's studies. In one he investigated the effects of mood on people's interpretations of pictures from the Thematic Apperception Test (TAT). In these tests people are shown pictures with

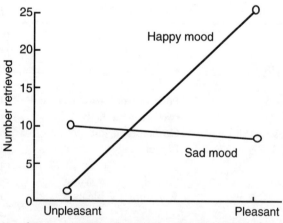

Figure 1.7 Results of Bower's study of people's memories from before the age of 15. The figure shows the number of items recalled by subjects when a happy or sad mood had been induced by hypnosis. When in the happy mood they remembered many more of the memories they had previously categorized as pleasant. When in a sad mood they recalled slightly more unpleasant memories.

meanings that are ambiguous, and asked to describe them. So, for instance one subject with a happy induction said of a picture of a woman looking out over fields: "This lady is looking over the beautiful country. The lady has wandered here from a campsite nearby and is soaking in the beauty of the surroundings. She has never felt as good as this before . . ." (Bower, 1981). In another experiment subjects had happy or sad moods induced and read a story which involved two protagonists, one happy and one sad, getting together and playing a friendly game of tennis. Then next day they recalled the story in a neutral mood. The people who had read the story while happy identified with the happy character in the story, and recalled more facts about him than about the other. Those who read the story when sad identified with the sad character, and remembered more facts about him.

The experiments of Isen and Bower not only show that emotions can have quite large effects on memory, social interaction, interpretation, and so on. They have also prompted psychologists working on clinical issues to explore whether these mechanisms could account for the persistence of moods in psychiatric syndromes. The selective bringing to mind of sad incidents when in a sad mood may have important effects in the persistence of depression (see chapter 11) as well as offering clues as to what kinds of therapy might be able to affect persistent moods (see chapter 12).

Erving Goffman and Arlie Russell Hochschild: the dramaturgical perspective

Create alarm
> Slogan on an office wall of a debt-collecting agency

Erving Goffman proposed that when Shakespeare wrote "all the world's a stage" (in *As You Like It*, 1623) this was not just metaphor: we literally give dramatic presentations of ourselves to each other, and create the social reality in which we live as a kind of performance. From such performances moral worlds are created, in them we derive our own selfhood, and from them others derive their sense of who we are.

For understanding emotions, perhaps Goffman's most instructive work is the essay "Fun in games," published in his book *Encounters* (1961). It is one of the most important analyses since Aristotle of the nature of happiness. It is also a reworking in social terms of Freud's *The Psychopathology of Everyday Life* (1901). It explores the psychology of role and the way in which we misunderstand emotions if we think of them as merely individual: they are frequently, perhaps predominantly, social.

We can think of each kind of social interaction, in a shop, in the workplace, in the family, as like a game, says Goffman. It is as if the various games that have been invented – chess, Monopoly, tennis – are simplified versions of types of social interaction. Within each kind of game we can experiment, making mistakes and trying again without the consequences that mistakes have in real life. When we enter into any kind of interaction, in a game or real life, it is as if we pass through a membrane into a little world with its own rules, its own traditions, its own history. We take on the role that is afforded to us in that kind of interaction – in a game of tennis perhaps we serve first, in ordinary life perhaps our role is to be a student. Within the membrane, then, we give a certain kind of performance to sustain our role, following the outline rules or scripts that are relevant within that membrane. So in tennis we try to hit the ball over the net, as a student we try to learn. These performances are viewed by ourselves and others as good or bad of their kind, as correct, incorrect, or partially correct. They invite commentary from others – including suggested modifications, blame, and praise. In other words the distinctive rules within each kind of membrane provide for moral worlds which are the subject of much of our conversation: "He needs to work on that backhand," or "Isn't it great? She got an A average this year!"

Now comes Goffman's insight into emotions: as well as giving a more or less good performance we can ask how strongly engaged we become in a role. Games are fun because they are social interactions in which we can easily become wholeheartedly engaged. By extension we can see that happiness occurs more generally when we are engaged fully in what we are doing. But in much of life there can be inner conflict: we can follow the rules, enact the script, but not be engaged. We might prefer to be doing something else. Then occur some of the painful and unsatisfying aspects of our lives.

Arlie Hochschild went to Berkeley to work as a graduate student, and was influenced by Goffman. In her work she explores the tension that may occur when the person is in conflict about the role he or she plays, when there are questions about who one is in oneself, and the performance one is giving.

Hochschild's parents were in the US Foreign Service, and she describes how at the age of 12 she found herself passing round a dish of peanuts at a diplomatic party and wondering whether the smiles of those who accepted her offerings were real. Her parents had an interest in gestures, and would discuss and interpret the "tight smile of the Bulgarian emissary, the averted glance of the Chinese consul, and the prolonged handshake of the French economic officer" (Hochschild, 1983, p. ix). These gestures did not just convey meaning from one person to another – they were messages between governments. Had the 12-year-old just passed peanuts to actors playing prescribed diplomatic roles? Where did the person end and the job begin?

As a graduate student Hochschild continued searching for answers to this problem: do sales people sell the product, or their personalities? She developed a theory of "emotion rules." They can be private and unconscious, or socially engineered in occupations that require us to send signals to others to influence their emotions and judgments.

Hochschild studied the training of Delta Airlines cabin staff, which includes learning how to operate the aircraft, how to act in emergencies, how to serve food, and so on. But what Hochschild described was how in becoming a Delta

stewardess one had to learn to give a particular kind
trainee had to learn to play a role, much as she would if
The main aim of this role is to induce a particular kind of
the passengers: "Trainees were exhorted: to 'Really work on y
your smile is your biggest asset'" (Hochschild, 1983, p. 105). They
to think of a passenger as if he were a 'personal guest in your living
workers' emotional memories of offering personal hospitality were c
and put to use, as Stanislavski would recommend" (p. 105). The appro
that of method acting: both the technique of practicing particular express
and recalling memories to aid performances are part of the exacting training fo
a part that Stanislavski (1965) recommended to professional actors. It is easier
to give a convincing performance if one fully enters into the part.

Work which involves constructing emotions in oneself in order to induce
them in others is quite widespread: Hochschild calls it emotional labor. She
calculated that in 1970, 38 percent of all paid jobs in the USA required
substantial amounts of emotional labor. Within the job categories that called
for such labor there were roughly twice as many women as men. The purposes
served are social. The job of secretary requires amiability, cheerfulness,
helpfulness: its purpose includes providing pleasant emotional support for the
boss. Many jobs requiring emotional labor are at interfaces between companies
and customers. As in the airline business, often their purpose is to sell more of
the company's product.

Not all jobs requiring emotional labor are intended to induce pleasant
emotions. Being a debt collector is something like the opposite of being an
airline stewardess: "Create alarm" was the motto of one debt-collecting agency
boss (Hochschild, 1983, p. 146).

Though Goffman, in an echo of Spinoza, may convince us that being
engaged wholeheartedly in what we are doing is the secret of happiness,
Hochschild raises a question. What if the performance we are paid to give in
our job is at variance with anything we can become fully engaged in?

Drawing together some threads

In this first chapter we have started some lines of thinking about emotions.
This chapter is not intended as the first actions in a story – these come in the
next chapter. Its function is to lay out some of the intellectual furniture of this
area.

Lots of readers of the literature on emotions remark on its diversity, throw
up their hands, conclude that the field is too heterogeneous to make sense of.
We (the authors) do not see it like this. There is diversity, but we hope to show
that these approaches complement each other, and that a unity can be
discerned.

We believe also that it can be helpful for you, as reader, to start by
identifying with just one or a few pioneers, whose interests and insights accord

your own intuitions. What we hope to have done here is to provide a sufficient array of such pioneers to make this possible for you. Then the insights of one of these can be used as a starting point. You can assimilate new information in relation to it, and start to build a structure from this base.

Not everyone who has been a pioneer appears here. We have chosen just some who have initiated a genre of research or thinking, not necessarily those who have made it important. So for instance, John Bowlby and Mary Ainsworth have arguably been more important than anyone else in the last 20 years to our understanding of emotional development in infancy. Their work derives from Freud's, and they do not appear in this chapter, but their research is treated fully in chapter 7. Some who have been most formative for the writers personally, for example, Herbert Simon, Michael Rutter, and George Brown, similarly are not met until later chapters. The story of this book proper starts with the next chapter: are emotions different or the same in different kinds of society?

Summary

In this chapter some of the men and women who laid foundations for understanding emotions in the Western intellectual tradition are introduced, each with some of their most important ideas. There are many different approaches to understanding emotions: the founders included among their methods naturalistic observation (Charles Darwin), proposing and testing theories by examples and counterexamples (William James), and listening carefully to what people say about emotional experiences (Sigmund Freud).

Many insights into emotions have been described and communicated not by people with any aspiration to be scientists, but by philosophers such as Aristotle, René Descartes and Baruch Spinoza, and by novelists such as George Eliot. Modern emotion research is represented in many disciplines of natural and social science: as well as psychologists (Magda Arnold, Sylvan Tomkins, Alice Isen, Gordon Bower), researchers in anthropology (Erving Goffman), in sociology (Arlie Hochschild), in medicine (John Harlow), and neurophysiology (Walter Hess), have each started important new approaches – as indeed have people in other disciplines. We are unlikely to be able to understand emotions or their significance without paying attention to the multidisciplinary nature of understanding.

Further Reading

The best general and comprehensive introduction to emotions, with chapters on interdisciplinary foundations of research in emotions, biological bases, psychological processes, social processes, and selected specific emotions, is:

Michael Lewis & Jeannette M. Haviland (Eds.) (1993) *Handbook of emotions.* New York: Guilford.

A book that ranges across the diverse approaches to emotions that we have introduced in this chapter – including sociology, psychology, philosophy, narrative literature – while integrating these different approaches is:

Thomas J. Scheff (1990). *Microsociology: Discourse, emotion, and social structure*. Chicago: University of Chicago Press.

For a brief history of emotion research:

George Mandler (1984). *Mind and body: Psychology of emotions and stress*. New York: Norton, chapter 2 "The psychology of emotion: Past and present."

For an engaging general account of emotions and their properties:

Nico Frijda (1988). The laws of emotion. *American Psychologist*, 43, 349–358.

Cultural Understandings of Emotions

Figure 2.0 Two bronze figurines from the Han dynasty in China, made more than 2,000 years ago, probably representing people from alien northern tribes.

... there is a kind of universal language, consisting of expressions of the face and eyes, gestures and tones of voice, which can show whether a person means to ask for something and get it, or refuse it and have nothing to do with it.

Augustine, *Confessions*, 1–8

The cultural context

There is a suspicion in Western culture that there is something wrong with emotions. The idea goes back at least to Plato (375 BCE) who thought that emotions are to be distrusted because they arise from the lower part of the mind and pervert reason. The distrust was brought into the modern era by Darwin (1872) who implied that, in human adults, expressions of emotions are obsolete, vestiges of our evolution from the beasts and of our development from infancy.

It is not difficult to detect a disparaging attitude to emotions within Western culture: if in a discussion you want to dismiss what another person says you can say that person is just being "emotional," meaning in this context "irrational." Emotions are often considered as out of control and destructive, in comparison with the constructive products of thoughtful consideration. Emotions are also sometimes seen as primitive and childish rather than civilized and adult. But, contradicting all this, and in the end even more tellingly, emotions are seen as the very guarantee of authenticity, our best guide to our true selves. As Solomon (1977) has put it: "Emotions are the life force of the soul, the source of most of our values" (p. 14).

Both distrust of emotions and affirmation of their value are constructions of Western culture. We see this from the fact that neither the distrust nor the affirmation, nor their paradoxical mixture that we in Western society are brought up with, is universal. In some other societies emotions are seen differently. So we present some scenes from emotional life in which there are similarities with present-day Western societies, and some differences. We will do this in two ways, with some historical materials so that we can see how some Western beliefs and experiences of emotion emerged, and by comparison with contemporary non-Western cultures.

Romanticism

Let us look at some recent cultural history to get some hints as to how present-day Western ideas about emotions arose and have been maintained. The eighteenth century in Europe was an age of enlightenment, when scientific understanding of the universe advanced with Newton's laws, and when intolerance began to be an object of shame in public life, a process that led to its reduction. Civilized reason became the ideal. Kant (1784) expressed it like this: "Dare to reason, have the courage to use your own minds" (p. 263).

By the time Kant wrote this another change was occurring, more or less in self-conscious reaction to enlightenment themes – it was called "romanticism." In Europe and America, despite potential contradictions of some of our cultural beliefs about emotions, "romantic" is probably still an appropriate term for Western cultural style. Romanticism is an affirmation of emotions and their implications in personal life, in politics, in literature, in philosophy. By 1800 romanticism had become firmly part of Western culture, more or less inseparable from ideas of individual freedom.

It was Jean-Jacques Rousseau (1755), an impoverished citizen of Geneva, who is generally credited with the articulation of the romantic spirit. That his ideas found ready acceptance meant that people were prepared for the shift in values that he proposed. He it was who first published the idea, now considered obvious, that religious sensibility is based on how you feel rather than on authority, or on scripture, or on arguments for the existence of God. He it was who began to attack cultivated pursuits as artificial and corrupting: he proposed instead that education should be natural, and that people's natural emotions indicate what is right – they have merely to be alive to the feelings of their conscience. His ringing phrase from the beginning of *The Social Contract* (1762) "Man is born free, and is everywhere in chains" became a rallying call for the Jacobins in the French Revolution, and such thoughts also crossed the Atlantic to help fuel the American War of Independence.

Romanticism inspired writers, who can be thought of as continuing to articulate the cultural changes that were occurring. The romantics were fascinated by the natural. Wild scenery, previously thought frightening and barbarous, began to be valued. Writers began to explore the worlds of ordinary life, rather than the lives of aristocrats. They explored childhood, dreams, far-away places, the exotic. Writing itself became a way of discovering inner emotional truths. And, rather than reason, it was emotion, experienced and accepted, that became the ideal. Emotions were expressed by poets, novelists, and dramatists, as well as by painters, and musicians. Readers, audiences, viewers, listeners, too were moved; they too experienced emotions. Remember George Eliot's new social science (discussed in chapter 1) in which the experience of emotions became central.

Rather than giving a history of romanticism let us consider just one romantic novel – by Mary Shelley, daughter of the famous feminist Mary Wollstonecraft and the social reformer William Godwin. At the age of 16 she eloped with the poet Percy Bysshe Shelley. When she was 18, Mary with Percy, her step-sister Claire, Lord Byron, and another friend, were on holiday during an "ungenial" summer in the Alps. Incessant rain confined them to the house for days. They read a great deal, and had long conversations on literature, philosophy, and biology. One day Byron suggested that each should write a ghost story. Retiring to bed Mary Shelley could not sleep. Prompted by a conversation about experiments in which electricity was used to stimulate muscle movements in dead creatures, there rose to her mind an image of a scientist with a powerful engine beside him, kneeling over a hideous phantasm

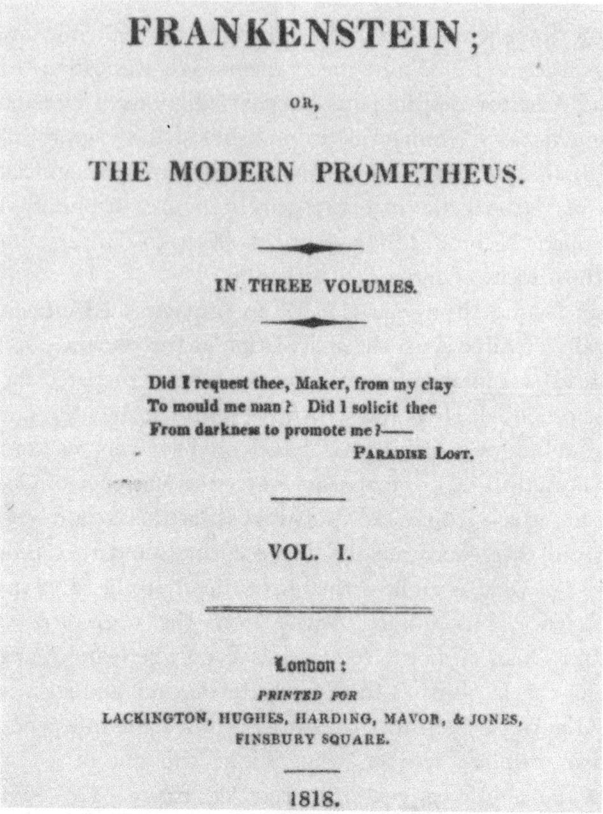

> # FRANKENSTEIN;
>
> OR,
>
> ## THE MODERN PROMETHEUS.
>
> ———
>
> IN THREE VOLUMES.
>
> ———
>
> Did I request thee, Maker, from my clay
> To mould me man? Did I solicit thee
> From darkness to promote me?——
>   PARADISE LOST.
>
> ———
>
> VOL. I.
>
> ———
>
> London:
> PRINTED FOR
> LACKINGTON, HUGHES, HARDING, MAVOR, & JONES,
> FINSBURY SQUARE.
>
> ———
>
> 1818.

Figure 2.1 Title-page of Volume I of the first edition of *Frankenstein*, written by Mary Wollstonecraft Shelley but originally published anonymously – it was one of the first novels of the English romantic period, stressing emotions and their effects.

of a man that he had put together. Her story became *Frankenstein* (1818), one of the earliest English romantic novels, and one of the world's first science fiction stories.

Box 2.1 Mary Shelley's romantic novel *Frankenstein*

The novel is about Victor Frankenstein, an idealistic scientist who discovers how to imbue dead matter with life. He collects body parts from charnel houses and constructs an artificial man, eight feet tall. He had meant him to be beautiful but "his yellow skin scarcely covered the work of the muscles and arteries" (p. 105). After years of hard work driven by the excitement of research he infuses the spark of life – then rushes from the room in disgust as the thing begins to move. In exhaustion he tries to sleep – he dreams joyfully of meeting his loved one in the street, and they kiss: with this gesture her lips "became livid with the hue of death, her features appeared to change, and I thought that I held the corpse of my dead mother in my arms" (p. 106).

With this surprisingly modern image of an incestuous abuse of nature, Frankenstein wakes. He goes upstairs again to his laboratory. The creature rises and stretches out its hand as if to detain its creator. Frankenstein again rushes from the room. When the creature's face was at rest it was ugly, but with animation it became a vision from Hell.

After two years and a long illness Frankenstein returns to his family in Geneva to find that a child, his brother, has been murdered. He glimpses his creature in the woods, and guesses that it had done the deed. A servant girl is convicted of the crime, and dies for it. In a torment of guilt Frankenstein tries to find solace by escaping to the Alps, but the creature finds him amid the majestic scenery. The creature declares devotion to his creator. He tells of his escape from Frankenstein's laboratory. In his first meetings with humans he has been repelled in fear and loathing. He took refuge in a disused hovel that leant against the wall of a peasant's cottage. Through a chink he observed the cottagers, a young woman, a youth, and a blind old man, a sister and brother with their father. When the old man smiled at the young woman with kindness and affection, the creature "felt sensations of a peculiar and overpowering nature, such as [he] had never before experienced, either from hunger or cold, warmth or food, and withdrew from the window, unable to bear these emotions" (pp. 153–154).

Over the months, while keeping concealed, the creature collects wood and does other tasks for the family. Painstakingly he learns their language and social customs. In an innocence that reflects Mary Shelley's close reading of Rousseau, he comes to feel natural benevolence and love for the cottagers in their simple life. After a year he visits the blind old man when the others are out. He starts to explain that though he looks frightening he wishes them only well; he is their "good spirit" who has helped them, he desires their friendship. The old man listens – but the others return and are horrified. The youth beats the creature, who rushes off in impotent despair. Next day the family abandons their cottage. That night during a gale, the creature rages and sets fire to his hovel and to the cottage.

The creature wanders that winter in bitterness, but in the spring feels benevolence returning. He decides to find his creator. In Geneva he comes across a small boy, and approaches him thinking that the child would be too young to feel prejudice. But the child is alarmed, calls him an ogre and threatens that his father, "Monsieur Frankenstein," will punish him. The creature strangles the boy – prompted by rage at hearing the family name of the man who has been responsible for his disfigurement.

Days later the creature catches up with Frankenstein in the Alps. He says he will always be shunned by human beings. He owns that he has become wicked, but it is because he is utterly wretched; it is intolerable to be so despised. His emotions of kindness have turned to rage in response to the hatred directed at himself. So his creator must make another creature, a female, equally deformed, with whom he can live in sympathy. "If any being felt emotions of benevolence towards me," the creature says, "I should return them a hundred and a hundredfold . . . cut off from all the world our lives will not be happy, but they will be harmless . . ." (p. 191).

Frankenstein is horrified by his dilemma: should he risk creating another monster so that two of them could wreak havoc, or should he gratify the wish of this creature who seeks the indulgence of his creator?

Frankenstein is still an exciting novel to read; thought-provoking in these days of robots and artificial intelligence, of our exploitation of natural resources and the construction of ever more clever but risky technological systems (Perrow, 1984). In the novel are many of the themes of romantic thought: settings amid wild scenery, appeal to emotions as causes of action, the emphasis on the natural, distrust of the artificial, and apprehension of humans arrogantly overstepping their boundaries.

The values of romanticism were not those of European culture before the eighteenth century. In Shelley's novel we can see many of these values made explicit; they are still with us. We experience emotions as reasons for much of what we do.

Comparing ourselves with people of other cultures

There are several windows onto culture. One is historical, reading documents from the past – comparing writings such as those of Mary Shelley with what came before, and with what we believe now. Another is from travelers such as anthropologists who bring back news of contemporary cultures different from our own. Yet another is by studying socialization, how children acquire the beliefs and skills of society. In this book we will take "our" cultural history to be that of North America and Europe, since that is the tradition in which the authors of this book (one English and the other American) have been brought up, and about which we have first-hand knowledge. To understand emotions – your own, those of the other people you know well, those of people in different societies – you need to locate yourself within your own cultural tradition. Since the majority of readers of this book will be North American and European, we begin with Western culture. But it is only a starting point, and a crude one at that because Europe and America house a great many cultures. We do not think our culture preeminent. If we were Japanese or Indian we would write this chapter and some other sections of the book differently. There is no fixed point on which to stand outside cultural tradition.

Nor are we arguing that culture contradicts rationality: rather, among the many values that any human society can adopt, some are chosen rather than others. For instance, we have suggested that North America is still in many ways romantic. In the last 20 years environmentalist concerns have become strong. They fit closely with romantic attitudes and values affirming the natural, but this does not mean these concerns are irrational.

East and West

Let us consider the emotional atmosphere of a non-Western society, Japan, which is based, like the Western one, on a money economy. Differences are not due to different degrees of industrial progress, literacy, or suchlike: nevertheless Euro-American and Japanese emotional climates do differ. The main contrast noted both by Western and Japanese observers is in the nature of the self. In the West we conceptualize the self as an "I-self" (Lewis, 1992), an autonomous entity, the source of decisions, thoughts, and actions, as well as the center of experience of emotions. This self is separate from other selves. In this society it is important to become independent, to assert the self, to contend against other selves if necessary.

By contrast, in Japan and many non-Western cultures, although this account is no doubt oversimplified, many commentators have described the self as a "We-self," deriving from connections with family, colleagues, and the social group. It is more important to fit in with others and live in harmony with them (Markus & Kitayama, 1991). Lest we think that the independent "I," deriving authenticity from its individual desires and emotions, is natural, we should reflect that this emphasis on the natural is itself part of the Western cultural heritage (see the previous section on romanticism). In terms of world cultures it is the individualistic self that is unusual (Geertz, 1975).

In every society children develop a sense of themselves as physically separate from the world. Neisser (1988) has proposed that this physical aspect should be called the "ecological self." In addition, people everywhere probably have a sense of a private mental life, including a stream of conscious thoughts, feelings, and dreams. But some other aspects of the self differ and affect emotional life. With an interdependent or We-self, thoughts and feelings focus not on being separate but on overlapping with others. Even in our individualistic society you can get a sense of this: when you fall in love you can experience the boundaries of yourself expanding to include the other person in your primary concerns, and becoming more of a "We" than an "I."

Anger in the West is an emotion of independence and self-assertion. In Japan, although it is thought appropriate between people from different social groups, for instance in the tradition of Samurai warfare in feudal Japan, Markus and Kitayama (1991) report that anger is considered highly inappropriate between relations or colleagues. By contrast, anger between Americans who know and like each other is relatively common and accepted. Averill (1982) found in Massachusetts, by means of people keeping diaries structured like questionnaires, that incidents of anger occurred about once a week. Most concerned someone the subject knew and liked (e.g., a spouse, parent, child, friend). Most (63 percent) subjects said the reason for their anger was to assert authority or independence, or improve their image. Miyake et al. (1986) found different effects of interpersonal anger in America and Japan from early in life. The experimenters showed interesting toys to American and Japanese infants of 11 months, pairing each toy with the mother's voice expressing joy, anger, or fear. Measuring the time it took for the infants to start moving towards the toy after hearing the mother's expression, American and Japanese infants were no different in how soon they moved after the sound of their mothers' joyful or fearful voices. After their mothers had spoken in an angry voice American infants started moving towards the toy an average of 18 seconds later, but Japanese infants took significantly longer, an average of 48 seconds, to start moving. Japanese babies were probably more inhibited by their mother's angry expressions because these were rare events.

Turning to a more positive emotion: in Japan there is an emotion *amae*, for which there is no simple translation in English (Morsbach & Tyler, 1986). *Amae* is an emotion of interdependence, arising from a kind of symbiosis, from comfort in the other person's complete acceptance. It is not that this emotion is unrecognizable in other cultures, or that it lacks universal significance. Rather, it has no clear place in adult Western life. Its original Chinese ideogram was of a breast on which the baby suckled. But as Westerners imagine this emotion, they know that one ought to have grown out of it. In Japan this is not so: this is an emotion of an accepting relationship within the family, and it is also valued as a mutual dependency between lovers. It has its own special word, and special cultural significance. In the West it would be considered regressed. It is an emotion not of separateness, but of merged togetherness.

Heelas (1986) takes readers on what he calls a Cook's tour of emotions in different societies. He proposes that in some cultures a particular emotion or cluster of emotions is recognized, has special names, and is the subject of social discussion. Such emotions are "hypercognized" (Levy, 1984), they are culturally emphasized. By contrast certain emotions seem to occur rarely or not at all in some cultures; they are not conceptualized or commented upon. They are "hypocognized." So emotions of dependence such as *amae* are hypercognized in Japan, hypocognized in America.

In the West our folk theory tends towards hypocognizance and suppression of fear. One source for such theory is advice manuals for parents: Stearns and Haggarty (1991) surveyed 84 such manuals published between 1850 and 1950, as well as popular literature aimed at children. Before 1900 three features stood out: warnings to parents about dangers of arousing fear in their children; silence on the subject of dealing with childhood fears; boys' stories aimed at inspiring courage in being ready to act properly despite fear. Then a change occurred: "Twentieth-century parents were told not only to avoid frightening their children as a disciplinary device but also to master their own emotions lest they give disturbing signals" (Stearns & Haggarty, 1991, p. 75). Dr Spock (1945) in his influential manual described childhood fears as requiring careful management. Separations from toddlers arouse fears, and are to be avoided. If fears occur they should be met with patience and affection. By the 1940s the boys' stories of acting well despite fear had disappeared, to be replaced by adventures in which tough guys felt no fear at all. In American society controlling fear has been important, first because it prevents one from being a good citizen, and latterly because it prevents one becoming an effective individual. As President Franklin Roosevelt famously put it in his 1933 inaugural address: "The only thing we have to fear is fear itself." In a transformation of the medieval idea of the last judgment, the Hollywood film *Defending your Life* depicts events after an earthly death in terms of a courtroom trial with lawyers. Instead of sin it is the judgment that fear has ruled a person's life that determines whether the person goes onwards, or back.

In the West it is thought that emotions, except for fear, are largely involuntary and that it is generally best to express them. Health risks are thought to attend suppression of other emotions and we become suspicious of someone who seems too emotionally controlled. By contrast, in Japan many emotions and bodily states are cultivated in some circumstances, but controlled in others. Matsumoto et al. (1988) found that Americans believed fear could be influenced. As compared with the Japanese, Americans thought anger and disgust were more involuntary.

In America individuals have rights. In interdependent cultures people have duties, and they experience themselves most completely in fulfilling them. As the anthropologist Benedict (1946) explained in a book written in the last year of World War II and commissioned by the US Government to help understand the Japanese who were the adversaries, to be sincere in America is to act in accord with one's innermost emotions. In Japan, the concept usually translated as sincerity, *makoto*, means something different: doing a social duty not according to inner feelings, but doing it completely, with expertise, without inner conflict. The concept may seem odd to some, but bridges can be built to this ideal: the concept of complete absorption in what one is doing has attracted Westerners to Zen, in which this ideal is cultivated. It is one of the several forms of Buddhism that flourish in Japan, see for instance Watts (1957).

In 1945, the Japanese in their surrender that ended World War II offered the condition that the Emperor would remain the head of state, but would be directed by the American administration. This was accepted. The Americans worked through existing Japanese government channels, and the Japanese were told by their Emperor that the war was finished, that militarism had been a mistake, and that they should now get on with the next task. They did indeed absorb themselves in this task. That the Japanese could do this astonished many Americans. In the West under such circumstances one might expect grudges, resistance, sabotage – continuations of an inner cause. But as Benedict explains, it was not astounding to the Japanese to take up their new duties. Japanese culture continued, and people continued to do their duty.

Emotions may provide a basis for human interaction, but differences such as those between America and Japan can lead to difficulties of communication. While Japanese can find American directness and assertion alarming, Americans can find the Japanese inscrutable. Now Japan has become the world's most successful industrial economy, we no longer see Americans trying to understand Japanese culture in order to see how to wage war. Instead we see Western business people trying to understand Japanese feelings and customs in order to trade, and to compete economically.

Emotional climates

The term "emotional climate," coined by De Rivera (1992), describes the mood of a cultural group or nation. It affects not only how one feels, but what can and cannot be done. For instance, in certain South and Central American countries people have been subjected to climates of fear by random acts of assassination and "disappearance." In such climates distrust multiplies, cooperation ceases. Even the interpretation of everyday objects changes: "a red traffic light which should mean 'stop', may no longer mean stop because it is when one stops that one is an easy target for gunfire" (De Rivera, 1992, p. 201).

In most industrialized countries the prevailing climate is one of inter-personal cooperation, conducive to the activities of urban societies: for the most part people who do not know each other interact peaceably. In this respect Japanese and American cities are similar. If you as a Westerner, never outside your own society, were transported to the middle of Tokyo with some travelers' checks, but without even a word of Japanese, you could live happily for a week there. You would be surprised by the absence of graffiti or vandalism, pleased that there was no threat of mugging (Tasker, 1987), surprised to see respectable young women walking alone without concern through the city at night, but much would be familiar. You could find your way, interact with people, and recognize much of what was going on. By contrast, if you were transported to a nonindustrialized society, more would be unfamiliar. Much more than travelers' checks would be needed.

Emotions on Ifaluk

One of the nonindustrialized societies that has been studied to understand its emotional life is that of Ifaluk, a tiny Pacific atoll about one fifth the size of New York's Central Park, with a population of 430 people. It was visited for nine months by Lutz (1988). She wrote that she wanted to see: "if and how it was possible for people to organize their lives in such a way as to avoid the problems that seemed to me to diminish American culture, in particular its pervasive inequality of both gender and class and its violence" (p. 17).

Ifaluk is a highly interdependent society. People have come to rely on each other on this island which has its highest point just a few yards above sea level and where typhoons not infrequently sweep the huts away, destroy the taro gardens, and deplete fish in the lagoon.

In her portrayal of Ifaluk, Lutz has been successful in three important ways, the combination of which is unprecedented in the anthropological literature. First, she went specifically to study not kinship, not religion, not economic relations . . . but emotional life. Secondly, because of her cultural sensitivity and her skill as a writer, she has been able to give what Geertz (1973) has called a "thick description," not just of what emotions occur but of the settings from which they arise with the cultural significance that derives from them. Thirdly, because none of us can become a member of another culture in a short visit during adulthood, Lutz does not describe how it feels to be an Ifalukian, but she developed another method. Instead of simply suffering from culture shock she made use of it. She herself was "an American female at a particular point in historical time" (p. 15). By paying attention to misunderstandings that arose between her and the Ifalukians, and on their emotional effects, she saw how cultural rules operated both in her own society and that of Ifaluk.

Here is an illustration of the American I-self and the Ifalukian We-self encountering each other. During her first weeks on the island Lutz asked some young women visiting her hut: "Do you (all) want to come with me to get drinking water?" (p. 88). Their faces fell. Lutz writes that it was not till later that she realized what had gone wrong. By addressing them as "you" she had implied a separation between them and her own decision-making I-self. She writes that a more correct form, indicating the We-self, would be something more like: "We'll go and get water now, OK?" implying that such decisions are collective.

Figure 2.2 An Ifaluk woman smiles as she makes an impromptu head-dress for her small son, while she rests after grating coconut. This kind of socially responsive smiling is of a lower intensity, and signals something different from *ker*, meaning "excited happiness," of which people on Ifaluk are suspicious because it implies ignoring the presence and needs of others.

There are noticeable differences between social meanings of emotion in America and Ifaluk. Take the Ifaluk *ker* for instance. Lutz translates this as "happiness/excitement." In America people believe that it is a truth self-evident that there is "a right . . . to the pursuit of happiness" (American Constitution). On Ifaluk people do not think they have any right to the pursuit of *ker*. They think instead that they should avoid it. *Ker* is not contentment or interpersonal pleasantness, which are common on Ifaluk. A person feeling *ker* is likely to be too pleased with him or herself. It can lead to showing off, perhaps even to rowdiness, behavior of which the Ifalukians disapprove. By contrast one should be "*maluwelu*, gentle, calm and quiet" (p. 112).

One day, sitting with another woman Lutz watched a five-year-old girl dancing and making silly faces, showing a bit of *ker*. Lutz thought this little girl was rather cute. "Don't smile at her," said her companion, "she'll think that you're not *song*" (p. 167). The woman was indicating that the girl was approaching the age at which she should have "social intelligence," the concern for others that is so valued on Ifaluk. The woman was indicating another of the tenets of emotional life on Ifaluk, that if Lutz were to look *song* (justifiably angry at a breach of social rules) the girl would stop displaying *ker* and showing off, with its risk of misbehavior. The girl should sit quietly, as good, socially intelligent people do. So *song* is not anger as we in the West tend to experience it, arising from violation of a right. It is people's social duty to express *song* if they notice anything that might disrupt social functioning. *Metagu* is the natural response to *song*, an anxious concern for others.

The differences between her own and Ifalukian culture caused Lutz to make many social mistakes. One night she was frightened by a man entering the doorless, individual hut that she had negotiated for herself. Her scream awakened her adopted family who came to see what was wrong. They were asleep a yard or two away in their communal hut, with each one's sleeping mat touching others so that no one would be lonely. The man had fled, and the family laughed hilariously when they heard Lutz had been alarmed by such an event. She said that she had been on the island long enough to know that men sometimes called on women at night for a sexual rendezvous. But she had imported the American idea that an uninvited visit from a man inevitably meant harm. On Ifaluk, Lutz says, although men may very occasionally seem frightening in public if drunk, so that others may fear that a disagreement might break out between them, interpersonal violence is virtually nonexistent, and rape unknown. Hence a night visitor means the very antithesis of fear. The incident became a topic of conversation. Though no one could understand why she had been frightened, Lutz sensed that her adopted mother showed some satisfaction in the story of the event because, although the anxiety that Lutz displayed was inappropriate, it was anxiety: her adopted mother thought that this meant that at last Lutz was capable of showing this valued emotion!

The most valued emotion, however, is *fago*, translated as "compassion/love/sadness." It is the primary index of positive relationships, including those with children, relatives, and sexual partners. It is felt particularly when loved ones are in need in some way, including when they are absent, since in this absence they will be separated from those on whom they depend. It expresses the sadness that a needful state implies, and the compassion that has transmitted this sadness to the more resourceful one.

Are there human universals of emotions?

The emotional climate of Ifaluk is different from New York, and from Tokyo. One of the difficulties in reading cross-cultural studies of emotion is to decide whether differences that ethnographers describe are deep or superficial. Two schools debate this question: universalists believe that fundamental emotions occur in all humans, relativists believe that emotions are specific to the cultures in which they occur. Relativists, who include Harré (1986), Heelas (1986), and Lutz (1988), find differences between cultures interesting and concentrate on them. Universalists, who include Ekman (1989), Brown (1991), and Shaver, Wu, and Schwartz (1992), find similarities more compelling.

Lutz says her book was meant to show that emotions on Ifaluk are different from those in America, cultural rather than natural – hence her book's title, *Unnatural Emotions*. She says that on Ifaluk people experience emotions not individually, as in America, but primarily as mediating social relationships. Although one can see differences, Shaver, Wu, and Schwartz (1992) compared concepts of emotion in the USA, Italy, and China. They put an argument for similarity. Just as on Ifaluk, in America too most emotions mediate social relationships – for instance love, happiness, anger, sadness; fear too is sometimes interpersonal. Lutz writes that on Ifaluk if some interpersonal problem is unresolved a person "will go to another with the express purpose of 'saying my thoughts/emotions so that they will leave me'" (p. 99). But the idea of speaking one's emotions to the person whom they concern occurs also in the West, where most emotions that are sufficiently salient to be remembered are spoken about to others (Rimé et al., 1991).

Part of the case for emotions as universals is that they can be recognized cross-culturally. Lutz's own emotions during her visit to Ifaluk, such as her smile when she watched the little girl make silly faces and her fear when a man came into her hut at night, were recognized by her hosts. And she recognized the emotions of Ifalukians: she saw the faces of the young women fall when she asked if they wanted to get water, and she made translations of Ifalukian emotional concepts for her English speaking readers.

The question is how fundamental are the similarities; how radical the differences? Partly it is a matter of emphasis. In reading and thinking for this book we have concluded that although there are substantial differences in emotional life in different cultures, and although in some cultures some emotions are hypercognized while others are hypocognized, emotional commonalities among peoples are larger than the differences.

If there were no cross-cultural commonality, if all emotions were culturally idiosyncratic, it would be hard to see how any emotional understandings could be possible between people of different societies. Trying to understand emotions in another society would be like a person trying to understand colors although suffering from the kind of color blindness that allows seeing only in black and white.

The fact that as writers of this book we have come to think there is a universal emotional basis does not mean that we devalue differences among cultures. It means that the old idea that one had to opt either for universalism or relativism is past. Just as there are universal anatomical traits of humanity such as a skeleton that supports upright walking, so there are universal psychological traits such as attachment between mothers and offspring, the ability to learn language, the sharing of food (Brown, 1991). In the realm of emotional life we no longer ask: "Is this due to nature or culture?" And, although popular in the days of behaviorism, the idea that the human mind is a *tabula rasa*, on which cultures can write anything whatsoever, is no longer tenable. Humans are genetically provided with a start-up program of innate patterns, distinctive abilities, and biases. In trying to understand emotions, we believe that there are innate bases, and we ask how they are built upon and differentiated by cultures.

Next, therefore, we consider some ways in which emotions might be similar or different among cultures and how hypotheses about similarities and differences might be tested.

Differences of elicitors and interpretations in different cultures

Although some emotions, for example, fear on meeting a bear or wild pig, might be universal others might be culturally specific. Some institutions in one society have no equivalent in another. Prison is seen as barbarous by members of some societies, and without police and prisons the emotions associated with them would not occur.

More subtle are emotions like jealousy (Salovey, 1991; Van Sommers, 1988). In the West jealousy tends to be felt when the sexual attention of a primary partner turns towards someone else. It is hard, perhaps impossible, to find societies in which jealousy does not occur at all, but at the same time social arrangements in different societies are various. As Hupka (1991) points out, in Western society marriage (leading to the two-parent family) is a social key to establishing one's adult status, economic security, housing, rearing of children, adult companionship, and sex. A sexual interloper threatens this whole structure, so in Western society such a person is jealously feared and hated. In some other, more clan-based, societies however, the sense of a We-self is more extended, cooperative effort supports everyone including the elderly, child-rearing is distributed among several people, adult companionship derives from many relatives, and extramarital recreational sex may be customary. So a sexual interloper would not threaten such a large and important structure. Hupka

(1991) discusses how when at the beginning of this century the Todas of India were visited by anthropologists, they lived in a society of this kind. They were not jealous when marriage partners had lovers from within their social group. But Toda men did become jealous if a wife had intercourse with a non-Toda man, and they became distressed in a similar way if a second-born son got married before the first born.

Like other emotions, jealousy depends on some universal characteristics. Hupka suggests that this universal is that people become jealous when something they value very much, and which has been hard to achieve, is threatened by an interloper. So for most Westerners deeply held values and beliefs are threatened by sexual infidelity. For Toda men comparable values are invested in their first-born child. Sexual intercourse is not private to marriage, and these deep beliefs are not, therefore, threatened by extramarital relationships.

So, although there may be emotional universals, what is universal may not be so obvious. It may lie at the level not of complex emotions like guilt, embarrassment, and jealousy, because the way in which events are interpreted can be so different. More possibly commonalities lie at the level of more basic emotions like fear, or interpersonal warmth and affection. There certainly are cross-cultural differences in emotions. What is appropriate in one society can be regarded incredulously in another — as was Lutz's fright when a man entered her hut at night.

There have been few systematic or quantitative comparisons of how emotions are elicited in different cultures. One that was aimed at investigating whether there may be some basic emotions, was by Boucher and Brandt (1981). They started with six terms derived from America, "anger, disgust, fear, happiness, sadness, and surprise" (p. 274) and with six corresponding emotion terms in Malay, "*marah, bosan, takut, gembira, sedeh*, and *hairan*" (p. 274). There was evidence that in Malay there were clusters of concepts around each of these terms — all these were hypercognized. Furthermore they were judged to be adequate translations of the English terms. The experimenters next asked 50 American students and 50 young adult Malay informants each to describe two situations in which one person caused another to feel each of the six emotions. Those that were not clearly interpersonal were excluded. The Malay situations were translated into English. From their pool of 1,200 eliciting situations, Boucher and Brandt randomly selected 96, with the constraints that only one situation could come from each informant and that there would be 16 situations for each emotion, half from American informants and half from Malaysian. The emotional situations from both cultures were then read by 18 students of the University of Hawaii. Of judgments of American situations, 65.8 percent were as intended by the original informants; of Malaysian situations, 68.9 percent were recognized as intended. In situations from both cultures occasions for fear and happiness were the most easily recognized (approximately 80 percent as intended), and occasions for anger the least easily recognized (53 percent as intended). Limitations of this study were that only two cultures were compared, and just a few emotions sampled. Moreover, the Malay culture was not completely isolated from Western influence.

In a more recent study Frijda and Mesquita (1994) describe how people from Turkey, from Surinam, and people of European Dutch origin, all living in the Netherlands, understood certain kinds of events, such as an acquaintance being inconsiderate, and a partner or intimate friend being inconsiderate. One might assume that universally such events cause negative emotions. As compared with the European Dutch, the Turkish and Surinamese respondents evaluated such incidents much more socially: they thought the offender would be more aware of the impact of the behavior, be more likely to have done it on purpose, be more likely to profit from the behavior. Frijda and Mesquita interpret this in relation to Markus and Kitayama's (1991) hypothesis that European culture stresses individuality – Dutch people believe that colleagues or even partners have their own plans and ideas and so might be unintentionally inconsiderate. In more interdependent cultures, such unawareness of the social effects of actions would be much more unlikely.

Display rules

One way of dealing both with universals and cultural variation has been postulated by Ekman (1972) in his neurocultural theory, the best known of the so-called "two-factor" theories of emotion (Fridlund, 1994), which derive from Tomkins' proposals (1995). One factor is universal and biological: there is a small set of fundamental emotions, such as happiness and anger, which can be experienced. If unimpeded they are expressed naturally in motor programs that include smiles, frowns, and so on. The other factor is specific to cultures: a set of display rules regulating when and where each expression should be intensified, suppressed, neutralized, or masked.

The basis for the display rule idea is a much-cited experiment by Ekman and Friesen. Because the experiment was published only in part, Fridlund (1994) reconstructed it from a preliminary report in Ekman's (1972) paper, and from Friesen's (1972) PhD thesis. Subjects were 25 American and 25 Japanese males, each in his own country. In Phase 1 subjects were alone and watched film clips of a canoe trip, a ritual circumcision, a suction-aided delivery of a baby, and nasal sinus surgery. In Phase 2 a graduate student from the subject's own society entered the room, and interviewed the subject briefly about his experience while viewing. In Phase 3, the interviewer remained, sitting with his back towards the screen and facing the subject, while the very unpleasant clip of nasal surgery was replayed and the interviewer asked the subject: "Tell me how you feel right now as you look at the film" (Fridlund, 1994, p. 288). In each phase subjects' facial expressions were videotaped, although they did not know this.

The reported results were that when they were alone, in Phase 1, American and Japanese subjects made similar facial expressions of fear and disgust at the same points in the films. But in Phase 3, facing the interviewer and the screen, the Japanese subjects smiled more and inhibited their negative expressions more than the Americans. When viewed in slow motion, the videotapes showed Japanese subjects beginning to make a facial expression of fear or disgust, but then masking it with a social smile in which they turned the corners of their lips upwards. Fridlund (1994) is critical of these conclusions. He argues that to be convincing the experimenters would have needed evidence that the Japanese subjects experienced the same emotions as the Americans while watching the film clip in Phase 3, while exaggerating smiles and suppressing negative expressions. Fridlund prefers the explanation that the Japanese subjects were more polite: they tended to look more at the interviewer rather than the film, and they smiled more at the interviewer.

Other researchers have postulated cultural rules for suppressing emotions, but they have derived their conclusions quite differently. Among the Chewong, a small group of aboriginal hunters and shifting cultivators in Malaysia, Howell (1981) concluded that prohibitions exist against all emotions with the exception of fear and shyness. Instead of emotions prompting people to act in this way or that, as seems to occur in many societies, the Chewong have explicit behavioral rules about what to do and what not to do in different circumstances. Penalties of severe bodily ills are believed to occur if rules are broken. The result is a society in which Howell says the people, though confident in their interactions with the environment, are emotionally inexpressive with each other. "They rarely use gestures of any kind, and their faces register little change as they speak and listen" (pp. 134–135). Howell concluded that emotions and their display are suppressed, and one gains the impression also that suppression involves the emotion of fear of consequences of expressing an emotion, though other anthropologists, such as Heelas (1986), suggest that emotions are not a salient part of life among the Chewong; because they are hypocognized they simply may not occur at all frequently.

Cultural construction and the social functions of emotion

The third category of cross-cultural distinctiveness is the most radical. It is that of cultural construction: the idea that because they derive from human meanings which are necessarily cultural, emotions are cultural products just like languages or works of art. One of the arguments, made strongly by Wierzbicka (1994), is that social scientists' ideas about emotions have been ethnocentric: Western researchers have tended to think about emotions like anger and love as they occur in their own culture, and then enquire about whether they exist or not in other cultures. But equally we could imagine a cross-cultural psychologist from Ifaluk or Japan visiting New York and enquiring about *fago* or *amae*.

Are all emotions cultural products? There are certainly some human universals, walking on two legs, using language and tools, but perhaps there are no universal emotions with equivalence across cultures. The argument is, for instance, that *fago* is distinctive to Ifaluk. Although it can be hinted at by describing how it arises, and indicated by a composite of English terms (compassion/love/sadness) you cannot experience the Ifaluk emotion *fago* unless you are a member of that society. Similarly, as Averill (1985) argues, you could not experience falling in love, with its mixture of sexual attraction, perception of the other person's beauty, a feeling of altruism, and the making of a commitment, unless you have been enculturated in the West.

This postulate is among the most controversial in cross-cultural studies of emotions. The difficulty with coming to any considered judgment is that universalists and relativists focus on different evidence, and on different interpretations of the same evidence. Russell (1991a), in a wide-ranging survey of concepts of emotion in different cultures, has concluded that there are cultural differences in such concepts, but also strong cross-cultural similarities: people in the societies that have been studied think of an emotion as something distinctive, perhaps internal, that occurs when some particular kind of external event occurs. But as Russell points out, most anthropological research is on concepts, not directly on experience, causation, or physiology of emotions. Moreover, although researchers have devised partial experimental tests of culture-specific elicitation, and of cultural display rules, so far social constructionists have not created unequivocal demonstrations of emotions being entirely socially constructed. We believe, however, that they have made a more important contribution than any such demonstration: they have been in the forefront of showing how emotions function within societies to mediate social relationships. In the last part of this chapter we show how sexual love functions in this way.

Passionate love

If we were to use Lutz's way of indicating a culturally specific emotional concept, we might call being in love in the West something like "sexual attraction/adoration/exclusiveness." This love is the most valued emotion in the USA. It occurs only between actual or potential sexual partners. It is not money, not power, not youth, not health – but love in marriage that was found in Freedman's (1978) survey of 100,000 Americans to be what they thought was most strongly associated with happiness.

Passionate sexual love (sometimes also called romantic love) is culturally widespread. Jankowiak and Fischer (1992) propose that it consists of sexual attraction with a biological core, perhaps involving increased levels of phenylalanine in the brain (Liebowitz, 1983). It is experienced as joyful and energizing, and it is enacted as courtship. Jankowiak and Fischer have surveyed the anthropological literature to see whether either in the writings of anthropologists or in folklore there was evidence of this kind of love in a sample of 186 cultures described in 250 books and articles. They dropped 19 cultures from their survey because the writings provided no evidence about courtship, marriage, or sexual behavior, and one on which the two authors could not agree. In the remaining 166 societies, they counted this kind of love as being present if the writer made a distinction between love and lust and noted the presence of at least one of the following attributes of love occurring within the first two years of a couple meeting, irrespective of whether they married or not: (a) personal anguish or longing, (b) love songs and the like, (c) elopement due to mutual affection, (d) indigenous accounts of passionate love, or (e) the anthropologist's affirmation that love occurred.

Jankowiak and Fischer found that at least one incident of passionate (romantic) love was described in 147 of the 166 cultures that met their criteria (88.5 percent). Here is an example from the !Kung who are hunter-gatherers in Southern Africa. Nisa, a !Kung woman, said: "when two people come together their hearts are on fire, and their passion is very great. After a while the fire cools" (Shostak, 1981, p. 269).

Falling in love

The European idea of being in love involves the attributes that Jankowiak and Fischer used in their coding. But arguably it is more distinctive: Western culture seems to have taken the universal pattern, and embellished it further. Here, for instance, is a newspaper story, like an anthropological report from home.

> On Monday Cpl. Floyd Johnson, 23, and the then Ellen Skinner, 19, total strangers, boarded a train at San Francisco and sat down across the aisle from each other. Johnson didn't cross the aisle until Wednesday, but his bride said, "I'd already made up my mind to say yes if he asked me to marry him." "We did most of the talking with our eyes," Johnson explained. Thursday the couple got off the train in Omaha with plans to be married. Because they would need to have the consent of the bride's parents if they were married in Nebraska, they crossed the river to Council Bluffs, Iowa, where they were married Friday. (Cited by Averill, 1985)

This story is striking because it so closely represents a Western cultural ideal. Averill (1985) showed it to a sample of American adults, and 40 percent of them said they had had experiences conforming to the ideal embodied in the story. A further 40 percent said their experiences of love definitely did not conform to it, basing their responses on an unfavorable attitude to this ideal plus any single departure they had felt from it. In responding in this way, they too indicated that they were influenced by this ideal.

Medieval courtly love

Love of this kind – meeting with a stranger, the special experience of falling in love, commitment to the other as the core of adult life, rearrangement of all other plans and relationships – is more specific than the pattern found cross-culturally by Jankowiak and Fischer. In this form it may not always have been with us. One appealing account is that the Western version of falling in love started its development in medieval Europe, crossed the Atlantic, was eagerly taken up in Hollywood, and only more lately emerged in such striking forms as the encounter between Ellen Skinner and Floyd Johnson on a train from San Francisco.

According to this account the germ of the Western idea of falling in love was courtly love, created in Provence in the eleventh century. The word "courtly" originally meant occurring at a royal court; the later meaning of "courtship" is derived from it. The idea was that a nobleman might fall in love with a lady and become her knight, devoting his life to her service, doing whatever she might wish, however dangerous or however trifling.

Although conceived as a kind of aristocratic game, although it probably existed more in literary forms than in real life, and although courtly love was by no means the only form in which love was described in medieval literature (Robertson, 1972), the idea flourished. For several hundred years it was the subject of some of Europe's greatest poetry. Prototypical was the story of Lancelot and his love for Guinevere, the queen and wife of King Arthur at his court in Camelot – told by the French poet Chrétien de Troyes in *The Knight of the Cart* (Chrétien de Troyes, 1180). Later came the *Romance of the Rose* (1237–1277). The first part, written by Guillaume de Lorris, is an extraordinary psychological allegory, in which the lovers are represented as a set of emotions and psychological characteristics, each of which is a distinct actor in

Figure 2.3 The origin of the culturally distinctive version of romantic love that occurs in the West is generally traced from courtly love in medieval Europe. The most famous book depicting this was *Roman de la Rose*, for which this was an illuminated illustration for a Flemish edition published about 1500. It depicts the garden of courtly love, with its pleasures and delights.

the drama. The poem begins with the lover, a young man, falling asleep and dreaming. As interpreted by C.S. Lewis (1936) the reader experiences the story through the young man's eyes. He strolls by the river of life, then enters the beautiful garden of courtly love. As the wooing proceeds, his consciousness is represented by the appearance in turn of distinct characters, Hope, Sweet Thought, Reason, and so on. The lady also does not appear as a whole. She too is a cast of characters: Bielacoil (meaning "fair welcome" from the Provençal *belh aculhir*) is something like the lady's conversational self, pleasant and friendly, and it is, of course, via this aspect that the young man must first approach.

Then there is Franchise (her sense of aristocratic status), and Pity. But then also there are others: Danger, Fear, Shame. When the young man sounds a false note, Bielacoil disappears for hours, and only Fear or one of these others is present. Then, in addition, there is Jealousy, and the god of Love, not permanent characteristics of either the young man or the lady but able, in a somewhat unpredictable way, to take over either of them. As the young man reaches towards the Rose in the center of the garden, it is the god of Love who fires arrows at him, and makes him Love's servant.

From the beginning the idea of being in love was full of contradictions. This love had to occur outside marriage; at the same the knight was to be a paragon of Christian virtues. And the very idea of worshipping a lady, or worshipping Love, was close to blasphemy. The reason courtly love was extramarital was that the lady had to be high-born. The knight had to offer his service and worship her: one can only do this for someone superior to oneself. If the couple were to marry she would become inferior to her husband, bound to obey him, thus making impossible the courtly ideal.

Some people are sceptical that the idea of "falling in love" derives from medieval courtly love. In the Hebrew tradition, for instance in Genesis, chapter 29, the story of Jacob and Rachel is told. Quotations are from Rosenberg's translation (Rosenberg and Bloom, 1990), based on a reconstruction of the original text probably written between 950 and 900 BCE. Jacob met his cousin, the shepherdess Rachel, and fell in love, seeing her as "finely formed, a vision." He asked her father for her hand, offering in return to work for him for seven years. Rachel's father agreed. The seven years "seemed in [Jacob's] eyes a few days, in the grasp of his love for her" (p. 108). When the seven years were completed, a marriage was arranged. "But that night it was the daughter Leah who was brought in fulfillment" (p. 109). The father of Leah and Rachel explained to Jacob that it was the custom for the firstborn daughter to be married first. "Finish the bridal work for this one [Leah]; then we can give you the other also" (p. 109). "This Jacob did, finishing the work for this one. Then [Rachel's father] gave his daughter Rachel to him as a wife . . . So he entered as well Rachel; he was in love with Rachel instead of Leah. He worked with him seven more years, starting again" (p. 109). Here is a story of perceived beauty, of strong preference, of a waiting period with arduous work to complete, of the gift by the father into lifelong marriage. Certain elements are comparable to some in medieval stories of knights and ladies, and also to some more recent Western traditions.

All the same, some wise people have seen something distinctive in postmedieval Western love: La Rochefoucauld (1665) said: "Some people would never have fallen in love if they had never heard of love" (Maxim 136). Averill and Nunley (1992) go further: they doubt whether anyone would fall in love if they had not heard of it. Maybe you think that they go too far. Perhaps what they mean is that in each culture there are some universal elements, and also something quite distinctive.

In Europe and America a really good job of falling in love is thought to happen suddenly, unexpectedly, involuntarily. The state engenders altruistic feelings, including the other within the boundary of a We-self. It enables a couple to overcome social difficulties and allows them to break previous ties. Rombouts, cited by Frijda (1988), has found in a Dutch survey that in addition the lovers must be open to this experience, and that after the initial meeting there needs to be a period when fantasies can build. Then, at a sign of acknowledgment from the other which, as between Floyd Johnson and Ellen Skinner, can be as insubstantial as a meaningful look, the two people fall in love.

In-love as a transitional social role

Averill (1985) argues that falling in love, like many emotions, acts as a temporary social role. It provides an outline script for the role of "lover" in which it is permissible for other social roles to be suspended, for instance in relation to parents, or to former loved ones. The emotion "in love" accomplishes a transition, from one structure of social relationships to another. Ellen Skinner and Floyd Johnson had to cross a state border to Iowa, where they did not require the consent of the bride's parents. Here is a plain statement of how previous patterns of social obligation are broken.

Even in its modern form this Western ideal has its contradictions – which perhaps is part of its charm, since each pair of lovers must meet the challenge of resolving these for themselves. The most pressing modern contradiction – which also shows the cultural function of this kind of love at its clearest – is that love, a rather temporary emotion arising on short acquaintance, must be transformed into lifelong commitment. Now the ideal is not adultery, though for some this is not excluded and the original secrecy of this kind of love seems never far away. Opening of the bud of the rose is consummation in marriage, both partners in thrall to Love. Mysteriously the individual "I," center of decisions, captain of the soul, comes to be part of a mutually constructed "We." There follows cohabitation, economic interdependence, the raising of children.

In Western culture, with its suspicion that there is something wrong with emotions, falling in love occurs as its most valued personal experience. The experience of passionate love may, as Jankowiak and Fischer (1992) propose, be universal. But this briefish emotion with its admixture of fantasy, as the basis for lifelong commitment in a two-adult family, is probably not universal. In the next chapter we approach the question of universals in emotional life from another direction, that of human evolution.

Summary

Emotions are strongly affected by cultural ideas. In Western culture emotion is rather distrusted, as compared with reason; but at the same time it is valued as the basis of authenticity. We can recognize our own cultural ideas more acutely by making comparisons, both with historical materials, and with contemporary cultures. Historically we in the West still seem to be living in an age of romanticism, which has lasted nearly 250 years. As compared with many other cultures worldwide, present-day Euro-American culture is strikingly different in its emphasis on the autonomy of the individual, and on the individual's rights. In such a culture emotions like anger occur at the infringement of such rights. By contrast many other societies, including Japan, see the social group as the basis of selfhood. They define themselves in terms of duties, and of "We" rather than "I," and some emotions of togetherness are hypercognized. Many cultures stress how emotions mediate relationships – probably Westerners believe this too because we know that love, happiness, sadness, anger, all tend to concern our relations with others. But our emphasis on individuality makes us also believe that emotions are individual states. Testing the bases of cultural differences is not easy. Certainly the value placed on different emotions, the situations that cause emotions, the names for emotions, and the extensiveness of the vocabulary of emotions, all vary cross-culturally. The question of how far emotions are universal, and how far they are socially constructed by cultures is more difficult. Passionate love, for instance, seems to occur in many cultures. Our own Western culture has a form of it which is not only distinctive, but has particular functions just in our kind of society.

Further Reading

If you do not like the idea of reading Mary Shelley's *Frankenstein*, perhaps you would prefer the most famous European romantic novella of the eighteenth century, a semi-autobiographical piece by the scientist-novelist-playwright:

Johann von Goethe (1774) *The sorrows of young Werther* (translated by M. Hulse). Harmondsworth: Penguin (1989).

A book based on living with an Inuit family, including two winters in an igloo – one of the classics of emotional life and customs:

Jean Briggs (1970). *Never in anger: Portrait of an Eskimo family.* Cambridge, MA: Harvard University Press.

A comprehensive recent review article on emotions as they occur in different cultures is:

Batja Mesquita & Nico H. Frijda (1992). Cultural variations in emotions: A review. *Psychological Bulletin, 112,* 179–204.

An article on cultural differences in emotions in terms of how far the self is regarded as independent, as in Europe and North America, or interdependent, as in Japan, is:

Hazel Rose Markus and Shinobu Kitayama (1994). The cultural construction of self and emotion: Implications for social behavior. In S. Kitayama & H. R. Markus (Eds.), *Emotion and culture: Empirical studies of mutual influence* (pp. 89–130). Washington, DC: American Psychological Association.

CHAPTER *3*

Evolution of Emotions

Contents

Figure 3.0 About ten minutes before this photograph was taken these two male chimpanzees had a fight that ended in the trees. Now one extends a hand towards the other in reconciliation. Immediately after this they embraced each other and climbed down to the ground together.

Le coeur a ses raisons que la raison ne connaît point.
(The heart has its reasons of which reason knows nothing.)

Blaise Pascal, *Pensées*, 4, 277

Emotional expressions: are they natural but obsolete?

In 1860, on hearing that humans are descended from apes, the wife of the Bishop of Worcester is said to have remarked: "My dear, descended from the apes! Let us hope it is not true, but if it is, let us pray that it does not become generally known" (Leakey & Lewin, 1991, p. 16). Though we are not exactly descended from them we do share common ancestors with present-day apes. The line that led to modern humans is thought to have diverged from that leading to modern chimpanzees some five million years ago. And the theory of our evolution from other animals has become generally known.

As has often been remarked, Darwin (1859) dethroned human beings from their place as unique creations in the image of God. A piece of Darwin's evidence was the similarity of human emotional expressions to those of lower animals. Evidence of our relatedness to other animals is now extensive. Anatomical and behavioral correspondences provide qualitative indications, and now analyses of proteins, immunological reactions, and genetic material, have allowed quantitative estimates of the degree of similarity between species (Washburn, 1991), though the accuracy of such estimates is controversial (Marks, 1992). Closest of our animal relatives are chimpanzees, from whose genetic material our own is estimated to differ by about 2 per cent.

Darwin (1872) argued that human emotional expressions have a primitive quality, keeping us firmly grounded in the animal world. Fridlund (1994, p. 14) cites Darwin as having written, in a letter to Alfred Wallace in 1867, that in his book on emotional expression he wanted "to upset Sir C. Bell's view . . . that certain muscles have been given to man solely that he may reveal to other men his feelings." His hypothesis that emotional expressions are behavioral vestiges was described in chapter 1: "some expressions, such as the bristling of

Table 3.1 Human relatedness to other primates, expressed in terms of differences in DNA and estimates of the time before the present at which divergence from human stock occurred

Humans to . . .	Chimpanzees	Gorillas	Orangutans	Gibbons	Monkeys
% unshared DNA	1.8	2.4	3.6	5.2	7.7
Millions of years since divergence	5*	7*	10	12	20

*We have changed Sibley's figures of 4 and 5 million years respectively since divergence of humans from the line that led to chimpanzees and gorillas, because of more recent estimates. Leakey (1994) estimates an even longer time of 7 million years ago as the origin of upright walking.
Source: Sibley & Ahlquist (1984)

the hair under the influence of extreme terror, or the uncovering of the teeth under that of furious rage, can hardly be understood, except under the belief that man once existed in a much lower and animal-like condition" (Darwin, 1872, p. 12). Vygotsky (1987) caught the sentiment nicely by saying that Darwin gave the impression that among human psychological characteristics emotions were a "dying tribe." As humanity moves forward they will become less prominent, and finally extinct.

Emotions, reflexes, action patterns, and biases

Darwin's and Wallace's theory of natural selection, to explain evolution, has become the foundation of biology (Dawkins, 1986). Because the theory is based on so many kinds of evidence, emotions are less important to biologists as evidence for evolution, but they have become much more interesting for themselves. The current belief is that emotions have not been superseded like the appendix. The focus has come to be on how human emotions have been selected, how they too fulfill functions. But how are these functions fulfilled, and how are they related to evolution?

The answer that has become widely accepted is that emotions provide outline patterns for certain kinds of behavior, especially social behavior, that underlie the human adaptation to the world. Bases of this patterning are passed on genetically. To speak of genetics does not mean we are rigidly determined. It means we are born with certain potentialities for behavior. You can think of these potentialities as something like inherited start-up programs – like computer programs, although in this case provided by our genes – which give us the initial bases for walking, for learning language, for emotions, and so forth, which are then elaborated and given content by experience.

In this book we consider three kinds of inherited patterning in which emotions are involved: (a) expressions, which are small discrete actions, (b) more extensive species-characteristic programs for action, and (c) biases towards one set of emotions or another. Expressions and species-characteristic patterns (a and b) are inherited by everyone. They are part of what it is to be human, and it is here that we see what Darwin noticed – our relatedness to all humans and to other animals. Biases (c) are different: each individual has different biases, so one person may be biased towards social anxiety; we would call this person shy. Another may be biased towards anger; we would call this person aggressive. Part of the engine of evolution is that variability is necessary among individuals, so that some people and the genetically based traits they carry can be selected while others are not. A bias that is subject to favorable selection can, many generations later, become a universal for the species. We introduce the idea of individual biases briefly in this chapter in the section entitled "The social lives of our living primate relatives" but our main treatment of the issue is in chapter 7 which is entirely about individual differences in emotionality.

Brief biography: Charles Darwin

Not everyone is fortunate enough to have a family that is both illustrious and well off: Charles Darwin was fortunate in this way. His father's father was the famous biologist Erasmus Darwin, and his mother's was Josiah Wedgwood the potter. His own father was a doctor, his mother died when he was eight. At 16 he was sent to Edinburgh University to study medicine, but he would skip classes to collect specimens of invertebrate animals along the shores of the Firth of Forth, developing his strong interest in natural history. In despair about the failure of Charles's medical studies, his father sent him to Cambridge to study theology. Again, he was not fully engaged with his courses: he was more interested in collecting beetles, and in hunting. He obtained an ordinary BA in 1831, and seemed headed for a life as a country parson with the hobby of natural history. He had not been idle at Cambridge however. He had won the esteem of a number of scientists and, at the age of 22, he was appointed naturalist on the *Beagle*, a British Navy ship with a mission to chart coastlines in South America. On his return from this five-year voyage, with independent means, Darwin wrote up his findings. From 1837 his notebooks show him struggling to understand the change of one species into another, and his notes about emotions were prominent in this period. In 1842 and 1844 he wrote sketches of his theory of evolution by natural selection. He asked his wife to arrange that, in the event of his death, the 1844 sketch should be given to an editor to be published along with the supporting evidence from his notebooks, and he proposed a sum of £400 to pay for this work. He himself proceeded slowly, gathering more and more evidence, and finally starting to write a compendious work. But in 1858 Alfred Wallace independently developed this same idea, and sent a paper on it to Darwin asking for his opinion. Greatly perturbed at the problem of priority, Darwin consulted friends who had read his own earlier sketch. They arranged that the paper by Wallace, and a hastily prepared revision by Darwin of his sketch, would be read at the same meeting of the Linnaean Society – in the absence of both authors. Neither paper mentioned evolution of humans, and neither attracted much attention outside a small circle, but the incident at last spurred Darwin towards publication of a book that could be appreciated by the educated public. A year later *The Origin of Species* appeared. Darwin did not stop there: his book on emotional expression is the foundation of the study of emotions, and his paper in the journal *Mind*, in which he describes observations of his son William's emotional and cognitive development, is one of the first contributions to developmental psychology. (Biographical information from Bowlby, 1991, Gruber & Barrett, 1974).

Whereas in chapter 2 we concentrated on how emotions are different in different human societies, in this chapter we discuss mainly the inherited patterns that are similar, not just among humans, but between humans and other animals.

Pancultural recognition of facial expressions of emotion

An important principle of evolution is that a feature with a function at one stage of evolution can be built upon. Old anatomical and behavioral features can be captured and pressed into service in new ways. Andrew (1963, 1965) uses this principle to propose how facial expressions in primates, including humans, were developed from reflexes.

A reflex is a relatively simple pattern in which an event known as a stimulus releases an action. An example is that we blink when something looms closely in our vision: this mechanism is inherited, wired into our nervous systems.

Many animals have a reflex in which they flatten their ears and/or retract their scalp when startled. This reflex also occurs when an animal approaches another member of its species. Its original function was to protect the ears. But as well as being protective the pattern is easily recognized by others: if we think a dog looks friendly part of this look is due to the flattened ears. Humans are unable to retract their ears or scalp, but raising of the eyebrows seems to derive from this same movement, and Eibl-Eibesfeldt (1970) has shown, by

Figure 3.1 Frames from a cine film taken by H. Hass of a French woman greeting a friend with an eyebrow flash that is universal. In these frames in (a) the face is neutral, in (b) and (c) the eyebrows are raised for about one third of a second, and in (d) a smile occurs.

inconspicuous filming in many different cultures, that a brief raising of the eyebrows, lasting a fraction of a second, occurs when people approach one another during greeting, and in flirting. It is probably a human universal.

Andrew argues that emotional expressions of smiling, frowning, and so forth, may have started far back in our evolutionary past as reflexes that originally had functions that were not primarily emotional. Then new evolutionary steps occurred, as tendencies arose for these actions to be recognized. Then these tendencies were selected, and over many generations the reflex actions became available as stimuli that could elicit further expressions in others. They became prelinguistic bases for signaling intentions, and for setting up certain kinds of interaction. The emotions they express can set the tone for an interaction, friendly, flirtatious, wary, antagonistic, fearful, and so forth.

So according to this idea, an emotional expression is a reflex pattern of the face, voice, and so forth, that is distinctive for a particular emotion. How could one show that such expressions are universals, and hence part of the inherited equipment of us all? One line of evidence is from children born deaf and blind, cut off from learning expressions. Eibl-Eibesfeldt (1973) found that such children do make facial expressions such as laughing, smiling, crying, frowning, surprise or startle, and pouting. They also show distinctive emotional postures, such as the sagging shoulders of sadness, the clenched fists of anger. Where expressions involve vocal sounds the children made these too. Facial and vocal expressions were similar to those of normal children, but sometimes lacked subtlety.

With the exception of happiness, facial expressions of emotions are not easy to identify if all clues other than the expressions themselves are removed (Wagner, MacDonald, & Manstead, 1986), but certain aspects of facial expressions can be captured and frozen in time as photographs. Then selected expressions can be recognized. Izard (1968) was the first to show that photographs of facial expressions of happiness, sadness, anger, and so on, were recognizable in different cultures. There is now a very large quantity of research on recognition of facial expression of emotions (Camras, Holland, & Patterson, 1993), as well as on electrical recording of the activities of facial muscles (Cacioppo, Bush, & Tassinary, 1992).

Probably the best known evidence of universals of emotional expression was from a bold attempt made by Ekman and his colleagues who journeyed to New Guinea to study a group called the Fore, a neolithic people who until 12 years previously had been isolated from all external influences, and were unlikely to have seen Western photographs, movies, or the like. Principal papers are by Ekman, Sorenson, and Friesen (1969), and Ekman and Friesen (1971), as well as a paper and a book by Sorenson (1975, 1976).

In their 1969 paper Ekman, Sorenson, and Friesen reported data from New Guinean Fore people who had some contact with Westerners. From 3,000 photographs of Americans, the experimenters had selected 30 showing "pure" expressions of six emotions. They showed these pictures, one at a time, to Fore subjects. For each photo the subject had to choose from a set of translated emotion words the one that most closely corresponded to it. Recognition of American happy faces was reported as 99 percent for subjects who spoke some Melanesian pidgin, and 82 percent for those who spoke only the Fore language. For negative emotions recognition was less good (56 percent or less) and subjects tended to see American faces intended for sadness as angry.

Taking part in the second study (Ekman & Friesen, 1971) were 189 Fore adults and 130 children who had had minimal contact with anyone outside their society. The standard method of having subjects choose from a fixed set of verbal labels did not work as well as had been hoped. So tiny stories were constructed by Fore informants to correspond to the facial expressions in the photographs: the story for the happy face was "His (her) friends have come, and he (she) is happy" (p. 126); the story for the fearful face was longer and was about meeting a wild pig in the hut when alone. To each subject, a Fore assistant told each story while the Western researcher held up three pictures of American faces, and looked at the tape recorder to avoid giving any clues. For each story the adult subject had to indicate, by pointing, which of three picture faces corresponded to it. For the story designed for the happy face 90 percent or more subjects chose the happy picture as compared with all other photos, and for the stories of sadness, anger, and disgust, the correct face was chosen by between 69 and 89 percent of subjects. The Fore adults were no better than chance in discriminating the picture for fear from that of surprise. Results from Fore children were similar to those of adults (children were asked to choose between just two faces).

The difficulties of such cross-cultural experiments are extreme. Ekman, Sorenson, and Friesen have been criticized because they did not speak the Fore language and therefore could not monitor their Fore-speaking assistants (Van Brakel, 1994). Sorenson (1976) wrote that inadvertent clues to subjects may have been given because the convention of experimental testing without "leakage" was "quite incomprehensible to the Fore and alien to their view of language" (p. 139) as a cooperative activity. But subjects' failure to discriminate fear from surprise argues against inadvertent clues being responsible for all the results.

Ekman and Friesen then asked the New Guinean Fore people to make facial expressions appropriate to the six emotion stories, and videotaped these expressions. Later, after returning to San Francisco, they found that 34 American students made between 46 percent and 73 percent correct judgments on four of the six faces made by the New Guineans (see figure 3.2) but were not correct for fear or surprise (Ekman, 1972).

Ekman proposed at first that facial expressions of happiness, surprise, sadness, anger, fear, and disgust are human universals; he later added contempt (Ekman & Friesen, 1986). As we explained in chapter 2, Ekman's is a two factor theory – he calls it *neurocultural*: an innate neural patterning of expressions is accompanied by culturally variable display rules that regulate when each expression can be made.

Ekman's work has become the subject of intense controversy. In a long critique, Russell (1994) pointed out that studies of people choosing from a fixed set of pictures and matching them to a fixed set of emotion terms may overestimate the accuracy of recognizing expressions as specific emotions. Russell described some demonstrations in which subjects were asked to choose from a fixed set of labels deriving from his own theory (Russell, 1980), which is very different from that of Ekman. Taking a photograph from a set published by Ekman to represent anger, Russell found that when given a choice among his proposed labels of happiness, surprise, contempt, fear, and interest, 80 Canadian subjects labeled this picture as contempt on 76 percent of occasions. When given a picture intended by Ekman to represent sadness, and a choice among the labels joy, fear, relaxation, surprise, excitement, and interest, 74

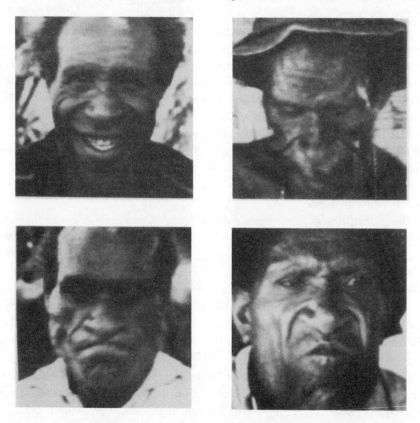

Figure 3.2 Members of the Fore community in New Guinea, who had not seen the photographs for the earlier recognition experiment, enact facial expressions appropriate to stories of emotion (Ekman, 1972): (a) "Your friend has come and you are happy," (b) "Your child has died, and you feel very sad," (c) "You are angry and about to fight," (d) "You are looking at something that smells bad." (The story fragments are from Ekman & Friesen, 1971.) Russell (1994) has criticized experiments on recognizing faces that represent stories because although the researchers hypothesize that a face indicates emotion, it might be recognized as appropriate to a situation: face (d) might not mean disgust but might be made when something smells bad.

percent of Russell's subjects' choices were for fear. So, a researcher necessarily gives subjects choices according to the theory he or she believes to be correct, but forced choices restrict subjects' options. When subjects choose freely a word for an expression in a photograph, different results can occur. For instance Sorenson (1976) asked three groups of Fore subjects (those who had most contact with Westerners, those with some contact, and those with hardly any contact) to give names to photographed facial expressions. All groups predominantly saw the happy face as happy, the anger face as anger, the fear face as fear, but more than half the subjects in all groups saw the sad face as anger, and the most common responses to the surprise and the disgust faces were not as predicted from Ekman's theory.

Russell (1994) lists eight hypotheses as fitting available cross-cultural data. One is Russell's (1980, in press) own view of a dimension running from positive to negative, and another from aroused to unaroused. Emotions can be arranged in a circle as follows (in clock notation): 12 o'clock "arousal," 3 o'clock "pleasure," 6 o'clock "sleepiness," 9 o'clock "displeasure." In this scheme positive and aroused emotions like "excitement" occur around 1.30 on the clock face, negative and unaroused emotions like "depression" are at 7.30, the negative and aroused emotions of stress are at about 10.30.

The most prominent hypothesis is still Ekman's neurocultural theory that distinct expressions correspond to basic emotions, which are subject to cultural display rules. He has defended his theory (1994) from Russell's (1994) critique.

Another theory is Eibl-Eibesfeldt's (1973), that certain innate expressions of greeting, laughing, crying, and so forth are seen in many cultures, and in deaf and blind children. Notice that what is universal in this account are expressions, not emotions; tears for instance can be shed with sadness but sometimes too with laughter, and also with pain – which most researchers do not consider an emotion. As compared with recognition of photographs there has been little research on tears and reasons for them, though see Neu (1987). For laughter and its evolutionary value, see Weisfeld (1993); and for blushing see Leary et al. (1992).

A further hypothesis is that individual components of expression, such as drawing the eyebrows together, wrinkling the brow, baring the teeth, and so forth may be the universals (Ortony & Turner, 1990). For instance, in Ekman and Friesen's (1971) experiment in which subjects chose a photograph appropriate to meeting a wild pig, they may have responded to raised eyebrows in the picture rather than a composite expression of fear (see also figure 3.2 and its caption).

Perhaps the most radical hypothesis is that of Fridlund (1994): expressions, he argues, can be understood in terms of evolution of the signaling of intentions and the coevolution of abilities of recognition, but these expressions probably do not map in any one-to-one way onto inner emotions.

Some of these theoretical positions will be discussed further in the next chapter. The best evidence is that the smiling face of happiness and/or welcome is made and recognized universally, but recognition of negative facial expressions is more problematic. Russell's argument is that cross-cultural studies have established that there are universals in human facial expression. But the research does not yet allow us to distinguish sharply among available theories of exactly what the universal aspects of expression are.

Species-characteristic patterns of action

For the most part, when we think of an emotion, we think of something more extensive than a smile or a frown. The older term used in biology for a genetically based, extended, pattern of action is "instinct." William James wrote near the beginning of his chapter on emotions in his famous textbook (James, 1890): "Every object that excites an instinct excites an emotion as well" (vol. II, p. 442).

What does this mean? Think back to chapter 1 where we described Hess and Brügger's (1943) discovery of patterns of attack made by cats when a part of their hypothalamus was stimulated electrically. We can infer that the electrical stimulation made the cat angry. In this state of the brain a complicated pattern of attack – recognizable as distinctive to cats – was directed at a nearby target such as the experimenter. This is not just a reflex, but a whole pattern. In the older terminology it is an instinct. It is clear from Hess's and later studies that it is a pattern for which the start-up program is genetically given. Usually the actions are elicited by some appropriate event in the environment, and they become more skilled with learning.

It used to be thought that lower animals' actions were based on instinct, while human actions were based on intelligence and learning. Research over the last 60 years has shown this to be quite wrong. Not only do nonhuman mammals learn very well, but human behavior is strongly influenced by genetic patterns in the same way that that of other animals is. So if we feel bereft from the loss of a parent or lover, our feelings, postures, and actions are based on genetically based tendencies called "attachment." In the following sections we hope to explain these ideas. In the next chapter we will propose a more exact definition of emotions.

A large step in the study of instincts was made by Lorenz (1937) who demonstrated their genetic basis by showing that, like anatomical features, they are characteristic of a species. One of the first instinctive patterns to be studied in the new way was described by Lorenz and Tinbergen (1938). It was part of the repertoire of maternal caregiving in greylag geese. If an egg gets out of a goose's nest she extends her neck towards it and stays in that position for several seconds. Next, apparently grudgingly, she gets up. With her neck still extended she approaches the egg and touches it with her beak. Then, after sliding her beak over the top of the egg, she quivers, then bends her neck and starts rolling the egg back towards her feet while backing towards the nest. She steers the egg carefully up and over the incline of the nest. This pattern occurs even in geese who have had no opportunity to learn it.

These patterns, called by Lorenz "instincts," had several components. The first was called by Lorenz a "fixed action pattern." A joke among biologists is that the concept is fine so long as you realize that these things are neither fixed, nor actions. Since Lorenz's time biologists have shown that instinctive actions are not fixed. They develop during the animal's life, and are highly responsive to features of the environment. So the actions of egg rolling depend on the shape of the nest and the egg.

Fixed action patterns, and indeed the whole notion of instincts, have been replaced in the language of most biologists, who now speak of "species-characteristic" or "species-typical" patterns. Two concepts have replaced the idea of fixed sequences. One is of goal-directed behavior. The knowledge of how to achieve the goals that are accomplished by species-characteristic actions is not consciously accessible, and it is not acquired by the individual; during evolution it has been compiled into the brain as a set of outline procedures. The function of egg retrieval by geese is to make the survival of goose genes more likely. When a discrepancy from the goal, or desired state, is perceived, "egg out of the nest," a goal-directed, plan-like set of actions brings the errant egg toward the nest until the goal state "all eggs in the nest" is reached. The second theoretical concept is the idea of a script, imported by Schank and Abelson (1977) and by Tomkins (1979) from the theater. The idea is of an outline sequence of actions, which again achieves a goal. Schank and Abelson's example is of getting a meal in a restaurant. To do this a set of actions has to be performed – order food, eat, pay – the ways in which each of these are done varies considerably, but people who are familiar with restaurants know and can perform this outline. The restaurant script, of course, is learned; the idea of species-characteristic actions is that some outline scripts, for important functions in humans, like maternal caregiving, mating, aggressive conflict, are provided by our genes.

The second component of an instinct according to Lorenz was the perceptual pattern that triggers it, sometimes called an "innate releaser," or "sign stimulus." It is comparable to the idea of the "adequate stimulus" in understanding reflexes, or the "cue" in visual perception. As Lorenz and Tinbergen's experiments showed, even crude features are often effective, and the term "stimulus" is still used. For some species-characteristic patterns an unnatural stimulus does even better than the natural one: and is called a "super-normal stimulus." For instance Tinbergen (1951) showed that oyster catchers prefer eggs much bigger than their own. They cannot manage to retrieve these eggs, but they try unremittingly to do so. Some film stars and models act as super-normal stimuli for us humans, drawing us towards them even though they can mean nothing to us personally. Other stimuli, for instance the sight of someone very different from ourselves in some way, may repel us. This idea of responding to such stimuli quite irrationally is thoroughly disturbing. The question that is difficult to avoid is: "How much of our behavior is like this?"

The third component of species-characteristic patterns is motivational. Without it the actions do not occur: in geese, egg retrieval only occurs during incubation. It will not occur, for instance, after hatching.

Species-characteristic patterns are easily triggered, but less easily modified by the individual. In his book of 1872 Darwin described an experiment upon himself that nicely illustrates this point:

> I put my face close to the thick glass-plate in front of a puff-adder in the Zoological Gardens, with the determination of not starting back if the snake struck at me; but, as soon as the blow was struck, my resolution went for nothing, and I jumped a yard or two backwards with astonishing rapidity. My will and reason were powerless against the imagination of a danger which had never been experienced. (Darwin, 1872/1965, p. 38)

Origins of the emotional characteristics of humankind

So how do we find out about the species-characteristic bases of human emotions? There are various kinds of information on which we can draw. In this section we will consider three and hope, by a kind of triangulation, to catch a glimpse of the origins of our emotional lives:

- study of our close relatives the chimpanzees as compared to us;
- study of prehistoric evidence of early humans and of human ancestors;
- study of contemporary human societies living in ways thought to be like those of humans when they first became the distinct species of which we are part.

The social lives of our living primate relatives

Jane Goodall (1986) and her colleagues have spent many years observing 160 or so common chimpanzees in Gombe, Tanzania. Gombe is an area of 19.4 square miles of rugged forest, roughly the size and shape of Manhattan, with a shoreline on Lake Tanganyika, and with deep valleys made by streams running down to the lake. The chimpanzees were frightened of Goodall at first, so she could not get near them. But they gradually habituated to her. She encouraged their habituation by making fruit available to them at her camp, later a research center. After habituation, observers could sit a few yards away from groups of chimpanzees, or follow an individual for many days taking notes and photographs.

Goodall's work is an account of the social lives and personalities of chimpanzees. We discuss it here because it is also an account of their emotional lives. For Goodall the predominant tone is of affectionate sociability. Here is a description, derived from following individuals and noting their behavior.

> Melissa and her daughter Gremlin have made their nests [in the trees] some 10 meters apart. Melissa's son Gimble still feeds on *msongati* pods . . . Gremlin's infant, Getty, dangles above his mother, twirling, kicking his legs, and grabbing at his toes. From time to time Gremlin reaches up, idly, tickling his groin. After a few minutes he climbs away through the branches, a tiny figure outlined against the orange-red of the evening sky. When he reaches a small branch above Melissa's nest, he suddenly drops down, plop, on her belly. With a soft laugh his grandmother holds him close and play-nibbles his neck . . . He goes back to his mother and lies beside her, suckling, one arm on her chest . . . Suddenly from the far side of the valley come the melodious pant-hoots of a single male: Evered, probably in his nest too. It is Gimble who starts the answering chorus, sitting up beside Melissa, his hand on her arm, gazing toward the adult male – one of his "heroes." (Goodall, 1986, p. 594)

Not all chimpanzee life is so calm. The animals have dominance hierarchies. The so-called "alpha male," to whom all others defer, wins his position by defeating the previous holder in fights or by making threats, sometimes with the help of allies (Goodall, 1992). He usually holds his position for several years. Other males have a status in a rough hierarchy below him. Females too have a parallel hierarchy and animals of both sexes defend their position, or challenge to rise in the hierarchy, usually by angry threats sometimes backed by overt fights, which often occur after two animals at about the same level in the hierarchy have not met for an interval.

Goodall has categorized fights into three levels of aggression. At the lowest is a hit, push, or kick, in passing. Levels 2 and 3 she calls "attacks." Level 2 includes dragging, pounding with a fist and suchlike; it lasts for less than 30 seconds. Level 3 is like level 2 and lasts longer than 30 seconds. Attacks (levels 2 and 3) were about 15 percent of all fights; of these about a quarter were serious in that blood flowed or injury resulted. Sometimes a fight would snowball as more individuals joined in to support friends or relatives. Males fought more than females. Goodall calculated from 4,900 hours of observation in which 13 individuals were followed during two separate years, and excluding darkness or when the followed animal was alone or only with dependent offspring, attacks at levels 2 and 3 occurred on average every 62 hours by males, and every 106 hours by females. There were large individual differences: one male averaged an attack every 27 hours (of 207 hours total). One female did not attack at all in 230 hours. In another year, the alpha male averaged an attack once every 9 hours.

Chimpanzees eat mainly fruit, but they also hunt opportunistically, killing small mammals such as cebus monkeys or piglets when they come across them in the forest. Males are more usually involved in the hunt than females. When chimpanzees have made a kill they often squabble for the meat, though sometimes they distribute it as a favor that will elicit future reciprocity (Weisfeld, 1980). High-ranking animals tend to get hold of it even if they took no part in the catch and they usually only allow certain others (relatives and allies) to share the meat (Nishida et al., 1992). Neither group-eating from trees, nor distribution of meat is equivalent to the universal pattern of human communal sharing of food.

Emotional bias: a basis of individual differences in dominance

Raleigh et al. (1991) have shown that serotonin mechanisms in the brain have a substantial effect on whether an animal becomes dominant. They experimented on vervet monkeys, who lived in 12 small species-typical social groups, each with a dominant male (the alpha male), two other males, a number of females, and offspring. From each of the 12 social groups one of the nondominant males was selected at random. Six were given drugs that enhanced serotonin activity in the brain, and six drugs that reduced it. Those with enhanced serotonin function all became dominant. In the groups of those whose serotonin function was reduced, the original alpha male retained his position. Then the animals who had been given serotonin-reducing drugs were given drugs to increase their serotonin, and vice versa. Now all six animals with newly enhanced serotonin systems became dominant in their groups.

Although it is clear that serotonin mechanisms are not the only ones important in dominance, this experiment is striking for several reasons. It is the first to show experimentally that a manipulation of the brain's chemistry can enhance dominance in a setting similar to a naturalistic one. Secondly, this kind of mechanism could be the basis of genetic biases, that affect individual differences in social-emotional relations. Thirdly, the behavioral process of becoming dominant in these monkeys does not just involve aggression. It involves affiliation and grooming with females, without whose support a male does not become dominant. Fourthly the recently much publicized, and effective, antidepressant drug Prozac is one that increases serotonin function in humans. According to Kramer (1993) it does much more than that: it increases social confidence and enthusiasm for life. So a genetic bias towards social confidence, or the reverse, may operate by means of serotonin function.

Sexuality in common chimpanzees and pygmy chimpanzees

Sexually chimpanzees are promiscuous. A female is not sexually mature until 15; she advertises her sexual receptiveness by a large pink patch of sexual skin (the labia), about the size of a large bread roll, which is highly visible from behind. In common chimpanzees it is swollen for about 10 days during a menstrual cycle of about 36 days. During this time she may copulate several dozen times a day, with all or most of the adult males in her social group. Alternatively she may go off with a single male consort, away from the rest of the community. When pregnant or lactating, however, she is not sexually receptive. Because weaning of infants does not occur till they are about five, this means that for fertile females a few 10-day periods of sexual activity alternate with five-year intervals of sexual inactivity.

Just as interesting as the common chimpanzees studied by Goodall are pygmy chimpanzees or bonobos. This species is rare; the pygmy chimpanzee is thought to be our closest living relative. Pygmy chimpanzees are similar to common chimpanzees, but more slender. Kano (1992) and his associates studied a group of wild pygmy chimpanzees in Wamba, Zaire, for about 10 years. Whereas adolescent female common chimpanzees are unattractive to males for several years after starting to show sexual skin but before becoming fertile, pygmy chimpanzee females are sexually active for about five years before becoming fertile, they are receptive for more than half the time in each menstrual cycle, and they are sexually inactive only from a month before giving birth to about a year after it. They seem to remain sterile while lactating, because, as with common chimpanzees, the birth interval is about five years.

Sexual activity among pygmy chimpanzees includes females copulating with many of the adult males in their immediate social group. These males tend not to interfere when others copulate. Sexual advances are made both by males, who display an erection and perhaps touch the female with a hand to draw attention to themselves, and by females who will present their sexual region. Females also choose whom to mate with (Furuichi, 1992). Aggression seems not to be involved with sexuality, and refusals are accepted by males without demur. Copulation involves face-to-face positions as well as the more common primate position from behind. Homosexual relations as well as heterosexual relations are common. Females rub their genital areas together. Adults, adolescents, and juveniles all become fascinated and watch copulations and female genital rubbing. Males become excited and erect. Insertion by young males is accepted by females other than their mothers, often after sex with an adult, in what might be thought of as sexual initiation play.

So among common and pygmy chimpanzees, mating is promiscuous. Females tend to travel with their offspring. Overt cooperation occurs among adult males who forage and hunt together and contribute to the group by maintaining the borders of a range against intruders. Adolescent females tend to leave a group, and join another one.

Among olive baboons, by contrast, a quite different mode of organization occurs (Smuts, 1985). Although they are also promiscuous, and forage as a troop, females form long-lasting friendships with two or three males, involving grooming and keeping close. These friendships are marked by emotions such as jealousy that seem similar to ours. Friendships function for the females in protecting them against aggression from males (who are twice as large as they), and for the males in being groomed and in being more often accepted as mating partners during periods of sexual receptiveness. In this species it is the male who leaves one social group to join another; his success in joining depends on being accepted on a friendly basis by females in the new group.

Are chimpanzees emotional?

There seems to be no difficulty in seeing aspects of chimpanzee life as being based on patterns of action that are characteristic of the species. In closely related species, as with anatomical characteristics, there are strong similarities but some differences. So, between chimpanzees and us there are similarities and differences. Though we humans know in ourselves that patterns of aggression and sexuality are highly emotional, how are we to think about them in chimpanzees? Do they too get angry in dominance disputes, and become lustful when copulating? If so the bridge between them and ourselves can be built more strongly.

To such questions Hebb (1945) said that there is no problem in identifying chimpanzee emotions because they are so like ours. Goodall agrees: "the emotional states of the chimpanzee are so obviously similar to ours that even an inexperienced observer can interpret the behavior" (Goodall, 1986, p. 118). She says it is easy to see when a youngster has a temper tantrum by hurling himself to the ground, hitting it, and screaming, or equally when a youngster plays joyfully around its mother, turning somersaults, rushing to her, tumbling in her lap, and requesting to be tickled. She lists (pp. 118–119) adult chimpanzee emotions and the situations in which they arise: apprehension at a stranger, fear at an aggressive interaction, distress when lost, annoyance at a bothersome juvenile, anger in a fight. She also describes displays. Intimidation displays, for instance, involve a male charging, pulling branches, throwing stones, and making a great din. Then, in reconciliation after an aggressive incident, there is body contact such as one reaching out a hand and the other responding by touching, patting, embracing, kissing. So close is the resemblance to human emotional life that a series of films have been made of some Gombe chimpanzee families by Hugo van Lawick, with voice-over by Donald Sutherland; the plot, the actions, the emotions, are almost indistinguishable from those of soap opera.

Goodall lists distinctive facial patterns in chimpanzees indicating fear, distress, threat and playfulness, and describes how during excitement (sexual or aggressive) the hair stands on end indicating arousal, and how it becomes sleek during calm times, when grooming, after copulation, and during reconciliations. Similarly Goodall (1986, p. 127) provides a table of the many emotional vocalizations, including the following: the pant-grunt indicates social apprehension, squeaking and screaming indicate fear, a bark indicates anger, whimpers indicate distress, copulation squeals occur during sex, laughter and panting accompany the enjoyment of body contact, food grunts accompany enjoyment of food, pant-hoots and roars accompany social excitement, and grunting accompanies sociability.

Lutz (1988) wrote of the people in Ifaluk that "their emotional lives *are* their social lives" (p. 101, emphasis in original); and Shaver, Wu, and Schwartz (1992) argued that the same is true for Americans. Reading the accounts of Goodall and Kano it is clear that Lutz's phrase is also true of chimpanzees. What this means is that relationships are primarily emotional relationships. Like us, chimpanzees are intensely social. Like us they have friends and relations, alliances, and positions in power hierarchies. Since most or all social interactions have an emotional tone, often expressed very obviously by displays of the face, by postures, gestures, vocalizations, a plausible inference is that emotions and their expressions are the bases for distinctive patterns of interaction. So, when they find a tree with a lot of fruit on it, chimpanzees pant-hoot. Others come to the spot, and they eat together with obvious enjoyment. During copulation they may be calm, or may utter distinctive squeals. At the sight of sexual activity males become aroused and await their turn to copulate. In maternal–infant interactions, in play, and in reconciliation there is affectionate body contact, touching, stroking, and hugging. During mutual grooming, there is quiet concentration and enjoyment. When a mother or an infant dies, the bereaved one becomes sad, and mourns. An orphaned infant becomes immobile and may die, even if able to forage for itself. In aggressive encounters, anger is shown in threats, and fear in submission. Other animals watch fights with great interest, and may on occasion join in. If an animal is hurt, it screams in a distinctive SOS call; the effect is to summon others to its aid. During a hunt and after a kill there is high excitement. When patrolling their range, groups of males are tense and alert to sounds, and they become excited when they attack an animal from outside their community.

Validity of everyday concepts of emotion

Our concepts of emotions such as fear, anger, and love, are fundamental for understanding behavior. But how far might these be simply based on folk theories of Western society? Hebb (1946) has proposed an answer, with an account of what happened when he joined the Yerkes Laboratories with its colony of chimpanzees. This took place during the days of behaviorism – it had been forbidden to refer to emotions or any other such mentalistic terms because they were then thought unscientific. So in the notes that attendants were required to keep only behaviorist terms were allowed. But this made some of the animals unpredictable, even dangerous. Hebb describes two animals, Bimba and Pati who would occasionally attack an attendant, and says that no description that confined itself merely to behavior could describe or predict these attacks. But by using the folk-theoretical terms of emotion these animals became understandable. Bimba was friendly and responsive, but would become angry and attack an attendant if she were slighted. Pati, on the other hand, seemed to hate humans, and would sometimes appear friendly, then attack an attendant who was taken unawares. Hebb says that by allowing animals to be described using "concepts of emotion and attitude . . . a newcomer to the staff could handle the animals as he could not safely otherwise" (Hebb, 1946, p. 88).

One important hypothesis about emotions, then, certainly not firmly established but held by many researchers, is that at least some emotions and our concepts of them form bridges between ourselves and our nearer animal relatives. They also form bridges between one human culture and another; they help us understand other cultures. Without concepts of emotions many stories from other cultures or from the past, and most narrative accounts of our actions in the present would be incomprehensible.

The bonds of social interaction, then, are emotions and moods which link individuals together in scripts: of mutual affection, of sexual intimacy, of dominance and submission, of group excitement in an attack, of group apprehension when there is danger. Individuals make expressions that act as releasers to trigger appropriate moods and behavior in those who see or hear them.

Emotional modes can set the tone for whole communities, or even for whole species. Pygmy chimpanzees, for example, take great interest in sex, and the sounds they make imply that females as well as males experience orgasm. Sex is not just reproductive (De Waal, 1995; Kano, 1992): female pygmy chimpanzees are sexually receptive for long intervals when they are not fertile, and both males and females take part in homosexual relations. It is as if sex has become an activity that can be shared, it has an enjoyable emotional tone, and it produces social bonding. While aggression and jockeying for dominance are prominent among common chimpanzees, among the more sexually active pygmy chimpanzees aggression is rare and sexual activity seems to defuse conflict. Sex defusing conflict is not unknown among humans; and of course, we have potentially many other activities beside sex that can be enjoyably shared.

Evidence of human ancestry

An idea that has become important is that human emotions are based on mechanisms enabling us to react to distinctive situations that have recurred often during human evolution (Nesse, 1990). But emotions and patterns of action that are characteristic of the human species were evolved to suit a physical and social environment – called the environment of evolutionary adaptedness – that was quite different from the towns and cities in which so many of us now live. One set of clues to the origins of human emotions might be found in studying the origins of humankind. So what is known about this?

Calculations of rates of mutation allow the small differences in the RNA of modern people from all over the world to be traced back to a point of convergence. While several species of human-like primates that have existed in the last few million years have become extinct, all modern humans may have had a common ancestor, a woman who lived about 200,000 years ago in Africa (Wilson & Cann, 1992). According to this hypothesis (which is controversial) we are all descended from this African Eve. She wasn't alone, of course, but a member of an interbreeding population of perhaps 10,000 – her descendents are the modern humans who have migrated to populate every part of the Earth except Antarctica.

It is less controversial that in the last several hundred thousand years the earth's climate fluctuated between warm periods such as that in which we now live and ice ages, when glaciers spread south of the Great Lakes in America and across northern Europe making the sea level 400 feet lower than now.

Developing the technologies of clothing and shelter, probably much like those of Inuit people, and surviving the Arctic cold, the forebears of all the native peoples of America probably crossed the land bridge between what are now Siberia and Alaska in a period of glaciation, perhaps 40,000 to 50,000 years ago. Then Australia and New Guinea were joined, and separated by only 40 miles from Asia. Early humans (but no other mammals) were able to cross the water, later to be isolated as sea levels rose again when the glaciers began to melt, to live as the aboriginal hunting and gathering peoples of Australia and New Guinea (Stringer & Gamble, 1993).

The usual answer to the question of what is most distinctive about humans, or what separates us from other animals, is language. Perhaps a better answer would be culture – of tools, skills to use them, concepts – of which language is a part. Recently Savage-Rumbaugh et al. (1993) have brought up a pygmy chimpanzee, Kanzi, like a human child. He seems just on the border between humans and other primates. He can understand human spoken speech and uses a symbol-board to utter words and phrases. He can also receive instruction in using implements. In general he behaves at about the level of a human two-year-old. Attributes of symbolic language, or activities such as the deliberate making and retention of tools, have never been seen in apes in the wild. By contrast, human culture has included behavioral skills like deliberate tool making (starting about two-and-a-half million years ago); deliberately preserving or making fire (starting about 700,000 years ago); social skills like sharing food, division of labor and exchange; as well as the language arts of informing, disputing, gossiping, planning, story telling. All of these are human universals. A more complete list is provided by Hockett (1973). All are cultural inventions that mark us off from other living primates. All are social. Many have an emotional basis, such as the distinctive warmth and acceptance of sharing food and the grateful cooperativeness of exchange. Other emotions may have evolved to support long-established human activities such as the fascination of staring at a fire, and the engrossment of making something.

The invention of agriculture, and of cities for trade, occurred in several parts of the world about 10,000 years ago. In the domestication of plants and animals, the evolution of human cultures overtook the evolution of species. If we take Wilson and Cann's estimate of 200,000 years ago as the time when the common ancestor of all living human beings was alive, the 10,000 years of settlement and of the civilizations in which most people now live is only 5 percent of that time; this same period is less than a quarter of one percent of the time from the divergence of humans from apes. For much of the time in which our emotional responsiveness was being shaped by natural selection, most researchers propose that these environments – our environments of evolutionary adaptedness – were of extended family groups of hunter-gatherers, rather than the conditions of modern city-dwelling. The likelihood is that if we were able to bring back a human baby from 10,000 years ago, before there were cities, it would have the same repertoire of social and emotional responsiveness as we do. It would take on the modern culture into which it was adopted and be indistinguishable from modern humans.

Hunter-gathering ways of life

We can get another glimpse of the origins of human emotions by asking what is known about existing cultures of hunter-gatherers. In Australia and in the savannas of southern Africa there is archeological evidence that the hunter-gatherer way of life has existed for several thousand years. Until its recent erosion by Western influences, this was the way of life of the Bushmen (also known as San) of the Kalahari who include the !Kung and the G/wi. (Their languages include clicks: ! designates a click made by drawing the tongue sharply away from the roof of the mouth, and / is made by drawing the tongue away from the front teeth, like the "tsk" of scolding.) Lorna Marshall and her family lived among them in the 1950s (Marshall, 1976; Thomas, 1989). In the 1960s and 1970s, Lee (1984) and other Harvard anthropologists visited these peoples.

!Kung and G/wi peoples have lived in a semidesert land, traveling over a range of several hundred square miles which they know intimately. Thomas describes the G/wi as small and lithe, living in extended families. In their travels they meet other families to whom they are related by blood or marriage. Round a fire, the G/wi scoop out shallow impressions in the ground to sleep in. The women especially are expert botanists: they gather roots and other vegetable foods from the land, obtain fluid from tsama melons. The men hunt and shoot animals with bow and arrows tipped with a poison made from a grub. They may have to follow a shot antelope for a day before it dies. It is brought back to camp, and there are complex rules about how it is divided. Nothing is wasted. The society of these people is cooperative and nonhierarchical.

Origins of the family

Among chimpanzees, although a mother lives within a community, she raises infants more or less on her own, and usually travels around with just her offspring. Babies are born singly, with a birth interval of about five years. Each infant clings to its mother's belly or rides on her back, and does not impede travel or foraging. Juvenile offspring travel with their mother. Males make contributions to the community, but not to individual offspring. In the human adaptation, child rearing is difficult for a single person: optimally it requires the resources of two or more adults for children to progress from weaning to adulthood, the period of highest mortality.

According to the hypothesis of male provisioning (Lovejoy, 1981), upright walking allowed the possibility of carrying things – the bag may have been the first important piece of human technology. Division of labor arose as a substantial proportion of the diet was obtained from the meat of larger animals. With increasing brain size prehumans needed to be more immature at birth for

Figure 3.3 Two groups of Bushmen camping together, under the shade of the same small tree.

the large head to pass through the birth canal, so infants had a longer period of dependency than those of apes. At the same time the baby cannot cling to the mother, as ape babies do. Even with a sling for carrying babies, travel is impeded. Division of labor became established. Women took primary care of infants during the extended period of immaturity, and they traveled less. Because females became sexually active throughout their menstrual cycles, a male and a female could maintain exclusive sexual interest in each other. Division of labor meant that men could hunt and bring home meat, while sexual bonding enabled them to make a specific economic contribution to one female and her offspring.

Lovejoy's hypothesis was that all these adaptations were interdependent, and arose about the same time as upright walking. More recent opinion favors a more gradual evolution. The first upright walking creatures five to seven million years ago were apelike, with ape-sized brains, and there was a large difference in size between males and females – a difference associated with a common form of mammalian social organization in which males compete with each other for access to females. Certainly, too, monogamy is not exclusive to humans – it is unusual but not unique among primates. The heterosexual friendships of olive baboons, discussed earlier, provide another kind of example of long-lasting heterosexual friendships in which the females prefer particular males, although they do not mate with them exclusively.

Despite these reservations, however, evolutionary biologists continue to argue that monogamy is important among humans. It allows males to have a reasonable probability of knowing that offspring to whom they contribute economically are their own (Lancaster & Kaplan, 1992). Although the proportion of societies (like Western ones) where monogamy is official policy is only 16 percent among a total of 853 societies sampled (Van den Berghe, 1979) and although extramarital activities are not uncommon in most societies, in practice monogamy is overwhelmingly the most usual sexual pattern, amounting to a human universal. Even in societies where one male can have several wives, this pattern is practiced only by a few men who have large resources.

It is a universal too that the central structure of human life is the family: a group which often includes both sexes and individuals of all ages, living with a female and her offspring. In the group there is usually at least one adult male. He may be the woman's sexual partner, perhaps father of her children, but at some times and in some societies the male of the family may be a father, brother, or son. The extended family group typically includes other relatives, such as siblings, older offspring, and their sexual partners who have joined the family from other groups. (A taboo on incest, and social mechanisms for people to marry outside the family, are other human universals.)

It is probable, therefore, that our environment of evolutionary adaptedness, the way of life of the earliest modern humans (say) 200,000 years ago, was in seminomadic hunter-gatherer groups of 10 to 30 people living face-to-face with each other in extended families, much like the G/wi and !Kung. Most of our emotions, then, are probably adapted to living in this kind of way; cooperating, though with division of labor, in hunting and gathering, in preparing and sharing food, in rearing and protecting children. Perhaps also, as we will discuss in chapter 10, we are adapted to competing with other groups similar but noticeably different from ourselves, whose ecological niches have overlapped with ours, such as the Neanderthals. This species, perhaps because of the aggressive success of our ancestors, has become extinct (Stringer & Gamble, 1993).

Evolutionary bases of emotions

Tooby and Cosmides (1990) have proposed that from an evolutionary standpoint, human life is based on information and on using it in plans. Emotions are based on genetically based mechanisms that have been responsive to informational events in the environment that have recurred frequently over many hundreds of generations. These recurrences have enabled adaptations, genetic changes, to occur that have become design features of our planful relation to the world. Emotions arise largely with problems to be solved. So for recurring problems like escaping from predators, responding to strangers, meeting aggressive threats, caring for infants, falling in love, and so on, we are equipped with genetically based mechanisms that provide outline scripts for behavior that has been successful in the past, and has therefore been selected. Each kind of emotional pattern is triggered by distinctive cues. Each makes ready patterns of action appropriate to solving the problem that has arisen.

Table 3.2 Recurring situations and emotional responses in relation to members of the same species, other species, and inanimate objects

Relation	Recurring situation	Emotion
Attachment	Joining, being with an attachment person	Happiness, love
	Interruption of attachment	Distress, anxiety
	Resumption of attachment	Relief (and maybe anger)
	Loss of attachment	Sadness, despair
Caregiving	Assisting others, including infants	Caregiving love
Cooperation	Formation of relationships and plans	Happiness
	Completing plans	Happiness
	Exchange	Gratitude
	Sex, grooming	Happiness, love
	Loss of relationship, failure of plans	Sadness
Competition	Achieving/defending position or resources	Anger
	Defeat	Fear, shame
Predation	Hunting	Excitement, happiness
	Being hunted	Fear
Inanimate	Finding resources	Happiness
	Physical danger	Fear
	Toxins, contamination	Disgust

Nesse (1991) has argued that the characteristic feelings associated with these patterns are typically functional even when they are unpleasant, just as is the feeling of pain.

What, then, are these recurring features of the environment, and the adapted emotions that have been selected? Several authors have made suggestions (Bowlby, 1971; Oatley, 1992; Plutchik, 1991) and some of these suggestions are indicated in table 3.2.

Attachment in humans and other primates

The psychological aspect of the concept "mammal" – an animal that is live-born and is suckled by its mother – is attachment. As well as being able to suckle, infant mammals must stay close to their mothers, they become fearful when separated, and their cries summon the mother. Attachment is quite clearly a species-characteristic pattern. It is by now perhaps the most researched of all such complex patterns.

It was John Bowlby who realized that this pattern of attachment is central to human emotional development: "What is believed to be essential for mental health is that the infant and young child should experience a warm, intimate and continuous relationship with [his or her] mother (or permanent mother substitute . . .) in which both find satisfaction and enjoyment" (Bowlby, 1951,

p. 11). The inverse is maternal deprivation: Bowlby thought that children deprived of maternal love would grow up unable to form satisfying emotional relationships in adulthood, and that love in the early years was as important for emotional development as proper nutrition is for physical development.

Mary Ainsworth worked with Bowlby on attachment in London, then moved to Uganda and there undertook a naturalistic anthropological study of babies and mothers in a culture different from her own (Ainsworth, 1967). She discerned a set of behavior patterns that young children showed when they were with their mothers, which they did not show with anyone else, see table 3.3.

Each is a specific attachment pattern. When the mother is present there is a sense of security, and a distinctive set of actions occurs. When she is absent quite different actions occur. So, in widely different cultures attachment patterns can be seen. They are best thought of as emotional. In humans we talk about them in terms of love. Infant love and fear of separation are human universals. They serve the vital function of keeping the mother nearby able and willing to care for the infant.

Origins of the idea of attachment

In 1935 Lorenz had described an instinctive pattern. Baby goslings follow, then stay close to, almost any object that moves around and makes sounds. The process is called imprinting. Lorenz proposed that there is a critical period – in goslings at about two days of age – during which a biological mechanism is set to recognize characteristics of the mother: but objects acceptable to this mechanism are not closely specified. If no real mother appears, characteristics of the first crudely plausible moving object that appears are learned instead. In

Table 3.3 Ainsworth's (1967) list of attachment behaviors

1   Differential crying (i.e. with mother as compared with others);
2   Differential smiling;
3   Differential vocalization;
4   Crying when the mother leaves;
5   Following the mother;
6   Visual motor orientation towards the mother;
7   Greeting through smiling, crowing and general excitement;
8   Lifting arms in greeting the mother;
9   Clapping hands in greeting the mother;
10 Scrambling over the mother;
11 Burying the face in the mother's lap;
12 Approach to the mother through locomotion;
13 Embracing, hugging, kissing the mother (not seen in Ugandan infants but observed frequently by infants in Western societies);
14 Exploration away from the mother as a secure base;
15 Flight to the mother as a haven of safety;
16 Clinging to the mother.

Lorenz's studies this object was often himself. The effects are irreversible; geese imprinted in this way do not recognize other geese, but make social signals to whatever they have been imprinted on. When Robert Hinde and Julian Huxley introduced Bowlby to the idea of imprinting and to the works of Lorenz and Tinbergen he quickly realized that in ethology and Darwinian evolution theory lay the key: "attachment theory's main structure emerged whole in this first flash of insight and gave coherence to all that followed" (Ainsworth, 1992).

As well as studies of imprinting, Bowlby was also impressed by ethologists' descriptions of genetically based patterns such as that of egg retrieval by the greylag goose, which we discussed above and said was well described as goal-directed. In attachment, the goal state for mother and baby is to be close to each other. If the mother moves away this is a releasing stimulus for the baby to cry, and the crying is effective in getting her back, achieving the goal.

Experiments on artificial rearing of monkeys

In a series of experiments Harlow (1959) demonstrated in monkeys that attachment behaviors toward a parent were based on an infant's need for comfort. Harlow separated infant monkeys from their mothers within 12 hours of birth and supplied two artificial mothers made so that the baby monkeys could cling to them. One was made of wire topped with a crude head. The other was made similarly but its wire frame was covered with terry cloth and it had a different shaped head. In Harlow's first experiment four baby monkeys got their milk from a bottle attached to the wire mother, and four others got milk from the cloth mother. During the first 5.5 months of their lives all eight monkeys spent an average of 14 to 18 hours per day clinging to their cloth mother. Even when milk was obtained entirely from the wire mother, infants spent less than an average of two hours a day on her. The idea that closeness to a mother was secondary to feeding was thoroughly refuted. Preference of all the infants for the cloth mother was one measure of a primary motivation for comfort: another was shown when a large toy spider was introduced to the cage. The infant monkeys were terrified and rushed to the cloth mother rather than the wire one (see figure 3.4) irrespective of which they had obtained their milk from. When the baby monkeys were placed in an unfamiliar room they tended to cower and hide in a corner. With the cloth mother in the room they were not frightened, but clung to her, then used her as a base for explorations.

At first the theory of attachment included the idea, derived from imprinting, of a critical period in early infancy (Bowlby, 1951). It was thought that uninterrupted experience of an affectionate relationship with one person, usually the mother, was necessary. If, in human babies, such an experience did not occur between the ages of about six months and three years, Bowlby thought that the negative effects would be irreversible. Such consequences of attachment failure were evident in Harlow's work with monkeys. In his 1959 article he had drawn conclusions that now seem strange. He thought his artificially reared monkeys would mature normally given nutrition, housing,

Figure 3.4 A baby monkey in Harlow's experiments clings in terror to the cloth mother when a large toy spider is introduced into the room. Even if the baby monkey has obtained all its nourishment from the wire mother, it uses only the cloth mother to calm its anxiety.

and the simple comfort of cloth mothers. He wrote: "All our experience, in fact, indicates that our cloth-covered mother surrogate is an eminently satisfactory mother ... available 24 hours a day ... she possesses infinite patience, never scolding her baby or biting it in anger. In these respects we regard her as superior to a living monkey mother" (p. 94). Not till later did Harlow realize that monkeys reared with surrogate mothers were damaged in almost every way, emotionally, socially, and intellectually.

Kraemer (1992) summarized the effects of baby monkeys being reared with artificial mothers. As they grow older they do not eat or drink normally. They stare into space, show repetitive and stereotyped behavior like body rocking. They viciously bite their own limbs, alternating this with self-clasping. They are poorer in many cognitive tasks. Most of all, when introduced to other monkeys they act in socially inappropriate ways. They make mutually exclusive expressions of fear and threat at the same time. They alternate between reclusiveness and aggressively attacking other monkeys from adult males to juveniles, as well as inanimate objects. They are sexually incompetent, male mounting and female presenting are disrupted, and if a female is artificially impregnated she will ignore, maim, or kill, her infant. Damaging effects are most marked in monkeys who are reared with an artificial mother in their first six months of life. Monkeys who have been reared in this way, and then have some "therapeutic" experience of peers who will cling to them, groom with them, and so forth, recover some aspects of normal social functioning (Suomi & Harlow, 1972). As Kraemer points out, however, what is at issue in attachment is not just survival, but building an inner model of interactions with another individual. With no such individual, no such inner model is built. Although monkeys who were maternally deprived but had "therapy" with peers seemed to be rehabilitated in many of their day-to-day interactions, these rehabilitated monkeys remained abnormal in reacting to stress or conflict. They also had persisting neurobiological defects in brain transmitter metabolism, and in the anatomy of some nerve cells.

The socioemotional patterning of attachment is innate. What this means is that species-characteristic mechanisms are like sets of building bricks. In primates, including ourselves, growing up with parents and others of our own species allows these bricks to be assembled into meaningful and useful structures. Running the genetic program without social interaction, as happened to the monkeys raised as social isolates with artificial mothers, is like dumping the bricks in a heap on the ground. Even then some, though not all the bricks, can be later assembled into more meaningful patterns with care and persistence. But these do not reinstate the processes that were missed. Rather, alternative pathways are developed to enable some of the goals of social interaction to be met. Despite this, vulnerabilities to stress remain.

Primate attachment, then, offers us an important example of a process that is characteristic of the species. Such processes are innately provided for, but not rigidly determined. They do not develop normally without the proper emotionally based interactions with others.

Emotions as bases of social relationships

Human emotions are the language of human social life – they provide the outline patterns that relate people to each other. The smile – the best established universal signal of emotion – is the sign of social affirmation; happiness is the emotion of cooperation. The frown signals something not going well; anger is the emotion of interpersonal conflict, and so forth. What verbal language has done is not to replace emotions, but to allow us to communicate yet more elaborately about what is most important to us – our emotional relationships.

Intentionality of emotions

During evolution, and during individual development, emotions have become – as philosophers say – more intentional. The idea of intentionality is that conscious mental states in humans are about something: humans have beliefs about things, desires for things, and so forth. Intentionality in this philosophical sense means "aboutness." In adults, just as with other mental states, most emotions are intentional: usually we are angry about something, we fear some possibility, and so forth.

Most, perhaps all, mammals have emotions which then prompt behavior. For instance, when a predator is detected fear occurs, and it prompts avoiding actions which have a species-typical character. In more sophisticated animals emotion comes to have more specific content, so Cheyney and Seyfarth (1990) describe how vervet monkeys have three species-typical patterns of fearful response appropriate to their three main predators. When an eagle appears a monkey hides in undergrowth, when a leopard is seen the monkey climbs a tree, if there is a snake the monkey rears on its hind legs and looks downwards. Moreover fear does not just affect the individual brain, it is spread socially: these monkeys make three different kinds of alarm call, one for each kind of predator, each invoking the specific kind of fear in other monkeys and inducing them to take the appropriate evasive action. So we can say that among these monkeys fear has some specific intentional content.

Human infants are perhaps like lower mammals. Although we can see their emotions are mostly caused by events, some occur for no obvious reason. So for infants all emotions may be more like moods, without much intentional content. By the age of one-and-a-half children begin to talk about their feelings and, as we will discuss in chapter 6, three-year-olds know distinctly what they feel, and why. By adolescence most emotions are fully intentional.

This kind of development is reflected in the English lexicon which has some 600 emotion terms: many not only indicate a basic feeling state but also imply what it is about, often what kind of event caused it. Our hypothesis is that in all the languages of the world, many emotion terms have this kind of structure, referring both to some kind of feeling and implying something about its object. So in English "frightened" means being fearful and implying that the fear has an object.

Social emotions

Existing in most languages are emotion terms that are usually called "complex." They refer to emotions not primarily of survival, not to biologically based relationships such as attachment (see table 3.2), but to social comparison (Ben Ze'ev & Oatley, in press). In English all such terms involve the self, most often in relation to some social concern (Johnson-Laird & Oatley, 1989). Thus, regret is sadness arising as we compare results of an untaken decision with the current social circumstance of the self (Landman, 1993). Envy is hatred arising from a comparison of oneself with another person, and the emotion prompts destructive thoughts or actions towards the other. *Schadenfreude* is a German term; the emotion occurs in English culture too, although without a one-word translation. It is related to envy, and it means taking pleasure in another person's misfortune. It too arises from a comparison of the self with another (Ben-Ze'ev, 1992).

Figure 3.5 Three different kinds of fearful response by vervet monkeys to three kinds of predator.

In evolutionary terms two families of complex emotions are important to humans; they are absent from simpler mammals, but the beginnings of some aspects are present in chimpanzees. The first of these is based around gratitude. Weisfeld (1980) discusses how the roots of this emotion are seen among chimpanzees as they share food with a friend, in alliances, and in mutual grooming. The effect of this emotion is to set up a desire to reciprocate. It provides a basis for a continuing cooperative relationship with a distinct individual. Along with empathy, sympathy, and pity – emotions that Adam Smith (1759) called the "moral sentiments" because he believed that they made human society possible – gratitude does not just have an object, it sets up a relationship that includes friendliness and future obligations. Gratitude is essential to human life. It is the prototype of exchanges that are universal in human societies, perhaps the basis for modern economic relations.

The second interesting family of complex social emotions with evolutionary significance is that of embarrassment, shame, guilt, and social anxiety. Darwin (1872) devoted a chapter to them, pointing out that one expression of this family – blushing – is both unique and universal to humans. Eales (1992) on reviewing the large ethological and cross-cultural literature on this topic has concluded that gestures of appeasement and submission are inherited universals among higher primates including humans. They include looking downwards, hunching the body, averting or lowering the gaze, immobility, and facial expressions of fear. They occur in recognizable circumstances of threat from a dominant individual, from having made some social transgression, from social rejection, and also in some sexual interactions especially among the young. At one level we can see such gestures as complementary to dominance. Like gratitude and empathy they do not just have objects – they set up a certain kind of relationship, originally functioning to allow peaceful coexistence at the price of lowering an individual in a persisting dominance hierarchy. There is evidence that embarrassment and the more serious emotion of shame can be distinguished from their displays (Keltner, 1995).

Hierarchy among humans is so common as to be almost a universal, but human hierarchies are usually achieved not by fights, but symbolically (Weisfeld, 1980) for instance by achievements, and by egregious displays of possessions and other resources (Veblen, 1899). Probably the best way of thinking about complex emotions is in terms of presenting the self to others and of being able to imagine what those others might think and feel towards us. This was the field pioneered by Goffman (1959), in which the self is seen as predominantly social, dependent on a history of interactions with others, based on being able to sustain a certain kind of performance that is seen by others and oneself as morally worthy. From this kind of analysis, shame is perhaps the most human of emotions, the opposite of social confidence. It is the emotion around which the story of the Garden of Eden revolves: Adam and Eve acquired knowledge – let us say they left the state of simple nature and started on the path to civilization. In so doing they had to become selves among other selves, presenting and comparing themselves to these others. The result is the possibility of respect, but also the possibility of shame. In this story we could say that the important thing that has changed from the ancestral conditions of dominance hierarchies, such as those seen in chimpanzees, is that with the emergence of a sense of self now we can feel inferior according to our own internalized standards (Lewis, 1993). Such standards can, of course, also lead to guilt – but this emotion tends to concern more specific breaks with the conventions of society that signal a need for repair; shame and guilt can be explicitly distinguished by children before the age of 12 (Ferguson, Stegge, & Damhuis, 1991).

Despite its importance shame, as Scheff (1990) points out, is usually so successfully managed by most of us, most of the time, that it is barely visible. So this experience is relatively rare. Incidents of shame are spoken about to confidants, but the delay before telling others is longer than for other emotions (Rimé et al., 1991).

Shame or humiliation imposed by others can give rise to immoderate anger. As Anderson (1994) points out, the adolescents about whose feuds one reads in headlines like "Teen killed in drive-by shooting" have no money and very few other resources in the predominantly wealthy society of America. Their self-esteem is correspondingly fragile. Respect, as in many ancient societies, has become the code to live by. For many street kids the worst thing you can do is to show disrespect – a stare may be enough. Such a slight will easily lead to violence, and respect is built on the reputation for being tough; death is feared less than dishonor.

Humiliations can be felt by whole nations. Scheff (1990) has shown that the lever by which Hitler in the 1920s and 1930s moved Germany towards war and the Holocaust was to evoke shame at the humiliating terms of the Treaty of Versailles that concluded World War I, then draw from responsive hearers eager echoes of his own fury.

For us human beings – groups as well as individuals – although overt dominance disputes no longer permeate social life as they do among male chimpanzees, not far beneath the surface such disputes never seem far away. For the most part in the societies of the West we try to cultivate alternatives: respect in actions of kindness and competence rather than in threats, bravado, and killings. Behavior is constructed to avoid shame, hence binding the self to norms of politeness and society (Elias, 1939), while positive complex emotions of affection, gratitude, sympathy, empathy, compassion, provide the most important social glue.

The uniqueness of human relationships

We have yet to make explicit the most important fact about the social life of chimpanzees and humans. It is this. Emotions are felt not just towards other members of the species, but to specific individuals. For Goodall (1986) to carry out her research, she had to recognize each individual chimpanzee at Gombe, give him or her a name for purposes of remembering and talking to other researchers, find who were each individual's relations, friends, enemies, who above and who below in the hierarchy. Without this none of her research would have been possible. In lower mammals individuality has not yet emerged: a mother rat for instance looks after her litter of pups, she does not recognize each one as an individual.

In human social life this issue becomes not just important, but all-important. Each of us, as we discussed in the previous section, achieves an identity, meaning a social identity. And for each of us our particular mother and father, our particular sexual partner, our particular children, are each unique, irreplaceable. This makes us uniquely vulnerable, because if anything should happen to any of these, we can be emotionally devastated.

R. I. M. Dunbar (1993) has argued that the enormous growth of the human brain during the last five million years of evolution, and its large ratio of cortex to the rest of the brain (about four to one), is concerned not with being more skilled at technical tasks like tool making, but from having more complex and more numerous social relationships, alliances, and antipathies with individuals, each with its own history, each with its implications for other relationships. Dunbar does not write about emotions as such, but in our terms the relationships he describes are emotional ones with individuals whom we love, feel affection for, feel vengeful towards, feel grateful to, and so forth. Dunbar has calculated that chimpanzees interact successfully with about 65 individuals. When a group gets larger, it divides. Humans can manage to know and interact successfully with a maximum of about 150 individuals. So human villages often have around this number. What we see in hunter-gatherers such as the !Kung is that individuals live together in groups of about 20, and have relationships with about 150 people whom they know and meet from time to time as they travel across a large territory (Lee, 1984).

So human emotions not only have objects who are usually people, but these "objects" are specific individuals: John feels affection for Mary, Jane is angry with Joan. Ape and human relationships are mostly cooperative. To start with, no doubt, the genetic basis of altruism was in parents caring for offspring: the genes were selected that were shared by mother and offspring. They prompted behavior that made the offspring's survival more likely. In apes and humans altruism has extended beyond genetically related individuals on the basis of gratitude and reciprocal obligations. Friendships and alliances are maintained by grooming, and in pygmy chimpanzees by sex. Chimpanzees spend up to about 20 percent of their total time grooming in pairs, but they cannot do anything else while they do this. Dunbar hypothesizes that language evolved as social grooming – we talk not primarily to communicate about food, or tools, or hunting, but to cultivate our relationships. Unlike the grooming of chimpanzees, it has the advantages that we can do it with more than one person at a time, and also while we are doing something else like preparing food or walking.

So what do we talk about? R.I.M. Dunbar found from recording conversations from 19 social groups in a college refectory, that in 453 thirty-second samples of conversation in which males spoke, 64.7 percent of the talk was about personal relationships, personal experiences, or social plans. In 617 samples in which women spoke, 74.4 percent were about these matters. In a study of married couples, Shimanoff (1984) found that the two most commonly named emotions in conversation were very clearly social: love and regret (including guilt and sorrow). And if we ask about emotional experiences that are sufficiently salient to be memorable, Rimé et al. (1991) found that between 88 and 96 percent of subjects in different populations, irrespective of sex or age, talked about these emotional experiences to someone else. In talk we cultivate, define, and redefine, ourselves and our relationships by presenting our experiences to others – we elaborate our emotional bonds and antipathies with specific people we know.

Figure 3.6 Among chimpanzees grooming occupies a large amount of time, and it functions to maintain affectionate relationships with specific individuals. In humans, although body contact remains very important, R.I.M. Dunbar (1993) has proposed that some of the functions of social grooming have been taken over by verbal language.

Summary

Evolution has selected outline patterns of action – previously called instincts but now referred to as species-characteristic patterns – compiled outline programs for them into networks of nerve cells, and passed these on to individuals. As Darwin found, some of these patterns, especially those that express emotions, show human relatedness to nonhuman animals. Aspects of them, including attachment, play, affectionate interaction in small groups, coming to the aid of those in distress, grief at the death of close relatives, interindividual aggression in dominance hierarchies, and sexuality, can be seen in the lives of our primate relatives, the chimpanzees. Evidence from hominid evolution during the last few million years indicates that the human family, based around a group of children and their mother, with a male emotionally bonded to her and providing economic support, has been distinctive for the human adaptation. During perhaps most of the last 200,000 years humans are thought to have lived mainly as hunter-gatherers, seminomadically, and for many of those who continue this way of life, the emotional tone is cooperative and egalitarian. One development especially important to humans is that emotions have become more specific and, as philosophers say, more intentional, including emotions that involve the development of a sense of self, social comparisons of this self with others, and the cultivation of emotional relationships with particular individuals.

Further Reading

An introduction to evolutionary theory as it affects emotions is:

Randy M. Nesse (1990). Evolutionary explanations of emotions. *Human Nature, 1,* 261–283.

For the debate about whether there is pancultural recognition of emotions in human facial expressions:

James Russell (1994). Is there universal recognition of emotion from facial expression? A review of methods and studies. *Psychological Bulletin, 115,* 102–141, plus replies by Paul Ekman, *Psychological Bulletin, 115,* 268–287 and Carroll Izard, *Psychological Bulletin, 115,* 288–299.

For an accessible account of the social and emotional life of chimpanzees:

Frans de Waal (1982). *Chimpanzee politics.* New York: Harper & Row.

For readable discussions of human evolution:

Richard Leakey (1994). *The origin of humankind.* New York: Basic Books, or

Mary and John Gribbin (1993). *Being human: Putting people in an evolutionary perspective.* London: Dent.

What is an Emotion?

Contents

Figure 4.0 Bernini: St Teresa (detail from the altar of Santa Maria della Vittoria, Rome, 1644–1647). Of this sculpture Gombrich (1972, p. 345) says Bernini has "carried us to a pitch of emotion which artists had so far shunned."

Everyone knows what an emotion is, until asked to give a definition.

Beverly Fehr and James Russell, 1984, p. 464

Definitions and examples of emotions

It has been difficult to define emotions, and this difficulty continues. We will be rash and start this chapter with a working definition of a kind that has been gaining acceptance. It goes something like this.

1   An emotion is usually caused by a person consciously or unconsciously evaluating an event as relevant to a concern (a goal) that is important; the emotion is felt as positive when a concern is advanced and negative when a concern is impeded.
2   The core of an emotion is readiness to act and the prompting of plans; an emotion gives priority for one or a few kinds of action to which it gives a sense of urgency – so it can interrupt, or compete with, alternative mental processes or actions. Different types of readiness create different outline relationships with others.
3   An emotion is usually experienced as a distinctive type of mental state, sometimes accompanied or followed by bodily changes, expressions, actions.

An example: you are talking with a friend as you walk. As you start to cross the street there is a screech of brakes. You stop your conversation, jump back onto the sidewalk. You find your heart pounding, thinking you could have been hurt, and you determine to be more careful, not to get so deeply involved in conversations. The event is evaluated as important, priorities are changed, interrupting your previous actions. You are shaken bodily, and you make plans about what to do.

The definition derives mainly from Frijda's (1986) book which in our view remains the best modern discussion of psychological research on emotions. There are other approaches. Mandler (1984) complained that "too many psychologists still fail to accept today, that there is no commonly, even superficially, acceptable definition of what a psychology of emotion is about" (p. 16), and Van Brakel (1994) provides a table of 22 recent definitions of emotion. We believe, however, that a consensus is developing that allows us to write this book.

We need not worry that this definition may not be quite right, or that some people might disagree. Definitions in science are really working definitions. They provide an orientation, but they are subject to change whenever anything relevant is discovered. The approach we take in this chapter, starting from this definition, is to discuss properties and examples of emotions, to show how they are caused and how they can be measured. This fills out our understanding of how emotions derive from matters that are important to us (concerns) make us ready for the next action. If you find evidence that does not f definition, you will need to modify the definition.

The reason we can treat a definition as merely a starting point is this: there is no simple or agreed definition of a sentence but this does not impede research or understanding in linguistics. The aim is not to discover such definitions. What we seek is not, in the end, to define emotions but to understand them.

When William James, in 1884, asked his famous question "What is an emotion?" he implied that the answer was not obvious. Why is this? Usually people are not in much doubt about what emotions are – in an important sense we are all experts: a parent knows how to recognize an emotion in a child, friends and lovers are sensitive to the emotional tone of exchanges between them.

Fehr and Russell (1984) showed that people could give examples very easily. They asked 200 undergraduates in Vancouver, Canada, to spend one minute writing down as many terms as came readily to mind from the category "emotion." The researchers merged syntactic variants (e.g., sad, sadness, sadly) and found 383 different examples of emotions, 196 mentioned by at least two subjects. Most frequent was "happiness" mentioned by 152 subjects; the next most frequent were "anger," "sadness," and "love," each mentioned by more than half the subjects.

Though examples are easy, definitions of emotions are difficult. They need specification of what philosophers call necessary conditions (without which an emotion would not exist) and sufficient conditions (so that if these occurred we could be certain that an emotion was present). Frijda proposed that the necessary condition of an emotion is the change in readiness for action. Frijda's proposal, now widely accepted, is an important scientific step, one that was not obvious. It does not offer a sufficient condition because we can imagine people getting ready for an action, making sure they have money ready to go shopping for instance, without this being emotional.

Concepts of emotion based on prototypes

Fehr and Russell (1984) used the terms they collected in six further studies. Their results showed how everyday concepts are different from scientific ones. Everyday concepts of emotion were represented as prototypes – as typical examples that everyone knows. In general (not just with emotions) people rarely think in terms of necessary and sufficient features (Lakoff, 1987). Instead, prototypes are fundamental to everyday human thinking.

The argument is this: for some concepts we can fairly easily give a correct definition with necessary and sufficient features – so "a grandmother" is "a mother of a person who is a parent." For most concepts exact definition is difficult or impossible because the natural world is not so neatly divided into categories, and for many objects we just do not know enough. So when you say

kind of thing called "tree" of which we all know typical
which, if need be, those scientists in the Botany
us more.

hought have the wonderful property of allowing people
d quite well even when we do not know very much. To
ting with prototypical examples which the hearer can
am, 1975). Then we can specify modifications if need
pe for tree might include the concept "large" you
it is a tiny tree that has been grown in a pot and

the idea that people's everyday prototype of an
script (a characteristic outline of a sequence of
er 3). You can think, for instance, of a typical
does something hurtful → angry feelings →
remedy the situation. Russsell (1991b) has suggested
gh in ordinary life we think with prototypical examples with no
snarp boundaries dividing off good from less good examples, in science we need
to understand defining characteristics of emotions. We will continue to give
examples that have prototypical features; at the same time we try to understand
the defining conditions of emotions.

The process of emotion

Emotions do not usually happen all at once. They are usually caused, then run
through a process, then have consequences. A widely accepted proposal has
been made by Frijda (Frijda, 1986; Mesquita & Frijda, 1992) of an emotion as
a set of stages, as follows:

appraisal → context evaluation → action readiness →
physiological change, expression, action.

So Fehr and Russell's (1984) idea of our folk-theoretical understanding of
emotion as a kind of script with several steps converges with this scientific
theory of Frijda.

Stein, Trabasso, and Liwag (1994) have proposed slightly different stages to
those of Frijda, in which beliefs, inferences, and plans are emphasized. These,
slightly modified from their account, are as follows:

1   An event, usually unexpected, is perceived that changes the status of
    a valued goal.
2   Beliefs are often challenged; this can cause bodily changes and
    expressions to occur.
3   Plans are formed about what to do about the event to reinstate or
    modify the goal, and the likely results of the plans are considered.

These stages are captured in the questions: "What happened? What can I do about it, and what might then happen next?"

Stein, Trabasso, and Liwag (1994) give an example of a five-year-old, Amy. Her kindergarten teacher had just told the class that she had a paint set for each child, and that after painting pictures for Parents' Night the children could take their paint sets home. When the children had been given their paint sets, Stein et al.'s research assistant noticed Amy looking apprehensive. She asked why. Amy said: "I'm jittery. I'm not sure why she wants to give me the paints. So do I have to paint all of the time at home? I really don't want to do this. I didn't think teachers made you paint at home. I don't like painting that much. Why does she want me to paint at home?"

Here we see that Amy has a goal which has been violated (1): she doesn't want to paint. The idea of being given something to do at home violates a belief about what teachers do (2). The conversation continues with Amy's plans (3).

> Research assistant: What will you do Amy?
> Amy: I don't want to take the paints home. I want to know why I have to do this.
> Research assistant: Well Amy, what are you going to do about this?
> Amy: I'll take the paints home, but when I get home, I'll ask my Mom why I have to do this.

Two weeks later the research assistant talked casually to Amy. She was still worried about the paints. She said she had used them only once. But she has not told the teacher, fearing that the teacher might be mad at her.

Stein, Trabasso, and Liwag (1994) propose that how a person sees an event – the frame they use which depends on the person's goals and values – will determine how the event is perceived and remembered. Different people, for instance Amy's teacher, would have different frames: indeed when the teacher was asked, she did have a different view. She said that Amy did not have to paint at home if she did not want to, and that she had given paint sets to everyone so that the children would not fight over them. The value of investigating such matters in young children is that we can perhaps see some of the fundamental processes in an unelaborated form. Stein, Trabasso, and Liwag (1993) have found that these same features occur regularly in emotion processes in adults as well as children.

Frijda's and Stein et al.'s stages are similar. Their proposals indicate a converging set of understandings of the stages of emotion being reached by different researchers. The headings of the following sections follow Frijda's scheme.

Appraisal

Emotions can be caused in a number of ways (Izard, 1993), but the usual first step is appraisal – the recognition of an event as significant, an idea introduced by Arnold and Gasson (1954), and discussed in chapter 1. It corresponds to point 1 of our working definition, and to the first stage in both Frijda's and Stein, Trabasso, and Liwag's schemes.

Modern research on appraisal has tended to be in two families. In one, called the componential approach because emotions are seen as having components, researchers have asked people to remember an episode of emotion or to consider a story or vignette, and then asked them to rate it on a number of features. Ellsworth and Smith's (1988) appraisal features or components were:

- pleasantness;
- anticipated effort;
- attentional activity;
- certainty;
- human agency;
- situational control;
- perceived obstacle;
- importance;
- predictability.

Some researchers prefer fewer features. Roseman (1991), trying to identify the essential, proposed five. Others, striving for completeness, have included 15 dimensions, or vectors, of appraisal (Scherer, 1993). Following Arnold and Gasson (1954) profiles of features for each kind of emotion have been produced by many researchers. So, with Ellsworth and Smith's scheme, happiness is the emotion that is pleasant, associated with low effort, high certainty, and high attention. These features can be thought of as constituting a core meaning of a prototype for happiness. We can imagine that the event that Amy was concerned about with the paints would include ratings of: unpleasant, attention provoking, uncertain, little control of the situation, important, and unpredictable. These imply, on Ellsworth and Smith's scheme, a case of fear or anxiety.

Appraisals in lists such as Ellsworth and Smith's do not all indicate what has caused the emotion. Attention, for instance, is a result of the emotion, not its cause. So another family of theories, called goal-relevance theories, has concentrated only on causes in relation to goals or concerns. Stein, Trabasso, and Liwag's (1993) theory is in this group, as is that of Oatley and Johnson-Laird (1987). A good summary of the idea of appraisal as relevant to a goal has been given by Lazarus (1991) – he calls it primary appraisal, and suggests that it has three features:

- whether or not there is *goal relevance* – only if an event is relevant to a concern or goal will an emotion occur;
- *goal congruence* or incongruence – moving towards a goal causes positive emotions, moving away causes negative ones;

- the type of *ego involvement* in the event, its value for the person; for instance, if the event involves self-esteem then pride and anger will be possibilities.

What is implied in research on appraisal is that emotions are typically caused by events and are (in the philosophical sense) intentional – they have an object of some sort (Reisenzein, 1992b). For example, one does not just love, one loves somebody, and usually one is not just afraid, but afraid of something.

There are some difficulties with the idea of appraisal. One is that all the evidence comes from people's reports about themselves, often about past episodes or about prototypical stories. There is relatively little observational evidence of emotions being caused by events that can be objectively classified as involving anticipated effort, or being goal-congruent, ego-involving, and so forth. Although, as we discuss in chapter 6, observations of children confirm that events congruent with goals cause happiness, that threats cause fear, and so

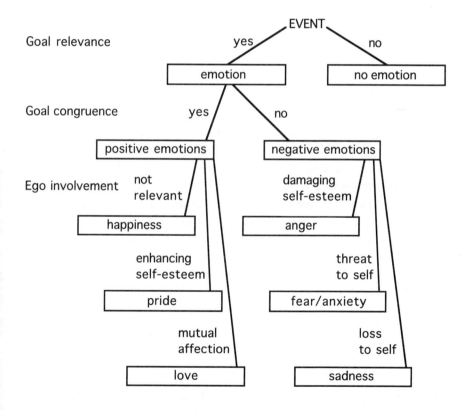

Figure 4.1 Decision tree of primary appraisals based on three features (goal relevance, goal congruence, and ego involvement), plus the kinds of emotions that can occur with these appraisals, derived from Lazarus (1991). Further differentiation among emotions occurs in secondary appraisals.

on, the very idea of emotions as events that link inner and outer worlds make them methodologically difficult. The answer is to put together evidence from different sources.

Another problem identified by some researchers is that appraisals can seem "cold," like a kind of checklist, whereas emotions are "hot" (Zajonc, 1980). The idea is this. Imagine you are seeking a boyfriend or girlfriend. You could make a list of characteristics: "likes movies, sense of humor, non-smoker . . ."; this is a bit like the appraisal idea. Or you could just meet someone and find that you like them a lot without – apparently – any intervening processes.

There is a long tradition of work on emotions in which a principal postulate is that emotions involve a feeling which cannot be reduced or analyzed any further. Wundt (1897) supposed that there were just two such feelings, pleasure and pain, corresponding to the appraisals of goal congruence or incongruence in figure 4.1.

Other authors, following Descartes (1649), whose ideas were discussed in chapter 1, have thought that a small number of specific emotions are basic and hence not reducible. Those who follow this line of thinking generally list at least happiness, sadness, anger, and fear, as distinctive and irreducible basic emotions (Stein & Oatley, 1992). The proposal is that sadness and fear, for instance, feel quite different, and are not just states appraised as unpleasant, caused by different kinds of event, requiring different amounts of effort, and so on.

The causation of emotions is not necessarily conscious, and appraisals need not be conscious either, let alone cold. Look again at figure 4.1: imagine evaluating something hurtful or inconsiderate that someone has done to you. Though it damages a concern for your self-esteem, you cannot look within yourself to see the mechanism of the process. Nor can you directly alter it – so it could be experienced as "hot." Appraisal does not mean that an emotion is caused by a person deliberately and consciously checking off "yes" or "no" answers to: "is this relevant to a goal?", "is it congruent?" . . . and so on. The conscious aspects of emotion typically do not come until the next stage.

Context evaluation

Thoughts are salient in our experience of emotions. If you are newly in love your thoughts tend towards your loved one; if you feel anxious it is hard to stop worrying about what might befall; if you feel angry your thoughts include plans for retribution. These thoughts are about the context: thinking about plans and how to cope with the event that caused the emotion. This is the second stage in Frijda's process and the second and third in Stein, Trabasso, and Liwag's. Lazarus (1991) calls this secondary appraisal.

A good method for capturing the thoughts of this stage is to note them down in a special diary. One of the first to do this was Joanna Field (1934), who wanted to see what it was in her life that made her happy. Here are some of her thoughts after falling in love, thinking about the man she would marry. "June 8th. I want us to travel together, exploring, seeing how other people live . . . sleeping at country inns, sailing boats, tramping dusty roads together . . ." (p. 48). Here the thoughts take the form of plans of activities in a shared life of new experiences with the loved one.

In anxiety the thoughts are quite different. Here is Joanna Field again:

Oughtn't we to ask those people to tea? That's best, say, "Do you ever have time for a cup of tea? Will you come in any day?" Say we are free all the week, let them choose, will the maid answer the door? will she be too busy? what shall we give them? go into town and buy a cake? will they expect it? Can't afford these extras, but bread and jam won't do, what does one give people for tea . . .? (p. 114)

In this anxious little train of thought, Field wonders how to approach some people who are wealthier than she, rehearsing different forms of invitation, worrying about how she would feel if she calls and a maid tells her that the person she wants to see is too busy. Recent uses of the method of having subjects keep emotion diaries have yielded many examples. Oatley and Duncan (1992) report a 20-year-old woman, Abigail, who had had an angry argument with her boyfriend about preferences for different kinds of music. The argument lasted two and a half hours, but intrusive thoughts continued for three days, and kept her from sleeping for three nights. She said: "I just couldn't get through to him." Her thoughts included: "Is this going too far? If it goes too far, it [the relationship with the boyfriend] would end." Memories came to mind: the argument "reminded her of an ex-boyfriend" and made her "wonder if it [the relationship] was worth it" (p. 275).

These examples of being in love, mild anxiety, and anger, illustrate the energetic mental activity that emotions prompt. If changes of priority are to occur as a result of the event that caused the emotion, then many considerations must be canvassed. The preoccupied thoughts of emotion may be necessary, constraining attention, trying to make meaningful sense of events that challenge beliefs, recalling similar situations for comparison with the current problem, making plans for the future. If our human adaptation depends on our understanding the unexpected and on making new plans, then the preoccupation of emotions, as we decide on the meaning of what has happened and how to cope with it, is essential.

Part of this process involves attribution, deciding how an emotionally significant event was caused. As Wiener and Graham (1989) have shown, some distinct emotions depend on "attributions," the explanations of the causes of events that people give. Wiener and Graham describe how children between the ages of 5 and 11 were given little vignettes and asked to decide what emotion would occur. One was this:

This is a story about a boy named Chris. Chris's teacher gave a spelling test and he got all the words right. Chris received an "A" on the test. (Wiener & Graham, 1989, p. 407)

If the children were told that Chris had studied all the words the night before (implying that the cause of his success was his own action) they tended to say that he would feel pride, but if the cause was that the teacher gave an easy text (a cause external to Chris), then the children, especially the older ones, thought Chris would not feel pride. Comparable results were found with guilt: if an event that caused damage could have been controlled, the children thought the person causing it would feel guilt, but if it was an accident, the older children thought the person would not feel guilt.

Are the thought patterns of emotions adaptive? Some patterns that revolve endlessly in anxiety, self-denigration, or bitterness, do not seem so (Lyubomirsky & Nolen-Hoeksema, 1993). They are classified as symptoms of mental illness. With a view to capturing such patterns, Beck et al. (1979) recommend a form of diary in which a patient notes down incidents that lead to emotions, the emotions themselves, and the thoughts that occur. The thoughts are interpretations of the event. Part of Beck's therapy is to ask the patient to generate alternative thoughts as well as the ones that actually occurred. These alternative thoughts in turn might lead to different emotions. Here is an example from a medical records librarian who worked in a hospital (abbreviated from Beck, 1979, p. 165).

Event	*Emotions*	*Thoughts*	*Alternative thoughts*
The charge nurse in the coronary care unit was curt and said "I hate medical records" when I went to collect charts for the medical review committee.	Sadness Slight anger Loneliness	She does not like me.	She is foolish to hate medical records. They are her only defense in a lawsuit.

At the center of Beck's therapy is the ancient idea of Aristotle that emotions *are* evaluations, and that because we can to some extent choose how we evaluate events we can change our emotions. In this case the sadness, anger, and loneliness of the medical records librarian were caused by the thought that the coronary care nurse did not like her. But if in her context evaluations she were able to interpret the event differently, in terms of the nurse needing the records in case of a lawsuit, she might feel differently. Cognitive therapists hypothesize that depressed and anxious people have acquired habits of mind that produce sad and fearful emotions. The therapists then work with patients to discover different evaluations of events that do not lead to sadness and fear.

According to Frijda a change in action readiness is the central core of an emotion. This is point 2 of the working definition at the head of the chapter, Stage 3 in Frijda's schema. To explore this Frijda, Kuipers, and ter Schure (1989) started with 32 names of emotions (e.g., happiness, sadness, anger, etc.) and asked student subjects to remember episodes of emotion corresponding to each of these names. For each remembered episode each subject was asked to check a seven-point scale of intensity for each of 19 dimensions of appraisal (similar to those given in the section on appraisal). We can imagine that if Abigail were rating the incident that led to her angry argument with her boyfriend she would have rated it "very unpleasant," "very goal obstructive," and so forth.

Then the same incident was rated for each of 29 dimensions of action readiness. Here is a selection of the action readiness dimensions, and the items to test for them, which were to be rated from "not at all" to "very strongly."

Dimension	Action readiness item
Antagonistic	I wanted to oppose, to assault, hurt or insult
Approach	I wanted to approach, make contact
Avoidance	I wanted to have nothing to do with someone or something, to be bothered by it as little as possible, to stay away
Exuberant	I wanted to move, be exuberant, sing, jump, undertake things
Helplessness	I wanted to do something, but I did not know what; I was helpless
In command	I stood above the situation; I felt I was in command; I held the ropes
Inhibition	I felt inhibited, paralyzed, or frozen
Rest	I felt at rest, thought everything was OK, felt no need to do anything

Frijda, Kuipers, and ter Schure (1989) found that patterns of their 29 items of action readiness correctly predicted 46 percent of the names of the emotions about which the subjects had been asked – this percentage would no doubt have been higher had some of the emotion names not been synonyms (for instance, sadness, sorrow, upset). The success of predicting emotions from the appraisal items was similar but slightly lower (43 percent).

Profiles of action readiness are, therefore, at least as good in characterizing emotions as profiles of appraisal. Moreover appraisals were meaningfully related to states of action readiness (with an average 0.55 multiple correlation overall). Looking at individual groups of emotions, therefore, meaningful patterns emerge. For instance, positive emotions (such as pride, relief, enthusiasm) all show "pleasant" and "self-agency" as appraisals, and "exuberant" as the state of action readiness. Anger and rage involved "unpleasant" and "other-agency" as appraisals, and "antagonistic" action readiness.

Stein, Trabasso, and Liwag (1993) argue that traditionally in research on emotions, too little attention has been paid to the role emotions have in prompting plans, so they stress this aspect in Stage 3 of their version of the emotion process. From the age of three children know that an emotion poses a problem, and needs to be followed by some action that might solve it. And, from this age, a good deal of mental activity goes into thinking: "What to do about it." So Amy, who did not like to paint, immediately considers refusing to take the paints home, then considers taking them home but enlisting her mother's support. Abigail, who had the argument with her boyfriend, spends a good deal of time wondering how to get through to him and – more seriously – whether she should end the relationship.

Emotions, then, mark the junctures in our actions. Something has happened that is important to us. Emotions are the processes that allow us to focus on any problem that has arisen, and to change course if necessary. And if we ask what the readiness is about, or what the plans are about, for the most part they concern other people.

Expression, bodily change, action

Thoughts are private, and so to some degree is action readiness and the plans we review. So how do we recognize emotions in others? As Frijda (1986) has put it, we often recognize an emotion in others when their "behavior seems to come to a stop. Effective interaction with the environment halts, and is replaced by behavior that is centered, as it were, around the person himself, as in a fit of weeping, or laughter, anger or fear" (p. 2). These bodily and expressive effects are indicated in the third component of the working definition at the head of the chapter. They are parts of Frijda's final stage in the emotion process, and of Stein, Trabasso, and Liwag's Stage 2. Exactly where such effects occur in the emotion process is a controversial matter in the history of research on emotions. We will discuss expression, bodily change, and action, in turn.

Expression

Darwin proposed a taxonomy of emotional expressions (table 1.1), and supposed that each emotion is a discrete state, with an expression by which it can be recognized, sometimes an action, sometimes as in the case of tears or perspiration a physiological event. The term "expression" indicates something within that is externalized – "expressed." This idea corresponds to a common intuition that emotions are inner states, like substances that a person can bottle up or let out. Some implications of this idea might be misleading (Hinde, 1985) but the term has stuck.

Since Darwin's time, and especially since the work of Tomkins and his followers Ekman and Izard, research has focused on the face as the principal site of expression and the place on which objective measurements may be made. If expressions were to vary from culture to culture then although we might be able to say that they were emotional, at best we would end up with dictionaries of expressive signs, like words in different languages. Along these lines Birdwhistell (1970) had argued: "There are probably no universal symbols of emotional state . . . We can expect them [emotional expressions] to be learned and patterned according to the particular structure of particular societies" (p. 126).

There are indeed nonverbal signs of emotion which are language-like. Morris et al. (1979) have provided a dictionary of a small group of them together with their meanings and geographical distribution. You could use it, if you liked, when traveling in Europe as an addition to your phrase book, especially if you want to express contempt. For instance, the gesture of extending the index finger and little finger of one hand towards someone (see figure 4.2) indicates contempt in Italy and Spain, but it is largely unknown in Britain and Scandinavia. In Britain the equivalent gesture is raising the first and second fingers of one hand with the palm facing towards the sender, and it is largely unknown elsewhere. In America the equivalent gesture is raising the middle finger, and in Australia it is raising the thumb. All four gestures have comparable meanings as insults with a coarse sexual connotation, but except for being made with fingers they share few morphological features: they are like a

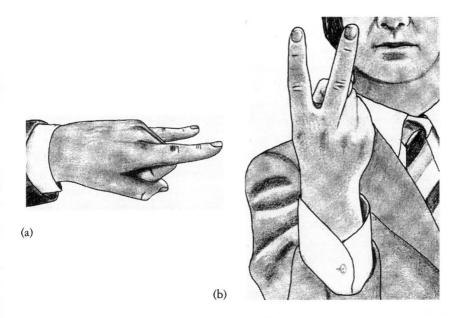

(a)

(b)

Figure 4.2 Two coarse gestures of contempt: (a) seen in Italy and other Mediterranean countries, but not in Northern Europe; (b) seen in Britain, but not in Southern Europe. Such gestures are based on learned conventions like words (Morris et al., 1979).

word in four different languages. Politicians wanting to show a common touch and believing in the universality of such gestures sometimes get them wrong: so there are news photographs of US President George Bush raising his thumb on a visit to Australia, evidently intending a sign meaning "OK," but seen quite differently by Australians. Birdwhistell's proposal was that emotional expressions of the face and voice also are of this kind: nonverbal terms that are specific to culture.

To establish the alternative, that there are some emotional expressions that could be classified in a universal taxonomy, several moves were necessary. The first was to show that among all expressions only some express emotions as such. Ekman and Friesen (1969) described five categories of nonverbal expression: (a) "emblems," more usually known as gestures, such as the coarsely insulting ones described in the previous paragraph; (b) "illustrators" that accompany speech and that vary with the degree of excitement, such as waving the arms or clenching the fist; (c) "regulators" such as nods used in adjusting the flow of conversation; (d) "affect displays," expressions such as smiling and frowning; and (e) "adaptors" or body manipulators of self-grooming, self-touching, and so forth, which often occur as what ethologists call displacement activities, signs of anxiety and inner conflict (Maestripieri et al., 1992).

The second move was to find whether any of these were species-typical, like reflexes, indicating emotions: only those of category (d) (affect displays) were potentially of this kind. The studies on pancultural recognition of photographs discussed in chapter 3 were aimed at discovering what these were.

The third move made both by Izard and his colleagues and Ekman and his colleagues was to produce coding systems for classifying facial expressions of emotion. Izard's systems MAX (Izard, 1979), and AFFEX (Izard, Dougherty, & Hembree, 1983), are based on the idea that there is a discrete set of basic emotions; his coding systems define features that best discriminate among them. Ekman's system, Facial Action Coding System (FACS) (Ekman & Friesen, 1978), catalogs facial muscles (more specifically "action units"), and their visible movements. An addendum, EM-FACS (Ekman & Friesen, 1984), describes configurations of these actions thought to be expressions of specific emotions. It takes several months' training to learn the often subtle discriminations of these systems. The technique itself is time-consuming: for a skilled FACS coder each second of video tape of a fully visible face takes at least 100 seconds to code. Progress has been made on a computer expert system for interpreting manual measurements of photographed facial expressions (Kearney & McKenzie, 1993); and Pilowsky and Katsikitis (1994) have described a computer facial recognition system working directly from video recordings which is quite successful in classifying emotional expressions posed by actors, particularly happiness which the system can classify correctly in 70 percent of the poses.

To indicate how the FACS system works, consider the smile of happiness. The coding system designates each distinct facial movement as an action unit (AU). In figure 4.3 (a) is neutral, with no facial actions, and (b) shows a face in which three action units have operated. AU6 is a contraction of the *orbicularis oculi*, the muscle that encircles each eye: it has contracted on both sides, raising the cheeks and gathering the skin inwards towards the bridge of the nose. In older people, loss of elasticity of the skin and repeated contraction of this muscle will have caused wrinkles that radiate outwards from the corner of each eye, and which become easily visible when smiling, but in this young subject wrinkles have not formed. Secondly AU12, contraction of the *zygomaticus major* muscles has occurred, pulling the corners of the lips upwards. Thirdly AU25 has occurred, not a contraction of a muscle but a relaxation that allows the lips to part while leaving the teeth closed. The muscles for AU6 and AU12 have been indicated on the right side of the photograph (b), with the contractions pulling the skin towards the circled numbers.

Humans have good voluntary control over the muscles around the mouth, perhaps because they are used in talking: so people can voluntarily curve their lips upwards. But the other part, the smile of enjoyment, involves contracting the *orbicularis oculi* muscle AU6 which is not easily controlled voluntarily. Simply to move the lips in an upward curve looks phony. It may merely

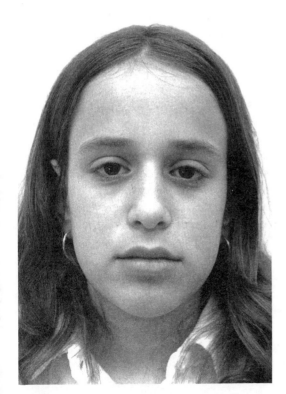 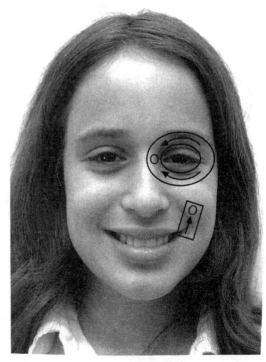

Figure 4.3 Camras's photographs of facial expressions of emotion: (a) neutral, and (b) happy. In (a) the facial muscles are relaxed, and in (b) the coding in terms of FACS action units is AU6 + AU12 + AU25. The pure Duchenne smile, such as this, is the combination of AU6 and AU12 with no action units associated with negative emotions.

indicate someone trying to cover up some other emotion, for example, anxiety. Ekman and his colleagues have shown that people who are lying may try to mask negative feelings by performing this voluntary part of smiling, but traces of anxiety may leak out. Ekman and O'Sullivan (1991) found that, with the exception of secret service agents, almost nobody can detect lying just from the face. This suggests that such subtle signs are not important in ordinary communication, but Ekman has had success in training people such as detectives and customs officers to recognize signs of anxiety leakage as clues to deception.

Ekman has called the innate pattern of enjoyment (the simultaneous contraction of the *zygomaticus major* and *orbicularis oculi*) the Duchenne smile (Ekman, Davidson, & Friesen, 1990), after the French researcher who first described it, and who was the first to take photographs of emotional expressions (Duchenne de Bologne, 1862). Ekman and Davidson (1993) have shown how, in the electroencephalogram (EEG) this Duchenne smile is associated with a different pattern of brain activity than attempted smiles made voluntarily but without contraction of the muscles round the eye.

The voice is also important for expression (Pittam & Scherer, 1993). Here too some aspects may be universal. Van Bezooijen, Van Otto, and Heenan (1983) had four male and four female native speakers of Dutch say the words *twee maanden zwanger* (meaning "two months pregnant") in a neutral voice and in voices expressing nine emotions (disgust, surprise, shame, interest, joy, fear, contempt, sadness, and anger). Audio recordings of the phrases were then played to Dutch subjects, and to subjects in Taiwan and Japan who were unfamiliar with Dutch and had little contact with any Western language. The Dutch subjects did significantly better than the others at correctly identifying neutral and emotional tones. The sad voice was well recognized by all groups (53 percent by Taiwanese, 70 percent by Japanese, 73 percent by Dutch), as was the fearful one (47 percent for Taiwanese, 40 percent by Japanese, 70 percent by Dutch). Happy tones of voice were not recognized well by Taiwanese (24 percent) or Japanese listeners (20 percent).

Although the face has been the object of overwhelmingly the largest amount of research on expression, this research has not concentrated on how important this and other cues are in recognizing emotions in real life. Planalp, DeFrancisco, and Rutherford (in press) have asked people who live with someone else to record the cues they used to tell when this other person was having an emotion. They found that a very large variety of cues was used, in some incidents people listed as many as 12. Most people (97 percent) used two or more cues to recognize any one emotion. The most frequently used cues were vocal (in two thirds of incidents), and over half the incidents were recognized using a combination of facial, verbal, and contextual cues.

Bodily change

As discussed in chapter 1, James's answer to his own question "What is an emotion?" was that just as we have systems of seeing, hearing, touch, and so on, that detect events in the outer world so there is another system aimed at events within the body. For James, and many people subsequently, feeling is not a metaphor; an emotion *is* the feeling of what is going on inside our body. This idea that emotions arise as sensations in the body has become known as the peripheral theory, in contrast to the idea that emotions arise in the brain (Cannon, 1927), the central theory.

Brief biography: William James

William James was born in 1842, eldest of five talented children. William's father, a dreamer, a bit of a crank, a man of leisure with independent means, had inherited from his own Irish immigrant father a large house in New York, where William was born. William's mother Mary was the practical one of the family. His brother Henry, born in 1843, became one of the world's great novelists, while his only sister Alice, as talented as her brothers, was not able to overcome the barriers to women in that period, and declined into invalidism. The family led an affectionate but chaotic life, with a pot-pourri of educational experiences for the children, including a procession of governesses and tutors, long stays in Europe, periods in private experimental schools. At the age of 18, William studied art for a year, then took up chemistry. Two years later he changed to medicine, gaining an MD degree in 1869. He obtained an instructor's post in physiology at Harvard in 1872. In 1878, a turning point occurred: he met Alice Gibbens, who introduced a degree of organization into his life, shared his interests, and helped him concentrate his energies. From then on his hypochondria, which had been disabling, decreased. In 1885 James became Professor of Philosophy. He was the principal founder of American psychology, as well as a considerable influence on the philosophical school of Pragmatism, whose adherents included John Dewey. An amiable, tolerant, widely read man, with a gift for thoughtful literary expression, James's *Principles of Psychology* is regarded still as the best textbook that psychology has had; besides this book his theory of emotions is the work for which he is best known.

James's idea had intuitive appeal and promised to ground emotions in physiology. It made predictions that could be tested: for instance that decreased sensation from inside the body should decrease the intensity of emotions. Conversely inducing certain bodily changes should cause emotions.

This first prediction was tested by Hohmann (1966). He interviewed 25 adult men who had suffered injuries of the spine. They had lost all sensation below the injury. The subjects had all completed high school, and none had psychiatric problems. Hohmann conducted the interviews, and says that the fact that he was himself paraplegic allowed him to establish rapport. He asked the men about sexual feelings, fear, anger, grief, sentimentality, and overall emotionality. Most of the men reported decreases in sexual feeling since their injury. Those with injuries at the neck level reported large decreases: before injury, one single 29-year-old described his previous feelings in sexual encounters: "a hot, tense feeling all over my body," but said that since the injury "it doesn't do anything for me" (p. 148). A 33-year-old was typical of paraplegic men with injuries in the lower back: "I believe the pressure I feel for sex is just a bit less. It's hard to tell because now I'm married, and of course the emotional part of it is greater because I want to please my wife, and that makes it confusing to try and say what my own feelings inside myself are. I used to be always on the hunt, maybe to make a conquest and reassure myself. All told there seems to be less tension and pressure for sex" (p. 149). Hohmann also reported decreased feelings of fear. One man had his injury at the high chest level. One day he was fishing on a lake when a storm came up and a log punctured his boat. He said: "I knew I was sinking, and I was afraid all right, but somehow I didn't have that feeling of trapped panic that I know I would have had before" (p. 150).

Along with such decreases in sexual feelings, fear, and anger, most subjects reported an increase in feelings that Hohmann called sentimentality, feeling tearful and choked up on occasions such as partings. As one reads Hohmann's descriptions, questions come to mind: What is the effect of disablement itself on people's reactions to emotion-inducing events? What is the effect of simply getting older – the time lapse since the injury ranged from 2 to 17 years with a mean of 10 years? Were Hohmann's results affected by the subjects' or the interviewer's beliefs of the dependence of emotions on the body?

One subject talking of anger said: "Now I don't get a feeling of physical animation . . . Sometimes I get angry when I see some injustice. I yell and cuss and raise hell because if you don't do it sometimes I've learned that people will take advantage of you, but it just doesn't have the heat in it. It's a mental kind of anger" (p. 151).

None of these questions is easy to answer, but a replication of Hohmann's study was carried out by Bermond et al. (1991). They reported interviews with 37 subjects who had suffered spinal injuries during the previous one to nine years (mean of 4.5 years). The interviewers were carefully trained. To avoid bias they were told that both peripheral and central theories of emotion are valid.

Subjects were asked separately about the intensities of physiological disturbances and about the subjective intensities of the emotional experiences. They were asked to remember two experiences of fear that were similar in what caused them and in their concerns for the subject, one from before and one from after the injury: 23 subjects could remember a pair of such incidents. Contrary to James's prediction, they reported subjective experiences of fear following the injury as significantly increased ($p < 0.05$). They found that purely physiological disturbance in the postinjury emotion had diminished, as would be predicted by the injury, and that the extent of this was correlated with loss of sensory input, but that this did not have a noticeable effect in decreasing the experience of emotions.

Subjects were also asked to remember two similar incidents of anger, one before and one since their injury: 32 subjects could remember such incidents. For these responses there was a slight increase in the subjective experience of anger, but no change in the remembered bodily experience of anger.

Bermond et al. also asked their subjects to rate fear, anger, grief, sentimentality, and joyfulness, on scales indicating increases and decreases since their injury. Neither in the whole group, nor in the 14 subjects with injuries in the neck region and hence the greatest sensory loss, was there any general decrease in rated emotional intensity – most subjects reported no change on most scales, though some reported some increases in intensity since their injury.

Hohmann's subjects often spoke of intense mental emotions while saying that the bodily aspect had decreased, and because of this Bermond et al. point out that their own results may therefore not be as discrepant from Hohmann's as they seem. How people experience emotions may depend on how they interpret them, on the extent to which they believe emotion to be affected by body sensations. We have to remember that both studies are based on memory. But if the memories are accurate, the results of the more recent and systematic study seem, at least, to make difficulties for James's hypothesis.

What about approaching the problem from another direction? What if bodily changes were made deliberately? Could any of these actually produce emotions? Lange (1885) in his version of the James–Lange hypothesis emphasized changes produced by the autonomic nervous system – the part of the nervous system that controls involuntary processes such as heart rate, the size of blood vessels, and sweating. But, as Andalmann and Zajonc (1989) point out, though James also emphasized these autonomic effects he did not exclude feedback from muscles, joints, and skin. So perhaps one might induce emotions by making particular body movements.

Zajonc, Murphy, and Inglehart (1989) proposed that some facial expressions have emotional effects by constricting flow through blood vessels in the face. In turn, these constrictions affect blood flow through parts of the brain, which then produce temperature changes that are experienced as positive or negative. Zajonc, Murphy, and Inglehard have performed experiments to show that merely contracting certain muscles had these effects. German speakers read four 200-word short stories, two of which had a high frequency of the vowel "ü," and two of which had none of these vowels. The German "ü" sounds like the French "u" as in *sur*, and is somewhat like the English "oo." It requires vigorous action of the muscles round the mouth, protruding the lips, rather in the opposite way to smiling. Reading the two "ü" stories subjects (as compared with reading the two "no-ü" stories) gave rise to an increase of facial temperature, and also a dislike of the "ü" stories, although all four stories were similar. In another experiment, subjects simply pronouncing the vowel "ü," as well as other vowels, liked the other vowels more. In another unobtrusive manipulation Strack, Martin, and Stepper (1988) found that getting subjects to hold a pen in the mouth, thus making the muscle movements characteristic of a smile without the subjects realizing it, gave rise to judgments of cartoons as more funny than for subjects not contracting these muscles; and Larsen, Kasimatis, and Frey (1992) induced subjects to draw their eyebrows together in a way that mimicked those of a sad face. They found that subjects' judgments of pictures was more sad, although they did not know that their eyebrow pose had implied sadness.

So there is suggestive evidence that facial changes can cause or intensify emotions, though the intensity of these emotions remains low. As Zajonc, Murphy, and Inglehart (1989) have said: "We would not expect someone who has just learned that he has cancer to turn his grief to joy by the mere contraction of the zygomatic muscle" (p. 412).

Action

Plans and actions are closely associated with emotions. Some kinds of emotional action are widely recognized. In their study of self-reports on emotional incidents by students in 27 nations, Wallbott and Scherer (1986) found actions specific to emotions, and that differences between responses as a function of the different countries of the respondents were small: "moving toward" was associated with joy, "moving against" was associated with anger, and "moving away" was associated with all negative emotions.

One might expect that during the days of behaviorism there would have been a focus on actions in relation to emotions but, of course, during these days emotions had been outlawed. So in a well-known work, *Frustration and Aggression* (Dollard et al., 1939), although relations between the amount of frustration and the probability of aggression were established, anger was not seen as causally involved. It was mentioned only once in the book (obliquely, in a footnote, where a study of increased irritability in old age is cited, p. 77). In more modern versions of this idea, however, Berkowitz (1993) has shown experimentally that aggressive responses do follow from the induction of anger.

Emotions implied by patterns of action are recognizable to others: Sogon and Masutani (1989) filmed two Japanese actors and two Japanese actresses from behind, so that viewers of the films could not see their faces. The filmed actions depicted a range of emotions (joy, surprise, fear, sadness, disgust, anger, contempt) and three "affective-cognitive structures" (affection, anticipation, acceptance) with the actors performing from scripts they were given. American and Japanese subjects watched the filmed scenes, and chose from a list of words the one that best corresponded to each scene. Recognition was 52 percent for Americans and 57 percent for Japanese. Some patterns – fear, sadness, disgust – were well recognized by both groups. Some of these, such as slumping shoulders and slowly sitting in sadness, may be universal. Others, such as the low bow to authority, can indicate fear, but it is certainly affected by culture – bowing is a conventionalized form of greeting and parting in Japan. See also Weisfeld and Beresford (1982) for a discussion of posture as an indicator of pride and dominance, Cunningham (1988) for information about how people act when they have an emotion or mood, and Montepare, Goldstein, and Clausen (1987) for recognition of emotions from gait.

As well as such individual actions, societies also provide culturally specific rituals for communal action on important emotional occasions. Funerals allow a bereaved person to express grief, to withdraw from the usual actions of life, to receive support and recognition from relatives and friends. Celebrations provide socially scripted occasions for rejoicing. And, as several writers have remarked, the rhetoric and music that accompany such rituals have a quality of arousing and sustaining the appropriate emotions in groups of people acting in concert, a quality often referred to when described in societies other than our own as "magic" (Collingwood, 1938).

Relations among elicitors, experience, expressions, and bodily changes

According to many theories of emotion, one would expect the different aspects of an emotion all to occur together. Happiness would be expected to have one kind of elicitor, one kind of experience, one type of facial expression, one set of bodily accompaniments; anger should have a different set, fear another set, and so forth. The most influential theory of coherence among these aspects is that of Tomkins (1962):

> Affects are sets of muscle and glandular responses located in the face and also widely distributed through the body, which generate sensory feedback which is either inherently "acceptable" or "unacceptable." These organized sets of responses are triggered at subcortical centers where specific "programs" for each distinct affect are stored. These programs are innately endowed and have been genetically inherited. They are capable of simultaneously capturing such widely distributed organs as the face, the heart, and the endocrines and imposing on them a specific pattern of correlated responses. (pp. 243–244)

James (1884) too predicted that specific bodily changes correspond to specific emotions. But there are also quite different kinds of theory, for instance Cannon (1927) had argued against James's peripheral theory; and proposed that bodily changes are produced by the brain, and that they are similar during different emotions such as anger and fear (1929). According to this idea, quite different emotions involve exactly the same general activation of a part of the autonomic nervous system – its sympathetic division. This so-called arousal response includes release of the hormone adrenaline. The effects of this sympathetic-adrenal response are a shift of bodily resources to prepare for action, including fight, flight, and sexual behavior.

Elicitors, experience, and bodily changes
The relation of emotions to bodily changes has been much researched. An early study was by Dysinger and Ruckmick (1933) who showed films to pre-adolescent children, adolescents, and adults, while recording their skin

conductance (a measure of imperceptible sweating). Love scenes produced changes in skin conductance, and the viewers most affected were the adolescents. Relations have also been found between events and bodily changes in other circumstances: for instance, the heart rate of physicians has been found to rise when performing difficult procedures like passing a catheter into the heart (Ira, Whalen, & Bogdanoff, 1963). The heart rate even of experienced pilots on scheduled flights rises by 50 percent on takeoffs, and sometimes even more on landings, especially when there is a complication such as poor weather (Smith, 1967). Yet other matters can touch the heart more closely: Harrer and Harrer (1977) monitored the heart rate of the famous conductor Herbert von Karajan. He flew his own private jet. His heart rate rose when landing his plane at Salzburg Airport. It rose further when he was told to make an emergency takeoff just after landing, but not so much as when he was conducting emotional passages of Beethoven's "Leonora Overture No. 3."

But are such bodily changes specific to particular emotions? Ekman et al. (Ekman, Levenson, & Friesen, 1983; Levenson, Ekman, & Friesen, 1990) asked 12 professional actors and four scientists to pose facial expressions corresponding to each of six emotions (surprise, disgust, sadness, anger, fear, and happiness). The subjects' faces were video recorded, and four bodily measures were taken (heart rate, hand temperature, skin conductance, and forearm muscle tension). Then posing instructions were given in steps, for example, "first raise your brows and pull them together," "now raise your upper eyelids" and so on. Subjects were not told the emotions to which each pose corresponded; after each pose they were asked to describe any feelings, memories, or sensations that occurred during the pose. Then after a short rest a new pose began. It was found that each posed expression was accompanied by a somewhat specific bodily pattern. Low heart rate was characteristic of poses corresponding to happiness, disgust, and surprise. High heart rate was characteristic of sadness, anger, and fear. Also, angry expressions were differentiated by high skin temperature from those of fear and sadness which had low skin temperature.

After the experiments with posing, subjects were asked to relive remembered episodes of the six emotions, and to rate the intensity of each on a 0 to 8 scale, with 8 representing "as intense as ever experienced." Data were only used when these ratings were at or above the midpoint on the scale, and measurements like those following directed facial action were made. With imagery neither heart rate nor finger temperature differentiated among emotions, though skin conductance showed some differentiation.

In a different approach, Stemmler (1989) had 42 women students undertake a procedure in which they were connected to a polygraph by which eight bodily measures were recorded. The procedure had control conditions, and many stages. It included three real life inductions of emotion: one of fear (listening to the terrifying ending of *The Fall of the House of Usher* by Edgar Allan Poe accompanied by scary music and then – unexpectedly – all the lights going off for one minute), one of anger (being required to solve insoluble anagrams, while being told brusquely to shout "I don't know" louder, because the sound equipment was not working well), and one of happiness (being told all the recordings had been successful, that there was a short rest, and that the payment for taking part in the experiment had been increased). There were also two emotional imagery inductions, asking subjects to recall an episode of fear and an episode of anger. For each induction subjects completed scales to indicate the intensity of specific emotions, and were also asked in an interview to say what they experienced. The averages on the response scales showed that both the real life and imagery inductions worked well, and produced similar subjective responses, though the interviews indicated that one third of the subjects did not experience the intended emotions. For the real life inductions, some bodily measures (such as skin conductance and head temperature) did discriminate between fear, anger, and happiness. Some other measures found to discriminate in other studies (such as heart rate) did not. In the imagery conditions, none of the bodily measures discriminated among the emotions.

In understanding the relation of emotions and bodily changes, Cacioppo et al.'s (1993) discussion is helpful. They have carefully reviewed many studies, proposed methodological criteria, and concluded that it is unclear whether specific bodily changes correspond to the experience of specific emotions. Most measures of bodily change (e.g., skin conductance, facial temperature, etc.) have not been found to correspond reliably in a one-to-one fashion with specific emotions in different studies: the most reliable measure is heart rate, but even here results have not been clear. In 10 comparisons of happiness and anger in different studies, half showed significant differences between the two emotions, but half did not.

Cacioppo et al. conclude that there is evidence for at least three kinds of association between bodily change and experienced emotion. One, common to both James and Tomkins, is correspondence between specific bodily changes and specific emotions. The second is Cannon's idea of bodily activation being general rather than specific, and occurring when the body prepares for vigorous activity. The third is that some patterns of bodily change might be ambiguous. We know that visual figures can be ambiguous (see figure 4.4), so it is easy to imagine that a pattern of bodily response could be too: someone on a roller coaster can alternate between happy excitement and near panic. Experimentally this kind of ambiguity was the basis of the influential study of Schachter and Singer (1962, discussed in more detail in chapter 9) who found that the same state of arousal could be interpreted either as happiness or anger, depending on the social situation; this kind of effect has become the basis for Mandler's (1984) theory. Cacioppo et al. also propose different kinds of relationship at different phases of processing: first perhaps a generally positive arousal associated with approach or a generally negative effect associated with avoidance may occur, then, with more cognitive processing, more specific effects, or ambiguous effects, may take place.

Figure 4.4 Ambiguous figure, after Jastrow (1900). Exactly the same pattern of lines on the paper can be seen either as a duck's head or a rabbit's: similarly, if emotions depend on perception of bodily patterns, some patterns such as arousal could be experienced in two ways, for instance as excitement or fear.

Elicitors, experience, and expressions

What about the mapping of eliciting situations onto experience and facial expression? Do these aspects occur together? The most elaborate experiment so far is that of Rosenberg and Ekman (1994). They studied 20 women undergraduates who watched short films calculated to evoke disgust. One was of an amputation; in the other a rat entered the mouth of a sleeping man. While subjects watched the films individually on a large color screen, their faces were surreptitiously videotaped. Later their facial expressions were coded using the FACS system. After watching the film, subjects saw it again on a small black and white screen, and indicated where they had experienced emotions during their first viewing. The experimenters found some correspondence between disgusting parts of the film, subjects' reports of the emotions they had experienced, and their facial expressions of disgust – but only 50 percent of facial expressions of emotion were accompanied by subjective feelings. A comparable lack of exact correspondence was reported in another study of watching unpleasant films, by Tomarken and Davidson (reported in Davidson, 1992b). Subjects often reported fear while showing facial expressions of disgust, but not fear.

Yet more challenging results have been reported by Kraut and Johnson (1979). They unobtrusively observed and filmed people playing or watching sports events, and found little relation between events that would make people happy and their facial expressions. One study was in a bowling alley; in observing 1,793 rolls of the ball they found that smiles were quite unrelated to how well the bowler had done on each roll. In a more acute test, Kraut and Johnson watched 116 rolls of the ball, and counted a good score for a strike or spare, and a bad score for other outcomes. One observer was stationed unobtrusively behind the pins with binoculars, observing the face of the bowler as he or she watched the ball hit or miss. Another observer sat behind the bowler and recorded expressions as the bowler turned to face his or her friends. According to theories of coherence among emotion measures, happiness should be elicited by a good score, and we might expect it to be displayed in a smile, perhaps enhanced when the bowler faced his or her friends. With a poor score one would predict frustration, expressed perhaps in a frown or angry expression. Kraut and Johnson found something quite different. When they were facing the pins, bowlers smiled only 4 times in 116 rolls, only once when a good score was made (out of a total of 26 occasions when there were good scores). But they frequently smiled when they turned to face their friends. They smiled in this way after 36 rolls – and here is the thought-provoking observation: there was no difference in the frequency of smiling following a good score or a bad score. Taking this idea further, Jones, Collins, and Hong (1991) filmed 10-month-old babies as they played with a group of interesting toys, and as they turned round to look at their mother who was seated behind them. The babies did smile nonsocially at the toys, but they smiled much more at their mothers. On occasions when the mothers had been instructed to attend to the infant, the frequency of the infant's smiling at her was higher than when she had been asked to remain passive (see figure 4.5). If facial expressions are principally communicative it would of course make sense for smiles to be made primarily to other people.

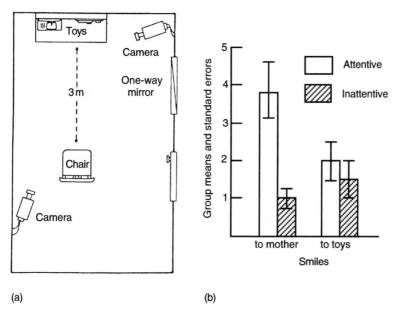

(a)   (b)

Figure 4.5 (a) The experimental setting for Jones et al.'s (1991) experiment. When playing with the toys the infant had his or her back to the mother who was seated on the chair. In (b) are shown the means and standard errors of the numbers of smiles, defined in terms of activation of the FACS AU12 (zygomatic muscle). More smiles were made toward the mother than toward the toys, and this effect was larger when the mother was asked to be attentive. However, even in these cases the majority of smiles were started by the child, while turning towards the mother, and before she came in sight.

Fridlund (1994) takes failures of expression to correspond closely with elicitors as evidence against some theories of emotion, especially Ekman's (e.g. 1994) neurocultural version of Tomkins's theory. Fridlund's alternative, which he calls the behavioral ecology view, is that expressions are not of emotions at all, but of intentions. Expressions have coevolved with abilities to recognize them. So some expressions signal welcome or friendliness, others signal preparedness to attack, and so forth. None of these expressions can be understood outside the social context of their intentions and recognition by others. They aid the negotiation of social encounters.

Separate functions of cognitive, bodily, and expressive systems

What, then, are we to make of the relations among elicitors, subjective feelings, physiological changes, and expressions? With all the objective measures one might think this should be the clearest aspect of research on emotion; instead it is one of the most confusing. We believe, tentatively, that the best answer is the one proposed by Lang (1985, 1988). He pointed out that after psychological therapy, patients' anxiety might be reduced on some measures, for instance on verbal self-report scales, but remain high on bodily measures.

Lang postulated three separate response systems that are not closely tied together: the cognitive-verbal, the bodily-physiological, and the behavioral-expressive. Correlation of changes in one system with those of another have typically been found to be low, sometimes not even positive.

We can extend Lang's argument by postulating that each of the three systems (cognitive-verbal, bodily-physiological, behavioral-expressive) has its own functions. The argument goes like this: the system with which most theories of emotions are concerned is the cognitive-verbal system. We can experience some aspects of it, and according to these experiences an episode of emotion usually lasts between a few minutes and a few hours (Frijda et al., 1991). These are the emotions we notice, the emotions we can refer to when we think back over the last few hours, the emotions we discuss with other people: "I was happy to find that book in the used-book store," "I was angry that John had arranged the meeting without telling me," "When my child had not come home I was terrified she might have had an accident." What each of these states does is to let us know about something important to our concerns, our goals. The function of this cognitive-verbal system is that each emotion, as Frijda has said, is a state of readiness which gives priority and commitment to one set of goals and plans, rather than to another – eagerness to read the book we found, preparedness to remonstrate with John, vigilance for the child's arrival.

By contrast, expressions of the face and bodily changes last just a few seconds – and most pass unnoticed. Moreover, people are not, in general, accurate in reporting their own bodily changes (Rimé, Philippot, & Cisamolo, 1990). Bodily systems have their own functions, which may include complex adjustments among different organs. Where a change occurs over minutes, as when a pilot's heart rate rises when landing in bad weather, its function may be based on switching bodily resources for energetic action, anticipating an emergency. This switch may be partly genetic, partly learned – it is known that bodily systems easily become classically conditioned to expectations. The function of this system is to make ready, and to regulate, bodily resources for different kinds of action.

As well as the measures of short-term bodily changes we have discussed so far in this chapter, measures have also been taken over longer periods, comparable to those during which people become subjectively aware of emotions. In such studies more specific relations have been found. Elmadjian et al. (1957), for instance, studied levels of the hormone nor-adrenaline (also known as nor-epinephrine) and its relation to anger, and the level of the hormone adrenaline (also known as epinephrine) and its relation to anxiety or fear in several situations. In one they had professional ice hockey players give urine samples both before a game, and three hours later when the game was over. Ice hockey involves a good deal of competitive aggression. The average levels of nor-adrenaline in the urine of 20 forwards and defensemen were on average six times higher after a game than before; in the goaltender they were three times higher. In two players who, after physical examination by the trainer were not allowed to participate, nor-adrenaline levels remained the same. Increases of adrenaline were higher in the goaltender, and in the two players who had to watch from the bench. Elmadjian et al. attribute the nor-adrenaline increases to anger and aggression: they were not due to physical activity, because they did not occur in some subjects who performed hard physical activity for two hours, but they did occur in the goaltender who does not move much during a game. Wagner (1989), reviewing the history and recent studies of the physiology of emotions, concludes that there is reasonable evidence for differentiation in hormonal accompaniments of fear and anger, though differentiation among other emotions is less clear. According to the three-systems view, coherence in studies such as Elmadjian's occurs because experience, expression in aggressive interaction or in anxiety, and bodily change, all occur together, and they occur over similar periods of time.

A three-systems account, of the kind suggested by Lang, helps to explain why imagined or remembered emotions produce smaller and less differentiated bodily responses than real life events. This kind of result, as in Ekman et al.'s (1983) and in Stemmler's (1989) studies, is widely found. It argues against emotion-specific bodily changes, but it is explained on a three-systems view because in imagery there is no need for mobilization of bodily resources. Cacioppo et al. (1993) point out that emotions are caused not just in one way (e.g. by bodily change) but in several ways. Sometimes strong subjective emotions occur with no bodily change at all. Sometimes one kind of emotion has been found to correspond to several different kinds of bodily change. Sometimes one kind of bodily change has been shown to accompany quite different emotions.

The system of facial expression also has its own functions: it is largely social. So, as Kraut and Johnson (1979) found, we do not usually smile unless there is someone to smile at. Once again, therefore, by postulating separable systems, as Lang has done, we can make sense of their functions. If the functions of expressions are largely of communicating intentions in joint activity then sometimes there will be coherence with experienced emotions, sometimes not. Usually, like many bodily changes, facial expressions are fleeting; people are barely aware of them. But if their function is largely social, largely in regulation of moment-by-moment interaction – a smile of encouragement, a frown of frustration – there is no reason to suppose that such expressions necessarily correspond exactly with the longer-lasting states we become aware of in ourselves or others, such as the happiness of a shared activity among friends, or the anger of a quarrel.

So what are emotions really?

We have considered conceptualizations and aspects of emotions. So what are emotions really? To answer this question we propose a hypothesis. Emotions have traditionally been regarded as extras in psychology, not serious mental functions like perception, language, thinking, learning. Our survey of the literature for this book leads to a different conclusion: emotions are not extras. They are the very center of human mental life. Campos et al. (1994) put it like this: emotions are those processes which "establish, maintain, change, or terminate the relation between the person and the environment on matters of significance to the person" (p. 285). In other words emotions link what is important for us to the world of people, things, and happenings.

Let us approach this neuropsychologically. Remember Phineas Gage (discussed in chapter 1), the railroad construction foreman whose frontal lobes were damaged when an iron bar was shot through them by an accidental explosion, and who became unable to organize his life. Hanna Damasio and colleagues (1994), using computer methods with Gage's skull, determined that the region of his brain that was destroyed was the lower middle part of the frontal lobes. Antonio Damasio (1994) and his colleagues have now studied many patients with this kind of damage to their frontal lobes and have noticed that, like Phineas Gage, their emotions seem blunted. Along with the emotional deficit, frontally damaged patients have great difficulties in planning ordinary life: they make disastrous social decisions – such as associating with the wrong kinds of people – while dithering endlessly over issues that are inconsequential.

Antonio Damasio (1994) proposes the following hypothesis. For patients with damaged frontal lobes the deficits in emotions and in planning have a common cause. Emotions are necessary because when we plan our lives, rather than examining every option, some possibilities are emotionally blocked off. We do not even consider decisions that would be socially punishing. Some other directions are emotionally attractive, so we search more extensively for solutions in those directions. Damasio proposes that it was this socioemotional guidance system that was affected in the brains of the original Phineas Gage and of the modern Phineas Gages he has studied.

For Damasio, the guidance system is the body itself: emotional events are experienced as bodily reactions – "somatic markers" as he calls them. These markers can be learned so that in thinking of possible decisions, any outcome of a kind that has previously been bad for you "you experience as an unpleasant gut feeling" (1994, p. 173). Automatically, based on conditioned avoidance, you then tend not to make decisions leading to this kind of punishing event. Similarly you tend to be attracted to events that have been associated with reward.

Damasio's hypothesis is that although the origin of emotions is bodily, as they become learned and established they can occur entirely within the brain, no longer needing the feedback loop via the body. As we have discussed above, the bodily bases of emotions remain unclear, so this aspect of Damasio's hypothesis may remain controversial. More important, we believe, is the deeper issue that Damasio discusses – the relation of emotions to real-life planning.

First consider a slight amendment to Damasio's idea, a metaphor: think of decision making about your life as exploring within a landscape in which height indicates emotional difficulty. Mountains make progress in some directions hard: you might have to climb against steep gradients of fear, or potential loss. Fertile valleys are attractive and indicate easier going, helped by familiarity, by roads, by signposts, by people, and other aspects of culture.

Simon (1967) argued that we humans are limited by our embodiment: we can only be in one place at a time. We are limited too by being able only to know a tiny amount about the world. Being only able to see as far as the next hill, or curve in the path, we never know enough to predict exactly what will happen. So our knowledge and exploration of such landscapes is forever incomplete. We will often encounter the unexpected. Oatley (1992) has extended Simon's postulate by noting that full rationality in human life is limited not just by our partial knowledge and finite resources, but because we often have goals that cannot be fully reconciled: for some people, for instance, a career and a satisfying sexual relationship conflict. Moreover most of our concerns involve other people. Though we humans are good at cooperation with others, these others often also have goals that we do not share.

In real life, purely logical search through all possibilities is not possible (because of limitations of resources, multiple goals, and problems of coordination with others). Nevertheless we must act and, as the great dramatists of Western culture have shown, herein are the roots of human tragedy: despite our limitations we must take responsibility for our actions, and suffer their effects. This is why emotions or something like them are necessary to bridge across the unexpected and the unknown, to guide reason, and to give priorities among multiple goals.

So emotion is not something opposed to reason. Emotions and their potentiality for guiding and managing thought in a general way are more basic. They complement the deficiencies of thinking. And perhaps most important of all, as we stressed in chapter 3, emotions provide the infrastructure for social life: the plans they prompt are largely plans that involve others. This is something that appraisal theories, goal-relevance theories, studies of bodily changes and expression, do not deny but tend to neglect. The readiness that emotions induce provides outline structures for particular modes of relating: emotions of happiness and affection provide for cooperation, sadness allows for withdrawal from social interaction and the seeking of help, anger provides for conflict with others, and anxiety makes for wariness and deference.

What emotions really are, therefore, are the guiding structures of our lives – especially of our relations with others.

The affective realm: emotions – moods – dispositions

Many terms have been used to indicate emotions. The term "feeling" is a synonym for emotion, although with a broader range. In the older psychological literature the term "affect" was used. It is still used to imply an even wider range of phenomena that have anything to do with emotions, moods, dispositions, and preferences. In figure 4.6 we show this spectrum in terms of the duration of each kind of state.

Part of the difficulty of answering the question "What is an emotion?" is that "emotion" and the adjective "emotional" are sometimes used in the same way as "affect" to imply a whole range of states and conditions. But as research has proceeded it has become clear that it is merely frustrating to offer the same explanation for states that are different. It is better to use terms and concepts more selectively (Ekman & Davidson, 1995).

Episodes of emotion
A consensus is emerging: the term "emotion" or "emotion episode" is generally used for states that last a limited amount of time. As indicated in figure 4.6, facial expressions and most bodily responses generally last from 0.5 to 4

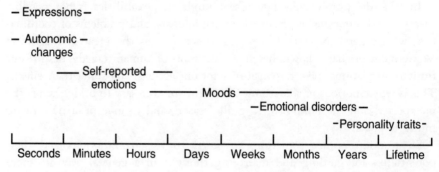

Figure 4.6 A spectrum of affective phenomena in terms of the time course of each.

seconds. The states of which people are conscious and can report, can be conveniently measured by asking people to keep structured diaries of these episodes recording their duration, intensity, eliciting circumstance, and so forth, as described above, or by getting people to remember episodes and then to make appraisals of suggested features of them. Emotions recorded in these ways are typically described as lasting between a few minutes and a few hours.

Moods

The term "mood" refers to an emotional state that usually lasts for hours, days, or weeks, sometimes as a low intensity background. When it starts or stops may be unclear. Whereas episodes of emotion typically have an object (they are intentional in the philosophical sense), moods are often objectless, free-floating. Frijda (1993a) has suggested that this distinction may be the best way of differentiating emotions and moods. Both involve readiness: an emotion episode tends to change the state of readiness for action, moods maintain such states and resist change. When in a sad mood, for instance, an invitation to go out and enjoy oneself is resisted. We do not always try to create an affective state that is most pleasant (Parrott, 1993).

Measurement of mood has become increasingly popular: an early study was by Nowlis and Nowlis (1956) to see if drugs such as amphetamines, barbiturates, and antihistamines had effects on mood in experiments where groups of people had to interact with each other. Moderate doses of the three kinds of drug had effects on mood as well as on people's behavior. But the effects were not simple: they depended on the subject's mood before taking the drug, and on the moods of others. Though everyone knew that such drugs had effects on mood, when these studies started this was not thought of as their primary effect. Now, as Nowlis and Nowlis pointed out, many drugs are used mainly to modify moods. Alcohol is the mood-altering drug that is probably the most widely used in Western society. Its primary effect is to decrease anxiety. Mood change is also the main target of prescription drugs classed as antidepressants and tranquillizers. So moods are relatively long-lasting emotional states, and they can be altered in ways that do not involve appraisals of external events.

Nowlis and Nowlis used a method called an adjective checklist to measure mood. Their list is not much used now; more recently, examples of checklists to assess positive and negative moods have been offered by Green, Goldman, and Salovey (1993), for example:

cheerful	blue
contented	depressed
happy	downhearted
pleased	gloomy
satisfied	sad
warmhearted	unhappy

The principle is to make up sets of adjectives that are synonyms of the moods in which you are interested (in the above cases happy and sad, or positive and negative). Then scramble all the adjectives and ask the subject to check any that apply to him or her. You count one point for each adjective from each set.

A second method is to offer statements like: "I am feeling sad and dispirited." Then ask people to indicate agreement on a scale – a common five-point scale is "strongly agree, agree, not sure, disagree, strongly disagree." Alternatively you can make up a scale indicating the extent to which each statement "Describes me."

A third method is to use a scale like the following:

Circle a number on the scale below to indicate how sad you feel.
Not at all 0–1–2–3–4–5–6–7–8–9–10 The most intense I have felt in my life

The ends of this kind of scale are marked with verbal expressions called anchor points, with which the subject can compare his or her current experience.

Green, Goldman, and Salovey (1993) give a good survey of mood scales, and show that different scales introduce different kinds of bias, for instance in an adjective checklist a person may check all the adjectives indicating sadness, and thus score six out of six (on the above checklist) although not feeling intensely sad. It is often a good idea, therefore, to use several of the above methods together, and perhaps add the scores to make composite mood measures.

Emotional disorders

For emotional states that last longer than moods, different terms are used: "emotional disorder" is a term used for the two most common psychiatric syndromes – mood disorder (depression and mania) and anxiety disorder (which has many different forms). Emotional disorders last for weeks or months, some for many years. Such disorders are now routinely assessed by research interviews, which relate them to categories in the *Diagnostic and Statistical Manual of Mental Disorders*, DSM-IV (American Psychiatric Association, 1994).

Thus in DSM-IV major depression is a mood disorder that includes depressed mood, or loss of interest or pleasure in most activities, lasting at least two weeks, accompanied by at least four of the following further symptoms that continue or occur nearly every day:

- significant weight loss or gain (without deliberate dieting);
- insomnia (not being able to sleep) or hypersomnia (sleeping too much);
- agitation or being markedly slowed down (observable by others, not just subjective);
- fatigue or loss of energy;
- feelings of worthlessness or inappropriate guilt;

- lack of concentration or indecisiveness;
- recurrent thoughts of death or plans for suicide.

Clearly not all these are emotional (for example, weight loss) but it is a matter of considerable research interest to find what relation episodes of depression have to normal episodes of sadness. We will take up this issue further in chapters 8 and 11. Diagnosis indicates categories of disorder. Intensities of disorder are often measured by questionnaire scales: for depression the Beck Depression Inventory (Beck, Steer, & Garbin, 1988) is probably the most widely used. Here is Item 10 from this inventory. To the left of each statement are scores given for each response option:

0 I don't cry any more than usual.
1 I cry more now than I used to.
2 I cry all the time now.
3 I used to be able to cry, but now I can't cry even though I want to.

The scale has 21 items; a score of 10 to 15 is usually taken as indicating mild depression, and 20 to 29 as indicating moderate to severe depression.

Personality

In a further step along the spectrum, there are terms used to describe aspects of personality which can last a lifetime. Many aspects have an emotional component, for example, shyness implies a tendency to social anxiety. The term "trait" is used to designate any long-lasting aspect of personality.

Although people behave differently in different situations, so that it is important to recognize person–situation interactions (Mischel, 1968), there is also consistency of some emotionally based aspects of behavior across time. We discuss long-lasting temperamental differences, and traits of personality, in chapter 7.

Here we give an example from the widely used State–Trait Anxiety Inventory (Spielberger & Krasner, 1988). Part of the inventory assesses current state – anxious mood – by offering statements and asking for extent of agreement with them, as described above. To assess an anxious personality trait, questionnaire items have been selected that do not overlap with the current mood state of anxiety, for example:

I worry too much over something that really doesn't matter.
I get in a state of tension or turmoil as I think over my recent concerns and interests.

For such items, subjects indicate one of the following: "almost never, sometimes, often, almost always." Responses are respectively given scores of 1,

2, 3, 4, and the scores are summed for 20 items that the test constructors have identified, to give the person's total trait anxiety score.

Relationships among parts of the emotion spectrum

The relationship between emotional phenomena on different parts of the spectrum of figure 4.6 can be complex. In general the relationships of episodes of emotion, moods, psychiatric symptoms, and traits are not well understood. Some relationships are known: for happiness Diener, Sandvik, and Pavot (1991) have shown that it is the frequency of positive moods, rather than their intensity, that predicts whether a person is generally happy as measured by various psychometric tests. We will take up the issue of the relation of emotion and moods to personality and to emotional disorders in later chapters.

Components or basic emotions

One of the main purposes of theory is to reduce complexity to manageable proportions, to see emotions as composed of parts that are more understandable than the whole array of emotional phenomena. As Reisenzein (1992a) has put it, these attempts take two main forms: either theorists reduce emotions to parts that are not themselves emotions (e.g., appraisals or dimensions), or they argue that the diverse set of emotions can be reduced to basic emotions, with the many different forms being complexes involving these basic emotions.

Most researchers agree that there is a biological basis for emotions. Some theorists take the view represented in the left half of table 4.1, and see emotions as based on parts that are put together, so that emotions are talked about in different ways by different cultures according to which features are emphasized. For these a common metaphor is that there is an inherited, biological, basis of emotion just as there is for human language, which is a human universal. Specific emotions derive from patterns of parts, just as specific human languages derive from patterns of words. In the world of emotions such patterns reflect styles of life and socialization in the cultures from which they arise.

The alternative, indicated in the right-hand column of table 4.1, is that whole emotions (not just components) are universals. There are some basic start-up programs of emotions derived from evolutionary selection. Following the principles that have been found in attachment which we discussed in chapter 3, these programs require interactions with others for their development, and considerable differences can be produced in different societies, and in different individuals.

In order not to sit on the fence, we should say that in our current assessment of the evidence for this book we favor the view that some basic emotions are human universals – though we also see the attractions of the other view; and on the question of the coherence of experiential, bodily, and expressive components, we incline (as discussed above) towards the view of Lang that these systems are separable. The issues are by no means settled, and we could imagine changing our minds. The metaphor we prefer is that emotions are not indefinitely various like human languages; they are more like musical notes. In most systems of music there is just a small set of discrete notes, repeated at octave intervals. Just so, we believe, there is a finite set of emotions. They can be repeated at different intensities, so happiness can occur with quiet engagement in some activity, as cooperative pleasure in another's company, as joy, as ecstasy. The same emotion can have different qualities, just as middle C on a piano and a trombone sound different. Sequences of emotions can follow each other in patterns that are distinctive to cultures, just as notes follow one another in melodies. And they can occur in mixtures, as notes do in chords. In this metaphor emotions of different cultures are like distinctive musical genres: the choir song, the string quartet, the country ballad, jazz. Each genre is distinctive (each is indeed produced as a particular cultural form). In each a small range of the same basic elements like the 12 notes of Western music, equivalent to basic emotions, occur in forms, sequences, and combinations, that are quite different.

Table 4.1 Two sets of elements in two leading families of emotion theories. The papers cited are examples in which an aspect of the respective theory is discussed, and/or data are critically reviewed with a conclusion favoring one alternative

	Componential theories	*Theories of basic emotions*
Underlying idea	Emotions based on reflex-like components (Ortony & Turner, 1990)	Emotions derive from genetically derived species-characteristic programs (Tomkins, 1962)
Appraisal	Based on features (Ellsworth, 1991) or dimensions (Russell, 1978)	Based on goal-relevance (Oatley & Johnson-Laird, 1987)
Significance evaluation	Emotion concepts, including self-talk, are culturally variable (Harré, 1986)	Unfolding emotion episodes follow basic patterns (Stein, Trabasso, & Liwag, 1993)
Action readiness	Culturally variable (Mesquita & Frijda, 1992)	Derived from evolutionarily based programs of readiness (Tooby & Cosmides, 1990)
Expression	Expressions vary with social context and may not indicate emotions (Fridlund, 1994)	Facial expressions are fixed human universals and correspond to basic emotions (Ekman, 1992)
Physiological changes	Low correlation with other aspects of emotion (Lang, 1988)	Coherence between expression, physiological, and experiential aspects (Levenson, Ekman, & Friesen, 1990)

The debate between those favoring a componential view and those favoring basic emotions is energetic. To the readers and writers of this book it reflects a challenge – there can be several interpretations of complex phenomena. Like ambiguous figures, there can be mutually excluding views. For readers this can be confusing. It may require the suspension of belief in any idea that a "correct" theory on some aspects of emotion is yet possible. For researchers, this state is as it should be at the growing edge.

Overall we believe that though a firm definition of emotions may not yet be possible, the idea that emotions are states that relate events to what is important for a person, that they prompt plans and provide outline structures for relations with others, will allow us to appreciate their functions, and act as a basis for understanding.

Summary

Ordinarily we think of emotions in terms of prototypes, typical examples, though scientifically emotions need to be defined. Emotions might best be considered as processes, with identifiable stages: first events are evaluated for their relevance to what is important to us, next comes an evaluation of the context – what can be done about the event. An emotion is a state of readiness for action, setting priorities and prompting plans. Accompanying it are components of bodily change, expression, and actions, or urges to action. Research on the relations between these components of emotion has shown that although they do sometimes occur together, their linkage is loose, sometimes an emotion experienced subjectively is accompanied by bodily changes and expression, sometimes not. One possibility is that the cognitive, bodily, and expressive aspects of emotion have different functions. The central aspect of emotions, however, is change in readiness, that gives priority to some goals and plans rather than others, and that mediates social relationships. Different emotional phenomena have different time courses. Facial expressions and many bodily changes are usually complete within a few seconds. The emotions we notice and talk to others about usually last minutes or hours. Moods last hours, days, or weeks. Emotional disorders such as depression and anxiety states last for months or years; personality traits also have an emotional quality, and can last a lifetime. One of the unresolved issues in emotion research is what emotions are made up of. One view is that they are made up of components that are not themselves emotions, such as appraisals and pieces of expression. If this were the case it would help understand how different cultures prioritize and name different bundles of such components. The other view is that there is a small set of biologically given basic emotions, and that these are elaborated by culture to produce the large set of emotions that people experience.

The best recent book, written for a nonspecialist readership to explore a bodily based answer to William James's question "What is an emotion?" is:

Antonio R. Damasio (1994). *Descartes' error*. New York: Putnam.

For a cognitive account of emotions, their nature, and their implications for life and health, see the long and scholarly book:

Richard S. Lazarus (1991). *Emotion and adaptation*. New York: Oxford University Press.

Alternatively, a more popular book with the same themes is:

Richard S. Lazarus & Bernice N. Lazarus (1994). *Passion and reason: Making sense of our emotions*. New York: Oxford University Press.

For an account of the prototype approach to emotion concepts, comparing it with necessary and sufficient conditions, see:

James A. Russell (1991). In defense of a prototype approach to emotion concepts. *Journal of Personality and Social Psychology, 60,* 37–47.

On the question of the differentiation between emotions and moods see:

Nico H. Frijda (1993). Moods, emotion episodes, and emotions. In M. Lewis & J. M. Haviland (Eds.), *Handbook of emotions* (pp. 381–403). New York: Guilford.

Brain Mechanisms of Emotion

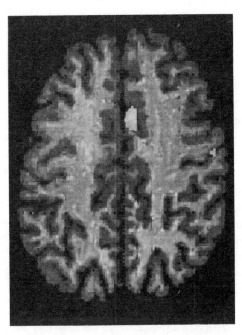

Figure 5.0 Image from Positron Emission Tomography (PET, one of a range of new technologies for visualizing brain activity) of a transverse scan through a human brain in an experiment on the emotional effects of contracting muscles in the left side of the face which induce a negative mood. This scan shows a region – the brighter area on the right side near the midline – in the anterior cingulate gyrus in which there is greater blood flow, indicating greater nerve-cell activity, following left-sided as compared with right-sided contractions

*Herein too may be felt the powerlessness of mere Logic . . . to resolve these problems
which lie nearer to our hearts.*

George Boole, 1854, An Investigation of the Laws of Thought, p. 416

How do brain mechanisms of emotion work?

The human brain is calculated to have about 100,000,000,000 nerve cells; typical cells have perhaps 10,000 synapses, some as many as 150,000 (Kandel, Schwartz, & Jessell, 1991). Imagine making sense of how the brain works. We can study anatomy using techniques that show nerve pathways and individual nerve cells, and we can use new scanning techniques to indicate where metabolism is going on as different psychological activities occur. We can study effects of accidental damage, or of lesions made deliberately in the brains of animals for experimental purposes. We can stimulate parts of the brain electrically or with substances that affect the chemical mechanisms of neurons, applied either generally as drugs or locally to small regions of the brain, and relate effects to knowledge of biochemistry and cell biology. And we can record the electrical activity of single nerve cells or groups of them. That is it: anatomy, lesions, stimulation, recording.

The brain is unlike a computer in many ways, but if it were a computer it would be vastly more complex than any that now exists. If we were trying to find out how a computer worked, say one that was running a program that held conversations with a human being, these techniques would amount to looking at the wiring diagrams, observing effects of exploding tiny bombs inside the machine, seeing what happened if we applied electrical currents to one region or another, recording voltages from different parts while the program was running. You can see that although biology and neuroscience are treated as hard sciences in comparison with the softer disciplines of psychology and anthropology, this does not mean that their evidence gives easy access to understanding. Making any valid inferences from such evidence about psychological processes involves many steps, and it is difficult to get the inferences right.

With such complexity, understanding how the brain works to generate and recognize emotions seems daunting; without a conceptual schema, or without energetic collaboration between brain scientists and social scientists, it would be. The schema that allowed us to start making sense of brain mechanisms and emotion was due to Descartes (1649). The mechanism he proposed was called the reflex. It works like this. Events (stimuli) are able to excite sensory receptors, and these start messages along the sensory nerves to the brain where, via a set of switches, they are rerouted along motor nerves to work the muscles. The system is arranged so that the rerouting of messages produces a response more or less appropriate to the stimulus. Descartes thought sensory stimuli pulled little strings that ran inside the sensory nerves to open tiny valves which would let fluid from a central reservoir run down the motor nerve tubes to inflate muscles. Nowadays, of course, we know the brain does not work by strings and hydraulics. The history of neurophysiology has been largely that of showing how the mechanisms proposed by Descartes occur by means of messages carried by electricity and chemicals.

Researchers have asked what are the pathways of nerve messages? Where do they go? How do they diverge and converge? In figure 5.1 you can see some of the areas thought to be important for nerve messages concerned with emotions. They include the striatal region, the hypothalamus, and the limbic system, which are in the lower and central regions of the brain. Then there is the neocortex, which includes the frontal lobes that are thought to be especially important for emotions.

Descartes's idea of the reflex has the environment controlling what happens via a set of switches. But the idea rather leaves out the brain's influences on these pathways. For understanding emotions there have been two important modifications. The first is the idea that actions prompted by emotions are not merely responses. They are generated by self-regulating systems based on

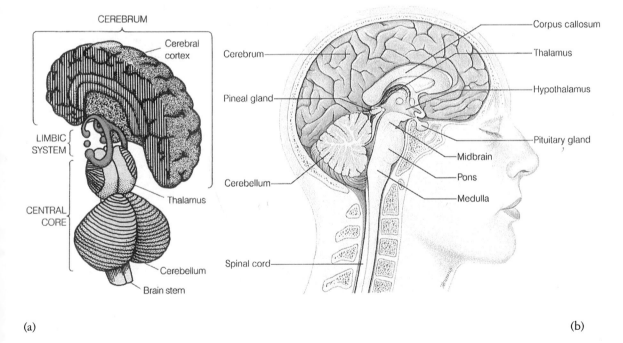

(a)

(b)

Figure 5.1 (a) Exploded view of the human brain. The largest part in this diagram is the right side of the cortex; the left side is not shown. The frontal lobes are at the left of this diagram, and the area where visual information arrives in the cortex is on the right of the diagram. This diagram also shows the limbic system, on both sides. The hypothalamus (not shown) lies in front of and below the thalamus. (b) Diagram of the human brain as it would be seen if sliced in the midline. Here the hypothalamus and pituitary gland to which it connects can be seen, but the main parts of the limbic system cannot because they lie to the side of the midline.

internal representations of goals and the comparison of events with these goals – primary appraisals. The second modification is that animals and people do not just make reflex responses to events, they generate plan-like patterns of action that are characteristic of the species.

Early research on brain lesions and stimulation

The first substantial theory of the brain mechanisms of emotion was proposed by Cannon and Bard. Research in Cannon's laboratory in the 1920s, particularly by Bard (1928), indicated that cats deprived of their neocortex (see figure 5.2) were liable to make sudden, inappropriate, and ill-directed attacks. The phenomenon was called "sham rage" (Cannon, 1931). If they were fed artificially and carefully tended, cats without any neocortex could live for a long time. Bard and Rioch (1937) described a cat kept alive for a year with no forebrain except for a small piece of the diencephalon and a shred of striatum. It would not feed itself, and showed no other spontaneous movements, except for one instance of claw sharpening. It showed no sign of pleasure reaction, but it did show undirected angry behavior, "sham rage," when provoked. Such observations prompted Cannon to propose that the thalamus is a center for the expression of emotions in response to stimuli, and to infer that the cortex usually acts to inhibit this expression. As we described in chapter 1, it was Hess (Hess & Brügger, 1943) who complemented the research on lesions with experiments using electrical stimulation that showed angry behavior to be

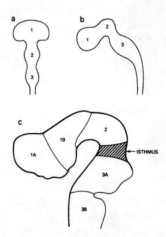

Figure 5.2 MacLean's diagrams of the development of the brain in the human embryo. The upper diagrams (a and b, from the back and side respectively) represent the parts of the brain as they appear at four weeks, with the forebrain (1), midbrain (2), and hindbrain (3), being evident. In the lower diagram (c, shortly thereafter) the forebrain is beginning to differentiate into 1A, the telencephalon (which includes the neocortex, the limbic system and the striatal region), and the diencephalon 1B (which includes the hypothalamus).

elicited not from the thalamus, as Cannon had supposed, but from the hypothalamus which lies just below it.

Cannon and Bard's idea was really the continuation of the nineteenth century hypothesis of the nervous system proposed by Hughlings-Jackson (1959, discussed in chapter 1). This was that at the lowest level of the brain are simple reflex pathways including such functions as reactions to simple stimuli, posture, and movement. At the next level are more recently evolved structures, including those of emotions, that modulate these functions. And, at the highest and most recently evolved level, the cortex controls all levels below it. According to this argument, children are full of uncontrolled excitement and emotions until their cortex develops sufficiently to inhibit their lower functions. Similarly, according to Jackson, one can see the dissolution of the nervous system to lower levels of evolution in various ways: not only does this occur when there is damage that affects higher functions (as with poor Phineas Gage), but one can see it in drunkenness, which by diminishing the activity of the higher regions releases the lower ones from inhibition.

A better supported theory of the relation of parts of the brain to evolution was put by MacLean (1990, 1993). He describes his work as having been started by a speculative paper of Papez (1937). Papez had argued that whereas the hypothalamus (diencephalon) was important for the expression of emotion, other regions connected to it were responsible for the experience of emotion. Guided by Descartes's idea of the reflex arc, Papez argued that sensory impulses from the body and outside world reach the thalamus and split into three main pathways. One goes to the striatal region, the stream of movement. One goes to the neocortex, the stream of thought. One goes to the limbic system with its many connections to the hypothalamus, the stream of feeling. His main evidence for the limbic system being concerned with emotion was that in patients with rabies the virus has attacked the limbic system, and the patients sometimes experience extreme terror, whereas tumors in this region sometimes cause a loss of feeling and of memory.

MacLean has taken the argument further. He has argued that the human forebrain is largely made up of three distinct systems, somewhat similar to Papez's three pathways. Each system developed initially in a distinctive phase of evolution. Then each region evolved further by accretion to what already existed. Each older structure developed links with later-evolved structures but also continued to fulfill its original functions and remained dependent on its original mechanisms.

The new element in MacLean's argument was that each newly evolved pathway did not just control lower reflex pathways. Rather, he argued, the brain provides repertoires of species-characteristic actions of the kind we discussed in chapter 3. In vertebrates there have been three large steps of brain evolution. Each has added a species-characteristic repertoire to fulfill new functions; each is based on a distinctive brain network. If this is so it has indeed been fortunate for neurobiological researchers, because it means that the brain is partly modular. Removing one part of it can simply remove the function it serves, leaving the rest largely intact. It also means that stimulating an area electrically or chemically should have the effect of producing the behavioral function for which that area is responsible. This, therefore, has become the main strategy for discovering where functions are localized in the brain. To proceed in this way means gathering evidence that a lesion of some particular area removes some piece of behavior while lesions in other areas do not affect it, and also that electrical stimulation of the particular area causes the behavior.

The striatal system

Apart from the hypothalamus, the earliest and most basic part of the forebrain is called the striatal region. This area became enlarged with the evolution of reptiles, argues MacLean, and it provides the basis for all animal behavior evolved from this stock. It is devoted to scheduling and generating outline scripts for daily life, and for behavior based on modifying these activities in response to actions of other members of the species. Based on the work of several researchers MacLean (1990) describes reptilian behavior as seen in modern lizards. It includes preparation and establishment of a home site,

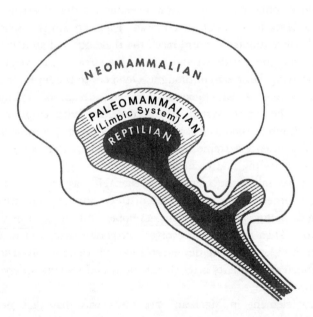

Figure 5.3 MacLean's diagram of the three major divisions of the forebrain. In embryological development the forebrain is in two parts, the diencephalon (which includes the hypothalamus) and the telencephalon. Evolutionarily the oldest part of the telencephalon is the reptilian brain (including the so-called corpus striatum). It exists in reptiles, birds, and mammals. Next is the part of the brain that evolved in the earliest mammals, the paleomammalian limbic system which includes the amygdala and septum. Last is the neocortex, which MacLean calls "neomammalian."

marking and patrolling of territory, formalized fighting in defense of territory, foraging, hunting, hoarding, forming social groups including hierarchies, greeting, grooming, mating, flocking, migration. Activities are scheduled by a master routine or script that each day involves waking and slow emergence, basking in the sun to increase body temperature, defecating (usually in the same place each day), local foraging, an inactive period, foraging further afield, return to the shelter area, and finally retirement for the night.

MacLean also lists four communicative displays to other members of the species: the signature display (a "this-is-me" display performed when an animal has moved to a new position and in various social contexts), the challenge display often made in relation to territory, the courtship display, and the submissive display. In addition, six other kinds of behavior occur: routinizing (learning a routine and being able to repeat it), imitation or mimicry, tropisms (moving towards specific features), repetitious behavior, reenactments, deceptive behavior. Birds (probably descended from dinosaurs) and mammals (including ourselves) share these behavior patterns with reptiles.

MacLean and his associates have been concerned to make as complete an inventory as possible of the behavioral repertoire of lizards, and in order to do this have made two moves. The first was to localize the mechanisms that generate species-typical behavior patterns. In the lizard the striatal region is the largest part of the forebrain. The limbic system and neocortex had not evolved substantially when the line that led to lizards branched off from the stock that led to mammals. To investigate whether the behavioral mechanisms seen in reptiles are still subserved by the striatal region of higher animals, MacLean (1990) studied a distinctive species-typical greeting display in monkeys. This display has elements of signature, challenge, and courtship, and it is given by a monkey when a new monkey comes into sight, and also (usefully for experimentation) when the monkey sees a reflection of itself in a mirror. Removal of part of the striatal brain area in monkeys results in them failing to give the mirror display, whereas removal of other parts of the midbrain and forebrain leave the display intact.

So the hypothesis is that the striatal region is involved in scheduling species-characteristic behavior patterns in mammals that are comparable to those of reptiles: when striatal areas are damaged in humans we see here also effects that are suggestive of this scheduling function. One kind of damage occurs in a hereditary disease called Huntingdon's chorea which has effects only later in life: patients become unable to organize daily activities. They tend to sit and do nothing, though they are happy to join in activities that are scheduled for them.

The limbic system

The next move that MacLean (1993) made was to ask: "What do mammals do that reptiles do not?" There are just three additions: maternal caregiving with infant attachment, vocal signaling, and play.

MacLean writes that it is particularly significant that structures in the limbic system of mammals are concerned with self-preservation in the behaviors of eating and competing with others for resources, and with continuation of the species in the activities of mating, caregiving, and infant attachment. These latter functions add a principle of sociality to the lives of mammals which is largely absent from reptiles. Reptiles do interact with one other, but they hatch from eggs and start life on their own. In many species of reptiles infants have to escape as soon as they hatch to avoid being eaten by parents. Though some species form aggregations, for the most part their lives are solitary. By contrast, every mammal is born in close association with another, and broadly speaking mammals are interdependent. Reflect on how silent are turtles and lizards: the earliest vocalizations of the vertebrate world, says MacLean, may have been the cries of separation distress in the earliest mammals that function to summon a parent. There is no equivalent among reptiles. Most mammals never lose the social component of their life. Among mammals we humans are the most social of all. Most of our accomplishments and much of our lives depend on people doing things, ranging from conversation to producing every kind of useful object, that individuals cannot do alone.

What is known of the second-evolved major area of the forebrain? It was MacLean who called it the limbic system. It has close connections with the hypothalamus (MacLean, 1949), which not only controls the autonomic nervous system (the part responsible for bodily changes such as heart rate and sweating, which are important in several theories of emotion) but via the pituitary gland that is an extension of it, it controls also the body's hormonal system. MacLean (1993) argues that the limbic system underwent a new evolutionary enlargement with mammals, with the branching of their line from reptiles.

A study that has formed the foundation for much subsequent work was by Klüver and Bucy (1937). They described the effects of a neurosurgical operation to remove the temporal lobe of the neocortex and large parts of the limbic system in wild monkeys housed in a laboratory. Instead of their fear of humans and their normal aggressiveness, immediately after their operation the monkeys were docile, and they were without facial expression. The monkeys repeatedly examined every object, even harmful ones such as broken glass and live flames, putting all such things in their mouths. Moreover, though ordinarily eating only fruit, they would now eat raw meat and fish, as well as feces. There were sexual changes: the monkeys continually manipulated their genitalia, and indiscriminately tried sexually to mount other monkeys, male or female, and even inanimate objects. Together these effects are known as the Klüver–Bucy syndrome. It is now known that this syndrome only occurs if an area called the amygdala is removed or damaged. This area is a smallish region, shaped like an almond (*amygdala* is Greek for almond); the Klüver–Bucy syndrome does not occur if it remains intact (Weiskrantz, 1956).

The amygdala was not originally included in Papez's circuit. As LeDoux (1993) has pointed out, the idea of the limbic system which MacLean derived from Papez's circuit is vague, because as studies of the Klüver–Bucy syndrome have shown, many of its presumed emotional functions can be more specifically localized to the amygdala. Following most current usage we will in this book speak of the limbic system as including the amygdala.

Since this early research, much work on emotions has used the techniques pioneered by Hess (as we discussed in chapter 1) of implanting electrodes into the brain, then stimulating parts of the brain when the animals have recovered from their operations, and are moving around normally again. To understand what is happening in such experiments, think of the electrode as a fine needle, insulated except at the tip. When electrical stimulation is applied, several thousand nerve cells near the tip of the electrode are set into action and nerve impulses from them spread through surrounding networks. As the artificially initiated impulses pass from neuron to neuron, they become patterned in a way that is characteristic of the network. So, for instance, Hess showed that with such stimulation in the hypothalamus, cats would start an angry attack on some object in their vicinity. Since Hess's work it has been found that one brain area of cats is involved in quiet biting attacks characteristic of hunting prey, and another in angry aggression characteristic of fear and of fighting with other cats (Siegel & Brutus, 1990; Siegel & Pott, 1988).

In 1954, experimenting with rats who had been implanted with electrodes, Olds and Milner discovered, more or less by accident, a phenomenon called "self-stimulation." When a rat went to one corner of a large experimental box the experimenters delivered electrical stimulation to its brain — the rat kept returning to this corner. Or if put in a box with a lever that switched on the stimulation, rats would press this lever repeatedly. In these experiments the rats were neither hungry nor thirsty, but with placements of the electrode tips in the septal part of the limbic system, they would press a lever continuously for about 75 percent of the time, for up to four hours a day to deliver this stimulation. Evidently the electrical stimulation was rewarding: rats would learn instrumental tasks to receive it. Exploring different regions of the brain with this technique Olds (1955) reported the results of electrode implantations in 76 rats. With 35 out of 41 electrode sites within the limbic system, rewarding effects were obtained. Of 35 electrode placements outside the limbic system, only two showed rewarding effects.

At around the same time, reporting studies of human schizophrenic subjects, Heath (1954) described how electrical stimulation in the septal region produced various experiences, including some of pleasure, or a lessening of fear or anger, or glowing feelings. In 1956 Olds came straight out and called the limbic regions from which self-stimulation could be obtained: "pleasure centers."

How then should we understand the limbic system? In some areas within this region stimulation has been found to induce different patterns of action such as angry attacks, and also eating and drinking. Would animals with electrodes placed in much the same areas deliver rewarding stimulation to themselves? Following a clever set of experiments, Valenstein, Cox, and

Kakolewski (1970) questioned the prevalent conception of these studies, which was that electrical stimulation in the limbic system activated circuits of specific drives such as aggression, hunger, and thirst. They found in their rats that exactly the same electrode with exactly the same pattern of stimulation could elicit eating if food were provided, drinking if water were provided, or gnawing if blocks of wood were provided. The stimulation did not produce specific actions, nor even did it activate specific drives, such as hunger or thirst. Rather the effect was dependent on the combination of stimulation and what was available. So here again is evidence that species-characteristic patterns are not fixed, but responsive to the environment. In another set of experiments, Valenstein, Cox, and Kakolewski also found electrode placements that would support self-stimulation. The rats would go to a particular place in an experimental box, interrupting a photo-beam to turn the stimulation on. But if instead of providing for self-stimulation the same rats in the same box were provided with pieces of wood, erasers, and food pellets at one end of the box, then with the onset of stimulation applied by the experimenter, the rats would begin carrying these objects to the other end, actions typical of hoarding at a home site, or of nest building.

Valenstein, Cox, and Kakolewski argued, therefore, that the organization of the hypothalamus and limbic system involves networks on which species-typical actions are based. If these networks are artificially stimulated, the nerve impulses around the tip of the electrode become patterned by the organization of the network and by the currently perceived environment. The effects of this patterning give rise to recognizable species-typical scripts, such as eating, drinking, grooming, or hoarding, not directly but via something like inducing a more general readiness, or a tendency to approach. Von Holst and Von Saint Paul (1963) wrote that the effect of such stimulation was like activating a mood, so that the behavior that occurs reveals species-characteristic patterns and something of their interrelation to each other, as well as their responsiveness to the environment, when facilitated by that mood.

Glickman and Schiff (1967) proposed the most comprehensive theory of the effects of brain stimulation. They proposed (a) that not only does stimulation activate the mechanisms responsible for species-typical patterns, but that (b) when these mechanisms are activated the pleasurable or displeasurable qualities associated with the activation (as revealed by self-stimulation) depend on whether the action is generally to approach, or to withdraw. In other words, if the mood produced by some kinds of electrical stimulation is based on approach, it encourages curiosity and exploration. And if food, water, or a mate are there, feeding, drinking, or sexual behavior will tend to occur. In animals that are predators, attacking prey involves a similar tendency to approach. Perhaps also actions in protection of home territory are based on an approach mechanism. Patterns based on withdrawal, however, involve different areas of the limbic system, and the species-characteristic actions here include escape from painful encounters, freezing or flight from predators, avoidance of bad tastes or smells. For a more recent version of this theory see Vaccarino, Schiff, and Glickman (1989).

As well as the evidence from animals there is evidence from humans: a patient with damage to the amygdala had a record of defective social decision making, and was very poor at recognizing emotional expressions (Adolphs et al., 1994). Moreover, in humans the limbic system is thought to support the subjective experience of emotions. The best evidence, MacLean argues, is from a form of epilepsy – temporal lobe or psychomotor epilepsy (Gibbs, Gibbs, & Fuster, 1948). In epilepsy nerve cells in a part of the brain all start firing together in a self-sustaining wave-like pattern, and the disturbance spreads to involve a progressively larger area. These discharges can last from a few seconds to a few minutes, and the sufferer may lose consciousness. In psychomotor epilepsy discharges do not spread outside the limbic region, and this finding is evidence that the region is physiologically separate. This kind of epilepsy is common. It can occur because of damage to the limbic system during birth, or from the attack of a virus, or for other reasons. With an epileptic attack in this area there is first an aura, a subjective state that often includes strong emotions. The Russian novelist Dostoevsky, who suffered from epilepsy, wrote of the aura of his attacks: "a feeling of happiness such as it is quite impossible to imagine in a normal state and which other people have no idea of . . . entirely in harmony with myself and with the whole world" (Dostoevsky, 1955, p. 8). As well as emotional changes during the aura, people who suffer from this kind of epilepsy often suffer changes of personality, for instance becoming less interested in sex but more socially aggressive, in ways that do not occur with epilepsy affecting other regions of the brain (Bear, 1979).

MacLean (1993) lists six kinds of emotions as occurring in psychomotor epileptic auras: feelings of desire, fear, anger, dejection (sadness), gratulant feelings (feelings of happiness, insight, or achievement), and feelings of affection. Often, as in the feeling described by Dostoevsky, there is a sense of complete conviction. MacLean goes on to say: *Significantly, these feelings are free-floating, being completely unattached to any particular thing, situation, or idea"* (p. 79, emphasis in original). The feelings are often associated with some motor automatism, for instance "pugilistic behavior, with the arms flailing somewhat like those of a fighting chimpanzee" (MacLean, 1993, p. 79), or showing affection to anyone present. For example, Gowers (1881) described a 20-year-old woman for whom: "each slight seizure was followed by a paroxysm of kissing." Feindel and Penfield (1954) were able to produce emotional effects by electrically stimulating the brains of their patients at sites that were thought to be damaged and to be responsible for the epileptic attacks.

Epileptic seizures of this kind are usually accompanied by a loss of consciousness and of memory for the events occurring as the attack began. This suggested to MacLean that emotions might depend on memory and on a continued sense of self. And, separating the functions of the limbic system from those of the neocortex in which the mechanisms of language are located, MacLean has proposed that the limbic system functions to bring stimuli from

143

the outside world together with those from inside the body. This system operates in terms of emotions, and "eludes the grasp of the intellect because its animalistic and primitive structure make it impossible to communicate in verbal terms" (MacLean, 1949, p. 348). Though this quotation catches the tone of the first-hand descriptions, for example, from Dostoevsky, it now sounds a little old fashioned – it is clear that emotions are not unsophisticated. But the idea involves the hint that emotions may have had a primary function, only later built upon by culture and language.

Emotions and the neocortex

The third large step in the evolution of the human brain is distinctive to higher mammals. The neocortex (often referred to as the cortex) reaches its largest development in human beings: in us about 80 percent of the whole brain is taken up by it. The cortex (meaning "outer layer") of the brain is between 0.06 and 0.12 in. thick, but it is deeply folded. If spread out flat it would have an area of about 310 square in. In humans the cortex is greatly enlarged compared to that of our closest animal relations. The frontal lobes of the cortex have shown the largest relative increase in size. It was this area, remember, that was damaged in Phineas Gage (discussed in chapter 1). The frontal lobes have close connections with the limbic system.

Right-sided superiority in recognition of emotional expressions

In humans information from the outside world crosses over to the opposite side of the brain. So if you look directly at something vertical such as the edge of a door, then information about the world to the right of that edge is relayed via the thalamus to the visual regions at the rear of the cortex on the left side, while information about things to the left of it are similarly relayed to the right side. In a comparable way the neural pathways of action are crossed. So if you reach out with your right hand, this action is controlled from the left side of the cortex, from the motor areas which are about equally distant from the front and back of the brain. If a person has a stroke (a hemorrhage due to a blood vessel bursting which causes brain damage) on the left side he or she may lose the use of language along with becoming paralyzed on the right side of the body. By contrast, with right-sided brain damage a person will not be impaired in language, but may be unable to recognize emotions of other people. Look at figure 5.4 to see how sensory pathways cross on their way to each side of the cortex.

The right side of the cortex has been found to be more closely associated with the processing of emotional events. As well as the findings that patients with damage to the right side of the cortex often have difficulty in recognizing facial expressions of emotion, there are three kinds of evidence for this (Etcoff, 1989).

First, patients who have had a surgical operation to sever connections between the two sides of the cortex to prevent the spread of epileptic discharges

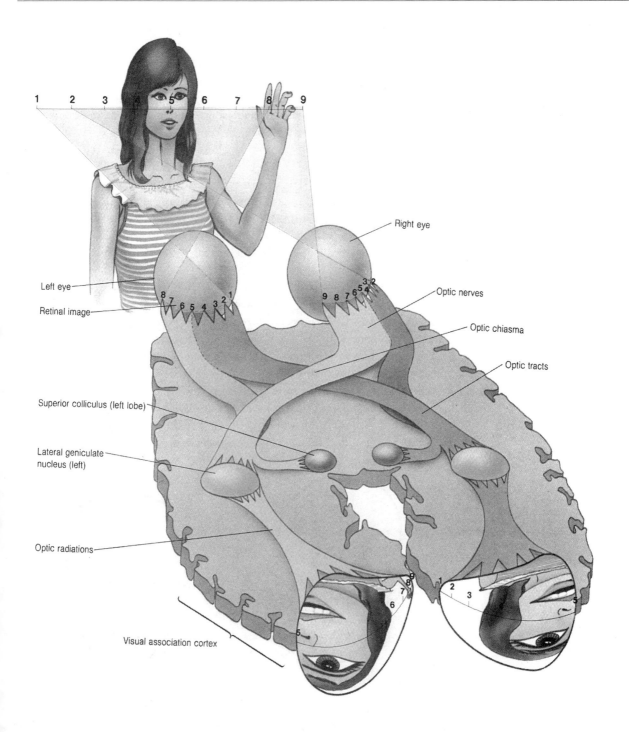

Figure 5.4 Diagram to show the projection of information from one side of the visual world to the opposite side of the brain. There is a pathway to a part of the midbrain (superior colliculus), and a pathway to the visual area of the neocortex (where you can see the projection of the woman's face). In split-brain patients the two sides of the cortex, though not the limbic system and midbrain, are severed.

from one side to the other – so-called split-brain patients – can recognize emotionally significant events when films are shown only to the right side. Thus Gazzaniga (1988) reports on a split-brain patient to whose right cortex was shown a film clip of a person being thrown onto a fire. This patient could not describe what she saw since verbal language depends on the left side. She said: "I don't really know what I saw; I think just a white flash. Maybe some trees, red trees like in the fall." Then she continued, speaking to Gazzaniga: "I feel kind of scared. I feel jumpy. I don't like this room, or maybe it's you getting me nervous" (p. 235). The film seen by means of the right cortex had evidently frightened her. The experience of fear presumably also involved the limbic system which was intact below the level of the operation, but neither the right cortex nor the limbic system operates in terms of words. The fear signals reached the verbally able left cortex but, knowing nothing of their cause, a search started for verbally specific reasons: ". . . maybe it's you getting me nervous."

Second, normal people shown faces which have the upcurved lips of a smile on one side of the face and the downcurved lips of sadness on the other side tend to interpret the expression in terms of the part relayed to the right side of the brain. Look at figure 5.5. One face looks happier than the other, probably because one side of the brain is relatively more important than the other in processing emotional expressions.

Third, when pictures of faces are flashed quickly onto a screen, recognition of emotional expressions is better for faces in the left visual field (relayed to the right cortex) (Strauss & Moscovitch, 1981). The difference is not large, though it is more pronounced for difficult discriminations. So again here is evidence of

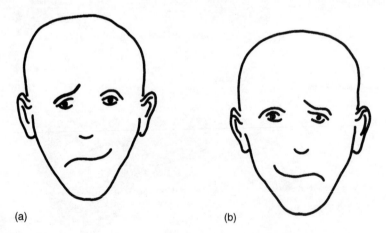

(a)   (b)

Figure 5.5 Chimeric faces. These caricatures have expressions of happiness on one side and sadness on the other. Look at the nose of each face and see which face you think looks happy, and which sad. If you are right-handed, you are likely to see (b) as happier than (a). The probable explanation is that more of the left side of any picture or visual scene is processed by the right side of your brain where recognition of emotional expression is thought primarily to occur in right-handed people.

a superiority of the right side of the cortex in recognizing emotional expressions.

Etcoff et al. (1992) have tested ability to detect lying. Recall Ekman and O'Sullivan's (1991) study of people's ability to detect lying from subtle facial clues of anxiety (discussed in chapter 4). In Etcoff et al.'s experiment, patients with damage to their left cortex were significantly better than those with damage on the right, and than normal people, in detecting lying. Etcoff et al. explained this by saying that subjects who attend to language were more likely to be misled by words, while subjects with poor language ability, but whose sensitivity to facial expressions of emotion was intact, relied on facial clues.

As Etcoff (1989) points out in her review, right-brain superiority in recognizing facial expressions of emotion is separate from effects of recognizing the identity of faces. Etcoff also reviews recognition of emotion by tone of voice and other nonverbal aspects of speech. These abilities are separable from visual recognition of emotions, as well as from processing verbal meanings with emotional significance. Moreover, lesions in a region of the right frontal area can affect emotional aspects of the production of speech and gestures (Ross, 1984). As Etcoff points out, it is not that the right hemisphere globally processes everything emotional. Rather, there are specific mechanisms for recognizing and producing emotional expressions that have greater representation in the right cortex for right-handed people.

Taking a more global view Tucker and Frederick (1989) have argued that the right side of the cortex has closer connections to the amygdala, develops earlier during infancy, and is generally attuned for emotional processing, perhaps especially in activities that involve relations with others. The functions of this side of the cortex, as described by Tucker and Frederick, sound close to those described by Epstein (1993) as the experiential self system, based on emotions, operating wholistically, analogically, and with immediacy in terms of experience. By contrast the left cortex is specialized for processing which is verbal, symbolic, and analytical. One problem for us human beings is to integrate these two kinds of processing, given the indications that they are somewhat separate. One indication of separateness, found by Lois Bloom (1989), is that in infancy the more emotional expressions babies make, the later they start to talk. When the babies she studied started speaking around the age of 13 months, their emotional expression as they said a word was neutral; emotional and verbal expressions were statistically independent of each other. Only by around 19 months were the infants able to say a word and at the same time express an emotion in a coordinated way.

Experience and expression of emotions: positive emotions are more strongly represented on the left side and negative emotions on the right

Whereas the perceptual areas are at the back of the cortex, experience and expression are represented towards the front. For experience there is no overall right-sided superiority for emotional events as compared with nonemotional ones. Instead at least some mechanisms concerned with the experience and expression of positive emotions are situated on the left side, and those for negative emotions are on the right. Two kinds of evidence have been gathered (Davidson, 1992a).

The first concerns experience and expression of specific episodes of emotion (those at the short end of the time-spectrum, figure 4.6). For negative emotional episodes there is more activation on the right side of the cortex; for positive episodes there is more activation on the left. Davidson et al. (1990) had subjects individually watch four short film clips. Two amusing films were of animals playing. Two gruesome ones were training films for nurses, one showing a burn victim and the other an amputation. While each subject watched, electroencephalogram (EEG) recordings were made from four positions on each side of the scalp, and facial expressions were videotaped. Expressions of happiness (indicated by Duchenne smiles as described in chapter 4) and disgust (indicated by wrinkling of the nose) were found. While the subjects were making happy expressions there was a significant average increase of activation in the left frontal region of the cortex as compared with the right frontal region. When expressing disgust there was greater right-sided activation in the frontal region. For each subject the experimenters calculated an index of asymmetry of frontal activation. Every subject showed more activation on the right for episodes in which their faces had showed disgust as compared with episodes in which they had showed happiness.

Davidson (1992a) has reviewed a number of other studies from his laboratory including one of adults playing a video-type game in which they either gained monetary rewards or suffered monetary punishments for actions, and one in which 10-month-old infants were approached either by their mother or by a stranger. In both studies similar patterns were found in the EEG: positive emotions were accompanied by more left-sided activation in the frontal region and negative emotions by more right-frontal activation. The explanation he offers is this: the frontal region of the brain is specialized for intention, self-regulation, and planning. In most people, moreover, approach to something often involves using the right hand to reach out, and this is controlled by the left side of the brain; the positive emotion of happiness is part of an approach tendency. Negative emotions such as disgust and fear are associated with withdrawal, and activation is controlled in the right frontal and temporal regions. In left-handed people one would expect the activation patterns to occur on the opposite sides, but too few studies have been made on left-handed people.

Davidson's studies are correlational; experimental confirmation of the lateralization of emotional experience has been found by Schiff and Lamon (1989, 1994). They found that having people contract the muscles of the left side of their face, or having them squeeze a rubber ball in their left hand as hard as they could for four periods of 45 seconds interspersed with 10-second pauses, induced negative emotions, principally sadness. Contracting facial or hand muscles on the right produced emotions that were more positive, and sometimes assertive. In these inductions nothing explicit or verbal was said concerning emotions, so different emotional effects occurred independently of subjects' conscious knowledge. Emotions were measured in a number of ways, but most strikingly Schiff and Lamon asked subjects to tell stories about ambiguous pictures from the Thematic Apperception Test (Bellak, 1986) that are known to be sensitive to mood. Independent raters, who did not know which kind of induction the subject had received, counted the number of emotionally positive, negative, and neutral propositions in the transcribed stories that the subjects told. Following contractions of the left side of the face or the muscles of the left hand (presumably activating the right side of the brain) subjects wrote stories with significantly more emotionally negative propositions. With contractions on the right side there were fewer negative propositions. More informally, Schiff and Lamon report on what people said spontaneously. One subject after the contractions said:

Left hand contraction: "I felt teary in my eyes. It felt like being a sulking child."
Right hand contraction: "I felt aggression, anger towards my brother. Lots of determination." (Schiff & Lamon, 1994, p. 253)

The asymmetries of brain activation described so far concern short-term emotions. But what about longer-term episodes, moods, temperaments, psychiatric syndromes? Patients who have suffered left-sided strokes that damage the frontal regions have a high probability of becoming clinically depressed, while symptoms of mania are more common when a stroke damages the right frontal region (Starkstein & Robinson, 1991). Henriques and Davidson (1991) have found that patients who are depressed (without brain damage) have less activation in the left frontal regions than nondepressed people.

Genetically based asymmetries of function have been called by Davidson (1993) "affective styles"; he describes a study performed with Kagan and others (Davidson, 1992a). At 31 months of age 386 children were tested in pairs with their mothers during 25-minute sessions in a large playroom with toys that included a play tunnel. Ten minutes after starting the session an experimenter came in with a remote controlled robot that moved towards each child and spoke. After three minutes the robot said it had to take a nap, and it was removed. Twenty minutes after starting, a stranger came into the room with a tray of interesting looking toys, invited the children to play with them, and left three minutes later. From these sessions three groups of children were selected. In an inhibited group the children (a) spent more than 9.5 minutes of the 25-minute session near their mothers, (b) did not touch a toy, (c) did not speak until more than three minutes after the start, (d) did not approach the robot, (e) did not approach the stranger, and (f) did not enter the play tunnel.

Then there was an uninhibited group. These children spent less than 30 seconds near their mother and did all the other activities (b to f) readily. There was a middle group of children who fell in between on these measures. Twenty-eight children were selected for each group, approximately balanced by sex. Seven months later, these children were tested for their resting EEG patterns. As can be seen from figure 5.6, there was a substantial difference. The inhibited children had much higher right-sided activation, the uninhibited much less. Children of the middle group were in between.

Results on lateralization of positive and negative emotions in the human cortex agree with the theory of Glickman and Schiff (1967) originally proposed to account for experiments on animals. When species-typical actions, including some aggressive patterns, include approach they are positively toned and pleasurable. By contrast patterns of withdrawal are negatively toned. Anatomically the mechanisms of approach and avoidance are separate in the limbic system. In humans this separate grouping of approach-related and withdrawal-related brain mechanisms is continued on different sides of the cortex, and is associated with positive and negative emotional experience.

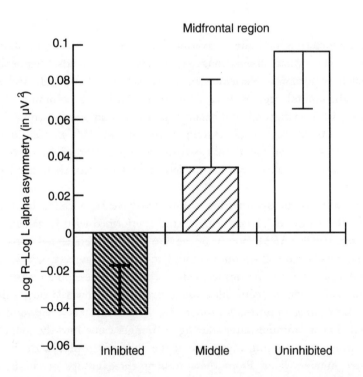

Figure 5.6 Mean scores at age 38 months on an index indicating relatively more EEG activation on the left as compared to the right hemisphere of children who at age 31 months had been classified as inhibited, middle, or uninhibited in a 25-minute play session (Davidson, 1992a).

The studies discussed so far indicate where the mechanisms are that generate certain aspects of emotion. But what is the brain doing to produce emotions? The foremost hypothesis is LeDoux's (1993). He has argued that the amygdala is the central emotional computer for the brain, evaluating sensory input for its emotional significance – performing the functions of primary appraisal, as we described in the previous chapter. The evidence is complex, but it includes the following. The amygdala has connections to the right places to fulfill this role. It receives inputs from regions of the cortex concerned with visual recognition of objects and from regions concerned with recognition of sounds. The amygdala also has close connections with the hypothalamus, which from the work of Hess onwards has been known to be concerned with emotional behavior. Rewarding self-stimulation can be demonstrated in the amygdala (Kane, Coulombe, & Miliaressis, 1991), and components of emotional behavior and autonomic responses can be elicited by electrical stimulation in this region (Hilton & Zbrozyna, 1963).

The most distinctive part of LeDoux's hypothesis is that as well as inputs from the visual and auditory cortex, the amygdala receives visual and auditory inputs directly via the thalamus – not via routes that result in the recognition of objects or distinctive sounds. Experiments by LeDoux et al. (e.g. 1990) use Pavlovian conditioning, which is considered to be the basic mechanism of learning about the emotional significance of events that signal something pleasant or unpleasant. It is thought of as learning the temporal structure of what causes important events related to goals. The standard arrangement involves two stimuli. One is called the conditioned stimulus – it is the one whose significance will be learned – perhaps a flashing light or an auditory tone. Before the experiment it has no significance other than being noticeable. Then there is the unconditioned stimulus that has biological significance – something rewarding like delivery of meat powder into the mouth of a hungry dog as in Pavlov's original experiments (Pavlov, 1927), or something nasty like an electric shock. What is learned in Pavlovian conditioning is not a response as such, and not the association of two stimuli. It is an emotion about what signals the important event: readiness for something pleasant (happy anticipation), or for something unpleasant (fear or anxiety). Such emotional effects are expressed as species-typical actions, for example, a dog jumping, wagging its tail, and salivating when it sees its meal being prepared, or the same dog freezing, slinking, cringing, struggling to escape, when threatened. In primates emotional conditioning can occur purely by observation: monkeys not originally frightened of snakes observing another monkey reacting fearfully towards a snake, then become themselves permanently frightened of snakes (Mineka & Cook, 1993). Emotional conditioning for negative stimuli is quick to be learned and slow to extinguish – one of the reasons why anxiety can be such a severe and long-lasting clinical disorder.

What LeDoux and his collaborators have found is that with conditioned stimuli of simple auditory tones or flashing lights, and with an unconditioned stimulus of an electric shock to the feet, rats will learn an association so long as the amygdala and the thalamus are present. This learning occurs even if the cortex has been removed. LeDoux interprets this as meaning that the amygdala can receive sensory information that has not been processed by the cortex. Based on the simplest features of stimuli, such as intensity, emotional learning can occur.

LeDoux has proposed that the amygdala is the core of a central network of emotional processing. In humans it can receive information from the cortex depending on verbal meanings. Equally it can receive less detailed information via a pathway that, as MacLean would argue, evolved before the networks of processing by the cortex. Modifying Weiskrantz's (1956) suggestion that the amygdala is responsible for assigning motivational significance to stimuli, LeDoux argues that it is responsible for assigning emotional significance to events – for appraisal. He proposes that in emotions such as eager anticipation or fearful avoidance the amygdala sets up species-typical action systems, and modulates the activity of many other parts of the brain, affecting arousal as originally postulated by Lindsley (1951), and directing attention.

Neurochemicals, modulation, and the emotions

If the most important discovery yet made about the nervous system was that nerve fibers work by electricity – this was Galvani's finding, part of Mary Shelley's inspiration in writing *Frankenstein* (Tropp, 1976) – then the next most momentous event was finding that chemicals are the messengers from nerve cell to nerve cell. It was discovered when Otto Loewi was conducting experiments of electrically stimulating the vagus nerve of a frog; this stimulation slowed down its heart (Brazier, 1959). If during stimulation Loewi bathed the frog's heart in fluid, and then applied this fluid to the heart of a second frog, then this second frog's heart slowed down too. He inferred that some chemical substance was released into the fluid by the nerve endings of the first frog, and was then responsible for slowing down the heart of the second.

The substance discovered by Loewi was acetyl choline. Subsequently more than 50 substances have been discovered that are released by nerve cells and have effects on other nerve cells, or on muscles. Various distinctions have been made: one is that some neurochemicals have small molecules which diffuse rapidly, while others (more recently discovered) have larger molecules made up of short chains of amino acids. They are like small fragments of protein, and they are called peptides.

Neurochemicals can be thought of in three functional families, which merge into each other. The first family is of transmitter substances released into the synapses of nerve cells. There is a limited number of such substances, most with small molecules. As well as acetyl choline they include nor-adrenaline, dopamine, serotonin, gamma-amino butyric acid. Some simple amino acids act as transmitter substances, most importantly glutamine, the chemical (in the form of monosodium glutamate) that is often used as a taste enhancer. Transmitter substances work by being released by nerve impulses at the end of a nerve cell's axon, and rapidly diffusing across the tiny synaptic gaps between cells to excite or inhibit the receiving nerve cell or muscle fiber.

Secondly, there are hormones, substances carried round the body by the blood to affect organs that are sensitive to them. They usually take longer to begin to act than transmitter substances, and they also continue their effects for longer. They include both small molecules like adrenaline and cortisol, and also peptides. The gland that controls most hormonal systems is the pituitary, which is joined to and largely controlled by the hypothalamus. Similarly, other glands remote from the brain release hormones that have effects on the body, and in some cases also on nerve cells in the hypothalamus.

Thirdly there is a group of substances which are neuromodulators. Many of them are peptides. Their significance is only beginning to be guessed at, but endogenous opiates (chemically similar to addictive drugs like opium and heroin) modulate the pain system, and other peptides (such as cholecystokinin) have important emotional effects. Some peptides are transmitters, but when they act as neuromodulators they are released by some nerve cells, and diffuse some distance to affect many thousands of other nerve cells.

Reasons why the chemical effects in the brain are so important for understanding emotions are, first, that separate emotional systems seem to employ specific chemical messengers – so systems are distinguished not only anatomically but also chemically. Secondly, an effect of this arrangement that has been useful for researchers and clinicians: some chemicals introduced into the body (by mouth or injection) can diffuse via the bloodstream throughout the whole body, including the cerebro-spinal fluid that surrounds nerve cells. Because of the different chemical messengers used by brain systems, these drugs affect some systems rather than others. This is the basis for all drugs that have effects on emotions, moods, arousal, and other psychological states. For instance a drug may induce fear (as in a bad trip, one of the lesser risks of certain recreational drugs), another may reduce fear (as is intended for tranquillizers, antianxiety drugs), another may induce happiness (a high), and yet another may reduce feelings of despair (as antidepressants are designed to do).

Restoration of transmitter function in the striatal region

One of the most striking effects of manipulating the brain's chemical systems, which bears on MacLean's hypotheses about the scheduling functions of the striatum and the emotional effects of the limbic system, comes from Sacks's (1973) book *Awakenings* on the survivors of the sleeping sickness (*encephalitis lethargica*) that started in Europe in the winter of 1916–1917 and spread throughout the world. It continued for more 10 years, affecting five million people. It was due to a virus that attacked the striatal regions of the brain. Victims fell into a suspended state – "they were as insubstantial as ghosts, as passive as zombies" (Sacks, p. 32), sitting motionless and speechless all day, observing but doing nothing. A few remained alive in hospitals for up to 50 years. Then, in 1969, the drug L-Dopa was discovered, a precursor of the transmitter substance dopamine. With the administration of L-Dopa, transmitter functions in the striatal system were restored: Sacks described how people experienced awakenings. They were again able to act spontaneously and schedule their own daily activities.

With this restoration not only did there arise emotions of joy and excitement as these people emerged from decades of lethargy, but administration of the drug gave rise to a range of excitements, mood swings, and other emotional effects. Neural messages started to traverse long-dormant nerve pathways. In the case of Frances D, Sacks writes, there occurred:

> . . . certain violent appetites and passions, and certain obsessive ideas and images – [that] could not be dismissed by her as "purely physical" or "completely alien" to her "real self" but on the contrary were felt to be in some sense releases or exposures or confessions of very deep and ancient parts of herself . . . prehistoric and perhaps prehuman landscapes whose features were at once utterly strange to her, yet mysteriously familiar. (p. 77)

Such emotions, passions, and strong appetites, sexual and otherwise, were common with the administration of L-Dopa in the cases Sacks describes. One may suppose that the effects occurred because the neural activity caused by the drug in the severely damaged striatal regions was not exactly the same as the activity of normal coordinated functions, and as well as restoring partial function to the damaged striatal region gusts of nerve impulses were sent to the nearby limbic system where, according to MacLean, experiences of emotions arise. Such experiences were partly characteristic of normal functions, but partly they were strange transformations of those functions.

Peptide effects on fear

To illustrate the role of peptides we will describe some work on panic. Panic attacks are sudden onsets of fear usually lasting 15 to 30 minutes, only rarely for an hour or more (American Psychiatric Association, 1994). Unlike phobias, which are fears of some recognizable object or situation, a panic is unexpected and occurs without it being clear what has caused it. A panic attack typically includes cognitive symptoms such as intense apprehension, and bodily symptoms such as shortness of breath, dizziness, or the heart beating rapidly. Bradwejn et al. (Bradwejn, 1993; Harro, Vasar, & Bradwejn, 1993) have found that a peptide called cholecystokinin (CCK) induces panic attacks – without any external cause. Like many other peptides this one seems to work by modulating effects of transmitters. In its most active form it has four amino acids, with this structure:

$$Trp\text{-}Met\text{-}Asp\text{-}Phe\text{-}NH_2$$

The main elements in this structure (Trp, Met, etc.) are single amino acids, and this peptide is often referred to as CCK_4 to indicate its four components. In 97 percent of patients who were subject to panic attack, and in 60 percent of normal subjects who were not subject to such attacks, injections of 25µg or 50µg of CCK_4 reliably induced anxiety, apprehension, or fear, with other symptoms such as dizziness and depersonalization being common. Symptoms of fear have also been found in monkeys and rats with injections of CCK. Moreover, when the activity of the human brain was studied by positron emission tomography (PET scanning), and magnetic resonance imaging (MRI), increases in blood flow in the limbic system were found. Using PET scanning this region has also been implicated in anticipatory anxiety (Reiman et al., 1989).

Researchers on pharmacology set themselves several conditions before a specific action of a neurochemical is accepted, so for a specific effect of CCK in inducing fear, they require that:

- it reliably produces the effect of fear or panic;
- patients recognize the symptoms as like those of their usual panic attacks;
- patients susceptible to such attacks have greater sensitivity to the neurochemical than those who are not susceptible;
- there is a dose–response relationship so that a placebo produces no effect and larger doses of the drug give rise to more symptoms in a greater proportion of subjects;
- effects occur in double-blind studies in which neither subject nor experimenter knows whether an injection is drug or placebo;
- effects are neutralized or reduced by agents known to antagonize the effect of the specific neurochemical at sites on the nerve cells;
- effects are not reduced by agents that antagonize other systems.

CCK has passed all these tests. It seems therefore that this peptide neuromodulator may be responsible for spreading the effects of fear through the brain, with processes of particular importance being localized in the limbic system.

Integration of neurochemical and anatomical information in emotional behavior

As Panksepp (1993) has put it, it is highly likely that brains contain a small number of emotional mechanisms common to many species. Each system has its own distinctive brain organization, and when activated each gives rise to a pattern of emotion-relevant action which provides a script that is characteristic for each species. So there are systems for anger, fear, attachment, maternal nurturance, anticipatory eagerness, play, and sexuality. Each system is somewhat localized anatomically, so that it is differentially susceptible to lesions and stimulation. Moreover, each system employs its own transmitter substances, neuromodulators, and in some cases hormones, so that it is also differentially affected by neurochemical manipulations such as drugs.

Maternal behavior

According to MacLean (1993) the most distinctive attribute of mammalian life is the emotional structure of maternal–infant interaction. Here, then, is an area in which we can look not just at single variables in individuals but at interactions: interactions between a mother and her offspring, between genetically specified mechanisms and learning, and between brain circuits and neurochemicals.

The animal that has been most studied is the rat. Rat infants, or pups, are born blind and immature in litters of 6 to 12. They live in a nest constructed by the mother. When the pups are born the mother licks them all over. The pups have the motor mechanisms to suckle at the mother's teats, and also to emit high pitched squeaks if they get separated from the nest. These squeaks have the effect of alerting the mother, who retrieves the pups and puts them back in the nest. Pups' distress vocalizations are distinctive; and differentiations have been made between separation mechanisms and those of other kinds of fear (Panksepp, Newman, & Insel, 1992). Being able to signal separation distress depends on the integrity of the limbic system, but not the cortex. Moreover, calling can be modulated by specific neurochemicals, although in different species different chemicals affect the system.

Fleming and Corter (in press) have reviewed what is known of the mechanisms supporting maternal behavior in rats, with some of the studies having been performed by Fleming and her associates. As the mother rat reaches the end of pregnancy there are changes that include increases of the hormones estradiol and prolactin, against a background of declining progesterone. In addition, while giving birth there is a rise of the peptide oxytocin which may also facilitate the early expression of maternal behavior. Oxytocin is involved in producing milk let down in nursing mothers. It has also been proposed as reducing separation distress in young animals, and in other aspects of social bonding as well (Panksepp, 1993).

As Fleming and Corter point out, the hormones that reach high levels in mother rats about to give birth have effects on behavior as well as on physiological mechanisms. For instance, within 30 minutes of giving birth a new mother rat has pulled off the amniotic sacs, eaten the placentas, and licked her pups all over to clean them. She will have gathered all the pups together into a nest, and adopted a nursing posture over them. She does this without any prior experience of pups, so we can assume that these actions are genetically based. If virgin rats – without any of the hormonal changes associated with birth – are presented with a nest full of pups, they show none of this maternal behavior. In fact virgin rats are fearful of rat pups, and actively avoid them. So the hormonal changes that occur with giving birth induce in mother rats an emotional state that switches off their fear of pups, and switches on an attraction to them. We know this is caused by hormones acting on the brain, because if rats are administered a set of hormones designed to mimic those circulating at the time of giving birth, virgin females do behave maternally if they are presented with a litter of foster pups: they show retrieval, licking the pups, and adopting a nursing posture.

Now consider the adaptational problem: the hormones involved in giving birth and beginning milk production, which have the emotional effects of starting maternal responsiveness, quickly decline to lower levels after birth has occurred. Clearly it would not be adaptive for the mother rat to lose interest in her pups at this point. What happens is that the initial hormone-dependent mechanism of inducing maternal behavior is complemented by, and then replaced by, another mechanism based on learning. The mother rat learns about her litter of pups; they become rewarding to her. This can be seen in two kinds of experiment described by Fleming and Corter. In one, foster pups are given to virgin female rats, untreated with any hormones. Though avoiding them at first, after one to two days the virgin female becomes willing to lie down with them, and after five to ten days she starts to show maternal behavior towards them. So, it seems the normal process is that there is a hormone-induced start-up of maternal behavior, and this is followed by an experience-produced maintenance of the behavior.

What does the mother rat become attracted to? Odor, it seems is a primary cue. So, for instance, rats who have just given birth but who have not yet had any experience of their pups will choose nest material taken from the nest of a new mother rat and her pups rather than from the nest of a nonmother female. Virgin female rats show no such preference, though virgin females treated with birth-related hormones do show it (Fleming et al., 1989). It may be that the sounds that pups make also have similar effects: certainly these sounds wake up mother rats, although they do not awaken virgin rats. Mother rats are attracted to a whole litter, not specifically to their own litter, and they do not distinguish individual pups.

Where are the mechanisms for these effects? Fleming and Corter describe the main regions that have been implicated, principally the preoptic region of the hypothalamus, an area known to be responsive to some of the hormones of giving birth (estradiol and prolactin). Moreover if activity of neurons, as measured by the production of new proteins, is monitored while mother rats learn about their pups, specific anatomical effects are found. The experiment showing this involved new mother rats. There were four groups: one spent an hour with their new pups, one spent an hour with another adult rat, one spent an hour with a new food, and one had no new stimulation. The highest level of brain activation, indicated by new protein production, was in the group with pups; the activation was found mainly in the preoptic area of the hypothalamus and in the amygdala. These effects were seen to be specific to the pups, because some other areas of the brain were equally activated both by pups and being with another adult rat.

What we see in maternal behavior therefore is a complex orchestration: the components include species-characteristic actions (like adopting the nursing posture), the networks of which are anatomically localized, emotional repulsions and attractions (like the female rat's fear of pups turning to attraction), and sensory cues (like odor). The mechanisms are genetically based, affected by hormones, but subject to change by learning. Other emotion-based systems use a similar set of components. Such systems provide bases for goal-directed sequences of action which are important to the individual and for the propagation of genes – sequences that are then elaborated by individual experience.

Summary

Since the work of Darwin it has been clear that many animals express emotions. In reptiles the issue is not so clear, though these animals do show interindividual displays such as those of courtship and aggression. Very clear emotions arose in evolution with the development of the limbic system in early mammals, as these animals developed adaptations based on maternal care of the young, social lives that involved interdependence rather than mere association, and the behavioral patterns of play. The social qualities of lives of mammals and birds make their lives more complex than those of reptiles. Mechanisms are required to provide outline scripts for social interactions – in cooperation and competition – and for changing behavior in response to the unexpected. These are the functions in which the limbic system provides a repertoire of species-specific actions, some of which have emotional properties, such as the positive emotion of attraction to particular individuals, or negative properties of withdrawal from them. With the evolution of the neocortex these mechanisms continue to be important, but they are supplemented by learning, and in higher primates by increased sophistication of identification so that inter-dependencies can begin to be based on cooperation with particular individuals, and on actions carried out planfully together.

Further Reading

The best paper we know linking evolution of emotions to brain anatomy is:

Paul MacLean (1993). Cerebral evolution of emotion. In M. Lewis & J. M. Haviland (Eds.), *Handbook of emotions* (pp. 67–83). New York: Guilford.

The best known neurophysiological theory of emotions is LeDoux's. See for example:

Joseph LeDoux (1994). Emotion, memory and the brain. *Scientific American, 270* (June), 50–57.

For a wide-ranging and thoughtful review of emotion and cortical lateralization:

D. M. Tucker & S. L. Frederick (1989). Emotion and brain lateralization. In H. Wagner & A. Manstead (Eds.), *Handbook of social psychophysiology* (pp. 27–70). Chichester: Wiley.

An excellent and wide-ranging introduction to the functions of transmitter substances, peptides, and hormones in emotional functioning is:

Jaak Panksepp (1993). Neurochemical control of moods and emotions: Amino acids to neuropeptides. In M. Lewis & J. M. Haviland (Eds.), *Handbook of emotions* (pp. 87–107). New York: Guilford.

Development of Emotions

Contents

Figure 6.0 This picture of a four-year-old girl was taken after her father had photographed her sister in her confirmation dress. Finally this little girl jumped forward and shouted: "I want to have my picture taken too." The picture shows a characteristic angry expression (eyebrows raised, square mouth) and posture with fists clenched.

Why is every critical moment in the fate of the adult or child so clearly colored by emotion?

Vygotsky, 1987, p. 335

Emotional development

Emotion is the first language of us all. Within seconds of birth the human baby makes its first emotional communication – a cry. According to MacLean (1993) such sounds during evolution were momentous. They signaled the beginnings of a new kind of adaptation as mammal-like reptiles started to become mammals. Social activity and cooperation began to emerge among vertebrates. Understanding the development of emotions involves understanding how biologically based patterns of vocal sounds (Papousek, Jürgens, & Papousek, 1992) and visible expressions enable infant and parent to communicate, and how these patterns later take on the forms of culture and individuality.

In this and the following chapters we sometimes use the term "caregiver" to indicate any parental figure. We write of mothers more than fathers, not because we believe that fathers are less important in infants' emotional development but just because most of the research on infants has been done with mothers, although this is now starting to change.

Differential emotions versus dynamic systems theory

What develops during emotional development? Let us consider this by way of two theories, to sharpen the questions and give point to the observations.

The first is the theory of differential emotions, a version of the idea that there is a small set of basic emotions as discussed in chapters 4 and 5. In research on infant development its best known proponents are Izard (e.g. 1991) and Malatesta et al. (1989a). It is derived from Tomkins's (1962) idea that each innate emotion comes as a package: there is a specific emotion with a set of bodily changes and a distinctive facial expression, the feedback from which amplifies the emotion. Emotional expressions then are outward and visible signs of inner programs. They undergo modification during development. Studying emotions in infants is informative because the emotions are displayed before the modifications of culture have occurred.

The second kind of theory is that of dynamic systems. Principal proponents are Fogel and his colleagues (1992), Camras (1992), and Marc Lewis (1995). Here, there are no innate neurophysiological programs, no read-outs, no core aspect of emotion such as facial expression. Rather, a number of genetically derived components become organized into patterns of interaction. This theory has affinities to those discussed in chapter 4, that emotions are made up from components. But there is a difference: in componential theories of adult emotions components occur together because they are elicited by features of the environment that occur together (Ortony & Turner, 1990). In Fogel's developmental view the components become linked together, responsive to features of the environment, but also constraining each other as the whole system develops. Fogel proposes that in interactions of such systems with the social world, further interdependencies occur. The whole system of person-with-other becomes self-organizing, and emotions occur as modes of interaction among components and external events. Such modes have distinctive time courses – for instance the rise and fall of an episode of laughing. Many biological systems have self-organizing properties, and there are mathematical theories of such systems. It is plausible too that neural networks and their interactions with the environment derive from several interacting constraints – remember from the previous chapter the experiments of Valenstein, Cox, and Kakolewski (1970) who found that the very same electrical stimulation of the brain elicited different patterns of action, depending on what was available in the environment. Fogel's hypothesis has three principles: (a) emotions are based on self-organizing dynamic systems; (b) these depend on continuously evolving sequences of action in particular environments, not just on internal programs; (c) categories of emotions are constructed from gradients of timing and intensity of vocal, gestural, and other features. According to this view emotions emerge – they derive from the interactions of lower level processes that are not themselves emotions.

As you might imagine there are many other views, some intermediate between theories of these types. To start with, however, let us keep the theories separate, since this will help us discern the significance of the evidence that has been collected. Let us look first at the debate around whether and when discrete emotions appear in childhood. Do infants get angry? When they show that they are angry does it imply the same thing as in an adult?

Expression of emotions in the first year

There is little argument that in early infancy some emotions look discrete. The facial expression of disgust, for instance, has been seen in newborns in response to sour tastes (Steiner, 1979). This clear response to an appropriate elicitor indicates that newborns do express disgust.

One kind of study has been to ask adults to look at photographs of infants' faces and to say what emotions are expressed. Adults are good at seeing happiness in the faces of 2- to 12-month-old babies (Emde et al., 1985). Such infant smiles have also been rated as indicating happiness by experts trained in one of the facial action coding schemes (Oster, Hegley, & Nagel, 1992) as described in chapter 4.

Although small babies do smile, the relationship of these smiles to appropriate elicitors is less clear (Sroufe & Waters, 1976; Wolff, 1987). In the first weeks of life smiles are made in the phase of sleep during which vivid dreams occur (rapid eye movement, or REM, sleep). After the first month smiles begin to occur with gentle stroking, and by two months they occur frequently in interaction with a caregiver (Malatesta et al., 1989a). So if smiling is an index of emotion, then happiness can occur within hours of birth; but if REM sleep merely elicits smiling as a reflex without any internal state of happiness, then clear signs of happiness do not emerge till after the first month or two (Sroufe, 1978).

Certainly by the time children are three months old they smile in response to the same kinds of events that make older children and adults happy – attention, invitations to play, and suchlike. Lewis, Alessandri, and Sullivan (1990) have also shown that smiling occurs when infants master skills. They placed babies in an infant seat and attached a string to their arms. For babies in one condition pulling the string turned on a short period of music: infants of two, four, six, and eight months soon learned to start the music by pulling the string. They showed higher levels of interest and smiling than those for whom the music came on irrespective of their string pulling. As in adults, mastery of a skill made the children happy.

One function of infants' smiles is to make adults both interested and happy. Malatesta and Haviland (1982) found that when infants showed interest in playing with their parents, the parents' expressions of interest also increased. Huebner and Izard (1988) showed pictures of infants' facial expressions to

Figure 6.1 Photographs of babies showing emotional expressions: (a) a positive or happy expression, (b) a negative expression.

mothers: the mothers said the expression of positive emotion or of interest would make them feel good, that they would talk, play, and interact with the baby, and show love. So, even before infants can direct expressions at specific people, their smiles function to draw adults into affectionate interactions with them. Whether such smiles really indicate happiness or are reflex facial movements is less important than their function of facilitating a positive relationship.

Evidence for the early expression of differential negative emotions is more problematic. Some researchers such as Oster, Hegley, and Nagel (1992) argue that babies' negative expressions show only undifferentiated distress, whereas others such as Izard and Malatesta (1987) argue that expressions of fear, anger, and sadness can all be seen from early infancy. As we described in chapter 4, there are two schemes for analyzing facial expressions: Izard's MAX (Izard, 1979) with its later modification AFFEX (Izard et al., 1983), and Oster's Baby-FACS (Oster & Rosenstein, in press), an adaptation for infants of Ekman and Friesen's (1978) FACS. Oster, Hegley, and Nagel (1992) took 19 photographs of infants that had been rated on the MAX system as discrete negative emotions (anger, sadness, disgust) and rerated them using Baby-FACS. Only 3 of the 19 were rated on the FACS as indicating the same emotion as that indicated by the MAX. With this low level of agreement studies using different coding systems are likely to come to different conclusions as to which emotions emerge in development and when.

Some researchers simply code the child's facial expression – if it meets coding criteria then specific negative emotions are inferred. In this way, researchers using the MAX system have seen expressions of anger, sadness, and pain-distress in three-month-olds during play with their mothers, during separation, and at reunion (Malatesta et al., 1986). Izard, Hembree, and Huebner (1987) videotaped infants at two, four, six, and eighteen months of age, while they were given routine injections to inoculate against diphtheria and other diseases. All the two-month-olds showed distress-pain expressions, 96 percent showed anger, and 44 percent showed sadness.

Others too have also seen anger expressions in the first year. Remember that in the experiment by Lewis, Alessandri, and Sullivan (1990) one group of babies turned on music for a short period by pulling a string attached to their arm. Two-month-old babies in this condition showed more anger and fussiness when their string-pulling no longer turned the music on, than when they could turn the music on. Anger is what we would expect in response to frustration and this is what was seen. However, babies also showed increased fear, sadness, and fussing in response to this frustration. Now this finding raises a problematic theoretical issue. When we see a facial expression that looks like fear, but we see it in response to something that is not thought of typically as a fear-inducing event, can we call it fear?

This has led some people to argue that the "real" test of whether young babies experience discrete emotions is if babies show a specific facial expression in response to an appropriate elicitor. These are exacting criteria for the presence of discrete emotions: an emotion is not just a facial expression, but it is an expression in the appropriate context.

An elegantly designed study by Hiatt, Campos, and Emde (1979) gives us insight into the link between internal states, facial expressions, and elicitors. They presented 10- to 12-month-old babies with six eliciting conditions. The hypotheses were that either playing peekaboo or allowing the child to play with a toy would elicit happiness; confronting a visual cliff (see figure 6.2) or seeing the approach of a stranger would elicit fear; seeing an object vanish (by means of a tachistoscope and mirror) or a piece of mild conjuring where a toy was hidden and substituted for another one, would elicit surprise. Components of infants' facial expressions were coded using features described by Ekman and Friesen (1978). To conclude that discrete emotions exist two criteria were to be met:

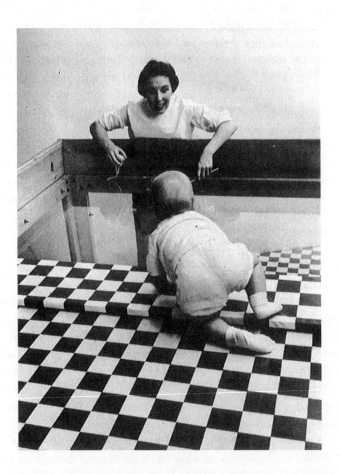

Figure 6.2 Picture of the visual cliff. What appears visually to the baby is a steep drop – notice the finer grain of the chequer-board pattern to the right of the baby's right knee – but a plate of thick glass supports the child safely when it crawls towards its mother (Gibson & Walk, 1960).

- the predicted expression should occur more often than any non-predicted expression in response to the specific elicitor, for instance an expression of fear must occur more often than surprise in response to the visual cliff and to approach of the stranger;
- the predicted expression must be displayed more often in its appropriate eliciting circumstances than in nonpredicted eliciting circumstances, for instance the fear expression must occur more in response to the visual cliff and the approach of a stranger than in response to the vanishing object or to the substitution of a toy.

Hiatt, Campos, and Emde found that babies do express happiness: both criteria were met. Fear met the criteria least well. In response to stimuli intended to elicit fear, infants showed a wide range of expressions, and significantly more nonpredicted expressions than expressions of fear. However, one of the fear conditions did elicit fear more often than either the happy or surprise conditions. For the situations designed to elicit expressions of surprise, the predicted expressions were seen more often than nonpredicted ones, but surprise was elicited just as often by elicitors hypothesized to elicit fear and happiness. So happiness met the criteria for a discrete emotion more than the other emotions.

This evidence suggests that there is some difficulty arguing that a wide range of discrete emotions are present in young infants. Certainly different expressions are present, but it seems as if these different expressions may not have a direct mapping onto internal emotional states, except for happiness.

Some naturalistic data illustrate this issue further. Camras (1992), a researcher in the emotion field, made video recordings of her daughter Justine's facial expressions in the first year of her life. She also kept careful notes about the circumstances in which each expression occurred. Using Izard's AFFEX coding scheme Camras found that Justine showed expressions of disgust, fear, distress-pain, and anger, in her first months. Her expressions often did not occur with expected elicitors, however. For instance Justine showed the fear expression when she was protesting being fed. Although it is possible that she was feeling frightened, her mother thought that this was unlikely given the circumstances. She showed a sadness expression when eating a sour vitamin. Why should this event cause sadness? Camras provides many such observations of episodes when the eliciting circumstances do not seem to be compatible with the child's emotional expression.

If infants are not showing a range of discrete emotions in infancy that correspond to discrete internal emotion experiences, how can we interpret these different expressions? Some argue that infants experience undifferentiated distress (Oster, Hegley, and Nagel, 1992) although this may be experienced at different levels of intensity. Camras (1992) has elaborated this view: most negative expressions of infants can be coded as distress-pain, as anger, or as blends of discrete expressions. When making negative expressions infants often contract their *orbicularis oculi* muscles and close their eyes. According to

AFFEX the only difference between codings of expressions of distress-pain and anger is that in anger the eyes are open. In young infants negative expressions certainly occur, but at different intensities: at high intensity the expression is coded by AFFEX as distress-pain, at slightly lower intensity as anger, and at low or waning intensity as sadness. As development proceeds changes in facial expressions occur. Camras suggests that emotions are communications that are modified as the needs of the child change. She supports Fogel's dynamic systems view: in adulthood distinctive patterns of emotions are visible, but they are not present in infancy. During development these distinctive patterns coalesce into their recognizable forms as a function of inner constraints and interactions with other people.

We started this section with two theories: Izard's (1991) theory of differential emotions, and Fogel's dynamic systems theory. These theories offer us different emphases about how emotional development occurs. One of the difficulties in evaluating them is that crucial tests are hard to construct. What looks like a piece of disconfirming evidence to an opponent is a piece of supporting evidence to the proponent of the theory, when viewed from a different vantage point – see a commentary by Fogel and Reimers (1989) and the subsequent reply by Malatesta et al. (1989b). We know from the above discussion that infants can show differentiated expressions in the first year, corresponding to adult conceptions of what specific facial expressions of emotion look like. However, we do not know whether these facial expressions are a valid indication of internal experiences of corresponding emotions. Without being able to talk to babies, we do not know what they are feeling. Our best way of guessing is to present them with something that should elicit an internal experience of a particular emotion: for instance the visual cliff should elicit fear. If babies respond to this elicitor with an unexpected emotion there are two possibilities. One is that there is not an invariant relationship between internal emotional experience and facial expression, and such an interpretation would argue against a differential emotions perspective. The other explanation, however, is that the situation that we thought elicited an internal experience of fear did not do so in all babies. Some babies might be surprised or frustrated. Either theory is just as plausible. Even though crucial tests of these theories are not forthcoming, the theories do orient us in different directions. Differential emotions theory orients us towards the maturation of innate, prewired, packaged structures. Dynamic systems theory orients us towards person–environment transactions in which links between internal experience and external expression are not predetermined.

Our own conclusion is that negative emotions are not well differentiated from one another in infancy. We think that it is unlikely that there are one-to-one linkages between internal experiences of emotion and their expression in babies. In the course of development internal states do become more discrete and more organized, as well as being expressed within individuals and cultures in characteristic ways. Internal experiences of emotion are about action readiness and as such these internal states are associated more often than not with particular patterns of expressive behavior: facial expressions, voice tone and so forth. But environmental influences are important in shaping both internal experiences and the way in which action readiness is expressed. Dynamic systems theory becomes attractive where the emphasis is on the relationship between the individual and the environment in the creation of these patterns of responsiveness.

Before leaving this debate think for a moment about the function of emotions in the lives of infants. A baby's smile makes a caregiver happy and interested – as if the baby's happiness were directly communicated. A baby's expressions of negative emotions signal that something is not right. A parent is then likely to pick the baby up, give comfort, offer food, and consider a range of other reasons for the distress. In the first year before the baby is mobile, there may be no point in a caregiver discriminating more than positive and negative emotions. Instead, the parent pays attention to the context to make sense of the baby's signals: how many hours since the baby was fed (Richards & Bernal, 1972)? Has the baby been hit by her sister? Has a stranger come into the room? Has she rolled onto a sharp toy? Only when the baby starts to move around and function at a distance from the caregiver would finer discrimination among negative emotions become important.

Developmental changes in elicitation of emotion

As well as changes in children's capacities to signal different emotions, there are also marked changes, as children get older, in the kinds of events that elicit emotions. Scarr and Salapatek (1970) performed experiments documenting some of these changes in the first two years. They exposed infants between two months and two years to strangers, a visual cliff, a jack-in-the-box, a moving toy dog, loud noises, and someone wearing a mask. Few children under seven months showed marked expressions of fear or distress to any of these. With increasing age up to two years, children showed more fearful avoidance of the visual cliff, and more fear of strangers and masks. Their fear of loud or sudden movements, and of unfamiliar toys, showed a different pattern: for these fear began around seven months, reached a peak at the end of the first year and then declined in intensity, see figure 6.3.

Later in childhood further developments occur. Preschoolers are mainly frightened by imaginary themes: monsters, ghosts, frightening dreams. In the early school years fears surrounding bodily injury and physical danger predominate (Bauer, 1976). In adolescence, social fears take over (Bamber, 1979).

Some events are universally frightening. Distress on separation from the attachment figure is one such and, as Bowlby (1973) points out, its development is accompanied by a growing wariness of strangers – of people who are not attachment figures. Separation distress begins in the second half of the first year, reaching a peak between 15 and 18 months, then declining, so that by three years of age very distressed reactions to separation are rare.

Although this pattern of fear is universal it depends on context. If babies crawl or walk away from the parent themselves, they show much less distress than when it is the parent who leaves (Rheingold & Eckerman, 1970). Infants

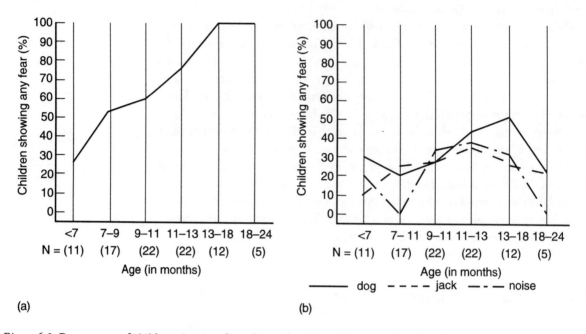

(a)

(b)

Figure 6.3 Percentages of children showing fear of (a) the visual cliff, and of (b) dogs, noises, and a jack-in-the-box, as a function of age (Scarr & Salapatek, 1970).

Figure 6.4 Percentages of children who cried during separations: These graphs show the course of separation distress in children of the African Bushmen, the Guatemalan Indians, lower-class families from Antigua, Guatemala, and infants from an Israeli kibbutz (Kagan et al., 1980).

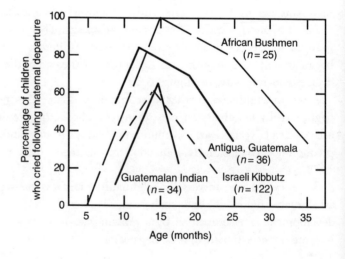

are also less distressed if their parent leaves a house through the door by which they usually leave than through an unusual door (Littenberg, Tulkin, & Kagan, 1971). Thus infants appraise events, and unfamiliarity is one determinant of a distress and avoidance response.

Infants' abilities to discriminate and react to emotions in other people

Let us now consider what information babies have and how early they perceive emotions in other people. What effects do other people's emotions have on the baby?

One of the challenges of developmental research is to find whether infants know something – when they are little one cannot ask them directly. A well-established method has been to use habituation, based on the finding that infants look at new patterns for longer than familiar ones. So if infants are presented with a happy face they look at it for a long time, then turn away. If presented with another happy face we might expect them only to look briefly because the expression is not new. But if they are now presented with a sad face, we might expect them to look at it for a long time, as this expression would be new for them. We are able to tell from this methodology what kinds of discriminations infants are able to make about emotions.

Field et al. (1982) used this method to see whether newborn babies could discriminate emotional expressions. Infants who were 36 hours old saw an adult who made expressions of happiness, surprise, and sadness. The infant first habituated to one expression, then saw a new one. When the infant had habituated to the second expression, a third was presented. Infants did habituate and dishabituate to the three different expressions. They also showed some ability to imitate the expressions they saw. They showed more widening of the mouth and of the eyes in response to the adult's expression of surprise, more pouting of the lips in response to the adult's expression of sadness, and more widening of the lips in response to the adult's expression of happiness. Haviland and Lelwicka (1987) confirmed these findings in babies who were 10 weeks old.

The conclusion was that before much opportunity for learning has occurred infants can discriminate among emotions shown by the same adult, and they can imitate some aspects of them. This implies a genetically specified mechanism of recognition and production of expressions, perhaps explicable in terms of differential emotions theory. But it may be that a step was omitted in drawing this conclusion (Nelson, 1987): perhaps infants habituate to aspects of the face other than those which truly indicate emotions. Remember how complex are the discriminations in AFFEX or FACS necessary for identifying facial expressions. Remember too how subtle is the cue distinguishing a real smile involving contractions of the muscles round the eyes from a phony smile in which only the mouth moves.

Caron, Caron, and Myers (1985) have demonstrated that young infants probably cannot differentiate emotional expressions as such. They presented four- to seven-month-old infants with pictures of women showing angry and happy, toothy and nontoothy expressions. Infants could discriminate the toothy from the nontoothy faces, but if both angry and happy expressions showed teeth, they could not discriminate between them.

Thus infants can recognize salient features of the face, but these features need not correspond to those that discriminate among emotions. Caron, Caron, and Maclean (1988) have gone on to examine when infants do discriminate critical aspects of emotional expression. They habituated infants to an emotional facial expression and voice sound of six different adults. Then infants saw and heard two new adults presenting both a new expression and an expression that was familiar to them. When habituated to a happy or sad expression and then presented with a new expression (sad or happy) made by a new adult, five-month-olds could discriminate the expressions as such, but four-month-olds could not. Five-month-olds could not discriminate happy and angry, but seven-month-olds could. When the experimenters investigated further by removing the voice and just showing the adults' faces, the five-month-olds could still discriminate happiness from sadness, but even at seven months they could not discriminate happiness and anger from faces alone. Hence, babies do not discriminate different emotional expressions made by different people before

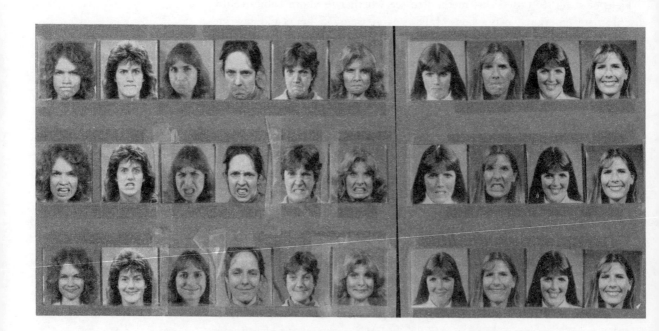

Figure 6.5 Stimuli used in the experiment of Caron, Caron, and Myers (1985); children habituated to toothy anger did not dishabituate when new faces (on the right) showed toothy smiles.

four months, and they probably discriminate emotion in the voice before they can make the same discrimination visually.

The voice is important for emotional communication, and Fernald (1989) has shown that adults use a different voice in talking to infants than in talking to adults. Infants pay more attention to this special voice of "motherese" and show more positive emotion during speech intended for them. From five months they can discriminate affective messages indicating approval or prohibition, either in their parents' language, or in a language their parents do not speak. Infants showed more positive affect to approvals, and more negative affect to prohibitions (Fernald, 1993).

By seven months babies can match facial and vocal expressions. Walker-Andrews (1986) presented five- and seven-month-old infants with filmed expressions of happiness and anger, and recorded the voices that went with them. In the film the mouth of the person was obscured so the infant could not match mouth movements with the voice. By seven months of age babies spent longer looking at the film clips of visual expressions that matched the sounds than at expressions that did not match, but at five months of age infants could not make this discrimination.

What is clear is that within their first few months babies do have skills of expression and perception suitable to their interpersonal needs. They can signal distress from the beginning, and soon afterwards they can signal happiness. They can also recognize aspects of their parent's emotional state, particularly from tones of voice. The stringent requirement that recognition must be demonstrated across several people is not necessary to most babies who have just one or two primary caregivers. It may be, moreover, that imitative abilities that babies show from the first few hours of life have important emotional effects for them. Melzoff (1993) has demonstrated these abilities, and suggested that infant facial actions imitating adult emotional expressions could evoke emotions in the child. This could occur either because there are discrete neural programs of emotions which start up when any part is activated, in which case the emotion evoked would be the same between parent and child, or because making a particular expression contributes to a particular mode within a dynamic self-organizing system. In either case this could mean that babies' imitative expressions are important in sharing affective states with caregivers (Stern, 1985; Trevarthen, 1979). By one year of age skills have developed that allow infants to take part in complex interactions.

Construction of the child's relationship with others

How do emotions function in constructing relationships? Emotions show that an interaction is going well or that adjustments need to be made. Here, for instance, is a description of a mother of a three-and-a-half-month-old baby responding to emotional signals and regulating her own behavior to fit in with that of her baby, who is blind, sitting in an infant seat. This excerpt is taken from Als, Tronick, and Brazelton (1980).

> . . . the mother comes in with a friendly somewhat throaty "Hi peanut, Hi peanut," Marci moves her face even more toward the mother, opens her mouth and points her index finger toward her. She is very still, her face open to the mother. The mother leans in very close, touches Marci's right hand and with her face, almost touches the infant's face. She says in a warm, playful crooning voice, "What are you doing?" She repeats "What are you doing?" several more times and nuzzles the infant with her face. Marci lies back, still absorbing every touch and sound . . . The mother taps Marci's nose. Marci immediately fusses and pulls back, tongues and opens and closes her mouth. The mother lets go of her and says, "Yeah!" She sits farther back and says softly, "You had a fun ride! You had a fun ride in!" At this Marci stills again and raises her eyebrows opens her mouth and is hooked on the mother. The mother now walks her fingers up Marci's arm and stomach, saying playfully, "What are you doing? What are you doing?" Marci brings her face closer to the mother's. The mother switches to moving her own face closer to and farther away from Marci's face, saying "Ha-booh! Ha-booh! Ha-booh!" in rhythm with her movements. Marci's mouth is wide open. Her shoulders are lifted toward the mother, and her right arm moves in rhythm to the mother's voice. Then she breaks into a wide smile, staying fastened onto her mother with her body and face. The mother acknowledges this saying in a gurgling voice, "That's a pretty smile! Ha-booh!" She says "Ha-booh!" once more. She then shifts Marci's whole body into midline. Marci's face changes. The mother resumes the Ha-booh! game immediately moving her face even closer to Marci's face than it was before. Marci relaxes once more, opens her mouth wide, lifts her right arm, raises her eyebrows and begins to smile again. (Als, Tronick, and Brazelton, 1980, p. 30)

We see a finely tuned interaction in which the mother watches the baby's emotional state, and gears her own responses to it. To start with the mother engages the baby with "motherese," making big shifts in intonational pattern which capture the baby's attention (Fernald, 1989). She moves close to the baby and nuzzles her. Stimulation gradually increases as the mother touches the baby and speaks. The mother is sensitive to the baby's level of arousal so that when the baby fusses, she withdraws a bit, then tries again more slowly. The mother plays a sound-and-touch game. Marci signals enjoyment of this game to her mother with a smile. When her mother moves her in her seat, Marci signals that she doesn't want the game to stop. When the mother restarts the game, Marci again signals her pleasure. Stern (1985) too has made similar findings, that when a baby smiles, the parent very often mirrors the happy expression but in a different way, for instance with their voice: "Oooohh. That's a nice smile." Field (1994) suggests that the caregiver helps regulate arousal, by reading a baby's signals, keeping in time with them, and altering the environment to maintain the best level of stimulation for the baby. This keeping-in-time is called "attunement." It affects the baby's well-being; without it the baby's behavior can become disorganized.

The role of emotion in regulating interactions between mothers and young babies has also been demonstrated experimentally. Cohn and Tronick (1983) established the important role of emotion in mother–infant interaction by examining what happened when mothers showed no emotions to their babies. Twelve baby girls and twelve baby boys took part. The mother sat face to face with her infant who sat in an infant seat. In one condition (called flat affect) mothers were asked to direct their gaze at their infant, speak in a flat uninteresting monotone, keep their face expressionless, minimize body movement, and not touch their infant. This was contrasted with three-minute periods of the mother acting normally. Babies were videotaped. When mothers demonstrated flat affect, infants showed more wary expressions, made more protests and showed more brief positive expressions, were much more disorganized, and were more likely to enter a negative state. During normal interactions infants were likely to cycle between play, brief positive expressions, and monitoring. Once this positive cycle had started they were less likely to enter a negative state.

So even in children of only three months emotions function to regulate interaction. Infants' expressions of happiness signal that their goals are being achieved; negative expressions signal that the interaction is not going well for them. From the description of the mother's interaction with Marci we can see that the mother attends to her baby's signals, interprets them as messages about the interaction, and alters her own behavior accordingly. Tronick, Cohn, and Shea (1986) call this the mutual regulation model: emotional messages are exchanged so that each partner achieves his or her own goals in coordination

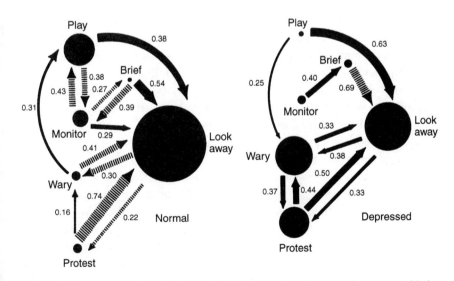

Figure 6.6 State transition diagrams for infants when their mothers were (a) in a normal condition, and (b) when depressed. The proportion of time spent in a state is indicated by the size of circles. The thickness of arrows represents the conditional probabilities, with numerical values shown next to them. Striped arrows indicate conditional probabilities with $p < 0.05$ (Cohn & Tronick, 1983).

with those of the other. Emotions are communications: the infant signals to the parent, the parent signals to the infant, each alters behavior accordingly.

This progression in meaningful communication is captured by Wolff's (1963) careful ethological studies of babies in their homes in the first six months of their lives. He observed 22 infants for an average of 30 hours during their first one, three, or six, months of life. Even in their first weeks infants smiled more to their mother's voice than to the voice of the investigator. In the first six weeks they smiled more at voices than faces, but after six weeks this pattern changed with infants smiling more to faces.

Smiling then decreased over the months, as vocalizations increased. The time it took infants to begin a smile on hearing their mother's voice also got longer as they approached three months. This was because they began to look around for the source of the voice and smiled only when they found it. So early in the relationship, infants show parents how much they matter, pulling parents in with emotional communications that are specific to them. There is also growth in infants' ability to time their emotional responses, so that these become truly communicative. Instead of smiling to a disembodied voice, the infant smiles when someone else can receive their message.

The sophistication in the communicative process can be seen in how anger is expressed in the first year. Stenberg and Campos (1990) examined where infants targeted their angry expressions. One-, four-, and seven-month-old babies were placed in an infant seat. To elicit anger, one investigator sat on one side of the child and restrained the child's arms. The mother sat on the child's other side. When the babies' arms were restrained, only the four- and seven-month-olds showed angry expressions. Whereas the four-month-olds look more at their restrainer or at the restrainer's hands, the seven-month-olds looked at their mothers after making facial expressions of anger. This suggests that the older infants were developing some notion of anger being used as a communication to their mothers. Vocalizations followed arm restraint immediately, before the negative facial expressions, as if vocal expressions were being used to capture attention. So, the expressions are not just read-outs of inner states: increasingly they are targeted towards specific people. The sequence of vocalizations and expression suggests that infants try to get the attention of the mothers, and then signal their distress.

In the first year not only do babies change their emotional signals as their relationships develop, but they acquire skills of using information from caregivers to alter their own actions, for instance if there is something ambiguous in the environment. These skills have been called "social referencing." For instance Sorce et al. (1985) exposed one-year-old babies to a visual cliff adjusted to a height that did not evoke clear avoidance. Seventy-four percent of babies crossed the cliff when mothers showed a happy expression, but none crossed when their mother showed a fearful expression.

Infants older than 10 months, as compared with six- to nine-month-olds, are more likely to look at a parent's face for emotional information than at other parts of the body, and it is only the older babies who look at a parent before taking action with respect to an ambiguous elicitor (Walden & Ogan, 1988). Thus from the end of the first year babies begin to alter their own behavior on the basis of their parents' appraisals and emotions, and this influences how they themselves appraise and react to the world.

Cooperative action and the goal-corrected partnership

As we discussed in chapter 4, emotions can function to allow people to cooperate in complex plans. Bowlby (1971), the founder of attachment theory, proposed a version of this idea he called "the goal-corrected partnership," the mutual cooperation between two people that allows them to achieve their goals. (In chapter 3 we discussed goal-directed behavior: behavior directed towards the achievement of a goal.) "Goal-directed" (a term we introduced in chapter 2) and "goal-corrected" are equivalent. Bowlby preferred the latter, and was mainly concerned with how goal-corrected partnerships came about between parents and children, but also saw this as the basis of cooperative relationships throughout life. Early in life the infant knows little about their parents' goals, but with increasing cognitive maturity and through repeated interactions, the child develops a model of the other person's desires and intentions, allowing for a partnership in which parents and children collaborate in the fulfillment of each other's goals. We discuss the work of Bowlby in the next chapter; here our concern is with the important changes in cognitive development that allow for the development and elaboration of cooperative action.

Differentiation between self and others

The ability to form a partnership relies on the ability to differentiate self from others. Developmentalists have argued that children's recognition of themselves as separate from others is only rudimentary during the first year (Stern, 1985), and it depends on cognitive maturation. Remember too, as we discussed in chapter 2, that in some cultures distinctions between self and other are minimized as compared to Western individualistic societies. During the second year, differentiation between self and other becomes more established. At this point we see the emergence of emotions that rely on such a differentiation: empathy and embarrassment.

Newborn babies respond to the cries of other infants by crying themselves. Some have argued that this early indication of emotion contagion is an important precursor of later empathy, but others argue that the response may be more like a reflex, with the baby confusing another person's cry with their own. As early as six months, however, babies show much clearer interest in others' emotions, by leaning towards a peer who shows distress, by touching, and so forth (Eisenberg, 1992).

Between 12 and 24 months children respond to another's distress by comforting, bringing a parent, offering an object (Zahn-Waxler et al., 1992). They do react with concern – but they tend to offer comfort in the way that they themselves like to be comforted. When our daughter Hannah was 14 months old another baby was crying in our apartment. Hannah had some shoes that she particularly liked. When she heard the baby crying she walked over, watched her for a moment, then tried to offer her own shoe to the baby. Dunn and Kendrick (1982) give another example:

> [This] occurred when a 15 month old was in the garden with his brother. The 15-month-old Len was a stocky boy with a fine round tummy and he played at this time a particular game with his parents which always made him laugh. His game was to come towards them, walking in an odd way, pulling up his T-shirt and showing his big stomach. One day his elder brother fell off the climbing frame in the garden and cried vigorously. Len watched solemnly. Then he approached his brother, pulling up his T-shirt and showing his tummy, vocalizing and looking at his brother. (Dunn & Kendrick, 1982, p. 115)

These scenes show how children perceive distress and feel motivated to do something about it. But they offer comfort in the way that they like to be comforted, rather than being able to think about what the other person might find comforting.

By the time children are three years old, the ways they offer comfort are more appropriate to the needs of the other person. For instance, children comfort a child in distress by fetching the mother of the crying child. Also, as children get older, they are more likely to respond with concern to the distress of another child if they have not themselves caused this distress (Zahn-Waxler et al., 1992). This shows the older child's increasing ability both to think about the event from other points of view and to start, perhaps, experiencing guilt.

We can see the crucial role of the child's sense of herself or himself in different displays of empathy. Hoffman (1984) has outlined four stages in this development that depend on children's increasing ability to differentiate themselves from others. Global empathy is when a child's feeling of distress is triggered by another person's distress through contagion or imitation. Egocentric empathy occurs when a child knows that the other is in distress, but reacts as if they themselves were in distress. In the third stage, the child's empathy for others' feelings involves understanding that the others' feelings can differ from his or her own. The final stage is empathy for another's life experience, which involves knowing that different experiences lead to different reactions over the course of someone's life.

What would cooperative endeavors be like without empathy? When we see that another person is sad or angry in response to our actions, we usually feel some motivation to modify our behavior and reassess our own actions. And, from early in life, experiencing emotions that are similar to those of someone else provides us with a stepping stone to the other's internal world. With increasing cognitive capacity our ability to understand that world will become more complex and allow for more appropriate responses to the other person.

Other complex emotions are intimately tied to the child's dawning recognition of self. Embarrassment for instance has been called a complex emotion. This is because it is not evident in infancy and relies on the development of the differentiation of self, which comes with cognitive maturity. Embarrassment is experienced when we feel ourself to be the object of unwelcome attention. Lewis et al. (1989) compared the ability of children to feel embarrassment with their ability to feel fear, arguing that fear is a more basic emotion, not dependent on self-recognition. To test reactions to fear they introduced a stranger. They tested self-recognition by putting children in front of a mirror, having surreptitiously placed some rouge on their noses. The children who recognized that the reflection was of themselves showed this by touching their own noses. To test for embarrassment the researchers did such things as overcomplimenting the child, and asking him or her to dance. The researchers' prediction was that though all the children would show fear, only those who recognized themselves in the mirror would be able to experience embarrassment.

The relationship between self-recognition and embarrassment can be seen in table 6.1. Children were much more likely to experience embarrassment when they could recognize themselves in a mirror. But there was no significant

Figure 6.7 Child becoming interested in a mirror: children who have developed a sense of self know it is a reflection they see in the mirror and will touch a red patch that has been surreptitiously put on their nose or forehead, even though they cannot see this part of their body except by reflection.

Table 6.1 Numbers of children who showed embarrassment as a function of whether they recognized themselves from the rouge-on-the-nose test

	Showed self-recognition	*Did not show self-recognition*
Showed embarrassment	19	5
Showed no embarrassment	7	13

Source: Lewis et al. (1989)

relationship between self-recognition and showing fear. The conclusion is that embarrassment is experienced mainly when a sense of self has developed.

The self, however, is not just an isolated object: the very concept of self is social. It would be better described as self-in-relation-to-other, so that when we start to form a conception of ourselves we do not do so as some isolated Robinson Crusoe, alone and independent of society. The self is that aspect of personality that allows us to know how to interact with others. In the studies on empathy we see something of its development: the self-with-other-in-distress. And in studies of embarrassment, the self which is embarrassed is the self with too much attention from others. So in Western societies the ideal self is not a self cut off from society. We conceive ourselves not as isolated but as self-reliant, not dependent. In Asiatic and other "We-based" societies, the ideal self is thought of as interdependent. So in the West emotions are appropriate to how well we achieve independence, despite needs for others; perhaps in the East they are appropriate to how well interdependence is maintained, despite physical separateness.

The language of emotions in cooperative action

Naturalistic studies have shown how children learn emotion words and how much they know about emotions – Bretherton et al. (1986) have written a comprehensive review. Children start talking about internal states around 18 months, and the proportion of time they spend talking about emotions gradually increases with age. Dunn and her colleagues (Dunn, Bretherton, and Munn, 1987; Dunn, Brown, and Beardsall, 1991) recorded talk of feeling states between mothers, children, and their siblings in their homes when the children were three years old. The commonest themes for mothers and children were pleasure and pain, but 5 percent or more of turns taken by mothers involved specific emotional issues such as anger, distress, concern, sympathy, and disgust.

Learning to discuss emotional experiences has several important consequences for cooperative action. The most common early function of talking about emotions is simply comment (Dunn, 1987). But by the time children were three, Dunn, Brown, and Beardsall (1991) found that half of the conversations about emotions were about the causes of the feelings, and they show the complexity of children's knowledge. For instance 28-month-old children understand common antecedents of distress – "You sad mommy. What did daddy do?" – as well as how an emotion of one person can affect actions of another: "I cry, lady pick me up and hold me" (Bretherton et al., 1986). Here, rather than just comment, emotion talk can become part of the negotiation of relationships.

Mothers markedly increase their talk about internal states to children between 13 and 28 months old, presumably responding to their children's grasp of such matters. By the time children are 28 months, 60 percent of their mothers' speech to them involves references to internal states (Beeghly, Bretherton, & Mervis, 1986). Through their talk, parents implicitly teach children how to represent their internal states, how emotions function between people, how they are expressed, controlled, and so forth. (In chapter 7 we discuss such socialization in more detail.)

We see that children are engaged in understanding their own and other people's emotions. By learning to talk about emotions and their causes they move well beyond the simple communication system that facial expression and voice tone allow. Language about emotions enables the development of shared meanings about internal states (Stern, 1985). A new degree of relatedness is possible. Children can talk about a feeling, give their version of its cause, refer back to emotions, alter their understanding of them. And, crucially, instead of a model based only on the child's experience, parents can offer their understanding to be put together with those of the child. Similarly, parents can understand an event from their child's perspective. The shared meanings that are created become part of that relationship and its shared history. Dunn and Brown (1991) provide wonderful examples; here is a conversation in which a 21-month-old child initiates a conversation with his mother about an event that happened at breakfast (p. 97).

Child: Eat my Weetabix (breakfast cereal). Eat my Weetabix. Crying.
Mother: Crying weren't you? We had quite a battle. "One more mouthful, Michael." And what did you do? You spat it out!
Child: (Pretends to cry).

They go over the event with the child naming the emotions – "Crying" – and then doing a reenactment. The mother learns that the child has been thinking about the event, and the child learns why his mother thought it had happened. Maybe he is apologizing, maybe he is trying to find out whether she is still angry with him, maybe he is wondering about what next breakfast time will be like. They have shared an experience together and are in the process of constructing a shared representation of that experience that gives each of them a better model of the other. Simple empathic experiences link people together; with language shared meanings become possible, facilitating the process of cooperative action.

Children's understanding of the causes of emotion

Between two and three years of age comes a great growth of language, including emotion terms and the ability to communicate with others about emotions. From this point forward it is clear that children think about what causes emotions, consider how they can be controlled, and so on. They construct, as we might say, their own theories about emotions.

Adult understanding of emotions makes implicit reference to people's desires: "He wanted that truck so he was angry when it was taken away," or beliefs: "He was surprised when he saw her because he thought that she had left." It has been argued that children under four are not capable of such representations. Consequently, their ideas of emotions are more "behavioral" than "mentalistic" (Harris & Saarni, 1989). The argument goes that young children are more likely to describe emotions as facial expressions or behavior rather than as internal feelings, and as caused by external situations rather than being provoked by mental entities such as what a person wanted or believed. Our daughter, Hannah, at age three provided us with an example after being reprimanded for doing something by Jenny. Her face crumpled and she started to cry. After a moment she burst out with: "See what you've done to my face." We could say that her theory of emotions at that time was: "What someone shows *is* what they feel."

Yet there are now many counter-examples that indicate that children as young as two or three can talk about emotions in ways that look convincingly mentalistic, as if they understand that internal mental states drive their actions. Wellman (1995) reports on an intensive study of the language of five children starting when they were two years old. He asked whether children have the concept that one kind of situation elicits only one kind of emotion, arguing that if children understand that situations elicit different kinds of emotional reactions in different people, then they have some conception of emotion as an internal mental state. He found that between two and three years of age children speak about the same object eliciting different emotions in different people:

> Adam (age 3): Shaving. I don't like shaving cream . . .
> Mother: You don't like shaving cream.
> Adam: No. Daddy like shaving cream. Daddy like shaving cream. Mommy wipe it off. (Wellman, 1995, p. 296)

By three to four years old children give plausible reasons for experiencing emotions in which they make reference to the goal states (or desires) of other people. Stein and Levine (1989) read three- to six-year-old children stories in which the goals and consequent outcomes varied for different protagonists: in one story a child wanted something and got it. In another the child wanted something but did not get it. In yet another the child did not want something but got it. If children understand that specific emotions are consequences of having goals (i.e., mental states drive the experience of the emotion) then we would expect children to predict negative and positive emotions on the basis of the protagonist's goal. Three-year-old children were able to do this, and they were also able to generate explanations involving reference to the protagonists' goals. Further evidence for preschool children explaining the causes of emotion with reference to mental states comes from Harris et al. (1989). They told children between three and six years old a story about Ellie the elephant who likes only milk. Then a monkey came and poured the milk out of the milk jug and replaced it with Coke. They were then asked how will Ellie feel when she tastes the Coke? Children of four, though preferring Coke themselves, said that Ellie would feel fed up when she found the Coke. Four year olds were able to predict an emotion on the basis of the other's desire. In both of these studies age did make a difference: as children became older more of them made predictions that took into account the goals of the protagonist.

In naturalistic circumstances, preschool children frequently explain the emotions of other children by making reference to the desires and beliefs of the other child. In a study by Fabes et al. (1991) observers noted details of incidents of emotion in three-, four-, and five-year-olds, at a nursery school. A child who was the closest to each incident, but not involved in it, was asked what emotion had occurred and what had caused it. These children made external attributions by referring to behavior such as "He's mad because she took his toy." To be rated as providing an internal explanation a child had to make explicit reference to an internal or psychological state, such as: "She's sad because she misses her mom," or "She's mad because she thought it was her turn." The majority (55 percent) of explanations of negative emotions given by three-year-olds were external, but 45 percent were internal – mainly involving explanations around a child's goal not being met. Negative emotions received more internal explanations than did positive ones. Children also made more internal explanations for intense emotions, both positive and negative. So negative emotions and intense displays orient children to seeking for explanations of a more mental kind. This research shows that in everyday life preschool children start to think about the internal worlds of other people. If emotions are communications in a social world it makes sense that negative emotions and intense emotions provoke thoughts of the other's inner states: they signal a need for attention, a possibility that a participant's behavior needs changing in some shared activity.

We have seen that preschool children explain emotions by making reference to the mental states of the protagonist: in the form of his or her goals or desires. Certainly children's ability to do this increases with age, but for many children we see evidence for this by age three. These developments in understanding the causes of emotion are early indications of the child's theory of mind: understanding that their own mental states are distinctive and may change, and that others have mental states that can be different from their own (Astington, 1993; Harris, 1989).

This development in children's ability to represent other people's mental states is an important development for cooperative partnerships. When children can begin to conceptualize other people's desires, goals, and beliefs, they can negotiate plans in the world knowing what the other person wants and believes. Astington and Jenkins (1995) found that children with a fuller understanding of how beliefs can affect behavior showed more joint planning during make-believe play with other children.

Understanding the masking of emotion

If emotions are, at least in part, mental the question arises: what about concealing emotions? As adults, we recognize a difference between what we feel inside and what we express or how we act. We might modulate our expression of anger if we think that demonstrating open anger might have negative consequences. Sometimes we even try to show one emotion although we feel another one inside. We do these things both for ourselves and for others, for instance to maintain positive interactions with people who are important to us. Sometimes we feel extremely sad about an event but instead of allowing ourselves to think about it, we make ourselves think about something else. When can children make distinctions between showing and feeling something, and how might controlling emotions help them in carrying out cooperative plans?

Conscious modulation of emotion, or substitution of one emotion for another, begins in the early school years. P. L. Harris et al. (1986) read stories to children of four, six, and ten years old, about children who feel a certain way but for whom an unwelcome consequence would follow if they expressed an emotion or other feeling. Children were asked how the character really felt and what feelings they would show. For instance, "Diana wants to go outside but she has a tummy ache. She knows that if she tells her mom that she has a tummy ache her mom will say that she can't go out. She tries to hide the way she feels so that her mom will let her go outside." The child is then asked "How did Diana feel when she had a tummy ache? How did Diana try to look on her face when she had a tummy ache?" Six-year-olds consistently made a distinction between what a child felt and what they showed. This distinction was just beginning in four-year-olds in relation to hiding negative feelings but not positive ones. Although four-year-olds understood that real and apparent emotion need not correspond, they showed a less systematic understanding of this issue than the older children.

What children think about stories, such as those read to them by Harris and his colleagues, and what they can do to modulate their emotions in everyday life, may be different. Saarni (1984) arranged an event in which she thought children would modulate their emotions in response to social pressure. In the first session six- and ten-year-old children received an age-appropriate present following the performance of an unimportant task. In the second session their present was a baby toy. Would the children show their disappointment at receiving a baby toy? Their expressions were videorecorded, and coded as negative, positive, or transitional (defined as suggesting uncertainty or tension). Differences between the expressions following the age-appropriate gift and of the baby toy were calculated. Children's ability to mask disappointment increased with age, although this skill was seen to a limited extent in six-year-olds. Girls did more masking of their emotional expressions than boys did.

Terwogt, Schene, and Harris (1986) also examined the extent to which children could manipulate their feelings. They read a sad story to one group of six-year-olds and told them not to let it affect them. Another group were told to let the story affect them. Before and after the story they were tested on a memory task. Those who were told to let the story affect them showed some impairment in memory and a self-rating of increased sadness, as compared to the group who were told not to let the story affect them. Girls were much better than boys at intensifying and attenuating their emotions. Of interest is the finding that few of the children could say anything about the strategies they used to do this, suggesting that a conscious understanding of the process occurs even later than this.

We might imagine that children would gain a more rapid understanding of the distinction between real and apparent emotions in societies that emphasized external control of emotion. Hess et al. (1980) found for instance that Japanese mothers expect their children to control emotional expression earlier than mothers in North America. This corresponds to the idea, discussed in chapter 2, that Japanese people generally regard emotions such as anger and disgust as more controllable than American people (Matsumoto et al., 1988). Gardner et al. (1988), however, using Harris's methods of asking children about emotions experienced by characters in stories, found no differences for the age at which Japanese and Western children have a conscious understanding of the distinction between inner and displayed emotions.

Conscious awareness of controlling emotions in a wide range of circumstances is unlikely to emerge before about the age of six. This corresponds to the finding, discussed in chapter 2, that parents in many cultures expect children to behave — more or less — according to the social standards of adult society by this age (Briggs, 1970; Lutz, 1988).

Being able to mask their emotions may help people to cooperate in a social world in which they and other people have multiple goals. Sometimes goals conflict with one another and we may need to prioritize one goal rather than another. A child feels disappointed to receive an inappropriate present, but knows that showing disappointment will make another person feel badly. When children begin to understand this process in themselves and others, they are drawing on a more elaborate — actually a better — model of understanding other people. Skills in constructing such models equip people for negotiating complex situations in which the goals of another person are understood to be multiple, sometimes contradictory, sometimes obscured. Through masking emotions, people's feelings can sometimes elude even themselves – a process that we discuss in chapter 12.

Children's concepts of ambivalence

Ambivalence is having two conflicting emotions at the same time. Children's ability to understand ambivalence represents their growing ability to make more complex models of their own and other people's mental states.

As with the masking and modulation of emotion, children show ambivalence before they are consciously aware of it. For instance some one-year-olds react to reunion with their mother after a separation by wanting to be close to her while also angrily trying to push her away (Ainsworth et al., 1978). It is, however, not until children are nearer 10 years old that they explicitly understand that they can experience two opposite emotions simultaneously. Harter and Buddin (1987) asked 126 children between four and twelve years old to sort pictures of four negative emotions and three positive emotions into two piles. Children selected two pictures either from the same pile or from different piles, and were asked whether they could have the feelings indicated in the pictures at the same time towards the same thing, or towards separate things. They found a developmental sequence: some of the youngest children said you cannot experience two emotions at the same time. At the next stage, children said you could experience two positive, or two negative, emotions at the same time towards different objects: "I'd be happy that I got a motorcycle and glad that I got a race car." The next stage was experiencing two emotions of the same valence towards the same target: "I was happy and proud that I hit a home run." Then children said you can experience two emotions of different valence towards different targets: "I was glad that I was seeing *Star Wars* but sad that I was missing the ball game." Finally children could talk about emotions of different valence toward the same object: "I was happy that I got a bike for Christmas but sad that it was only a 3-speed." Children's examples moved further along this sequence as they got older, so that the mean age of reaching the last stage was 11.3 years.

The recognition of ambivalence is an important step in understanding the multiplicity of goals that both we ourselves and others have in everyday life. Moreover, experiencing an emotion is not just a matter of experiencing the workings of a biological mechanism like a sneeze. Genetically given bases of emotion become elaborated into complex social skills and are elements, not final products, in the construction of our inner theories of our selves, of others, and of social relationships.

Summary

Emotions are central to how parents and children relate, and to how they develop their relationship. Through emotional expressions parents and children come to learn about each others' desires and beliefs. Children's own experience of emotions signal what is working or not working for them in an interaction. Even very young babies alter their own behavior in response to another person's negative and positive emotional expressions, so emotions are essential components of babies' experience of others. The emotional communication system starts simply, as children signal negative states such as distress, and positive states by smiling and eye contact. Differentiation of emotional expressions (e.g., of happiness, surprise, fear, anger) and the targeting of these expressions to specific people, develop somewhat gradually during the first year. Similarly, over the course of the first year infants come to discriminate different emotions in adults at first by tone of voice, and later also by adults' facial expressions. Babies and caregivers develop a dance together in which the emotions of one are treated by the other as important communications that affect their actions and understanding of the other. Emotional expressions orient children to thinking about and constructing a model (or inner theory) of the internal world of others. The emergence of talk about emotion allows for the development of shared meanings around emotional experience. Such shared meanings become part of the fabric of relationships. Metacognitive skills allow for elaborated models of other people. We humans become oriented to the fact that people have multiple goals, and that sometimes these goals conflict. Human responses to such dilemmas include masking emotions, and experiencing ambivalence. Without elaborated models of other people, that become a keen focus of discussion in older children and adults, joint cooperation would be more difficult.

Further Reading

The best general introduction we know to the development of emotions is:

Paul L. Harris (1989). *Children and emotion: The development of psychological understanding*. Oxford: Blackwell.

For an account of children's early expressions:

Carol Z. Malatesta and colleagues (1989). The development of emotion expression during the first two years of life. *Monographs of the Society for Research in Child Development, 54* (1–2, Serial No. 219) 1–103.

On the significance of children's emotions and their understanding in family interaction:

Judy Dunn & Jane Brown (1994). Affect expression in the family, children's understanding of emotions and their interactions with others. *Merrill Palmer Quarterly, 40*, 120–138.

A good summary of the development of complex emotions that involve the self:

Michael Lewis (1995). Self-conscious emotions. *American Scientist, 83* (Jan–Feb), 68–78.

CHAPTER 7

Individual Differences in the Development of Emotionality

Figure 7.0 A mother picks up her child after an absence. Notice the child clasping the mother and pushing away the baby-sitter.

Contents

A child forsaken, waking suddenly,
Whose gaze afeared on all things round doth rove
And seeth only that it cannot see
The meeting eyes of love.

George Eliot

Introduction

As we saw in chapter 6, infants' emotions are their earliest means of communicating with caregivers. Such communications are functional within the parent–child relationship. They signal the need for food, warmth, closeness, love. Although emotions have universal aspects, based in our need to communicate with others and receive care and protection in infancy, different emotions are experienced and displayed differently by different individuals. Some children are cheerful and contented much of the time, and they continue in the same kind of way as adults. Others are easily frustrated and grumpy. Yet others are often sad, or fearful. Such individual differences in emotions are central to personality. How do they come about?

In this chapter we concentrate on two main themes. The first, which we discuss in the first half of the chapter, is that only through understanding the child in the context of his or her relationships can we really understand individual differences in emotionality. Patterns of emotionality are, in part, a distillation of the history of the child's close relationships with parents, peers, teachers, siblings, and others. As well as there being many different relationships that are important to the child's emerging emotionality, there are also many different processes within relationships that are important to how children experience and express emotions. The second theme, discussed in the second part of the chapter, is that infants bring their own emotional constitution to interactions with their caregivers, and others. Even within the first few months of life infants vary greatly in their emotionality. Some are easily comforted by being picked up and hugged. Others are difficult to console. Such innate differences are described as "temperament."

Emotion regulation

Perhaps one of the most pervasive ideas about individual differences in emotionality is that children experience emotions, and individual differences emerge in how they regulate these emotions. Patterns of emotional expression are, for instance, strongly affected by the child's age, and developmental stage. Crying lasts for longer and is more intense in infants than in toddlers. Temper tantrums are most common in the second year and decline in intensity subsequently (Goodenough, 1931). So with both crying and tantrums, we can imagine individual differences developing in how successfully children come to regulate these expressions.

Children's ability to use language is an important factor affecting how they regulate their emotions. When children learn to speak they can talk about what distresses or angers them, rather than communicating merely through facial or gestural expressions (Kopp, 1992). Being able to talk about emotional issues may have an important impact on children's relationships with parents, as they start to be able to "argue rather than resort to physical violence, to wait rather than wail, to contain their impatience rather than explode in tantrums" (Dunn & Brown, 1991, p. 89). Mobility also has an important effect: when infants begin to move about and can start to satisfy some of their own desires, their need for a very intense signaling system lessens (Campos, Kermoian, & Zumbahlen, 1992). Developmental changes in neurophysiology also contribute to the changes in emotional lability and control over arousal (see Thompson, 1994, for review).

One view is that regulation starts with the modulation of expressions, initially fostered by the caregiver, and then becoming internalized by the child. Kopp (1989), for instance, has argued that the regulatory function begins with the parent soothing the child. Crying has a very insistent effect on parents, and they try to lessen it, modulating the emotion by picking the infant up, soothing, rocking, and so forth. The metaphor here is of containment, the building of trust, and intimacy; based on this the infant becomes able to soothe himself or herself.

Cicchetti, Ganiban, and Barnett (1991) elaborate different stages or tasks involved in emotion regulation. Failure at one stage has implications for the successful regulation at other stages. In the first months the task is to achieve stability in functioning. When the infant becomes too distressed, he or she needs to regain a state of being able to function. This is achieved through being able to signal distress and the parent responding to help calm the infant. In the next few months, emotions are expressed so that social interaction between parent and child becomes central. Neurological systems are developing so that the baby can inhibit some expressions, and at the same time be able to sooth the self. At the end of the first year, attachment becomes the central issue. At this point affect, cognition, and behavioral systems become organized to ensure the caregiver is close by and emotionally available. Mental representations are formed of interactions with the caregiver, of when, where, and how she or he is available. So both child and caregiver regulate their emotions to what can be expected from the other. The next phase is the development of the self system, and of self-regulation. At this point the child begins to develop a notion of an autonomous self. Processes of regulation have moved from being largely sensorimotor, to becoming symbolic. Children start to think about events, to find different ways of interpreting them, to calm themselves with a thought.

In these formulations the role of the self in being able to manage distress is emphasized. Children become progressively less reliant on caregivers to regulate emotions. Yet to think of emotion regulation as an entirely internal event by the preschool period or even by the end of childhood would be a mistake. As we will see in subsequent chapters, one of the most important factors in helping both children and adults to maintain emotional equilibrium is the presence of supportive people in their lives. Disorganizing emotions are alleviated by being with loved ones. So we should not think that maintaining emotional equilibrium is a task for the individual alone.

Having considered developmental changes in the intensity with which children experience and show emotions we turn to a harder question. What exactly is emotion regulation? The concept has been used in many different ways. Some researchers have used it to refer to individual differences in intensity, frequency, and duration of emotions. So, for instance when a goal is blocked, one person may become extremely angry, shouting and looking angry for several minutes, while another may feel mildly inconvenienced, look momentarily angry, and then forget about it. Others researchers, such as Cassidy (1994), use the concept of emotion regulation to refer to the balance of emotions displayed by an individual. For instance one person may show a propensity to anger rather than sadness or show few emotions altogether.

Emotion regulation is also used to refer to the processes involved in modifying emotional reactions: the coping processes that lessen or augment the intensity of experience. If you are sitting in a traffic jam on the way to catch an airplane, you might try various means to feel less anxious: turn on the radio, think that you can always get on another plane, take deep breaths and try to relax. Regulatory processes affect every stage of the emotion process: appraisal of the event, evaluation of the context, the suppression of urges, as well as the selection and control of various kinds of expression and action (Frijda, 1986). Thompson (1994) has defined emotion regulation as "the extrinsic and intrinsic processes responsible for monitoring, evaluating, and modifying emotional reactions, especially their intensive and temporal features, to accomplish one's goals" (p. 27). As an example of such a process, Rothbart, Ziaie, and O'Boyle (1992) have shown how infants regulate arousal by shifting attention away from objects or people that are causing a high level of arousal.

Dysregulation of emotion follows from definitions of regulation in which the emphasis is on the individuals' ability to modulate the expression of a more fundamental or basic internal experience. "Dysregulation" is what happens when people cannot modulate or control their emotions. When this term is used synonymously with psychopathology (Garber & Dodge, 1991) the implication is that the cause of psychopathology is a deficit in the individual's ability to modulate internal experience. If children are depressed this means that they cannot regulate the experience of sadness. If they have an anxiety disorder, they are not able to modulate their experience of fear, and it leads to avoidance of certain circumstances.

This concept of emotion regulation is a confusing one. It has been used to refer both to a pattern of emotionality (e.g. showing high levels of intense anger), and to the hypothesized processes that may operate on our expressions of emotion (e.g. trying to distract oneself). The implicit notion, common to both meanings, is that everyone has certain emotions, and that there are optimal levels at which these emotions should be experienced and expressed. Quite different notions might give better descriptions. For instance, if we treat emotions as communications between parent and child we might want to talk about the effectiveness of a communication, but would we want to talk about its regulation? Or if we consider emotions to be made up of components interacting with each other in a dynamic self-organizing system as we discussed in chapter 6 (Camras, 1992), then whether an emotion is experienced or how intensely it is felt will derive from a pattern that has developed in response to constraints in the child and the environment. For instance, a parent does not like it when his or her child cries. The parent encourages the child to speak instead of yell, and not to care about little things that do not go the child's way. Over time the child cries less, partly because she or he appraises events differently, and partly because crying does not work to help the child achieve her or his goals. Is this best described as regulation, or as components of emotion becoming organized in relation to the constraints of the self and the environment? We have also seen that emotions are experienced differently by people in different cultures. Is it best to think that some emotions have been so completely "regulated" as to be unknown in some cultures, or might it be better to suppose that to function within a particular society, we need to become skilled at making certain signals to communicate?

Attachment

Whether they favor the concept of emotion regulation or not, most researchers in this area agree that environmental and constitutional effects are both important in explaining individual differences in emotionality. We will discuss these in terms of emotional biases: some individuals for reasons of upbringing, or genetics, or both, come to have a bias towards experiencing and expressing certain emotions more than others. For some researchers, aspects of the parent–child relationship, such as attachment, are primary (Cassidy, 1994), forming the basis of the most important emotional biases. For others, inborn factors within the child play a stronger role (Kagan, 1994). Our discussion starts with attachment.

Protection from threat and the "Strange Situation"

Attachment theory provides us with perhaps the most developed and influential view about how the relationship between parent and infant affects biases and patterns of emotionality. The attachment system operates within the parent–child relationship so that parent and infant stay close to one another. Emotions function as signals: the infant cries, signaling fear and a need for protection; this brings the parent closer. Bowlby (1971) saw attachment as an evolutionarily derived aspect of the parent – child relationship that is activated when the infant experiences a threat. It keeps the mother close to the child in the first few years of life. It is as important psychologically as the mother's milk is physically. Through interaction with the caregiver at moments of fear, the infant builds up a model of whether or not the caregiver can be trusted. If the baby has an expectation that the caregiver will be there to give protection, the baby will feel secure to explore the world, and learn new skills.

A decisive step in research was taken when Ainsworth brought attachment within the two most distinctive and favored paradigms of research psychology: she made attachment simultaneously a subject for experiments and for the identification of individual differences. She developed a test of infants' responses to a situation that was strange to them – the "Strange Situation" test – based on observations of infants' emotional reactions to brief separations from their caregivers, and of their behavior when the caregiver returns.

Using this test, Ainsworth et al. (1978) recognized three distinct styles of attachment. The first is "securely attached." Infants with this style are distressed at separation but when their caregivers return they seek them, and can be comforted. The second style is "ambivalently attached." When caregivers of these infants return after separations the children want to be near them, but at the same time will not be comforted, and show a great deal of

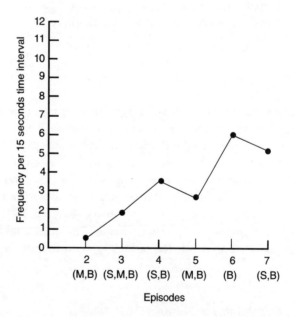

Figure 7.1 The frequency of crying per 15 seconds of observation, in different episodes of the "Strange Situation" test. Along the x-axis are the episodes as follows: (Key: M = Mother present, B = Baby present, S = Stranger present) 2. Mother sits quietly with Baby; 3. Stranger enters and sits quietly, at the end of this episode Mother leaves unobtrusively; 4. Stranger tries to interact with Baby; 5. Mother returns and Stranger leaves unobtrusively, then at the end of the episode Mother leaves saying "bye-bye"; 6. Baby alone; 7. Stranger returns to interact with baby (Ainsworth and Bell, 1970).

angry and resistant behavior. The third style is "avoidantly attached." Infants with this style make no effort to interact when their caregivers return.

Each attachment style has a specific pattern of emotionality, a bias, associated with it. Secure infants show both positive and negative emotions, as well as neutrality. Ambivalent infants show more negative emotions, and avoidant infants show fewer emotions of all kinds (Goldberg, MacKay, & Rochester, 1994).

Some researchers (Cassidy, 1994) have argued that the child's style of attachment itself gives a clue to the history of how the parent has responded to expressions of emotion, and to how the child has come to cope with the caregiver's style of responding. Secure babies demonstrate a range of negative and positive emotions, it is argued, because their parents have been responsive to all their emotional expressions. And indeed, Goldberg, Mackay, and Rochester (1994) found that, when mothers returned to their babies in the Strange Situation, the mothers of secure infants responded to a wider range of emotions than mothers of ambivalent or avoidant babies. Responsiveness was defined as the mother saying or doing something in response to the baby's emotion and included behaviors such as distracting, prohibiting, and encouraging the baby. By contrast, it is thought that ambivalently attached infants have been responded to only inconsistently, so that they have developed a strategy of noisy expression of negative emotions in an effort to get parents to respond to them; Goldberg, Mackay, and Rochester found that mothers of ambivalent babies were most responsive to negative affect, and were least responsive to positive affect. Avoidant babies are thought to have experienced repeated rejections; Goldberg, Mackay, and Rochester found that mothers of these babies were the least responsive to their babies' negative emotions. So it is thought that although avoidant babies feel negative emotions these babies have adopted a strategy of infrequently showing them. Evidence comes from a study by Spangler and Grossmann (1993) who measured heart rate and levels of an adrenal cortical hormone (cortisol, which is released in stress) during and after a Strange Situation test. Although avoidant babies showed fewer facial and vocal displays of emotion than secure babies, they had similar levels of heart rate during the test, and higher cortisol levels after it. This implies that, despite their lack of expression, for them the Strange Situation was as stressful at the time and, according to the cortisol measures, more stressful afterwards than for the securely attached babies. These effects are not conscious – remember we discussed in chapter 6 how conscious masking of emotions does not occur until much later in childhood. So masking of emotion by the avoidant babies may help maintain the attachment relationship: to show more negative emotions would threaten it.

Studies carried out in English-speaking countries with middle-class subjects generally find that about 65 percent of infants show secure attachment in the Strange Situation test, as compared with 15 percent who are ambivalent, and 20 percent who are avoidant. In other countries these proportions are quite different. In Israel, Sagi et al. (1985) found that a very high proportion of babies showed the ambivalent style in the Strange Situation: they showed marked distress on separation, and anger and sadness when the mother returned. For many Israeli babies, the Strange Situation procedure had to be shortened because the babies became inconsolably distressed. In Germany the Grossmanns and their colleagues (1985) found that nearly half of the babies were avoidant: they showed little emotional reaction to either the mother leaving or the mother returning. In Germany as compared with the USA, parents were less encouraging of close bodily contact and more encouraging of independence as soon as the child became mobile. In Japan, Miyake, Chen, and Campos (1985) found no avoidant babies. Such differences among children in different societies are thought to result from children being more or less used to separation from parents, so the separation and reunion procedure varies from being terrifying to being commonplace. Also possible is that some cultures may value early independence, whereas others discourage this. Another possibility is that in some cultures the expression of fear and sadness is encouraged, but in other societies it is discouraged, leading to different emotions being expressed during the Strange Situation procedure.

Internal working models of attachment

Bowlby hypothesized that through experiences during infancy and early childhood, the baby builds up an internal working model of relationships. This is a mental model about what to expect in an intimate relationship. Can the other person be trusted at times of stress? Can one expect to be comforted? The idea is that these models are set up before the child learns language, but if it could be spelled out in words, the model of a secure child would be something like "When I am in danger, I can trust my parent to protect me." For an avoidant child it would be something like: "When I am in danger, be wary, rely only on myself." So, it is thought, such internal models form the basis of a persisting emotional bias. The reason Bowlby proposed them is that such biases persist through time. They start in early relationships with caregivers, they are somewhat resistant to change, and they affect all later intimate relationships (Bowlby, 1988). So, for instance, children who were classified as securely attached at age one were, later in their preschool years, found to be more sociable and communicative with adults (Lutkenhaus, Grossmann, & Grossmann, 1985; Main, Kaplan, & Cassidy, 1985), to have better problem-solving skills, and to be more compliant (Londerville & Main, 1981; Matas, Arend, & Sroufe, 1978), as well as to have better relationships with other children (Sroufe et al., 1984).

If internal working models are important, and if they do influence later relationships, we would expect the experience that adults had during their own childhood to influence their parenting when they had babies of their own. In the earliest work in this area, George, Kaplan, and Main (1985) developed the Adult Attachment Interview to examine how people think about their early attachment relationships: people are asked about their relationship with their parents when they were children and in the present. The interview covers what they remembered doing when they were upset in childhood, whether they were ever rejected, and so forth. On the basis of this interview, adults are classified into secure/autonomous, preoccupied, or dismissing, and these categories are thought respectively to derive from secure, ambivalent, and avoidant attachment in infancy. Autonomous adults are those who talk about their childhood experiences with objectivity and balance. They give a coherent account of difficulties in their childhood, experiences that may have been good or bad. Adults are rated as preoccupied when they give incoherent accounts of their experiences and still seem overwhelmed by their memories of their often traumatic childhood. Dismissing adults give a very distanced account of their childhood, characterized by inability to recall events, idealization, or over-rationalization, with little show of emotion. One question is: "How do adults with these different styles affect the attachment styles of their own babies?"

To answer this question Fonagy, Steele, and Steele (1991) assessed women on the Adult Attachment Interview during their pregnancy, then measured the attachment style of their babies at age one in the Strange Situation test: 75 percent of the secure/autonomous women had securely attached one-year-olds, and 73 percent of preoccupied or dismissing women had insecurely attached one-year-olds (ambivalent or avoidant). This evidence tells us that adults do have relational styles that are measurable, and that something of these styles is passed on from generation to generation. Similar findings have been made by others (Van Ijzendoorn, 1992). We should not conclude from these data that this concordance is due only to the way that the parent relates to the child. As we will discuss later, parents and children show similar patterns of emotionality, in part because of genetic transmission. A parent who finds social interaction unrewarding for reasons of temperament may have a child who shares this lack of sociability, leading both to be classified as dismissive (in adulthood) or avoidant (in infancy).

Until recently, there was no direct evidence linking people's status on the Adult Attachment Interview to their attachment style in infancy. The adult classification, though aimed at childhood, could merely have been a measure of how each person thought about relationships, and the intergenerational findings of Fonagy and others may have reflected how this style generalized to children. Waters and colleagues (1995) carried out a follow-up of people whose attachment status was assessed at age one. At 20 years old these people were interviewed using the Adult Attachment Interview. They found there was substantial continuity from attachment status at one year to classification on the Adult Attachment Interview at age 20, see table 7.1. Notice the continuity, as seen in the cells of the table that run from top left to bottom right, in how the child responded on reunion after separation from the adult caregiver at age one, as compared with their attitude towards relationships as seen in the Adult Attachment Interview. Two-thirds of the securely attached and avoidant children maintained their style into early adulthood, but less than one half of ambivalently attached children maintained their predicted style.

Table 7.1 Numbers of people classified as secure, ambivalent, or avoidant in the Strange Situation test at age 12 months, who were later classified as secure/autonomous, preoccupied, or dismissing, on the Adult Attachment Interview at age 20

Status on Adult Attachment Interview at age 20	Status on the Strange Situation test as infants		
	Secure	*Ambivalent*	*Avoidant*
Secure/autonomous	20	3	2
Preoccupied	3	4	2
Dismissing	6	2	8

Source: Waters et al. (1995)

Although the concept of working models has been essential in explaining continuities, it should not be thought that these models rigidly program behavior; changes in children's environments have been associated with changes in attachment behavior (Vaughn et al., 1979). And even people who have experienced early attachment failures can recover from them, to build satisfactory attachment relationships later in their lives, as we shall see in the next chapter.

Factors affecting style of attachment

In our treatment of attachment so far, we have preserved Bowlby's original conception with its rootedness in evolutionary theory. According to this idea the attachment system is a specific one, based on babies' expressions of fear and distress which keep the mother close to the baby, and summon her to the baby's aid. Maternal responding to distress has been found to affect attachment style. So, Ainsworth et al. (1978) conducted an extensive study in which they visited the homes of mothers and their babies every three weeks during the first year. Among other observations, they noted how rapidly mothers responded to their babies crying. Mothers who responded to their babies rapidly and consistently were more likely to have babies who were classified as secure in the Strange Situation at one year.

But the evidence also shows that mothers' responsiveness to distress is not alone in affecting attachment style. For instance, Crockenberg (1981) assessed mothers' responsiveness to distress when their babies were three months old, and then tested their attachment style at one year. She found that the mothers' responsiveness was only associated with their babies' later attachment style under some conditions, for instance when the mothers had little support from spouses and others – there was no association when mothers were well supported. In another study of a similar kind, Bates, Maslin, and Frankel (1985) were able to demonstrate only a weak relationship between mothers' responsiveness to distress when their babies were six months old, and the babies' attachment style at one year. So it seems that a mother's responsiveness to distress does contribute to the baby's experience of trust, and hence to security of attachment as judged in the Strange Situation test, but that the influence is not as strong as had been thought (Goldsmith & Alansky, 1987). Other influences on the child's attachment status are also important.

General maternal sensitivity

Ainsworth et al. (1978) hypothesized that infants developed a sense of trust and security as a result of parents being sensitively responsive to both distress and positive emotion signals. This concept of maternal sensitivity already takes us a long way away from Bowlby's argument about the evolutionary value of maternal responsiveness to distress. Ainsworth and colleagues observed mothers while interacting with their babies. Mothers were rated on behaviors such as: appropriately interpreting the infants' signals, behaving in an accepting way towards the infant, respecting the baby's autonomy, being accessible to the baby, being tender. These ratings of the interaction were all found to be associated with security. Others have confirmed these findings, but the relationship between maternal sensitivity ratings and attachment has not been found to be as strong in other studies (Goldsmith & Alansky, 1987). Grossmann et al. (1985), for instance, found that mothers who were more sensitive during their babies' first year had infants who were more securely attached at the end of the year, although this relationship was not found at all measurement points during the year.

Synchronization

A further elaboration of the concept of maternal sensitivity is "synchronization." As we saw above, maternal sensitivity has been measured by observers making a global rating of how in tune the mother seemed to be with the child. Others have tried to examine this concept of maternal sensitivity with much finer-grained research tools: looking at moment-by-moment interactions. Remember in chapter 6 we described in detail an interaction between a mother and her blind baby, Marci. This mother and baby were synchronized with each other, each responding to the other, the mother keeping in time with the baby in a kind of dance. Isabella, Belsky, and Von Eye (1989) defined a measure of this kind of behavior, and separated mothers into two categories. The mothers who were synchronized kept in tune and in time with their babies: when the babies vocalized they did too, when the babies wanted to gaze at the mother's face the mother gazed back, when the baby wanted to explore, the mother assisted this, and so on. The interactions of the pair were reciprocal and mutually rewarding. By contrast, nonsynchronized mothers would vocalize or try to stimulate when their babies were asleep or being quiet, remain quiet and unresponsive when the babies vocalized, and so forth. Isabella, Belsky, and Von Eye found that mothers who kept more closely in time with their one-month-old and three-month-olds during interactions with them had babies who were more likely to be securely attached at one year.

This concept of synchronization has strayed even further away from Bowlby's evolutionary theory in which crying functions to elicit parental caregiving and protection. It involves the way parents respond to positive emotions as well as negative ones, as well as whether emotional states of mothers and babies are in tune with one another. Researchers in the "attachment" field have used attachment concepts more broadly than was intended by Bowlby (Bretherton, 1985; Hinde, 1976). In our view this broadening of the term has been theoretically confusing. In the next section we will elucidate some of the mechanisms within the parent–child relationship that are important in children's developing emotionality, that involve more than the activation of the attachment system. Indeed we return to some of the processes that we have already discussed, such as synchronization, to see how other people, who work outside of the attachment theory framework, interpret the significance of such processes for the development of individual differences in children's emotionality.

Socialization of emotions within relationships

As we saw in chapter 2, across societies different emotions are emphasized and there are differences in what expressions mean. The same is true of families: one family may be full of laughter, another earnest, another avoiding all displays of anger, and so forth. In this section we will examine how families, peers, and adults outside the family socialize the display of emotions in children. What kinds of processes are involved in children experiencing and expressing certain emotions more than others?

Synchronization revisited

Let's think again about synchronization: when mothers and babies are attuned to one another and engaged in a mutually satisfying dance. Several people have argued that attunement is important for babies to build up a representation of whether their goals will be met in relationship, which will in turn affect the emotions that are expressed (Stern, 1994; Tronick, 1989). As we saw in chapter 6, these researchers suggest that in the expression of emotions, infants are expressing goals. Even small babies have goals: to share a moment of pleasure, to explore their environment, to vocalize and elicit a response. When goals are expressed they can either be fulfilled, or not fulfilled. If a mother is too preoccupied with matters other than her baby then she may not pay attention to her baby's bid to engage her. If this experience is repeated over and over again, and is the main experience that some babies have in their relationships, then these babies may come to feel that their goals cannot be met in their relationships. In interactions babies build up representations of their own goals. If their goals are not met, they will experience anger or sadness more frequently. As they get older, they will build up expectations about what to expect from relationships. We return to this issue shortly.

Warmth

Warmth and affection are probably especially important in human development. MacDonald (1992) points out that warmth is associated with happiness, whereas fear and distress, which trigger the attachment system in Bowlby's formulation, derive from a quite different emotional system. We have discussed different emotional systems in chapters 4 and 5, but one indication specific to this discussion is that babies seeing their mothers approaching with open arms showed joy and an activation of the left side of the cortex, whereas distress on separation in the Strange Situation activated the right side of the cortex (Fox & Davidson, 1987). MacDonald also points out that although attachment occurs among all primates only some species form affectional bonds. So there is no reason to suppose these two systems are the same.

In humans too, the indications are that caregivers in some societies can be strong in attachment behavior but show relatively little warmth to their infants. In fact, the society in Uganda which Ainsworth (1967) first studied to outline the range of attachment behavior patterns was like this. For instance the Ugandan mothers did not try to elicit hugging or kissing from their babies. It is not that Ugandan mothers were without warmth, for instance occasional nuzzling was seen. Rather, their warmth was not the same as responsiveness to distress; Ainsworth concluded that American mothers are warmer, but their responsiveness to their children's distress was less than the Ugandan mothers. So, according to MacDonald's hypothesis, warmth is a separate system from attachment. The two systems typically operate together, with some societies giving more priority to one, some to the other. The system of warmth and affection, rather than being based on preventing separation of infant from mother, is built on positive reward. This evolved to create and maintain bonds of affection, which are characteristic of humans. This system may be particularly relevant when societies are organized around predominantly monogamous sexual relationships, in which the males make an economic contribution to a specific family (Lovejoy, 1981), as we have discussed in chapter 3.

In their original study to determine the maternal antecedents of attachment status, Ainsworth et al. (1978) also measured mothers' affection in their interactions with their babies in the first year – this too predicted whether babies would have a secure or insecure style of attachment at age one. So it seems possible that even if the Strange Situation measures babies' sense of trust, in Western society at least, this trust does not come purely by being attended to when fearful, and not just because mothers have responded to babies' signals. Parenting that is warm and affectionate makes a difference too. There are two reasons why this distinction between the basic theoretical idea of attachment theorists (mothers' responsiveness to babies' signals) and the alternative idea of warmth and affection may matter. One is that parental warmth and affection have been found in a range of studies to affect very many aspects of a child's development — not just style of attachment. Warmth and affection affect childhood friendships, and many other aspects of later emotional well-being (Maccoby & Martin, 1983). The second issue has more to do with the research community. Attachment has become a "catch all" term for the parent–child relationship, as well as socioemotional development. When differences across babies are found in attachment status, an implicit assumption is that these differences arise out of differences in maternal responsiveness or sensitivity to the infants. Clearly, other types of processes are also important for understanding emotionality. In the following sections we elucidate these processes.

Learning to speak about emotions

Among the processes that are important in the patterns of emotional expression that we develop consider for instance the role of language. Through the learning of emotion language, parents and other caregivers structure a world that will contribute to the emotional experience of children. Parents do this in several ways. One way is to talk to children about the kinds of events that evoke emotions in their society. For instance, on one occasion, a father says to his daughter who is recoiling at the sight of a big dog: "You don't need to be scared of him." On another occasion she wanders into the cycle path, and a bicyclist narrowly misses her. Her father rushes to her and says, "That's dangerous! You really frightened me." Such emotional communications teach children about what events appropriately elicit emotions in their community, inducting the child into the cultural rules of emotional expression. Emotion talk also structures the child's own internal experience, and lets the child know about the internal experience of others.

Dunn and her colleagues (Dunn, Brown, and Beardsall, 1991) have demonstrated the importance of talk about emotions in relation to later emotional understanding. They recorded talk of feeling states between mothers and children, and with siblings, when the children were three years old. The average number of conversations (defined as two or more speaker turns between the child and another family member) was 8.4 per hour; some families had as few as 2, others as many as 25 such conversations per hour. They found that such talk about feelings has long-term consequences for children's understanding of emotional communications. The more mothers talked to their children about feeling states at three years of age, the more skilled the children were in making judgments about the emotions displayed by unfamiliar adults when they were six years old. Discussion of negative feelings was most strongly related to an increased ability to understand and identify emotions in a standardized task. We see this kind of talk as helping children to develop explicit models of their own and others' goals, plans, and emotions.

Consider for instance when a mother talks about why she is angry. She makes clear her motivations and intentions; the child can construct a model of what makes the mother angry and why. When a mother does not explain herself, the child's information is less complete, more likely to be incorrect. Zahn-Waxler, Radke-Yarrow, and King (1979) found that parental explanations and reasoning (delivered at intense emotional levels) were associated with increased displays of empathy in children. When children were given better information about internal states of others through language, they were better able to respond with understanding and concern to others.

We can see effects of certain kinds of extreme family experience on emotion talk from work by Cicchetti and Beeghly (1987). They compared talk about mental and other internal states of a group of maltreated children with that of a group of children of similar socioeconomic background who had not been maltreated. Toddlers who had been maltreated used fewer words for bodily states such as hunger and thirst; and about negative emotions, such as hatred, anger, disgust. Presumably, maltreated children had either not much opportunity to discuss internal states or were frightened to do so because of negative consequences.

Effects of modeling

Any time a parent enacts some piece of behavior, drying the dishes or speaking angrily to the cat, this person acts as a model for children in the family. These children are then more likely to perform the same kinds of behavior, and this process is thought to be very important in passing on messages about what emotions to display, and how. Families differ on the type and frequency of emotions that are displayed to their children. Malatesta and Haviland (1982) found that most mothers display negative emotions to their infants only rather rarely. In six-minute periods of mother–baby interaction, mothers showed an average of 21 enjoyment expressions to babies, 0.5 sadness expressions, and 0.2 anger expressions. So mothers showed their children 100 times more enjoyment than anger and 40 times more enjoyment than sadness. As their children got older parents displayed more negative emotions to their babies, but these expressions still remained very infrequent. As we will see in chapter 8, some parents, when experiencing major stress, discord in their marriage, or psychiatric problems such as depression, show many more negative emotions to their children.

Over time infants become more similar to their mothers in terms of their expressions of emotion (Malatesta & Haviland, 1982). If their own mothers' expressions include more anger than those of other mothers, then by six months the infants too show more anger than do other infants. If their mothers display more happiness, then by six months the infants show more happiness. The way that children can produce the same emotions as people they observe has also been called emotion contagion (Hatfield, Cacioppo, & Rapson, 1994). As we saw in chapter 6, this occurs early in development.

Responding to some emotions but not others

As babies develop language, they have many different ways of communicating about internal states. As they see their infants having more flexible ways of expressing their needs, parents change the ways in which they respond to their children's emotions. One way of doing this is to pay attention to acceptable modes of expression, and to ignore other modes of expression. Brooks-Gunn and Lewis (1982) found that mothers responded more to crying in their babies' first six months than in their second year. But they increased their responding to their child's vocalizations and efforts to speak; see table 7.2. Such behavior says to the children: "I'll pay attention to you when you talk to me, but not just when you cry." They also found that mothers responded less to the crying of boys than to the crying of girls. We see that even by two years old mothers are inducting their children into a culture in which it is less acceptable to cry to achieve goals, and less acceptable for boys to show sadness than girls.

From another study carried out by Dunn, Bretherton, and Munn (1987), we also have evidence that parents change the way in which they respond to emotions as children get older. They found that mothers' references to feeling states following a child's distress decreased as the child grew from 18 to 24 months. Presumably the mothers were trying to de-emphasize negative emotions by not discussing them.

We might think from our discussion about attachment and parental responsiveness that the best thing for parents to do as soon as a child is distressed is to respond immediately and sympathetically. Indeed, we talked about one study carried out in an attachment theory framework in which it was found that mothers of secure infants responded to a wider range of infant's emotions than mothers of insecure babies (Goldberg, Mackay, and Rochester, 1994). But as we see from the way that parents selectively attend to emotions, it is clear that parents' goals are more complex than simply protecting or comforting children, particularly as children get older. Imagine for instance a three year old who whines whenever another child reaches over to play with his toy. The likelihood is that a parent watching this may comfort, but will also explain about the need to share. If the whining and refusal to share escalate, the parent may resort to power-assertive tactics such as "You won't be able to play with those toys if you are going to whine like that." As infants become

Table 7.2 Percentages of mothers' responses to different kinds of expression by their babies at different ages

| | Maternal responses to infant behaviour | |
Child's age	*To infant vocalizations*	*To infant crying*
2 to 7 months	13	21
8 to 16 months	35	8
17 to 27 months	50	6

Source: Brooks-Gunn and Lewis (1982)

toddlers, parents make complex evaluations about how distressed their child is, what the context of their expression is, how important the situation is in teaching a long-term lesson, and so forth (Dix, 1991).

Not surprisingly given the complexity of these interactions, we know relatively little about the kinds of parental responses that are associated with different emotional outcomes in children beyond infancy. Two kinds of outcomes are typically investigated: the frequency of expression of certain negative emotions (e.g., anger) and whether children are liked by their peers (social competence). Roberts and Strayer (1987) examined parental responsiveness to emotion in three- to five-year-old children. They found that most parents responded to children with firmness, but also helped the children with what had caused the distress, thereby communicating that they understood the child's goal. A medium level of parental responsiveness was associated with higher levels of social competence in children; however, a high level of responsiveness was not. Some parents were too responsive to negative emotions; these parents had children who were less competent in their interactions with others. Other work also points to the delicate balancing act that parents need to achieve when responding to their children's emotions. Eisenberg and Fabes (1994) found that parents who were higher on trying to control or minimize their children's display of negative emotion, by, for instance, telling a child to go to another room when he or she started to cry, had children who showed less anger in their peer group. However, these investigators also found that being more sympathetic and comforting when children showed negative emotions was associated with children showing less anger in their peer group.

It may be that when children get older, responding sympathetically to their negative emotion displays without also giving some coaching on a way of communicating anger or distress that is developmentally, socially, and culturally acceptable, may reinforce the negative emotion expression. Snyder and Patterson (1986) have found that certain kinds of parental responses to anger can reinforce it, thereby making it more likely that children will respond in an angry or aggressive way on another occasion. Patterson (1982) observed that when children are aggressive, other people in the family tend to withdraw or lessen their demands, thus giving the child what he or she wants, and providing a reward for a display of aggression. This is associated with increases in aggression.

What influences on the parents might contribute to how they respond to their children? One factor may be how the parents have dealt with emotional issues in their own lives. Earlier in this chapter we talked about how parents and children show concordance in their attachment styles. Perhaps one of the mechanisms contributing to this concordance is that parents train emotional styles that are acceptable to them. One way to investigate this is to ask parents about their own views about the expression of anger and sadness. Hooven, Gottman, and Katz (1995) have called this "meta-emotion" – what people think about feelings. They interviewed parents about meta-emotion when their children were aged five. They found that at the age of eight the children of parents who were both aware of their own sadness and anger, and coached their children in the meaning of such emotions and how to deal with them, showed less evidence of stress, showed less negative emotion in play with their friends, better achievement at school, and fewer behavior problems.

It is unlikely that there is any formula for how best to respond to children's emotions. There is also no formula for the best mode of emotion expression that a child can show. In our view all emotions, both negative and positive, serve communicative purposes in interactions. We can only tell if some pattern of emotional expression is working against the person, by analyzing the expression within the context. Maybe what parents are doing is helping children understand their emotional expression in context: whether the expression was appropriate given the eliciting circumstance and culture, how it affected those to whom it was directed. If this view is correct then parental behaviors that encourage children to consider their emotional expressions in the context of their interactions will be most effective. Beyond infancy, this will not always mean being sympathetic and responsive. Sometimes it will mean ignoring a child. Sometimes it will mean displaying intense emotional reactions and power assertion to impress upon a child that his or her mode of expression is unacceptable to others. It is also important to remember that when we are talking about parental responses to children's emotions we are talking about a discrete aspect of the parent–child relationship. If power-assertive behaviors occur in an overall context of warmth and affection, they have a very different meaning to a child than when they occur in a context of hostility and neglect. Thus the overall emotional tone of the parent–child relationship may influence how parental responses to emotion are understood by children.

We have considered the impact of parental responsiveness to children's emotions at length. What about how other significant people in children's lives react to their emotions? Less is known about this area of emotion socialization. Strayer (1980) observed four- and five-year-olds playing with one another and documented how children's emotional expressions were responded to by their peers. During interactions children most frequently showed happiness (34 percent), then sadness (30 percent), then anger (22 percent), and least commonly hurt (13 percent). For the most part their companions just let them pass. Hurt was most often ignored, followed by anger, then sadness, then happiness; so the emotions that were most often displayed were also those that were most often responded to by other children. Children gave more empathic responses to happy expressions than to all other emotions combined, and fewer in response to anger than to all other emotions combined. When emotions were responded to, the responses were different for different emotions: happy displays usually met with happiness, sad displays usually met with an attempt to share an activity or a toy, angry expression most often met with verbal or physical acknowledgement like moving out of the way, and hurt expressions met with reassurance or a question such as "Are you OK?" So different emotions are responded to very differently by children.

It is important to note that these reactions alter with the age of the child. For instance, Denham (1986) found when she observed two- to three-year-old children that they were more responsive to other children's anger than they were to their sadness, a quite different result from that found by Strayer. It may be that as children get older they get better at responding to lower intensity emotions (like sadness) in other people. In any case, such differential responding probably affects children's expressions of emotion with their peers. Children learn what results when they are angry, when they are sad, and so forth within the context of their age group; they alter their own expressions accordingly.

How cultures affect the development of emotionality

Let us situate such influences in a broader cultural framework. Families exist within societies and are influenced by patterns of emotion within that society. As we shall see in chapter 10, among the Yanomamö anger and aggression are valued. Children and adults who are not fierce find it hard to exist in this society and the upbringing is designed to foster aggression (Eibl-Eibesfeldt, 1979). Patterson (1985) puts the same argument about children's aggression in coercive families. When others are hostile, to protect oneself one also must use escalating angry aggression. In a quite different kind of society, Briggs (1970) described her observations of an indulgent style of early upbringing in an Inuit family: by the age of six Inuit children show little or no anger. In yet other cultures upbringing is designed to make children tough, and show low levels of fear or sadness. Thus Harkness and Super (1985) described the Kipsigis, in a small community in Kenya. When a child aged two cries, the mother waits for the child to come to her. She comforts the child but also quickly offers distraction. With the first sign of calming, the child is returned to the care of siblings. These children are socialized to disregard any internal experience of sadness and pain. At adolescence girls will undergo clitoridectomy and boys circumcision as rites of passage into adult life. During these painful procedures they must not cry, or else they bring disgrace onto themselves and their family with very unfortunate consequences.

These cultural beliefs about emotions and their display have profound influences on emotionality in children. More extreme measures of emotionality are also affected. Different cultures have very different rates of certain kinds of emotional disorders in childhood. In Thailand (Weisz et al., 1987), children who are referred to clinics are low on disorders based on anger – involving aggression, hostility, stealing, and lying – when compared with children in the USA. Thai children live in a Buddhist culture in which a high value is placed on peacefulness and deference in order to avoid disturbing others. But the Thai children show higher rates of problems with fearfulness, anxiety, and psychosomatic symptoms than their US counterparts.

Our conclusion is that children develop schemas, or mental models, about emotions within relationships. These schemas are similar to Tomkins's (1979) "scripts," discussed in chapter 4. They are representations of sequences of action, of the meanings of emotion, and of how emotions function. As each of us interacts with others, in our family and outside it, we come to know how and where some emotions are appropriate, while others are not. We know that some will serve our goals, while others will not. We know that we can express anger in one setting without bad consequences, while in another setting, or with certain people, the expression would be problematic. So our emotion schemas are distillations of what is to be expected, and they are based on our previous experience of emotions in relationships (Baldwin, 1992). These schemas include representation of the self, of the other, and of the self and other in interaction (Mitchell, 1988).

Stern (1994) has described how we develop a variety of schemas of "being with another person" based on our early experiences. At the core of such schemas is a representation of our goals in interaction. The baby wants something to happen, and looks to the parent to join in with him or her to fulfill this goal. The goal, and the emotions associated with it, unfold over time, leading us to different representations of what it is like to "be" with another person. Stern describes how a baby might interact with a mother who is depressed. First the baby invites the mother to play, by being animated, trying to elicit a response. But the depressed mother fails to attune to her. In another attempt to be with the mother, the baby takes on and shares the mother's depressed mood. The baby moves from being animated to being sad as she joins in the mother's sad emotions. Next, the baby may also look to herself, rather than her mother, for engagement and arousal, while still experiencing her distanced mother in the background. Perhaps then, the mother starts to feel stronger; she may force herself to engage with her baby. The baby experiences her as animated, but slightly out of tune with her because the interaction is a forced one. Now another kind of schema may emerge, from this false interaction: a "false self" with a "false mother." Stern postulates that these are all "schemas of being with" that, as the child gets older, are then experienced with other people. From childhood, and from subsequent relationships, we carry forward with us emotional schemas of how to take part in interactions, based on the kinds of relating we have experienced.

This is one view of the way in which information about relationships and emotions are built into our schemas or models. Each different tradition of research has its own way of describing how early experiences of emotion in relationships affect later relationships, and how an emotional response learned in one setting may be carried through to another (Baldwin, 1992). At least six kinds of process have been proposed in the development of individual differences in emotionality: (a) growth of trust and a sense of self from being responded to when distressed; (b) warmth and affection; (c) modeling and similar effects; (d) reinforcement, with more frequent occurrence of expressions that have been rewarded and less frequent occurrence of those that have been ignored; (e) coaching, meta-emotion and learning how to talk about emotions; (f) mutual goal structures with each person playing a part. We are still far from understanding what such models are like, but we do know that something like models or schemas is necessary to explain how we develop patterns of emotional responding with one set of people, which are reenacted at other times, in other places, and with other people.

Temperament

In the sections above we have discussed effects on the socialization of emotions. Now we turn to those aspects of emotionality that have their origins in the constitutional make-up of the child – we have already mentioned some of these effects in our discussion of how styles of attachment are formed.

From the very first hours of life children show marked individual differences in their behavior and emotions. Some babies are placid and easily calmed when upset. Others are more passionate; they become upset easily and intensely. Some babies enjoy social interaction and engage with other people easily. Others become distressed when people try to play with them; they attempt to withdraw. Such differences are called "temperament."

Temperament is defined as those aspects of behavior and emotions that are constitutional, that are stable over time and across situations, that have a neurophysiological underpinning, and that have some degree of heritability (Goldsmith, 1993). There are many different conceptualizations of what temperament is and, within these different conceptualizations, emotions play a more or less prominent role.

Biases of emotion at the core of temperament

Campos et al. (1983) have argued that temperament is based on an innate structure that organizes the expression of emotion, and that most of the dimensions of temperament form part of a system for how emotions are expressed. They give a table, from which our table 7.3 is adapted, to illustrate this by showing how temperamental dimensions, proposed by principal temperament theorists, map onto the discrete emotions that we have discussed in chapters 4 and 6.

In this chapter we treat the concept of temperament as the important component of emotionality that is biologically based, typically inherited, that influences emotionality and personality. Some researchers limit temperamental dimensions to those for which heritability has been established (Buss & Plomin, 1984). Unfortunately, when it comes to measuring temperament such clear-cut distinctions can not easily be maintained. The measurement of

Table 7.3 Mapping of dimensions of temperament onto aspects of emotions, for two well-known schemes of temperament: Buss and Plomin's (1975) with four dimensions, and Rothbart's (1981) with six dimensions

Dimensions of temperament	Aspects of emotion into which each dimension maps
Buss & Plomin (1975)	
Emotionality	Fear, anger, and distress
Activity	General arousal of the motor system
Sociability	Interest and positive emotions expressed towards people
Impulsivity	Time taken to express emotion or activity
Rothbart (1981)	
Activity	General arousal of the motor system
Smiling and laughter	Happiness or pleasure
Fear	Fear
Distress to limitations	Anger
Soothability	Recovery time from negative emotions when soothed
Persistence	Duration of interest

Source: adapted from Campos et al. (1983)

temperament involves parents rating their children on how quickly they are roused to anger, or the amount of fear that they show in a situation. Alternatively, observation of temperament may involve the amount of negative emotional expression that children show during an assessment period. Such measures are assessing what we have referred to in this chapter as children's emotionality and derive both from the environment and the individual's constitution.

Even individual differences in infant emotionality present in the first few months of life are not only constitutional, as a study by Belsky, Fish, and Isabella (1991) shows us. They examined changes in infants' negative and positive emotionality between three and nine months as a function of characteristics of their families. As compared with children who remained low in negative emotionality, children who changed from low to high negative emotionality had fathers who were less affectively oriented towards others, less positive about their marriages before their infants were born and more discrepant with their wives in the amount of involvement they had with the baby. As compared to infants who remained high in negative emotionality, those who changed from high to low negative emotionality had mothers who were high in self-esteem, who experienced less negativity in their marriages, and who showed more harmonious, complementary, and responsive interaction with their infants. Stability and change in infants' emotionality over time are therefore affected by the emotional tone of the family environment.

One of the criteria of temperament is stability over time. Stability over six months and one year is fairly high, particularly when parental reports are used to assess temperament. Rothbart (1986) reported correlations between parents' ratings of smiling/laughter, fear, and distress to limitations, taken at six and nine months of r = 0.48, 0.37, and 0.51 respectively. Worobey and Blajda (1989) reported on correlations between two months and one year of 0.46 for positive reactivity and 0.50 for negative reactivity (irritability). Continuities spanning many years have also been found. Chess and Thomas (1990) assessed a group of people as adults who had had ratings of temperament made each year in the first five years of their lives. They found few significant correlations between their nine individual dimensions of temperament and traits in adulthood. But when they combined ratings into an overall score of easy versus difficult temperament, the correlations were higher. Easy versus difficult temperament in years three, four, and five showed the following correlations with the same measure in adulthood: r = 0.31, r = 0.37, r = 0.15.

Even using measures of emotionality that are only based on how frequently children show certain facial expressions of emotion, continuities across time are evident. Hyson and Izard (1985) videotaped children during brief separations from their mother during Ainsworth's "Strange Situation" procedure at 13 months and 18 months, and their facial expressions were coded using the MAX system. Continuity across the interval between the two tests was extremely high for expressions of interest (r = 0.90), for anger (r = 0.61), and for total negative expressions (r = 0.90), but sadness had low continuity. Comparable results were found using Lewis's procedure of having infants pull a string attached to their arm to turn on music; Sullivan, Lewis, and Alessandri (1992) compared effects of the same conditions at two-month intervals for infants of two to eight months old. High continuity was found in the frequencies of expressions of anger, interest, joy and surprise, but low continuities were found for sadness and fear.

The studies mentioned in the previous paragraph were based on the same elicitors on two occasions. An even more convincing demonstration comes from the work of Malatesta et al. (1989a) in which eliciting circumstances were more varied. Babies' facial expressions were coded while their mothers played with them and again on reunion after a brief period of separation. Between seven and twenty-two months of age infants showed continuity of negative expressions of anger (r = 0.32) and sadness (r = 0.37). Continuity was not found for positive expressions.

Shyness is another dimension of temperament. Very shy children have a high stable heart rate, and greater sympathetic reactivity, suggesting a lower threshold for limbic-hypothalamic arousal to unexpected changes in the environment, and these physiological measures also show continuity over time (Kagan, 1982). Davidson and Fox (1989) were able to predict how much babies would cry when separated from their parent from greater electroencephalogram

(EEG) activation of the right, as compared with the left, side of the cortex during a baseline period. Kagan, Reznick, and Snidman (1988) followed up children from two to seven years of age who were extremely inhibited at age two – these were children who, in response to unfamiliar adults and children, clung to their mothers, stopped speaking and did not interact with the unfamiliar person for a long time. About 7 percent of an unselected sample of two-year-olds were classified in this way. At age seven ratings of behavioral inhibition were again made; behavior was coded as the children were observed entering a situation with 10 other same-aged, same-sex children. Frequency of spontaneous comments, and periods of standing apart were measured. Continuities were only evident in that small group of children who were found to be extremely shy at age two, not in the total sample of children, but at age seven these extremely shy children approached other children less, and were less talkative with the researchers. Continuities in shy behavior have also been found by Rubin (1993) who followed up socially inhibited children from the age of four until midadolescence. Preschool ratings of shyness did not predict social behavior at age 14, but ratings of shyness at 7 predicted loneliness ($r = 0.5$) and lack of integration with the peer group ($r = 0.4$) at age 14.

So using both parental ratings and facial expressions, it has been found that children have some characteristic styles of emotionality. Some biases that can be observed in infancy influence typical emotional patterns during childhood and later in life.

Genetic basis of temperament

Most temperament theorists argue that temperament is partly inherited (Buss & Plomin, 1984) and studies on twins have been carried out to estimate the size of this influence. Identical, or monozygotic (MZ), twins who share all their genes, and non-identical, or dizygotic (DZ), twins who share half their genes, have been compared on parental ratings of temperament, and in some studies on observers' ratings made in a laboratory. Other designs to investigate genetic effects have involved comparing natural and adopted siblings with one another.

There is evidence for genetic effects on the main dimensions of temperament (Campos et al., 1983) although estimates of heritability vary depending on whether the measure is based on observation or parental report, the design of the study, and the dimension of temperament being assessed. Table 7.4 is adapted from a review by Plomin (1988) summarizing some studies on twins. Look at the columns headed "Results." You will see pairs of correlation coefficients, for example 0.37 vs 0.13. The first coefficient in each pair is the concordance (correlation on the particular dimension) for the monozygotic twins, and the second is for the dizygotic twins. A genetic influence is indicated by concordances being higher for the monozygotic than for the dizygotic twins, and the size of the genetic influence is measured by a difference in concordances. So these studies show that emotionality is affected by genetic factors, as in all instances concordances are higher for MZ than DZ twins. Goldsmith (1993) found that, based on parental report, activity level, fear, and distress in response to limitations, all showed strong genetic influences. Other factors, such as soothability, showed only slight genetic influences: see in the bottom line of table 7.4, there was a very small difference in the concordances for soothability.

In an investigation by Emde et al. (1992) emotionality was more broadly defined than just measures of temperament. Two hundred pairs of 14-month-old twins, half monozygotic and half dizygotic, were studied. Some measures of emotionality and temperament of the children were assessed by parental report, some by independent observers, and some by both. Genetic influence was evident for behavioral inhibition (as measured by observation), and for the very similar construct of shyness (as measured by both parental report and observation). Parental reports of temperament and negative emotion also indicated genetic effect. There was, however, no evidence for genetic effects from observational measures of negative and positive emotion, overall mood, or frustration. Some results conflicted for measures purporting to measure the same construct; when negative emotionality was rated by parents, heritability estimates were high, but when rated by observers, heritability estimates were low. In summary, twin studies indicate that genetic influences play a role in children's emotionality, although the extent of this role is not clear. Part of the problem is with measurement; and there is still a long way to go before we know which measures are the most valid measures for the constructs of interest. Studies of adoption, in which emotional characteristics of parents and their

Table 7.4 Summary results of some behavioral genetic studies of emotionality in twins; in each set of results the first figure is the concordance for monozygotic twins, and the second for dizygotic twins

Authors of study	Measure	Results	
		At six months	At two years
	Parental interviews on:		
Matheny et al. (1981)	hurt feelings	—	0.37 vs 0.13
	frequency of temper	0.39 vs 0.26	0.41 vs 0.15
	irritability	0.45 vs 0.29	0.46 vs 0.28
	crying	0.62 vs 0.51	0.59 vs 0.39
Matheny & Dolan (1975)	Ratings of emotionality in a playroom after mother has departed		0.66 vs 0.30
Goldsmith & Campos (1982)	Parental ratings of:		
	fear		0.66 vs 0.46
	distress to limitations		0.77 vs 0.25
	soothability		0.71 vs 0.69

Source: adapted from Plomin (1988)

biological and adopted children have been made, have shown less strong evidence of the heritability of emotional styles (Plomin, 1988).

Temperament in relation to style of attachment

Bowlby and others (Hinde, 1976) stressed the importance of reciprocity in constructing the emotional relationship of parent and child. Just as the baby has to fit in with the parents, the parents must learn to fit in with the baby's temperament. It has been a fact of life for parents that some infants are more difficult than others; some stretch the adaptive abilities of parents to their limits. Some researchers argue that a baby's differences in reaction to separations and reunions in the Strange Situation are less affected by parents' responsiveness or sensitivity, and better explained by temperament – for instance by how easily babies become angry, and by how interested they are in objects as compared with people (Kagan, 1987). For instance, a temperamentally unsociable baby may take little notice of her mother leaving or coming back into the room. This pattern of response would result in her being classified as insecurely attached.

Support for the role of temperament in attachment comes, for instance, from Miyake, Chen, and Campos (1985) who found that babies who were irritable as newborns were more likely to be insecurely attached at 12 months, and from Fox and his colleagues (Aaron, Calkins, & Fox, 1990; Calkins & Fox, 1992) who found that ambivalent attachment status was best predicted by a neurophysiological measure of early infant reactivity to only mildly stressful events. Thompson, Connell, and Bridges (1988) found that difficult temperament was related to the intensity of babies' distress on separation, and to how the babies reacted on reunion. As to babies' interest in objects, Lewis and Feiring (1989) found that babies who at three months were more interested in objects than people, were most avoidant at 12 months. There is also an indication that as children get older their attachment style is more influenced by these innate factors (Vaughn et al., 1992).

It seems intuitively plausible that parents respond differently to babies who have different temperaments. For instance, one might think that parents would react to babies who are irritable and hard to comfort by withdrawing from their babies, to protect themselves from feelings of helplessness and disappointment. Crockenberg (1986) reviewed research findings, and concluded that there is support for this hypothesis, but it is not strong. In some studies mothers were found to withdraw more from temperamentally difficult children (Peters-Martin & Wachs, 1984), but in others mothers were more involved when infants were temperamentally difficult (Bates et al., 1982). Some investigators have tested the more complex hypothesis that negative temperament is only associated with a negative outcome if parents are not flexible enough to adapt to the child's temperament, and become drawn into negative parenting. This notion of a contingent relationship between temperament and characteristics of parents is called the "goodness of fit" model (Thomas & Chess, 1977). Manglesdorf et al. (1990) examined this issue. They found that proneness to distress at nine months did not in itself predict babies' attachment styles four months later, and neither did characteristics of the mothers' personality. But infants who were high on distress more often had insecure attachments to their mother when their mothers were rigid and traditional. No such relationship was found among babies who were not prone to distress. So here we see evidence for a contingent relationship: temperament is only important to the attachment relationship when the mother is somewhat rigid. Although it seems very plausible not all studies have found support for the "goodness of fit" model (Windle & Lerner, 1986).

So attachment status depends on the interplay between parental caregiving behaviors and the baby's temperament. Goldsmith and Alansky (1987) carried out a meta-analysis of studies, examining parental caregiving and temperament in relation to babies' attachment style. Maternal caregiving and temperament were found to have similar degrees of influence on attachment status, and for both the degree of effect was modest.

However, what is a relatively small statistical effect may not be insignificant in the meaning that it has for parents and the quality of the parent–child relationship. Parents who are struggling with their difficult babies can welcome the acknowledgment from a clinician that they have a baby who would stretch the caregiving capacity of any parent. The concept of temperament can make all the difference to some parents who are seeking help for themselves and their babies. It can help them to renew their efforts to cope with the idiosyncrasies of their baby.

Affective biases – responses to the environment

In summary, over time emotional patterns become established both within the infant and between the infant and the caregiver. If we think of specific emotions, then some of these may come to predominate. If we think in terms of a dynamic system, specific modes may be molded by repetitive kinds of interactions, and develop a continuity through time. Whichever theory you prefer, it is clear that emotions come to be organizing structures in a child's interaction with the world and with other people.

Some continuities are adaptive: a child learns characteristics of the social world to establish useful expectations and patterns of interaction that work well. Moreover if a child is somewhat emotionally predictable, the caregiver can anticipate her or his reactions and adapt the environment to lessen the possibility of the most distressing of these reactions. Next we show how the child's emotionality has an organizing effect on the child's life, leading to wide-ranging consequences in adulthood.

Patterns of childhood emotionality that extend to adult life

When we discussed continuities (above), we referred to patterns of emotional response that remained similar over time. How do patterns established in childhood affect adults? Thirty years after an initial assessment as children, Caspi, Elder, and Bem (1987, 1988) followed up people who had been (respectively) ill-tempered or shy at age eight.

Caspi, Elder, and Bem found that those who had temper outbursts at age eight were more likely to be ill-tempered as adults. Ill-tempered boys were less likely to stay in school and as men had a more erratic work life. This led them to have lower occupational status and more downward mobility than their even-tempered counterparts. Effects of ill-temperedness in women were evident in their home lives. They married below their social class expectations, divorced more often, expressed less satisfaction in marital relationships, and were perceived by their husbands and children as more ill-tempered in parenting than women who were even-tempered at age eight.

Men who had been shy as children were slower to marry, become fathers, and establish a stable career, than the nonshy men. Their slowness to enter the work-force was in turn related to how much they subsequently achieved in their jobs and to how stable their jobs were. By contrast, shy women continued to be shy as adults but with less deleterious consequences. They were not slower to marry or have children, but they did spend less time in the workforce. They were married to men who achieved higher career status, maybe because shy women were prepared to stay at home and make fewer domestic demands on their spouses.

This research gives us an insight into the ways in which continuity in emotional functioning occurs. It is not just that responses remain stable over time, but patterns in emotional responding, established in childhood, continue to affect choices that people make throughout their lives.

Personality dimensions and traits

Most dimensions and traits of personality, almost by definition, are emotional and social. We have discussed how some are genetically based, and how some extend from childhood into adulthood. Genetically based traits of personality are like species-characteristic patterns, such as those discussed in chapter 3. Some species-characteristic patterns provide for rather specific patterns of behavior, such as attachment, and maternal caregiving. But other genetic influences are not so specific. They may be expressed as biases, such as warmth and affection, shyness, or a susceptibility to anger. We know that variability is an essential part of the evolutionary mechanism so, for instance, although all humans have capacities for fear, some individuals are very shy, others are less so. For each of us, such biases are built upon by individual experience and culture.

Perhaps most intriguing of the apparent genetically determined biases of this kind are indications that a constellation of factors that include interpersonal warmth, affection, and ease of social interaction within the family (discussed earlier in the chapter) has a genetic basis (Plomin & Bergeman, 1991). So, in behavioral genetics, it is not that genes only provide bases for species-characteristic behaviors such as infants trying to remain in close proximity to their caregivers. They provide too for variability in the form of biases, for being more or less shy, more or less affectionate, and so forth. Invariably, the measures on such matters as warmth and affection show only a proportion (generally between 20 and 50 percent) of the variation accounted for by genetic factors.

Figure 7.2 Most three- to five-year-olds are shy with strangers: notice this boy clinging to his mother and looking apprehensive. Extreme shyness in childhood can continue into adulthood.

Personality has usually been measured by questionnaire tests of people's responsiveness to situations, to see which of people's attitudes, proclivities, and tendencies cluster together, and persist through time. This approach to personality was well established, with a number of different concepts of personality, each producing its own collection of traits, until Mischel (1968) argued that personality was not just dependent on inner dispositions: in one kind of situation a person could behave in one way, in a different situation he or she would behave in another. Though this is acknowledged, we can take the concept of personality to be the extent to which a person does tend to act in a characteristic way over time, and across situations. In some imaginative studies, results from self-reports have been compared with evidence from spouses (Costa & McCrae, 1988), and have been found to be stable for at least six years. It is likely that personality becomes more set with age (Wiggins & Pincus, 1992), perhaps as people's jobs, partnerships, friendships, life circumstances, and skills, crystallize out from an array of possibilities, and are then supported by the environment that has been created.

The consensus of personality theorists has tended to recognition of the so-called "big five" dimensions of personality (John, 1990; McCrea, 1992; Ozer & Reise, 1994): Neuroticism (including traits of anxiety, hostility, and depression), Extraversion (including warmth, gregariousness, and tendencies to positive emotions), Openness (to fantasy, esthetics, feelings, ideas), Agreeableness (including trust, straightforwardness, and compliance), and Conscientiousness (including achievement striving, self-discipline, and dutifulness). Neuroticism and Extraversion are clearly straightforwardly emotional, Openness also has an emotional quality, and Agreeableness is close to the emotional idea of warmth and affection.

Neuroticism in the "big five" corresponds to a dimension with the same name proposed by Eysenck. He has argued that it is based in the limbic system (Eysenck, 1990). Remember how in chapter 5 we described the limbic system's involvement in classical conditioning of stimuli that signal punishment to the response of fear. Eysenck's theory is that people vary in the ease with which their nervous systems acquire such associations, including the prohibitions of socialization and the formation of conscience. In easily conditioned nervous systems fear tends to be intense and can have substantial effects, so people have a tendency to be often fearful and to arrange their lives to avoid occasions for fear.

For the factor of Extraversion, Eysenck has an explanation based on a different part of the nervous system. Different people, he argues, have different background levels of arousal of the brain, mediated by the reticular activating system. People try to maintain their arousal at some optimal level. Extraverts are people who are generally underaroused. To maintain their ideal level, they seek excitement from social interaction and external stimulation. Introverts already have quite enough inner arousal. They try to ensure this does not get added to by external factors, so they tend to prefer quietness and self-organized activities.

To the extent that personality dimensions are stable, we might expect them to be inherited. Current estimates from studies of monozygotic and dizygotic twins are that extraversion and neuroticism do show substantial heritability (Plomin, Chipuer, & Loelin, 1990). The biological basis of these factors is far from fully accepted: it is strongest for the dimension of Extraversion (Eysenck, 1990).

An approach by Gray (1991), based mainly on research on learning in animals, has led to a comparable hypothesis of two biologically based dimensions. One is a tendency to anxiety, based on sensitivity to signals of punishment, nonreward, and novelty. This dimension is similar to Eysenck's "Neuroticism" but according to Gray it derives from a behavioral inhibition system, based in the septum and hippocampal regions of the brain. Gray's other dimension, rather different from Eysenck's "Extraversion," is an independent system of impulsivity.

Overall it is clear that although we are different in different situations, and with different people, there is for most of us a continuity in our personality. Much of this continuity has an emotional quality, and involves our relationships with others: are we generally affectionate, melancholy, shy, aggressive? Structures that carry forward our style of emotionality have been postulated: emotional schemas. These are certainly affected by emotional biases with which we start life – temperamental characteristics – but these are modified substantially by the history of our close relationships. In the next chapter we consider what happens when children have extreme forms of such schemas.

Summary

Individual differences in emotionality have two main sources: the effects of close relationships, usually starting with those of the family, and a genetic patterning of behavior and emotions, called temperament. The most researched kind of early emotional relationship is that of attachment, the relationship of infant to parent, in which a sense of trust is built upon the parent's responses to the baby's fear. Three styles of attachment have been recognized: secure, ambivalent, and avoidant. There is evidence that some aspects of these styles continue from age one to adulthood, and can be transmitted from parents to their offspring. Such continuities may be affected by temperament as well as experiences within relationships. But other aspects of parental caregiving are also important, particularly warmth and affection. Parents shape the emotionality of their children in various ways, by language, by modeling particular emotional patterns, and by responding to some emotions rather than others. Temperament is usually thought of in terms of a genetic bias towards one or another form of emotionality, for instance, susceptibility to negative emotions. There is evidence that some of these biases, especially when present in an extreme form, persist from early to later childhood, and even into adulthood. In adulthood, continuing patterns of emotionality are usually discussed in terms of personality, and modern personality theories tend to recognize five dimensions: Neuroticism, Extraversion, Openness, Agreeableness, and Conscientiousness. The first four of these are straightforwardly emotional. Probably the best way of thinking about individual differences in emotionality is that people form emotion schemas, based partly on experience, partly on temperament, on which propensities to particular styles of emotional responding in relationships are based.

Further Reading

A classic which is still stimulating in its thoughtful and wide-ranging treatment of fundamental issues of emotions in our human condition:

John Bowlby (1971). *Attachment and loss, Volume 1. Attachment.* London: Hogarth Press (reprinted by Penguin, 1978)

Perhaps the best book on the emotional and interpersonal life of the very young:

Daniel Stern (1985). *The interpersonal world of the infant.* New York: Basic Books.

The argument for emotional schemas of social interaction, with a review of how this idea has been approached from different perspectives:

Mark Baldwin (1992). Relational schemas and the processing of social information. *Psychological Bulletin, 112,* 461–484.

On continuities of emotions through the life span:

Carol Magai (previously Carol Malatesta) & Susan H. McFadden (1995). *The role of emotions in social and personality development.* New York: Plenum.

Emotions and Psychopathology in Childhood

Figure 8.0 In childhood boys are more prone than girls to psychiatric disorder, and the most worrying kinds of disorder are based on anger and aggression which can cast a long shadow over their lives: Boys who are frequently and violently aggressive in childhood are at risk of becoming delinquents in adolescence, and criminals in adulthood.

... we are obliged to pay as much attention in our case histories to the purely human and social circumstances of our patients as to the somatic data and symptoms of the disorder. Above all, our interest will be directed towards their family circumstances.

Sigmund Freud, 1905, p. 47

Emotions in child psychopathology

Psychopathology is the study of mental states in which people can no longer cope successfully with their lives. Much of this area is concerned with extremes of emotional experience – with intense and long-lasting states of anxiety, of depression, or of anger. Such states occur in childhood: they are often referred to as "disturbances" or "disorders." Our aim in this chapter is to understand the relationship between normal emotions and psychopathology. Although the commonest psychopathological conditions in childhood have emotions as major components, a disorder is not just an extreme emotion. A child who is very sad is different from one who is depressed.

In chapter 7 we saw that children develop emotional schemas, and that these can persist. Here we suggest that sometimes these schemas become less flexible as children get older and as they establish repetitive patterns of interaction with others.

The case of Peter

How do emotions and psychopathology overlap? To get a sense of this we describe a boy with conduct disorder. He is a composite of several boys that have been seen in the course of clinical work and research interviews by one of us (JJ). We have developed this composite to maintain anonymity and to illustrate the range of issues in the child, in the family, and in the community, that we discuss in the rest of the chapter.

Peter, aged 11, lived in an apartment building with one older sister, one younger sister and his parents. He was often in trouble at school and recently he was suspended for several days, because he had been in a fight with another child. A teacher came to intervene and he picked up a chair and threw it at her. He screamed and swore at her, and only stopped being aggressive when he was restrained by two adults who came into the classroom. This outburst was worse than previous ones, but for the last year the principal had been complaining to Peter's parents that he was defiant, rude, verbally aggressive, and truanting. His behavior was similar at home. Whenever his mother asked him to do anything he refused, screamed at her and occasionally raised his fist to her. He fought regularly with both his sisters and recently his youngest sister had complained that he had twisted her arm and it had remained sore for several days. Peter's mother found money missing from her bag on several occasions in the last few months, although Peter denied taking it. She felt she had lost control of her son. Peter's father had ignored his behavior recently, because the last time he had disciplined Peter he had become enraged and hit Peter harder than he had intended. The family was frightened to come to the clinic. By the time they were seen, Peter had been showing significant disturbance for more than 18 months.

In terms of his emotional state, this boy is very angry. Whenever his parents speak to him he replies in a hostile tone. His facial expression is often angry when he is with others. But he also describes feelings of sadness and loneliness. At times he is frightened, particularly recently when he was suspended and his parents were so angry with him. We see a child who is hostile towards others, while his own emotional experience also includes loneliness and fear.

Classifying childhood disorders

Peter's pattern of disturbance is not unusual. Many boys, and a smaller number of girls, show similar patterns. Mental health workers have developed classification systems for such clusters of behavior. The main system is that of psychiatric diagnosis, in which cases are identified, usually by means of an interview, on the basis of certain criteria derived from the clinical experience of psychiatrists, psychologists, social workers, and other mental health professionals. They are descriptions of pieces of behavior and of emotions such as "excessive or unrealistic worry about future events." To make a diagnosis, some set of behavior patterns, experiences, or emotions need to occur for a specified period within an age range. Psychiatric diagnosis is based on the so-called "disease model." Someone is classified as a "case" if he or she meets the criteria for a disorder. The importance of this idea is that people at the case level are handicapped in their functioning: for children this may mean that family and school relationships become extremely strained, or that the child's symptoms stop him or her from leading a normal life.

The current scheme used to classify psychiatric problems of adults and children in North America is DSM-IV (American Psychiatric Association, 1994). It was devised by a working party of the American Psychiatric Association and it is constantly being revised as researchers and clinicians accrue information about disorders. Another widely used psychiatric classification scheme is ICD 10 (World Health Organization, 1992). These schemes have similar criteria for diagnosing disorder.

The other way of conceptualizing psychopathology, often preferred by psychologists, is that there are no sharp distinctions between having and not having a disorder. Instead there is a continuum; the method of assessment typically uses checklists of symptoms or behavior patterns, and sometimes questionnaires, which a parent or teacher completes for a particular child. Checklists and questionnaires provide continuous measures. Clusters of behaviors (similar to what psychiatrists call syndromes) are determined by factor analysis, which shows which behaviors group together. Designations of children as disturbed are made statistically to include the extreme 5 or 10 percent of a population. Though agreement of this kind of measure with psychiatric diagnoses is far from perfect (Jenson et al., 1988), conclusions about factors that cause psychopathology are similar using either method of assessment.

Using either method, researchers have found that childhood disorders that involve emotions occur in two broad categories. One is externalizing disorders defined by anger, hostility, aggression, stealing, and lying. The other is internalizing disorders based on emotions of sadness and anxiety, along with a tendency to withdrawal.

How does child psychopathology involve emotions?

The two main externalizing disorders of childhood are called oppositional defiant disorder and conduct disorder. The criterion for oppositional defiant disorder is that the child frequently displays four or more of the following behaviors over a six-month period and that this pattern leads to an impairment of social, academic, or occupational life:

- loses temper;
- argues with adults;
- defies or refuses adult requests or rules;
- deliberately does things to annoy other people;
- blames others for his or her own mistakes;
- is touchy or easily annoyed by others;
- is angry, resentful, spiteful, or vindictive;
- frequently swears or uses obscene language.

The criteria for conduct disorder are similar but include more seriously antisocial behavior such as truanting before age 13, stealing, firesetting, sexual assault, physical fights, physical cruelty to people or animals, use of weapons. Peter, whose case we gave at the beginning of the chapter, would be diagnosed as having a conduct disorder, based on six months of defiance, stealing, fighting, and truanting. Although actions rather than emotions are the descriptors of oppositional defiant disorder and conduct disorder, these actions indicate anger, aggression, and perhaps contempt.

As to internalizing disorders, the two main types are anxiety and depression. Central to the description of anxiety disorders is an experience of fear that is abnormal in intensity, duration, and how it is elicited. One disabling syndrome is overanxious disorder, in which there is excessive or unrealistic anxiety or worry, with marked tension, for at least six months across a range of areas: future events, feelings of incompetence, self-consciousness, concerns about previous performance. Separation anxiety disorder is a different pattern, defined as excessive anxiety for at least two weeks about separation from the child's main attachment figures: worry about harm befalling them, refusal to go to school or to sleep because of separation, clinging, and so forth.

In a major depressive episode a child feels either very low in mood or has no interest in anything for at least two weeks, and this must be different from how the child has previously felt. For a diagnosis the child must also have five symptoms of the kind described in chapter 4, such as weight changes, sleep disturbance, fatigue, feelings of worthlessness, inability to concentrate, and recurrent thoughts of death or suicide.

So emotional experience is central to how we define certain types of psychopathology in childhood. Missing from these descriptive criteria, however, and from our more general knowledge of disorders, is an understanding of how the different levels of emotional experience relate to one another. Remember from chapter 4 we elaborated a continuum of emotional experience and expression. At one end are emotional expressions lasting for seconds, and emotional episodes lasting for minutes or hours. Near the other end are psychopathologies like conduct disorder or depression, in which prolonged emotional states drastically affect everyday life. Psychopathology is an aggregate concept like personality, and the level of description is different from that of emotions which last for a few minutes or hours. Now our task is to consider how the shorter-term emotions relate to the longer-term aggregate notion of psychopathology. Although work in this area has begun, understanding is still preliminary (Cole, Michel, & O'Donnell-Teti, 1994). We present some of the possibilities, though as yet there is not enough evidence to choose among them.

Hypotheses about the relation between emotions and disorder

One hypothesis about the relationship between emotion and psychopathology is that when a person has a disorder one emotion becomes prominent in the emotional organization of the individual. This was proposed by Tomkins (1962, 1963). This might be operationalized as depressed people experiencing more sadness than other emotions, or perhaps experiencing sadness more often than other people. Tomkins argued that an emotional bias in which one affect is more prominent than another can develop in response to events in life; he gives an example of a girl separated from her parents when taken into hospital (Tomkins, 1979). This event elicits great fear and sadness. Memories of it, including who was there, and how it happened, are incorporated into a mental schema. Subsequent events that have any similarity to the initial eliciting circumstances then trigger the same emotions, magnifying and amplifying them. So whenever this girl is separated from her parents memories of her previous separation are re-evoked. A man with a white coat, whom she sees when she is not with her parents, reminds her of a doctor at the hospital, and again she is afraid. So painful emotions are elicited by a broader range of events than for other children. Tomkins is not arguing that single events elicit long-term disturbance, but that later affective events amplify the effects of earlier events, such that over time a pattern of responsiveness emerges.

Another view about the relationship between short-lived emotions and psychopathology is that children with psychopathology react to events with deviant emotional responses in ways that others would not: laughing when someone else is distressed, crying when nothing has happened, being angry when someone makes an affiliative gesture. Their emotional responses are unusual and other people can make no sense of them. In this view it is not that children show more of one emotion than another, but that the pattern of elicitation and response seems unusual or inappropriate to other people.

Another possibility, and one that was discussed in chapter 7, is that children with psychopathology have emotions that are not properly regulated – emotions that are more intense, that last longer, and that interfere with ordinary life. According to this idea, we might expect children with psychopathology to have emotions that are higher in intensity and last for longer than the emotions of nondisordered children.

What aspects of the emotion process are deviant in children with psychopathology?

As we discussed in chapter 4, there are many components of the emotion process: having a goal, appraising events in relation to the goal, facial expressions, bodily change, actions, and so forth. Now we turn to the question of how these different elements of the emotion process have been found to be deviant in children with psychopathology.

Appraisal biases have received most attention. In a study by Dodge and Coie (1987) aggressive and nonaggressive children were read vignettes or shown videotapes in which something negative happened – one child bumped into another or one child refused to let another child play – then they were asked to say whether the perpetrator was being deliberately mean. The aggressive children were more likely to say that the perpetrator was being intentionally hostile. Hostile attribution biases (as this bias in appraisal has been named) are not specific to children who are overly aggressive. They have also been found to characterize the thinking of depressed children when compared to non-depressed children (Quiggle et al., 1992). Another appraisal pattern is the "depressogenic" attribution style. Depressed as compared with nondepressed children are more likely to make attributions for negative events that are stable (it will always be this way), internal (it is my fault), and global (all situations will be like this) (Bodiford et al., 1988). We consider the theory that explains this depressogenic style in chapter 11. This pattern of appraisal has not been found with externalizing disorders; it may be specific to depression (Quiggle et al., 1992).

Other aspects of the emotion process have also been found to be deviant in children with psychopathology. Children with externalizing disorders differ from their nondisordered peers in their goals when interacting with others: they place more value on gaining control over another child who has thwarted them (Boldizar, Perry, & Perry, 1989). Evaluations of the consequences of emotion expressions have also been found to differ in children with psychopathology. Children with externalizing disorders evaluated aggressive solutions more positively than their nonaggressive counterparts (Boldizar, Perry, & Perry, 1989). Boys are more likely than girls to think that aggression enhances self-esteem (Slaby & Guerra, 1988) and this may contribute to the gender differences in aggression. Casey and Schlosser (1994) found that children with externalizing disorders also showed less understanding of their emotions than children without externalizing disorders. They gave less sophisticated reasons for why their feelings occurred and were less able to remember elements of events that had elicited emotions. Among children with internalizing psychopathology, those with depression have been found to value withdrawal such as quietly leaving the scene of a conflict, more than nondepressed children (Quiggle et al., 1992).

Dysfunction

To say that emotions are deviant simply means that they are different from those of the majority of children. But do emotions in psychopathology impede a person's functioning? In this book we argue that emotions are largely functional in relating people to their world. So how can we make sense of a syndrome like conduct disorder, in which anger and aggression so frequently get children into trouble? How do we explain depression, in which feelings of sadness can be so overwhelming that people think about killing themselves? Such patterns of emotional experience seem far from functional.

One way to think about this is that atypical emotions emerge from atypical environments. Some emotional response, though deviant in a whole community, may be functional in the situation in which it arises. How can extreme emotional expressions be functional? Patterson (1982) has found that a frequent consequence of anger is that the person expressing anger achieves his or her goal, as we saw in chapter 7. Children who are aggressive tend to live in homes with aggressive parents. In such settings anger and aggression may be the best means for children to achieve their goals. Later in this chapter we shall consider a study showing that depressed affect suppresses aggression from other family members. Thus, one way to look at the functional significance of emotions in psychopathology is that these deviant expressions develop within families in which they do have beneficial consequences, but they do not transfer well to other environments.

Prevalence of psychopathology in childhood

In understanding the development of emotions in childhood, observation and experiment have been the main methods — in understanding psychopathology some of our most important findings have come from psychiatric epidemiology. Epidemiology is the study of how many people show a particular disorder in the population, statistically relating disorder to factors in people's lives. Two kinds of statistic are important. Prevalence is the proportion of a population suffering from some disorder over a particular time period. Incidence is the number of new onsets of a particular disorder in a given time.

The prevalence of psychiatric disorders among children in Western societies is between 15 and 22 percent. These estimates are based on studies in different countries using instruments based on the criteria of DSM-III or ICD 9 (Anderson et al., 1987; Earls & Young, 1987; Offord, Boyle, & Racine, 1989; Richman, Stevenson, & Graham, 1982). One factor contributing to differences in prevalence rates is whether the degree of handicap caused by a disorder is taken into account.

Externalizing disorders and anxiety disorders are the most common psychiatric problems of childhood including adolescence (Kashani et al., 1989; McGee et al., 1990). Over a six-month period, between 6 and 9 percent of the child population meet the criteria for oppositional defiant disorder. Conduct disorders are rarer – between 1 and 5 percent of the child population. Separation anxiety disorder occurs in between 3 and 5 percent of children, overanxious disorder in between 1 and 3 percent and simple phobias in between 2 and 9 percent of children. Depression, and its milder version called dysthymia, are less common and occur in between 1 and 5 percent of children.

To show how these prevalence figures were obtained here are the methods used in the first major study in child psychiatric epidemiology, carried out by Rutter, Tizard, and Whitmore (1970), and known as the Isle of Wight study. Parents or guardians of all the 10-year-old children living on the Isle of Wight, an island off the south coast of England, were contacted. Children were first screened by asking their parents and teachers to complete a questionnaire about their behavior and emotions, which included behaviors indicating psychiatric disorder such as the child showing very low mood, being frequently aggressive with siblings or peers, and so forth. Children showing a lot of problems were then contacted for an interview to see what, if any, psychiatric diagnosis was to be made. Some children who showed few problems on the questionnaire were also interviewed to see how many showed psychiatric disorder which had been missed by the questionnaire. In this way an estimate was made of the true prevalence of disorder in the population. Parents were also interviewed about many aspects of their own lives as well as about their child's history, family, and school. Because all children in the whole population were subjects of study, we can obtain an accurate picture of how many suffered from disorders as well as why they suffered. It is no good just basing prevalence estimates or findings about causation on people who find their way to clinics – these are invariably just a proportion of those suffering. Moreover, certain kinds of people are overrepresented in clinic samples, for instance, children who have externalizing disorders and people who are skilled at getting health care systems to work for them. As we saw with Peter, problems were present for a long time before he attended a clinic. In fact only 10 to 30 percent of children with psychiatric disorder receive any help for it (Esser, 1990; Richman, Stevenson, & Graham, 1982).

Epidemiological methods were a breakthrough in understanding origins of disorder, and they have helped plan services for children. Psychological instruments (for instance interviews) assessing the presence of psychopathology have been developed for use with parents, teachers, and children (Edelbrock & Costello, 1988; Rutter, Tuma, & Lann, 1988). In these, the criteria for disorders have been defined so that two people interviewing the same child, or the same parent about the child, agree closely about whether or not the child has a disorder.

Diagnoses differ, however, according to whether the informant is a parent, a teacher, or the child. Who is most in touch with the behavior or emotional state in question? Children are more likely to report fears and anxieties than parents; parents are more likely to report externalizing behaviors than children (Achenbach & Edelbrock, 1984). The reliability of children as respondents increases with age, suggesting that some of the discrepancy in reporting is simply because young children are cognitively immature (Edelbrock et al., 1985). Another factor is that children's emotional states and behavior depend on the situation they are in. At school a child can be tearful, self-deprecatory, and withdrawn; may find interaction with other children difficult, feel rejected and lonely, and be seen in need of some help by a teacher. At home the same child may be lively, feel comfortable, and be seen by parents as unproblematic. So some differences may indicate real differences in children's behavior across situations.

Externalizing disorders

Children show more externalizing behaviors, such as destroying property, screaming, cruelty to animals, than internalizing behaviors such as sadness, anxiety, and withdrawal, when they are young. Achenbach et al. (1991) surveyed parents of 2,500 children between 4 and 16 years of age, drawn from different communities across the United States and making up a representative sample. Each parent completed a questionnaire about one child, and children in the community sample were matched with a group of children receiving treatment in clinics. The questionnaire had 215 items of behavior, and parents scored the frequency with which their child showed each one.

The items were based on the behaviors and emotional states commonly used in assessing psychiatric disorder. Examples were: "screams a lot," "shy or timid," "teases other children," "swears," "physically attacks people." Within externalizing behaviors, patterns of expression changed with age. Aggressive behaviors decreased and delinquent behaviors increased as children got older (Achenbach et al., 1991).

The same patterns are seen using measures of psychiatric disorder based on DSM-III criteria. Oppositional defiant disorder is most common in early childhood, but conduct disorder is more common as children get older (Offord et al., 1987). This may reflect an increased opportunity for seriously antisocial behavior as children grow older, for example, greater access to weapons, and increased knowledge of how to cause harm.

Boys show more externalizing behavior than girls throughout childhood (Achenbach et al., 1991), and the difference in levels of aggression is evident by the age of two (Prior et al., 1993). From an early naturalistic study on anger and aggression in children, Goodenough (1931) reported that angry outbursts in children decline sharply in the second year. For girls, however, the decline is much sharper than it is for boys. Different rates of aggressive behavior in males and females have been found in many societies (see chapter 10), and in other primate species (see chapter 3). As to diagnosable externalizing disorders, boys show much greater prevalence than girls (Anderson et al., 1987). Graham (1979) estimated a 3:1 ratio of boys to girls in prevalence of conduct disorder and this has been confirmed in more recent studies (Bird, Canino, & Rubio-Stipec, 1988; Fleming, Boyle, & Offord, 1993).

Anxiety disorders

Anxiety generally increases with age during childhood (Achenbach et al., 1991). Richman, Stevenson, and Graham (1982) found a ninefold increase in maternal reports of children's worrying from three to eight years. Between middle childhood and adolescence the prevalence of diagnosable anxiety disorders remains fairly constant (McGee et al., 1990), or may even drop a little with age (Velez, Johnson, & Cohen, 1989). The forms that anxiety disorders take, however, change with age (Bernstein & Borchardt, 1991). Separation anxiety disorder is more common in early childhood, but overanxious disorder affecting many aspects of life is more common in adolescence (Kashani & Orvaschel, 1988).

Girls are more likely than boys to show single symptoms of anxiety (Achenbach et al., 1991) and disorders of anxiety (Anderson et al., 1987; Costello, 1989). This sex difference is consistently found but relatively slight. It is not uncommon for a child to show two different types of anxiety disorder (Last et al., 1992). Anxiety disorders also frequently occur with depression: Anderson et al. (1987) found that 17 percent of preadolescents with anxiety disorder were also depressed; by adolescence Kashani and Orvaschel (1990) found that this figure had risen to 69 percent.

Depressive disorders

Both normal low mood and depression become more common as children get older (Angold, 1988). Larson and Lampman-Petraitis (1989) asked pre-adolescents and adolescents to rate their moods through the day when signaled by a beeper. Adolescents' emotions were no more variable than younger children's but their mood was generally lower. In a population study of preadolescents and adolescents in Germany, Esser (1990) found a similar phenomenon – 11 percent of eight-year-olds reported depressed mood or had it reported by parents, compared to 30 percent of 13-year-olds. For diagnosable depression findings are also similar. Rates of depressive disorders increase dramatically in adolescence (Costello, 1989; Weissman, Gammon, & John, 1987) with some studies showing as much as a tenfold increase between childhood and adolescence (Rutter et al., 1976).

In childhood, boys and girls are about equally likely to suffer from depression. By late adolescence and adult life, as Angold (1991) has shown, females are twice as likely as males to be depressed, with more adolescent girls becoming depressed as they get older and reach adulthood. But this is not the case for boys, whose level of reported symptoms remains constant from earlier childhood through adolescence.

As we see from the above, marked gender differences are evident in the ways that boys and girls express disturbance. Reasons for this are still far from understood. Socialization practices are likely to play some role. Parents may be more allowing of expressions of fear and sadness in their girls than in their boys. They may find the expression of anger in their boys more acceptable than in their girls (Golombok & Fivush, 1994). Biological factors are also likely to play a role in the gender differences. Across societies and species aggression is more common in males. The consistency of this finding when socialization and environmental factors vary widely, makes it likely that biological factors contribute to aggressive behavior, an issue that we return to in chapter 10.

Continuity of disorders

We have seen in normal development that children show some continuity of emotional response over time. What about people with more extreme emotional responses? Is there continuity in types of disturbance from early childhood onwards?

Continuities of disorders over time are high. In a general population sample Richman, Stevenson, and Graham (1982) found that 60 percent of children with a disorder when they were three had a disorder at eight. The highest continuities are for children with externalizing problems (Verhulst, Koot, & Berden, 1990). In a follow-up of the Isle of Wight study Graham and Rutter (1973) found that 75 percent of children who had conduct disorder at 10 still had it at 14. Robins (1978) found continuities over a much longer period: 50 percent of children with an externalizing disorder in childhood went on to show personality disorder as adults. Magnusson (1988) found that boys who showed a combination of aggression, hyperactivity, and poor peer relationships in childhood were five times more likely than children without such problems to become criminals or to abuse alcohol as adults.

Stability in aggression is almost as high as the stability of IQ (Olweus, 1979). Huesmann et al. (1984) carried out a follow-up over 22 years. Boys and girls who were nominated by their peers at age eight as particularly aggressive were also the most aggressive 30-year-old men and women. They had more criminal convictions, were aggressive towards their children, and were more abusive to spouses. Once a style of aggressive behavior has developed it persists over time.

In general population studies, continuities for internalizing disorders are less than those for externalizing problems (Esser, 1990). Offord et al. (1992) found that between 70 and 75 percent of children with diagnoses of internalizing disorder when first interviewed were free of disorder at follow-up.

For the specific disorder of depression, however, follow-up studies on children seen at clinics showed that recurrences of psychopathology were high. Harrington et al. (1990) followed up one group who had been depressed as children and another group, matched for age and sex, who had a psychiatric disorder other than depression as children. Those who had been depressed as children were much more likely than the others to be depressed as adults. Kovacs et al. (1984) followed up a sample of children 8 to 13 years old after their first episode of major depression. Within two years after recovery, 40 percent of them had a recurrence.

Changes from internalizing disorders to externalizing disorders are more uncommon than persistence in the same type of disorder. Children from the Isle of Wight study were followed up four years after they were first seen. No children went from showing an internalizing to an externalizing disorder, although children with conduct disorders occasionally developed internalizing difficulties subsequently (Graham & Rutter, 1973). Fleming, Boyle, and Offord (1993) followed up a general population sample of children in Ontario, Canada. They found that a quarter of those diagnosed with a depression when first seen were depressed four years later. None went from being depressed to showing

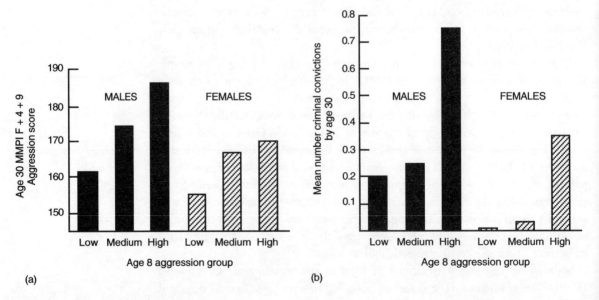

Figure 8.1 In (a) mean aggression scores on the Minnesota Multiphasic Personality Scales for aggression at age 30 for people who were nominated by their peers as aggressive at age 8. In (b) are the mean numbers of criminal convictions by age 30 for this same group. (From Huesmann et al., 1984.)

antisocial personality disorder. Adolescents with conduct disorder when first seen were much more likely than depressed adolescents to show antisocial personality disorder as adults, and they were six times more likely to be abusing drugs. A small number subsequently developed depression.

Gender has an important influence on the persistence of problems and on whether problems continue to be expressed in the same way. Preschool boys followed up into middle childhood were much more likely to show persistence in disorders than girls (Richman, Stevenson, and Graham, 1982). Externalizing disorders show much higher continuity for boys than for girls, and internalizing disorders show much higher continuity for girls than for boys (McGee et al., 1990). There are preliminary indications that the small percentage of girls with externalizing problems in childhood are more likely to change and become depressed in adulthood (Quinton, Rutter, & Gulliver, 1990; Robins, 1986). It is as if gender stereotypes about appropriate emotions influence prevalence and the persistence of certain kinds of problem.

This evidence on the continuity of the type of disorder that a child has, either an internalizing or an externalizing disorder, is further evidence for the concept of emotion schemas that we discussed in chapter 7. Children develop emotion orientations that persist over time. They may go in and out of disorder, particularly internalizing disorders, but on the whole they remain true to the type of emotional orientation that they first show.

We should not, however, think that continuities persist solely within the person (Lewis, 1990). Adverse environments are of central importance in the development of disorders, and many environments remain stable over time. The environment that causes a disorder in the first place often continues to elicit the same disorder over time. For example, Richman, Stevenson, and Graham (1982) investigated continuities in a group of families drawn from the general population. Over the years when children were between three and eight years old, half their mothers who were depressed when children were three, were still depressed when children were eight, and 60 percent of parents in a conflictual marriage at the beginning still had a conflictual marriage at the end. If relationships in the family were positive at the beginning, they were likely still to be positive at the end.

Risks and causes of psychiatric disorders in children

In this section we discuss why children develop internalizing or externalizing disorders. Processes involved in the development of psychopathology are often just more extreme versions of those processes that structure normal emotionality. So the role of temperament and the way that emotions are expressed in families are central, just as for the individual differences of personality. Disorders in children are rarely caused by only a single factor: factors combine to increase or decrease the risk of disorder in children.

Let us return first to Peter, the boy whose case we described at the beginning of the chapter, and think about the factors in his life that may have contributed to his problems. Peter had never been an easy child. His mother said he was difficult to soothe as a baby, and he did not usually want to wait for anything. She found him hard to cope with. As he got older, family life became more and more tense. His father was an unskilled worker who was made redundant from several jobs. His parents had no savings and, although periods of unemployment were relatively short, the family was very stressed during these periods. When she had her third child Peter's mother could no longer cope and had a period when she became clinically depressed, and she considered leaving the family. The parents' relationship later became more and more angry, so that by the time Peter was seven screaming fights were common. On one occasion Peter's father left home for a month, but he returned because he was concerned about the children. Peter's relationship with both his parents was difficult. When his mother asked him to do anything he yelled at her not to bother him. She screamed back at him, but would then leave it because it was not worth the fight. Peter's father said that he was sometimes so mad that he hit Peter hard without meaning to. Peter's sisters have always been closer to each other than to him. They exclude him from their play so he often feels lonely and left out.

This kind of situation is not unusual for a child with psychopathology. Not just one, but many things go wrong in Peter's life. He was temperamentally difficult. His parents had financial struggles, the demands of a large family, and difficulties in their own relationship. He was exposed to extremes of emotional expression, including parents being very angry with one another and with him. Here, already, are seeds of a tragic life, since Peter has no very positive relationships with anyone. In the following section we review how such factors in children's lives contribute to disturbed behavior. In the Isle of Wight study Rutter, Tizard, and Whitmore (1970) identified several key factors, including some of those in Peter's life, that were associated with increased risk of psychiatric disorder in children. We will now discuss those that are illuminating about the relation between emotions and emotional disorders.

Conflict between parents

Children who are exposed to serious and prolonged conflict between their parents are at increased risk of developing externalizing disorders (Grych & Fincham, 1992). Such children, particularly boys, show aggression and anger to parents and to other children. One of the important mechanisms is exposure to overt expression of hostility – parents angrily shouting at one another. Jenkins and Smith (1991) examined three aspects of poor marital relationships: frequency and severity of angry arguments, discrepancy over child rearing issues, and periods of silent tension. It was frequency and severity of angry arguments that was associated with an increase in child psychopathology. Open and severe quarrelling was also associated with more parenting problems, such as monitoring children less, and being critical of them. After controlling for these aspects of the parent–child relationship, the effect of seeing parents shouting at one another remained associated with externalizing problems in children.

In the early days of trying to explain why children become delinquent, parental divorce was thought to increase the risk of children's psychopathology. But it is now clear that externalizing problems occur before marital separation occurs, and that they are related to parental conflict before divorce (Block, Block, & Gjerde, 1986; Cherlin et al., 1991). Similarly, children's psychopathology after their parents have divorced is most strongly associated with continuing parental conflict (Emery, 1988).

The studies mentioned above are correlational. To investigate causal influences experimental studies have been conducted. Cummings (1987) arranged for pairs of children to play together and, while they were doing so, to see two adults whom they did not know conversing in a friendly way, and then later having an angry verbal argument. Children increased their aggressive behavior after the adult argument, as can be seen in figure 8.2. Exposure to the anger of strangers may have quite different significance to being exposed to the

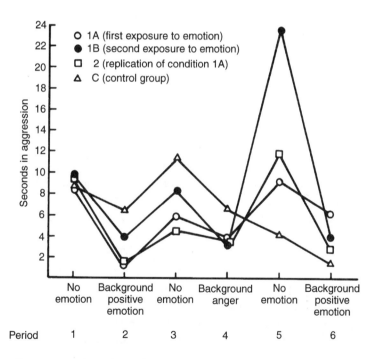

Figure 8.2 Mean number of seconds of aggression between two children who have witnessed an angry adult argument in the study by Cummings (1987). Note that in period 5, the children who were exposed to adult anger have increased amounts of aggression, and this is especially so for the children who were exposed to adult anger for a second time. In contrast the control group, who have not been exposed to adult anger, show a declining level of aggression.

anger of one's parents. Nevertheless, adding experimental results to epidemiological findings suggests that hostile and negative emotion between adults can cause children to be aggressive themselves.

Witnessing negative expressions of emotion may increase the risk of children developing externalizing behavior in several ways (Emery, Fincham, & Cummings, 1992). Through modeling, children may learn from their parents that negative emotional expression is the way to deal with conflict. They may become aroused by anger, and their behavior may be influenced by this increased arousal. Seeing negative emotion expressed between parents may alter children's expectations about relationships such that they interpret neutral behavior of other people in a negative light (Jenkins et al., in press). These are direct effects of marital disharmony. Indirect effects of parental conflict on childhood disturbance also occur, because relationships between each parent and the child may suffer (Fauber & Long, 1992).

Parental psychiatric disturbance

Epidemiological studies have repeatedly shown that psychiatric problems in a parent are associated with increased risk of disorder in the child (Bird, Canino, Rubio-Sripec, 1988; Richman, Stevenson, & Graham, 1982). Often children show a similar type of disorder to that shown by their parents. So for instance, parental depression is more strongly related to internalizing disorders than to externalizing ones (Dowdney & Coyne, 1990; Williams et al., 1990). Hammen et al. (1990) found that when children of depressed parents show a disorder, this disorder too is likely to be depression. Children of parents who suffer from an anxiety disorder are most likely themselves to show anxiety symptoms (Rosenbaum, Biederman, & Gersten, 1988). Children who live with parents with antisocial disorders (including aggression) are more likely to show externalizing disorders than other types of disorder (Huesmann et al., 1984; Rutter & Giller, 1983).

The increased risk of disorder in children of psychiatrically disordered parents comes about through adverse genetic and environmental effects – both play a role in the development of disorder (Rutter, Tizard, & Whitmore, 1970). Heritability estimates for at least some measures of negative emotionality have been found to be significant, as we discussed in chapter 7. In the environment too, there are contributory causes: children with a depressed parent are exposed to sad and irritable emotions more often than infants of nondepressed mothers (Cohn et al., 1990; Field et al., 1990). Such children are more likely to show anger and sadness themselves. For instance, Cohn et al. found that during interactions with their depressed mothers infants spent 6.7 percent of their time showing sadness and 7.6 percent of their time showing anger, compared to infants with their nondepressed mothers who spent 0.2 percent of their time showing sadness and 0.8 percent showing anger. Modeling may account for some of this association. It is also likely, however, that infants' goals during interactions with depressed or irritable parents may be thwarted, leading them to express more negative emotions (Tronick, 1989).

In interaction with a depressed caregiver the child learns how to respond to the emotions of their caregiver, how their caregiver's emotions elicit emotions in them, and how their own communications affect their caregiver. Through their experience they begin to construct a schema about their own and their caregiver's emotions. Field et al. (1988) compared interactions of babies with depressed mothers and babies with nondepressed mothers. Babies were videotaped playing with their mothers and then with a stranger. The stranger did not know whether the babies had a depressed mother or not. With their own depressed mothers, babies showed more gaze aversion and were more negative generally. The behavior of the infants carried into the interaction with the stranger. The stranger was less active, made fewer vocalizations, and played

Figure 8.3 Depression is relatively common in mothers of young children. It involves a loss of hope, made more likely by adversities, shortages of resources, and lack of support from a spouse – and of course, it affects children.

less with infants of depressed mothers than with babies of nondepressed mothers. So, in the first three months of their lives, infants develop patterns of responding based on adapting to their mothers' affective states, that they carry with them into new interactions.

Such interactions may lead babies to feel untrusting of their caregivers, disturbing the development of the attachment relationship. Children with depressed mothers have been found to be more likely to develop insecure attachments (Lyons-Ruth, Alpern, & Repacholi, 1993; Radke-Yarrow et al., 1985).

The child also learns about the effect of emotions on interactions, from watching their depressed parent interact with other members of the family. Hops et al. (1987) observed patterns of interactions in families in which the mother was depressed. They found that the mothers' depressed moods resulted in the suppression of fathers' and children's aggression towards the mothers. The mothers' moods therefore served the function of winning the mother a respite from the anger of other family members. When the fathers and children did express anger to the mother, this temporarily suppressed her depressed mood. What do children learn about emotions from this kind of experience? They learn that being sad stops other people from getting angry, and that getting angry activates other people and pulls them out of depressed states. Another interesting finding emerged: when fathers suppressed their anger with their wives, they became more angry with their children. So children may also learn that people do not necessarily express the emotion they feel towards the person whom it concerns.

Another consequence of living in a family with a depressed parent may be that children are exposed to negative appraisals of the world that they use subsequently in their own appraisals of events. Zahn-Waxler and Kochanska (1990) found that mothers with depression were more likely to say things that induced guilt and anxiety in their children, and to express feelings of disappointment than did nondepressed mothers. Garber, Braafladt, and Zeman (1991) found that depressed mothers were more critical of their children than nondepressed mothers. Negative evaluations of the child by parents may encourage the development of the appraisal patterns that we discussed earlier: attributing negative events to the inadequacies of the self. So in ways such as those we have reviewed here, children develop emotional reactions that become habitual, and are compiled into emotion schemas. Though initially these may be adaptive in their home environment, these schemas continue forward in life, and into other settings.

The parent–child relationship

As we discussed in chapter 7, difficulties of the parent–child relationship are important for understanding children's patterns of emotionality. Here we review just three of the several types of difficulty that are associated with disorders in children.

Attachment failures

In Bowlby's early formulations of attachment theory he proposed that children who did not have the opportunity to form a primary attachment relationship early in childhood would be permanently damaged (Bowlby, 1951). The reason for this was because Bowlby hypothesized that parental love was as important to the child's development as food. Research of Harlow and Harlow (1962) and others reviewed in chapter 3 supports this idea. Follow-up studies of children who have been reared in institutions allow us to examine the long-term impact of being without a primary attachment relationship in early life. Tizard and Hodges (Hodges & Tizard, 1989a, 1989b; Tizard & Hodges, 1978) followed up children who had entered institutions before age two and who left them between the ages of two and seven. Staff working in the institutions provided good physical care, cognitive and language stimulation, but the children experienced multiple caretakers (an average of 50) and did not establish any specific attachment relationship.

Between two and seven years old, the children were either restored to their biological family, or were permanently adopted. The restored families had fewer resources and more children living in the home; they felt more ambivalent about the children returning. Adoptive families were generally very keen to have the children, made a lot of effort to build the relationship with the child, and were willing to tolerate marked dependency early in the relationship. Restored and adopted children were compared with children of the same age who had been in the continuous care of their parents.

When children were 8 and 16 years old, those who had been in institutions were more likely to show psychopathology than children who had experienced continuous parental care. Both groups of ex-institutionalized children were regarded by their teachers as showing more symptoms indicating psychopathology – attention seeking, restlessness, unpopularity, quarrelsomeness, and aggression – than their noninstitutionalized counterparts. Relationships with peers were also less good.

The picture at home was different. Here, the restored children and the adopted children differed in relationships with other family members as well as psychopathology, as reported by their parents. The restored children were much more disturbed, with higher rates of psychopathology, less strong attachments, and more conflictual and difficult family relationships. The children who had been adopted, however, were reported by their parents to be functioning well. They were said to have intimate and warm relationships with other family members. The quality of their attachment did not differ from the quality of attachment of children who had been in the continuous care of their parents. These adopted children did not show higher levels of psychopathology.

These findings suggest that institutionalized children who have not experienced a primary attachment relationship early in their childhood do find it more difficult to get along with their peers. Both teachers and peers perceive this and withdraw from the children. However, in families that are committed to these children, family members make a special effort. Maybe early on in the relationship they tolerate peculiarities, giving the children a chance to be loved and to experience intimate relationships. Perhaps with this experience children's distrust diminishes. But, of course, the parents of adopted children may rate their children as less problematic, not because they actually are, but because they perceive them in that way. However, there is convergent evidence from another study suggesting that warm and supportive relationships in later life can ameliorate the negative effects of early emotional deprivation.

In this study, children who had been in institutions as children were followed up into adulthood, when they were interviewed and observed interacting with their children (Quinton, Rutter, & Liddle, 1984; Quinton & Rutter, 1988). As adults, 33 percent of ex-care women were found to have a handicapping psychiatric disorder in their adult life, compared with 5 percent of noninstitutionalized women. Clearly, being without a primary attachment figure in early childhood does put people at risk. On the basis of attachment theory and the findings in relation to surrogate-reared monkeys, we would expect such women to be incompetent in caring for their own children. These mothers did indeed have significant problems in parenting, being insensitive, lacking in warmth, harsher with their children, and showing inconsistent or ineffective control. Some women, however, who had very poor early experiences functioned well as parents. These women were differentiated from the others by having a supportive spouse: in whom they could confide and on whom they could count for help. This study by Quinton et al. and the one by Tizard and Hodges, show us that attachment failures in childhood do have deleterious effects on mental health and the ability to relate to others, but children and young adults who find love show a remarkable ability to recover from their early institutional experiences. They can form new models of themselves with others, new emotion schemas – a topic to which we return in chapter 12.

Another kind of attachment trauma occurs when a child loses a parent through death. This, too, is associated with increased risk of psychopathology both in childhood and adulthood. In the short term, children who lose a parent show grief reactions comparable to those shown by adults (Van Eerdewegh et al., 1982). They show more sadness, more tempers, poorer appetite, sleep difficulties, and more withdrawal. Though such symptoms are generally less pervasive after one year, they are still evident in some children. Most children do not show continuing grieving throughout their childhood as a result of such loss. They are, however, more likely to show depressed symptomatology as adults (Brown & Harris, 1978). From the point of view of attachment theory, the quality of care that children receive after they have experienced the loss is a stronger predictor of psychopathology than the loss itself (Harris, Brown, & Bifulco, 1986). We discuss this evidence in chapter 11. The point here is that children develop psychological well-being through close and warm relationships with parents. When children do not experience this love, or if they lose it, although they are certainly more at risk than people who have not experienced such stresses, all is not lost. Other close relationships throughout life can make up for early negative experiences.

Attachment style

Though Bowlby's attachment theory was formulated to explain gross deviations in caregiving, for instance in institutional care, Ainsworth et al. (1978) extended the theory to link parent and child behavior in the normal range. As we explained in chapter 7, relatively minor variations in mothers' sensitivity were related to specific styles in the "Strange Situation" test. Attachment has seemed so basic to many researchers that the question has arisen of whether these styles – secure, ambivalent, avoidant – predict psychopathology. There have been many studies, but the relationship between attachment style at age one and subsequent psychopathology has been found to be inconsistent and weak. So in one study an association between attachment status and psychopathology in preschool and school-aged children was found for boys but not girls (Lewis et al., 1984), in another study it was found for girls but not boys (La Freniere & Sroufe, 1984), in another it was found for behavior in one setting but not another (Oppenheim, Sagi, & Lamb, 1988). In other studies it was found not to be associated with psychopathology at all despite sound methodology (Fagot & Kavanagh, 1990; Goldberg et al., 1989). This inconsistency suggests that insecure attachment style is, at best, a weak predictor of psychopathology.

There is one category of attachment however, that has been found to be strongly associated with psychopathology in children. This is the category of disoriented/disorganized attachment, that was added to the three existing styles (secure, ambivalent, and avoidant) by Main and Solomon (1986). Children with this style respond to reunion with their parent with disorientation and contradictory behaviors. They do not have a coherent and organized response to their parent at times of stress. This pattern of attachment has been found more frequently in children at risk. In a middle-class population it occurred in 13 percent of infants (Main & Soloman, 1990), rising to 54 percent amongst the infants of low income mothers suffering from depression (Lyons-Ruth et al., 1990) and 82 percent in a sample of abused children (Carlson et al., 1989).

This category of disorganized attachment has been found to relate strongly to psychopathology. Lyons-Ruth, Alpern, and Repacholi (1993) followed up a group of children from 18 months to five years; these children were exposed to multiple risks including poverty, maltreatment, and a history of maternal psychiatric illness. Of these children, 71 percent who had significant levels of hostility at age five had been classified as disorganized at 18 months, and only 12 percent had been classified as secure. Prospective predictions were not so good: about half of those who were disorganized at 18 months did not develop psychopathology. This study confirms that children in very disturbed environments are at risk of developing psychopathology, and early signs can be traced to emotional responses at 18 months. It is not clear, however, what the specific environmental or temperamental antecedents are to this pattern of response.

So secure, ambivalent, and avoidant styles of attachment at age one are not important predictors of psychopathology. The disorganized style is related to psychopathology, but this style is so strongly associated with major risks in the child's environment that it seems likely that these factors, rather than lapses in maternal sensitivity, are the risks. As compared with extreme hostility, abuse, and neglect, which we now discuss, small variations in maternal sensitivity have only insignificant effects on psychopathology.

Differences in the quality of relationship between parent and child

Hostility and criticism in the parents' relationships with their children have consistently been identified as important predictors of psychopathology in childhood, particularly onsets of externalizing disorders (Olweus, 1980; Patterson, 1982; Stubbe et al., 1993). For instance, Richman, Stevenson, and Graham (1982) interviewed families when children were three and eight years old. Warmth and criticism were rated on the basis of the mother's tone of voice and content during a two-hour interview when she talked about her children. As compared with children who did not have any psychiatric disturbance, three-year-olds who had a disturbance were four times more likely to have a mother who was critical of them, three-and-a-half times more likely to have a mother low in warmth towards them, and three times more likely to have a mother who hit them. Patterns with fathers were similar.

Physical abuse of children results in wide-ranging developmental, cognitive, emotional, and social consequences (Cicchetti, 1990). In relation to psychopathology, children are likely to develop externalizing disorders and problems around aggression (Simons et al., 1991). Internalizing symptoms, particularly depression, have also been reported (Sternberg et al., 1993).

Children in abusive homes develop hostile appraisals of other people's actions. Dodge, Bates, and Pettit (1990) investigated children in the general population. Six months before the children entered school their parents were interviewed about the frequency and severity with which they gave physical punishment to their children. On entering school, the children's aggression with peers was assessed by sociometric interviews in which all children in the class were asked to nominate children who were mean and fought a lot. Frequency and severity of physical punishment in the home were associated with more aggression towards peers in school. Children were also asked to make attributions of intent about neutral stimuli. Children who had been subjected to high levels of physical punishment were more likely to attribute hostile intent to other children's neutral actions than nonabused children. Their cognitive appraisals of the intentions of others partially explained the relationship between the children's home experience and levels of aggression with peers. Thus, as a result of living in an abusive home children were more likely to see their peers as having hostile intentions toward them and consequently to respond aggressively.

It is not only exposure to negative affect that puts children at risk for psychopathology. A lack of positive affect in the parent–child relationship is also associated with increased psychopathology in children. Pettit and Bates (1989) carried out home observations of parent–child interaction when babies were 6, 13, and 24 months old. Mothers were rated on the positive affect that they showed towards their children: affectionate contact (6 months), affectionate teaching (13 months) and verbal stimulation (24 months). When children were four years old, psychopathology was assessed. Lower levels of positive maternal affect in the first two years predicted internalizing and externalizing problems when the children were four years old. Lack of positive maternal affect was a stronger predictor of children's problems than was negative affect.

As with marital conflict and parental depression, the mechanisms involved in the association between children living in highly critical or physically abusive homes and developing problems with aggression are probably various. They include matching of high levels of anger, learning negatively biased appraisal systems, and learning emotion sequences in which a range of emotions are responded to with anger. The absence of warmth is also important in predicting patterns of emotionality that children develop. We do not yet know enough about why an abusive upbringing results sometimes in externalizing disorders, sometimes in internalizing disorders. Constitutional factors such as sex and temperament may play some role in this.

Poverty

Poverty is strongly related to a raised prevalence of psychiatric disorder (Costello, 1989). Boyle (1991), reporting on a general population sample of children in Ontario between 4 and 16 years old, found that the prevalence of disorder amongst children whose parents earned over $50,000 per year (in 1983) was 14 percent. Among children whose parents earned below $10,000 per year it was 35 percent. The concept "poverty" gives us little understanding of how children are at increased risk of disorder. In industrialized society poverty means having few resources; levels of stress are higher in homes where resources are fewer (Rutter et al., 1975). This in turn is related to a higher frequency of expressions of negative emotion towards children (Radke-Yarrow, Richters, & Wilson, 1988), to rates of parental psychiatric and personality disorder, and to marital disharmony. But poverty may also have a direct effect on the development of problems: particularly externalizing ones. Poor children may feel themselves to be blocked in their goals: via the media and in other ways they are exposed to objects, activities, attainments, available to others, but not to them.

Combinations of risks

Think back to the case of Peter, introduced at the beginning of the chapter. As we saw, several stresses occurred together in his life. His mother was depressed for a time, his parents were in conflict, and the family experienced poverty. Several groups of epidemiological researchers have demonstrated that children are most at risk when several such stresses occur together (Rutter, 1979; Williams et al., 1990). Rutter describes six family factors that put children at increased risk of child psychopathology. We have discussed four: parental depression, parental marital disharmony or separation, removal of a child by some statutory authority, and poverty – the factors best understood in terms of the involvement of emotions. We have not discussed Rutter's two other factors: large family size and parental criminality. The first of these may operate, like poverty, by scarcity of valued resources including access to parents, hence increasing the frequency and intensity of negative emotions; the second may be associated with more negative parenting practices such as increased hostility to children, as well as poorer supervision of them (Patterson, 1986). Rutter et al. (1975) found that in urban, as compared with rural, areas twice as many children had disorders, largely because of the increased presence of the six risk factors mentioned above.

Now here is an important conclusion, seen in figure 8.4. Children with any one of these six risks do as well as those with none. But with each additional risk the chances of a child suffering a disorder multiply sharply. Two stressors rather than one increase a child's risk of developing psychopathology fourfold. Four stressors increase the risk 20 times.

Bidirectional and reinforcing effects in the environment

Although we have described parents affecting their children, it is most unlikely to be as simple as this. Children who are more difficult make their parents more angry, and this in turn is likely to make children's behavior more difficult (Lytton, 1990). Patterson (1982) has written about mutually coercive patterns in aggressive homes. In response to an aggressive action by a child, a parent responds with an escalated aggressive action, that can provoke further

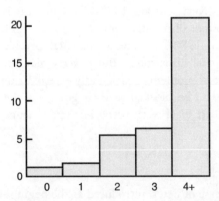

Figure 8.4 Rutter's (1979) diagram of effects of risk factors on developing a psychiatric disorder in children. Children with just one risk factor are no more likely to develop a disorder than those with none, but then with each added risk factor the prevalence of psychiatric disorder multiplies.

aggression by the child, and so forth. Emotions are communications to others. Within sequences of emotional communications, attributing an emotional expression to an individual has its problematic aspect. The more a person refuses to talk with his or her spouse, the more frustrated and angry this spouse may feel. The more angry the spouse becomes the less the original person feels like talking. Describing the emotion within the individual does not do justice to how it was caused or how it is sustained.

Here we have concentrated on families associated with particular types of psychopathology. Peer groups also play a role in maintaining psychopathology, particularly externalizing disorders. Patterson, Capaldi, and Bank (1991) suggest that children learn antisocial behavior patterns in the home, then take them to school. Such patterns lead to rapid rejection by other children (Coie & Kupersmidt, 1983), making it more likely that the children continue to behave aggressively.

Constitutional factors related to psychopathology

In the previous chapter we discussed the role of temperament in emotionality. Temperament was conceived of as one element that contributes to emotional bias. Early temperamental characteristics are modestly related to the probability of developing psychopathology and to the type of psychopathology (Bates, 1987; Maziade et al., 1990). Rende (1993) reported on a representative sample of 164 children. Temperament was assessed at ages one and two, and then in years three and four. Behavioral problems were assessed at age seven by mothers completing a questionnaire. In boys, emotionality in infancy explained 4 percent, and emotionality in early childhood explained a further 4 percent, of the variance of seven-year-olds' anxiety and depression. Prediction in girls was higher; infant emotionality explained 9 percent, and early childhood emotionality explained a further 8 percent, of the variance of later anxiety and depression. Attentional problems in boys were predicted by early ratings of the activity dimension of temperament, with 20 percent of the variance of attentional problems at age seven being explained by early ratings of activity. So temperament makes some contribution to the development of behavioral problems in children. Perhaps it is only when adverse temperament interacts with a negative environment that psychopathology develops. For instance, when temperamentally difficult children lived in dysfunctional families, Maziade et al. (1990) found that they were more at risk of subsequent psychopathology than when they lived in well-functioning families.

There has been a great deal of interest recently in genetic influence on psychopathology. We do not discuss it in detail here, not because it is unimportant, but because there is more understanding of the link between emotion and environmental risks for psychopathology, than emotion and genetic risk for psychopathology. Methods for investigating genetic hypotheses have improved in the last 15 years, and there have been several comprehensive reviews of findings for childhood disorder, including one by Rutter et al.

(1990). Some childhood disorders, notably autism, must primarily be approached from a genetic point of view. Rutter et al. concluded that although there is evidence for genetic effects on externalizing and internalizing disorders in childhood, it is difficult to know how strong these effects are. Patterns of results across studies are sometimes puzzling. For adult criminality, for instance, there is strong evidence of a genetic effect, but the evidence for a genetic influence on childhood conduct disorders and delinquency is not strong. Given that adult criminality is almost always preceded by earlier conduct disorder, this seems surprising. It may be that persistent delinquency has a stronger genetic basis than delinquency that remits before adulthood, but this is not yet known. For internalizing disorders of childhood, Rutter et al. concluded that although it is a fair inference that genetic factors are involved, there was at the time of their review no direct evidence from properly conducted twin studies. We take up the issue of genetic influences in psychopathology again in chapter 11.

Some constitutional factors that are important in increasing risk of disorder in children, and may or may not operate via emotional factors, are developmental delays and cognitive impairments. Children with lower IQ (Anderson et al., 1987; Rutter, Tizard, & Whitmore, 1970), language delay (Richman, Stevenson, & Graham, 1982), and mild cognitive impairments associated with premature birth (Minde et al., 1989) are more likely to develop psychiatric disorder later in childhood.

Protective factors

Just as stresses combine with each other to increase risk, some other factors can combine with risks to make things better (Rutter, 1992). One of the important questions in child psychopathology is why some children develop emotional and behavioral disorders while others exposed to the same risks do not. Think about Peter again. Why did he show disturbance, while his sisters, growing up in the same family, did not? Peter's sisters had each other, they were easier babies, and they each had a better relationship with their mother. The fact that they were girls is also significant – girls are less vulnerable than boys to developing certain kinds of psychopathology.

What factors have been identified in children's lives that protect them from disorder? Children in highly stressful circumstances have fewer problems if they have siblings whom they are close to (Jenkins, 1992), grandparents who are very involved with them (Jenkins & Smith, 1990; Werner & Smith, 1982), or have had experiences of achievement at school (Quinton, Rutter, & Liddle, 1984). Such factors can make the difference between enabling the child to function well despite stress, and succumbing to the effects of stress by developing a disorder. An example of this comes from a study by Jenkins and Smith (Jenkins & Smith, 1990), who interviewed parents and children from homes in which there was a high level of conflict between parents, together with children in a matched sample of families where parental conflict was low.

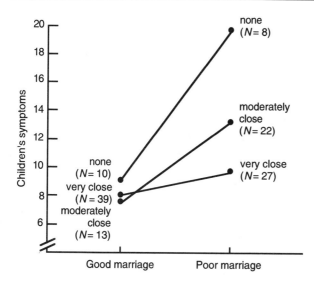

Figure 8.5 The mean number of psychiatric symptoms in children whose parents had good or conflictual marriages, as a function of whether the child had a close relationship with an adult outside the family (Jenkins & Smith, 1990).

By looking at figure 8.5 you can see that children in conflictual homes who had a close relationship with an adult outside the family (usually a grandparent), had lower levels of psychopathology than children without such a relationship. The presence of a grandparent was not a predictor of psychopathology amongst children who did not experience stress. This suggests that grandparents can sometimes compensate for problems in a child's environment.

Schools can also do a lot to protect children from deleterious consequences of stressful home environments (Rutter et al., 1979). One of the most impressive examples has been work done by Comer (1988), a child psychiatrist concerned to improve the life chances of children at high risk both of psychopathology and of failing at school. He began working with two schools in the poorest areas of New Haven, Connecticut. His hypothesis was that black children experienced school failure because of alienation from school. The values of their parents and the values of the school were discrepant. He worked to change the structure of the schools, so that parents were involved in their management and running. A mental health team was set up in the schools to help teachers understand disturbed behavior and to intervene early with children showing disturbance. The schools built links with the community and ran social events at which school personnel and parents from the community got to know one another in nonthreatening circumstances. Before this program started the two schools in which Comer and his team worked had the lowest achievement levels of any in New Haven. Children were frequently expelled for difficult behavior. Ten years later, without any change in the socioeconomic level of the schools' parents, the schools ranked third and fourth highest in the city on mathematics and reading achievement tests – and there have been no serious behavioral problems in the schools for 10 years. This is an important and heartening example of how the lives of children at risk can be significantly improved.

Diathesis–stress: a model of disturbance

What models do we have in psychopathology and in normal emotional development to account for the evidence reviewed in this chapter? In the diathesis–stress model it is proposed that physiological and environmental variables interact to produce psychopathology. Some people are more vulnerable than others to developing psychopathology because of their constitution – including genetic vulnerability, cognitive deficits due to injury at birth, or temperamental factors. Such factors can constitute a diathesis, meaning a predisposition.

Then in people's lives, events and difficulties make demands they cannot cope with. These are the stresses. Children may experience loss of a parent, or a parent not caring for them, or two parents fighting all the time. If a child is without inner resources, or resources in the environment, to cope with such stress, that child's emotional state and behavior can become disordered. When protective factors are present they operate by supporting the person in coping with adversity. Such a model implies factors at different levels: constitutional, familial, and societal, combining with one another to cause or protect from disturbance.

In chapter 7 we saw that constitutional and environmental factors influence the development of patterns of emotional expression. This patterning can be seen as a diathesis. It can be a bias towards particular emotions – for instance, tending always to respond angrily or by withdrawing in dejection or anxiety – when events become stressful. Such emotional biases do not predict when a child will show disturbance, but they are probably important in the type of disturbance that occurs.

Think back once more to Peter. Although other children experience similar risks in their lives, the order in which they occur, their timing, their intensity and the internal experience of these events, make each person's experience unique. Such effects interact to cause an outcome that is much more than the sum of the individual effects. It is quite comprehensible, then, that in studies of psychopathology, when we consider multiple risk factors, we are rarely able to predict more than about 25 to 30 percent of the variance in child psychopathology.

This takes us back to our discussion of dynamic systems that we raised in chapter 6. Emotional development occurs through the interaction of many effects within an individual, and between the individual and the environment. The individual system does become organized in particular ways. Some children are more oriented towards anger, some towards sadness, some towards anxiety. But multiple influences have contributed to this organization. Although we can identify the most severe of these influences, our ability to predict the outcome for individuals remains limited – which is perhaps as it should be. The study of child psychopathology in the last 30 years has made much clearer what the severe risks to children are, and even what can be done effectively to ameliorate them. Yet in the end each person makes her or his own way in the world, and no one can exactly predict the outcome.

Summary

Emotions are involved in child psychopathology because the disorders that constitute the disturbance are themselves emotional: externalizing disorders are characterized by anger and aggression, depression is characterized by sadness, and anxiety is characterized by fear. In many ways the principles of causation of these disorders are similar to those of the causation of smaller emotions. But there are differences between emotions and disorders. Perhaps the principal one is that emotional disorders are usually based on patterns of emotional response rather than single emotions, and the patterns of response reduce children's ability to function in their everyday life. We have argued that these patterns of response are influenced by emotional expression in the family environment: the emotions that children see as well as emotional communications that are directed at them, meanings given to emotional events, as well as how family members respond to the emotional expressions of children. Externalizing disorders are most frequently shown by boys, depression about equally by boys and girls, and anxiety is slightly more frequently shown by girls. Some disorders have quite high continuity, some extending into adulthood. Six principal stresses, or risks for childhood psychopathology, have been identified: (a) conflict between parents; (b) parental depression or other psychiatric problems; (c) neglect, abuse and other such features of parents' relationships with their children; (d) poor socioeconomic circumstances; (e) large family size; (f) and parental criminality. One of these factors on its own does not increase a child's risk of disorder, but two together increase it by a factor of four, four together by a factor of 20. Temperamental and other genetic factors also play a role in increasing risk, and one needs to think about how factors within children combine with environmental events to produce disturbance. At the same time, some factors in children's lives can be protective against stresses – having a sibling with whom a child has a close relationship, having a grandparent with whom the child is close, and being able to do well in some aspect of school life. In general, genetic and other factors produce emotional biases which contribute to predispositions (diatheses) for particular kinds of disorder, and events and difficulties can act as stressors which can trigger and maintain a disorder.

Further Reading

Child psychiatry has a large and useful handbook; see particularly chapters 12 and 13 on the adversities of children and 18, 19, and 20 on the externalizing and internalizing disorders:

Michael Rutter, Eric Taylor, & Lionel Hersov (Eds.). (1994). *Child and adolescent psychiatry: Modern approaches* (3rd ed.). Oxford: Blackwell.

For an excellent introduction to development and the problems of children:

Michael Rutter & Marjorie Rutter (1992). *Developing minds: Challenge and continuity across the life span.* Harmondsworth: Penguin.

A clearly written article about children's vulnerability and resilience:

Emmie Werner (1989, April). Children of the Garden Island. *Scientific American, 260,* 106–111.

For a helpful treatment of the topic of regulation in children:

Pamela Cole, Margaret Michel, & Laureen O'Donnell-Teti (1994). The development of emotion regulation and dysregulation: A clinical perspective. In N. Fox (Ed.), *The development of emotion regulation. Monographs of the Society for Research in Child Development, 59* (2–3, Serial No. 240), 73–103.

CHAPTER 9

Functions and Effects of Emotions in Cognition and Persuasion

Figure 9.0 What is going on in this famous painting? Pierre Auguste Renoir used it to illustrate a story, by Lhote, about an artist seeking to persuade a young woman to model for him. In the painting we see the man thrusting his face eagerly towards the young woman, and grasping her possessively. We also notice from her ring that she is married. Keeping her polite social smile, she turns away: Renoir "Dance at Bougival" 1882–1883 (detail).

Contents

. . . the doctrine of natural selection and the study of natural materials shows that in the absence of anything that could be called a voluntary, human, purpose mechanisms with definite functions can arise, and that the distinction between function and purpose is by no means clear.

Kenneth Craik, 1966, p. 153

Functions of emotions

Perhaps more than anything else the study of emotions has been put on a strong and lasting basis by the recognition of functions. None of the nineteenth century founders of research in the area thought emotions were purposeful. For Darwin, emotional expressions were patterns of action that once had functions, but in adult humans they occurred whether or not they were any use. James thought that emotions were perceptions of inner states, but with no immediate effect on action because they occurred when the real business of producing behavior was over. Freud concentrated on how emotional states could be actively dysfunctional. But within these early approaches are seeds of more recent understandings. Prompted by Darwin's work we now believe that by eliciting species-characteristic outline patterns in situations that have recurred during evolution (Tooby & Cosmides, 1990) emotions have helped adapt humans to the physical and social world. From James's thinking about emotions as perceptions of bodily processes, we can ask how they could serve a monitoring function that could be important. And by Freud drawing attention to dysfunctional aspects, we are reminded to ask about the functions of emotions in everyday life.

Functions of emotions are important not just in terms of evolutionary significance (discussed in chapters 3 and 5) but during individual development as our actions are coordinated with those of other people (as discussed in chapters 6 and 7). In this chapter we extend the argument by discussing two main cognitive properties of emotions: the management of action and the structuring of the cognitive system into distinct modes of organization. The effects of this structuring are to modify perception, to direct attention, to give preferential access to certain memories, and to bias thinking. In the next chapter we discuss functions of emotions in adult social interaction.

Cognitive functions

The movement called cognitive science, growing up in the 1960s, has profoundly altered the way in which researchers think about mental life. The principal method of this new movement is the construction of mind-like processes in computers. The question for cognitive science is this: if one had to design a mind, what problems would have to be faced, what principles embodied, what considerations included – not just for humans, but for any intelligent being? If we can discern some of these general principles then they will be important to understanding human psychology.

In an influential paper Simon (1967) argued that emotions, or something like them, are not just biological. Emotions would be necessary in any intelligent being; in a human, in a Martian, or – if we were ever able to create it – in an intelligent computer. In other words emotions are not just a biological quirk. They are a solution to a general problem. Simon's argument takes Darwin's theory of evolution a step further, applying it to emotions in a way that Darwin did not. Simon asks: what would it take for any cognitive system to be adapted to a complex world, what principles must be embodied in the design of beings that work as we human beings do? "The proper study of mankind," Simon has said, "is design." The challenge to discover design principles is at the heart of cognitive science.

One of the principles had been the subject of a theoretical proposal by Tomkins (1995, discussed in chapter 1): it is that we have many different motivations or goals, and that emotions set priorities among them. Simon argued that as we begin to develop computer programs that have not one but many goals, events will occur that must interrupt what the program is doing. In animals interruptions occur when something happens that is loud or unexpected or that warns of danger, when some physiological need becomes urgent, or when certain cognitive associations alert us to an important meaning. All such events affect our attention – and as Simon said "all the evidence points to a close connection between the operation of the interrupt system and much of what is usually called emotional behavior" (Simon, 1967, p. 36).

This hypothesis of Tomkins and Simon forms a foundation of most modern cognitive approaches to emotions. Emotions function to manage our multiple motives, switching attention from one concern to another when unforeseen events affecting these concerns occur in the world, in the body, or in the mind.

As Mandler (1984) has shown, ideas about the association of emotions with interruptions go back at least to the French psychologist Paulhan (1887). More recently they were proposed as important in the influential book by Miller, Galanter, and Pribram (1960) and in an article by Mandler (1964). Nor was it new to focus upon actions as having effects that might be unpredictable, or on how multiple motives might interfere with one another. These themes had been the focus of classical Greek dramas, of some of Aristotle's work, and much of Freud's. What was new in the era of cognitive science was the idea of just how important emotions (or something like them) are, not just for human beings but for any complex intelligent system that has several motives and which operates in a complex world. Emotions are not just by-products of our biological origins. They point to the fundamental problematics of action in a world that is imperfectly known, and can never be fully controlled.

A cognitive theory that starts from this idea, and integrates the data we have reviewed in chapters 3, 4, and 5 of this book, is that of Oatley & Johnson-Laird

(1987, 1995) who proposed the communicative theory of emotions, based on two different kinds of signaling in the nervous system. One kind is informational. It is the kind with which psychologists and neurophysiologists are familiar. These messages carry information about events, and carry commands to specific destinations. But another, evolutionarily older, and much simpler kind of signal occurs which has been less frequently discussed. It does not carry specific information. It simply controls the brain by setting it into particular modes of organization. These distinctive modes, one for happiness, one for sadness, and so on, underlie emotions and moods. A signal that sets up one of these modes can be started in a number of ways (Izard, 1993). As LeDoux (1993) found in his conditioning experiments, eliciting an emotion does not require participation of the cortex or any conscious awareness. Consider the signal for fear. It spreads through the brain. In humans, it interrupts the ongoing action. It makes ready physiological mechanisms and a repertoire of actions for flight or for defensive fight. It directs attention to the environment for any sign of danger or safety, and it induces checking of the results of actions just completed. In this mode, we can think of the brain as having been simplified, and resources marshaled, to respond to danger. The emotion signal has a control function of turning on this mode, or in moods such as anxiety, which is an extended state of fear, of maintaining the brain in this state despite events that might tend to switch it into some other mode.

Usually, the emotional control signal is accompanied by a signal of the informational kind; so we usually know what started an emotion. Often it is some consciously recognized event: you are embarrassed when you become conscious of being the center of unwelcome attention. But such conscious, intentional, knowledge is not necessary for all emotions. Oatley and Duncan (1992) found that in everyday life subjects reported some incidents of happiness, sadness, anger, and fear, without knowing what caused them. Such emotions – let us call them free-floating emotions – without consciously known causes were rare. Only 6 percent of incidents were free-floating. But the fact that they happen at all is significant because it means that emotions of some kinds can take place without our knowing consciously what caused them, or what their objects are. From the work of Bradwejn (1993) it is known that the neurochemical agent cholecystokinin can give rise to all the symptoms of free-floating fear. It is also known that drugs such as antidepressants and tranquillizers can modulate moods of sadness and anxiety without anything happening in the external world to cause these changes. Moreover the auras of temporal lobe epilepsy, as discussed by MacLean (1993) also indicate that certain emotions can occur without the person who experiences them knowing what started them.

All such evidence indicates that to understand emotions we must think in terms of two kinds of signal. One indicates what has caused the emotion or to whom it is directed. The other controls brain organization and has an emotional tone (happiness, sadness, fear, etc.) but no other content. Normally the two kinds of signal occur together to produce an emotional feeling with a consciously known object. But they can occur separately. Figure 9.1 is a diagram of the two kinds of signal.

Oatley and Johnson-Laird (1987) argued that the function of the control signal is to change the organization of the cognitive system to respond to a distinctive kind of event that has recurred frequently during evolution. There is just a small number of such basic emotional signals, each of which sets up a

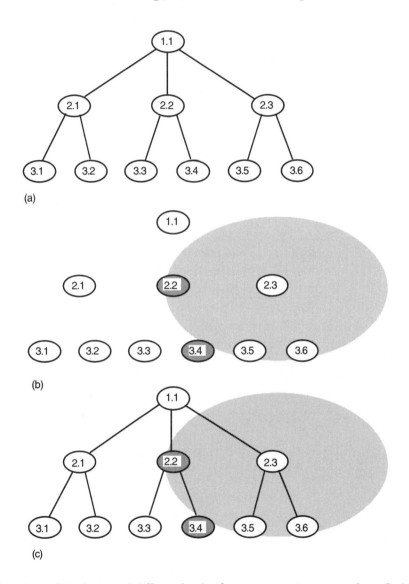

Figure 9.1 Diagram of modules of the brain and different kinds of messages passing among them. In (a) the signals are informational, traveling along particular pathways carrying sensory input, specific commands, and so forth. In (b) is depicted the emotion control signal spreading out diffusely from one of the modules (2.3), turning some of the other modules on, and other modules off. Normally (c) these two kinds of signals occur together, but they can be dissociated (Oatley, 1988).

distinctive mode of brain organization. The number of such modes is less important than the hypothesis that each kind of emotion has specific functions in the life of the species, and that mechanisms have evolved to fulfill these functions.

The primary functions of the basic emotional signals are related to action. So, when some plan is going well, with progress towards some goal and with new events being met with available resources, a signal to continue that line of action spreads, and the emotional tone is happy. We become absorbed in what we are doing, disregarding events that are irrelevant to this activity, or that might run counter to it. The tendency is generally to approach, and to continue. For negative events, interruptions of ongoing activity occur, and there is more differentiation: into emotions of sadness, anger, fear, and perhaps some others. Table 9.1 summarizes the functions and effects of nine basic emotions postulated by Oatley and Johnson-Laird (1995).

Both for the emotions that can occasionally be free-floating, and for those that always have an object, there are usually two parts – the basic emotion control signal that sets up a mode of readiness to act in a particular way, and some information about what elicited the emotion.

Table 9.1 Nine basic emotions, with the functions they perform and the transitions they accomplish. Emotions in the first group can occur without the experiencer knowing what caused them; those in the second group always have an object. In this analysis, plans are goal-directed sequences of action

Emotion (mode)	Eliciting event or object of emotion	Actions to which transition occurs
Emotions that can occasionally be free-floating		
Happiness	Subgoals being achieved	Continue with plan, modifying if necessary; cooperate; show affection
Sadness	Failure of major plan or loss of active goal	Do nothing; search for new plan; seek help
Anger	Active plan frustrated	Try harder; aggress
Fear	Self-preservation goal threatened or goal conflict	Stop current plan; attend vigilantly to environment; freeze and/or escape
Emotions that always have an object		
Attachment love	Caregiver	Keep contact; talk
Caregiving love	Offspring	Nurture; help; support
Sexual love	Sexual partner	Engage in courtship; sexual activity
Disgust	Contamination	Reject substance; withdraw
Contempt	Outgroup person	Treat without consideration

Source: Oatley and Johnson-Laird (1995)

It is not accepted by everyone that emotions can be grouped into basic functional families as in table 9.1. The core of this hypothesis is that there is a limited number of such signals, each based on a specific system that has evolved to set the brain into a state of readiness appropriate for a recurring kind of important event in the life of the species. These mechanisms are based in the limbic system: but in humans each instinctual pattern also comes to have its own meanings within a society, and is modified – using the processing of the cortex – by culture and individual development.

Rationality and emotions

Think of the functions of emotions as midway between very simple and very complex control of behavior (De Sousa, 1987; Oatley, 1992). In very simple animals behavior is controlled by reflexes. The behavior of the female tick, for instance, is controlled in this way (Von Uexküll, 1934). After mating, she climbs a tree and hangs at the end of a lower twig. When she detects a particular stimulus – the smell of butyric acid – she lets go. Because butyric acid is released into the air in small quantities by mammals, letting go the branch in response to this stimulus gives a fair probability of falling onto the back of a passing mammal, such as a browsing deer brushing beneath the branch on which the tick is hanging. If the tick lands on a mammal's back, another stimulus comes to control behavior: warm temperature causes the tick to climb through the fur towards the warmth. When she reaches the mammal's skin, another stimulus triggers burrowing into it, to suck the mammal's blood, which will be necessary for laying her eggs.

The tick's behavior is understandable, even rational. But the tick's world is a very simple one. All complexity is missed. The perceptual system is tuned just to a few kinds of event. And in the tick's world there is no hint of emotionality.

Now imagine a different kind of being at the other end of the scale of complexity, one vastly more intelligent than ourselves, perhaps a god. A god is often conceived of as omniscient and omnipotent – or as a cognitive psychologist might say, having a perfect mental model of the universe and no limitations of resources. Such a being, then, could predict the results of its actions even in a complex universe. Again there is no place for emotions. Everything is known, everything anticipated.

We humans and other mammals are somewhere in between ticks and gods. Our world is complex and we act with purposes – but our actions sometimes produce effects we did not anticipate. We have limitations of resources and knowledge, so sometimes we need prompting to continue with what we were doing, or to switch goals and change plans. Because we are not self-sufficient we cooperate with other people in many of our more important goals, but our communication with these others is not perfect. All this means that for us human beings events occur – small successes, losses, frustrations, threats – for which we have no ready prepared response, no skill or habit that works, not enough knowledge to be completely certain what to do next. And when such events occur, emotions signal them. They do not tell us exactly what to do next, we typically do not know enough. What they do is prompt us in a way that on average, during the course of evolution and assisted by our own development, has been better either than simply acting randomly or than becoming lost in thought trying to calculate the best possible action.

An emotion, then, is based on something like a built-in inference about what has happened and what to do next. The philosopher Peirce called such inferences "guesses" or "abductions," and among these he included emotions. Without abductive abilities, said Peirce, "the human race would long ago have been extirpated for its utter incapacity in the struggles for existence" (quoted in Sebeok & Umiker-Sebeok, 1983, p. 17). Thus fear is a kind of inference in response to specific kinds of event, implying that these events are dangerous, and it prompts particular kinds of actions: to interrupt the current action, to freeze, to prepare to flee or fight, and so forth. During evolution such mechanisms of recognition and response have been compiled into the nervous systems of animals including ourselves. Emotional abductions have therefore become implicit (Polanyi, 1966). They occur without our needing to say to ourselves, "this situation is dangerous." Instead, we simply feel frightened, and the brain becomes specialized to respond to that kind of situation.

Emotions as heuristics

Why might such simplifications be adaptive? The reason is that the world is a complex place. Even the cleverest of us, equipped with libraries, skills, technology, and all the other knowledge amassed over the last three thousand years could not know it fully or predict it entirely. Another way to put this is that only very seldom can human beings act completely rationally – seldom can we know enough to predict the best course of action. Moreover, we often have goals that are incompatible with each other, so there is no course of action that would satisfy them all. But this complexity does not remove the necessity for acting. What evolution has equipped us with, therefore, is a set of emotional states that organize ready repertoires of action. Although not perfect, emotions are better than doing nothing, or than acting randomly, or than becoming lost in thought. Emotions are heuristics.

A heuristic is a method of doing something that is usually useful when there is no guaranteed solution. In problem solving (Polya, 1957), or in computing, it can be compared with an algorithm that guarantees a solution. Except for certain technical problems, there are few algorithms in human life – mostly we rely on heuristics, and emotions provide us with our basic package of them, for coping with some of the problems that arise.

Emotions in the management of action

The following paragraphs briefly sketch, without many qualifications, the emotions that Oatley and Johnson-Laird (1995) propose as basic, to indicate their nature, their elicitation, and their functions within the individual – in chapter 10 we concentrate on the function of emotions between people.

Emotions that can occasionally be free-floating

Four basic emotions can be free-floating (nonintentional); this happens only rarely, when the emotion control signal on which they are based occurs without the person knowing what has caused it. Usually, however, the control signal occurs with another signal indicating what caused the emotion. Because these four emotions can be free-floating, even in normal life, they are also the basis of moods: enjoyment, depression, irritability, and anxiety.

Happiness

Happiness is the emotion or mood of achieving subgoals, of being engaged in what one is doing. When happy, as Isen and her colleagues have shown (see table 1.2), the brain is more flexibly organized. In one of Isen's demonstrations (Isen et al., 1987) subjects were made happy, or left in their previous emotional state, by watching a funny or a neutral film. They were given a problem: to use only a box of tacks, a book of matches, and a candle, and fix the candle to a cork-board wall so that it could be lit. The tacks were not long enough to pass through the candle, and in any case they just broke it when pressed into it. The solution was to empty out all the tacks, and pin part of the box to the wall as a holder for the candle. After watching the neutral film 20 percent or fewer people found this solution in 10 minutes, but in one experiment 75 percent, and in another 58 percent, of subjects who had watched the funny film solved this problem in 10 minutes. Isen explained this by arguing that happiness makes cognitive organization more flexible, and produces more unusual associations. Happiness has been found to prompt people to aim for higher goals (Hom & Arbuckle, 1988), as well as to continue in what they are doing, and to resist change to some other state. When happy we are also more helpful and cooperative. Some activities are entered into merely to enjoy them – games, vacations, reading novels, conversations. It is not that during such activities other emotions are absent; rather, we become happily engaged in what we are doing, without distractions, and are able to cope easily with what happens as it occurs.

Sadness

Sadness is an opposite of happiness. It is the emotion of losing a goal or social role, and knowing it cannot be reinstated. As compared with fear, which looks towards the future, sadness looks towards the past. As compared with anger, there is resignation about the event that caused it, rather than taking up arms against it. It is related to grief, to depression, to remorse, to regret, all of which imply some internal reorientation. In sadness we come to focus on the self, and reassess ourselves in relation to what has happened. As Stearns (1993) points out, however, the emotion has been understood differently in former historical periods. Sad derives from the term "sated." In former European societies, moreover, it had a more culturally valued meaning of something like dignified, bearing troubles with acceptance and patience. In other cultures too there are differences. Thus Lutz (1988) describes how on Ifaluk the term *fago* means compassion/love/sadness – a highly valued emotion felt towards those who are cared about, and might be lonely or needy in any way. In our more achievement-oriented society, when sadness is occasioned by a loss, it functions to prompt disengagement from that goal. When the loss that caused it is the death of someone close, it is accompanied by societal rituals to mark and facilitate mourning, but when prolonged it is seen as pathological, as depression.

Anger

Anger is the emotion of asserting ourselves in dominance. More generally it is the emotion of frustration with anything we are trying to do, or with anyone who impedes us or who shows lack of consideration. If a goal that is obstructed looks as if it could be reinstated, anger makes us try harder. If some remedy for our frustration seems possible, anger makes us become aggressive and vengeful. As Berkowitz (1993) has shown in many experiments, anger can be induced by subjecting people to restraints or to pain, and it prompts aggression either towards the person who is being frustrating, or to someone else who happens to be a convenient target. At the same time, as Averill (1982) has shown, angry arguments often lead to renegotiation when expectations we have of friends, relations, or associates, have been disappointed.

Fear

Fear is the emotion of anticipated danger. With a threat in the environment, a conflict between our own goals, or a lack of resources, fear sets the system into a mode of readiness to cope with the danger; it promotes vigilance for the feared event, and it monopolizes attention. Fear may involve a family of responses; Kalin (1993) has shown three kinds in baby rhesus monkeys. One occurs when they are left alone: the infants coo, a sound that functions to call their mothers. Another is to freeze: this functions to avoid detection by a nearby predator, and it can be elicited by a human standing outside their cage, but not looking at them. A third is to make a threatening display. The function is to scare off a potential attacker, and it can be elicited when a human looks directly at the infant monkey. Each of these has its own neurochemical mechanism, and it is selectively affected by different pharmaceutical manipulations. We think of fear as highly unpleasant – and indeed people suffering fear in panic attacks sometimes say this feeling is worse than any other experience. But this does not mean it is dysfunctional. Like pain that functions to protect the body from further injury, the intense unpleasantness and exclusion of other issues means the matter is important.

Emotions that always have an object

Five other basic emotions (the emotions of love and rejection) are always felt towards a goal of some kind. In psychological terms they are said to have objects; in philosophical terms they are always intentional. We can ask what the nature of these objects is. The object of emotions of love and rejection is a person seen by means of a mental model. The reason for thinking that there is a mental intermediate between our feeling and the relevant person or thing in the world is that, as Darwin (1872) pointed out, all these emotions can be elicited not just by the person or thing itself, but by a mere idea. So we can feel attracted to a film star who can mean nothing to us personally. In all the object-based emotions there is an element of our projecting qualities onto the object which it may or may not have: in love we idealize, in rejection we denigrate.

Attachment love

Attachment love is the emotion of an offspring for its mother or other caregiver. It is shown by gazing, following, wanting to be with the caregiver, being more animated in her or his presence than when with others, being able to use this person as a secure base from which to explore; conversely, being anxious when this person is absent, and sad if she or he is lost. In attachment, the infant builds a model of the caregiver and the extent to which she or he can be trusted, that allows recognition of this person, and later allows retention of an idea of the caregiver even when absent.

Caregiving love

Caregiving love is the reciprocal of attachment – love of a parent, or other caregiver, for an offspring. Parents must fall in love with their babies to sustain the concern, preoccupation, care, time, and other resources that need to be lavished on a baby. Without this emotional attraction, the degree of commitment that children require would be too great: children produce more preoccupation and require more resources than any other single kind of object in human life, with the possible exception of acquiring food. Caregiving love can also be felt for others, such as sexual partners.

Sexual love

When people fall in love, typically, they are attracted to their idea of the other person. It may take years to adjust to the reality. This emotion too has a biological basis. It has been described in most cultures (Jankowiak & Fischer,

261

1992), and it has elements that are clearly derived from courtship and mating in other animals.

Disgust

Disgust is the emotion of revulsion and of avoidance of anything that makes one sick, literally or metaphorically. Rozin et al. (Rozin & Fallon, 1987; Rozin, Haidt, & McCauley, 1993) have traced disgust from an innate rejection of substances because they are decayed, infectious, or toxic. The mechanism is one in which revulsion is easily learned and associated with a taste or smell. The distaste for taking something into our mouths is accompanied by a feeling of nausea. In humans, not just sights and smells cause this emotion, but ideas. So there is disgust for contamination by objects that might be touched, or even thought about, for example sexual practices that we find objectionable. People are disgusted at a plastic fly in their drink, even though they know it is quite clean, whereas they do not object to a stirring stick made of the same material.

Contempt

Contempt is the emotion of interpersonal rejection, particularly as it concerns members of outgroups. A term often used in this context is prejudice: rejection of and discrimination against another person purely on the basis of an idea. The idea can occur as one switches from a positive evaluation of a person to a negative one. It can also occur when one does not know the other person at all – one merely has an idea of the person as being of opposite gender, as of a different race, as having a handicap one does not share. None of these need be based on the actual person.

Why not just think of emotions as positive or negative?

Classifying emotions as positive and negative, or pleasant and unpleasant, is often useful and it has been the center of several influential treatments of emotions and moods (Russell, 1980; Watson & Tellegen, 1985). Positive and negative dimensions can be mapped onto approach and avoidance. According to functional arguments, however, just a positive–negative dimension makes some emotions confusing. Consider anger: although the majority of incidents of anger feel bad (Averill, 1982), it is nevertheless an emotion of approach, and even of reconciliation on a new basis. Our position is that positive evaluations arise from subgoals being likely to be achieved (including the goals of being close to a loved one) and generally involves approach; negative evaluations arise when a goal is less likely to be achieved than expected, and often prompt withdrawal. But during evolution, more differentiation has occurred than implied by just approach–avoidance, or pleasure–displeasure. Differentiated emotions prompt more appropriate classes of behavior and brain organization than could just pleasantness and unpleasantness.

Effects of moods and emotions on cognitive functioning

We can think of moods and emotions as having two kinds of effect on the individual. One that we have just discussed is immediate: the core of an emotion is a change in readiness, making available a repertoire of actions that have previously been useful in that circumstance. But emotions usually last for a while, and they sometimes extend into moods. As well as effects in changing readiness, emotions prompt the search for possible plans; by changing cognitive organization they help guide this search.

We can all smile knowingly at the idea that executives offer free lunches with a view towards inclining their guest favorably towards a business proposition. As discussed in chapter 1, Isen (1990) has found in experiments since 1970 that small gifts and anything that causes mild happiness have measurable effects on a range of cognitive and social processes (see table 1.2). Happiness, like other basic emotions, is a distinctive mode of organization of the brain. It produces a simplification of the full set of possible brain processes and operations, and has been evolutionarily selected to deal with things when activities are going well. What are these changes in cognitive organization caused by happiness and other emotions? In the following sections we will focus on just three such effects: on attention, on memory, and on thinking.

Perceptual effects

One consequence of the idea that there may be basic emotional modes is that the influence of these modes could be detected in perception. Etcoff and Magee (1992) have demonstrated such an effect. They argued that if there were basic emotions, then facial expressions would be recognized in categories. All happy faces would be sorted into one category, angry ones into another, and so forth. Perception of these expressions should be comparable to certain phenomena in the perception of speech. What distinguishes a spoken "b" from "p" in words like "bit" and "pit" is the time between the mouth opening and the onset of sound made by the larynx, called "voicing onset time." People are bad at making discriminations of voicing onset time on either side of the b-p boundary, but they are excellent at discriminations across this boundary, indicating that time differences of a few milliseconds are sorted into functional categories to define "b" and "p." Etcoff and Magee did an experiment on faces: they created several series of faces ranging between pairs of states: happy to neutral, happy to sad, angry to disgusted, and so forth. To do this they traced faces from expressions of six basic emotions and a neutral face in photographs taken by Ekman and Friesen (1975) and used the caricature-generating computer program of Brennan (1985). For each pair of states they created 11-point scales with exactly equal increments of transition. You can see the series of 11 faces from happiness to sadness in figure 9.2. They found that for these series there were abrupt shifts in discriminability between the faces,

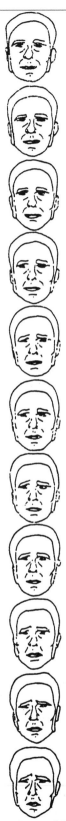

Figure 9.2 Series of faces in equal increments from happy to sad.

indicating a boundary between, for instance, happy and sad, angry and disgusted, and so forth. On either side of the boundary, people were not good at telling the difference between, for instance, the second and fourth faces in such series, but across the boundary, for instance between the fourth and sixth faces in the series, they were good. This experiment implies that functional categories of basic emotions affect discriminability of facial expressions.

What about effects of mood on perception? Are we more tuned to perceiving things that are congruent with our mood? Such effects have been difficult to demonstrate. An explanation for this difficulty, offered by Niedenthal and Setterlund (1994), is that previous attempts at demonstrations have used a positive–negative dimension. In two experiments they found an effect of selective perception of specific emotions of happiness and sadness, but not of a generally positive and negative dimension.

Niedenthal and Setterlund induced happy and sad moods by giving their subjects earphones and playing music throughout the experimental session. To put people in a happy mood they played pieces such as the allegro from Mozart's *Eine Kleine Nacht Musik*, and parts of Vivaldi's Concerto in C Major. To induce sadness they played pieces such as *Adagietto* by Mahler, and the adagio from the Piano Concerto No. 2 in C Minor by Rachmaninov. The task subjects performed was standard in experimental psychology: a lexical decision task. Strings of letters were flashed on a screen: some were words, some were nonwords (strings of letters that do not appear in the dictionary but that can be pronounced in English, like "blatkin"). Subjects were asked to work as quickly as possible to press one button if the string of letters was a word, another if it was a nonword. In this study words were from five categories: happy words such as "delight," positive words but unrelated to happiness such as "calm," sad words like "weep," negative words unrelated to sadness like "injury," and neutral words like "habit."

Niedenthal and Setterlund found that the music did indeed put people into happy or sad moods. Overall, subjects made decisions more quickly for happy than for sad words; and moreover, when in a happy mood they were quicker at identifying happy than sad words. Conversely when sad, they were quicker at identifying sad than happy words. But the effects of happy and sad moods did not extend to the positive or negative words that were unrelated to the specific emotions of happiness or sadness.

Attentional qualities of emotions

William James, in his textbook of psychology (1890, vol. 1, p. 402) wrote: "My experience is what I agree to attend to." It is also what we attend to even when we do not consciously agree to it. Emotions affect attention. The effects range from largely unconscious processes of filtering incoming information to conscious preoccupation of the kind that we have when we worry.

The most fully researched effects of emotions on attention concern anxiety: it is clear that anxiety narrows attention. When people are fearful or anxious they focus mainly on what they are afraid of, or on safety from this thing, and they disregard almost everything else. Many effects of anxiety on attention can be demonstrated in the laboratory. Mathews and others (Broadbent & Broadbent, 1988; Mathews, 1993) have used a method in which two words are flashed, one above the other, on a screen, then these are replaced by a dot. One of the words is threatening like "failure" or "disease." The other is neutral, like "table." Subjects are instructed that when the dot appears they should press a button. Some subjects are anxious, as indicated by a scale of trait anxiety; others do not have an anxiety trait. When the dot appears in the position where the threat word was, anxious people have a shorter reaction time to its appearance than nonanxious people. When the dot appears in the position of the neutral word, there is no difference between the anxious and the nonanxious people. The explanation offered by Mathews is that reaction time is shorter when the dot appears in the position of the word that the subject was actively attending to. Anxious subjects are much more likely to be looking at the threat word rather than the neutral one. This kind of finding has been replicated with clinically anxious patients as well as with people with an anxious trait of personality.

A similar kind of experiment is based on the so-called emotional Stroop test. Stroop (1935) found that if subjects were asked to look at words such as "red," "yellow," "blue," that were printed in different colors, and to name the color of the *print* for each word, they were slowed down when the color of the print and the color word were different – they were slower if the word "red" were printed in blue ink and they had to say "blue," than if it were printed in red ink and they had to say "red." The meaning of the word involuntarily captures attention, distracting subjects from naming the ink color. This idea of the emotional Stroop test is that words are shown that are neutral or that have emotional significance, to see if people are slowed down in naming the colors in which words with emotional significance are printed.

Foa et al. (1991) found that people who had been the victims of rape were slowed down in naming the print-colors of words that were related to rape. People who had coped with their trauma better showed less interference. Mathews (1993) summarizes the conclusions of the many experiments that have been conducted with this technique: the slowing of color naming is greatest with words that correspond to the subjects' greatest anxiety. Thus people who have a social phobia are slowed by words about confidence, people with eating disorders are slowed by words for food, and so forth. Mathews and Klug (1993) found that the words did not have to be threatening to produce this effect: the issue was whether they were emotionally significant. If the emotional words included such terms as "confident" or "healthy" then people who were socially anxious or were anxious about disease would be slowed in naming color-printed positive words, but only when these positive concepts were related to their own specific anxiety. These results are illustrated in figure 9.3. Look at this figure, and compare the two right-hand bars of the histogram with all the other bars. You can see that the subjects who were anxious were slower than control subjects in naming the colors of those words that were related to their specific anxieties, whether these words were positive or negative.

A number of explanations have been put forward for these effects of attention. The most straightforward is that when people are fearful – either because of some immediate fear, or because they are suffering from an anxiety state that makes them fearful for much of the time – their nervous system is switched into a particular mode of processing. This mode is one in which attention is narrowed, and directed to cues in the environment about threat and safety. It is even more specifically tuned for cues related to particular objects of a person's anxiety. For instance, people who believe themselves vulnerable to cancer are induced to worry whenever they experience anything, including very uncancerlike bodily symptoms, that reminds them of their vulnerability (Easterling & Leventhal, 1989).

In the normal course of events the mechanism of fear and anxiety has no doubt been invaluable for our survival but, it seems, it can get switched on almost permanently, occupying people's cognitive resources, making the world a frightening place, undermining confidence, and preventing the sufferers from concentrating on much else. We will discuss this further in chapter 11. One issue that several researchers have pointed to is that emotions exist at a number of levels – at the level of basic reflex-like mechanisms, at the level of more complex emotional schemas, and at the level of our concepts of our emotions and their effects (Leventhal, 1991). A continuing problem is how we can use

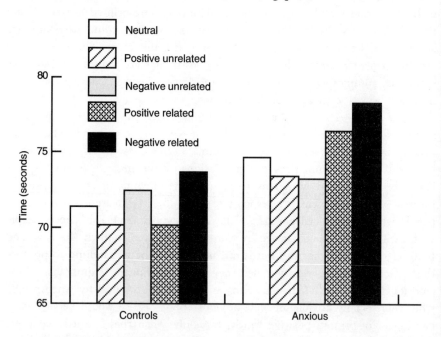

Figure 9.3 Mean times for anxious and control subjects to name colors in which words were printed. Words were neutral, related to the anxious subjects' specific anxieties, and threatening words unrelated to their anxieties (Matthews & Klug, 1993).

our conceptual understandings of ourselves to modulate lower level processes such as those of anxiety (Bandura, 1988).

Emotions and memory

To understand the effect of emotions on memory, we need first to say something about how memory in general works. One can make a strong case that the most important study of memory so far completed has been that of Bartlett (1932). He gave people meaningful material such as pictures or stories to remember, then asked them to reproduce it as exactly as possible, both immediately after being presented with it, and at intervals up to several years later – see box 9.1.

Box 9.1 Bartlett's study of remembering

Bartlett (1932) had people read an American Indian folk story, collected by Franz Boas. The story starts like this:

> One night two young men from Egulac went down to the river to hunt seals, and while they were there it became foggy and calm. Then they heard war-cries, and they thought: "Maybe this is a war party." They escaped to the shore, and hid behind a log. Now canoes came up, and they heard the noise of paddles, and saw one canoe coming up to them. There were five men in the canoe, and they said:
> "What do you think? We wish to take you along. We are going up the river to make war on the people."
> One of the young men said: 'I have no arrows."
> "Arrows are in the canoe," they said.
> "I will not go along. I might be killed. My relatives do not know where I have gone. But you," he said, turning to the other, "may go with them."
> So one of the young men went . . .

There follow 11 lines about how the young man who went took part in a fight in which he was shot but did not feel sick, and thinks "Oh, they are ghosts." The story ends like this, after his return home.

> He told it all, and then he became quiet. When the sun rose he fell down. Something black came out of his mouth. His face became contorted. The people jumped up and cried.
> He was dead.

After reading the story through twice people were asked to reproduce it. Here is is the start of the first reproduction by Subject H, 20 hours later.

> Two men from Edulac went fishing. While thus occupied by the river they heard a noise in the distance.

"It sounds like a cry," said one, and presently there appeared some men in canoes who invited them to join the party on their adventure. One of the young men refused to go on the ground of family ties, but the other offered to go . . .

Notice what has happened. Some material is lost – forgotten, like the number of men in the canoe, and one young man saying he could not go because he had no arrows. Then there are other more subtle changes, including a change in style, so that now phrases like "on the ground of family ties" appear; now also the young men were fishing not hunting for seals, the war party is an adventure, and one of the young men "offers" to go whereas in the story he just goes with no mention of an offer.

Next, here is a reproduction by Bartlett's subject P, who had been asked to reproduce the story several times in the first months after reading it, but had then not thought of it for two and a half years:

Some warriors went to wage war against the ghosts. They fought all day and one of their number was wounded.

They returned home in the evening, bearing their sick comrade. As the day drew to a close, he became rapidly worse and the villagers came round him. At sunset he sighed: something black came out of his mouth. He was dead.

In this version much is lost – such as the whole introductory sequence about the two young men going hunting for seals – and also much is changed. Now the man dies at sunset rather than sunrise. But the single striking detail "something black came out of his mouth" is preserved here, as it was in most of the reproductions that Bartlett reported.

What Bartlett concluded is that when we remember a verbal account the words are never exact. What happens is that what we perceive is assimilated into our own structure of meaning, that Bartlett called a schema, which includes a great deal of general knowledge. Then when a recall is asked for, the subject takes a few significant remembered details and a general emotional attitude to the story, and from the schema constructs what the story must have been. So style becomes the subject's style, details such as "to hunt seals" become "fishing," and things happen in ways appropriate to the culture of the person remembering, such as dying in the evening rather than at sunrise.

Bartlett notes that his subjects did the experiment towards the end of World War I when in Britain the anxiety-provoking issue of separation from family was very salient. Men had either been to the war, or were faced by the probability of going. In one group of subjects, half male and half female, 10 out of 20 people in their early reproductions omitted mentioning that one of the young men said he could not go on the war party because he had no arrows, but only two forgot the excuse about relatives. In later reproductions the whole issue of excuses tended to be forgotten.

Loftus and Loftus (1980) gave people the following two statements and asked them to say which better described their belief about how memory worked.

(a) Everything we learn is permanently stored in the mind, although sometimes particular details are not accessible. With hypnosis or other special techniques these inaccessible details could eventually be recovered.

(b) Some details that we learn may be permanently lost from memory. Such details would never be able to be recovered by hypnosis or any other special technique because these details are simply no longer there.

Loftus found that 69 percent of the general public believed statement (a) – it is a kind of folk belief in our society, the kind of thing that might change on learning about Bartlett and the psychology of memory. This issue has come into prominence recently with the many cases now being discussed in the media about adults reporting that after being unable to remember being sexually abused in childhood, with the help of a therapist they could now remember such incidents. The issue is very controversial: on one side are those such as Bass and Davis (1988) who argue that memories of emotionally traumatic abuse can be repressed and then recovered; on the other side are those who argue that the memories are false and have been induced by suggestion at the hands of therapists who believe in the phenomenon (Ofshe & Watters, 1994). One relevant finding is that the proportion of people working in the mental health field who believe statement (a) above was 84 percent, much higher than the proportion of the general public.

There is no evidence that people can remember scenes in perfect detail, and with perfect accuracy, as if they were stored in some internal video recording. Though memory is often good, even people with the most accurate memories make some mistakes. Moreover, there is evidence that features introduced after the event – for instance mentioned by other people or suggested by leading questions – are incorporated into memories, so that as far as the subject is concerned these become indistinguishable from the real memory. As Bartlett said, remembering "is an imaginative reconstruction, built out of the relation of our [emotional] attitude towards a whole active mass of organized past reactions or experience, and to a little outstanding detail . . . It is thus hardly ever really exact . . . and it is not at all important that it should be" (1932, p. 213).

In some cases it is important to be exact, for example, when giving evidence in a court of law. So here is the issue for research on emotions: do intense emotions increase or decrease the accuracy of what is remembered? Let us start this with a brief passage by the Russian novelist Esther Salaman (1982) in an essay about autobiography.

I have a memory of being bitten by a dog when I was three. I have always remembered this. I am standing outside the closed front door when suddenly I see a big dog bounding towards me, his broken rope trailing on the left; there is no snow or mud, the season is late spring . . . The moment that came back after fifty years was this: the dog has knocked me over, and I am actually turning my head away and burying my face in the earth while the dog is searching between my petticoats and the long black stockings on my left leg for bare flesh to dig his teeth into. It is like a picture in slow motion. Today I am writing only a memory of a memory, but at the time it came back to me I actually was that child of three; the "then" was "now," and time stood still. (Salaman, 1982, p. 56)

Salaman discusses other such incidents of events of her own life, and from other writers including De Quincy, Martineau, and Proust, memories that arise involuntarily, often after many years. She says they are always associated with emotions, and give the sense of reliving the past. The sense of conviction in such memories can be overwhelming, unshakable, but what about their veracity – a quite different question needing a quite different approach. It needs studies with independent corroboration.

We can start to answer some of the questions with a study by Linton (1982) that she conducted on her own memory. For six years she wrote down brief descriptions of at least two significant events each day on filing cards. On the reverse of each card she wrote its date. She also rated each event on a scale of emotional salience. At the end of each month she sampled pairs of events from the whole pool of memories collected until then, to see if she could remember the order in which they had happened, and she re-evaluated each event's emotional salience. She found that events that seemed distinctive at the time were completely lost from her memory at the rate of about 5 percent a year. To be well remembered as a discrete memory, she concluded, an event had to be not only distinctive at the time but unique – for instance the first time she did something emotionally significant to her. An example was that she was delighted to be elected to a distinguished board that met occasionally at a distant city; a significant event was the first meeting she attended. When events of the same type were repeated, their distinctiveness was lost, and replaced by more general information. So as she continued going to meetings of the board she came to know the layout of the airport of the city they met in, the styles of members of the board at meetings, their relationships to each other, but without being able to remember what had occurred at which meeting. For events that became part of the pattern of her life, distinct episodic memories were lost and became transformed into semantic memory.

Linton concluded that emotional events that remain in memory as distinct episodes must have the following features.

1 The event must be salient and perceived as strongly emotional at the time it occurs (or it must be "rewritten" shortly thereafter).

2 Your life's subsequent course must make the target event focal in recall; the event must be a turning point, the beginning of a sequence, or instrumental in later activities.

3 The event must remain relatively unique. Its image must not be blurred by subsequent occurrences of similar events. (Linton, 1982, pp. 89–90)

You can begin to see from Linton's conclusions why particular events that have emotional significance are also remembered well as discrete episodes. Exactly those features which give emotional impact to an event – their importance to a goal, their unusualness, their unpredictability, the absence of preexisting skills to deal with them – make the event distinctive in memory. Note too that Linton says that the event must be "strongly emotional at the time," or that it must be "rewritten" shortly thereafter. Some events, perhaps meeting a new person, may not seem significant immediately, but if we were to fall in love we would start to think about that person a lot, and the mental preoccupation caused by the emotion would also act to rehearse the events of the first meeting, so that they would remain memorable.

Waganaar (1986) repeated Linton's study. In his main series of incidents he recorded an event from his own life every day for four years. He had made up standard forms, and for each event he wrote whom it concerned, what it was, where it happened, and when. He also described a critical detail about each event, and he rated the event on three scales: salience (how frequently events such as this occurred, from every day to once in a lifetime), emotional involvement, and pleasantness. A colleague transcribed all the events into typewritten booklets, so that on recall he could be given one, two, three, or all

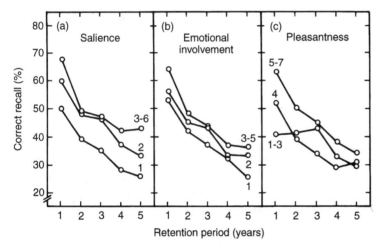

Figure 9.4 The results of Waganaar's study of his own autobiographical memory, with a four-year period of recording events, followed by a year of recalling them. In each graph the percentage of events correctly recalled when all the cues were given is shown as a function of three variables over five years. In (a) the variable is salience; the line marked 3–6 indicates events of the kind that happen once a month to once in a lifetime, 2 indicates the kind that happen once a week, and 1 indicates the kind that happen once a day. In (b) the variable of emotional involvement has a line marked 3–5 for moderately to extremely involving, one marked 2 indicating little involvement, and one marked 1 meaning no involvement. In (c), the variable of pleasantness, the line marked 5–7 means pleasant to extremely pleasant, 4 means neutral, and 1–3 means unpleasant to extremely unpleasant.

four, of the recall cues (who, what, where, when) in order. His task was to recall all the other cues, and when all four had been given, also to recall the critical detail. If he were unsuccessful in all these the event was scored as completely forgotten. Over a period of five years, the numbers of events forgotten were about 20 percent. Waganaar found that in general emotionally involving events were remembered better than uninvolving ones, and pleasant events were recalled better than unpleasant events, see figure 9.4. This result was predicted by Freud – that we do protect ourselves somewhat from unpleasant thoughts.

Emotional involvement and eyewitness testimony

What if you are an eyewitness to a crime, how will your memory for that event be affected? Psychologists know from Bartlett's (1932) principles (discussed above) and from specific research (Loftus & Doyle, 1987), that eyewitness testimony usually has mistakes. Neither certainty nor vividness guarantee that "remembered" details are correct. In Britain the Devlin Report (of an official committee set up to examine cases of wrongful conviction for crimes) recommended that it is not reliable to convict someone on the basis of eyewitness testimony unless the circumstances are exceptional or the testimony is corroborated by evidence of some other kind.

There has now been a large amount of research on memory for emotional events (Christianson, 1992). Here is an influential study. Five months after a thief had held up a gun shop in a suburb of Vancouver, Yuille and Cutshall (1986) were able to reinterview 13 witnesses, previously interviewed by the police, about the event. The thief had tied up the owner of the shop, and left with money and several guns. The owner had freed himself, taken a revolver, and gone out to take the thief's car number. The thief had not yet departed and, in full view of several people, he shot the shop owner twice. After a pause the shop owner fired all six rounds of his revolver at the thief, who died. The shop owner recovered. Because the thief was dead, and there were no legal complications, Yuille and Cutshall were able to gain access to police files, to reconstruct events from the rather complete forensic evidence of the event, including police photographs, and from the testimony of the witnesses where they corroborated each other. Yuille and Cutshall made up a list of details of actions, of people present, and of objects.

In their research interview, Yuille and Cutshall found that witnesses who had contact with the store owner or the thief rated themselves as very stressed by this event, and had had difficulty sleeping for several nights after it, though other less involved witnesses were not so stressed. Witnesses were fairly accurate about the event, including incidental details such as the color of the thief's car and of the blanket that was used to cover his body. At the police interview the stressed witnesses correctly remembered 93.36 percent of the details, and at the research interview five months later 88.24 percent of details. The accuracy of the less stressed individuals was lower: approximately 75 percent in both the police interview and the later research interview. So for

Figure 9.5 The three versions of the critical eighth slide in the sequence used by Christianson and Loftus: scene (a) is neutral, (b) unusual, and (c) emotionally shocking.

emotionally involving events it seems likely that accuracy is increased. But such events are also subject to the processes of reconstruction that Bartlett discussed. Pynoos and Nader (1989) interviewed children who attended a school where a sniper had "shot repeated rounds of ammunition at children on an elementary school playground" (p. 236) from an apartment opposite the school in Los Angeles on February 24, 1984. One passer-by and one child were killed, and 13 other children and a playground attendant were wounded. In the accounts of 113 children who were interviewed between 6 and 16 weeks afterwards, characteristic distortions occurred. Children who had been wounded tended to have emotionally distanced themselves from the event, and five did not even mention their minor gunshot injuries when interviewed. By contrast children who were not at school that day, or who were on their way home, tended to place themselves nearer to the events.

Naturalistic studies do not allow full corroboration of an actual event, so such studies are supplemented by laboratory experiments even though, of course, the same degree of emotional shock and involvement is never attained. Together with general principles, however, such studies give valuable insights. Christianson and Loftus (1991) report five experiments in which 397 students in Sweden and the USA watched a set of 15 color slides of what a person might see leaving home and walking to work. In each slide there was a central detail, and a peripheral detail. There were three versions of the critical eighth slide – shown in figure 9.5. In a neutral version the central detail was a woman cycling along the road just in front of a car. In an unusual version a woman was walking in the road in front of a car carrying a bicycle upside down. In an emotional version a woman was lying at the side of the road evidently injured and bleeding, near an upturned bicycle and just in front of a car. In each case the woman's coat was either blue or beige. In all versions the peripheral detail was a Volvo 242 car in the distance, which was either white or orange. Christianson and Loftus found that subjects who saw the emotional version of the eighth slide remembered the central details of the woman and the color of her coat better than those who saw the neutral version. By contrast the peripheral detail for the emotional version was remembered less well than that of the neutral slide. The unusual version of the eighth slide was meant to control for the fact that emotional events are typically unusual: but as compared with the emotional version, subjects did not remember either its central or the peripheral details very well.

Half-way between an experiment and a naturalistic design is a study of Neisser and Harsch (1992) concerning the shocking explosion of the American space shuttle Challenger, at 11 a.m. on January 28, 1986. Overnight Neisser constructed a questionnaire asking subjects to write freely on how they heard the news, and then on the next page asking specific questions like where they were, what they were doing, who told them. Then he gave it to a class of 106 Emory University psychology students 24 hours after the event. Two and a half years later as many of the students as could be contacted (44) were given a similar questionnaire plus some scales to measure how confident they were about each answer. Neisser and Harsch matched each person's two-and-a-half-year-old account with that given 24 hours after the event, and gave it a score of 0 to 7 for accuracy (two points each for where the person was, who told the subject of the event, what the subject was doing at the time, and one point for correct minor details). Eleven subjects scored zero – their two-and-a-half-year-old memories were quite different from their 24-hour-old accounts. The mean score was 2.95. Nonetheless, people were generally confident of their memories, independently of how correct they were.

Overall we can conclude that, both in real life and in the laboratory, emotionally salient material is remembered better than neutral material. When the event is important to a person and when it is recounted in narrative form, using Stein et al.'s method described in chapter 4, Stein, Liwag, and Trabasso (1995) have shown that events can be recalled by children as young as three with considerable accuracy, and they can be resistant to alternative accounts of events given by adults. Even so memory is not perfect – it may still be subject to reconstructions and change after the event, especially if it is discussed and socially modified. The processes at work are those identified by Bartlett (1982) and by (1982) Linton.

If an event is important and unusual, the condition is set both for an emotion and for distinctive recall. And if the event is subject to being thought about often, or if traumatic flashbacks occur as they can do with severely traumatic events (American Psychiatric Association, 1994, p. 424), then the event itself will remain more salient in memory. The question of whether there is some special form of repressed memory is controversial: many psychologists who do research on memory do not discount the possibility but are sceptical (Loftus & Ketcham, 1994).

Mood effects on remembering

Since Bower's (1981) studies, discussed in chapter 1, there have been a large number of studies of the effects of mood on memory. Here is a laboratory

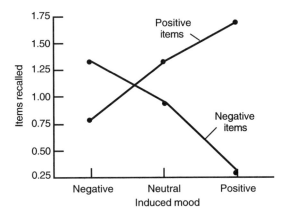

Figure 9.6 Mean number of positive and negative items mentioned in an interview by interviewers who were in a happy or despondent mood (Baron, 1987).

demonstration from the world of work in which effects of selective attention and memory on social judgment were examined. Baron (1987) brought pairs of people of the same sex together for a study in forming impressions. In fact, while one member of each pair was a student subject, the other was an accomplice of the experimenter. The student subject was, apparently randomly, chosen from the two to be an interviewer in a practice interview for a job as a management trainee, while the accomplice was chosen as interviewee. While the accomplice was (supposedly) studying the interview questions, the experimenter made the student subject happy or sad by giving them problems to solve, and telling them either that they had done much better than others, or had performed at an average level, or had done much worse than others.

In the interview the interviewer had to ask a prearranged set of six questions; the interviewee gave the same prearranged, but mixed, answers to the questions. One question was: "What are your most important traits?" In reply the interviewee would mention three positive traits saying: "I'm ambitious and reliable. Also I'm pretty friendly." He or she would also mention three negative traits: "On the minus side, some of my friends tell me I'm pretty stubborn and I know I'm impatient. Also, I'm pretty disorganized." After the interview the interviewer rated the interviewee on job-related and personal dimensions. When happy they tended to rate the interviewee more positively, and were more likely to say they would hire him or her, but when despondent they tended to rate the interviewee negatively, and said they would probably not hire the person (these effects were more marked for male than female interviewers). Baron also asked the interviewers to recall the things that the interviewees had said about themselves, presumably the base for their judgments. You can see the result in figure 9.6. Interviewers who had been made happy recalled significantly more positive things the interviewee had said and fewer negative things; those who had been made sad recalled more negative things and fewer positive things. According to the mood-dependent memory hypothesis, positive decisions about hiring would be influenced by more positive things being recalled by the happy interviewers, and negative decisions by more negative things being remembered.

The phenomenon of mood-dependent memory has, however, been found not to be as robust or wide-ranging as was at first assumed. It occurs more easily with happy rather than sad moods, better in lifelike situations than in artificial tasks, better when two moods are contrasted rather than when one mood is compared with a neutral state, better with strong moods than mild ones. Most important of all, the effects of mood on memory are most reliably obtained when what is remembered has emotional significance for the person who does the remembering (Ucros, 1989). In general, moreover, the effects are not, as Bower originally thought, well explained as a form of state-dependent learning in which anything learned, such as a list of words, in one state will be preferentially recalled when the state occurs again. Such effects are hard to demonstrate in adults (as in more recent studies by Bower), or in children (Duncan et al., 1985). A few laboratory demonstrations of modest effects of mood on remembering arbitrary verbal material do, however, exist (Eich & Metcalfe, 1989). The general conclusion is that most effects are better explained in terms of a hypothesis of mood congruence, which is that when a real incident of emotional significance occurs in a person's life, this incident is better recalled when the person again experiences the same emotion (Blaney, 1986).

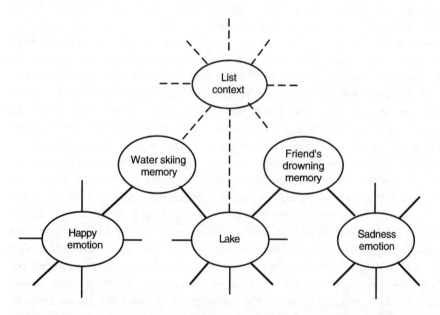

Figure 9.7 Diagram from Bower (1992) showing part of a memory network. The ellipses represent nodes in memory. If someone is asked to recall an incident from his or her life in response to the word "lake," then, if this person is in a sad mood the cue from the node "sadness" may prompt a memory of a friend who died by drowning, but if in a happy mood, the happy node may prompt memory of an occasion when he or she enjoyed water skiing.

Bower's (1981, 1992) hypothesis about such remembering is that each emotion is a distinctive mental state that forms a node in a memory network (see figure 9.7). When the emotion occurs again it can act as a cue to recall other parts of the network. We prefer an alternative explanation: moods are specific modes of brain organization, and so specific moods preferentially give access to memories of incidents experienced in the same emotional state (see figure 9.7). We link this idea to the explanation of Conway and Bekerian (1987) who found evidence that emotional knowledge is organized into groups corresponding to basic emotions: love/joy/happiness; misery/grief/sadness; anger/hate/jealousy; and fear/terror/panic. They found that, as compared with priming with an unrelated word, priming with any emotion term within one of these basic groups produced faster reaction times in a lexical decision task (like the one used by Niedenthal & Sutterlund, described above in the section on perception). In another study Conway (1990) found that when people were asked to generate an image in response to an emotion word, more than 60 percent of the images were of specific incidents that had occurred at a particular time in their life, that had emotional significance for them. By contrast other kinds of words had different effects. Images generated in response to self-referring personality traits were derived from lifetime experience but were not identifiable with any particular incident. Images generated in response to abstract words were semantic: they indicated pieces of knowledge which were not related to specific experiences. Conway suggests, therefore, that when we remember particular incidents many of them are indexed in memory under specific kinds of emotion. According to the idea of emotion modes, preferential access to the emotion-indexed set of memories of incidents occurs when we are in that same emotional state. The function of this mechanism, we believe, is to bring to mind incidents comparable to the one that started the current emotion, to provide examples of how we have dealt with that kind of problem in the past, as well as a sense of continuity of our own actions in situations that produce a specific kind of emotion.

Predictions made from the explanation in terms of emotion modes are not so different from those of Bower's network model. What the hypothesis of distinct emotion modes does, however, is to go beyond phenomena of memory. It is a step in a plausible explanation of effects of mood, such as those on attention, as discussed in the previous section, and on judgment as discussed in the next. It is preferred to the network model by some researchers (Mathews, 1993) for such reasons and it is, we believe, also more helpful for explaining some of the phenomena of emotional disorders, to be discussed in the next chapter.

Effects of moods on judgment

Gerald Clore made a striking remark in a paper in 1992: "The most reliable phenomenon in the cognition-emotion domain is the effect of mood on evaluative judgment" (Clore, 1992, p. 134). He was referring to evidence that when you are asked to judge something as good or bad, to approve or disapprove of someone, to accept or reject some course of action, to vote in this direction or that, you do not solely weigh facts. Usually life is more ambiguous. So we make judgments by combining what we know with how we feel.

In chapter 1 we described how Aristotle discussed the problem of speaking persuasively, for instance in a political speech or in a law court. He stressed the effects of emotions in the hearers. So how does this work? One way is suggested by research on why people change their minds under the influence of persuasion. Chaiken, Lieberman, and Eagly (1989) described two kinds of processing of arguments. One is systematic; the person carefully attends to the validity of the argument itself. The other involves short cuts; it is superficial, more careless, and involves responses to less essential aspects of the communication, for instance to the personality or reputation of who is presenting the argument, rather than to the validity of the argument itself. Petty and Cacioppo (1986) argue that people in good moods follow the short-cut route, and people in a neutral or negative mood tend to process arguments more systematically.

Worth and Mackie (1987) performed an experiment in which they measured (near the beginning and end of an experimental session) student subjects' ratings of agreement or disagreement with a proposal about controlling acid rain. After the first rating subjects took part in an apparently unrelated procedure that they thought was about risk taking. In fact the experimenters used this to put half the subjects into a good mood by allowing them to win $1, while the other half neither won anything nor knew there was anything to win. Then subjects were asked to evaluate a short speech about controlling acid rain, given at a student conference. Half the subjects had a speech that contained arguments that had previously been judged to be weak, and the other half had a passage with arguments previously judged to be strong. Then in a further split, half the students were told that the speech they read was made by an expert (an environmental studies major), and half were told the speech they read had been made by a nonexpert (a mathematics major).

Figure 9.8 shows the results of Worth and Mackie's study. Look first at the top graph, when no mood was induced (the neutral condition). Subjects changed their attitude toward the proposal about acid rain by nearly 1.5 points (on a nine-point scale) after reading the strong arguments, but they changed their attitude by only about half a point when they read the weak arguments. By contrast, when in a happy mood from having just won $1, they changed their attitude the same amount in response to both strong and weak arguments.

What were the people in the happy mood doing? The lower graph of figure 9.8 gives an indication. Whether the speech was said to have been given by an expert or nonexpert had no influence on the attitude change of people in the neutral mood. But people in a happy mood were more persuaded by the supposed expert than by the nonexpert.

Two years later, Mackie and Worth (1989) published a similar study although, presumably because of inflation, positive mood was now induced by subjects being given $2 rather than $1. When subjects were given a limited time to read the arguments for the proposal, the attitudes of those in a neutral mood shifted significantly more towards the proposal after reading the passage of strong as compared with weak arguments. But in a positive mood, attitude change was just as great with the weak as with the strong arguments, in fact slightly greater. With unlimited time, however, the happy subjects performed like those in a neutral mood. Mackie and Worth propose that this effect is attentional; perhaps the happy people were preoccupied with feeling good about having won $2 unexpectedly, and were therefore less inclined to concentrate on the arguments. When allowed as long as they wanted to read the arguments, those in the happy mood were less persuaded by the weak arguments.

So under at least some circumstances, how we feel can change our judgments for reasons quite irrelevant to the problem in hand: in Mackie and Worth's experiments mood was induced by a small gift of money which had nothing whatever to do with acid rain. We can imagine that this effect, if general,

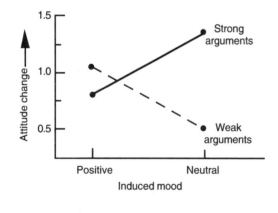

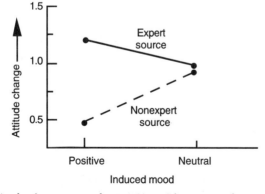

Figure 9.8 Attitude change towards agreeing with a proposal to control the effects of acid rain in happy and neutral moods, in response to strong and weak arguments, by experts and nonexperts (Mackie & Worth, 1987).

would give a handy formula to advertisers in magazines and television – perhaps one they already know without psychological experiments – if you can induce a happy mood and not give people too much time to think, you can incline a person favorably towards your product, independently of its merit or usefulness.

It turns out that the effect is rather general. Forgas and Moylan (1987) for instance, interviewed nearly 1,000 people leaving movie theaters after seeing a movie. The theaters chosen by the researchers were showing movies they had previously classified as happy, sad, or aggressive, in emotional tone. In the interviews subjects were asked about political figures, future events, crime, their own life satisfaction. In their responses people answered differently according to the emotions of the movie they had just seen. Other people interviewed before they went into the movie did not show such differences. Forgas and Bower (1988) and Forgas (1991) review a very long list of demonstrations that mood affects many kinds of judgments.

The hypothesis of Schwartz and Clore (1988) is that mood has an effect like an extra piece of information. Let us say you are being asked about the performance of your country's economy next year. Of course you don't know how it will perform. No one does. You could consider some information about current trends, but even if you are an expert you must still make a judgment on fragmentary knowledge. If you think that perhaps some experts know enough to be sure, you may like to reflect that the momentous collapse of the USSR was not predicted by the experts. In general, in all such judgments we have to make use of incomplete knowledge, and under such circumstances, other things enter the process of judgment. If you are feeling generally optimistic this will contribute to your judgment. We can add the effect (discussed in the previous section) that in a happy mood examples of happy events are more readily remembered. Good features and positive concepts are more readily available. And if one adds the effect that each episode in memory is tagged as having made us happy, sad, angry, and so forth, then, as we make a judgment our mood can act as a piece of information; it can combine with other incomplete pieces of information at our disposal. We mentioned the idea that emotions are heuristics – one well-researched effect of heuristics in thinking (Kahneman, Slovic, & Tversky, 1982), is that we make use of what is available. If an emotion is salient and available, we make use of it to help us over our uncertainty.

Misattribution

What is disturbing about all this, of course, is that mood can be manipulated quite independently of anything else. One might think that whether you get a job or not should not be affected by the mood of the interviewer. One might think that assessing an argument about what might be done about acid rain ought not to be influenced by whether you have just won $2. One might think that how you judge a political figure ought not to be influenced by what movie you have just seen. The intrusion of moods into these judgments are explained by some psychologists as misattributions: a mood derived from one context has spilled into another to which it does not belong. The prototype of misattribution was the famous study of Schachter and Singer (1962) who found that subjects injected with adrenaline, which has an arousing effect, felt and acted happily if they did not know the physiological effects of the injection, when they were put in a social context where they were encouraged to feel happy. They felt and acted angrily when put in an insulting and frustrating situation. The main prediction of Schachter and Singer's theory, that any arbitrarily chosen emotion can be produced by arousal along with an added cognitive or social interpretation, have not been substantiated (Manstead & Wagner, 1981; Reisenzein, 1983). But experimental studies have confirmed the misattribution effect, for instance in the engaging study of subjects who became more amorous after crossing a high and rather scary suspension bridge than those who had crossed a low and unarousing bridge (Dutton & Aron, 1974). Emotion, or arousal, acquired in one situation, can affect behavior and intensity of emotions in other situations, particularly if the people concerned do not know the source of their mood. Clore (1992) has shown that some effects of mood on persuasion also work in this way: if subjects' attention is drawn to the source of an induced mood, their judgments are less likely to be affected.

Mood effects on judgments about people

Many of the studies of effects of mood have involved judgments about other people, and also the subjects' own selves. Clark and Williamson (1989) have reviewed these studies, and concluded that at least six different kinds of influence occur, in the experiments and in real life. Four of these have been discussed in the previous sections: a mood may cue information that is congruent with that mood, a mood can create a general mode of thinking and responding such as happiness making one cooperative, a mood may itself act as a piece of information to the person who has it, and moods may be misattributed. Two other possibilities are that different moods may impose different limitations on the cognitive system, and that people may act to try to continue the mood they are in – so a happy person will keep bringing to mind material which will tend to continue that mood. They conclude that the fact that the influence can operate in several different ways may help to account for how pervasive the effects of mood are when we are thinking about ourselves or others.

Persuasion

Aristotle was clear on the issue of effects of emotions, but he argued in a different way from modern social psychologists. He thought there were exactly two kinds of case about which one had to make judgments. In one, say a problem in logic or mathematics, it is possible to have perfect or near perfect knowledge. Truth can be derived with certainty, and so judgments are clear.

But in the second case, when we do not know enough, we have to use methods that produce results that are better than average. In social judgments, politics, justice – and many other domains – we never have complete knowledge. There are no irrefutable demonstrations, no incontrovertible truths. Here is the domain for persuasive arguments that will approach the truth even if they do not get there.

If you remember back to chapter 1, you will recall how Aristotle said that in persuasive rhetoric a hearer is more likely to believe a good person than a bad one, more likely to be persuaded when emotions are stirred, and more likely to be persuaded by arguments that approach a truth or an apparent truth. Although according to social psychologists (Petty & Cacioppo, 1986) emotions are necessarily incidental, and are irrelevant to the evidence or argument to which we should attend, Aristotle does not see the effects of emotions here as warping judgment, but as aiding it.

According to the arguments of this book, emotions are among nature's heuristics – they prompt conclusions when we don't know enough, or don't have the time or other resources to decide exactly. What social psychologists have done is to tease apart the various components of judgment, as in Mackie and Worth's (1991) experiments in which the reputation of the person presenting an argument, time to process it, mood, strength of the argument, have all been shown to influence judgment. Mood can have effects quite independently of content. This might mean that some people use such effects, cynically, to be persuasive independently of whether we should believe them. But this does not mean that the mechanisms on which they are based are maladaptive; in general it is useful to believe people whom we trust.

Notice another thing, which Aristotle was clear about. In most cases of having to make judgments under uncertainty, each person is not an isolated decision maker, but takes part in a dialogue. We no longer believe that justice in legal cases can be approached by one person undertaking a witch-hunt; now one person speaks for the prosecution, another for the defense, yet others – judge and jury – decide what is to be done about the matter. By distributing cognition socially, in areas where individual knowledge is inadequate, or when cognitive processes are misleading, as when a person gets too attached to his or her own theory, we believe we can approach justice more closely. A similar distribution of roles occurs in science: one person proposes one explanation, which he or she likes and becomes attached to. The individual, despite what Popper (1962a) recommends, does not find it easy to look for ways of refuting his or her own arguments (K. Dunbar, 1993). It is another person, not liking that approach, who will propose an alternative – perhaps even taking part in angry controversy. Yet others, the writers of reviews and textbooks, will decide which view is more productive. If law courts and science are ways of approaching the truth, it is because limitations of individual thinking and emotions – both – are bridged by distributing knowledge and roles among different people.

Emotions, as part of the infrastructure of human cognition and interaction, are essential to this process. Here, for instance, is Quintillian (circa 90), a Roman writer on rhetoric, explaining how to argue for the defense in a law court.

> Suppose we are complaining that our client has been beaten. We must first speak of the act itself; we shall then proceed to point out that the victim was an old man, a child, a magistrate . . . and that the assailant was a worthless and contemptible fellow, or (to take the opposite case) was in a position of excessive power . . . the hatred excited by the act will be enhanced if it was committed in the theater, in a temple, or at a public assembly, and if the blow was given not in mistake or in a moment of passion or, if it was the result of passion was quite unjustifiable, being due to the fact that the victim had gone to the assistance of his father or . . . (p. 393)

Quintillian points out that the role of the plaintiff's counsel in a trial includes allowing those who will decide the case to feel what it was like to be this victim, and this must be done in all its individuality, with as vivid an elicitation of emotions appropriate to the incident as possible. It is the role of the defense to make a different case – so that we can feel that too. If the judge were a god, then she or he would know what happened, and what to do about it. But we are mere humans. We have to augment our limited human capacities by using emotional heuristics in interactions with others.

Summary

Though previous ideas about emotions stressed their disruptiveness, modern views are generally that emotions are, for the most part, functional. In the human adaptation, in which our knowledge is important although necessarily incomplete, in which our goals are many and sometimes incompatible, and in which we need to cooperate with other people, emotions serve important functions. They are heuristics, derived from our evolution, that help to bridge across those places where we do not know enough, or do not have sufficient resources, to decide how best to act. In general emotions seem to have two parts, an informational part which becomes conscious, so we typically know the objects of our emotions, and a control part that sets the brain into a mode that has been selected during evolution for coping with recurring kinds of situation, such as making progress towards a goal, losses, frustrations, threats, and so forth. In some emotions, of love and rejection, the object of the emotion is always known. Emotions and moods have been shown to have substantial effects on other mental processes. They can affect perception, and they usually constrain attention to events relevant to the emotion. Emotions, particularly positive ones, tend to enhance the memorability of events in our lives. They also affect judgment, especially of a social kind, and can be used in persuasion.

Where information is incomplete, other influences such as emotional ones can become influential.

Further Reading

A general review on function and dysfunction in emotions is:

Keith Oatley & Jennifer M. Jenkins (1992). Human emotions: Function and dysfunction. *Annual Review of Psychology, 43,* 55–85.

An excellent introduction to the philosophy of emotions, providing a basis for understanding the sense in which emotions are rational rather than irrational:

Ronald De Sousa (1987). *The rationality of emotions.* Cambridge, MA: MIT Press.

A useful review of experimental work on the effects of mood on memory and attention, including some of the clinical implications of the phenomena:

Andrew Mathews (1993). Biases in emotional processing. *The Psychologist: Bulletin of the British Psychological Society, 6,* 493–499.

A fine theoretical treatment of effects of mood on social judgments:

Joseph Forgas (1995). Mood and judgment: The affect infusion model (AIM). *Psychological Review, 117,* 39–66.

CHAPTER 10

Emotions in Social Relationships

Figure 10.0 Anger may be an important part of intimate relationships – one question is how to express it.

Contents

To be means to be for another, and through the other, for oneself. A person has no internal sovereign territory, he is wholly and always on the boundary; looking inside himself, he looks into the eyes of another or with the eyes of another.
Mikhail Bakhtin, Problems of Dostoevsky's Poetics, p. 287

Love and happiness: the emotions of cooperation

Here are two fundamental facts about human life. The first is that we rely on each other; the human adaptation is one in which we accomplish together what we cannot achieve alone. The second is that each of us inhabits a separate body; even when cooperating, even in the most interdependent societies, each can have somewhat different concerns. So when there are limited resources conflicts can occur with others for material or symbolic things.

Kemper (1990) traces the distinction between the emotions of love and aggression to two dimensions that provide, as it were, two coordinates like North–South and East–West, that allow us to locate ourselves at any moment in interpersonal geography. He traces them back to the Greek philosopher Empedocles (Wright, 1981), who called them "love" and "strife." Kemper gives them modern sociological names: "status" and "power." In this chapter we will use "affection" somewhat interchangeably with "status," and use "aggression" or "dominance" interchangeably with "power." What Kemper argues is that both in philosophical analyses, and in empirical studies of human interaction, these two dimensions keep being found. They explain something essential about what goes on between people. They have been found in studies of child development where they are called "love" and "control" (Sroufe, 1978), in anthropology where Triandis (1972) has called them "intimacy" and "superordination–subordination," in semantic analyses such as those of Osgood, May, and Miron (1975) where they emerge as evaluation (goodness) and potency, and in many other studies of social interaction (Kemper, 1978). Indeed, Kemper argues, these are not just dimensions. These may be fundamental explanatory concepts in understanding human interaction. So status or affection correspond (perhaps) to the states of calmness that Hess discovered could be released by stimulation of the forward part of the hypothalamus in the cat, and (we can say with more confidence) aggression corresponds to the angry attacks elicited by stimulation further back in the hypothalamus (as discussed in chapter 1). Perhaps, too, status and affection are more closely related to the emotions of sadness associated with activation of the right frontal cortex, and the emotions of assertion with activation of the left (see chapter 5).

So status or affection in this scheme concerns cooperation and acceptance of another. Power or aggression has to do with controlling another, independently of that person's will. Emotions then occur when one's position in this interpersonal geography changes. The emotions we feel when affection, love, support are given or received are those of happiness. Slightly modifying

Kemper's scheme, we can say that asserting power occurs via the emotions of anger and contempt; the emotions of being threatened by power are those of fear and anxiety.

The theory of evolution has previously been strong on issues of conflict. Because genes compete with each other, this has easily been translated into a fundamental concern with competition among animals, and it has spawned research on deception, manipulation, arms races, and so forth (Krebs & Dawkins, 1984). Recently theories of cooperation have also been developed within its framework (Axelrod, 1984).

Despite conflict, primates, rather like social insects, have found modes of life in which cooperation and interdependency are advantageous in reproducing the genes of individuals and those to whom they are closely related. Different primate species have evolved different modes of cooperation. Now, as well as explaining how modes of behavior promote reproduction of genes, we need to explain what induces individuals to act. This is the realm of motives and emotions.

As we discussed in chapter 3, a critical evolutionary move made by humans was for males to provide a specific parenting and economic contribution to the rearing of specific young (Lovejoy, 1981). It is a fair hypothesis that the emotion of this move, as suggested by MacDonald (1992), is affection or warmth. The move was accompanied by a tendency to form a long-lasting sexual relationship with a single individual. Human infancy is so long, and so demanding, that it strains the resources of a single caregiver. The human family — a woman, her offspring, and a male partner — are bound together by emotions of affection as well as more specific kinds of love and the mutual commitment that derives from them. Love functions to provide specific outline scripts for intimate relationships: attachment for dependency, caregiving love for the nurturance of children, sexual love for erotic activities.

As compared with the emotions of attachment the emotion of caregiving love is rather underresearched. We gave an account of some of its processes in chapter 5. It is clear from the work of Quinton, Rutter, and Liddle (1984) that in humans caregiving depends on the experience of having had a successful attachment relationship, either in infancy or later. It is also a fair hypothesis that in humans love between adult sexual partners is also based on attachment. Early experience provides a basic model not of just one but of two roles — of being loved and of being able to love (Shaver, Hazan, & Bradshaw, 1988).

In Western thinking it has been common to see personality as made up of parts. So Plato proposed that a person is like a charioteer (reason) driving two horses, one well-bred and the other ill-bred (*Phaedrus*). Freud saw life as orbiting round two centers, sexuality and death, which for him represented humankind's creative and destructive tendencies. Visions such as those of Plato and Freud have dramatic appeal. Perhaps more prosaically, we might say that the emotions of love, affection, and happiness draw people together creatively in cooperation. The emotions of anger, fear, and contempt set people in conflict. These two groups of emotions, then, create the two great fundamental modes of social interaction, and we base this chapter on them.

Intimacy and collaboration

The human experiences of loving and of being loved are thought by many to be what give life its principal meaning, and are much celebrated in fictional literature. Here for instance is Laura Esquivel in the novel *Like Water for Chocolate*:

> My Grandmother had a very interesting theory; she said that each of us is born with a box of matches inside us but we can't strike them all by ourselves . . . the oxygen would come from the breath of the person you love; the candle could be any kind of food, music, caress, word, or sound that engenders the explosion that lights one of the matches. For a moment we are dazzled by the intense emotion. A pleasant warmth grows within us . . . Each person has to discover what will set off these explosions in order to live, since the combustion that occurs when one of them is ignited is what nourishes the soul. (Esquivel, 1992, chapter 6)

For most people in Western society love is what is most important in life. As Freedman (1978) found in his survey of 100,000 Americans who responded to a magazine questionnaire, it was not wealth, not power, not youth, not health – but love in marriage that the respondents thought was the good that they most closely identified with happiness.

Principles of sexual love

A hypothesis that is receiving a great deal of attention is that patterns of infant attachment form a template for the love relations of adulthood. Try this little experiment on yourself. Think back to the patterns of attachment that we discussed in chapter 3, and perhaps look at table 3.3 where 16 of them are listed. Now imagine that instead of being patterns of interaction between an infant and a mother, these are descriptions of interaction between two adult lovers. Do the patterns fit? Do lovers show differential smiling and vocalization with each other, do they follow each other, gaze at each other, do they show distress at separation? If they do, might this confirm the hypothesis first put by Darwin that patterns of adult love relations are an echo of those of infancy.

In humans it is a fair hypothesis that a person who becomes the object of erotic love will have some characteristics that were learned in infant attachment (Hazan & Shaver, 1987). Human beings have a species-characteristic repertoire of actions such as caressing, and associated emotions and expressions such as feeling happy and smiling, based on their early relationships with caregivers. As we showed in chapter 7, the emotional tone of the relationship regulates what happens between a baby and a caregiver on whom that baby is dependent for comfort, safety, and emotional development.

Darwin (1872) supposed that the infant pattern of holding and being held is elaborated in adult caressing. To this idea Freud added the romantic notion that adult love is the return to the Eden of blissful merging with one's original love, with one's mother. It is helped onwards by developing sexual urges during adolescence. A principle of development is that new functions (like adult sexuality) do not arise out of nothing. They are elaborations, based on foundations of other functions earlier in life, which themselves derive from universal patterns.

In many societies falling in love is celebrated in literature as one of the most profound human experiences, but in few cases is it unproblematic, and perhaps this is true of emotions generally. An emotion is a response to a problem. It gives priority to one or a few goals related to the problem and concentrates attention on it. Because of such effects Dyer (1987, p. 337) has called emotions "locally rational judgments" often made quickly, without considering all implications. They have a certain feeling of involuntariness, of single-mindedness, which we enjoy and experience as authentic.

One of the profound ways in which we differ from most of our mammalian relations is that important people in our lives do not just fulfill roles – parent, infant, sexual partner – they become unique individuals. By the stage to which primates have evolved, so too has individuality. Goodall (1986) found that an infant chimpanzee who at the age of six had lost its mother, though able to forage for itself, would pine and die. It was a particular relationship with that individual which was lost. Since the individual was unique, she was irreplaceable. So too it is with us humans. Our parents are not just caregivers, but our own particular mothers or fathers. Our children are not just offspring to be tended, they are individuals. And when it comes to sexual partners, though sometimes we might get echoes of the way sexual life is among the chimpanzees of wanting merely someone amiable with whom to copulate, there is also the longing for that special someone, a particular individual.

Our love of unique others makes us uniquely vulnerable. Falling in love is momentous because a specific person is chosen for lifelong partnership. Of course that person may become ill, or die, or not turn out to be quite whom we expected. Sometimes we, or our chosen partner, may come to think that not the originally chosen partner but some other is that unique person who will make life worthwhile. This kind of issue is problematic not just in the West but in other societies where personal choice is the basis for marriage or its equivalent, for example, in a matrilineal society in Melanesia (Macintyre, 1986).

Although falling in love gives an impetus for change, the changes that are instigated by this and other emotions usually require working through. So, in the West love is the basis for commitment and for starting a family. But there are several kinds of love: caregiving, affectionate, friendly, as well as erotic (Berscheid, 1988). It is a question much pondered of how to accomplish the transition from the urgent, somewhat fantasy-based, temporary erotic state of being in love to the different state of permanent loving and caring for the other – and then to maintain a state of cooperative affection during the greater part of adult life. Jung (1925) has written a moving article about the psychological repercussions of withdrawing the fantasies on which being in love is based, and of the changing roles that occur as the life span is traversed.

In societies where an arrangement by parents is the basis for marriage, problematic issues are not avoided either (Seth, 1993). How in such a society does one treat love affairs as subsidiary to other matters, when emotions of erotic love are of such salience that they demand attention that might be insistent enough to relegate concerns for family and for other people?

Evolutionary perspectives on attachment and sexuality

Arguably, the processes that promote the reproduction of human life are the most important we possess, and as Shaver, Hazan, and Bradshaw (1988) propose, three main inherited systems are involved: attachment, caregiving of infants by parents, and the sexual relating that leads to reproduction. All involve at least two people cooperating to accomplish together what cannot be done alone. Thus child development typically requires a caregiver who is used as a secure base from which to explore; care for a baby involves becoming preoccupied with the child, its needs, and its welfare – and ideally, too, the economic contribution of a man based on commitment to an individual woman; ordinary sex clearly requires two participants. All these involve setting up lasting affectional bonds. As Bowlby has put it:

> Affectional bonds and subjective states of strong emotion tend to go together, as every novelist and playwright knows. Thus, many of the most intense of all human emotions arise during the formation, the maintenance, the disruption, and the renewal of affectional bonds – which, for that reason, are sometimes called emotional bonds. In terms of subjective experience, the formation of a bond is described as falling in love, maintaining a bond as loving someone, and losing a partner as grieving over someone. (Bowlby, 1979, p. 69)

Attachment provides behavioral mechanisms and an emotional tone of trust. This, and the more general tone of warmth or affection in interaction, are the keys to socialization. Together they profoundly affect how development will proceed. Should attachment and childhood affection fail in serious ways, a person may grow up on the margins of human existence.

The second of the instinctual bonding systems is caregiving. In parenthood what this means is that the mother, and preferably the father too, fall in love with their specific infant. This love will sustain them through the upheaval of their lives that child rearing demands. They will develop what Winnicott (1958) called "primary maternal preoccupation," and this state will allow them to develop the devotion that they will need for the baby to flourish. Klaus and Kennell (1976) described a process of the mother becoming bonded to her baby by body contact during the first days after delivery. They recommended this body contact as part of early infant care. Klaus and Kennell's work led to important changes in the organization of hospital maternity care, but their findings of widespread benefits to children's health and development with early maternal bonding have not all been replicated in subsequent studies (Svejda, Campos, & Emde, 1980; Svejda, Pannabecker, & Emde, 1982). Also their model of an early critical period for bonding was overstated: parents who, for whatever reason, are unable to have close contact with their babies in the first few days after birth do become perfectly good and loving parents, and their babies thrive just as well. Most tellingly, adoptive parents who have not had early contact make just as good and loving mothers and fathers as biological parents (Tizard & Hodges, 1978).

Early contact may help: not just mothers but fathers become bonded to infants. Fathers who were present at the birth of children (Peterson, Mehl, & Leiderman, 1979) show more intense attachment to their infants early on. As well as skin to skin contact, releaser patterns such as smiles, the high forehead, large eyes, and rounded face of the human baby easily elicit gazing and "ooh-ah" sounds from adults, and facilitate the growth of a loving relationship with the infant. But bonding to a child can involve a very wide range of mechanisms, not just early sensory and biological cues (Corter & Fleming, 1990, 1995).

In chapter 7 we reviewed evidence that a mother's responsiveness depends on her own attachment in infancy. Remember, too, the study of Quinton, Rutter, & Liddle (1984) discussed in chapter 8, which followed into adulthood a group of girls raised in institutions. Those who were institution-raised and who formed relationships with unsupportive men were liable to become poor mothers, but those who found supportive men became mothers who were as good as the women who had not been raised in institutions. An experience of being loved and cared for can be important in one's own ability to be a parent; early experiences can be supplemented by later ones.

Choosing a mate

In most human societies, genetically speaking, women choose males on the basis of their predicted investment in parenting, rather than (as in some species) from indicators of genetic prowess such as being very large or strong. The logic of males being trustworthily monogamous is what Maynard-Smith (1984) has shown to be an evolutionarily stable strategy – a strategy that does well in a population where most others are doing the same thing. It does, however, allow for a minority to coexist by deceptively only appearing to be trustworthy, while trying to further their genes with many women, without making a contribution to child rearing with any of them.

Since women make the main investment in bringing up children, the genetic aspect of male interest in mate selection is based on indications of a woman's abilities to rear children. Female attractiveness therefore, as many commentators have pointed out, includes visual indications of youth and healthiness. And what a wonderful irony it is that the visual aspect of women that is experienced as most erotic, that most boldly advertises sexuality in women, is not the sexual organs (as in chimpanzees) but the breasts – the organs whose primary function is to suckle the young. Humans are the only mammals in whom the organs of suckling are so prominent, and it may not be accidental that breasts as releasers of sexual interest for adult men were also objects of high significance to them as infants.

Shaver, Hazan, and Bradshaw (1988) discuss in detail what was hinted at by many authors from Darwin and Bowlby onwards, that falling in love is not only a parallel to forming bonds of attachment on infancy, but it is psychologically built on the same foundation. And caring for the person with whom one is in love is based on the caregiving patterns that one has received oneself. Falling in love, then, is not only a solution to mate choice, but it sets up patterns of mutual support. It is essential for two human mates to be caregivers for each other, as well as for children. Shaver, Hazan, and Bradshaw hypothesize that it is this element that may be the most vulnerable in marriage – when a partner ceases to feel cared for by the other.

Hazan and Shaver (1987) have suggested that adult sexuality tends to replay the patterns of infant attachment. Perhaps, then, among us human beings there is an element of repetition, and of hope of being able to regain the closeness of our first relationship, in someone who seems familiar – as if we had always known them. On the other hand, the taboos against incest and the social processes of exogamy that promote mating between unrelated adults, are human universals. The mechanism seems to include finding members of one's immediate family unattractive sexually: children raised in kibbutzim tend not to enter into sexual relationships with those they grew up with in the same kibbutz. As Bateson (1983) has said, and this may be the most we can say about the characteristics of people we fall in love with: we tend to choose as a mate someone similar to people we know, but not too similar!

Anger, fear, contempt: the emotions of competition

Emotions that underlie conflict are also celebrated in literature.

> . . . I came to myself as if out of a great sickness. There was something strange in my sensations, something indescribably new and, from its very novelty, incredibly sweet. I felt younger, lighter, happier in body; within I was conscious of a heady recklessness . . . a dissolution of the bonds of obligation, an unknown but not an innocent freedom of the soul . . .
>
> . . . This familiar that I called forth out of my own soul, and sent forth to do his good pleasure was a being inherently malign and villainous, his every act and thought centered on self, drinking pleasure with a bestial avidity from any degree of torture of another; relentless like a man of stone. (pp. 83, 86)

These passages are from Robert Louis Stevenson's (1886) *Dr Jekyll and Mr Hyde* – they describe the first sensations of Mr Hyde. Ordinary humans, according to this story, are mixtures of good and evil. Dr Jekyll has discovered a potion to fractionate out the purely evil part; the evil consists of liberation from "the bonds of social obligation" and as one might imagine, it is not long before this embodiment of asocial individuality commits a cruel murder.

Aggression

The portmanteau term for the emotions and behavior of conflict is aggression. In the history of Western thought anger, aggression, and revenge have been seen as the deep flaws in human character. The Stoics saw anger as the emotion that was most essential to master in themselves. In more modern times, first psychoanalysts and more recently ethologists have speculated on the origins of human aggression, and wondered what may be done about it. One does not need to be a social scientist to reflect on the devastating potential our species has to destroy its own members in political repression, ethnic hostility, and war.

Brief biography: Konrad Lorenz

The foremost figure in modern ethology was Konrad Lorenz. Born in Vienna in 1903, he died in 1989. Throughout his life he kept a menagerie of animals, and is remembered for the geese who followed him about. In the 1920s and 1930s he had no paid post and his father supported him until he married Greta Gebhardt, a physician, in 1927 – then she supported him! He finally obtained a professorship, but only held the job for a year when war broke out and he was drafted into the army as a doctor. He was in a Russian prisoner of war camp for four years where he kept himself healthy by eating insects and spiders. After the war, he was again without a job. In 1955 the Max Planck organization enabled him to set up an Institute at Seewiesen in Bavaria, and in 1973, with Niko Tinbergen and Karl von Frisch, he received a Nobel Prize.

When Hitler came to power, Lorenz went along with the Nazis. In 1940 he wrote a shocking article in which he proposed that people who had been overdomesticated should be eliminated as an act of public health. He regretted this appalling lapse for the rest of his life. But his theory that aggression was a "big drive," that "resembles a horse . . . which must have daily exercise to keep down its superfluous energy" (Lorenz, 1967, p. 77) made him an enemy of those who saw such arguments as justifying human militarism. While no one can excuse Lorenz's links with Nazism, one may note that after the war many of his friends believed his involvement to have been misjudgment rather than commitment. These friends included Tinbergen, who was sent to detention camp by the Nazis for protesting the dismissal of three Jewish faculty members from the University of Leiden where he worked. (Biographical information from Bateson, 1990)

In recent versions of this debate there have been views like those of Lorenz (1967), that aggression is an innate drive like hunger, and that human culture is in peril: aggression threatens to run out of control because technology and bureaucracy prevent humans from perceiving or responding to gestures of submission. Another well-known view was that of Ardrey (1966) with his idea of a "territorial imperative": that we are programmed for aggression in defense of territories ranging from a seat on the bus to a nation. The drift of such writing was that beneath the clothes of civilization there lurks a killer ape liable to burst out in irrational violence.

Lorenz and Ardrey certainly generalized beyond the evidence. Their ideas were attacked on the grounds that to propose instinctive repertoires of aggressive behavior seemed to justify human violence (Fox, 1991). But the opposing idea that violence is entirely cultural also has weaknesses; it involves an unfounded optimism in human malleability and perfectibility. Aggression is as much part of the repertoire of human behavior as, say, running. The relevant questions are how is it incorporated into human societies, avoided by some, celebrated by yet others? How might excesses of human violence be avoided? How might the clashes of cultures become less destructive?

Anger and submission within social groups: status and respect

In social mammals and birds, dominance hierarchies are common (Eibl-Eibesfeldt, 1970). In primates, including monkeys (Cheyney & Seyfarth, 1990) and apes (De Waal, 1982; Goodall, 1986), hierarchies have been described in detail.

Emotionally these hierarchies are negotiated by threatening displays of anger and complementary displays of deference, or by actual fights that have a winner and a loser. A position in the hierarchy won or defended persists through time. Alliances with relatives and others, formed and sustained by mutual grooming, also persist over time and during disputes an ally may intervene on another's behalf. High position in the hierarchy of many primate species is thought to benefit an individual by giving better access to food and sexual partners (Mason & Mendoza, 1993). In our species, high rank in males and its access to resources is sexually attractive. The species-characteristic mechanisms on which dominance is based may indeed be seeds of the individuality which has become so distinctive in Western society.

Not only do primates know their place in social hierarchies, and know who their relatives and allies are, but Cheyney and Seyfarth describe how a monkey beaten in a fight is more likely to become aggressive to a relative of the animal with whom it was fighting. Results such as this indicate that primates know others in the social group as individuals.

As important as aggression is reconciliation. Apes are not constantly antagonistic. Instead, after a fight or scuffle there is nearly always a reconciliation. In pygmy chimpanzees, this is initiated by the original aggressor on 61 percent of occasions, and in common chimpanzees on 44 percent of occasions (Visalberghi & Sonetti, 1994). Even high ranking and powerful males need allies. To defeat someone in a fight and leave it at that would produce a long-term opponent, who could muster support from elsewhere and become a threat. Alliances and relationships, then, are essential to the life of many primates. So we should see the typical aggressive sequence as (a) a phase of aggression, (b) a readjustment or acknowledgement of dominance position or resolution of some other issue, then (c) a reconciliation on the basis of the readjustment. As Visalberghi and Sonetti put it: in terms of either a species or an individual "aggression would be fatal if mechanisms to restore positive interactions were not present as well" (p. 66).

Mechanisms of eliciting anger

Anger, then, among the primates including ourselves, is the characteristic emotion of interpersonal conflict, and as a 50-year old formulation that became very well known has it: frustration causes aggression. Berkowitz, Cochran, and Embree (1981), for instance, had women student subjects evaluate the quality of suggestions about the functioning of a business made by another student to whom they were introduced – actually a confederate of the experimenters. The subjects sat in a cubicle, wearing earphones. Half had their arms immersed in cold water, at a painful 6 degrees C (43 degrees F). The other half had their arms in water at room temperature, 18 degrees C (65 degrees F), which was less painful. For each suggestion made by the other student the subject could give a reward, one to five nickels, by pushing the "reward" button one to five times, or they could ignore it by pressing an "ignore" button, or they could push a "punishment" button one to five times to deliver blasts of loud and very aversive noise. Cross-cutting the painfulness condition, half the subjects in the experiment were told punishment probably would help the other student's performance; the other half were told that it would probably hurt the other's performance. The suggestions made by the confederate were, of course, the same for all subjects – they had been tape recorded and were played through the subject's earphones. The results are shown in figure 10.1. In general subjects delivered more rewards than punishments, but the largest number of punishments was delivered by subjects who were in more pain and who had been told that punishment hurt the other person. Subjects in the more painful condition gave a significantly higher proportion of punishments to rewards than those in the less painful condition.

In general, Berkowitz (1993) has found that experimentally inducing pain, as in the above experiment, or causing discomfort by having subjects hold an arm horizontally for a long period, produces anger. This anger brings to mind not only emotionally similar memories, but it prompts a great deal of thinking to make sense of the situation, as well as planning. It prompts an aggressive urge to punish, which is visited on any convenient target person, irrespective of whether that person had anything to do with the pain or discomfort. This

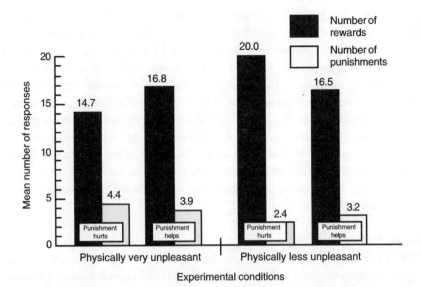

Figure 10.1 Mean numbers of rewards and punishments given by women students to other students for suggestions. In the very unpleasant condition the subjects had their arms immersed in very cold water, and in the less unpleasant condition they had their arms immersed in water at room temperature. The maximum number of responses possible for each subject was 50 (Berkowitz et al., 1981).

process seems to be a mechanism, with qualities that Darwin described as being automatic.

Cross-cultural variations in the management of anger

A fascinating aspect of the cross-cultural study of emotions is to see how each society regards anger. Some societies view anger as destructive, and think it should be avoided. One such is the Utku, an Inuit group living near the Arctic Circle. Briggs (1970) has written about the 17 months during 1963 to 1965 she spent living in the igloo or tent of her adopted family, which consisted of a couple and their children. The whole group she was with consisted of 35 people in eight families. They lived mainly on fish, and they trapped foxes which they exchanged for industrial goods at Gjoa Haven, a trading post 150 miles away. In winter they lived in an igloo village; in summer families dispersed to different camping sites.

What seemed most remarkable to Briggs was that Utku adults did not express anger interpersonally, and they did not use anger or threats in child rearing. Young children were treated with indulgence and were never scolded. By contrast the Utku found Briggs alarming in her propensity to anger. During her stay, which included months in a tiny confined space with other people, although she tried to suppress it she did become frequently angry with cold and physical hardship that she found difficult to bear, with children constantly wanting her supplies of raisins, and at many other events that we can easily recognize as irritating. Then, in the summer towards the end of her stay, there was a pivotal occasion. Some Canadian vacationers had come north from the city, had borrowed one of the two canoes owned by the Utku families, and had carelessly damaged it. The Utku response to this, as to all such events, was calm and smiling acceptance. Then the vacationers wanted to borrow the other canoe! Briggs confronted them angrily, on behalf of her adopted family who lived so precariously and with so few possessions, all of which were needed for survival. The result was that the Utku found it subsequently very hard to have anything to do with Briggs – with a person who could act in such an unstable and alien way. (In case any reader might think that Briggs is especially prone to anger one of us, K.O., who has met her, can vouch that by Euro-American standards she is charming and amiable.)

By contrast Chagnon (1968) went to stay for 19 months on three visits, between 1964 and 1968, with a group called the Yanomamö who live by hunting and growing vegetables in the forests of southern Venezuela and northern Brazil. The Yanomamö probably number perhaps 10,000. They conceive of themselves as a fierce people. They live in chronic warfare and shifting alliances between neighboring Yanomamö villages. Individual aggression is common, as is collective aggression when groups of men go on raiding parties to other villages intending to kill at least one man on each raid, and to abduct women if possible. Chagnon recorded that during the time of his fieldwork, one of the villages in which he lived was raided approximately 25 times (p. 2). He estimated that among the Yanomamö, while "54% of all adult deaths were due to malaria and other infectious diseases . . . 24% of adult males die in warfare" (p. 20).

Children, both male and female, are brought up to be fierce in their interactions with each other, and to hit with sticks in disputes. Eibl-Eibesfeldt (1979, p. 157) describes how he filmed an incident in which a small Yanomamö girl was instructed on how to hit and bite her brother in retaliation for some wrong. In his stay with the Yanomamö, Chagnon describes how his fieldwork was constantly difficult, as he had to find fierce ways of dealing with angry threats such as "Don't point your camera at me or I'll hit you" (p. 8). He became more skilled at angrily rebuffing such approaches, and at retaliating when his supplies were stolen.

The Yanomamö live in huts, each occupied by a family. For instance, the hut of Kaobawä, a village headman who was one of Chagnon's main informants, housed himself, his two wives and his children, as well as his brother who had helped him build the hut and who shared the younger of Kaobawä's wives. Huts are grouped together in the villages. The smallest size of village was about 40 people, and Chagnon estimates that the lowest size is set by needing to raise about 15 adult males for a raiding party. The largest villages were about 250 people, and seemed to be set by disputes becoming so frequent at this size that the village divides in two, with one party going off to start a new village elsewhere. Although only men take part in raiding and organized fighting, anger and fights are frequent among women too.

Figure 10.2 An adulterous affair prompts two Yanomamö men to fight together with clubs. Others watch the fight with interest.

Distinctive among the Yanomamö are several forms of duelling. The least destructive is chest pounding, in which one man stands while his antagonist delivers "a tremendous wallop with his fist to the man's left pectoral muscle, putting all his weight into the blow" (p. 114), raising a severe welt, causing the recipient to stagger and to cough up blood for several days afterwards. After one or several blows have been struck, roles are reversed and the hitter receives as many blows as he has delivered. In collective versions, as between members of two allied villages during a feast, champions from each side come forward, each stirred by the fight not having gone as well for their side as it might, and by the possibility of increasing his own reputation for fierceness.

Another common set-piece fight is with clubs eight to ten feet long, rather like double size pool cues, used for the adversaries to take turns in striking each other over the head with the thick end. Chagnon describes individual club fights starting within a village, for instance over a wife caught in a liaison with another man. As soon as blood begins to flow, these fights often enlarge to involve all the male members of a village getting their clubs, and joining in on one side or the other. "The tops of most men's heads are covered with long ugly scars of which their bearers are immensely proud" (p. 119).

Both the Utku and the Yanomamö are indigenous American societies, genetically related – but what of the currently dominant culture in the Americas, descended mainly from European colonists, and Africans forced to come here? In the industrial USA, anger leading to violence can be witnessed by any ordinary observer. The prevalence of serious violence is relatively high in the USA. Hammond and Yung (1993) have reviewed recent epidemiological evidence on violence among young people. In one national USA survey nearly 50 percent of adolescent boys and 25 percent of girls had been involved in at least one fight during the last year, with 23 percent of boys reporting taking a knife to school, and 3 percent reporting taking a gun. In another study, 20 percent of American high school students reported carrying a weapon in the previous 30 days, with a quarter of these (i.e. 5 percent of the total) admitting that the weapon was a gun. Young men are frequently injured in assaultive violence: about 8 percent of American males between 12 and 19 have experienced violent crime. In one of the less violent neighborhoods of Washington, DC, the city with the highest rate of homicide in the USA (703 homicides in 1990), Richters and Martinez (1993) interviewed schoolchildren and parents. They found 9 percent of children aged six and seven had witnessed a shooting, 13 percent had witnessed a stabbing, 16 percent had seen a dead body outside, and 25 percent had witnessed a mugging. Emotional effects of such events on children, and of living so close to violence, include feeling scared, having intrusive thoughts, and other symptoms of distress. These were significantly higher in those who had personally witnessed violence than in those who had not (Martinez & Richters, 1993).

Interdependence and individualism

Although patterns of anger and of lack of anger vary widely from society to society, we can recognize several recurring modes. One mode occurs in societies in which people live closely together in mutual dependence. Frequently in this kind of society, life is precarious and people depend on each other for survival. Within some of these societies, anger seldom arises, and aggression is rare. This kind of arrangement occurs among the Utku (Briggs, 1970), on Ifaluk (Lutz, 1988), and in one of the last isolated societies to be "discovered" by the West – an aboriginal group in the Philippines (Nance, 1975) whose first contact with anyone outside their own society was only 30 years ago.

We lack critical studies of how young children of such societies behave when frustrated, but one way of seeing the rarity of anger in them is that anger depends on how events are interpreted. As discussed by Markus and Kitayama (1991), in interdependent societies survival may depend on interreliance, and the self is experienced in terms of close interdependence, as a We-self rather than an I-self. Correspondingly, people do not see themselves as autonomously separate from others. Hence they do not experience themselves as thwarted or let down by others. If interpersonal anger were to occur, it would express disruption of the interdependent links among people, a sign of breakdown within the group. It would be like someone turning against himself or herself in an individualistic society, in self-mutilation or suicide. Such things do occur occasionally, but they are regarded as pathological. (Evidence of entirely nonviolent societies needs to be interpreted with care: reports of entirely anger-free societies have typically been on small groups over short periods.)

In individualistic cultures, by contrast, anger can come to play a predominant role, precisely because the self must be asserted against others. One mode, which seems to recur throughout history and across cultures, is male-dominated, aggression-based, power and revenge. This pattern is common, and much celebrated: we see it in Homer's *Iliad*, in Aeschylus and the classical Greek playwrights' themes of cycles of family revenge, in Viking sagas (Miller, 1994), in medieval European stories of valiant knights, in the anthropological accounts of unindustrialized warlike groups such as the Yanomamö, and in the history of industrialized warfare in this century. However dressed up by epic tradition, or by talk of chivalry and courage, the elements are surprisingly similar: rival males fight against each other with the spectacle, and even the story of a fight, creating high interest and excitement. Fighting occurs mainly in groups, but also individually. Campaigns are justified by vengeance for wrongs of others. Shifting alliances are based on economic necessity or military weakness. Some individuals emerge as heroes, their exploits marking them out. The resources they gain are displayed conspicuously (Veblen, 1899), and others admire rather than envy.

And, of course, there are cultures which share both these characteristics: of calm anger-free interactions in domestic relations, and warlike aggression with others outside the culture.

The role of anger in aggressive societies is that it fires people to perform deeds of which they would be otherwise incapable. Again and again, narrative accounts of aggressive exploits go to some lengths to explain how a man became angry, and to show how this anger created the courage and justified the slaughter which followed. So, in the ancient Greek *Iliad*, Achilles re-enters the war with Troy after his long sulk, in vengeful rage because his closest friend Patroclos was killed (Homer, c. 850 BCE). Erec, in Chrétien de Troyes' medieval story of Erec and Enide (Chrétien de Troyes, 1180) goes out looking for fights because his wife has shamed him by saying that people think he has become soft, and devoted himself to the pleasures of love. And Chagnon (1968), in his account of the Yanomamö, describes Damowa, who liked to seduce other men's wives. He was the head and fiercest man of Monou-teri village. He and his men set out in anger to raid Patanowa-teri village because its men had managed to recapture five of seven women Damowa's raiders had abducted. In the inevitable return raid, Damowa was ambushed while he was in his village garden with two of his wives and a child. He was shot with arrows and killed. Next his brother affirmed solidarity with allies, and organized the necessary return raid.

Fighting fuelled by anger, in our species as in certain other mammalian species, functions at least in part as the lever of individual power to control resources, including the resources of access to females who in aggressive societies typically have a rank inferior to that of men. It suspends fear and reduces consideration for other people. But as with love, the contradictions are evident. Anyone from a nonviolent society reading the violent history of Europe and America would be appalled, uncomprehending.

Vengeance is a frequent accompaniment of anger. Yet from a functional point of view it seems puzzling. As Frijda (1994) points out, it does nothing to right the wrong that was suffered, it is often harmful to the individual who wreaks revenge, and it is immoderate, often far exceeding the original offence. What seems to be going on is that as an emotion vengefulness is highly social: it restores a balance of power, and the threat of it can deter. As Axelrod (1984) has shown, tit-for-tat is a highly successful social strategy – it is not clear whether in some conflictual situations there is a better one – and this may be how it evolved. Moreover, if one is humiliated, then to take revenge means at least that the other does not enjoy the fruits of his or her act, and if revenge seems excessive, or to require plans that extend over months or years, then it may be because the social inequity seems so flagrant. At the same time, cycles of revenge have in many societies been seen as highly damaging to the social order. The Biblical law "an eye for an eye" is not the expression of cruelty, but a restraint on it. The world's great playwrights, including Sophocles and Shakespeare, have returned again and again to patterns of vengeance, and to the possibilities of replacing them with societal processes. Peaceable life in Western societies has included the control of feuding in which cycles of revenge and counter revenge, of triumph and shame, constantly escalate. Instead, responsibility to remedy wrongs is given to a suprapersonal agency, the police and the courts.

Anger and aggression in the adjustment of relationships

What has been achieved in modern Western societies is a state of public and interpersonal peace – more or less. In these societies, generally anger functions to readjust relationships without physical violence. In the most important study of its interpersonal functions in Western society (discussed in chapter 2), Averill (1982) distributed structured diaries to 80 randomly chosen married people, and 80 single university students. He has proposed that anger has a quality of the speech act of promising. To be angry with someone involves a commitment to seeing an argument through to some end. By contrast, annoyance has no sense of commitment, and may pass off quickly.

Most subjects (66 percent) reported an incident of anger once or twice a week, and 44 percent an episode of annoyance at least once a day. These are probably underestimates, because people tended to forget incidents. Events that made subjects angry were usually seen as caused by another person or a human institution, and people provoking anger were usually seen as doing something they had no right to do, or that they could have avoided by taking more care. Some 94 percent of anger-inducing events were described as frustrating but this was not the sole cause. Of the subjects who mentioned frustration, 96 percent also mentioned violation of important personal expectations or socially accepted ways of behaving, a loss of personal pride, possible or actual damage to property, or personal injury. Some people did not mention frustration but said their anger was caused by loss of self-esteem, violation of personal wishes or expectations or of accepted ways of behaving.

Anger was usually caused by people the subject knew and liked – parents, children, spouses, friends. Most of the subjects said that their motives included getting even for the present incident or for previous wrongs, but the most common reason for being angry, given by 63 percent of subjects, was to assert authority or independence, or to improve their image. Other common motives included trying to change the other person or to strengthen a relationship. Using anger to express dislike or to break off a relationship did occur, but it was infrequent as compared to strengthening or readjusting a relationship.

Averill also asked 80 students to keep similar structured diaries of incidents in which they had been targets of anger – 95 percent said that the other person's anger was caused by something they had done. But targets typically thought they had been justified or that the incident had been beyond their control. In the discussions that ensued most of the angry people re-evaluated the incident, usually reinterpreting the motives of the target.

Approximately two thirds of angry people felt their anger as negative, and targets mostly felt even worse. But despite this, 62 percent of angry people and 70 percent of targets rated the episode of anger as beneficial. Usually anger functions in long-term relationships to allow the participants to readjust something in that relationship, so anger usually starts with a sense of being wronged, and ends with both partners making some adjustment, and coming to a reconciliation on a new basis. One possible outcome, however, is harm to another, and breaking off a relationship. This can be followed by long trains of revenge as participants seek redress. Averill's formulation is that in Western society anger, like falling in love, is a temporary social role: the role of aggressor enacted by the one who has been wronged.

Cultural codes

Often in response to anger, the target also gets angry, in a symmetrical way. But a pattern that is complementary to anger is fear. Öhman (1986) has shown that although one pattern of fear evolved from escaping from predators, social fear is a separate pattern: a response in deference to social anger. We discussed in chapter 3 the family of emotions – embarrassment, shame, social anxiety – with which it is associated. In societies which are very hierarchical, or where power is frequently asserted, those who are not powerful need to be wary.

Although a capacity for anger may be a human universal, societies based on aggressive assertion and defense of hierarchical position are not universal (as discussed in chapter 2). And although division of labor between the sexes is universal, large differences in power or respect related to gender is not. Leakey and Lewin (1991) point out that male dominance and a corresponding lower position of women is somewhat associated with the proportion of food acquired by hunting. Where hunting is important men tend to occupy a higher rank associated with providing the group with meat and with joyful celebrations that occur with a catch. When humans hunt for a living it seems to be the men who do it. The Chambri (Gewertz, 1981) are a near exception; for them fishing is an important part of life, and women are the ones who do it.

In humans, anger is not as closely tied to asserting and defending hierarchical position as among other primates, though at least one recent and widely popular analysis has it that Western men relate to each other primarily by locating themselves in dominance hierarchies (Tannen, 1991), even when overt aggression does not occur.

Shweder (1990) has proposed that all societies are based on one of three ethical codes, though as we describe these you will see traces of the other codes in the one with which you are most familiar. In much of the West the code is of autonomy and individual rights. Its emotion is anger at moral trespass, resulting in social readjustment as individuals seek to establish their rights against any who infringe them. Its social enactment is the law suit. Not far beneath this, barely concealed, is the morality of the dominance hierarchy, where individuals acquire and defend position and resources, while others tolerate the inequities that result. A quite different kind of society is based on an ethics of divinity, on the idea of the self as a spiritual entity that has to be protected against contamination, from food and other pollutants. In such societies, as Rozin, Haidt, and McCauley (1993) have pointed out, the emotion at the center is disgust. Yet other kinds of societies are based on an ethics of duty, and for these Rozin et al. suggest that contempt is the emotion – or rather one of the twin emotions contempt and honor – that are at the center, as actions of the self as well as of other people are appraised and commented upon in terms of what is proper and what is improper.

Functioning within and between groups

In 1949 Sherif and Sherif (1953) performed an experiment that showed how human hierarchies need not involve anger. The researchers invited boys aged 11 to 12 to go on what was for them a standard summer camp in the country. The boys were selected to be culturally homogenous: they were white, healthy, well-adjusted, from stable lower-middle-class homes, and all had around average intelligence (a mean IQ of 105). The main data gathering was by participant observers who were graduate students, but who appeared to the boys as camp counselors. Apart from announcing activities, they abstained from leadership or decision making, and did not make notes in the boys' presence. Muzafer Sherif himself took the role of caretaker; this enabled him also to observe, and to ask the boys occasional naive questions. Activities were arranged to be interesting; the boys plunged into them without suspecting that they were being observed. In Phase 1 all 24 boys, who had not previously known each other, were housed together for three days. All activities occurred on a basis of personal interest and choice. The boys quickly formed friendships, and chose buddies.

In Phase 2 (five days), two evenly matched groups were formed, taking care to separate best friends. Each group now had its own cabin to sleep in. The pain of separation was assuaged by each group going on a separate hike and camp-out, which the boys found exciting. In this phase, kitchen duties, games, and all other activities were done in the separate groups, and all rewards were on a group basis. Each group quickly developed its own culture. In each a leader emerged and rough hierarchies formed with structures that were remarkably similar to those described by Goodall (1986) among chimpanzees. The difference was that the hierarchy of 12-year-old boys was formed mainly by the boys taking roles and suggesting decisions to the group – without fighting or threats.

The boys chose names for their groups, "Bulldogs" and "Red Devils," developed insignia, established territories, customs, and nicknames. The leader of the Bulldogs rose to his position "by his greater contribution to the planning and execution of common activities and by regulating and integrating the tasks and roles of the group members" (p. 252), including those for quite complicated activities such as improving the bunkhouse, building a latrine, and creating a secret swimming place. He praised others for their work, gave support, showed concern for other members including those of low rank in the group. Only once was he seen to threaten a group member (verbally, p. 262), though punishments included removing stones from the swimming place. These were seen as "fair." Each group achieved stability, and the predominant tone was one of interpersonal harmony, without competition with the other group. Bonding to the group and among its individuals was high. The choices of friends that had been made in Phase 1 were revised, and at the end of Phase 2 about 90 percent of the friendships were within the group.

The Bulldogs' solidarity occurred not by interpersonal competition, but by collaborating towards joint goals that all wanted to achieve. Although the focus of the study was not on emotions as such, the account of affection among the Bulldogs is striking. Although the Red Devils also achieved group cohesion, their style contrasted. They had greater distance between the more and less popular boys, the leader was cliquish, favoring his lieutenants. He "sometimes enforced his decisions by threats or actual physical encounters" (p. 259), and used "roughing up" as punishment. Despite this, he remained the "acknowledged leader and had great prestige within the group" (p. 259).

So, it seems, groups can function primarily on the basis of dominance (as with the common chimpanzees, or as the Red Devils did on occasion) or they can function on the basis of affection and shared activities, as with the pygmy chimpanzees' interest in sex, or with the Bulldogs' interest in organizing joint plans for agreed goals of the group.

Intergroup conflict

Both humans and chimpanzees are adapted to cooperating together in smallish groups: they do this in food gathering, in rearing young, in hunting, and in fighting. It seems to be an aspect of humankind's remarkable capacity for emotional bonding within cooperative groups that others outside these groups can become targets for hostility.

Perhaps the most extraordinary of Goodall's (1986) observations on the chimpanzees of Gombe occurred when she recognized the formation of a new community, when the original one divided. The smaller contingent, which had tended to range south of Goodall's camp, had six adult males. Though the two subcommunities met occasionally, for example, to get fruit at Goodall's camp, and though some interindividual contacts were friendly, in general the two groups were tense on meeting. They started to avoid each other. Finally southern males stopped visiting the camp. In 1974 violent episodes began. Northern males, who would patrol their borders, started to make incursions into the southern range. On one of these a group consisting of six adult males, an adolescent male, and a female came across a southern male on his own. He tried to flee but was caught by the northern males. While one held him, the other males beat him with fists for about 10 minutes, and one bit him several times. When they left him he was severely wounded, and although his body was never found, he was presumed to have died from his injuries. One by one all the other adult animals of the southern group, including a female, were killed in like manner. Adolescent females from the southern group joined the northern group. The human observers were in no doubt that in intercommunity attacks the intention was to kill. The attacks lasted longer than those within a community, and included biting and tearing flesh of the kind seen when eating animals of other species. Attacks were not caused by victims being strangers, because some of them had previously been friends of some of the attackers.

Observations indicated that there were no incursions of southern individuals into the northern range. Attacks were only made by roving gangs of males on individuals or on numerically weaker groups in the southern community. So, annihilating the southern community seemed not predominantly territorial. Hostilities seemed to have more to do with the southerners becoming an outgroup. They became "them." They were no longer "us."

The emotional preference for "us," and hostility to "them," is indeed a candidate for a biologically inherited human universal. The phenomenon of males acting together in groups, in teams, in patrols, that can turn into fighting parties to attack members of an outgroup, seems to be also a candidate for a universal shared by humans and chimpanzees. The instinctual bases of these activities are indicated by commonalities of pattern and the ease with which they can be switched on. They have, in other words, a close similarity to species-characteristic behavior that can be elicited by a crude feature of an eliciting stimulus, and they occur even when, as Darwin (1872) said, they "may not be of the least use" (p. 28). This can be seen in two groups of studies: one set by Tajfel and his colleagues, and one by Sherif and his colleagues.

Tajfel's studies have been discussed widely (Tajfel & Turner, 1979). They consist of assigning people, such as schoolchildren, to groups randomly and then showing that the people give preference to other members of the group of which they had been told they were members, the ingroup, even when they did not know who was in their own group or in the outgroup, and even when their actions and preferences had no effect on themselves.

Phases I and II of Sherif's studies (Sherif, 1956; Sherif & Sherif, 1953) on the formation of within-group relationships among boys at a series of summer camps are described above. In Phase III the investigators moved to studying relations between groups. They arranged a tournament of competitions between the two groups, the Bulldogs and the Red Devils, including tug-of-war, football, and baseball, with cumulating points and coveted prizes of camping knives for every member of the group that got the most points. Success of one group would mean failure for the other. At this point – though not before – boys started to make distinctions between "us" and "them." Accusations and name-calling began between the groups. Fights between members of one group and the other started to occur. Frustration increased angry attitudes and actions towards the outgroup. A proud self-glorifying attitude arose. Each group believed itself to be strong and fearless – each individual believed himself to possess all the strengths of the whole group. While an affectionate, interreliant attitude was present within the ingroup, the outgroup was seen to have very negative qualities.

After intergroup relations had deteriorated the investigators set about trying to improve them. One summer, with one pair of groups, they tried arranging for everyone to share a meal together. But one group arrived before the other and ate most of the food. The other group was furious: a fight occurred and the meal had to be abandoned. The method the investigators finally hit upon for reducing conflict was not meeting together but cooperating on joint projects. One such project was when the investigators arranged that the water supply to the camp was cut off. The boys had to search for the problem in the long pipeline coming into the camp, and then repair it. They could only do this by both groups cooperating. Another was when the boys were hungry and the investigators arranged that the truck, which was to go to town to get food, would not start. The boys used a rope – one that had been used in the tug-of-war competitions – to pull together to start the truck. Hostility did not cease immediately, but after a number of such cooperative activities it was much reduced (see figure 10.3).

It seems likely that the emotions of group coherence are part of a primate heritage that we share with chimpanzees. Though they are essential for human cooperation, without which as a species we would be nothing, they easily acquire, as their obverse, emotions of contempt and hostility to outgroups.

Violence between societies

When whole societies are disrupted, as has occurred when traditional societies have been invaded by industrial ones, violence has often become widespread. In North America, for instance, the cultures of native peoples, including hunter-

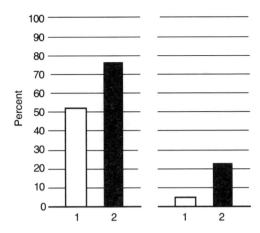

Figure 10.3 Hostility towards an outgroup in Sherif's study. On the left the open histogram shows the proportion of boys in group 1 who thought that *all* (rather than some or none) in group 2 were cheaters, sneaks, and so forth, while the solid histogram shows the proportion of group 2 who thought that all members of group 1 were cheaters, sneaks, and so forth. On the right are comparable histograms after harmony had been restored by cooperative activities.

gatherer groups, the alliance of independent nations of the Iroquois League, the city-based states of Mexico, Guatemala, and Peru, and many other kinds of society, were almost all destroyed (Wright, 1992).

On May 15, 1521, after the Aztec chief Montezuma had formally, and tearfully, signed papers making himself a subject of King Charles V of Spain, acquiescing to the invaders' demands, and after the Spaniards had ransacked his family's treasures, a group of Aztec nobles had asked permission to hold a spring festival that involved dancing. The Spanish leader Cortez had agreed, on condition that the nobles were unarmed. One of Cortez's lieutenants, Alvarado, took the opportunity of the unwary gathering to stage a massacre of the Aztec officers and noblemen. The following is from an account by an Aztec, written down by a Spanish missionary:

> They [the Spaniards] appeared suddenly [at the festival] in battle array . . . quickly they surrounded the dancers; then they rushed among the drums. They hacked at the drummer and cut off both his hands; they chopped off his head and it fell away. Then they ran the people through with iron spears, and slashed at them with iron swords. Some they cut open from behind and these fell to the ground with their intestines hanging out . . . The blood . . . ran like water, like slimy water, the stench of blood filled the air, and the entrails seemed to slither along by themselves. (Wright, 1992, p. 40)

Such scenes have been enacted time and again when societies have clashed. On the opposite side of the world, Dentan describes how the Semai became involved in a war with Communist troops in Malaya. People had thought the Semai would never make soldiers because they were such a nonviolent society, but when some of their people were killed then, outside the context of their culture, their behavior was different. One typical Semai veteran said: "We killed, killed, killed. The Malays would stop and go through people's pockets and take their watches and money, we did not think of taking watches and money. We thought only of killing" (Dentan, 1968, p. 59).

The relation of aggression to anger is not well understood. On the one hand, cycles of revenge occur in many societies, and are certainly associated with anger. But violent events such as these seem to go beyond anger to an appalling capacity of people in our species, usually acting in groups, to treat people of other cultures as nonhuman.

Disgust and contempt

Probably the best way to begin to understand these phenomena is to think not just in terms of anger, though this may also be involved, but in terms of the emotions of disgust and contempt. Though primarily taking impersonal objects, disgust can also be felt towards people. Here, for instance, is a description of the result of the Aztecs under Montezuma offering a gift of precious works of art in gold and other materials, hoping to buy off the aggression of Cortez and the Spaniard invaders.

> The Spaniards faces grinned: they were delighted, they were overjoyed. They snatched up the gold like monkeys . . . They were swollen with greed; they were ravenous; they hungered for that gold like wild pigs . . . They babbled in a barbarous language; everything they said was in a savage tongue. (Wright, 1992, p. 26)

The Aztecs, from whose eye-witness reports this is taken, observe the Spaniards' behavior with disgust, seeing those alien others as behaving not as people but as animals. As Rozin, Haidt, and McCauley (1993) have shown, disgust, though originally derived from taste, can apply to an idea. It extends from protecting the body from disease, to protection against contamination of all kinds, to anything that might harm our soul, or the social order.

If the Aztecs were disgusted in the above account, what are we modern people to say? Instead of the politeness with which a gift is received from an equal within a culture, the Spaniards behaved with contempt. Not just in the eyes of the Aztecs, but also in the eyes of we moderns, their behavior was appalling. This kind of behavior of utter contempt towards members of our own species is indeed a taint that we humans share.

Though in some ways similar to disgust, contempt is separate: it is the emotion of rejection of people who can be treated as members of outgroups. The term most often used in this context is prejudice. To see opponents as nonpeople is often a critical move in warlike relations. It allows others to be massacred, tortured, enslaved, without a thought. Hitler's Nazis were easily able to convince themselves that Jews, homosexuals, and other minority groups, were nonpeople who could be annihilated. In accounts of concentration camps aggressive cruelty often occurred, but the main killer was contemptuous indifference, the treatment of people as nonpeople, as things (Levi, 1958).

When different societies meet, a typical repertoire of emotions is elicited: first is an anxious distrust, perhaps hostility, perhaps a tentative friendliness. One can read about such reactions in the early European meetings with the native inhabitants of the Americas (Wright, 1992), in Captain Cook's meetings with native peoples of the Pacific, or in modern meetings with the few remaining groups previously untroubled by intercultural contact (Nance, 1975). What happens next is more problematic.

Wright makes the point in describing the European conquest of the Americas that both the Spaniards and the Aztecs were fierce and warlike peoples. The Europeans, however, had a secret weapon. To the New World they carried European infections and diseases – measles, influenza, smallpox, cholera – and malaria which Chagnon describes as now responsible for a high proportion of adult deaths among the Yanomamö. The invaders had resistance to these diseases, evolved over centuries. Native peoples of the Americas had none because these diseases simply had not existed there. In 1492 when Columbus landed in the New World, there were perhaps 100 million people living in the Americas, about a fifth of the world's population at the time. By 1600 successive waves of disease had reduced the native population to perhaps 10 million (Wright, 1992, p. 14). To grasp the scale of this, imagine that half the people you know, previously in good health, were to die within the next few years, including your parents, children, the knowledgeable, those in responsible positions. This aspect of the European invasion of the Americas is a tragedy.

Deaths from sickness were not at first deliberate, but infection was later used by Europeans as a means of killing native people. The term tragedy is not adequate for this and other deliberate aspects of the European conquest, forwarded by its firearms and metal-based technology, and characterized by its utter disregard of any human standard of behavior. In reading about this, we feel as we do when we read of the deliberate destruction of six million people by the Nazis because they were members of an outgroup.

The emotions of war may be yet more complex: sometimes impelled by material greed, very often fueled by angry revenge, almost invariably insulated from compassion for those who are killed in contempt, always fostered by close bonding within a male group which cultivates its traditions and heroes. In these ways warriors down the ages and across cultures have experienced their own emotional excitements. It may be, as Keegan (1994) says in what has been regarded as the best history of warfare yet written (one that includes anthropological evidence), that: "War is almost as old as man himself, and reaches into the most secret places of the human heart, places where self dissolves rational purpose, where pride reigns, where emotion is paramount, where instinct is king" (p. 3).

The warrior mentality is part of the human repertoire, but to be expressed it needs to be culturally cultivated, and cultures change. So, as Keegan points out, in medieval times the Vikings were universally feared round the coasts of Northern Europe, their name a synonym for ruthless aggression. Now the Scandinavians are known for peaceable neutrality and tolerance. Canadians were among the fiercest of fighters in World War II; now the Canadian army is known for its peacekeeping role. The striking and convincing aspect of Keegan's history is the evidence he gives that warfare is a cultural form which can and does wither when social arrangements no longer support it, but that its roots are not so much political as emotional. When these roots are watered by loyalties to an ethnic, religious, or other cultural group, and by emotions of revenge for privation, shame, or humiliation inflicted on that group, then the warlike mentality quickly springs up again in all its destructive force.

The most important question of understanding the past is how to construct the future. In the first part of the 1990s Eastern Europe has been in turmoil. Nationalistic aggression has been expressed in unspeakable ways; refugees and economic migrants have arrived in new societies. At the same time, in some countries multiculturalism is official policy. We need to find ways of understanding and valuing other cultures, even though one of the attributes of culture is to include some and exclude others. Western culture has not spread because its values are superior to those of other cultures. Far from it: the behavior of Spanish conquistadors in America was merely one example of a common and disgraceful European pattern against non-Europeans. European cultures and their American descendants have been among the most aggressive, and in numerical terms certainly the most destructive, that the world has seen.

But if emotions are to some extent universal, then as well as separating people they can build links. Just as empathy becomes an emotional foundation of children's sense of morality towards other children, emotional empathy for other people and other cultures can provide a foundation for an intercultural morality. If there were no universals of emotions, there would be no basis for concerted world action on anything, no human sympathy for the oppressed, no outrage against tyranny, no passion for justice, no concern for protecting or sharing the world's limited resources.

Anger and contempt in marriage

Human aggression and violence derive not from one but from several kinds of emotion. One can wound in anger – and also in contempt. In warlike relations there is a difference. In one kind of case there are rules, such as the Geneva Convention: despite their intention to kill, combatants maintain some rights in the eyes of the other. In other instances there are none: in death camps people are treated with contempt. Are similar emotions aroused in our more intimate relations? The answer is "Yes." Some of the forces seen in the clash of societies occur between individuals in sexual relationships. To complement the opening of this chapter on the factors that make for falling in love, we will close on the topic of staying in love, and of falling out of love.

Aggression can stem from anger and from the human equivalents of dominance disputes, or it can stem from contempt. In a series of studies over 20 years, Gottman and Levenson (1992) have asked married couples to come into their laboratory. As well as asking them to complete a range of questionnaires, the basic method was to have the couples discuss three topics after an absence from each other of at least eight hours. One topic was the events of the day. Another was a matter that was conflictual between the two spouses. A third was an agreed pleasant topic. Their facial expressions were videotaped and physiological variables were measured, including heart rate, skin conductance, finger pulse amplitude (an index of sympathetic nervous system activation). A few days after the discussion each spouse individually returned to the laboratory, was again connected to the physiological recording apparatus, and was asked to view a videotape of his or her discussion sessions. When doing so he or she was asked to move a pointer within the range "Extremely negative," through "Neutral," to "Extremely positive," to indicate how he or she remembered feeling at each moment of the videotaped discussion.

Gottman and Levenson (1992) studied 73 couples and on the basis of the content of their discussion about their conflictual subject classified them into 42 "regulated" and 31 "nonregulated" couples. Regulated couples were those for whom both spouses had a predominance of neutral or positive features. Unregulated couples had at least one spouse whose turns in the discussion had predominantly negative features.

The experimenters classified turns in the conversation in terms of five content codes. On each turn in the discussion, the speaker was given a score of one positive point for each of the following: problem description, task-oriented relationship information, assent, humor or laughter, and any other positive feature. Negative contents were coded by turns that included any of these eight codes, one negative point for each: complaint, criticism, talking of the relationship in negative terms, saying "yes-but," defensive maneuver, put-down, escalating negative affect, and any other negative feature. A balance score was calculated for each turn in the discussion by subtracting each speaker's negative from positive points. In figure 10.4 you can see examples of the balance scores of a regulated and a nonregulated couple.

Gottman and Levenson's nonregulated couples engaged more in conflict, were more defensive, more angry, more withdrawn as listeners, less affectionate, less interested in their partners, and less joyful in the interaction. The experimenters postulated that instability in a marriage – setting off on a path of becoming first dissatisfied, then seriously considering splitting up, then undergoing separation, and finally divorce – is predicted by couples failing to maintain at least a five-to-one ratio of positive to negative features in their conflictual interactions.

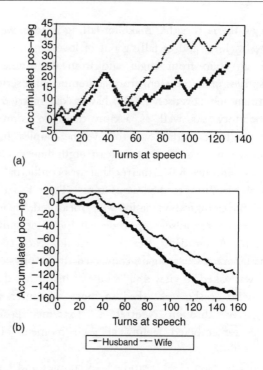

Figure 10.4 Cumulative graphs of two couples in Gottman and Levenson's (1992) study engaged in a discussion: (a) a regulated couple, (b) a nonregulated couple.

As Kemper (1990) might say: the issue in these couples is whether they become largely concerned with power, or are concerned with giving the other status and affection. Gottman (1993b), and in his self-help book (1993a), has proposed that stability involves maintaining at least a five-to-one ratio of positive to negative affect in interactions, though he does not consider the meanings of the concerns expressed. He has proposed a taxonomy. Some couples he calls "Validators": each member listens to, understands, and validates what the other is saying. "Volatiles" assented less but had a higher intensity of emotions both positive and negative. "Avoiders" minimized conflict and were generally less emotional than the other two groups. Instability in marriages, he proposes, is a feature of "Hostile" and "Hostile Detached" styles, in which at least one spouse does not manage to maintain the five-to-one ratio of positive to negative affect.

In verbal arguments between pairs of high-school students, Stein et al. (in press) have shown that students taking up opposing positions can reach compromises. Pairs who compromise are more likely to concentrate on making plans for the future, and to use a more accepting tones in considering the other's arguments. Those who take up a win–lose position are more likely to focus on the past, to make negative appraisals such as blame, and to express frustration, anger, and contempt.

In terms of a theory of emotions, it seems that anger, though people dislike it, and although it was less frequent in the stable couples studied by Gottman, is not the main corrosive force in relationships. According to Gottman, destructive elements are more expressions of contempt, more whining, more defensiveness, more stubbornness, more withdrawal, more stonewalling. Anger can be the expression of individuality, and although some marriages (such as Gottman's validators) are predominantly intimate in their "we-togetherness," others allow more individualism, and this inevitably involves more anger and conflict. But the volatile couples had ways of resolving these conflicts.

Confirming Averill's (1982) conclusion that most incidents of anger are seen as readjustment of a relationship, Jenkins, Smith, and Graham (1989) found in a study of 139 families that 79 percent of women interviewed about quarrels with their spouses that involved voices raised in anger for at least 10 minutes, thought that at least some good came from such quarrels. Though frequent, open and overheard parental quarrels are clearly not good for children's mental health, as we discussed in chapter 8, they may be important and functional in marriage where partners also wish to maintain some individuality. Gottman's hypothesis is that what is more problematic for continuance of marriage is something else: it is when partners come to view the other with contempt, the emotion that indicates that the other is no longer entitled to consideration or respect. In evolutionary terms it seems that contempt is the emotion of complete rejection, of unmodulated power, treating the other as a nonperson. Tooby and Cosmides (1990) argue that emotions enable us to glimpse something of our ancestral conditions. We can imagine that contempt may have been functional among our prehuman and early human ancestors, in confrontation with other human-like species, whom *Homo sapiens* finally displaced. It may also have been functional in seminomadic groups where huge tracts of land were available. If disputes arose and could not be resolved a group could divide and part. The two subgroups need seldom or never see each other again. In modern life divorce is a similar strategy for married couples. Here contempt functions, perhaps according to Averill's theory, as a temporary role, to produce separation. Continuing emotions of contempt, loathing, and hatred occur when there is mental withdrawal but physical proximity. In community relations it is seen as ethnic conflict. In marriages that have turned sour it is seen when couples remain together with predominantly negative rather than positive feelings for each other.

Summary

Love and anger, related to affection and power, are twin emotional poles of human social life. Love can perhaps best be thought of as having several aspects; one is the ordinary happiness of human relating based on warmth and affection, others are attachment, caregiving, and erotic love. In evolutionary terms, all of these are essential to the cooperation between people in pairs, and among people in groups, on which the human adaptation depends. The emotions of conflict within a group are anger and fear. In many primate species dominance hierarchies form, and these occur too in many human societies. Their emotions are anger and submissive fear. Anger, however, is typically an emotion that occurs between people within a community; though some interdependent societies avoid anger, in individualistic societies anger functions to enable assertion of the self in conflictual situations, and typically also the renegotiation of a relationship. By contrast with anger, the emotions of contempt are those of rejection of someone or some group from society, and they amount to treating others as nonpeople. Though anger and contempt both share a repertoire of aggressive action, there are good reasons for distinguishing them. Among societies, contempt enables outgroups to be denied human rights. Anger and contempt also occur within intimate relationships, for instance in marriage. Here it is not so much anger which is the corrosive force, but contempt, which make the relationship vulnerable to dissolution.

Further Reading

Among the several interesting books recently published on love, one with a number of useful articles is:

Robert J. Sternberg & Michael L. Barnes (Eds.) (1988). *The psychology of love*. New Haven, CT: Yale University Press.

Among the best single author works on love is a book by an anthropologist:

Helen E. Fisher (1992). *Anatomy of love*. New York: Norton.

The best general book on anger, in our view, is:

Carol Tavris (1982). *Anger: The misunderstood emotion*. New York: Simon & Schuster.

For the emotions of war one could scarcely do better than:

John Keegan (1994). *A history of warfare*. New York: Vintage.

CHAPTER 11

The Role of Emotions in Adult Psychopathology

Contents

Figure 11.0 Depressed woman. One of the striking results of psychiatric epidemiology is that the prevalence of emotional disorders is about twice as high in women as in men. By contrast men more frequently are dependent on alcohol and other drugs, and are much more frequently instigators of violent crime.

. . . human misery has awakened, stood before you, and today demands its proper place.

Jean Jourès (1897) cited by Kleinman, 1988, p. 53

Causes of emotional disorders

Into the lives of many people come periods of extreme emotion: hopeless depression or disabling anxiety – states referred to as psychopathology. Our objective in this chapter is not to cover the whole field – for that you need a book such as that of Oltmanns and Emery (1995). Here we aim to make sense of some of the roles emotions play in psychopathology. And whereas children seem to be primarily responsive to their immediate environment – for instance to a contented family or a distressing one – in adulthood people carry more of their lives with them, in their heads, from one setting to another.

Psychiatric epidemiology

How common are extreme emotional experiences in ordinary populations? To answer this question we turn to psychiatric epidemiology – the statistical study of how frequently disorders occur. The epidemiologist is a detective, finding out why some people suffer disorders, while others do not.

One might think that modern medicine owes its success to the discovery of drugs like antibiotics, and from advances such as surgery without germs but with anaesthetics. But history shows that infectious disease was receding before these innovations; really the advances that were most important in improving health were different. They were the epidemiological discoveries of how people caught infectious diseases, and the technical and social accomplishments of reducing infection by providing clean water and removing sewage from towns (Cartwright, 1977). Similarly in psychiatry, the discovery of drugs for depression, anxiety, and schizophrenia has been important, but more important will be prevention. From work in psychiatric epidemiology have come insights into who becomes psychiatrically disordered and why, and this lays the groundwork for reducing risk.

Psychiatric epidemiology has been slow to take its place alongside the epidemiology of physical medicine, mainly because it was difficult to agree on criteria for what constitutes a disorder, and because reliable psychological instruments (such as standardized interview schedules) had not been developed. Just as for the psychiatric epidemiology of childhood discussed in chapter 8, there are now suitable classification schemes and instruments for adults. Populations have been studied to find how common mental health problems are. In the most recent study in the USA, Kessler et al. (1994) used a research interview to make diagnoses and to determine risks in 48 states. Interviews were carried out with 8,098 people between the ages of 15 and 54, with a response rate of 82.6 percent.

Among the striking findings of this and of similar studies (Robins & Regier, 1991) was that depression and anxiety states, the two main emotion-based disorders, were nearly twice as common in women as in men. So in Kessler et al.'s study, as you can see from table 11.1, 21 percent of adult women have had an episode of major depression at some time in their life, as compared with 13 percent of men. Similarly women were much more likely (30.5 percent) than men (19 percent) to have had one of the five kinds of anxiety disorder diagnosed in the study.

As explained in chapter 8, percentages of people suffering from a diagnosed disorder over a specific time are called prevalences. By contrast with the higher prevalence for women of depression and anxiety, Kessler et al. found that 35 percent of men, but only 18 percent of women, had a disorder of alcohol or drug abuse or dependence at some time in their life. Men also had a higher prevalence (6 percent) of antisocial personality disorder, which is the adult equivalent of childhood conduct disorder, as compared with women (1 percent). These gender differences in how psychiatric problems are expressed are thought to continue a trend in childhood (see chapter 8), where boys are much more likely than girls to have externalizing disorders, and girls somewhat more likely than boys to have internalizing disorders. A change between childhood and adulthood occurs in depression. There is no gender

Table 11.1 Lifetime prevalences of psychiatric conditions in males and females in the 48 contiguous United States, using the Composite International Diagnostic Interview from which DSM-III-R diagnoses were made

Disorder	Male	Female	Total
Affective (depression related) disorder			
Major depressive episode	12.7	21.3	17.1
Manic episode	1.6	1.7	1.6
Dysthymia	4.8	8.0	6.4
Any affective disorder	14.7	23.9	19.3
Anxiety disorders			
Panic disorder	2.0	5.0	3.5
Agoraphobia without panics	3.5	7.0	5.3
Social phobia	11.1	15.5	13.3
Simple phobia	6.7	15.7	11.3
Generalized anxiety disorder	3.6	6.6	5.1
Any anxiety disorder	19.2	30.5	24.9
Other disorders			
Alcohol or drug abuse or dependence	35.4	17.9	26.6
Antisocial personality	5.8	1.2	3.5
Nonaffective psychosis	0.6	0.8	0.7
Any psychiatric disorder	48.7	47.3	48.0

Source: Kessler et al. (1994)

difference in prevalence of depression in childhood. Only in adulthood does the difference become large. Notice too the differences in prevalence as a function of income: people who had few material resources had more frequent disorder, see table 11.2.

The other major epidemiological study in the USA was the Epidemiologic Catchment Area study (Robins & Regier, 1991). Twenty thousand people were interviewed in five areas: New Haven, Eastern Baltimore, St Louis, Durham, and Los Angeles. This study shows patterns that were broadly similar to those of Kessler et al., in depression, anxiety, alcohol and drug-related disorders, and antisocial personality disorder. Robins & Regier, however, estimated lifetime prevalence of depression as 10.2 percent for women and 5.2 percent for men – lower than those reported by Kessler et al. (1994), probably because interviewers asked about some symptoms differently, and excluded some disorders if they were responses to particular events such as bereavements. Poverty was associated with increased risk of disorder overall, but this effect was not seen in the same disorders in both studies.

Differences in prevalence, such as those due to gender and poverty, are the clues the epidemiological detective starts with. Some are far larger than most of the differences that psychologists deal with. But the evidence is correlational; it does not tell us whether poverty makes depression more likely, or whether being depressed makes it harder to hold a job. So the next step was to find out what kinds of events and circumstances are related to becoming depressed. Could it be, for instance, that events of the kind that cause negative emotions also cause emotional disorders?

Table 11.2 Relative lifetime prevalences of psychiatric disorders as a function of sex and income. In each section of the table one group is assigned a rate of 1.00. For other groups within the section rates are expressed as multiples of this. For instance, in the first section, the rate for any affective disorder in women is 1.82 times that for men

	Any affective disorder	Any anxiety disorder	Any alcohol or drug disorder	Any disorder	Three or more disorders
Sex					
Male	1.00	1.00	1.00	1.00	1.00
Female	1.82*	1.85*	0.40*	0.95	1.24*
Income					
$0–19,000	1.56*	2.00*	1.27*	1.49*	2.46*
$20,000–34,000	1.19	1.52*	1.06	1.21	1.71*
$35,000–69,000	1.16	1.48*	1.06	1.21	1.55*
$70,000 or more	1.00	1.00	1.00	1.00	1.00

Note: In each group of figures an asterisk indicates a prevalence for which there was a significant difference ($p < 0.05$) from the prevalence with the standard value of 1.00. Not shown are relative prevalences by years of education: people who did not finish high school were no more or less likely to suffer affective disorder, but were significantly more likely to have anxiety disorders. Antisocial personality disorder was significantly associated with low income and with having completed few years of education.
Source: Kessler et al. (1994)

Life events and difficulties

One of the most important studies on why people develop disorders of anxiety and depression was carried out by Brown and Harris (1978). They interviewed 458 adult women in London, England, and found that in the previous year, 37 of them (8 percent) had suffered an onset of depression (some with anxiety) at a level that was disabling, the "case" level. In ordinary language such onsets are called "breakdowns." A further 9 percent of the women had a disabling psychiatric problem at the case level for more than a year (totalling 17 percent with a disorder during the year before interview).

In Brown and Harris's study, 89 percent of women with an onset of depression had a severely threatening life event or difficulty shortly before their breakdown. By contrast, of women who did not have any disorder at the case level, only 30 percent had suffered a severe event or difficulty. Severe events included bereavement, marital separation, job loss. Difficulties were long-lasting problems such as having to cope with a violent husband or looking after a demanding and chronically sick relative.

Brown and Harris developed a new method that gave stronger predictions of who would get depressed than had previously been possible, in the form of a semistructured interview (the Life Events and Difficulties Schedule). People

Figure 11.1 Poverty is a fundamental cause of depression which has hopelessness at its core, and contributes to other emotional disorders, and to antisocial disorders. In Western industrialized society being poor means having few or no resources to deal with life's adversities: not a mysterious concept, but one that does not get the attention it deserves in the psychiatry textbooks.

were asked about 40 areas of life – employment, finances, housing, children, relationships, and so forth. Interviews were audio recorded, and each stressful event or difficulty was written up as a brief vignette. This was later read to the research team who made a rating of the degree of long-term threat (lasting more than a week) that this event or difficulty would cause in a woman living in the described circumstances. Ratings of long-term severity of threat of an event or difficulty are made according to the intuitions of people (the researchers) living in the same society. At the same time these ratings pass the tests of being reliable. They are anchored over time by comparing them with previous ratings made by the research team over the years. The ratings are unbiased since the raters did not know the woman's diagnosis. They also are not dependent on the woman's own assessment of how distressing she found any event – which, of course, might be affected by how depressed she was.

People become depressed when extreme adversities occur. Here is the case of Mrs Trent, one of the women in Brown and Harris's study.

> Mrs Trent (not her real name) had three small children and was married to a van driver. Her apartment had two rooms and a kitchen. A year before the interview she had occasional migraine headaches, but she felt quite herself. Her third child was born eight months before the interview. Around that time her husband lost his job. She didn't worry too much, and he got another job quickly. But after two weeks he was fired from that job too, without explanation. Seven weeks later her worries had become so severe that she felt tense all the time, she felt miserable, did not sleep well, and became irritable with the children. She found it difficult to do the housework, became unable to concentrate, and her appetite declined. In the next two months these symptoms worsened. She would often cry all day. She got some sleeping pills from her doctor. Her relationship with her husband deteriorated. She lost all interest in sex and thought her marriage finished. Three times she packed and walked out but returned because of the children. She felt self-deprecatory, felt she could not cope, and thought that she might end it all. By three weeks before the interview things had started to get better. She still tended to brood, though her concentration was now good enough for her to watch television, which distracted her. Her sexual relationship with her husband had returned, and indeed was better than before. She had been depressed for five-and-a-half months. She had not consulted her doctor about depression, but about her migraines. It was for these, she said, that the sleeping pills had been prescribed. She thought it would have been wrong to bother her doctor about feeling depressed, since this was clearly related to her financial and marital worries. (Paraphrased from Brown & Harris, 1978, pp. 28–30)

In this case the severely threatening event was her husband's second occasion of being fired, which left the family without an income. Sleep disturbances, loss of weight, lack of concentration, self-deprecation, loss of interest in sex, and suicidal thoughts, were all symptoms of depression. In Brown and Harris's method Mrs Trent's marital difficulty was not counted as an event that could have caused the depression because it could easily have been caused by it. Others too have distinguished between events that people could have brought on themselves and those that were beyond their control. Shrout et al. (1989)

found that clinic patients suffering from depression were three times more likely than people in a nondepressed community sample to have suffered a negative and uncontrollable event. So depression is not necessarily irrational. It involves sadness and hopelessness, brought on by events that have serious implications for our lives and our views of ourselves.

Events that can cause depression are losses of what is most highly valued. Using life event interviews, Hammen et al. (1989) found that people who valued their relationships most became depressed when a social loss or social disruption occurred. Those to whom autonomy and work were most important were more likely to become depressed when a failure in achievement occurred.

Some people have argued that depression identified in community samples and related to life events is different in kind from the depression seen in clinics (Bebbington et al., 1981). The former has been called reactive depression and the latter endogenous depression. It has been assumed that endogenous depression is more biologically based, with a stronger genetic component. However, even in samples drawn from clinics of patients with repeated depression, and even in those with so-called endogenous depression, serious life events have been found to be related to onsets of depression (Bebbington et al., 1981; Frank et al., 1994). Brown and Moran (1994) have argued that for people with repeated episodes of depression, although subsequent episodes often occur without any obvious cause in their lives, their first episode was caused by a severe life event or difficulty.

Episodes of anxiety can also be caused by negative events (Monroe & Wade, 1988). In one study of a community sample, 2,902 men and women were interviewed using standardized measures to diagnose generalized anxiety and to assess life events occurring over the previous year (Blazer, Hughes, & George, 1987). Severe negative events were associated with a threefold increase of anxiety disorder in both men and women. Lesser events were associated with an eightfold increase of generalized anxiety disorder in men, but this relationship was not found in women.

Are anxiety and depression caused by the same kinds of event? Finlay-Jones (1989), using Brown and Harris's method, interviewed women attending a general practice: 85 percent of cases of anxiety, 82 percent of cases with depression, and 93 percent of cases with mixed anxiety and depression had suffered a severe life event as compared with 34 percent of those who were not suffering from any emotional disorder. Some events were future-directed, involving danger: receiving a diagnosis of a cancer, unwanted pregnancy, threat of eviction from home. Anxiety disorders were most often precipitated by such danger events. By contrast depressive disorders were most often precipitated by events which were losses. People who suffered from both anxiety and depression experienced events involving both danger and loss.

One specific type of anxiety disorder, posttraumatic stress disorder, has a severe adverse event as a criterion of diagnosis. Such events occur in war, when people have been in danger of their own lives, when companions have been killed and maimed (Grinker & Spiegel, 1945), also in natural and industrial disasters, as well as with assaults such as rape (Burnam et al., 1988). People's well-being is severely threatened. Symptoms involve intense anxiety, disturbed sleep, and compulsive replays of the trauma in flashbacks.

It is clear that most episodes of major depression and some types of anxiety occur when things go severely wrong in people's lives, and have serious long-term consequences. Like episodes of normal emotion, most emotional disorders are responses to events and circumstances. They let us know what is most important to us. When Mrs Trent's husband lost his job, she experienced feelings of defeat, and of dread about not being able to live adequately or to provide for her family.

So here is the first, perhaps the most important, relation of emotions to emotional disorders. Short-term emotions and moods are states of action readiness. Emotional disorders include emotions, but in a disorder these are described as more intense, longer lasting (see the time spectrum of emotional states in chapter 4), and as disabling. Mrs Trent experienced loss of her family's means of support, and lost hope. Her state was a severely decreased readiness, an inability to do normally the things that were most important to her, such as care for her children. Why the human condition is subject to such disabling states remains a puzzle for theories of emotions. Reflect, though, that we live in very different ways now than we did in our environments of evolutionary adaptedness; depression may, moreover, help people pull back or disengage from ongoing plans and commitments, perhaps prompting them to establish and organize new goals (Oatley, 1992).

Vulnerability factors

The conclusion that episodes of depression are usually started by some severe life event or difficulty is now widely accepted. Yet not everyone who experiences serious adversity suffers a breakdown. What is the difference between responding with an emotion or mood and responding with an emotional disorder of depression or anxiety? What makes one person more vulnerable than another?

Early experience: the value of being loved by a parent
A person who loses a parent in childhood, particularly a mother, is more likely to develop depression in later life (Brown & Harris, 1978). Originally it was thought that it was loss of the attachment figure that left the individual vulnerable. It now seems that it is not the loss as such, but the lack of parental care that is likely to follow such a loss which has the negative effect. Women who were neglected during childhood, or who experienced physical or sexual abuse, are at increased risk of both depression and anxiety as adults (Brewin, Andrews, & Gotlib, 1993; Brown & Harris, 1993).

In part, poor care in childhood makes people put themselves into situations of higher risk for life events. So Quinton, Rutter, and Liddle (1984, discussed in chapter 8) found that women who as children had been raised in institutions had earlier pregnancies, poorer sexual relationships, and more problematic parenting than normal. In other studies too, women vulnerable to depression have been found to bring more life events upon themselves; so Hammen (1991) found that women who had a history of major depression experienced more life events, even when not depressed, than women without a history of depression. Most such events were interpersonal, such as conflicts with a spouse or with children.

The vulnerability of early neglect may consist, in part, of damage in people's sense of themselves as being valuable and worthy of love. Negative emotion schemas of self-in-relationship can increase people's risk of depression by making more likely the kinds of situations that can turn out badly for them. People who have experienced lack of care may have yearnings for love, which prompt them towards hasty or early marriages. But with too unconsidered choices, the risk of such relationships being punitive is increased. This can confirm expectations of defeat and loss, which become part of the self-deprecating pattern of depression.

Whitbeck et al. (1992) found that when parents are depressed they are more likely to be rejecting of their children. The children are then more likely to develop difficulties, contributing further to rejection by parents. Sadly, these cycles of vulnerability within relationships are transgenerational. In chapter 8 we reviewed evidence showing that children were more likely to be depressed when they were in families with a depressed parent, than in nondepressed homes. Based on their own experience of the parent–child relationship, such children form schemas about themselves in relationships that they carry with them into their own adulthood.

Attributional style

The best-known clinical theory of cognitive vulnerability (Beck, 1983; Beck & Emery, 1985) identifies irrational thought patterns, carried over from childhood, as being associated with depression and anxiety. This thinking is overgeneralized and exaggerated, often set off by attending to events with negative connotations while events with positive connotations are not noticed. It involves jumping to conclusions arbitrarily, and seeing events as personal even when they may not have any personal significance. (We gave an example from Beck's work in chapter 4, of the medical records librarian upset by the attitude of the operating room nurse.) Attributional versions of the theory of learned helplessness (Abramson, Metalsky, & Alloy, 1989; Abramson, Seligman, & Teasdale, 1978) also take styles of thinking as predisposing to depression. The idea is that people become depressed if an event occurs over which they have no control when they see the event: (a) as having occurred for internal reasons, because of the self rather than anything external; (b) as global, happening in all situations rather than being local to just the current circumstance; and (c) as stable, meaning permanent rather than temporary.

Coyne and Gotlib (1983) have shown that Beck's theory and these attributional theories are very similar in their formulations and predictions.

Here is a recent study by members of the principal group of attribution theorists who work on depression (Metalsky et al., 1993). Students took a midterm examination. Their attributional style, their self-esteem, and their scores on Beck's Depression Inventory (BDI) were assessed before the exam and at several points after they received their grades. When the students received their grades, scores on the BDI were predicted only by how well they did, not by attributional style. Those who would continue to feel low beyond the first day after failing the exam, however, were predicted by their attributional style and self-esteem.

One caution: this study on students taking an exam is unusually good in that it tests a real event of importance to the participants. At the same time, like many other quasiexperimental studies, it takes changes on mood scales such as the BDI as indicating depression. Coyne (1994) has pointed out that changes on such self-report scales do not show that subjects are becoming clinically depressed. The epidemiological studies discussed at the beginning of this chapter, and those of Brown and his colleagues, use research diagnostic interviews to establish whether a person has (or had) a syndrome of major depression at the case level, and we know from this work that reasons for reaching the case level are much more serious than failing a midterm exam. Coyne points out that there is no evidence that lowering of mood on scales such as the BDI is an analog of clinical depression.

Self-esteem

For depression that reaches clinical proportions this theme of cognitive vulnerability has been taken up in research on self-esteem (Gotlib & Hammen, 1992). In a longitudinal study Brown et al. (1990) measured low self-esteem – a concept not too far from making internal attributions of failure – by counting the number of self-deprecatory remarks women made about themselves at a first interview. A year later among those who had suffered a severe event or difficulty, those who had made self-deprecatory remarks were more than twice as likely to have suffered major depression, as those who had evaluated themselves positively.

So, although early experience and later depression are linked, and from chapter 8 we know that some children show signs of depressive patterns that can continue into adult life, it is still not quite clear what aspect of cognitive or emotional functioning is affected. Thinking negatively about the self does seem to be involved in serious cases of depression, as well as in less serious cases of failure at some task.

Appraisal-based thinking

A new approach to the study of thinking style as a vulnerability factor, especially interesting to researchers on emotions because it is based on appraisals as described in chapter 4, comes from a research group who used narrative analysis to predict patterns of coping in people whose loved ones had died. Stein et al. (1995) followed up 30 people who were not themselves infected with Human Immunodeficiency Virus (HIV) but whose partners had died of AIDS from this virus. The subjects were interviewed two and four weeks after their loss, and then one year later. In the two earlier interviews, they were asked to talk about their partners, their experience of loss, what had happened at the time of their partners' death, and what helped them to cope. Appraisals were defined as evaluations about people, places, events, actions or outcomes that affected the status of their goals and well-being. Positive appraisals included talking about beneficial aspects of their relationship, or about how subjects felt they had been good caregivers. Negative appraisals included statements about fear of the future, and regrets about the quality of the relationship people had with their partners. The proportion of positive appraisals made in the narrative shortly after bereavement was a remarkably strong predictor of positive morale ($r = -0.63$) as well as self-reported depressive symptomatology ($r = -0.51$) one year later. Positive appraisals remained significant predictors of well-being at one year even after controlling for well-being or depression in the first month.

Social support

Close relationships have a huge effect on whether people develop major depression in response to adversities. Having an intimate relationship acts as a buffer. There has been a substantial amount of work demonstrating this relationship, first by Brown and Harris (1978), and subsequently by many others. So for instance, Parry and Shapiro (1986) interviewed women with low incomes and at least one young child. Of those who did not suffer any life event or difficulty 5 percent of those with an intimate relationship and 10 percent of those without one broke down with major depression. But of those who did suffer a severe event or difficulty, 10 percent of those with an intimate relationship, but 30 percent of those without one, broke down with major depression. In a study by Solomon and Bromet (1982) mothers with small children were studied after the severe event of the accident at Three Mile Island nuclear power plant in Pennsylvania, which released large quantities of radioactivity into the atmosphere. Here too there was a similar pattern, which you can see, along with other results in table 11.3. The general pattern is that social support has a small effect on its own, but it buffers against life events and difficulties when these occur (Cohen & Wills, 1985).

Most studies we have discussed so far have been carried out on women – this choice is made to maximize the number of cases found. But what about men? Is their vulnerability similar or different? In a cross-sectional study in Los Angeles, Anashensel and Stone (1982) did find a similar pattern for men as for women of becoming depressed when life events occurred, when the subject was without intimate social support – see table 11.3. There have been proposals that for men, being integrated into a community is the most important form of social support (Bolton & Oatley, 1987) but the data are not as extensive or reliable as they are for the protection of a single well-functioning intimate relationship for women.

Social support has been a very important concept in understanding the psychological impact of life events, but it is not a simple one. Typical social support measures include having a confidant, lack of interpersonal friction, interpersonal appreciation, integration in a social network, and practical assistance. Thoits (1986) has identified social support as assistance from other people in coping with the slings and arrows of life. Sarason et al. (1987) compared various measures of social support, and concluded that though they focus on different aspects of relationships, high social support generally indicates whether a person is accepted, loved, and involved in relationships where communication is open.

Table 11.3 Percentages of subjects suffering an episode of major depression, in several studies, as a function of whether or not they had a severe life event or difficulty, and whether or not they had social support in the form of an intimate relationship

		Intimacy of subject's closest relationship	
		High	*Low*
	Severe event or difficulty	*% depressed*	*% depressed*
Original study			
Brown & Harris (1978)	No	1	3
(*n* = 419, London, UK)	Yes	10	32
Replications			
Costello (1982)	No	5	7
(*n* = 386, Calgary, Canada)	Yes	21	57
Bebbington et al. (1984)	No	6	11
(*n* = 152, London, UK)	Yes	24	22
Parry & Shapiro (1986)	No	5	10
(*n* = 189, Sheffield, UK)	Yes	10	31
Similar studies			
Paykel et al. (1980)*	No	12	14
(*n* = 104, following childbirth)	Yes	24	82
Anashensel & Stone (1982)*	No	12	22
(*n* = 998, Los Angeles)	Yes	14	37
Solomon & Bromet (1982)	No	9	7
(*n* = 432, event was Three Mile Island nuclear accident)	Yes	12	21
Murphy (1982)	No	3	0
(*n* = 200 elderly people)	Yes	11	35

* includes chronic cases
Source: Oatley and Bolton (1985)

Despite adversities that undermine the sense of self, people with social support can experience themselves as continuing to achieve goals of interaction with others. In interactions with a supportive partner or friend, we do not experience the defeat or rejection that can occur in other aspects of life. In a supportive relationship we experience the other person as caring about what is important to us, and as helping us move forward with our aspirations and plans.

Genetic effects

In chapter 7 we discussed evidence that patterns of emotionality are genetically influenced. This is also true for psychopathology, as we mentioned in chapter 8. People inherit tendencies that raise the risk of depression and anxiety, both at the case level and at lower levels, that are more like personality traits (Kendler et al., 1986). People may inherit tendencies towards lower thresholds for certain negative emotions, maybe for experiencing more fear or sadness. One hypothesis is that a susceptibility to anxiety is biologically based (Hamm,

Figure 11.2 Woman off to work and day care. By the 1950s in the USA 50 percent of women with children were employed outside the home. In London, England, Brown and Harris (1978) found that a job outside the home was protective against depression when severe life events or difficulties occurred.

Vaitl, & Lang, 1990). A high genetic sensitivity of a mechanism that learns to associate certain cues to schemas based on anxiety may explain why some people are generally more fearful than others, despite not having experienced serious danger in their lives.

One way genetic effects are studied is by comparing frequencies of disorder between monozygotic (MZ) twins who share 100 percent of their genes and dizygotic (DZ) twins who share 50 percent. As we explained in chapter 7, a genetic effect is inferred when there is a much larger concordance (appearance of some feature in both members of each twin pair) for the MZ twins than for DZ twins.

Two kinds of environmental effects have also been found. Where the concordances between MZ and DZ twins are both similar and high for some disorder, then it is likely that shared environmental experience (for instance parents' marital conflict) has had a strong effect. Where concordance rates are similar and low for both MZ and DZ twins, then it likely that nonshared environmental factors were important, for instance one child receiving more love and attention than another.

Several recent studies have found genetic effects for major depression. Kendler et al. (1993b) examined 938 twins from a population registry at one point (Time 1) and then a year later (Time 2). At Time 1 concordance for MZ twins was 27 percent (i.e. in 27 percent of twins both members had the disorder) and for DZ twins concordance was 17 percent. The difference was slightly greater at Time 2 (28.9 vs 15.4 percent). These concordances are on the low side, indicating nonshared environmental factors such as the life events discussed earlier in this chapter, and such factors account for more variance in major depression than do genetic effects. But genetic effects, indicated by the difference in MZ and DZ concordances, were also substantial.

One way in which a genetic influence for depression could work would be in terms of bias – positive or negative – on social confidence and dominance, perhaps, as we discussed in chapter 3, mediated in part by mechanisms that use the transmitter substance serotonin – many antidepressant drugs work to increase the availability of this substance. The genetic influences on depression do not, however, only operate on biases toward depression itself. Plomin et al. (1990) examined life events in a twin population. They found that MZ twins were much more similar to each other than DZ twins in the number of events experienced during their lifetime. Kendler et al. (1993a) examined life events over the previous year in MZ and DZ twin pairs, and found that frequencies of life events were more strongly correlated in MZ pairs than in DZ pairs, with genetic effects being estimated to account for about 20 percent of the variance. One explanation is that personality is influenced by genes, and it can affect the occurrence of life events. Impulsiveness, for instance, may raise the rate of severe events. Plomin and Bergeman (1991) have reviewed studies that show how variables thought to be environmental (like life events) may be influenced by genetics – remember we have argued that some people can bring more severe events and difficulties upon themselves; such events show quite strong genetic associations. It is also easy to see that some people may be predisposed to forming more long-lasting supportive relationships than others. But in addition even uncontrollable events show a modest association with genetics.

The role of culture in depression and anxiety

Cultural factors play an important part in both vulnerability and patterning of emotional disorders (Kleinman, 1988). For instance, among 2,360 Australian aboriginal people Jones and Horne (1973) were able to find only one case of overt anxiety. If, moreover, you think about the people on Ifaluk described by Lutz (1988, see chapter 2) who spend their whole lives side-by-side with others, you will see that agoraphobia – a fear of being alone away from home – just would never occur at all.

To some extent such differences may reflect how communities are structured, the roles and opportunities open to people in different societies, and the resources that people can draw on. But other kinds of difference occur too. The World Health Organization (1983) carried out a study on depression in four countries: Switzerland, Canada, Japan, and Iran. The same diagnostic instrument was used throughout, and good reliability was established. The researchers found a core cluster of symptoms in each country: sadness, joylessness, anxiety, and lack of energy. Other symptoms, however, varied in frequency. For instance in Iran 57 percent of patients reported bodily symptoms, whereas only 27 percent of patients in Canada did so. Feelings of guilt and self-reproach were common in Canada and Switzerland (reported by 68 percent of patients) and less common in Iran (32 percent). So we could say that in different societies people have different ways of showing their depression.

Cultural differences emerged very clearly in a study by Kleinman (1982) of 100 people attending an outpatient psychiatric clinic in China with a diagnosis of neurasthenia. The pattern of symptoms consists of headaches, dizziness, and lack of energy. The symptoms sound physical, and this cluster has had meaning for centuries in China. The patients focused on pain as a predominant symptom – 90 percent suffered significant pain, such as headache, back pain, and chest pain. The majority believed their condition to be physical, though no physical cause is usually discoverable in this disorder. Other symptoms cannot be easily translated: for instance, a troubling symptom for some patients was a fear of excessive loss of semen with diminished vital energy. All 100 neurasthenic patients were also diagnosed using standardized psychiatric instruments developed in the West. With these, 87 percent received a diagnosis of major depression, and 69 percent also an anxiety disorder. So the ability to export the categories of these Western instruments seems to indicate an underlying universal. At the same time, just as culture shapes the experience of emotions, it shapes how psychiatric states are experienced and expressed.

A related issue is how symptoms function within a society. Mechanic (1982) interviewed patients, and for most of them (93 percent) symptoms functioned to communicate personal or interpersonal distress. In 74 percent of cases they functioned to manipulate interpersonal relationships. In 72 percent of cases they allowed for time off work or other social obligations. We can see, therefore, that in some societies some symptoms would be generally understood as having certain effects and functions, while others would not. An example of an interpersonal effect that is unusual in its explicitness (though not, we believe, in its generality) comes from the Andes in Ecuador, where an emotional state occurs called *pena*, meaning loss, sadness, or suffering (Tousignant & Maldonado, 1989). When intense it becomes a depressive illness. In that culture it is often taken to indicate a loss of reciprocity, so when a woman falls into *pena*, her kin become involved and investigate the condition, usually suspecting that the husband is not fulfilling his interpersonal obligations to her. They work to see how the problem can be corrected, even administering punishments to the offending person if necessary.

Relation of life events to normal emotions and emotional disorders

How can we conceptualize research on life events and depression in relation to normal emotions? We need to make two moves. One is to note that a major depressive breakdown is an intense emotional reaction, of sadness at a loss or disappointment, usually accompanied by intense anxiety about the future, sometimes by anger at what caused the event or difficulty. The difference between events that cause sadness, and those that cause depression, is that the ones which cause depression are much more severe. They are not just losses — they are devastating losses that undermine a person's whole sense of self and way of life. At the core of a depressive breakdown is the emotion of utter hopelessness.

We can conceptualize the idea of a severe life event by means of the diagram of figure 11.3. If an unexpected event or difficulty occurs, then if it makes a goal less probable it causes emotions. If it is severe, that is to say if the event threatens an important life goal or plan, then it may cause depression.

But depression is not just a bundle of intense or long-lasting emotions. For a diagnosis of major depression there must be depressed mood or loss of interest or pleasure lasting at least two weeks, plus four other symptoms, including weight-loss, specific patterns of sleep disturbance, and suicidal thoughts, that do not all easily derive from any current theory of emotions. So a second move is necessary to bring emotional disorders into register with our understanding of emotions. This second move is to include the concept of vulnerability. A general idea in psychopathology is that a disorder is explained by diathesis and stress — by predisposition and provoking event. For depression the diathesis is spoken of as vulnerability. Figure 11.3 shows how one vulnerability factor, lack of social support, might operate.

What sustains psychiatric disorders?

Much research on emotional disorders during the last 30 years has been on what causes depression and anxiety. Now we consider how such states are maintained over long periods of time.

Personal plans and interpersonal relationships

Some 60 percent of episodes of major depression last less than six months, but 20 percent become chronic and last for more than a year (Coryell et al., 1994). According to the diagram of figure 11.3, one of the main differences between an episode of depression resolving or becoming chronic is whether a person can find a new relationship, new plans, or a new life project, to replace what was lost, that enables that person to feel worthwhile and purposeful. Recovery is associated with fresh starts, with positive evaluations of self (Brown, Lemyre, & Bifulco, 1992), and with new plans coming to fruition (Oatley & Perring, 1991). We can think of depression as a refutation of the implicit theory that a person had based her or his life upon: it might be seen as prompting a rethinking of the person's life project. Though a breakdown is intensely

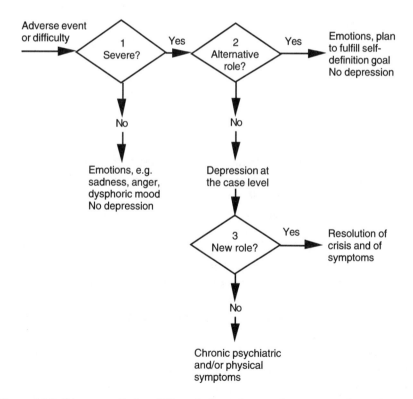

Figure 11.3 Diagram of the differentiation of normal emotions from depressive breakdowns (Oatley, 1988).

painful, it is a demand to rethink. But the outcome will depend on what resources are available.

An important mechanism in the maintenance of sadness and anxiety states is that these states themselves can make people more sad or anxious – they can set up vicious cycles that are self-sustaining, that make it more difficult to recover from the impact of the adversity. There are several kinds of process. One, shown by Hammen (1991), is that becoming depressed itself produces stress which, by its repercussions on relationships and in other ways, tends to prolong the course of an episode of depression. Another is that when difficulties that caused a depressive breakdown continue, the depression tends to continue too.

For some people after a breakdown, depression lifts, but a chronic anxiety disorder remains, which can also be self-sustaining. Fear makes one avoid certain situations. In disabling chronic anxiety disorders, such as agoraphobia and social phobias, the unfamiliar is avoided (Mathews, Gelder, & Johnson, 1981). This makes what is avoided more threatening, and further diminishes self-confidence. This in turn prolongs anxiety and avoidance.

A different kind of factor is the quality of the individual's social relationships. We have already discussed how supportive relationships can protect against negative life events. In contrast people who are prone to depression can create negative social networks for themselves, thereby increasing both their risk of depression, and the risk of depression being maintained. For instance, Coyne et al. (1987) found that 40 percent of spouses of depressed patients show clinically significant symptoms, compared to 17 percent of spouses of women not suffering from a disorder. Coyne, Burchill, and Stiles (1991) suggest that people who are susceptible to depression may choose partners who are themselves vulnerable. Poor relationships with caregivers in childhood may set people off on a trajectory in which they feel unconfident or socially unskilled, and hence make it harder to receive good social support in adulthood.

Gender – having a male or female role in society – has been shown in this chapter to be associated with large differences in the prevalence of emotional disorders. But interestingly, in the study of normal emotions such large differences between males and females are not typically found. So although in Western society women are expected to be more emotionally expressive, and men to be less so, Shields (1991) has concluded from a review of empirical literature that differences in emotionality, and in ability to recognize emotions, have generally been found to be small, and not reliable over different studies. Comparing such insubstantial results on normal emotions with the very large differences in prevalence of emotional disorders, what is going on? Shields has suggested that large differences in aspects of emotion in relation to gender occur mainly when the gender role itself becomes significant. A role difference becomes visible, for instance, in marriage where traditionally men are the primary wage earners, women the primary child rearers and homemakers. Hence problems within a marriage may fall particularly heavily on women whose homemaking provides their primary world. Weissman (1987) reported that 45 percent of women in conflictual marriages suffered from depression, compared with only 3 percent of women in satisfactory marriages.

Women may be more vulnerable to the negative effects of unsatisfactory relationships, which in turn may account for part of the gender difference in prevalence of depression. Bebbington et al. (1981) found that, for men, being married was protective against major depression or anxiety disorder: 2.6 percent of married men but 8 percent of single men had such a disorder. For women the effect of marriage was the reverse: 4.1 percent of single women had a depressive or anxiety disorder, but more than four times as many married women (18.4 percent) had one. Others have also shown that marriages increase the risk for women and decrease the risk for men of problems in mental health (Roberts, 1981; Weissman & Boyd, 1983), and in physical health (House, Landis, & Umberson, 1988). Reasons why marriages work often better for men than for women are various. Some have argued that women and men want different things from relationships. Men may have their emotional goals fulfilled — for instance a stable supportive background. Women may fail to achieve what they desire, perhaps an affectionate intimacy of relationship (McGoldrick, Anderson, & Walsh, 1991).

Poor marriages make episodes of depression longer-lasting, and more likely to recur. Miller et al. (1992) followed up psychiatric inpatients diagnosed as depressed. Those living in dysfunctional families showed a significantly higher level of symptoms a year after discharge than patients returning to functional families. Similarly, Hooley and Teasdale (1989) found that depressed patients were more likely to relapse within nine months of discharge if they reported marital difficulties and a spouse who was critical of them.

People who are depressed negatively affect their ongoing relationships — as compared with the nondepressed, they express more negative affect including sadness and anger (Biglan et al., 1985). Their negative emotions are aversive to other people, and this results in partners being more hostile to them (Coyne, 1976). Hokanson, Hummer, and Butler (1991) tracked mood and interactions between roommates at college. They had three groups of pairs. In one group one member of the pair showed a continuously high score on the Beck Depression Inventory (BDI). In the second group one person scored high on the BDI on one occasion but low subsequently, and in the third group one person had a continuously low score on the BDI. The roommates living with the continuously depressed people showed an increase in their own levels of depression over the course of the year. They reported becoming more managerial of their roommate, and saw their roommate as becoming more dependent.

Negative emotional interchanges between partners can become long-lasting where they serve a positive function in the relationship. Family therapists have convincingly argued that symptoms such as depression and anxiety, that have negative effects for the individual, may serve positive functions in nonobvious ways. For instance Byng-Hall (1980) argued that symptoms can function to regulate distance between people, and Haley (1963) has suggested that symptoms can be a way of gaining power in a relationship without admitting that this is the intention. Imagine a woman who runs the household without help or recognition from her spouse. When she becomes depressed her husband is forced to cook, clean, do the shopping. Her depression shields her from his demands, and makes him realize the nature of her usual activities. As her depression is not consciously adopted, he cannot reasonably object. Depression can reduce aggression from others, and elicit caregiving (Hops et al., 1987). So, although depression is personally painful, and though it sometimes also has negative interpersonal effects, it can also serve functions in relationships, and be maintained over long periods.

Cognitive factors maintaining depression and anxiety

Now we consider a quite different kind of process. Several theorists have seen thinking, memory, and attention, as contributing to aspects of depression (Gotlib & Hammen, 1992). There are several versions of this idea.

First, Brewin (1985) has argued that the evidence that attributional style is a cognitive vulnerability factor for depression (discussed above) is not as strong as was once thought. Much stronger is the evidence that this style (a tendency to make internal, global, and stable attributions for failures) is a symptom of depression, and that it prolongs depression. For instance, in a longitudinal study of recovery from diagnosed depression, Oatley and Perring (1991) found that attributions about the event that caused the breakdown were the largest predictor of whether symptoms remained six to eight months later.

A second hypothesis is coping and rumination. In the 1980s Folkman and Lazarus had defined several methods people use to cope with challenging events. Some methods were focused on the event or a relationship, others were focused on the emotion (Folkman & Lazarus, 1989). Subsequently, and growing partly out of this work, a style of thinking called "ruminative style" has been defined which is emotion-focused, specifically directed to negative emotions and their meaning. Women tend to have a more ruminative style; men are more likely to cope by distraction (Nolen-Hoeksema, Morrow, & Fredrickson, 1993), and this may contribute to the raised prevalence of depression among women. Nolen-Hoeksema and Morrow (1991) found that, as compared with people who did not ruminate, people who did ruminate about a natural disaster – the earthquake in the San Francisco Bay area on October 17, 1989 that killed 62 and left 12,000 people homeless – had lower mood 10 days after the disaster, and also at seven weeks after it. In a study of people who had a close relative who had recently died in a hospice, Nolen-Hoeksema, Parker, and Larson (1994) found that the mood of people with a ruminative style was no lower than that of others a month after bereavement, but six months after it their mood was still low, whereas that of nonruminators had started to lift.

A third kind of cognitive hypothesis, currently the most favored one for explaining prolongation of depression and anxiety, is that of cognitive biases (Williams et al., 1988).

It is an idea that links emotional disorders most closely to properties of normal emotions and moods – in chapter 9 we showed that emotions change the organization of the brain and hence produce biases of processing. Because depressed people have a tendency to recall memories of loss and failure, Teasdale (1988) has suggested that these memories in turn tend to lower mood, and prolong depression. Depressed people are usually capable of performing at normal levels in various tasks if they are given an appropriate strategy, but if left to themselves they may fail to discover such a strategy (Hertel & Hardin, 1990); they tend to lack initiative. They also tend to interpret the future in a more pessimistic way, focusing on negative events and rarely attending to positive events (Pyszczynski & Greenberg, 1987). If these biases extend to being less able to generate new life plans, then this lack of initiative too could contribute to lengthening periods of depression.

For depression, however, the vicious cycle hypothesis is not quite right, because as Blaney (1986) has pointed out, it explains too much. It is unclear how, once a sad or dejected emotion has occurred, discouraging memories would ever stop coming to mind, causing yet more dejection, causing more sad thoughts, and so on. Parrott and Sabini (1990) point out that people do not get trapped in such inescapable cycles for ever. People can regulate their mood, and some of the memories that come to mind are not depressing. We might say that as people start to reconceptualize their lives after an episode of depression they do review episodes of failure in the past, but they also tend to make plans for the future.

Biases of processing are also thought to help maintain anxiety states in vicious cycles, once they have begun – and anxiety states are more likely than depression to be chronic. Whereas the mechanism for sustaining depression is thought to be based on memory, the main mechanism sustaining anxiety is based on attention. For instance posttraumatic stress disorder involves large changes in attention. McNally et al. (1990) have shown that in people suffering from this disorder cues for threat are selectively attended to, and this may help

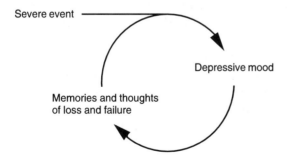

Figure 11.4 A vicious circle. Depression is typically elicited by a severe life event, and may then elicit memories of previous losses and failures, which in turn tend to make the person more depressed. This in turn tends to elicit more sad thoughts and memories, and so on.

explain how its repeated intrusive thoughts and images are maintained. People with more ordinary anxiety traits and disorders also have attentional biases towards events related to anxiety – especially towards their own particular anxieties (Eysenck, 1992; Mathews, 1993). So a person anxious about health attends to bodily events, thinking them to be symptoms, and will tend to notice newspaper items about health, and so forth, building up mental schemas and habits of mind that serve to make anxiety more likely, and to heighten its intensity. Here too, the cognitive organization set up by an emotional state is such as to bring to mind events that are likely to intensify and prolong that emotional state.

"Expressed Emotion" and relapse in schizophrenia

Whereas emotional disorders are largely provoked by the adversities of life, psychotic conditions such as schizophrenia are more closely determined by genetics. For instance, across twin studies Gottesman (1991) has estimated a concordance rate of 48 percent for monozygotic (MZ) twins and 17 percent for dizygotic (DZ) twins. In some studies the concordance for DZ twins was yet smaller: Onstad et al. (1991) found 4 percent in DZ twins, compared to 48 percent in MZ twins.

Symptoms of schizophrenia include delusions, certain kinds of hallucinations, very disorganized behavior, deteriorating relationships. For a DSM-IV diagnosis a disturbance has to last for at least six months, and to cause severe dysfunction socially and at work (American Psychiatric Association, 1994). The disorder has a variable course. Some people recover fully, some have frequent relapses, others never regain their previous level of functioning (Harding, Zubin, & Strauss, 1992).

In contrast with depression and anxiety, the lifetime prevalence of schizophrenia is low (about 1 percent) and there is little difference in the rate between males and females, or among dwellers in industrialized or developing countries (World Health Organization, 1979). However, the time course of the illness is generally shorter and with fewer relapses in rural communities of non-industrialized countries than in Western industrialized societies (Leff et al., 1992).

Although this disorder has a strong biological component, it seems that emotions affect its course and relapse rate – in the early 1960s Brown and his colleagues demonstrated a relationship between the emotional tone in the family and relapse in schizophrenics. Relapse in a patient returning from psychiatric hospitalization could be predicted from three features of an interview with a close relative (spouse or parent) about the patient who was returning home: (a) the number of critical comments, for instance "he just keeps smoking, smoking, smoking," (b) the degree of hostility both in non-verbal aspects such as tone of voice, and in content, for instance "I wish he were dead," and (c) the degree of overinvolvement, such as treating the patient as a child, as in "I'd lost so much weight, I couldn't sleep for worry" (Brown, Birley,

& Wing, 1972). These three (a, b, and c) were combined into an index that became known as "Expressed Emotion" (EE).

In a study that built on this work, Vaughn and Leff (1976) followed up schizophrenic patients who had been discharged from psychiatric hospital to see what factors predicted whether they would relapse and be back in hospital again within the next nine months. Frequency of critical comments was the best predictor from their interview. Two groups of families were defined: High Expressed Emotion families in which relatives made six or more critical comments, and Low Expressed Emotion families in which fewer than six such comments were recorded.

Results are shown in figure 11.5. For patients who returned to a family which was low in Expressed Emotion, irrespective of whether they took their antipsychotic medication, there was a low rate of relapse. But of those returning to a High Expressed Emotion family, who spent more than 35 hours a week with them, and who did not take their medication, 92 percent relapsed within nine months.

Since 1976, there have been many studies on Expressed Emotion (Goldstein, 1988). In a recent review paper in which the results of 23 studies were considered, Kavanagh (1992) found an average relapse amongst patients in high EE families of 48 percent, as compared with that of 21 percent among patients in low EE families. Studies have been done both in Western and Eastern cultures (Jenkins & Karno, 1992). The research also includes application of the concept of Expressed Emotion to families of people with other psychiatric conditions including bipolar affective disorder (Miklowitz et al., 1988) and conduct disorder in children (Stubbe et al., 1993). From such studies, it seems that Expressed Emotion is not just a risk for prolongation of schizophrenia, but operates more generally.

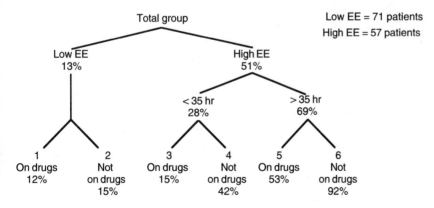

Figure 11.5 Percentages of schizophrenic patients relapsing within nine months of leaving hospital, as a function of High and Low Expressed Emotion of the families to whom they returned, of whether they spent less or more than 35 hours per week with this family, and of whether they took their medication (Vaughn & Leff, 1976).

Indices of Expressed Emotion are ways of taking the emotional temperature of a family. The index can vary with time, and in response to the patient's behavior. Patients' behavior certainly affects the amount of criticism, causing another kind of circular feedback path.

The idea of Expressed Emotion has met with criticism. It has been seen as the latest example of blaming the family for psychiatric problems (Hatfield, 1987), and as cross-culturally suspect – who is to say that the concept is not just the English trying to promote their view that family life, perhaps life in general, should be unemotional (Di Nicola, 1988)? Probably the most convincing replies to such criticisms have been the published therapeutic measures to reduce critical Expressed Emotion, reviewed by Leff (1989). All have had success in reducing relapse rate, and we discuss them in chapter 12. So Expressed Emotion is not a concept of blame. The research and therapy have enabled family members to cope with this distressing condition; those who see schizophrenia as an illness, and who can be more easy-going about the behavior of the patient, are the least likely to be hostile.

Different levels of Expressed Emotion have been suggested to account for the better outcome of schizophrenia in nonindustrialized countries. Kuipers and Bebbington (1988) considered the data on Expressed Emotion in rural and town dwellers near Chandrigarh, India (Wig et al., 1987). Here, although relapse rate was, as is generally found, much lower than in the West, particularly for country-dwellers, it was related to hostility of relatives. Kuipers and Bebbington performed calculations that suggest that the better outcome of schizophrenia in rural societies of developing countries might be accounted for by lower Expressed Emotion among relatives.

Theoretically, what seems to be at issue with Expressed Emotion is comparable to the conclusions we drew in chapter 8 about what sustains psychopathology in children: a potent factor in maintaining continuity of children's disorder was an environment that continued to provoke pathological emotional responses. Expressed Emotion is not just any emotion – it is interpersonal anger, contempt, and criticism of someone unable to escape: "she just follows me everywhere" said one patient (Kuipers & Bebbington, 1988, p. 905). It is the opposite of warmth and affection. It is known that schizophrenic patients (Sturgeon et al., 1984; Tarrier et al., 1988), and also children with disruptive behavior disorder (Hibbs et al., 1992), respond with increased measures of bodily arousal when high Expressed Emotion relatives, but not low Expressed Emotion relatives, are in the room with them.

There is no doubt that a psychotic relative is very difficult to cope with, and is a tremendous burden on carers. You can get something of the sense by reading a list of the DSM-IV symptoms of schizophrenia (American Psychiatric Association, 1994, pp. 274–278): deluded thinking, paranoid distrust, behaving inappropriately, unresponsive emotions. Imagine your spouse or other loved one starting to exhibit such behavior. A lesson of Expressed Emotion research is that with acceptance of the condition and some flexibility in coping with it, not only may the lives of families with schizophrenic members become easier, but the cycle of provoking the patient into ever more difficult behavior may be cut.

Psychosomatic illness

Emotions are related not only to psychiatric disorder but to physical illness. The relationship between emotions and disease is now called psychosomatic medicine. Stress, defined as threatening circumstances that elicit negative emotions, contributes to onset and maintenance of physical illness.

There are several traditions in psychosomatic research. One, based on psychoanalytic ideas, is that inner conflict can give rise to illness (Alexander, 1950). A more recent idea is that people who barely express or experience emotions – a trait known as alexithymia – are more susceptible to illness (Taylor, Bagby, & Parker, 1991). Events that cause emotions in others cause bodily symptoms in people with this trait – compare the way, discussed above, in which psychiatric problems are experienced in bodily ways in some societies. The main line of research on psychosomatic illness, however, has been based on the idea that any large change challenges the psychophysiological system. This is the idea of generalized stress, first proposed by Selye (1936). He thought that intense or long-lasting challenges may exhaust physiological resources and this would predispose to illness. The challenges he designed were for laboratory animals – cold, injury, electric shock, intense muscular exercise. In research on human subjects, rather than exposing subjects to cold and so forth, a stress score for each individual is derived from a checklist of adaptive changes he or she has recently experienced (Holmes & Rahe, 1967). A person taking the test checks which of 43 events have occurred recently – death of a spouse, divorce, marriage, change of residence, a vacation, and so forth. Each event has some number of points associated with it, and the total points for the person are correlated with the occurrence of illness (Rahe, 1972). The original checklist has been improved in second-generation instruments (Dohrenwend et al., 1990), and scores have also been used to predict depression, but these checklists now tend to be seen as less satisfactory than Brown and Harris's interview (Thoits, in press).

Stress and the immune system

Much of the research on psychosomatic illness now involves the immune system. This system extends throughout the body and includes the bone marrow, spleen, thymus, lymph nodes, and the white cells of the blood such as lymphocytes and macrophages. Useful introductory explanations of its parts and functions, and the aspects that are measured in studies of stress on disease, can be found in O'Leary (1990) and Maier, Watkins, and Fleshner (1994). The system evolved as one of several lines of defense against infection by bacteria, viruses, parasites, and fungi.

Two kinds of immunity are typically distinguished. One kind is innate. It consists of the acute response of inflammation and repair at a wound or infection and the migration of white blood cells called macrophages to ingest foreign particles and debris. The second kind is called acquired, because its effectiveness improves with contact with the disease: after contact with particular foreign invaders, recognition of their proteins (called antigens) occurs, then destruction of the invaders. Central to this response are white blood cells called T-lymphocytes; each has on its surface a receptor that recognizes and bonds to a single type of antigen. Since there are thought to be a million billion (10^{15}) different kinds of receptor, it follows that in any one person there can only be a tiny number of T-lymphocytes that can bond to any given antigen. The response includes proliferation of a clone of T-lymphocytes with receptors for the invading antigen, until there are enough to kill all the invaders with that antigen. It is enhanced by lymphocytes called helper T-cells; and it takes several days to develop fully. Once a response has occurred, memory T-cells for that antigen are created to give a faster response next time that antigen is encountered.

Other cells, B-lymphocytes, go through similar processes of recognition and proliferation to produce a different kind of response in the form of molecules – immunoglobulins – called antibodies that circulate in the blood and can bind to antigens and inactivate them. Another kind of lymphocyte, the natural killer (NK) cell, also proliferates during an immune response. NK cells can destroy virally infected body cells and some kinds of cancer cells.

There are three main kinds of effect of changes of immune function on illness (O'Leary, 1990). First, an impaired immune system can fail to recognize and destroy antigens. (This is also one of the effects of AIDS, where the body becomes susceptible to opportunistic infections normally kept at bay.) Second, an impaired immune system may fail to recognize and destroy malignant cancer cells – body cells that have undergone a pathological change (this too happens with AIDS which often includes cancers called Karposi's sarcoma). Third, changes can occur in the immune system's recognition of the body's own tissue. In some diseases, called autoimmune diseases, such as rheumatoid arthritis, this recognition fails, and it is suggested that T-cell function is impaired.

The idea that stress suppresses immune function is supported by many findings. So, astronauts re-entering the atmosphere at the end of a space flight (Kimsey et al., 1986), students taking an examination (Glaser et al., 1987), spouses in marital discord (Kiecolt-Glaser et al., 1988), people experiencing bereavement and marital separation (Kennedy, Kiecolt-Glaser, & Glaser, 1988), those who have continuing unemployment (Arnetz et al., 1987) have all been found to suffer changes of immune function as compared with those not suffering these stresses. These effects include lowered T-cell and NK cell counts, and diminished antibodies. Though this kind of result is common in the literature, its implications for actual illness are more problematic. In most studies only measurements of immune response are reported as outcomes. In some others self-reported illnesses are also measured: for instance Glaser et al. and Kiecolt-Glaser et al. found that with the immune changes they found, illnesses such as colds increased. In others (e.g. Arnetz et al.) there was no noticeable change in rates of self-reported illness, despite changes in immune system measures.

Interaction of brain and immune system in animals

In the last 15 years it has been established that in laboratory animals stress influences the brain, which in turn influences the immune system (Ader & Cohen, 1993). For instance, Fleshner et al. (1989) showed that male rats who were introduced into established territories of other rats, and were defeated by the alpha-males of those territories, suffered a decrease in antibody production. This decrease was associated with submissive behavior, not with being wounded; newly introduced rats who continued to fight and who suffered many wounds did not undergo a reduction of antibodies. In primates, Sapolsky (1993) has found that males who were high in the dominance hierarchy had more efficient, less potentially pathogenic, mechanisms involving adreno-corticoid hormones than low-ranking males when the hierarchy was stable. But the corticoid levels of high ranking animals rose after the defeat of a previous alpha male, during a period of stress when there were high levels of social conflict over rank with many fights.

In laboratory animals, it has also been found that the immune system can influence the brain. Maier, Watkins, and Fleshner (1994) reviewed evidence that this influence is responsible for heightened sensitivity to pain (perhaps by reducing peptides called opiates), and for effects similar to those of fear: reductions of activity, of eating and drinking, of exploration of novel objects, and of social interaction. Such effects then might have evolved as part of a repertoire of recuperative responses to illness.

Stress and cancer

As infectious diseases started to be controlled in the nineteenth century by the advent of public health, and in the second half of the twentieth century by the advent of antibiotics, cancer came more to be feared. Cancers arise when a certain line of cells in the body proliferates outside the control of the processes that build cells into body parts. So a glioma is a cancer of certain cells in the brain, a lymphoma is an abnormal proliferation of lymphocytes, and so on. Cancers that are benign tend to grow slowly, and are self-contained. Cancers that are malignant invade other tissues. Parts can detach and spread to other areas of the body where, if they start growing, they are called metastases or secondaries. By their growth into bodily organs cancers interfere with bodily functions, cause pain, and ultimately death. Ordinarily it is believed that cancer cells are formed all the time, but they are detected as abnormal by the immune system, and destroyed. With emotional stress, and with age, it is believed that either cancers are more likely to grow, or that they are less likely to be destroyed.

Cancers do not just happen because of genetics, or age, or luck, however; Doll and Peto (1981) have reviewed the epidemiology of cancers of many kinds, and shown that occurrence is highly affected by lifestyle or environment. For instance, the rate of breast cancer in Black American women is similar to that of White American women. It is more than three times higher than the rate for Black women in Nigeria to whom the American Black women are genetically related. The inference is that something about living in the USA has produced the difference. In this kind of way, up to 80 percent of cancers can be attributed to lifestyle or environment, and hence could be avoidable. Tobacco smoking accounts for 30 percent of the death rate in Western nations, mostly but not entirely from lung cancer. In addition, for reasons that are not well understood, perhaps associated with amounts of fat and fiber, diet contributes another 35 percent.

As we have explained above, it is known that there are neurohormonal mechanisms by which stress can affect immune function. The question is, how important are these processes: how much cancer can be explained by stress?

Let us consider breast cancer, which affects one in nine American women. A well-known early study was by Derogatis, Abeloff, and Melisaratos (1972), who reported on 35 women who had secondaries from breast cancer. As compared with those who survived for less than one year, those who survived for more than a year were angrier and more distressed; they were described as "capable of externalizing their negative feelings" (p. 1507). This seemed clear, and also corresponded to intuitions that in some way cancer is related to being emotionally inexpressive, to the personality trait of alexithymia. But subsequently a more sophisticated study by Cassileth et al. (1985) indicated that none of a range of psychological and social factors, including life stress and emotional adjustment to the diagnosis, had any effect in prolonging survival time in a variety of cancers.

In a recent study using Brown and Harris's Life Events and Difficulties Schedule rather than questionnaires and checklists, Ramirez (1988) interviewed 50 women with operable breast cancer who had relapses and 50 who did not. Each woman who had a relapse was carefully matched, on variables concerning operation, treatment, and progression of the disease, to a control woman who did not relapse. The number of severe life events and difficulties occurring between the date of the original operation and the recurrence, or an equivalent period for the controls, was determined. A severe event or difficulty significantly increased the risk of recurrence: nine pairs of women were found in which the woman with the recurrence had a severe event or difficulty while the one without a recurrence had not. Only one pair was found in which a woman without a recurrence had a severe event or difficulty when the woman with a recurrence had not. Levy et al. (1991) followed up 90 women after surgery for early breast cancer. Although mood did not predict who would have a recurrence, where recurrences did occur the women with more distressed mood and lower social support, had them earlier.

The literature on the effects of stress both upon cancer and upon infectious disease is very complex. There are many results in which some part of the proposed mechanism linking stress and disease has been demonstrated. For instance, in a meta-analysis Herbert and Cohen (1993) found 35 methodologically sound studies linking major depression to changes in immune function such as lymphocyte responses to antigens. The effects were found to be moderate to large. Also there are some results, such as those we have just mentioned for breast cancer, in which stress has been related directly to disease. But there are very few studies in which stress, intermediate immune mechanisms, and disease have all been convincingly linked. There are also a good number of findings that are negative or inconsistent: as Cohen and Williamson (1991) put it, much of the evidence is "provocative"; it may be some time before it is conclusive.

Personality and illness

While stress has been the principal focus of most studies of psychosomatic illness, a second kind of research has been on personality. If you think of life events and stresses as arising from the environment, you can think of personality as being based in the individual's propensities to interpret what happens, and hence respond emotionally, in a particular kind of way.

One set of studies was performed by Grossarth-Maticek et al. (1988). They defined four personality types. Type 1 (Understimulated) people were dependent for emotional well-being on some other person or on some highly valued activity and its withdrawal brought hopelessness and depression. Type 2 (Overaroused) people had highly valued goals, and felt angry if unable to reach them. Type 3 (Ambivalent) people tended to shift between reactions of Types 1 and 2. Type 4 (Autonomous) people had achieved a degree of emotional autonomy. The authors comment that Types 1 and 2 are dependent on "important objects that engage their emotions, but cannot remain autonomous when these objects withdraw or remain unattainable" (p. 480). In a prospective study of a random sample of 773 people in Heidelberg, Germany, they found that 17 percent of the Type 1 people died from cancer within 10 years of first contact with the researchers, 2 percent died from coronary heart disease, and 72 percent were still alive. Of the Type 2 people 6 percent died from cancer, 13.5 percent from coronary heart disease, and 16.5 percent from other causes. Of the Type 3 and Type 4 people (together totalling 74 percent of the whole sample) only 1.2 percent died within 10 years.

Grossarth-Maticek et al.'s Type 2 corresponds to the Type A personality (Friedman & Rosenman, 1959; Rosenman et al., 1975) characterized by impatience, competitiveness, and working to self-imposed deadlines, a pattern that had been linked to high incidence of coronary heart disease. Friedman and Rosenman's initial Type A categorization was seen by subsequent researchers as too heterogeneous, and has latterly been narrowed to one component: hostility. Shekelle, Gale, and Ostfield (1983) found, in a 20-year follow-up, that coronary artery disease was predicted by this component of hostility in their subjects at the beginning of the research project.

The nature of stress

Let us then consider the various responses – psychological, physiological, and immunological – to a stressor, say a marital separation or the death of a spouse. The psychological responses will include the sadness of loss, the fear of what will befall, perhaps anger at anyone who may have been in any way responsible. If the person is vulnerable – if the lost relationship was the only role that sustained the sense of self – then it is likely that the person will become clinically depressed. At the same time, physiological changes occur. One set, involving the sympathetic division of the autonomic nervous system, and the release of adrenalin from the adrenal medulla, includes an immediate response, part of mobilizing the body's response for fight or flight. Another response is that the hypothalamus stimulates the pituitary to release hormones that control the release from the adrenal cortex of adreno-corticoid hormones (in humans mainly cortisol). These hormones function to mobilize energy; but it is this corticoid response in animals that has also been found responsible for inhibiting the immune system (Maier, Watkins, & Fleshner, 1994; Riley, 1981). In humans this kind of effect is less clear.

In chapter 4 we discussed how experiential, bodily, and behavioral components of an emotional response are not always closely linked. We can think of the immune system as a fourth component. With it the problems of linking the various systems become yet worse. For example: in a previous section we discussed how events such as bereavement cause depression. Comparably, there is evidence that bereavement also increases the rate of death by cancer and other causes (Stroebe et al., 1982). It is also well established that some measures of immune function do change with depression (Herbert & Cohen, 1993), but despite such results, in some careful studies such as that of Zonderman, Costa, and McCrae (1989) in a large population sample, links were not found between episodes of depression and later onsets of cancer.

Even if the link from emotional distress following severe events to cancer and infectious illness were better established, puzzling questions would remain. Why should stress make us more prone to disease – why should we humans have evolved to carry a response which makes us less fit to survive?

Evolution of responses to stress

Maier, Watkins, and Fleshner (1994) suggest that suppression of immune function that occurs with stress may reflect its evolutionary ancestry. They argue that the innate immune response of acute inflammation is evolutionarily old. It occurs when there is a wound, or local invasion of bacteria. Within two hours macrophages capable of consuming foreign invaders move to the site, as do building materials to repair the breach. The process is expensive of bodily resources. The primary function of adrenal-corticoid hormones in this response is to mobilize energy for this process. In mammals part of this response is to raise body temperature, which is helpful in fighting disease. It comes about by chemical messengers (interleucins) from the macrophages affecting the hypothalamus to raise the body-temperature set point. In mammals these same chemicals decrease bodily activity and decrease social interaction. The adrenal corticoid hormones also act as the negative feedback, regulating this response.

Next occurring in evolutionary time, Maier, Watkins, and Fleshner argue, was the behavioral flight–fight response, in animals that could perceive and act to avoid or attack. Perhaps for such animals, during flight or fight it was advantageous to inhibit the inflammation response. To do so, adrenal corticoid hormones provided the mechanism; so flight–fight and the acute inflammation response would be linked. In fighting and fleeing, the peptides called opiates are also released, and these decrease sensitivity to pain. Only after energetic action does pain sensitivity increase; then if there is a wound the body is stilled with its feeling of illness and withdrawal. Its resources are devoted to repair – inflammation followed by healing can begin. In this process the adrenocortical hormones again act to mobilize energy, then to regulate the response.

The acquired immune response is yet more recently developed evolutionarily, Maier et al. argue. It occurs only in vertebrates. Whereas the acute inflammatory response takes hours, immune responses take days to develop, so the various flows of corticoid hormones and interleucins need to be seen as part of an intricately regulated process. The acquired immune response evolved from the innate response, and uses some of the same physiological components.

In reading and thinking about the effects of emotions and stress it is no good being too simplistic. In various studies of stress components are reported as increased or decreased; some of these changes may be deteriorations caused by disease, some may be aspects of complexly regulated processes.

Stress as loss of enthusiasm

As we described in chapter 3, the essence of success of the human adaptation was doing things together that cannot be done alone. Positive emotions of happiness and love are the emotions of interacting with others: following Tomkins's hypothesis, they amplify motivations to act. Putting it more simply, they make life worthwhile; they give life its vigor. So, perhaps, it is not surprising that when those bonds to others are lost, in bereavement or separation – the most severe kinds of stress, according to all the measuring instruments – we lose that motivation, the sense of worthwhileness, and possibility. "How weary, stale, flat and unprofitable" then become the uses of this world (Shakespeare, 1600, I, ii, 133). So we could even think of depression and susceptibility to illness not so much as negative states, but as the absence of that positive sense that makes life and its projects possible.

A gene for self-destruction?

Totman (1988) has proposed that the common link of stress studies is that when people lose their relation to their social group then increased susceptibility to illness makes them likely to die and hence no longer be a burden to that group. If the link between severe stress and illness were to be confirmed, this kind of explanation would only apply if the social groups from which we have evolved were genetically interrelated – a likely possibility. A gene for self-destruction among people living in unrelated groups could not reproduce itself. But, as Hamilton (1964) has pointed out, although genetically speaking you should not lay down your life for a friend, you can safely do so for two siblings (who each share 50 percent of your genes) or eight first cousins (who each share 12.5 percent). These others would be able to promote the survival of your genes just as well as one of you!

Whether the functioning of the interrelated social group has been important in evolutionary terms, so that single individuals who are not functioning within it become selected against, is a question that evolutionary biologists will ponder if the link between the stress of social disintegration and illness is substantiated. Meanwhile, realizing we are not just programmed by our genes, we may want to decide to continue to devote society's resources to promoting an emotional climate for psychiatric and physical health for as many people as possible.

Summary

Psychiatry textbooks typically start by describing patients suffering from different kinds of disorder, and then advance theories based on genetics or early childhood experience to account for these. The more recent approach is epidemiological, making psychiatric diagnoses of representative samples of people in the population. This approach has not suffered from the bias of making inferences only about people who find their way to clinics. Using an epidemiological approach it has been found that depression and anxiety are by far the commonest psychiatric syndromes, each affecting about a fifth of people in Western industrialized societies some time in their lifetime, and with women being nearly twice as frequently afflicted as men. By contrast men suffer more often than women from disorders of the abuse of alcohol, and from persistent antisocial behaviour that tends to continue from the externalizing disorders of childhood. As to the role of emotions in disorder: first, depressive and anxiety states include emotions or moods as principal symptoms. Second, these emotional disorders are most usually caused in the same kinds of ways as negative emotions, namely by adverse events. But emotional disorders are not just intense or long-lasting emotions. To become depressed people must typically also be vulnerable. Lack of social support is a common vulnerability factor; its absence can deprive a person of a sense of being worthwhile and loved. Through adverse early experiences, negative schemas about the self in relationship are formed. Genetic vulnerability may include a propensity to some emotions such as sadness or fear, and also may include personality factors making certain kinds of life event more probable, and making social support more difficult to maintain. Third, some properties of emotions help explain how some syndromes of psychopathology are prolonged. Fourth, just as with emotions and moods, the social world is the source of most causes of emotional disorder and, just as with emotions and moods, these disorders also affect people's relationships. For physical illness stressful life events are also thought to be important, though the relations are not so well established. Mechanisms by which emotionally significant stress increases adrenocortical hormones, which depress aspects of the functioning of the immune system, have been well established. There is suggestive evidence that these effects can make people more susceptible to infectious diseases and to cancer.

Further Reading

One of the most important books published in adult psychiatry, and engaging to read, is:

George W. Brown & Tirril Harris (1978). *Social origins of depression: A study of psychiatric disorder in women.* London: Tavistock.

Very useful for understanding depression is:

Ian Gotlib & Constance Hammen (1992). *Psychological aspects of depression: Toward a cognitive-interpersonal integration.* Chichester: Wiley.

An excellent review and theoretical exploration, including cross-cultural studies, of Expressed Emotion by Janis Jenkins (no relation to the author of this book!):

Janis Hunter Jenkins (1991). Expressed emotion and schizophrenia. *Ethos, 19,* 387–431.

The best comprehensive review we know of the effects of emotions and stress on immune function in infectious disease and cancer is:

Ann O'Leary (1990). Stress, emotion, and human immune function. *Psychological Bulletin, 108,* 363–382.

Psychotherapy, Consciousness, and Narrative

Figure 12.0 Ronald De Sousa used these pictures for the cover of his book
The Rationality of Emotions. They are from Thomas E. Hill's (1885) book
on etiquette – a making conscious of how to perform social customs.

Assuredly there is an art of healing the soul — I mean philosophy, whose aid must be sought not, as in bodily diseases, outside ourselves, and we must use our utmost endeavor, with all our resources and strength, to have the power to be ourselves our own physicians.

Cicero, Tusculan Disputations, III, 4

Psychological therapies and the emotions

Emotions can take over our lives. Sometimes they prompt actions for reasons of which we are not fully aware. Indeed emotions often have aspects that we do not completely understand. They can be mere beginnings of something vague and unformed, with meanings that only become clear as we express them to others. At the same time we sense that our emotions lie close to our most authentic selves. They are at the center of many religious practices and rituals, of drama and other literature, and of psychotherapy. It is as if, in the religions, literatures, and psychotherapeutic practices of the world, human consciousness has struggled to find a right relation with the emotions. And, if emotions are signals of events that affect our deepest concerns, we might expect that this would be so.

In the East the tenor of emotional life is thought to be best modulated by practices such as meditation, and by attitudes such as nonattachment to worldly things. In the West the idea of transformation of the self was of interest to the classical Greeks and to the Hebrews. Such ideas were attributed to ancient Egyptian sources. They flourished in dozens of sects in the Middle East. They were incorporated into Christianity, and became a driving force in the Renaissance (Jonas, 1958; Yates, 1964). Here is one version. At the core of each of us is a little piece of divine substance, the soul, that has been detached from God, and contained inside a human body. Our task on earth is to see through the veils of bodily existence, and undertake a spiritual journey. Helped by a mentor, we relinquish whatever obscures our vision, undergo spiritual rebirth, struggle out of the darkness to the light, so that our soul may reunite with the divine. Emotions are part of the obscuring veil, first to be recognized and owned, then transcended.

Consider the Catholic practice of penance and confession, as one expression of this theme. Early in the Christian tradition confession was made to a group of others. By early medieval times confession was performed privately, with just one priest, and this practice continues. Throughout, it has had several components. First comes a confession not just of general sinfulness but of some specific sin, perhaps an occasion of immoderate anger or of improper lustfulness. Second must come the emotions of shame and remorse for this sin. Third, some restitution for the wrong is necessary. A fourth part was then anticipated — the amendment of life. Confession was never something that could be done alone because the Church fathers were clear that an essential aspect was the presence of another person to induce the emotion of shame, understood to be an essential part of repudiating the sin.

In very many societies comparable elements exist, in practices that can be broadly classed as psychotherapeutic. The general pattern is this. Any of us can become disrelated with ourselves, with the society in which we live, or with the gods – and signs of this disrelation can include strong and disturbed emotions. Practices and rituals are applied, often including aspects of the disordered emotional state, which is itself perhaps part of the mind's own resources in healing. The societal practices may involve manipulating and interpreting particular states of consciousness or inducing them, by going to a special sequestered place, by privation, by meditation, and in some societies by drugs. There are typically meetings with others such as mentors, gurus, priests, shamans, and also with the members of the immediate community. The aim is healing (the root meaning of the Greek term "therapy") – which means making the self whole – and reintegration of the individual with society. As we might expect, many of these same elements exist in modern secular practices of psychotherapy.

In all the different tributaries of this stream, at the center of the process of change are the emotions (Greenberg & Safran, 1987; Neu, 1977). Let us first approach this topic from a direction that has become familiar in our culture – from the direction of psychoanalytic therapy, which stands in a long line of therapies from different cultures. The therapist tries to work with the client to make sense of symptoms, as compared to the more medical approach of trying directly to relieve suffering.

The basic idea of psychoanalytic therapy

Freud's first form of psychotherapy focused on traumatic events in a patient's earlier life. We presented a prototype in chapter 1: Freud's case of Katharina (1895). Therapy, using hypnosis or other means, was aimed at recalling the trauma, enabling it to become conscious, allowing the emotions associated with it to be expressed, thus freeing the patient from its continuing harmful effects. Not long after he had published his first papers on hysteria, however, Freud came to think that he had been mistaken in thinking that disorder was necessarily caused by sexual abuse in earlier life. The center of his new idea, formed in the final few years of the nineteenth century, was that neurotic people suffer from inner conflict, for instance, both feeling sexually attracted to someone and feeling inhibited by the prohibitions of society.

Almost from the beginning, psychoanalysis attracted both enthusiastic adherents and vituperative detractors. Detractors argued that psychoanalysis was less a therapeutic procedure, more a matter for the police! This debate continues: psychoanalytic therapy continues to flourish especially in the USA. The latest attacks are led by Frederick Crews (1994), a professor of literature who at one time was attracted to psychoanalysis, but who now argues that it is not only based on Freud's dishonesty, but that it is deleterious personally and for society. Probably the most respected recent treatment of the problems of psychoanalysis has been by Grünbaum, see the precis of his book (1986) along with commentaries that accompany it.

This is not the place to enter that debate. Whatever Freud's defects, and whatever the problematics of psychotherapeutic practice and theory, it is difficult to deny that Freud has left at least two positive legacies. First, it was he who proposed the therapy of listening carefully, with respect and attention, to patients suffering from psychiatric disorders. In Western psychiatric practice, all psychological therapies with individuals owe something to Freud. Secondly, and this is the aspect we wish to present here, Freud proposed the idea of transference, an idea that is likely to survive even if psychoanalytic therapy does not (Singer & Singer, 1992).

The idea of transference was discussed in his first full-length case history by Freud (1905). This therapy was conducted in the last three months of 1900 — when Ida Bauer, to whom Freud gave the pseudonym "Dora," came every day

---

Biographical note: Sigmund Freud

Sigmund Freud was born in 1856 to an impecunious wool merchant and his wife, and from the age of four until a year before he died he lived in Vienna. In 1938 he and his family fled from the Nazis to England. His last year was spent in London. He died of cancer in September 1939. A year after qualifying as a doctor in 1881, he had met Martha Bernays, fallen deeply in love, and begun a chaste four-year engagement, the frustrations of which may have contributed to his theories of sexuality. After various more or less unsuccessful attempts to make his way in biology and neurology, Freud had started treating patients by hypnosis, at which he said he was not very good, so he began the treatment that has become famous as psychoanalysis. Freud was promoted to professor extraordinarius (equivalent to associate professor) at the University in Vienna in 1902. Although he was always touchy about the

recognition he felt he deserved, in retrospect one can see that from this time his fortunes improved, and his influence spread until in his own lifetime he became the only psychologist whose name most people have heard. His work was foundational not only to psychology and psychiatry, but important in art and literature. He affected the very texture of twentieth-century thinking. Controversial throughout the twentieth century, Freud is nevertheless the founding figure of psychological therapy as it has been developed in the West because his idea was to understand the meanings of psychiatric symptoms, not just to try to relieve them. Now Freud's reputation is being questioned again in controversy surrounding cases in which people report having recovered memories that have been repressed. (Biographical information from Gay, 1988; Sulloway, 1979)

Figure 12.1 Almost all forms of therapy involve a therapist listening to and conversing with a client, making sense of that person's emotional life – practices that were begun by Freud.

except Sunday to see him at his consulting rooms at Berggasse 19, in Vienna (Bernheimer & Kahane, 1985). This was the case history in which he explained his new method, in which the patient was asked to lie on a couch, tell the story of her life, and say whatever else came to mind, while the analyst suggested interpretations to fill the gaps in the story. Transference is the manifestation of what we in this book have referred to as emotion schemas, mental models that embody rules and emotions of relating to others, derived from our intimate relationships.

"What are transferences?" asked Freud (1905). "They are new editions or facsimiles of the impulses and phantasies which . . . replace some earlier person [such as the mother or father] by the person of the physician" (p. 157). Emotional attitudes towards earlier figures are projected onto the therapist. Thus Dora, in Freud's case, said her father "always preferred secrecy and roundabout ways." Then, in her analysis, she treated Freud in the same wary fashion as she treated her father.

Or take the example of a modern patient, Tom (Singer & Singer, 1992): Tom's father had come from a well-off family, but had ended in a lowly job. He was verbally abusive to Tom, mockingly critical of him, and he dominated Tom's mother, who was a source of comfort to Tom. In therapy Tom described the following episode. In first grade he and the other children were given green pencils. Tom bent his to see how far it would go. It broke, and Tom asked for a new pencil. The teacher held up a brown pencil that she was going to give to Tom, and said, "'B' is for 'brown' and for 'baby'" (p. 518), shaming him in front of the class, and finally shutting him in a clothes closet at the back of the room, where Tom said he felt safe. The incident of this early memory did not, of course, begin Tom's psychological difficulties, but he felt it was emblematic of his life. Singer and Singer agree this was so. Though he had a degree and wanted to enter graduate school to train as an accountant, he worked at cleaning houses. Towards his therapist he maintained a distant air. The themes of Tom's life were dominated by an emotional schema of the fear of shame and humiliation; it had attracted him into a marginal and solitary occupation, where he could feel angry at other people but without having to confront them. In his transference towards the therapist, these same themes were reissued in a "new edition": he himself remained distant and uninvolved. He complained that the therapist was withholding, and somewhat covertly he expressed anger and disdain towards the therapist, as to all authorities.

The themes that people bring to therapy often have at their heart a profound conflict, so the themes generate self-defeat. For Tom the theme was that he would like to have a professional career, but he feared being humiliated. He would like to assert himself against authority figures, but he could do so only covertly. Slowly, with the therapist's interpretations, Tom began to recognize his fear that the therapist would criticize and reject him. At the same time he started to act more purposefully in the outside world. At the end of therapy he had completed his first quarter in a program in accountancy.

The reason why transference is important is that, as we have explained in this book, the emotional schemas that underlie people's styles of relating have typically been formed long ago, then have been elaborated and woven into many parts of life. It is not possible to undo childhood experiences, even if one knew clearly what they were. The idea of transference is that effects of the schema are brought directly into the therapeutic relationship. As Strachey (1934) has written, from the viewpoint of the therapist: "Instead of having to deal as best we may with conflicts of the remote past, which are concerned with dead circumstances and mummified personalities, and whose outcome is already determined, we find ourselves involved in an actual and immediate situation in which we and the patient are the principal characters" (p. 132). Then, as Strachey continues, there is the possibility that when the partly unconscious terms of the schema in which the client has been lodged become conscious, the person will be able to choose a new solution in the relationship with the therapist, and this kind of new solution can generalize to other relationships outside therapy.

As Singer and Singer (1992) point out, transference is a part of many relationships. Psychoanalytic therapy is a place designed to recognize emotional schemas, and perhaps to change them. But transference occurs in almost every consultation with a physician, as we find ourselves hoping he or she will look after us, make everything better, as once a caregiver could. It occurs, as even therapists who are not analysts admit, in almost every kind of psychological therapy. It occurs in teaching relationships, in encounters with people who have power or influence of some kind.

Most troublingly, transference occurs in intimate relationships. A direct demonstration of the persistence of the themes of early intimacy into adulthood has now been found in the longitudinal study (discussed in chapter 7) by Waters et al. (1995) in which the style of attachment at age one was transferred forward over 20 years into a distinctive kind of narrative account (autonomous, preoccupied, dismissing) given in the Adult Attachment Interview. Remember too Bartlett's (1932) theory of schemas, discussed in chapter 9? A schema is an organization of knowledge and propensity for action. New incidents are incorporated into emotion schemas just as they are into schemas of the kinds of knowledge that Bartlett studied. Thus Tom's incident of shame with the pencil in first grade gets incorporated into the life story he tells himself and his therapist. This schema, if spelled out in words, would include something like "I avoid all possibilities of humiliation by authority; they would lead to shame." This schema is the eyes through which Tom sees the world, the hands and feet with which he acts in it. It creates an unsatisfying world, and a supply of just those experiences that confirm it.

Emotional schemas that are problematic are often based on intense wishes together with closely held beliefs about what is wrong with them, or how they cannot be satisfied (Dahl, 1991). So people may have emotion schemas in which they know only bad things happen if they are angry; they may know they should not be frightened and feel ashamed if they are. Or they may feel it too dangerous to have any strong emotion because of the likelihood of losing control; or may long for intimacy but be terrified of being taken over.

According to most psychoanalysts, the main job of psychoanalytic therapy is the recognition and interpretation of transference, since here the terms and conditions of core emotion schemas are played out, as a kind of drama, in the relationship with the therapist. There have been a number of attempts to study transference empirically. In therapy the best known studies are those of Luborsky and Crits-Christoph (1990) who have devised a method of recognizing what they call Core Conflictual Relationship Themes in transference, and they have gone some way to showing that when therapists recognize and interpret occurrences of these themes, the patient makes better progress in therapy (Henry et al., 1994).

Different forms of psychotherapy and their effects

There are now several hundred forms of psychological therapy, and this must be the briefest discussion of them. Most involve a close relationship with a therapist, talk, and suggestions. Nearly all involve emotions (Greenberg & Safran, 1987, 1989). Therapy, then, is an interaction with another person in which we can discover some of the properties of our emotion schemas, and can change their terms to some extent. All forms of therapy do this by seeking to change the context in which the schemas operate. We have discussed psychoanalytic therapy, not because it is necessarily best at doing this, but because it came first. Its goal is to be able to provide the context of a relationship, in which emotion schemas of the client can be understandable. In the other forms of therapy, there are different approaches. Here we will use the rough division of types of therapy laid out by Bergin and Garfield (1994).

Experiential and humanistic therapies

Experiential therapies now include a very wide range of forms. Among them are gestalt therapy, known for its practices of pounding cushions in anger and speaking to empty chairs as if others to whom we would like to give a piece of our mind were sitting there (Perls, Hefferline, & Goodman, 1951); transactional analysis, known for the idea of the distressing games that people play (Berne, 1964); and psychosynthesis, known for guided imagery, inner helpers, and other subparts of the personality which need integration (Assagioli, 1965). All these were developed by psychoanalysts versed in Freud's methods, who transformed or abstracted one or more psychoanalytic ideas to create the new therapy.

The father of the experiential therapies in the USA is usually considered to be Carl Rogers (1951) with his client-centered therapy, which grew up quite outside the psychoanalytic tradition. In this therapy the aim is for the client to experience a relationship with the therapist that is genuine, emotionally empathetic, and nonjudgmental. The experiential therapies, though flourishing especially in North America, also resonate with European traditions of phenomenology and existentialism (e.g. Binswanger, 1963).

The central idea in this group of therapies is that people's emotion schemas have involved suppression or distortion to fit the self into some social framework acceptable to others, but denying the person's authenticity. A principal task in therapy, then, is to allow the client to experience emotions as they occur in primary appraisals, rather than denying, distorting, or suppressing them.

One way of thinking about these primary emotions – how they were lost, the effects of their being regained – is given by Scheff (1979). He refers to the process of regaining lost emotions as catharsis. This was a feature of many of Freud's earlier cases, such as that of Katharina, discussed in chapter 1. When people have experienced traumas such as cruelty, abuse, or deprivation in childhood, the loss of a loved one, failure in relationships or in work – events that lead to strong negative emotions – although such events are often remembered, the emotions associated with them may not have been expressed.

When in therapy a significant emotional event is remembered, it can come with a great deal of present emotion. Experiencing it can be important in liberating the person from an emotionally stultified, or overanxious, life. Scheff

(1979, pp. 14–17) describes this in a man who attended a psychotherapy group. He had been brought up to be a "real man," strong and silent. Between the ages of 16 and 40 he had cried only once. He was emotionally unexpressive, and he was subject to severe and frequent fits of migraine. At 40 he separated from his wife and children after many years of marriage. He was tense and lonely. In a psychotherapy group that emphasized the expression of emotions he had, at the suggestion of the leader, repeated the phrase, "I hurt." He had felt somewhat envious of other group members who had been able to cry. In the evening, discussing the group at the home of a friend, he repeated some of the phrases he had said, and began to cry. The crying lasted for 20 minutes, at first tense, then becoming more relaxed. Then, after a few minutes' rest he started to shake and sweat, violently like an earthquake – and this went on for about 30 minutes. Then after another brief pause he became tremendously angry, and started cursing – he sensed his friend was becoming concerned but she said she was all right, and he continued in this way for while. He said he had no idea what the anger was about. Then, after another pause, he found himself laughing, with strong exhilaration. About six months later he had another similar episode. For a year after the first discharge he cried almost daily. He experienced himself as having changed in fundamental ways, as becoming more emotionally open, less driven in his work, less impatient, more creative.

According to Scheff, when strongly emotional experiences occur, either early in life, or as we might say, following the work of Brown and Harris (1978), when in adulthood severe life events happen, these can be experienced either as overwhelming, or as rather distant. So grief – to take just one example – when it is overwhelming, involves intense sadness, but also headaches, nasal congestion, feelings of pervasive hopelessness. By contrast if we cut ourselves off from the event by overdistancing, not just sadness but other emotions tend also to be suppressed. So not only is the event itself not fully assimilated, but by being overwhelmed, or by overdistancing, distortions and side-effects occur. Only when experienced, as it were, at an appropriate distance does the event, or the memory of it, produce sadness and sobbing appropriate to it so that the event itself can be assimilated into our consciously acknowledged life story. So, therapy – perhaps especially experiential therapy – is a situation in which such emotions as happiness, sadness, anger, and fear, can be experienced in safety and at an appropriate distance, without distortion.

Behavior therapy

Perhaps the most firmly established form of therapy after psychoanalytic approaches, behavior therapy was first developed to apply principles of Pavlovian conditioning to anxiety (Wolpe, 1958). The technique developed by Wolpe was called desensitization. If disabling anxiety is a response of fear acquired by conditioning to events which in others do not generally cause fear, then conditioning principles could be applied to alleviate it. There is no easy way of just unlearning a conditioned association; what must be done is to learn a new association, which becomes more salient.

Take the condition of agoraphobia, which according to Kessler et al. (1994) has a lifetime prevalence of 5.3 percent (see table 11.1), higher in women and higher too if one includes cases in which panics occur. In this condition, a person fears leaving home, and indeed does everything to avoid this except when accompanied by an attachment figure, usually a spouse or parent. In desensitization, the client is taught systematically to relax, lying down, going carefully through each group of muscles of the body in turn, concentrating on breathing, letting worrisome thoughts slip away. Notice that the method focuses on bodily symptoms, and is in some ways similar to the techniques of meditation developed in Eastern religions (many practitioners indeed became interested in Eastern ideas). The induction of relaxation in response to suggestions of the therapist also shares many of the features of hypnosis. The idea is of pairing the fear-producing images with bodily relaxation, which is incompatible with a fully developed anxiety response, and that by continuing this procedure fear will subside. The client is then encouraged to take these techniques of relaxation out into ordinary life, and practice them while really leaving the house.

Figure 12.2 In the behavioral therapy of desensitization, the therapist (here Dr Arnold Lazarus) uses a hypnosis-like induction, getting the patient to relax and imagine pleasant scenes, then the therapist will try to use conditioning to pair anxiety-provoking images with these relaxed and pleasant scenes, in order to lessen the anxiety.

Behavior therapy has blossomed into many different practices, using many different techniques, for many different problems (Emmelkamp, 1994). Nowadays treatment of anxiety disorders is usually based not on imagery as Wolpe first recommended, but on exposure of the client to the actual feared situation. In facing the real life situations they have avoided, clients habituate to them, and experience them as being tolerable rather than intolerable (Mathews, Gelde, & Johnson 1981). The therapist, with a briefcase full of techniques and a style of encouragement and reassurance, persuades the client to undertake things that seem too hard. He or she generally succeeds in getting clients to experience themselves in new contexts, and in new ways. This kind of therapy can properly be thought of in terms of education, advice, coaching, making plans for more skilled actions in the world; the relationship of behavior therapist and client is like that of athlete and trainer.

Behavioral methods allow clients to experience themselves acting more effectively while being able to tolerate, and perhaps regulate, anxiety and other kinds of resistance to achieving their goals. These methods, therefore, are often thought of in terms of stress management and of mood regulation. Among recent pieces of advice, based on surveys of what people find helpful in managing bad moods, is the suggestion to alternate bodily relaxation with physical exercise (Thayer, Newman, & McCain, 1994).

Cognitive and cognitive-behavioral therapy

The best known, and most researched, form of cognitive therapy was developed by Beck (1976). It is a modern descendant of the Stoics' philosophical cure for the soul. It is based on teaching people how to recognize and avoid errors in context evaluations about the incidents that lead to emotions. Other kinds of cognitive therapy are based on similar formulations. The argument is that if people did not think in certain patterns, they would not reach despairing emotional conclusions, and would not become depressed.

To see how therapy would work in such cases consider again Beck's example, discussed in chapter 4, of the medical records librarian who had depressive feelings when the nurse from the operating room said to her: "I hate medical records." The client had been asked to write down such incidents, any emotions that occurred, the thoughts that accompanied them, and then some alternative thoughts, in a diary. She gained some distance on these emotion–thought sequences – these cycles of thoughts-causing-feelings which bring to mind thoughts that cause more of the same feelings (Teasdale, 1988). Writing, it turns out, has in all cultures that have used it become one of the main means for reflecting on, and becoming conscious of, the meaning of emotions. Also, in his therapy Beck (1976, 1979) has argued that the patterns that cause anxiety and depression involve contextual evaluations that are arbitrary, absolute, and personalizing. If clients can make evaluations of other kinds – attributions that are external rather than internal, local rather than global, impermanent rather than stably permanent – about events that trigger emotions, then different emotions can occur that will break vicious cycles. Cognitive therapy then allows revision both of core beliefs and of plans, changing the answer to the question that Stein, Trabasso, and Liwag (1994) propose as central to context evaluation: "What can I do about it?"

For depression Beck's cognitive therapy (sometimes called cognitive behavior therapy) has been found generally to have beneficial effects (Hollon & Beck, 1994). Effects have been comparable to those achieved with antidepressant drugs. In one of the largest trials of psychotherapy yet conducted, with 239 real patients in clinical settings (Elkin, 1994), it was found that Beck's cognitive psychotherapy did well. Another form of psychotherapy, and also anti-depressant drugs, did similarly well. But neither psychotherapy nor anti-depressants did much better than an inactive placebo pill plus supportive clinical management. The effectiveness of this placebo condition can be related to the finding that depression generally does remit as people find new projects in their life after a serious adversity. There was, however, some suggestion of a longer lasting effect with psychotherapy; there are also indications that for depression cognitive therapy of Beck's type is superior to other kinds of psychotherapy (Robinson, Berman, & Neimeyer, 1990). There is also some indication that some patients are more helped by cognitive therapy, others are more helped by antidepressant drugs, but no differences in the effects on the pattern of depression of these two forms of treatment have so far been found. This would be difficult to understand unless both kinds of treatment act by cutting into a vicious cycle of the kind postulated by Teasdale (1988).

Family therapy

For the most part, emotions occur not just to individuals – they occur in interaction with others. Family therapy is a branch of psychotherapy conducted not with an individual but by a therapist and a whole family, with the aim of understanding such patterns, and helping the family resolve them (Goldenberg & Goldenberg, 1991). A typical and well-known idea in family therapy is that of triangulation. When there is emotional conflict between a husband and wife which they are unwilling to express directly, they can nonetheless transmit to children in the family some of the anxiety of their relationship – making the children, for instance, anxious that their parents might separate. What can happen is that one child with a bias towards expressing anxiety in a bodily way, starts to develop physical symptoms which have the effect of maintaining the parents' attention on these symptoms. The symptoms cannot be understood except in terms of the structure of the whole family. Minuchin, Rosman, and Baker (1978) consider in their book children who develop anorexia, asthma, and psychosomatic forms of diabetes. All these illnesses have high capacity to monopolize the attention of the family, and all can be life-threatening for the child. The result is that the mother and father concentrate on their child's illness rather than on the conflicts of their own relationship. The threat of their dissatisfactions with each other recedes – but at the cost of having a chronically sick child. A form of family therapy called structural therapy consists of working with the whole family: for instance, getting the parents to talk with each other rather than remaining in emotionally overinvolved relationships with a child. This can help free the sick child from the burden of keeping the family together, allowing the parents to become aware of their conflicts and thus be in a better position to solve them.

Other kinds of family therapy draw on more behavioral methods of education and advice. Of these, let us consider just one kind, which arises from the research on Expressed Emotions discussed in chapter 11. Four recent intervention trials have used psychosocial education and family therapy with high Expressed Emotion families. All have had comparable results of reducing the relapse of psychotic symptoms. Here is the result of a trial in Pittsburgh by Hogarty et al. (1986). They started with 130 High Expressed Emotion families of schizophrenic patients. Of these, 90 families were prepared to accept the whole treatment package, and from them the investigators formed four groups:

- family treatment and medication for the schizophrenic patient (n = 21);
- social skills and medication (n = 20);
- family treatment, social skills, and medication (n = 20);
- medication alone (n = 29).

Family treatment consisted of an education workshop, plus sessions with each individual family at home. The aims were to increase education about the illness, to augment social networks, and help in coping with problems. Social skills treatment was conducted with the patients alone, and was aimed at helping them improve their social perception and to be more direct and assertive with their families.

The baseline relapse rate within a period of one year was 41 percent (12 of the 29 in the medication only group). In each of the two groups which had either family treatment, or social skills treatment, just five patients relapsed within a year. In the group with both family and social skills treatment none relapsed; these differences were significant. By a combination of relatives coming to express less hostility to the schizophrenic member of the family and by this person also becoming more emotionally direct, a less distressing – less pathogenic – family atmosphere can be set up.

Why emotions are the center of psychotherapy

Greenberg and Safran have given a sense of how to conceptualize different kinds of emotions in therapy. But why have emotions such a central role? Greenberg (1993) argues that making emotions explicit gives a sense of the schemas on which they are based, a sense of clarity and control in life, and a sense of where to focus. In the terms of this book we think the answer is threefold.

First, and perhaps most importantly, emotions point to goals or concerns. In the course of life we take on many goals, many projects. Some, like attachment, are formed without words. Others formed later may have arisen more explicitly, but without us realizing how our goals may affect each other, so some of their implications may be unconscious. Emotions signal that some goal or concern is affected. If it is only partly known, an emotion may be our best clue to the importance for us of this concern. One of the tasks of psychotherapy, then, is to work on such clues to build some consciously comprehended model of our goal structure as part of our sense of self.

Second, emotional habits are built up in life. We construct and inhabit a kind of inner theory, or schema, which makes sense of what happens to us and which informs us about what to do, especially in our relations with others. Severe life events and conflicts within ourselves are, as it were, challenges to our implicit theory, prompting us towards changing our beliefs, and making plans in different ways. Therapy is a place to become more aware of the terms and conditions of our schemas or theories, and perhaps to modify them.

Third, if there are basic emotions their noninformational parts can occur independently of what caused them, so they can appear as vague but disturbing disquiets. And, because some emotions (including love) can project now onto one object, now onto another, some emotions can be experienced as strange longings. Part of the task of therapy, and life, is that in expressing emotions with other people they become clearer. They crystallize into more comprehensible emotions and their origins and content become clearer; they become as philosophers say, more intentional, more conscious.

But does psychotherapy work?

In the sections above on cognitive therapy, and family therapy based on Expressed Emotion, we mentioned trials in which therapy had been successful. What about the many other kinds of therapy? Do psychological therapies work generally? Despite rumors to the contrary, the answer is "Yes." There have now been many hundreds of trials of different kinds of psychotherapy, assigning clients randomly to groups, comparing outcomes for people who received therapy with those in a control group: one of the best studies in the area is that of Sloane et al. (1975) who found that both behavior therapy and psychoanalytic therapy, with experienced excellent therapists, had positive effects on a number of measures as compared with a control group of people put on a waiting list for therapy. The effects of the two different kinds of therapy were not very different.

One of the first uses of the statistical technique of meta-analysis was to estimate the average effects of therapy, in a study by Smith, Glass, and Miller (1980). They found that in over 475 studies, the average effect size over a range of kinds of psychotherapy, including psychoanalytic and behavioral therapies, was 0.85 of a standard deviation. What this means is that the average person receiving therapy was better off than 80 percent of the members of control groups who did not receive therapy. Lambert and Bergin (1994) give an extensive review of meta-analyses of different kinds of psychotherapy, and come to similar conclusions, but with the addition that psychotherapy has been found to have effects lasting for months or in some cases for years. There has been a recent review of meta-analyses of psychotherapeutic trials, and also of educational interventions (Lipsey & Wilson, 1993), which broadly confirms these results. In comparison with educational interventions, a relatively modest amount of time in psychotherapy – typically of the order of a dozen sessions – is more effective than the majority of educational interventions designed, for instance, to produce more effective learning of mathematics.

These results are rather general, averaging across many clients. This does not mean that all therapy is effective, or that all therapists are helpful. Some therapists are clearly more effective than others. The worse news is that just as psychotherapy can do good, it can do harm. Lambert and Bergin (1994) have found studies in which therapists were either quite ineffective, or did active harm. Orlinsky and Howard (1980) for instance, reviewed case files of 143 women seen by 23 therapists. Six therapists were good: overall 84 percent of the clients they saw were improved at the end of therapy and none were worse. Five therapists were not good: less than 50 percent of their clients were improved, and 10 percent were worse. For these women clients, moreover, women therapists did markedly better – we might imagine an explanation based on empathy.

What about particular kinds of therapy? What you will find by looking at the literature are outcome studies for most older established therapies, usually with positive results. Despite partisan commitments, therapists of different persuasions often produce effects of similar size. Some results of therapy have been very striking, with effects that are not themselves psychological: Spiegel et al. (1989) found that patients who had metastatic breast cancer, randomly allocated to receive weekly supportive group therapy sessions, had their life prolonged by some 18 months, as compared with control subjects with similar pathology allocated to a condition with the same medical care but without group therapy.

Drugs, and in particular antidepressant and tranquilizing drugs which respectively decrease the intensity of sad and anxious moods, are still the treatments of choice for many psychiatrists. This response is an ancient medical one: to relieve suffering. The intent is different from that of most psychological therapies – including cognitive-behavior therapy – to understand the emotions that cause anguish.

Psychotherapy without professionals

Perhaps the most serious problem of therapy is its availability. Look at the prevalence of psychiatric disorder in the USA, described by Kessler et al.

(1994), that we discussed in chapter 11. Now consider the most common disorders, anxiety and depression. Now do some arithmetic: multiply the prevalence rates by the population of the USA, say 250 million, more than half of whom are between 15 and 54, the age-band of these prevalence figures. You will conclude that each year several tens of millions of Americans suffer from clinically significant anxiety or depression, or both. Even in this highly resourced society there are just not enough mental health professionals to go round. Kessler et al. (1994), indeed, found that in any year in which people suffered a disorder only about a fifth of them consulted a professional, and for only about half of those was this a mental health professional. Psychoanalysis, four or five times a week for several years, is obviously available only to the few. Even the shorter treatments such as behavioral and cognitive therapy typically involve a dozen or so sessions.

So what is the answer? One is that alongside ideas of individual therapy developed by Freud, his admirers and his critics, there was also another kind of therapy, always more populist, that involved people meeting in groups. Its founders included Jane Addams who opened a group social work house in 1889 and was later awarded a Nobel Prize, and Joseph Pratt who in 1905 discovered that tuberculosis patients whom he arranged to meet together in groups of 20 or so, formed supportive social structures among themselves, which had important therapeutic effects on the course of their illness.

At about the same time that group methods were being started in the USA, in the same city where Freud was beginning his individual psychotherapeutic practices, another therapeutic innovator was starting to work. This was Jacob Moreno, who as a medical student would meet with people in the parks of Vienna, in a format that was a cross between children's play and informal theater that has become known as psychodrama. In this form, protagonists reenact in fantasy some of the elements of difficult family and life situations. In 1921, he opened the Theater of Spontaneity in Vienna, and it was he who coined the terms "group psychotherapy," and "encounter" (Moreno, 1940).

In terms of outcomes, group therapy, like individual therapy, has generally been found effective (Tillitski, 1990). But as well as professionally led groups, there emerged particularly in the USA, a range of more populist group formats, such as encounter groups. Their popularity mushroomed in the 1960s and 1970s. Though they have declined they have not disappeared. These and many other forms had therapeutic aims, but most are somewhat outside mainstream psychiatric and psychological practice (Shaffer & Galinsky, 1974). These movements now include many self-help organizations based on group practices, such as Alcoholics Anonymous.

Even with populist group-based therapy there is still not enough to go round. It is therefore not surprising that when people are surveyed about the people they turn to in times of emotional crisis, they name a wide variety of persons, including priests, rabbis, doctors – but principally friends. Recall from chapters 8 and 11 that the factor most widely found to be protective against

Figure 12.3 In the 1970s encounter groups became very popular in the USA and Europe, and group therapy is still popular. One of the founders was Carl Rogers, seen with spectacles on the right-hand side of this picture of a group in progress.

emotional disorder, both in children and in adults, is relationships with other people – friendships, known technically as social support.

Among the most important aims of psychiatric health care, then, should be the aim of having society evolve so that it is harder for people to become socially marginalized. At the same time, where practices have been discovered by mental health professionals that have been helpful in therapy for emotional suffering, then arguably rather than distributing these services for fees, the job of mental health professionals might better be seen as giving them away, diffusing them into the community.

Emotional creativity

Emotions provide an important area for creativity. Averill and Thomas-Knowles (1991) have pointed out that just as intellectual areas and the arts are domains in which people can be creative, so too are the emotions. Although we have provided evidence in this book that emotions have a biological basis, they are anything but fixed. Rather they are like a painter's palette, the bases for elaboration. To use another simile: emotions are like modes of locomotion that we are innately given – creeping on all fours, walking, running, jumping – which allow for creative elaboration in dancing, skating, gymnastics, and so forth. Emotions have some aspects that are universal, but they vary from culture to culture. This tells us that they allow an important area for creativity, and for therapeutic development.

Averill and Nunley (1992) propose that one of the great examples of emotional creativity was the poet Dante. He fell in love with Beatrice in 1274. It does not seem an exaggeration to say that the European and American notion of falling in love, and being in love, has been affected by him and his writing ever since. Dante first met Beatrice when he was nine and she was eight – at that moment he immediately fell in love. They did not speak until nine years later, when one day they met on a street in Florence. She greeted him, and he was filled with joy. Dante's only contacts with Beatrice seemed to be in public places, and though she died at the age of 24, his love for her had become and remained the main preoccupation of his poetry.

Dante made love into the ultimate meaning. In his early poems in *The New Life* (1295) he writes of his love, and also of his despair. In one poem he writes about being mocked by other women for swooning in the presence of Beatrice, and how he resolved to seek peace of mind, rather than tormenting himself with Beatrice's goodness and beauty. The poem he wrote next after this resolve was, says Reynolds in her introduction to these poems, a turning point for Dante and for European literature: it "opened up vistas and depths in which the human experience of love was glimpsed as being ultimately one with the power by which the universe is governed" (p. 160). By the time he came to write his masterpiece *The Divine Comedy* (1307–1321) his love for Beatrice had become transformed into a pilgrimage first to the depths of hell – as we might say, into the human unconscious; then through purgatory, in which we reflect on our life and its meaning; and finally to paradise, where Beatrice becomes his guide.

Dante did not invent the romantic ideal of cultivating a love for someone idealized, and becoming good on her behalf, but he found a solution to the contradictions of courtly love that we discussed in chapter 2. Though his love was never consummated sexually, his writing had profound cultural implications. We could say his poetry began a new era.

For any of us in Western society the very existence of the erotic is an opportunity for a highly personal creativity. Some people may express this in poetry. Others are moved to different kinds of expressions that they have previously felt incapable of. Indeed in the West loving someone may be one of life's most truly creative events, responding to that change in which the self expands to include another, when doors of understanding may open. Building a self without this much mythologized experience may be yet more challenging.

Consciousness

Emotions can be mere stirrings, vague excitements, unshaped movements of the mind. We have presented evidence that there is a biological basis for them. But if we were to stop there we would stop with something like the emotions of our relatives the great apes. We human beings are born not just into the world, but into society. Each society includes traditions of skills and technology. It also includes individual people, to whom we become attached in friendship and other relations. And in every society, in every community, in every family, a history forms, with its characters, its traditions of custom and understanding about what we people are up to with each other. In such traditions, emotions and our understandings of them are the pivotal points.

As human beings we are conscious. By taking thought we can become conscious that we are conscious. But what difference does this make? What is it that we do that could not be done without being conscious? Many forms of therapy are based on the idea of making aspects of our emotional lives more conscious, and in previous sections of this chapter we have given reasons why this may be helpful. Leventhal (1991) has argued that emotions are represented at several different layers, as reflex-like phenomena, as schemas, and as concepts. Only concepts are open to consciousness and to (more or less) voluntary change, so an abiding question is what kinds of conceptual changes may occur, and which of these might also affect the lower level structures? Putting this differently, in what ways can we influence our mental and emotional lives (Wegner & Pennebaker, 1993)?

The question of why consciousness may be important is yet more general. One of the most striking facts about emotions is that they can cause a turmoil of conscious reflection. What is the significance of this?

The idea that we in part create ourselves by conscious reflection can be traced to Shakespeare. Harold Bloom puts it like this: the greatest of Shakespeare's originalities, one which was so original, but so complete in its cultural effects that we now do not notice it, or notice that someone began it, was "the representation of change by showing people pondering their own speeches and being altered through that consideration" (Harold Bloom, 1989, p. 54). If Bloom is right, for us moderns becoming conscious is an aspect of making us who we are. Let us therefore look briefly at how conscious reflection upon ourselves has emerged in the history of Western culture.

Becoming conscious of emotions in literature

"There is no history of mankind, there is only an indefinite number of histories of all kinds of aspects of human life," wrote Karl Popper. The history most of us learn at school, he continued, is largely "the history of power politics [which] is nothing but the history of international crime" (Popper, 1962b, p. 270). Among the many histories that would be more edifying — the history of ideas, the history of technology, the history of the family — might be counted the history of consciousness and of the emotions. This can be approached via written stories where emotions and their effects are typically at the center of narrative.

In the earliest history of the West there are generally taken to be four principal civilizations, from around the Eastern Mediterranean and in what is now called the Middle East, that contributed to the culture in which

Westerners now live and to our ways of thinking and feeling. Seemingly the oldest direct ancestor of our own civilizations is that of the Sumerians who lived in cities on the rivers Tigris and Euphrates in what is now Iraq. Some 5,000 years ago they invented writing, first based on little diagrams which then developed into a more abstract system called cuneiform that could also represent spoken syllables. The Sumerians' civilization was superseded by that of the Babylonians, with a different language, but who continued to preserve the Sumerian system of writing, as well as Sumerian mathematics and culture. More or less at the same time the great African civilization of Egypt arose, with a different system of writing. Starting later and deriving ideas and cultural practices from the Babylonians and Egyptians (Bernal, 1987) were the societies of the Greeks and the Hebrews, whose language and writing systems have continuity with modern languages, making their cultures more accessible.

From the Sumerians come epics dating from around 4,000 years ago about King Gilgamesh, and the troubles of himself and Enkidu, including an episode in which Gilgamesh becomes recognizably depressed at the death of Enkidu. From Egypt come many writings allowing a picture of ancient life to be drawn: among them is a famous one called "The dispute between a man and his soul," dating from about 3,700 years ago, in which a man complains of his misery, longs for death, and is answered by his soul saying that death will occur in due

Figure 12.4 Writing and reading allow us to make emotions conscious, and to reflect on them. This picture is of Christine de Pisan, a medieval writer. Before the invention of printing only a tiny number of people could read and write.

time (Lichtheim, 1973). From the Hebrews come the first five books of the Bible, the earliest parts of which were probably written about 2,800 years ago, with their theme of a family history in which the protagonists, Adam, Eve, Abraham, Sarah, Jacob, Isaac and the rest, oscillate between fear and hopeful dependence on their god Yahweh (Rosenberg & Bloom, 1990). From the Greeks comes the *Iliad*, contemporary with the first books of the Bible. Its first words are: "Of anger sing, goddess." It is a tale of the repercussions of Achilles's sulking during the long and angry war triggered by the abduction of Helen by the Trojan prince Menelaus (Homer, c. 850 BCE). So, from the first, we find writing in the West struggling to understand and reflect upon emotions and our consciousness of them.

In chapter 3 we argued that one difference between us and the apes was that our emotions have become more intentional, more conscious. The principal way in which we become conscious – at least conscious of ourselves – is in giving ourselves and others accounts in narrative form. In everyday life we tell stories of our emotional experiences to others (Rimé et al., 1991), allowing ourselves to explore these incidents consciously, in a context of a relationship. But we can also write about emotionally troubling issues. For instance Pennebaker, Kiecolt-Glaser, and Glaser (1988) had 50 students write either about such issues, or about superficial topics, for 20 minutes on four consecutive days. Those who wrote about the disturbing emotional issue showed improvements in immune function in the form of higher lymphocyte response to an antigen challenge, and fewer medical consultations at the University Health Center. Although they found the actual writing more distressing than that of the control subjects, three months later they were significantly happier than the control subjects and, looking back, they viewed the experience of confronting the emotional issues they wrote about as a positive experience. Pennebaker (1989) has found therapeutic effects of confronting traumatic experiences, by writing or by talking. He understands the process in terms of a debilitation caused by suppressing traumatic experiences, which is relieved by confiding and by confronting the experience and its emotions.

But what about reading or listening to narrative? Bruner (1986) has argued that understanding narrative is a special and distinctive faculty of the human mind, and that the essence of narrative is "human action and its vicissitudes." With equal justice he might have said: "human action, its vicissitudes, and emotional repercussions." Written narrative literature, from ancient times to the present, concentrates on our emotional lives and their problematics – as if story telling and story listening have always been attempts to understand these matters. The activity is satisfying because stories provide possibilities of vicarious action and pieces of solutions to the problems of how to act and how to be a person in the society that is depicted. Publicly available stories give members of society common exemplars of action and emotion. They help us to reflect on and become part of the cultural tradition in which we live.

Emotions and art

Since the beginning of the romantic era in literary theory discussed in chapter 2, the focus in theories of art in the West has fallen on the relationship of the artist to the work of art. A consensus has developed (Abrams, 1953); theorists agree that art is the expression by an artist of emotion in different media: music, poetry, novels, painting. In the English-speaking world Wordsworth was an early spokesman for this movement. In the preface to the second edition of the *Lyrical Ballads* (1802) he wrote:

> Poetry is the spontaneous overflow of powerful feelings: it takes its origin from emotions recollected in tranquility: the emotion is contemplated till by a species of reaction the tranquility disappears, and the emotion, kindred to that which was before the subject of contemplation, is gradually produced, and does itself actually exist in the mind. (p. 611)

This preface became a manifesto for romantic poets, and also for the novelists of the nineteenth century. It is fair to say that literary artists in the West still work in this tradition, and follow many of its principles.

Why is the idea that art is the expression of emotion so important for psychologists and others seeking to understand emotions? It is important because it points to emotions often being, as it were, protean, like raw material rather than finished products. Culture shapes these inchoate feelings. Parents explain them to children. In children's stories, as well as in the novels, plays, news, and movies, we are given examples of events leading up to emotions, and the consequences they have.

Because the biological bases of emotions have effects that are often powerful but loosely specified, it has seemed imperative to artists from the beginning of recorded time to articulate and express emotions creatively in their individuality. So emotions are given intentionality. Emotions emerge when we encounter problems, uncertainties in life, when we do not know how to act. They tell us something is happening to which we should pay attention. Often they demand a creative response. What artists do is to bring these vague feelings, the conflicts with others and within the self, the uncertainties that they represent, into awareness, giving them content and particularity by expressing them as works of art.

Emotions in drama, ritual, and psychotherapy

In many kinds of society, ritual, drama, and later literature, had a rather explicit function that we might broadly call therapeutic (Helman, 1984). In all societies people enact rituals that include such group activities as singing, dancing, processions. In all societies, then, there is theater or its equivalent. In all there is the telling of stories. With literacy came the writing down of these stories (Olson, 1994), and in some cultures, such as the Jewish one and that of the Christian Protestants after the Reformation, there is explicit understanding that the written text as such is sacred, to be interpreted and reflected upon. Just as emotions are at the center of the psychotherapies which are modern secular descendants of some of the rituals and societal practices of religion, emotions too are at the center of narrative literature. Just as catharsis, the experiencing of primary emotions, is a central event in therapy, so *katharsis*, as Aristotle called it – clarifying the relation of emotions to human action (Nussbaum, 1986, p. 391) – is central at the theater, or in listening to a story, or in reading a novel.

How do we understand this? One explanation is given by Scheff (1979). He argues that all these societal practices – explicit or informal therapy, ritual, drama, stories – have at their center the possibility not just of experiencing emotions but of experiencing them at what he calls a best aesthetic distance. Scheff argues that if emotionally damaging events or difficulties are experienced as overwhelming, or if we distance ourselves from them too much, then we accumulate a kind of emotional arrears, which distorts our emotional lives. What ritual, drama, narrative do, argues Scheff, is to provide memory cues that will bring emotions of our own to mind in a safe context where we can experience them at a best aesthetic distance.

> When we cry over the fate of Romeo and Juliet, we are reliving our own personal experiences of overwhelming loss, but under new and less severe conditions. The experience of vicarious loss, in a properly designed drama is sufficiently distressful to reawaken the old distress. It is also sufficiently vicarious, however, so that the emotion does not feel overwhelming. (Scheff, 1979, p. 13)

Scheff proposes that in experiencing emotions in this way – or, as Pennebaker suggests, in confiding and writing about them – we can assimilate them to our understanding with therapeutic effect. We have argued that the supply of therapeutic help in Western society is too limited to meet the need. But narrative, heard, read, or created, is not in short supply in any society. These forms, moreover, are more under the control of the client than are many kinds of therapy – we can use them as and when we wish.

Scheff's argument does not cover all the reasons for taking part in ritual, drama, and narrative. We might even conclude that most social practices in this domain – listening to music, taking part in or watching sport, going to the movies – occur largely for enjoyment, with no therapeutic aim whatever. Certainly people in general enjoy such practices even when the emotions that they experience are negative, as occurs when they pay to see a movie which is a thriller. We humans seem to prefer being in an emotional state to not being in one. Why do we find the experiencing of emotions entertaining? It is a question on which we can speculate; it remains unsolved.

A culture of understanding

In the nineteenth century, novels such as those by Gustave Flaubert and Émile Zola in France, by Jane Austen and George Eliot in England, by Leo Tolstoy and Fyodor Dostoevsky in Russia, by Herman Melville and Harriet Beecher Stowe in America, came to be means of enjoyment, ways of experiencing emotions so that they could be assimilated (as proposed by Scheff) and ways of identifying with others so that the experiences of taking part emotionally in lives beyond the boundaries of our personal lot could become, as George Eliot put it, "the raw material for moral sentiment" (Pinney, 1963, p. 270).

Soon after the close of the century a change began, prompted partly by movements within literature such as Marcel Proust's novel *Remembrance of Things Past* (1913–1927) in which the reader is invited to become the writer, and partly by the new movement of psychoanalysis, in which the client is asked "to give . . . the whole story of his life and illness" (Freud, 1905, p. 16).

By the 1920s novels had become more inward, and the idea – not new but beginning at least with Shakespeare – became common that becoming a whole person was wrapped up with being able to understand oneself in terms of a narrative of one's life. As Marcus has put it, in relation to psychoanalytic therapy, at the end of successful therapy "one has come into possession of one's own story . . . a fictional construction which is at the same time satisfactory to us in the form of the truth, and as the form of the truth" (Marcus, 1984, p. 62). By "fictional" here Marcus does not mean "untrue." He means, rather, that such a history of oneself necessarily is a construction, a creative interpretation from fragmentary elements, as Bartlett (1932) showed.

Marcus then continues with an extraordinary passage on the psychotherapy initiated by Freud:

> No larger tribute has ever been paid to a culture in which the various narrative and fictional forms had exerted for centuries both moral and philosophical authority and which had produced as one of its chief climaxes the great bourgeois novels of the nineteenth century. Indeed, we must see Freud's writings – and method – as themselves part of this culmination, and at the same moment, along with the great modernist novels of the first half of the twentieth century, as the beginning of the end of this tradition and its authority. (p. 62)

What then of the second half of the twentieth century and the eve of the twenty-first; what of postmodernism? We know that some fiction is read for its possibilities of reflection and the insights it prompts, not just as in action stories to get to the end to see what happens and stop feeling anxious (Cupchik & László, 1994). But today the reading of novels of any kind has been largely replaced with the watching of television (on average two hours a day per person in North America). From this perspective, so far as one can see, the notion "drama" typically means the evocation of fear in someone who has been threatened or whose rights have been infringed, followed by enactment of angry violence against the wrongdoer. This motif is so unchanging that it has all the properties of ritual with millions of ardent devotees, so one must suspect that in the West it is our new religion.

We the authors hope that other patterns of emotion are also recognizable within our culture – other plots in other narratives in which we can recognize human vulnerability and in which lives are related to each other in affection as well as in conflict. In such patterns life narratives turn round the fulcrum of emotion, not necessarily easily, but with a possibility of creativity and of understanding.

Summary

Psychological therapies in many forms have existed in the religious practices and rituals of many societies. In general they aim to reintegrate people who have become disrelated with their community. In such practices emotions play a central role. In the twentieth century secular practice of psychoanalytic therapy, a client tells the story of his or her life to a therapist within the structure of a relationship in which issues compiled into the client's emotion schemas are replayed in transference. There are, however, many forms of psychotherapy, and most have an emotional base that is more or less prominent. In some forms of therapy it is thought beneficial to express emotions, in others it is more important to understand habitual or defensive emotions, in yet others the aim is to allow new ways of thinking and acting that do not have the old and familiar emotional effects. Emotions are at the center of therapy because they point to our goals or concerns, including concerns of the deepest aspects of ourselves. And in therapy it is often possible to make fresh starts with some of the concerns that are most important to us. In general, benefits of therapy have been demonstrated empirically, though not every therapist is helpful with every client. It is clear from therapy, and from the narrative literature that has been written down during the last 4,000 years, that emotions are not just fixed, but are a matter for creativity. They arise when problems arise in individual lives, so as well as setting priorities they pose, as it were, challenges to how to deal with these problems. Most kinds of therapy involve clients telling the therapist some kind of narrative about their lives, narratives in which emotions are prominent. It may not be accidental also that the fictional literature of the world also consists of stories, the most common of which involve a protagonist who has some aim or concern, who forms a plan which then meets a problem of some kind, and results in the protagonist experiencing emotions, which may prompt a solution to the problem. Conscious understanding of our emotions involves becoming more knowledge-able about the narratives that we and others tell about the self and its doings.

Further Reading

Like other areas, psychotherapy has a useful handbook; it has chapters on outcomes of therapy, on different therapeutic approaches, and on therapy in different settings.

Allen Bergin & Sol Garfield (1994). *Handbook of psychotherapy and behavior change* (4th ed.). New York: Wiley.

For an engaging discussion about the relation of psychotherapy to autobiographical memory, emotions, and narratives of the self:

Jeff Singer & Peter Salovey (1993). *The remembered self: emotion and memory in personality.* New York: Free Press.

On emotions and creativity, see:

James R. Averill & Carol Thomas-Knowles (1991). Emotional creativity. In K. T. Strongman (Ed.), *International Review of Studies on Emotion* (pp. 269–299). Chichester: Wiley.

A review of the relation of psychology to literary criticism, and the role of emotions in reading and writing narrative literature:

Keith Oatley (1994). A taxonomy of the emotions of literary response and a theory of identification in fictional narrative. *Poetics, 23,* 53–74.

Glossary

This is a brief glossary, excluding terms found in any medium-sized English dictionary and concentrating on those used in this book that have a technical meaning. For a more complete glossary try Atkinson, R. L. et al. (1990). *Introduction to Psychology* (10th ed.). San Diego, CA: Harcourt Brace Jovanovich, or a dictionary of psychology.

Action readiness. A term proposed by Frijda as the core process of an emotion: giving priority and making ready to act in a certain kind of way.

Adreno-corticoid hormones. Hormones released from the outside part of the adrenal glands which mobilize energy, and which can suppress parts of the immune system.

Affect. A general, slightly old-fashioned, term used to include emotions, moods, and preferences. Affective disorder means depression or mania.

Aggression. Action of conflict with another, or of hurting, or intending to hurt: usually used in relation to physical violence, but used too as a metaphor, for example, an aggressive argument.

Amygdala. A part of the limbic system, implicated in emotions since experimental lesions of this region in monkeys were found to produce profound emotional changes.

Anxiety. A term used to designate a mood of fear, apprehension, or worry. Also a name for a group of psychiatric syndromes which include panic, agoraphobia, social phobia, specific phobia, obsessive-compulsive disorder, posttraumatic stress disorder, and generalized anxiety disorder.

Antidepressant. A drug designed to relieve the mood of depression by making certain transmitter substances, such as serotonin, more available for use at synapses.

Appraisal. A term meaning evaluation of an event on a number of criteria. A set of appraisals determines what emotion (if any) is produced by the event.

Arousal. Being alert, with the nervous system including the sympathetic division of the autonomic nervous system activated, and the body prepared for action.

Attachment. Behavioral system in which the infant and caregiver maintain an optimal degree of proximity to one another, for the safety of the infant. Crying is an emotional signaling system that functions to summon the caregiver.

Attachment style. Classification of children into secure, ambivalent or avoidant on the basis of Ainsworth's "Strange Situation" test; sometimes called attachment status.

Attribution. Assigning causes to an event. An internal attribution means assigning the cause to oneself; an external attribution means assigning it to something outside the self.

Attunement. Finely tuned interactions that occur between parent and infant, in which the emotions and actions of the parent are synchronized with those of the baby and vice versa.

Autonomic nervous system. The part of the nervous system aimed, as it were, at the inside of the body. There are two divisions: the parasympathetic division tends to promote rest, while the sympathetic division arouses the body, preparing it for sexuality, attack, or defense.

Basic emotions. A small set of emotions that is usually taken to include happiness, sadness, anger, and fear. The hypothesis of basic emotions is that humans are equipped biologically with a small number of such basic emotions, and that other emotions are elaborations of these.

Caregiver. The parent or other person responsible for the care of the infant.

Catharsis. Reduction of an emotion by expressing it in psychotherapy, in drama, or in ritual.

Cognitive. Having to do with the representation and use of knowledge.

Cognitive bias. Tendency towards a particular style of mental processing.

Complex emotion. An emotion with several parts, typically involving the self.

Componential theories of emotion. Theories that emotions are made up of components, such as features of appraisal.

Conditioning (classical or Pavlovian conditioning). Learning to associate some event with something pleasurable or painful.

Conduct disorder. Persistent pattern of behavior in childhood in which others' rights, or social norms, are violated. It includes aggression that causes or threatens harm to others, damage to property, deceitfulness, theft, and serious violations of rules.

Continuity. Term used in this book for patterns of emotional response, or emotional behavior, that continue over a period of months or years.

Cortex (neocortex). The outer part of the enlarged forebrain that is so prominent in humans.

Corticoid. see **adreno-corticoid hormones.**

Critical period. A period in the development of a human being or animal which is the optimal time of readiness for responding to particular stimùli or acquiring particular skills or abilities.

Cross-sectional study. A study done at a single point in time.

Culture. A pattern of ideas, custom, and tradition that characterizes a group of people who live together, or who share the same language.

Depression (or major depression). Psychiatric syndrome including a low or sad mood for at least two weeks, together with at least four symptoms such as: loss of pleasure, weight loss, insomnia, agitation or retardation, fatigue, feelings of worthlessness or guilt, difficulties of concentration, suicidal thoughts.

Diathesis–stress. Theoretical idea that psychiatric disorders are based on a personal vulnerability, genetic or learned (the diathesis), and a life event or difficulty (stress).

Diencephalon. Word used interchangeably with **hypothalamus.**

Differential Emotions Theory. Izard's theory of emotion in which there is a set of discrete emotions each with a specific neurophysiological basis.

Disorder (emotional or psychiatric disorder). Technical term for a persistent state of mind, or persistent behaviors, that are disabling, and make it hard or impossible for the person to function in everyday life.

Displacement activity. Apparently irrelevant behavior displayed by animals – and sometimes by human beings – when in situations of conflict.

Display rules. Theoretical term implying that a particular society has implicit rules about what emotions can be displayed to others, and when.

Diagnosis (psychiatric diagnosis). Recognition and naming of a particular medical (or psychiatric) condition.

Dynamic Systems Theory. Theory of emotional development in which emotions are made up of components that become organized as people interact with their environment.

Electroencephalogram (EEG). Electrical pattern recorded from the surface of the brain, summing the activity of many millions of nerve cells.

Elicitor. Event that starts off some emotion, or some action.

Emotion. A state usually caused by an event of importance to the subject. It typically includes (a) a conscious mental state with recognizable quality of feeling and directed towards some object, (b) a bodily perturbation of some kind, (c) recognizable expressions of the face, tone of voice, and gesture, (d) a readiness for certain kinds of action.

Emotional bias. Likelihood of responding with one kind of emotion more than another.

Emotion regulation. The implicit and explicit strategies that we use to increase or decrease the intensity and duration of emotional experiences.

Emotionality. Ways that individuals differ from one another on experience and expression of emotions; the emotional component of personality.

Emotion Schema Term used to indicate a pattern of emotional response based on previous experience of emotion in relationships, that we take with us into new circumstances.

Epidemiological psychiatry. The statistical study of psychiatric syndromes, such as depression, anxiety states, schizophrenia, and so on, in the ordinary population rather than among people who have found their way to a clinic.

Ethology. Study of human and animal behavior in natural settings.

Evolutionary adaptedness. State of having evolved by natural selection to fit a particular environment.

Expression. Charles Darwin's term for the more-or-less involuntary changes of face, voice, and posture that are observable signs of an emotion.

Expressed Emotion. Term used to indicate the amount of hostility or warmth, and overinvolvement, expressed in a family towards one of its members.

Externalizing disorder. A pattern of psychological disturbance in children characterized by antisocial behavior: opposition, destructiveness, sometimes aggression and delinquency. (See **conduct disorder,** one of the externalizing disorders.)

Facial feedback hypothesis. The idea that information from facial movements creates or intensifies emotions.

Folk psychology (folk theory). The ordinary understanding of psychological matters generally accepted, often implicitly, in any cultural group.

Forebrain. Most recently evolved part of the vertebrate brain.

Gesture. An expressive movement.

Goal. An aim or objective, not necessarily consciously known.

Goal-corrected partnership. Bowlby's term for the partnership that develops between child and parent, based on each being able to represent the goals of the other.

Goal relevance theories. Theories of emotion in which the determinant of emotion is the person's evaluation of whether a goal is being approached, or violated.

Habituation. A diminution of response with repeated exposure to a stimulus.

Heart rate. A measure taken to indicate emotional arousal.

Heritability. The extent to which a pattern of behavior is attributable to genetic transmission.

Heuristic. A strategy that can be used in different contexts when there is no guaranteed solution to a problem.

Hormone. Chemical substance that travels in the blood to affect the brain or other parts of the body.

Human universals. Characteristics shared by all human beings.

Hypothalamus. Part of the forebrain responsible for controlling the autonomic nervous system, and the pituitary gland – also implicated in species-characteristic behavior of eating, drinking, sex, and attack.

I-self. Version of the self, characteristic of Western culture, in which the self is experienced as autonomous.

Imprinting. A species-characteristic pattern of learning that occurs during a time-limited period in early infancy of some animals. For instance, when exposed to a moving, sound-producing object during this developmental phase, the animal subsequently follows this object.

Immune system. Part of the body's system of defense against infections, cancer, and other diseases.

Incidence. Term used in epidemiology to indicate the frequency with which new cases of some particular disorder occur in the population.

Individual differences. Differences among people on behavior, cognition, or emotional state.

Individualism. Cultural feature of Western societies: the individual is thought to be autonomous and independent; these features have acquired moral value.

Induction (mood induction). Causing a mood by watching a movie, listening to music, or in many other ways.

Instinct. An old-fashioned term, made popular by Lorenz, but brought into disfavor because of his descriptions of instincts as based on fixed action patterns controlled by hydraulic-like mechanisms. The term used now is "species-characteristic pattern."

Intentionality. Philosophical term describing mental states meaning (roughly) "aboutness," so beliefs, desires, and emotions are intentional when they are about something.

Internalizing disorder. A pattern of disturbance in children characterized by social withdrawal, anxiety, fears, and unhappiness.

Lateralization. Greater representation of a function on one side of the brain than the other.

Learned helplessness. A feeling of helplessness and lack of control over situations, and an inability to make connections between one's behavior and its outcomes; this attitude is thought to be learned from past experiences of failure.

Lesion. Damage to a part of the brain.

Life event. An event that happens in someone's life that demands some substantial change. A severe life event is the most serious type of event, such as a bereavement.

Limbic system. Part of the forebrain, including the amygdala, which is thought to be especially important for emotions.

Longitudinal study. Study in which measurements are taken at two or more points in time usually separated by several months, or even years.

Macrophages. White blood cells in the immune system, responsible for mopping up debris.

Meta-analysis. Statistical method applied to measures from a large number of studies, in which these measures are converted into a standard score and added in order to estimate the average effect of a particular intervention or kind of variable. An effect size of "plus one" tells us that the mean of the group of interest was greater by one standard deviation than the mean of the comparison group.

Metacognition. Thinking about thinking – planning, monitoring, and checking one's own cognitive processes.

Mood. A maintained state of emotion, or a disposition to respond emotionally in a particular way, that may last for hours, days, or even weeks, perhaps at a low level, and perhaps without the person knowing what started the mood.

Modeling. Process of learning that occurs through observation and imitation.

Mood congruent recall. Preferential recall of emotional episodes when the person is in the same mood subsequently.

Motivation. A state of having some goal, aim, or purpose.

Neocortex. See **Cortex**.

Neurochemicals. Generic term for substances such as transmitters, peptides, and hormones, that affect nerve function.

Neurocultural theory. Ekman's theory of biologically based emotions and cultural display rules.

Neurotransmitter. See **Transmitter substance**.

Object. Used in this book to denote the content of an emotion, as in the phrase "the object of my affections."

p. Probability – used in statistics to indicate how likely some research result is to have occurred by chance. Thus when the phrase $p < 0.05$ is used, this means that the result had only a 5 percent probability of occurring by chance, therefore making the explanation offered by the researchers more likely to be correct.

Peptide. Substance with large molecule made up of several amino acids, that diffuses to affect the function of the brain or other parts of the body.

Peripheral. In neuroanatomy: used in contrast to "central" – thus the peripheral nervous system is made up of the nerves running from the brain or spinal cord to muscles, and from the sensory endings to the brain or spinal cord.

Personality. Characteristic patterns of a person's behavior, thinking, emotions.

Phobia. An intense fear of a situation or object that leads to avoidance.

Prevalence. The number of people in the general population suffering from a disorder.

Prognosis. The likely outcome of a disorder or a disease.

Protective factors. Those factors in people's lives (like having a close friend) that keep them from developing mental health problems when they are undergoing major stress, but are not associated with the development of problems when the people are not under stress.

Prototype. A characteristic example of a concept.

Psychiatry. The care that medical practitioners provide for people's disordered emotions, thoughts, or behavior.

Psychoanalysis. The method of therapy initially developed by Freud, in which present behaviors and emotions are understood in the light of unconscious processes that have developed through childhood experience. The therapist listens and occasionally offers interpretations to make sense of what the patient is saying.

Psychopathology. Psychologically disordered states and the study and understanding of these states.

Psychosomatic illness. Physical illness that is initiated, maintained or exacerbated by psychological causes.

Psychotherapy (or psychological therapy). Therapy means healing (making whole); psychological versions involve one or more clients meeting with a therapist to discuss understandings of psychological distress or emotional disorder, sometimes to acquire insights, sometimes to receive advice, or better coping strategies.

r. Correlation coefficient – it ranges from 0 (meaning no relationship between two variables) to 1 (meaning that two variables correspond exactly when adjusted for the two different scales of measurement of each of them).

Reflex. Fairly discrete action, based on a neural pathway that connects a stimulus to a response.

Reinforcement. Reward that makes the behavior which preceded it more likely to occur again. Negative reinforcements (punishments and omissions of rewards) have more complex effects.

Role. Term derived from the theater, indicating a performance of a particular social function, like being a mother, or a student, or a friend. Performance in roles attracts comment from others, thus giving a basis for morality in any culture.

Romantic love. Term indicating the phenomenon of falling in love with someone who may become a sexual partner, and perhaps lifetime partner. It involves the idealization of the other, often expressed in terms of poetry or song, sometimes a certain amount of secrecy, and the suspension of some rules of ordinary conduct.

Romanticism (in the arts). A period starting in the late eighteenth century in Europe, stressing primacy of the natural and of the emotions, as compared with the artificial and with the dictates of convention.

Schema. Structure stored in memory that is a representation of people, events, and objects, that enable the person to take appropriate action.

Schizophrenia. A severe mental disorder characterized by disturbances of thought, emotion, and behavior. Delusions and hallucinations may be experienced.

Script. Stored outline of a sequence of actions that achieves a goal.

Septal region. Part of the limbic system.

Skin conductance. An electrical measurement of the minute amounts of sweat being produced by the skin. It indicates changes in the autonomic nervous system, which in turn indicate emotional changes.

Social support. Either the close friendships or the network of relationships that are supportive to the individual at times of stress.

Socialization. The ways that parents and teachers induct children into the appropriate behaviors and emotion display rules of the culture.

Socioemotional. Term used in development to imply the association between emotions and close relationships with others.

Species-characteristic pattern. An extended pattern of goal-directed behavior acquired genetically and characteristic of a species.

Strange Situation. Test developed by Ainsworth to examine infants' reactions to separation from and reunion with their caregivers.

Stress. An event that challenges a person's capacity to cope with the event and its consequences.

Striatal system. Part of the forebrain concerned with scheduling daily activities.

Symptoms (psychiatric symptoms). Individual pieces of emotional experience or behavior that are problematic for a person and are part of the criteria for determining whether a disorder exists.

Synapse. The junction at which a nerve impulse passes from one neuron to another.

Temperament. Aspect of behavior and emotions that is constitutional in origin, shows stability over time, and has a genetic basis.

Temporal lobe. Part of the cortex close to the limbic system.

Trait. Aspect of personality that is stable over time.

Transference. Patterns of a patient's behavior, emotional responses and beliefs, directed towards a therapist, that are thought to have their basis in relationships with others, such as parents.

Transmitter substance. Chemical substance secreted by nerve cells to communicate with other nerve cells. There are now known to be several dozen transmitter substances, examples are acetyl choline, noradrenaline, serotonin, dopamine. Many nerve cells have several of them, and sometimes they diffuse outside synapses to affect nerve cells over a local region.

Trauma. A damaging event of emotional significance, such as sexual or physical abuse in childhood, or a civil or military disaster, that closely affects a person.

Variance. Amount of variability of some measurements in a sample (technically: the square of the standard deviation of these measurements).

Vulnerability factors. Aspects of people's lives that make it more likely that they will succumb to psychiatric illness, when they are exposed to a major stressor.

We-self. Version of the self, characteristic of Eastern culture, in which the self is experienced as interdependent on other people.

References

References are for the most part cited in the format recommended by the American Psychological Association, except that for older books we cite the date of the original publication in the text, and in this reference list we generally give the date of a publication available in libraries and/or bookshops as (current edition 19xx) at the end of the reference. Citations in the text to papers with four or more authors are given by first author et al.; in this list of references they are generally given in full.

Aaron, N. A., Calkins, S., & Fox, N. (1990). Infant temperament and attachment predict behavioural inhibition at 24 months. *Infant Behavior and Development, 13,* 235.

Abrams, M. H. (1953). *The mirror and the lamp: Romantic theory and the critical tradition.* Oxford: Oxford University Press.

Abramson, L. Y., Metalsky, G. I., & Alloy, L. B. (1989). Hopelessness depression: A theory-based subtype of depression. *Psychological Review, 96,* 358–372.

Abramson, L. Y., Seligman, M. E. P., & Teasdale, J. D. (1978). Learned helplessness in humans: Critique and reformulation. *Journal of Abnormal Psychology, 87,* 49–74.

Achenbach, T. M., & Edelbrock, C. S. (1984). Psychopathology of childhood. *Annual Review of Psychology, 35,* 227–256.

Achenbach, T. M., Howell, C. T., Quay, H. C., & Conners, C. K. (1991). National survey of problems and competencies among four to sixteen year olds. *Monographs of the Society for Research in Child Development, 56* (3, Serial No. 225).

Ader, R., & Cohen, N. (1993). Psychoneuroimmunology: Conditioning and stress. *Annual Review of Psychology, 44,* 53–85.

Adolphs, R., Tranel, D., Damasio, H., & Damasio, A. (1994). Impaired recognition of emotion in facial expressions following bilateral damage to the human amygdala. *Nature, 22,* 669–672.

Ainsworth, M. D. S. (1967). *Infancy in Uganda: Infant care and the growth of love.* Baltimore, MD: Johns Hopkins Press.

Ainsworth, M. D. S. (1992). Obituary: John Bowlby (1907–1990). *American Psychologist, 47,* 668.

Ainsworth, M. D. S., Blehar, M. C., Walters, E., & Wall, S. (1978). *Patterns of attachment: A psychological study of the strange situation.* Hillsdale, NJ: Erlbaum.

Alexander, F. (1950). *Psychosomatic medicine.* New York: Norton.

Als, H., Tronick, E., & Brazelton, T. B. (1980). Affective reciprocity and the development of autonomy. The study of a blind infant. *Journal of Child Psychiatry, 19*, 22–40.

American Psychiatric Association (1994). *Diagnostic and statistical manual of mental disorders, Fourth edition: DSM-IV*. Washington, DC: American Psychiatric Association.

Anashensel, C., & Stone, J. D. (1982). Stress and depression: A test of the buffering model of social support. *Archives of General Psychiatry, 39*, 1392–1396.

Andalmann, P. K., & Zajonc, R. B. (1989). Facial efference and the experience of emotion. *Annual Review of Psychology, 40*, 249–280.

Anderson, E. (1994). The code of the streets. *Atlantic Monthly, 273* (5), 80–94.

Anderson, J. C., Williams, S., McGee, R., & Silva, P. A. (1987). DSM-III disorders in preadolescent children: Prevalence in a large sample from the general population. *Archives of General Psychiatry, 44*, 69–76.

Andrew, R. J. (1963). The origin and evolution of the calls and facial expressions of the primates. *Behavior, 20*, 1–109.

Andrew, R. J. (1965, October). The origin of facial expressions. *Scientific American, 213*, 88–94.

Angold, A. (1988). Childhood and adolescent depression: I. Epidemiological and aetiological aspects. *British Journal of Psychiatry, 152*, 501–507.

Angold, A. (1991). The effects of age and sex on depression ratings in children and adolescents. *Journal of the American Academy of Child and Adolescent Psychiatry, 30*, 67–74.

Ardrey, R. (1966). *The territorial imperative*. New York: Dell.

Aristotle (1984) *Complete works. Revised Oxford translation in 2 volumes* (J. Barnes, Ed.). Princeton, NJ: Princeton University Press.

Arnetz, B. B., Wasserman, J., Petrini, B., Brenner, S., Levi, L., Eneroth, P., Salovaara, L., Theorell, T., & Petterson, I. (1987). Immune function in unemployed women. *Psychosomatic Medicine, 49*, 3–12.

Arnold, M. B., & Gasson, J. A. (1954). Feelings and emotions as dynamic factors in personality integration. In M. B. Arnold & S. J. Gasson (Eds.), *The human person* (pp. 294–313). New York: Ronald.

Assagioli, R. (1965). *Psychosynthesis: A manual of principles and techniques*. New York: Viking.

Astington, J. W. (1993). *The child's discovery of the mind*. Cambridge, MA: Harvard University Press.

Astington, J. W., & Jenkins, J. M. (1995). Theory of mind development and social understanding. *Cognition and Emotion, 9*, 151–165.

Atkinson, R. L. et al. (1990). *Introduction to psychology* (10th ed.). San Diego, CA: Harcourt Brace Jovanovich.

Augustine (c 400). *Confessions* (Pine-Coffin, R. S., Trans.). Harmondsworth: Penguin. (current edition 1960).

Averill, J. R. (1982). *Anger and aggression. An essay on emotion*. New York: Springer.

Averill, J. R. (1985). The social construction of emotion: With special reference to love. In K. J. Gergen &. K. E. Davis (Eds.), *The social construction of the person* (pp. 89–109). New York: Springer Verlag.

Averill, J. R., & Nunley, E. P. (1992). *Voyages of the heart: Living an emotionally creative life*. New York: Free Press.

Averill, J. R., & Thomas-Knowles, C. (1991). Emotional creativity. In K. T. Strongman

(Ed.), *International Review of Studies on Emotion* (pp. 269–299). Chichester: Wiley.

Axelrod, R. (1984). *The evolution of cooperation*. New York: Basic Books.

Bakhtin, M. (1963). *Problems of Dostoevsky's poetics*. (C. Emerson, Trans.) Minneapolis: University of Minneapolis Press (current edition 1984).

Baldwin, M. (1992). Relational schemas and the processing of social information. *Psychological Bulletin, 112*, 461–484.

Bamber, J. H. (1979). *The fears of adolescence*. London: Academic Press.

Bandura, A. (1988). Self-efficacy conception of anxiety. *Anxiety Research, 1*, 177–98.

Bard, P. (1928). A diencephalic mechanism for the expression of rage with special reference to the sympathetic nervous system. *American Journal of Physiology, 84*, 490–513.

Bard, P., & Rioch, D. M. (1937). A study of four cats deprived of neocortex and additional portions of the forebrain. *Johns Hopkins Medical Journal, 60*, 73–153.

Baron, R. A. (1987). Interviewer's mood and reaction to job applicants. *Journal of Applied Social Psychology, 17*, 911–926.

Bartlett, F. C. (1932). *Remembering: A study in experimental and social psychology*. Cambridge: Cambridge University Press.

Bass, E., & Davis, L. (1988). *The courage to heal*. New York: Harper & Row.

Bates, J. E. (1987). Temperament in infancy. In J. Osofsky (Ed.), *Handbook of infant development*. New York: Wiley.

Bates, J. E., Olson, S., Pettit, G., & Bayles, K. (1982). Dimensions of individuality in the mother–infant relationship at six months of age. *Child Development, 53*, 446–461.

Bates, J. E., Maslin, C. A., & Frankel, K. E. (1985). Attachment security, mother–child interaction and temperament as predictors of behavior-problem ratings at age three years. In I. Bretherton & E. Waters (Eds.), *Growing points of attachment theory and research. Monographs of the Society for Research in Child Development, 50* (1–2, Serial No. 209), (pp. 167–193).

Bateson, P. (1990). Obituary: Konrad Lorenz (1903–1989). *American Psychologist, 45*, 65–66.

Bateson, P. P. G. (1983). *Mate choice*. Cambridge: Cambridge University Press.

Bauer, D. H. (1976). An exploratory study of developmental changes in children's fear. *Journal of Child Psychology and Psychiatry, 17*, 69–74.

Bear, D. (1979). The temporal lobes: An approach to the study of organic behavioral changes. In M. S. Gazzaniga (Ed.), *Handbook of behavioral neurobiology, Vol. 2. Neuropsychology* (pp. 75–95). New York: Plenum.

Bebbington, P. E., Hurry, J., Tennant, C., Sturt, E., & Wing, J. K. (1981). Epidemiology of mental disorders in Camberwell. *Psychological Medicine, 11*, 347–363.

Bebbington, P. E., Sturt, E., Tennant, C., & Hurry, J. (1984). Misfortune and resilience: A community study of women. *Psychological Medicine, 14*, 347–363.

Beck, A. T. (1976). *Cognitive therapy and the emotional disorders*. New York: Meridian.

Beck, A. T. (1983). Cognitive therapy of depression: New perspectives. In P. J. Clayton & P. E. Barrett (Eds.), *Treatment of depression: Old controversies, new approaches* (pp. 265–284). New York: Raven Press.

Beck, A. T., & Emery, G. (1985). *Anxiety disorders and phobias: A cognitive perspective*. New York: Basic Books.

Beck, A. T., Rush, A., J., Shaw, B. F., & Emery, G. (1979). *Cognitive therapy of depression*. New York: Guilford.

Beck, A. T., Steer, R., & Garbin, M. (1988). Psychometric properties of the Beck Depression Inventory: Twenty-five years of evaluation. *Clinical Psychology Review*, 8, 77–100.

Beeghly, M., Bretherton, I., & Mervis, C. B. (1986). Mothers' internal state language to toddlers. *British Journal of Developmental Psychology, 4,* 247–61.

Bellak, L. (1986). *The thematic apperception test* (4th ed.). Larchmont: Grune & Stratton.

Belsky, J., Fish, M., & Isabella, R. (1991). Continuity and discontinuity in infant negative and positive emotionality: Family antecedents and attachment consequences. *Developmental Psychology, 27,* 421–431.

Benedict, R. (1946). *The chrysanthemum and the sword: Patterns of Japanese culture*. Boston: Houghton Mifflin.

Ben-Ze'ev, A. (1992). Pleasure in other's misfortune. *Iyyun, 41,* 41–61.

Ben Ze'ev, A., & Oatley, K. (in press). Development of social understanding and constructive agents. *Behavioral and Brain Sciences*.

Bergin, A. E., & Garfield, S. L. (1994). *Handbook of psychotherapy and behavior change* (4th ed.) New York: Wiley.

Berkowitz, L. (1993). Towards a general theory of anger and emotional aggression: Implications of a cognitive neo-associationistic perspective for the analysis of anger and other emotions. In R. S. Wyer & T. Srull (Eds.), *Advances in social cognition*, Hillsdale, NJ: Erlbaum.

Berkowitz, L., Cochran, S., & Embree, M. (1981). Physical pain and the goal of aversively stimulated aggression. *Journal of Personality and Social Psychology, 40,* 687–700.

Bermond, B., Fasotti, L., Nieuwenhuyse, B., & Schuerman, J. (1991). Spinal cord lesions, peripheral feedback and intensities of emotional feelings. *Cognition and Emotion, 5,* 201–220.

Bernal, M. (1987). *Black Athena: The Afroasiatic roots of classical civilization, Vol. 1. The fabrication of ancient Greece, 1785–1985*. New Brunswick, NJ: Rutgers University Press.

Berne, E. (1964). *Games people play*. New York: Grove Press.

Bernheimer, C., & Kahane, C. (1985). *In Dora's case: Freud – hysteria – feminism*. New York: Columbia Universty Press.

Bernstein, G. A., & Borchardt, C. M. (1991). Anxiety disorders of childhood and adolescence: A critical review. *Journal of the American Academy of Child and Adolescent Psychiatry, 30,* 519–532.

Berscheid, E. (1988). Some comments on love's anatomy; Or, whatever happened to old-fashioned lust? In R. J. Sternberg & M. L. Barnes (Eds.), *The psychology of love* (pp. 359–374). New Haven, CT: Yale University Press.

Biglan, A., Hops, H., Sherman, L., Friedman, L. S., Arthus, J., & Osteen, V. (1985). Problem-solving interactions of depressed women and their husbands. *Behavior Therapy, 16,* 431–451.

Binswanger, L. (1963). *Being in the world: Selected papers* (J. Needleman, Ed. and Trans.). New York: Basic Books.

Bird, H. R., Canino, G., & Rubio-Stipec, M. (1988). Estimates of the prevalence of childhood maladjustment in a community survey in Puerto Rico. *Archives of General Psychiatry, 45,* 1120–1126.

Birdwhistell, R. L. (1970). *Kinesics and context*. Philadelphia: University of Pennsylvania Press.

Blaney, P. H. (1986). Affect and memory: A review. *Psychological Bulletin, 99,* 229–246.

Blazer, D., Hughes, D., & George, L. K. (1987). Stressful life events and the onset of a generalized anxiety syndrome. *American Journal of Psychiatry, 144,* 1178–1183.

Block, J. H., Block, J., & Gjerde, P. F. (1986). The personality of children prior to divorce: A prospective study. *Child Development, 57,* 827–840.

Bloom, Harold (1989). *Ruin the sacred truths: Poetry and belief from the Bible to the present.* Cambridge, MA: Harvard University Press.

Bloom, Lois (1989). Developments in expression: Affect and speech. In N. L. Stein, B. Leventhal, & T. Trabasso (Eds.), *Psychological and biological approaches to emotion* (pp. 215–245). Hillsdale, NJ: Erlbaum.

Bodiford, C. A., Eisenstadt, T. H., Johnson, J. H., & Bradlyn, A. S. (1988). Comparison of learned helplessness cognitions and behavior in children with high and low scores on the children's depression inventory. *Journal of Abnormal Child Psychology, 17,* 152–158.

Boldizar, J. P., Perry, D. G., & Perry, L. C. (1989). Outcome values and aggression. *Child Development, 60,* 571–579.

Bolton, W., & Oatley, K. (1987). A longitudinal study of social support and depression in unemployed men. *Psychological Medicine, 17,* 453–460.

Boole, G. (1854). *An investigation of the laws of thought.* Dover: New York.

Boucher, J. D., & Brandt, M. E. (1981). Judgment of emotion: American and Malay antecedents. *Journal of Cross-Cultural Psychology, 12,* 272–283.

Bower, G. H. (1981). Mood and memory. *American Psychologist, 36,* 129–148.

Bower, G. H. (1992). How might emotions affect learning. In S.-Å. Christianson (Ed.), *The handbook of emotion and memory: Research and theory* (pp. 3–31). Hillsdale, NJ: Erlbaum.

Bowlby, J. (1951). *Maternal care and mental health.* Geneva: World Health Organization (textual quotes from shorter version 1953 published as *Child care and the growth of love,* Harmondsworth: Penguin).

Bowlby, J. (1971). *Attachment and loss, Vol. 1. Attachment.* London: Hogarth Press (current edition Penguin, 1978).

Bowlby, J. (1973). *Attachment and loss, Vol. 2. Separation: anxiety and anger.* London: Hogarth Press (current edition Penguin, 1978).

Bowlby, J. (1979). *The making and breaking of affectional bonds.* London: Tavistock.

Bowlby, J. (1988). *A secure base: Clinical applications of attachment theory.* London: Routledge.

Bowlby, J. (1991). *Charles Darwin: A new life.* New York: Norton.

Boyle, M. (1991). Child health in Ontario. In R. Barnhorst & L. C. Johnson (Eds.), *The state of the child in Ontario.* Toronto: University of Toronto Press.

Bradwejn, J. (1993). Neurobiological investigations into the role of cholecystokinin in panic disorder. *Journal of Psychiatry and Neuroscience, 18,* 178–188.

Brazier, M. A. B. (1959). The historical development of neurophysiology. In *Handbook of physiology Section 1*, (Vol.1, pp. 1–58). Bethesda, MD: American Physiological Association.

Brennan, S. (1985). The caricature generator. *Leonardo, 18,* 59–87.

Bretherton, I. (1985). Attachment theory: Retrospect and prospect. In I. Bretherton &

E. Waters (Eds.), *Growing points in attachment: Theory and research. Monographs of the Society for Research in Child Development, 50* (1–2, serial No. 209) (pp. 3–35).

Bretherton, I., Fritz, J., Zahn-Waxler, C., & Ridgeway, D. (1986). Learning to talk about emotions: A functionalist perspective. *Child Development, 57,* 529–548.

Brewin, C. R. (1985). Depression and causal attributions: What is their relation? *Psychological Bulletin, 98,* 297–309.

Brewin, C. R., Andrews, B., & Gotlib, I. H. (1993). Psychopathology and early experience: A reappraisal of retrospective reports. *Psychological Bulletin, 133,* 82–98.

Briggs, J. L. (1970). *Never in anger: Portrait of an Eskimo family.* Cambridge, MA: Harvard University Press.

Broadbent, D. E., & Broadbent, M. (1988). Anxiety and attentional bias: State and trait. *Cognition and Emotion, 2,* 165–183.

Brooks-Gunn, J., & Lewis, M. (1982). Affective exchanges between normal and handicapped infants and their mothers. In T. Field & A. Fogel (Eds.), *Emotion and early interaction.* Hillsdale, NJ: Erlbaum.

Brown, D. E. (1991). *Human universals.* Philadelphia: Temple University Press.

Brown, G. W., Andrews, B., Bifulco, A., & Veiel, H. (1990). Self-esteem and depression 1. Measurement issues and prediction of onset. *Social Psychiatry and Psychiatric Epidemiology, 25,* 200–209.

Brown, G. W., Birley, J. L. T., & Wing, J. K. (1972). Influence of family life on the course of schizophrenic disorders. *British Journal of Psychiatry, 121,* 241–258.

Brown, G. W., & Harris, T. O. (1978). *Social origins of depression: A study of psychiatric disorder in women.* London: Tavistock.

Brown, G. W., & Harris, T. O. (1993). Aetiology of anxiety and depressive disorders in an inner-city population. 1. Early adversity. *Psychological Medicine, 23,* 143–154.

Brown, G. W., Lemyre, L., & Bifulco, A. (1992). Social factors and recovery from anxiety and depressive disorders: A test of specificity. *British Journal of Psychiatry, 161,* 44–54.

Brown, G. W., & Moran, P. (1994). Clinical and psychosocial origins of chronic depressive episodes. 1. A community study. *British Journal of Psychiatry, 165,* 447–456.

Bruner, J. (1986). *Actual minds, possible worlds.* Cambridge, MA: Harvard University Press.

Burnam, M. A., Stein, J. A., Golding, J. M., Siegel, J. M., Sorenson, S. B., Forsythe, A. B., & Telles, C. A. (1988). Sexual assault and mental disorders in a community population. *Journal of Consulting and Clinical Psychology, 56,* 843–850.

Burrow, J. W. (1968). Editor's introduction. In *Darwin's The Origin of Species* Harmondsworth: Penguin.

Buss, A. H., & Plomin, R. A. (1975). *A temperament theory of personality development.* New York: Wiley.

Buss, A. H., & Plomin, R. (1984). *Temperament: Early developing personality traits* Hillsdale, NJ: Erlbaum.

Byng-Hall, J. (1980). Symptom bearer as marital distance regulator. *Family Process, 19,* 355–365.

Cacioppo, J. T., Bush, L. K., & Tassinary, L. G. (1992). Microexpressive facial actions as a function of affective stimuli: Replication and extension. *Personality and Social Psychology Bulletin, 18,* 515–526.

Cacioppo, J. T., Klein, D. J., Berntson, G. C., & Hatfield, E. (1993). The psychophysiology of emotion. In M. Lewis & J. M. Haviland (Eds.), *Handbook of emotions* (pp. 119–142). New York: Guilford.

Calkins, S. D., & Fox, N. A. (1992). The relations among infant temperament, security of attachment and behavioral inhibition at twenty-four months. *Child Development*, *63*, 1456–1472.

Campos, J. J., Barrett, K. C., Lamb, M. E., Goldsmith, H. H., & Stenberg, C. (1983). Socioemotional development. In M. M. Haith & J. J. Campos (Eds.), *Handbook of child psychology* (pp. 783–915). New York: Wiley.

Campos, J. J., Kermoian, R., & Zumbahlen, M. R. (1992). Socioemotional transformations in the family system following infant crawling onset. In N. Eisenberg & R. A. Fabes (Eds.), *Emotion and its regulation in early development. (New Directions in Child Development No. 55)* (pp. 25–40). San Francisco: Jossey-Bass.

Campos, J. J., Mumme, D. L., Kermoian, R., & Campos, R. G. (1994). A functionalist perspective on the nature of emotion. In N. A. Fox (Ed.), *The development of emotion regulation: Monographs of the Society for Research in Child Development 59* (2–3, Serial No. 240), 284–303.

Camras, L. A. (1992). Expressive development and basic emotions. *Cognition and Emotion*, *6*, 269–283.

Camras, L. A., Holland, E. A., & Patterson, M. J. (1993). Facial expression. In M. Lewis & J. M. Haviland (Eds.), *Handbook of emotions* (pp. 199–208). New York: Guilford.

Cannon, W. B. (1927). The James–Lange theory of emotion: A critical examination and an alternative theory. *American Journal of Psychology*, *39*, 106–124.

Cannon, W. B. (1929). *Bodily changes in pain, hunger, fear and rage* (2nd ed.). New York: Appleton.

Cannon, W. B. (1931). Again the James–Lange and the thalamic theories of emotion. *Psychological Review*, *38*, 281–295.

Carlson, V., Barnett, D., Chichetti, D., & Braunwald, K. (1989). Disorganized/disoriented attachment relationships in maltreated infants. *Developmental Psychology*, *25*, 525–531.

Carnevale, P. J. D., & Isen, A. M. (1986). The influence of positive affect and visual access on the discovery of integrative solutions in bilateral negotiation. *Organizational Behavior and Human Decision Processes*, *37*, 1–13.

Caron, A. J., Caron, R. F., & MacLean, D. J. (1988). Infant discrimination of naturalistic emotional expressions: The role of face and voice. *Child Development*, *59*, 604–616.

Caron, R. F., Caron, A. J., & Myers, R. S. (1985). Do infants see facial expressions in static faces? *Child Development*, *56*, 1552–1560.

Cartwright, F. F. (1977). *A social history of medicine*. London: Longman.

Casey, R. J., & Schlosser, S. (1994). Emotional responses to peer praise in children with and without a diagnosed externalizing disorder. *Merrill Palmer Quarterly*, *40*, 60–81.

Caspi, A., Elder, G. H., & Bem, D. J. (1987). Moving against the world: Life course patterns of explosive children. *Developmental Psychology*, *23*, 308–313.

Caspi, A., Elder, G. H., & Bem, D. J. (1988). Moving away from the world: Life-course patterns of shy children. *Developmental Psychology*, *24*, 824–831.

Cassidy, J. (1994). Emotion regulation: Influences of attachment relationships. In N. A.

Fox (Ed.), *The development of emotion regulation: Monographs of the Society for Research in Child Development 59* (2–3, Serial No. 240) (pp. 228–249).

Cassileth, B. R., Lusk, E. J., Miller, D. S., Brown, L. L., & Miller, C. (1985). Psychosocial correlates of survival in advanced malignant disease. *New England Journal of Medicine, 312,* 1551–1555.

Chagnon, N. A. (1968). *Yanomamö: The fierce people.* New York: Holt Rinehart & Winston.

Chaiken, S., Lieberman, A., & Eagly, A. H. (1989). Heuristic and systematic information processing within and beyond the persuasion context. In J. S. Uleman & J. A. Bargh (Eds.), *Unintended thought: Limits of awareness, intention and control* (pp. 212–252). New York: Guilford.

Cherlin, A. J., Furstenberg, F. F., Chase-Lansdale, P. L., Kiernan, K. E., & Robins, P. K. (1991). Longitudinal studies of effects of divorce on children in Great Britain and the United States. *Science, 252,* 1386–1389.

Chess, S., & Thomas, A. (1990). Continuities and discontinuities in temperament. In L. Robins & M. Rutter (Eds.), *Straight and devious pathways from childhood to adulthood* (pp. 205–220). Cambridge: Cambridge University Press.

Cheyney, D. L., & Seyfarth, R. M. (1990). *How monkeys see the world: Inside the mind of another species.* Chicago: University of Chicago Press.

Chrétien de Troyes (1180). The knight of the cart. In D. Staines (Ed.), *The complete romances of Chrétien de Troyes* (pp. 170–256). Bloomington: Indiana University Press (1990).

Christianson, S.-Å. (Ed.) (1992). *The handbook of emotion and memory: Research and theory.* Hillsdale, NJ: Erlbaum.

Christianson, S.-Å., & Loftus, E. (1991). Remembering emotional events: The fate of detailed information. *Cognition and Emotion, 5,* 81–108.

Cicchetti, D. (1990). The organization of socioemotional, cognitive, and representational development: Illustrations through a developmental psychopathology perspective on Down syndrome and child maltreatment. In R. A. Thompson (Ed.), *Socioemotional development* (pp. 259–366). Lincoln: University of Nebraska Press.

Cicchetti, D., & Beeghly, M. (1987). Symbolic development in maltreated youngsters: An organizational perspective. *New Directions for Child Development, 36,* 47–68.

Cicchetti, D., Ganiban, J., & Barnett, D. (1991). Contributions from the study of high-risk populations to understanding the development of emotion regulation. In J. Garber & K. A. Dodge (Eds.), *The development of emotion regulation and dysregulation* (pp. 15–48). New York: Cambridge University Press.

Cicero (45 BCE). *Tusulan Disputations.* Loeb ed., Cicero vol. 18. (Ed. and Trans. J. E. King). Cambridge, MA: Harvard University Press (current edition 1927).

Clark, M. S., & Williamson, G. M. (1989). Moods and social judgments. In H. Wagner & A. Manstead (Eds.), *Handbook of social psychophysiology* (pp. 347–370). Chichester: Wiley.

Clore, G. L. (1992). Cognitive phenomenology: Feelings and the construction of judgment. In L. L. Martin & A. Tesser (Eds.), *The construction of social judgment* (pp. 133–163). Hillsdale, NJ: Erlbaum.

Cohen, S., & Williamson, G. M. (1991). Stress and infectious diseases in humans. *Psychological Bulletin, 109,* 5–24.

Cohen, S., & Wills, T. A. (1985). Stress, social support, and the buffering hypothesis. *Psychological Bulletin, 98,* 310–357.

Cohn, J. F., Campbell, S.B., Matias, R., & Hopkins, J. (1990). Face-to-face interactions of postpartum depressed and nondepressed mother–infant pairs at 2 months. *Developmental Psychology, 26,* 15–23.

Cohn, J. F., & Tronick, E. Z. (1983). Three-month-old infants' reaction to simulated maternal depression. *Child Development, 54,* 185–193.

Coie, J. D., & Kupersmidt, J. D. (1983). A behavioral analysis of emerging social status in boys' groups. *Child Development, 54,* 1400–1416.

Cole, P., Michel, M. K., & O'Donnell-Teti, L. (1994). The development of emotion regulation and dysregulation: A clinical perspective In N. Fox (Ed.), *Monographs of the Society for Research in Child Development, 59* (Serial No. 240), 73–103.

Collingwood, R. G. (1938). *The principles of art.* Oxford: Oxford University Press.

Comer, J. (1988 November). Educating poor minority children. *Scientific American, 259,* 24–30.

Conway, M. A. (1990). Conceptual representation of emotions: The role of autobiographical memories. In K. J. Gilhooly, M. T. G. Keene, R. H. Logie, & G. Erdos (Eds.), *Lines of thinking: Reflections on the psychology of thought, Vol. 2. Skills, emotion, creative processes, individual differences and teaching thinking.* Chichester: Wiley.

Conway, M. A., & Bekerian, D. A. (1987). Situational knowledge and emotions. *Cognition and Emotion, 1,* 145–191.

Corter, C. M., & Fleming, A. S. (1990). Maternal responsiveness in humans: Emotional, cognitive, and biological factors. *Advances in the Study of Behavior, 19,* 83–136.

Corter, C. M., & Fleming, A. S. (1995). Psychobiology of maternal behavior in humans: Role of sensory, experiential, and hormonal factors. In M. Bornstein (Ed.), *Handbook of parenting* (pp. 83–136). Hilldale, NJ: Erlbaum.

Coryell, W., Akiskal, H. S., Leon, A. C., Winokur, G., Maser, J. D., Mueller, T. J., & Keller, M. B. (1994). The time course of nonchronic major depressive disorders. *Archives of General Psychiatry, 51,* 405–410.

Costa, P. T., & McCrae, R. R. (1988). Personality in adulthood: A six-year longitudinal study of self-reports and spouse ratings on the NEO Personality Inventory. *Journal of Personality and Social Psychology, 54,* 853–863.

Costello, C. G. (1982). Social factors associated with depression: A retrospective community study. *Psychological Medicine, 12,* 421–435.

Costello, E. J. (1989). Developments in child psychiatric epidemiology. *Journal of the American Academy of Child and Adolescent Psychiatry, 28,* 836–841.

Coyne, J. C. (1976). Depression and response to others. *Journal of Abnormal Psychology, 85,* 186–193.

Coyne, J. C. (1994). Self-reported distress: Analog or ersatz depression. *Psychological Bulletin, 116,* 29–45.

Coyne, J. C., Burchill, S. A., & Stiles, W. B. (1991). An interactional perspective on depression. In C. R. Snyder & D. O. Forsyth (Eds.), *Handbook of social and clinical psychology: The health perspective* (pp. 327–349). New York: Pergamon.

Coyne, J. C., & Gotlib, I. H. (1983). The role of cognition in depression: A critical appraisal. *Psychological Bulletin, 94,* 472–505.

Coyne, J. C., Kessler, R. C., Tal, M., Turnbull, J., Wortman, C., & Greden, J. (1987). Living with a depressed person: Burden and psychological distress. *Journal of Consulting and Clinical Psychology, 55,* 347–352.

Craik, K. J. W. (1966). *The nature of psychology: A selection of papers, essays and other writings* (Ed. S. L. Sherwood). Cambridge: Cambridge University Press.

Crews, F. (1994, November 18). The unknown Freud. *New York Review of Books, 40,* 55–66.

Crockenberg, S. (1981). Infant irritability, mother responsiveness, and social support influences on the security of infant–mother attachment. *Child Development, 52,* 857–865.

Crockenberg, S. (1986). Are temperamental differences in babies associated with predictable differences in care giving? In J. V. Lerner & R. M. Lerner (Eds.), *New directions in child development: Temperament and social interaction in infants and children* (Vol. 31 pp. 53–74). San Francisco: Jossey-Bass.

Cummings, E. M. (1987). Coping with background anger in early childhood. *Child Development, 58,* 976–984.

Cunningham, M. R. (1988). What do you do when you're happy or blue? Mood, expectancies, and behavioral interest. *Motivation and Emotion, 12,* 309–331.

Cupchik, G., & László, J. (1994). The landscape of time in literary reception: Character experience and narrative action. *Cognition and Emotion, 8,* 297–312.

Dahl, H. (1991). The key to understanding change: Emotions as appetitive wishes and beliefs about their fulfillment. In J. D. Safran & L. S. Greenberg (Eds.), *Emotions, psychotherapy, and change* (pp. 130–165). New York: Guilford.

Damasio, A. R. (1994). *Descartes' error.* New York: Putnam.

Damasio, H., Grabowski, T., Frank, R., Galaburda, A. M., & Damasio, A. R. (1994). The return of Phineas Gage: The skull of a famous patient yields clues about the brain. *Science, 264,* 1102–1105.

Dante Alighieri (1295). *La vita nuova (The new life)* (Ed. & Trans. B. Reynolds). Harmondsworth: Penguin (1969).

Dante Alighieri (1307–1321). *La divina comedia (The divine comedy)* (Ed. & Trans. M. Musa). Harmondsworth: Penguin (1984).

Darwin, C. (1859). *On the origin of species by means of natural selection.* London: Murray.

Darwin, C. (1872). *The expression of the emotions in man and animals.* Chicago: University of Chicago Press (current edition 1965).

Davidson, R. J. (1992a). Anterior cerebral assymmetry and the nature of emotion. *Brain and Cognition, 20,* 125–151.

Davidson, R. J. (1992b). Prolegomenon to the structure of emotion: Gleanings from neuropsychology. *Cognition and Emotion, 6,* 245–268.

Davidson, R. J. (1993). The neuropsychology of affective style. In M. Lewis & J. M. Haviland (Eds.), *Handbook of emotions* (pp. 143–154). New York: Guilford.

Davidson, R. J., Ekman, P., Saron, C. D., Senulis, J. A., & Friesen, W. V. (1990). Approach-withdrawal and cerebral asymmetry: Emotional expression and brain physiology I. *Journal of Personality and Social Psychology, 58,* 330–341.

Davidson, R. J., & Fox, N. A. (1989). Frontal brain asymmetry predicts infants' response to maternal separation. *Journal of Abnormal Psychology, 98,* 127–131.

Dawkins, R. (1986). *The blind watchmaker.* New York: Norton.

De Lorris, G., & De Meun, J. (1237–1277). *The romance of the rose* (H. W. Robbins, Trans.). New York: Dutton (current edition 1962).

Denham, S. A. (1986). Social cognition, prosocial behavior, and emotion in preschoolers: Contextual validation. *Child Development, 57,* 194–201.

Dentan, R. K. (1968). *The Semai: A nonviolent people of Malaya.* New York: Holt, Rinehart & Winston.

Derogatis, L. R., Abeloff, M. D., & Melisaratos, N. (1972). Psychological coping mechanisms and survival time in metastatic breast cancer. *Journal of the American Medical Association, 242,* 1504–1508.

De Rivera, J. (1992). Emotional climate: Social structure and emotional dymamics. In K. T. Strongman (Ed.), *International review of studies on emotion* (Vol. 2, pp. 197–192). Chichester: Wiley.

Descartes, R. (1649). Passions of the soul. In E. L. Haldane & G. R. Ross (Eds.), *The philosophical works of Descartes.* New York: Dover (current edition 1911).

De Sousa, R. (1987). *The rationality of emotions.* Cambridge, MA: MIT Press.

De Waal, F. (1982). *Chimpanzee politics.* New York: Harper & Row.

De Waal, F. B. M. (1995, March). Bonobo sex and society. *Scientific American, 272,* 82–88.

Diener, E., Sandvik, E., & Pavot, W. (1991). Happiness is the frequency, not the intensity, of positive versus negative affect. In F. Strack, M. Argyle, & N. Schwartz (Eds.), *Subjective well-being: An interdisciplinary perspective.* Oxford: Pergamon.

Di Nicola, V. F. (1988). Expressed emotion and schizophrenia in North India. *Transcultural Psychiatric Research Review, 25,* 205–217.

Dix, T. (1991). The affective organization of parenting: Adaptive and maladaptive processes. *Psychological Bulletin, 110,* 3–25.

Dodge, K. A., Bates, J. E., & Pettit, G. S. (1990). Mechanisms in the cycle of violence. *Science, 250,* 1678–1683.

Dodge, K. A., & Coie, J. D. (1987). Social-information-processing factors in reactive and proactive aggression in children's peer groups. *Journal of Personality and Social Psychology, 53,* 1146–1158.

Dohrenwend, B. P., Link, B. C., Kern, R., Shrout, P. E., & Markowitz, J. (1990). Measuring life events: The problem of variablity within event categories. *Stress Medicine, 6,* 179–187.

Doll, R., & Peto, R. (1981). *The causes of cancer.* Oxford: Oxford University Press.

Dollard, J., Doob, L. W., Miller, N. E., Mowrer, O. H., & Sears, R. R. (1939). *Frustration and aggression.* New Haven: Yale University Press.

Dostoevsky, F. (1955). Introduction by D. Magarshak (Trans). *The Idiot.* Harmondsworth: Penguin.

Dowdney, G., & Coyne, J. C. (1990). Children of depressed parents. *Psychological Bulletin, 108,* 50–76.

Duchenne de Bologne, G.-B. (1862). *The mechanism of human facial expression* (R. A. Cuthbertson, Trans.). New York: Cambridge University Press (current edition 1990).

Dunbar, K. (1993). How scientists really reason: Scientific reasoning in real-world laboratories. In R. J. Sternberg & J. Davidson (Eds.), *Mechanisms of insight* Cambridge, MA: MIT Press.

Dunbar, R. I. M. (1993). Coevolution of neocortical size, group size, and language in humans. *Behavioral and Brain Sciences, 16,* 681–735.

Duncan, S. W., Todd, C. M., Perlmutter, M., & Masters, J. C. (1985). Affect and memory in young children. *Motivation and Emotion, 9,* 391–405.

Dunn, J. (1987). Understanding feelings: The early stages. In J. Bruner & H. Haste (Eds.), *Making sense: The child's construction of the world* (pp. 26–40). London: Methuen.

Dunn, J., Bretherton, I., & Munn, P. (1987). Conversations about feeling states between mothers and their young children. *Developmental Psychology, 23,* 132–139.

Dunn, J., & Brown, J. (1991). Relationships, talk about feelings, and the development of affect regulation in early childhood. In J. Garber & K. Dodge (Eds.), *The development of emotion regulation and dysregulation* (pp. 89–108). Cambridge: Cambridge University Press.

Dunn, J., & Brown, J. (1994). Affect expression in the family, children's understanding of emotions and their interactions with others. *Merrill Palmer Quarterly, 40,* 120–138.

Dunn, J., Brown, J., & Beardsall, L. (1991). Family talk about feeling states and children's later understanding of others' emotions. *Developmental Psychology, 27,* (3) 448–455.

Dunn, J., & Kendrick, C. (1982). *Siblings: Love, envy and understanding,* Cambridge: MA Harvard University Press.

Dutton, D. G., & Aron, A. P. (1974). Some evidence for heightened sexual attraction under conditions of high anxiety. *Journal of Personality and Social Psychology, 30,* 510–517.

Dyer, M. G. (1987). Emotions and their computations: Three computer models. *Cognition and Emotion, 1,* 323–347.

Dysinger, W. S., & Ruckmick, C. A. (1933). *The emotional responses of children to the motion picture situation.* New York: Macmillan.

Eales, M. J. (1992). Shame and guilt: instincts and their vicissitudes in human evolution. Unpublished manuscript.

Earls, F. J., & Young, K. G. (1987). Temperament and home environment characteristics as causal factors in the early development of child psychopathology. *Journal of the American Association for Child and Adolescent Psychiatry, 16,* 219–231.

Easterling, D. V., & Leventhal, H. (1989). Contribution of concrete cogntion to emotion: Neutral symptoms as elicitors of worry about cancer. *Journal of Applied Psychology, 74,* 787–796.

Edelbrock, C., & Costello, A. J. (1988). Structured psychiatric interviews for children. In M. Rutter, A. H. Tuma, & I. S. Lann (Eds.), *Assessment and diagnosis in child psychopathology* (pp. 87–112). London: David Fulton.

Edelbrock, C., Costello, A. J., Dulcan, M. K., Kalas, R., & Conover, N. C. (1985). Age differences in the reliability of the psychiatric interview of the child. *Child Development, 56,* 265–275.

Eibl-Eibesfeldt, I. (1970). *Ethology: The biology of behavior.* New York: Holt, Rinehart & Winston.

Eibl-Eibesfeldt, I. (1973). The expressive behavior of the deaf-and-blind-born. In M. Von Cranach & I. Vine (Eds.), *Social communication and movement* (pp. 163–194). New York: Academic Press.

Eibl-Eibesfeldt, I. (1979). *The biology of peace and war* (E. Mosbacher, Trans.). New York: Viking.

Eich, E., & Metcalfe, J. (1989). Mood dependent memory for internal versus external events. *Journal of Experimental Psychology: Learning, Memory and Cognition, 15,* 443–455.

Eisenberg, N. (1992). *The caring child.* Cambridge, MA: Harvard University Press.

Eisenberg, N., & Fabes, R. A. (1994). Mothers' reactions to children's negative emotions: Relations to children's temperament and anger behavior. *Merrill-Palmer Quarterly, 40,* 138–156.

Ekman, P. (1972). Universals and cultural differences in facial expressions of emotion.

In J. Cole (Ed.), *Nebraska symposium on motivation, 1971* (pp. 207–283). Lincoln, NE: University of Nebraska Press.

Ekman, P. (1989). The argument and evidence about universals in facial expressions of emotion. In H. Wagner & A. Manstead (Eds.), *Handbook of social psychophysiology* (pp. 143–164). Chichester: Wiley.

Ekman, P. (1992). An argument for basic emotions. *Cognition and Emotion, 6,* 169–200.

Ekman, P. (1994). Strong evidence for universals in facial expressions: A reply to Russell's mistaken critique. *Psychological Bulletin, 115,* 268–287.

Ekman, P., & Davidson, R. J. (1993). Voluntary smiling changes regional brain activity. *Psychological Science, 4,* 342–345.

Ekman, P., & Davidson, R. J. (1995). *The nature of emotion: Fundamental questions.* New York: Oxford University Press.

Ekman, P., Davidson, R. J., & Friesen, W. V. (1990). The Duchenne smile: Emotional expression and brain physiology II. *Journal of Personality and Social Psychology, 58,* 342–353.

Ekman, P., & Friesen, W. V. (1969). The repertoire of nonverbal behavior: categories, origins, usage and coding. *Semiotica, 1,* 49–98.

Ekman, P., & Friesen, W. V. (1971). Constants across culture in the face and emotion. *Journal of Personality and Social Psychology, 17,* 124–129.

Ekman, P., & Friesen, W. V. (1975). *Pictures of facial affect.* Palo Alto, CA: Consulting Psychologists Press.

Ekman, P., & Friesen, W. V. (1978). *Facial action coding system: A technique for the measurement of facial movement.* Palo Alto, CA: Consulting Psychologists Press.

Ekman, P., & Friesen, W. V. (1984). *Emotion facial action coding system (EM-FACS).* Obtainable from Paul Ekman, University of California, San Franciso.

Ekman, P., & Friesen, W. V. (1986). A new pan-cultural facial expression of emotion. *Motivation and Emotion, 10*(2), 159–168.

Ekman, P., Levenson, R. W., & Friesen, W. V. (1983). Autonomic nervous system activity distinguishes among emotions. *Science, 221,* 1208–1210.

Ekman, P., & O'Sullivan, M. (1991). Who can catch a liar? *American Psychologist, 46,* 913–920.

Ekman, P., Sorenson, E. R., & Friesen, W. V. (1969). Pan-cultural elements in the facial displays of emotions. *Science, 164,* 86–88.

Elias, N. (1939). *The history of manners: The civilization process, Vol. 1* (E. Jephcott, Trans.). New York: Pantheon (1978).

Eliot, G. (1858). *Scenes of clerical life.* Edinburgh: Blackwood (current edition Penguin, 1973).

Eliot, G. (1860). *The mill on the Floss.* Edinburgh: Blackwood (current edition Penguin, 1973).

Eliot, G. (1871–1872). *Middlemarch: A study of provincial life.* Edinburgh: Blackwood. (current edition Penguin, 1965).

Elkin, I. (1994). The NIMH treatment of depression collaborative program: Where we began and where we are. In A. E. Bergin & S. L. Garfield (Eds.), *Handbook of psychotherapy and behavior change* (4th ed., pp. 114–139). New York: Wiley.

Ellsworth, P. (1991). Some implications of cognitive appraisal theories of emotion. In K. T. Strongman (Ed.), *International Review of Studies on Emotion* (pp. 143–161). Chichester: Wiley.

Ellsworth, P. C., & Smith, C. A. (1988). From appraisal to emotion: Differences among unpleasant feelings. *Motivation and Emotion, 12,* 271–302.

Elmadjian, F. J., Hope, M., & Lamson, E. T. (1957). Excretion of E and NE in various emotional states. *Journal of Clinical Endocrinology, 17,* 608–620.

Emde, R. N., Izard, C., Huebner, R., Sorce, J. F., & Klinnert, M. (1985). Adult judgments of infant emotions: Replication studies within and across laboratories. *Infant Behavior and Development, 8,* 79–88.

Emde, R. N., Plomin, R., Robinson, J., Corley, R., DeFries, J., Fulker, D. W., Reznick, J. S., Campos, J., Kagan, J., & Zahn-Waxler, C. (1992). Temperament, emotion, and cognition at fourteen months: The MacArthur Longitudinal Twin Study. *Child Development, 63,* 1437–1455.

Emery, R. E. (1988). *Marriage, divorce and children's adjustment.* Newbury Park, CA: Sage.

Emery, R. E., Fincham, F. D., & Cummings, E. M. (1992). Parenting in context: The role of the family in child psychotherapy. *Journal of Consulting and Clinical Psychology, 60,* 909–912.

Emmelkamp, P. (1994). Behavior therapy with adults. In A. E. Bergin & S. L. Garfield (Eds.), *Handbook of psychotherapy and behavior change* (4th ed., pp. 379–427). New York: Wiley.

Epstein, S. (1993). Emotion and self theory. In M. Lewis & J. M. Haviland (Eds.), *Handbook of emotions* (pp. 313–326). New York: Guilford.

Esser, G. (1990). Epidemiology and course of psychiatric disorders in school aged children: Results of a longitudinal study. *Journal of Child Psychology and Psychiatry, 31,* 243–263.

Esquivel, L. (1992). *Like water for chocolate.* (T. & C. Christensen, Trans.) New York: Doubleday.

Etcoff, N. L. (1989). Asymmetries on recognition of emotion. In F. Boller & J. Grafman (Eds.), *Handbook of neuropsychology* (Vol. 3, pp. 363–382). Amsterdam: Elsevier.

Etcoff, N. L., Ekman, P., Frank, M., Magee, J., & Torreano, L. (1992). Detecting deception: Do aphasics have an advantage? Paper presented at conference of International Society for Research on Emotions, Carnegie Mellon University, Pittsburgh, PA, August.

Etcoff, N. L. & Magee, J. J. (1992). Categorical perception of facial expressions. *Cognition, 44,* 227–240.

Eysenck, H. J. (1990). Biological determinants of personality. In L. A. Pervin (Ed.), *Handbook of personality* (pp. 244–276). New York: Guilford.

Eysenck, M. W. (1992). *Anxiety: The cognitive perspective.* Howe: Erlbaum.

Fabes, R. A., Eisenberg, N., Nyman, M., & Michealieu, Q. (1991). Young children's appraisals of others' spontaneous emotional reactions. *Developmental Psychology, 27,* 858–866.

Fagot, B. I., & Kavanagh, K. (1990). The prediction of antisocial behavior from avoidant attachment classifications. *Child Development, 61,* 864–873.

Fauber, R. L., & Long, N. (1992). Children in context: The role of the family in child psychotherapy. *Journal of Consulting and Clinical Psychology, 59,* 813–820.

Fehr, B., & Russell, J. A. (1984). Concept of emotion viewed from a prototype perspective. *Journal of Experimental Psychology: General, 113,* 464–486.

Feindel, W., & Penfield, W. (1954). Localization of discharge in temporal lobe automatism. *Archives of Neurology and Psychiatry, 72,* 605–630.

Ferguson, T. J., Stegge, H., & Damhuis, I. (1991). Children's understanding of guilt and shame. *Child Development*, 62, 827–839.

Fernald, A. (1989). Intonation and communicative intent in mothers' speech to infants: Is the melody the message? *Child Development*, 60, 1497–1510.

Fernald, A. (1993). Approval and disapproval: Infant responsiveness to vocal affect in familiar and unfamiliar languages. *Child Development*, 64, 657–674.

Field, J. (1934). *A life of one's own*. Harmondsworth: Penguin (current edition 1952).

Field, T. (1994). The effects of mother's physical and emotional unavailability on emotion regulation. In N. A. Fox (Ed.), *The development of emotion regulation. Monographs of the Society for Child Development*, 59 (2–3, Serial No. 240), 208–227.

Field, T., Healy, B., Goldstein, S., & Guthertz, M. (1990). Behavior state matching and synchrony in mother–infant interactions of nondepressed versus depressed dyads. *Developmental Psychology*, 26, 7–14.

Field, T., Healy, B., Goldstein, S., Perry, S., Bendell, D., Schanberg, S., Zimmerman, E. A., & Kuhn, C. (1988). Infants of depressed mothers show "depressed" behavior even with nondepressed adults. *Child Development*, 59, 1569–1579.

Field, T., Woodson, R., Greenberg, R., & Cohen, D. (1982). Discrimination and imitation of facial expressions by neonates. *Science*, 218, 179–181.

Finlay-Jones, R. (1989). Anxiety. In G. W. Brown & T. O. Harris (Eds.), *Life events and illness* (pp. 95–112). London: Unwin Hyman.

Fisher, H. E. (1992). *Anatomy of love*. New York: Norton.

Fleming, A. S., Cheung, U. S., Myhal, N., & Kessler, Z. (1989). Effects of maternal hormones on "timidity" and attraction to pup-related odors in females. *Physiology and Behavior*, 46, 449–453.

Fleming, A. S., & Corter, C. (in press). Psychobiology of maternal behavior in nonhuman mammals: Role of sensory, experiential and neural factors. In M. Borstein (Ed.) *Handbook of parenting*. Hillsdale, NJ: Erlbaum.

Fleming, J. E., Boyle, M. E., & Offord, D. R. (1993). The outcome of adolescent depression in the Ontario Child Health Study follow-up. *Journal of the American Academy of Child and Adolescent Psychiatry*, 32, 28–33.

Fleshner, M., Laudenslager, M. L., Simons, L., & Maier, S. F. (1989). Reduced serum antibodies associated with social defeat in rats. *Physiology and Behavior*, 45, 1183–1187.

Foa, E. B., Feske, U., Murdoch, T. B., Kozak, M. J., & McCarthy, P. R. (1991). Processing of threat-related information in rape-victims. *Journal of Abnormal Psychology*, 100, 156–162.

Fogel, A., Nwokah, E., Dedo, J. Y., Messinger, D., Dickson, K. L., Matusov, E., & Holt, S. A. (1992). Social process theory of emotion: A dynamic systems approach. *Social Development*, 2, 122–142.

Fogel, A., & Reimers, M. (1989). Commentary: On the psychobiology of emotions and their development. In C. Z. Malatesta, C. Culver, J. R. Tesman, & B. Shepard (Eds.), *The development of emotion expression during the first two years of life. Monographs of the Society for Research in Child Development*. (Serial No. 219), 105–113.

Folkman, S., & Lazarus, R. J. (1989). Coping and emotion. In N. L. Stein, B. Leventhal, & T. Trabasso (Eds.), *Psychological and biological approaches to emotion* (pp. 313–332). Hillsdale, NJ: Erlbaum.

Fonagy, P., Steele, H., & Steele, M. (1991). Maternal representations of attachment during preganancy predict the organization of infant–mother attachment at one year of age. *Child Development, 62,* 891–905.

Forgas, J. P. (1995). Mood and judgment: The affect infusion model (AIM). *Psychological Review, 117,* 39–66.

Forgas, J. P., & Bower, G. H. (1988). Affect in social and personal judgments. In K. Fiedler & J. P. Forgas (Eds.), *Affect, cognition, and social behavior* (pp. 183–208). Toronto: Hogrefe.

Forgas, J. P., & Moylan, S. (1987). After the movies: The effect of mood on social judgments. *Personality and Social Psychology Bulletin, 13,* 465–477.

Fox, N., & Davidson, R. A. (1987). Electroencephalogram asymmetry in response to the approach of a stranger and maternal separation in 10-month-old infants. *Developmental Psychology, 23,* 233–240.

Fox, R. (1991). Aggression then and now. In M. H. Robinson & L. Tiger (Eds.), *Man and beast revisited* (pp. 81–93). Washington, DC: Smithsonian Institute Press.

Frank, E., Anderson, B., Reynolds, C. F., Ritenour, A., & Kupfer, D. (1994). Life events and the research diagnostic criteria endogenous subtype. *Archives of General Psychiatry, 51,* 519–524.

Freedman, J. L. (1978). *Happy people: What happiness is, who has it, and why.* New York: Harcourt Brace Jovanovich.

Freeman, W. (1971). Frontal lobotomy in early schizophrenia: Long follow up in 415 cases. *British Journal of Psychiatry, 119,* 621–624.

Freud, A. (1937). *The ego and the mechanisms of defense.* London: Hogarth Press.

Freud, S. (1901). *The psychopathology of everyday life. The Pelican Freud Library, Vol.5.* (J. Strachey, A. Richards, & A. Tyson, Eds. A. Tyson, Trans.). Harmondsworth: Penguin (current edition 1975).

Freud, S. (1905). *Fragment of an analysis of a case of hysteria (Dora). The Pelican Freud Library, Vol. 9. Case histories, II* (J. Strachey & A. Richards, Eds.),. Harmondswirth: Penguin (current edition 1979).

Freud, S. (1915–16). *Introductory lectures on psychoanalysis. The Pelican Freud Library, Vol. 1* (J. Strachey & A. Richards, Eds.). Harmondsworth: Penguin (current edition 1973).

Freud, S. (1920). *Beyond the pleasure principle. The Pelican Freud Library, Vol. 11. On metapsychology: The theory of psychoanalysis* (J. Strachey & A. Richards, Eds.) (pp. 1–64). Harmondsworth: Penguin (current edition 1974).

Freud, S., & Breuer, J. (1895). *Studies on hysteria. The Pelican Freud Library, Vol. 3.* (J. Strachey, A. Strachey, & A. Richards, Eds.). Harmondsworth: Penguin (current edition 1974).

Fridlund, A. J. (1994). *Human facial expression: An evolutionary view.* San Diego: CA Academic Press.

Friedman, M., & Rosenman, R. H. (1959). Association of specific overt behavior pattern with blood cardiovascular findings. *Journal of the American Medical Association, 169,* 1286–1295.

Friesen, W. V. (1972). *Cultural differences in facial expressions in a social situation. An experimental test of the concept of display rules.* Doctoral thesis, University of California, San Francisco.

Frijda, N. H. (1986). *The emotions.* Cambridge: Cambridge University Press.

Frijda, N. H. (1988). The laws of emotion. *American Psychologist, 43,* 349–358.

Frijda, N. (1993a). Moods, emotion episodes, and emotions. In M. Lewis & J. M. Haviland (Eds.), *Handbook of emotions* (pp. 381–403). New York: Guilford.

Frijda, N. H. (Ed.). (1993b). Appraisal and beyond: The issue of cognitive determinants of emotion. *Cognition and Emotion, 7*, 225–387.

Frijda, N. H. (1994). The Lex Talionis: On vengeance. In S. H. M. van Goozen, N. E. van der Poll, & J. A. Sergeant (Eds.), *Emotions: Essays on emotion theory* (pp. 263–289). Hillsdale, NJ: Erlbaum.

Frijda, N. H., Kuipers, P., & ter Schure, E. (1989). Relations among emotion, appraisal, and emotional action readiness. *Journal of Personality and Social Psychology, 57*, 212–228.

Frijda, N. H., & Mesquita, B. (1994). The social rules and functions of emotions. In S. Kitayama & H. R. Markus (Eds.), *Emotion and culture: Empirical studies of mutual influence* (pp. 51–87). Washington, DC: American Psychological Association.

Frijda, N. H., Mesquita, B., Sonnemans, J., & van Goozen, S. (1991). The duration of affective phenomena or emotions, sentiments and passions. In K. T. Strongman (Ed.), *International review of emotion* (Vol. 1, pp. 187–225) Chichester: Wiley.

Furuichi, T. (1992). The prolonged estrus of females and factors influencing mating in a wild group of bonobos (Pan Paniscus) in Wamba, Zaire. In M. Itoigawa, Y. Sugiyama, G. P. Sackett, & R. K. R. Thompson (Eds.), *Topics in primatology, Vol. 2. Behavior, ecology, and conservation* (pp. 179–190). Tokyo: University of Tokyo Press.

Garber, J., Braafladt, N., & Zeman, J. (1991). The regulation of sad affect: An information processing perspective. In J. Garber & K. A. Dodge (Eds.), *The development of emotion regulation and dysregulation* (pp. 208–240). Cambridge: Cambridge University Press.

Garber, J., & Dodge, K. A. (1991). *The development of emotion regulation and dysregulation.* Cambridge: Cambridge University Press.

Gardner, D., Harris, P. L., Ohmoto, M., & Hamazaki, T. (1988). Japanese children's understanding of the distinction between real and apparent emotion. *International Journal of Behavioural Development, 11*, 203–218.

Gay, P. (1988). *Freud: A life for our time.* London: Dent.

Gazzaniga, M. S. (1988). Brain modularity: Towards a philosophy of conscious experience. In A. J. Marcel & E. Bisiach (Eds.), *Consciousness in contemporary science* (pp. 218–238). Oxford: Oxford University Press.

Geertz, C. (1973). *The interpretation of cultures.* New York: Basic Books.

Geertz, C. (1975). On the nature of anthropological understanding. *American Scientist, 63*, 47–53.

George, C., Kaplan, N., & Main, M. (1985). The Berkeley Adult Attachment Interview. Unpublished protocol. Department of Psychology, University of California, Berkeley.

Gewertz, D. (1981). A historical reconsideration of female dominance among the Chambri of Papua New Guinea. *American Ethnologist, 8*, 94–106.

Gibbs, E. L., Gibbs, F. A., & Fuster, B. (1948). Psychomotor epilepsy. *Archives of Neurology and Psychiatry, 60*, 331–339.

Glaser, R., Rice, J., Sheridan, J., Fertel, R., Stout, J., Speicher, C. E., Pinsky, D. Kotur, Post, A., Beck, M., & Kiecolt-Glaser, J. (1987). Stress-related immune suppression: Health implications. *Brain, Behavior, and Immunity, 1*, 7–20.

Glickman, S. E., & Schiff, B. B. (1967). A biological theory of reinforcement. *Psychological Review, 74*, 81–109.

Goethe, J. W. von (1774). *The sorrows of young Werther* (M. Hulse, Trans.). Harmondsworth: Penguin (current edition 1989).

Goffman, E. (1959). *The presentation of self in everyday life*. New York: Doubleday.

Goffman, E. (1961). *Encounters: Two studies in the sociology of interaction*. Indianapolis, IN: Bobbs-Merrill.

Goldberg, S., Lojkasek, M., Gartner, G., & Corter, C. (1989). Maternal responsiveness and social development in preterm infants. In M. H. Bornstein (Ed.), *New Directions for Child Development, No 43*. (pp. 89–103). San Francisco: Jossey-Bass.

Goldberg, S., MacKay, S., & Rochester, M. (1994). Affect, attachment, and maternal responsiveness. *Infant Behavior and Development, 17*, 335–339.

Goldenberg, I., & Goldenberg, H. (1991). *Family therapy: An overview* (3rd ed.). Pacific Grove, CA: Brooks Cole.

Goldsmith, H. H. (1993). Temperament: Variability in developing emotion systems. In M. Lewis & J. M. Haviland (Eds.), *Handbook of emotions* (pp. 353–364). New York: Guilford.

Goldsmith, H. H., & Alansky, J. A. (1987). Maternal and infant temperamental predictors of attachment: A meta-analytic review. *Journal of Consulting and Clinical Psychology, 55*, 805–816.

Goldsmith, H. H., & Campos, J. J. (1982). Genetic influences on individual differences in emotionality. *Infant Behavior and Development, 5*, 99–115.

Goldstein, M. J. (1988). The family and psychopathology. *Annual Review of Psychology, 39*, 283–299.

Golombok, S., & Fivush, R. (1994). *Gender development*. Cambridge: Cambridge University Press.

Gombrich, E. H. (1972). *The story of art* (12th ed.). London: Phaidon.

Goodall, J. (1986). *The chimpanzees of Gombe: Patterns of behavior*. Cambridge, MA: Harvard University Press.

Goodall, J. (1992). Unusual violence in the overthrow of an alpha male chimpanzee at Gombe. In T. Nishida, W. C. McGrew, P. Marler, M. Pickford, & F. B. M. de Waal (Eds.), *Topics in primatology, Vol 1. Human origins* (pp. 131–142). Tokyo: University of Tokyo Press.

Goodenough, F. C. (1931). *Anger in young children*. Minneapolis: University of Minnesota Press.

Gotlib, I. H., & Hammen, C. L. (1992). *Psychological aspects of depression: Toward a cognitive-interpersonal integration*. Chichester: Wiley.

Gottesman, I. I. (1991). *Schizophrenia genesis: The origins of madness*. New York: Freeman.

Gottman, J. M. (1993a). *Why marriages succeed or fail*. New York: Simon & Schuster.

Gottman, J. M. (1993b). The roles of conflict engagement, escalation, and avoidance in marital interaction: A longitudinal view of five types of couples. *Journal of Consulting and Clinical Psychology, 61*, 6–15.

Gottman, J. M., & Levenson, R. W. (1992). Marital processes predictive of later dissolution: Behavior, physiology and health. *Journal of Personality and Social Psychology, 63*, 221–133.

Gowers, W. R. (1881). *Epilepsy and other chronic convulsive diseases: Their causes, symptoms, and treatment*. New York: William Wood.

Graham, P. J. (1979). Epidemiological studies. In H. C. Quay & J. S. Werry (Eds.), *Psychopathological disorders of childhood*. New York: Wiley.

Graham, P. J., & Rutter, M. (1973). Psychiatric disorder in the young adolescent: A follow-up study. *Proceedings of the Royal Society of Medicine, 66*, 1226–1229.

Gray, J. A. (1991). The neuropsychology of temperament. *Behavioral and Brain Sciences*, *14*, 105–128.

Green, D. P., Goldman, S. L., & Salovey, P. (1993). Measurement error masks bipolarity in affect ratings. *Journal of Personality and Social Psychology*, *64*, 1029–1041.

Greenberg, L. S. (1993). Emotion and change processes in psychotherapy. In M. Lewis & J. M. Haviland (Eds.), *Handbook of emotions* (pp. 499–508). New York: Guilford.

Greenberg, L. S., & Safran, J. D. (1987). *Emotion in psychotherapy*. New York: Guilford.

Greenberg, L. S., & Safran, J. D. (1989). Emotion in psychotherapy. *American Psychologist*, *44*, 19–29.

Gribbin, M., & Gribbin, J. (1993). *Being human: Putting people in an evolutionary perspective*. London: Dent.

Grinker, R. R., & Spiegel, J. P. (1945). *Men under stress*. New York: Blakiston.

Grossarth-Maticek, R., Eysenck, H. J., & Vetter, H. (1988). Personality type, smoking habit, and their interaction as predictors of cancer and coronary heart disease. *Personality and Individual Differences*, *9*, 479–495.

Grossmann, K., Grossmann, K. E., Spangler, G., Suess, G., & Unzner, L. (1985). Maternal sensitivity and newborn orientation responses as related to quality of attachment in northern Germany. *Monographs of the Society for Research in Child Development. 50* (1–2, Serial no. 209), 233–256.

Gruber, H. E., & Barrett, P. H. (1974). *Darwin on man: A psychological study of scientific creativity, together with Darwin's early and unpublished notebooks*. New York: Dutton.

Grunbaum, A. (1986). Precis of *The foundations of psychoanalysis: A philosophical critique*. *Behavioral and Brain Sciences*, *9*, 217–284.

Grych, J., & Fincham, F. (1992). Marital conflict and children's adjustment: A cognitive contextual framework. *Psychological Bulletin*, *101*, 267–290.

Haight, G. S. (1968). *George Eliot: A biography*. Oxford: Oxford University Press.

Haight, G. S. (Ed.) (1985). *Selections from George Eliot's letters*. New Haven, CT: Yale University Press.

Haley, J. (1963). *Strategies of psychotherapy*. New York: Grune & Stratton.

Hamilton, W. J. (1964). The genetical evolution of social behaviour. I. *Journal of Theoretical Biology*, *7*, 1–16.

Hamm, A. O., Vaitl, D., & Lang, P. J. (1990). Fear conditioning, meaning and belongingness: A selective association analysis. *Journal of Abnormal Psychology*, *98*, 395–406.

Hammen, C. (1991). Generation of stress in the course of unipolar depression. *Journal of Abnormal Psychology*, *100*, 555–561.

Hammen, C., Burge, D., Burney, E., & Adrian, C. (1990). Longitudinal study of diagnoses in children of women with unipolar and bipolar affective disorder. *Archives of General Psychiatry*, *47*, 1112–1117.

Hammen, C., Ellicott, A., Gitlin, M., & Jamison, K. R. (1989). Sociotropy/autonomy and vulnerability to specific life events in patients with unipolar depression and bipolar disorders. *Journal of Abnormal Psychology*, *98*, 154–160.

Hammond, W. R., & Yung, B. (1993). Psychology's role in the public health response to assaultive violence among young African-American men. *American Psychologist*, *48*, 142–154.

Harding, C. M., Zubin, J., & Strauss, J. S. (1992). Chronicity in schizophrenia revisited. *British Journal of Psychiatry, 161* (suppl. 18), 27–37.

Harkness, S., & Super, C. M. (1985). Child–environment interactions in the socialization of affect. In M. Lewis & C. Saarni (Eds.), *The socialization of emotions* (pp. 21–36). New York: Plenum Press.

Harlow, H. F. (1959, June). Love in infant monkeys. *Scientific American, 200,* 68–74.

Harlow, H. F., & Harlow, M. K. (1962). Social deprivation in monkeys. *Scientific American, 207,* 136–146.

Harlow, J. M. (1868). Recovery from the passage of an iron bar through the head. Reprinted in *History of Psychiatry* (1993), *4,* 274–281.

Harré, R. (1986). The social constructionist viewpoint. In R. Harré (Ed.), *The social construction of emotions* (pp. 2–14). Oxford: Blackwell.

Harrer, G., & Harrer, H. (1977). Music, emotion, and autonomic function. In M. Critchley & R. A. Henson (Eds.), *Music and the brain* (pp. 202–215). London: Heinemann.

Harrington, R., Fudge, H., Rutter, M., Pickles, A., & Hill, J. (1990). Adult outcomes of childhood and adolescent depression. *Archives of General Psychiatry, 47,* 465–473.

Harris, P. L. (1989). *Children and emotion: The development of psycholgical understanding.* Oxford: Blackwell.

Harris, P. L., Donnelly, K., Guz, G. R., & Pitt-Watson, R. (1986). Children's understanding of the distinction between real and apparent emotion. *Child Development, 57,* 895–909.

Harris, P. L., Johnson, C. N., Hutton, D., Andrews, G., & Cooke, T. (1989). Young children's theory of mind and emotion. *Cognition and Emotion, 3,* 379–400.

Harris, P. L., & Saarni, C. (1989). Children's understanding of emotion: An introduction. In C. Saarni & P. L. Harris (Eds.), *Children's understanding of emotion* (pp. 3–24). Cambridge: Cambridge University Press.

Harris, T. O., Brown, G. W., & Bifulco, T. (1986). Loss of parent in childhood and adult psychiatric disorder: The Walthamstow Study, 1. The role of lack of adequate parental care. *Psychological Medicine, 16,* 641–659.

Harro, J., Vasar, E., & Bradwejn, J. (1993). CCK in animal and human research on anxiety. *Trends in Pharmacological Science, 14,* 244–249.

Harter, S., & Buddin, B. (1987). Children's understanding of the simultaneity of two emotions: A five-stage developmental acquisition sequence. *Developmental Psychology, 23,* 388–399.

Hatfield, A. B. (1987). Taking issue: The expressed emotion theory: Why families object. *Hospital and Community Psychiatry, 8,* 341.

Hatfield, E., Cacioppo, J. T., & Rapson, R. L. (1994). *Emotional contagion.* Cambridge: Cambridge University Press.

Haviland, J., & Lelwicka, M. (1987). The induced affect response: 10-week old infants' responses to three emotional expressions. *Developmental Psychology, 23,* 97–104.

Hazan, C., & Shaver, P. (1987). Romantic love conceptualized as an attachment process. *Journal of Personality and Social Psychology, 52,* 511–524.

Heath, R. G. (1954). *Studies in schizophrenia.* Cambridge, MA: Harvard University Press.

Hebb, D. O. (1945). The forms and conditions of chimpanzee anger. *Bulletin of the Canadian Psychological Association, 5* 32–35.

Hebb, D. O. (1946). Emotion in man and animal: An analysis of the intuitive process of recognition. *Psychological Review, 53*, 88–106.

Heelas, P. (1986). Emotion talk across cultures. In R. Harré (Ed.), *The social construction of emotions* (pp. 234–266). Oxford: Blackwell.

Helman, C. (1984). *Culture, health and illness.* Bristol: Wright.

Henriques, J. B., & Davidson, R. J. (1991). Left frontal hypoactivation in depression. *Journal of Abnormal Psychology, 100*, 535–545.

Henry, W. P., Strupp, H. H., Schacht, T. E., & Gaston, L. (1994). Psychodynamic approaches. In A. E. Bergin & S. L. Garfield (Eds.), *Handbook of psychotherapy and behavior change* (4th ed., pp. 467–508). New York: Wiley.

Herbert, T. B., & Cohen, S. (1993). Depression and immunity: A meta-analytic view. *Psychological Bulletin, 113*, 472–486.

Hertel, P. T., & Hardin, T. S. (1990). Remembering with and without awareness in a depressed mood. *Journal of Experimental Psychology: General, 119*, 45–59.

Hess, R. D., Kashiwagi, K., Azuma, H., Price, G. G., & Dickson, W. P. (1980). Maternal expectations for mastery developmental tasks in Japan and the United States. *International Journal of Psychology, 15*, 259–271.

Hess, W. R. (1950). Function and neural regulation of internal organs. In K. Akert (Ed.), *Biological order and brain organization: Selected works of W. R. Hess* (pp. 17–32). Berlin: Springer-Verlag (current edition 1981).

Hess, W. R., & Brügger, M. (1943). Subcortical center of the affective defense reaction. In K. Akert (Ed.), *Biological order and brain organization: Selected works of W. R. Hess* (pp. 183–202). Berlin: Springer-Verlag (current edition 1981).

Hiatt, S., Campos, J. J., & Emde, R. N. (1979). Facial patterning an infant facial expression: Happiness, surprise, and fear. *Child Development, 50*, 1020–1035.

Hibbs, E. D., Zahn, T. P., Hamburger, S. D., Kruesi, M. J. P., & Rapoport, J. L. (1992). Parental expressed emotion and psychophysical reactivity in disturbed and normal children. *British Journal of Psychiatry, 160*, 504–510.

Hilton, S. M., & Zbrozyna, A. W. (1963). Amygdaloid region for defense reactions and its efferent pathway to the brainstem. *Journal of Physiology, 165*, 160–173.

Hinde, R. (1976). On describing relationships. *Journal of Child Psychology and Psychiatry, 17*, 1–19.

Hinde, R. A. (1985). Was "The expression of the emotions" a misleading title? *Animal Behaviour, 33*, 985–992.

Hochschild, A. R. (1983). *The managed heart: Commercialization of human feeling.* Berkeley, CA: University of California Press.

Hockett, C. F. (1973). *Man's place in nature.* New York: McGraw-Hill.

Hodges, J., & Tizard, B. (1989a). IQ and behavioural adjustment of ex-institutionalized adolescents. *Journal of Child Psychology and Psychiatry, 30*(1), 53–76.

Hodges, J., & Tizard, B. (1989b). Social and family relationships of ex-institutionalized adolescents. *Journal of Child Psychology and Psychiatry, 30*(1), 77–98.

Hoffman, M. L. (1984). Interaction of affect and cognition in empathy. In C. Izard, J. Kagan, & R. Zajonc (Eds.), *Emotions, cognition and behavior* (pp. 103–131). New York: Cambridge University Press.

Hogarty, G. E., Anderson, C. M., Reiss, M. A., Kornblith, S. J., Greenwald, D. P., Javna, C. D., & Madonia, M. J. (1986). Family psychoeducation, social skills training, and maintenance chemotherapy in the aftercare treatment of schizophrenia. One-year effects of a controlled study of relapse and Expressed Emotion. *Archives of General Psychiatry*, *43*, 633–642.

Hohmann, G. W. (1966). Some effects of spinal cord lesions on experienced emotional feelings. *Psychophysiology*, *3*, 143–156.

Hokanson, J. E., Hummer, J. T., & Butler, A. C. (1991). Interpersonal perceptions by depressed college students. *Cognitive Therapy and Research*, *15*, 443–457.

Hollon, S. D., & Beck, A. T. (1994). Cognitive and cognitive-behavioral therapies. In A. E. Bergin & S. L. Garfield (Eds.), *Handbook of psychotherapy and behavior change* (4th ed., pp. 428–466). New York: Wiley.

Holmes, T. H., & Rahe, R. H. (1967). The social readjustment rating scale. *Journal of Psychosomatic Research*, *11*, 213–218.

Hom, H. L., & Arbuckle, B. (1988). Mood induction effects upon goal setting and performance in young children. *Motivation and Emotion*, *12*, 113–122.

Homer (circa 850 BCE). *The Iliad*. (Ed. and Trans. M. Hammond). Harmondsworth: Penguin (current edition 1987).

Hooley, J. M., & Teasdale, J. D. (1989). Predictors of relapse in unipolar depressives: Expressed emotion, marital distress and perceived criticism. *Journal of Abnormal Psychology*, *98*, 229–237.

Hooven, C., Gottman, J. M., & Katz, L. F. (1995). Parental meta-emotion structure predicts family and child outcomes. *Cognition and Emotion*, *9*, 229–264.

Hops, H., Biglan, A., Sherman, L., Arthur, J., Friedman, L., & Osteen, V. (1987). Home observations of family interactions of depressed women. *Journal of Consulting and Clinical Psychology*, *55*, 341–346.

House, J., Landis, K., & Umberson, D. (1988). Social relationships and health. *Science*, *241*, 540–545.

Howell, S. (1981). Rules not words. In P. H. &. A. Lock (Ed.), *Indigenous psychologies: The anthropology of the self* (pp. 133–143). London: Academic Press.

Hsee, C. K., Hatfield, E., Carlson, J. G., & Chemtob, C. (1990). The effect of power on susceptibility to emotional contagion. *Cognition and Emotion*, *4*, 327–340.

Huebner, R. R., & Izard, C. E. (1988). Mothers' responses to infants' facial expressions of sadness, anger, and physical distress. *Motivation and Emotion*, *12*, 185–196.

Huesmann, L. R., Eron, L. D., Lefkowitz, M., & Walder, L. O. (1984). Stability of aggression over time and generations. *Developmental Psychology*, *20*, 1120–1134.

Hughlings-Jackson, J. (1959). *Selected writings of John Hughlings-Jackson* (J. Taylor, Ed.). New York: Basic Books.

Hupka, R. B. (1991). The motive for the arousal of romantic jealousy: Its cultural origin. In P. Salovey (Ed.), *The psychology of jealousy and envy* (pp. 252–270). New York: Guilford.

Hyson, M. C., & Izard, C. E. (1985). Continuities and changes in emotion expressions during brief separation at 13 and 18 months. *Developmental Psychology*, *21*, 1165–1170.

Ira, G. H., Whalen, R. E., & Bogdanoff, M. D. (1963). Heart rate changes in physicians during daily "stressful" tasks. *Journal of Psychosomatic Research*, *7*, 147–150.

Isabella, R. A., Belsky, J., & Von Eye, A. (1989). Origins of infant–mother attachment: An examination of interactional synchrony during the infant's first year. *Developmental Psychology*, *25*, 12–21.

Isen, A. (1970). Success, failure, attention and reactions to others: The warm glow of success. *Journal of Personality and Social Psychology*, *15*, 294–301.

Isen, A. (1990). The influence of positive and negative affect on cognitive organization. In N. Stein, B. Leventhal, & T. Trabasso (Eds.), *Psychological and biological processes in the development of emotion* (pp. 75–94). Hillsdale, NJ: Erlbaum.

Isen, A. M., Daubman, K. A., & Nowicki, G. P. (1987). Positive affect facilitates creative problem solving. *Journal of Personality and Social Psychology, 52,* 1122–1131.

Isen, A. M., & Geva, N. (1987). The influence of positive affect on acceptable level of risk: The person with large canoe has large worry. *Organizational Behavior and Human Decision Processes, 39,* 145–154.

Isen, A. M., Johnson, M. M. S., Mertz, E., & Robinson, G. F. (1985). The influence of positive affect on the unusualness of word associations. *Journal of Personality and Social Psychology, 48,* 1413–1426.

Isen, A. M., & Levin, P. F. (1972). The effect of feeling good on helping: Cookies and kindness. *Journal of Personality and Social Psychology, 21,* 384–388.

Isen, A. M., Rosenzweig, A. S., & Young, M. J. (1991). The influence of positive affect on clinical problem solving. *Medical Decision Making, 11,* 221–227.

Isen, A. M., Shalker, T., Clark, M., & Karp, L. (1978). Affect, accessibility of material in memory and behavior: A cognitive loop? *Journal of Personality and Social Psychology, 36,* 1–12.

Izard, C. E. (1968). The emotions and emotion constructs in personality and culture research. In R. B. Catell (Ed.), *Handbook of modern personality theory.* Chicago: Aldine.

Izard, C. E. (1979). *The maximally discriminative facial movement coding system (MAX).* Newark, DE: University of Delaware, Office of Instructional Technology.

Izard, C. E. (1991). *The psychology of emotions.* New York: Plenum.

Izard, C. E. (1993). Four systems for emotion activation: Cognitive and non-cognitive processes. *Psychological Review, 100,* 68–90.

Izard, C. E. (1994). Innate and universal facial expressions: Evidence from developmental and cross-cultural research. *Psychological Bulletin, 115,* 288–299.

Izard, C. E., Dougherty, L. M., & Hembree, E. A. (1983). *A system for identifying affect expressions by holistic judgments (AFFEX).* Newark, DE: University of Delaware, Office of Instructional Technology.

Izard, C. E., Hembree, E. A., & Huebner, R. R. (1987). Infants' emotion expressions to acute pain: Developmental change and stability of individual differences. *Developmental Psychology, 23,* 105–113.

Izard, C. E., & Malatesta, C. Z. (1987). Perspectives on emotional development I: Differential emotions theory of early emotional development. In J. D. Osofsky (Ed.), *Handbook of Infant Development* (pp. 494–554). New York: Wiley.

James, W. (1884). What is an emotion? *Mind, 9,* 188–205.

James, W. (1890). *The principles of psychology.* New York: Dover (current edition 1950).

Jankowiak, W. R., & Fischer, E. F. (1992). A cross-cultural perspective on romantic love. *Ethos, 31,* 149–155.

Jastrow, J. (1900). *Fact and fable in psychology.* Boston: Houghton.

Jenkins, J. H. (1991). Expressed emotion and schizophrenia. *Ethos, 19,* 387–431.

Jenkins, J. H., & Karno, M. (1992). The meaning of expressed emotion: Theoretical issues raised by cross-cultural research. *American Journal of Psychiatry, 149,* 9–21.

Jenkins, J. M. (1992). Sibling relationships in disharmonious homes. In F. Boer & J.

Dunn (Eds.), *Children's sibling relationships: Developmental and clinical issues* (pp. 125–136). Hillsdale, NJ: Erlbaum.

Jenkins, J. M., Franco, F., Dollins, F., & Sewell, A. (1995). Toddlers' reactions to negative emotion displays: Forming models of relationships. *Infant Behavior and Development, 18,* 273–281.

Jenkins, J. M., & Smith, M. A. (1990). Factors protecting children living in disharmonious homes: Maternal reports. *Journal of the American Academy of Child and Adolescent Psychiatry, 29,* 60–69.

Jenkins, J. M., & Smith, M. A. (1991). Marital disharmony and children's behaviour problems: Aspects of a poor marriage which affect children adversely. *Journal of Child Psychology and Psychiatry, 32,* 793–810.

Jenkins, J. M., Smith, M. A., & Graham, P. (1989). Coping with parental quarrels. *Journal of the American Academy of Child and Adolescent Psychiatry, 28,* 182–189.

Jenson, P. S., Xenakis, S. N., Davis, H., & Degroot, J. (1988). Child psychopathology rating scales and interrater agreement: II. Child and family characteristics. *Journal of the American Academy of Child and Adolescent Psychiatry, 27,* 451–461.

John, O. P. (1990). The "big five" factor taxonomy: Dimensions of personality in the natural language and in questionnaires. In L. A. Pervin (Ed.), *Handbook of personality* (pp. 66–100). New York: Guilford.

Johnson-Laird, P. N., & Oatley, K. (1989). The language of emotions: An analysis of a semantic field. *Cognition and Emotion, 3,* 81–123.

Jonas, H. (1958). *The gnostic religion: The message of the alien God and the beginnings of Christianity.* Boston: Beacon.

Jones, I., & Horne, D. (1973). Diagnosis of psychiatric illness among tribal aborigines. *Medical Journal of Australia, 1,* 345–349.

Jones, S. S., Collins, K., & Hong, H.-W. (1991). An audience effect on smile production in 10-month-old infants. *Psychological Science, 2,* 45–49.

Jung, C. G. (1925). Marriage as a psychological relationship. In J. Campbell (Ed.), *The portable Jung* (pp. 163–177). New York: Viking-Penguin (current edition 1971).

Kagan, J. (1982). Heart rate and heart rate variability as signs of temperamental dimensions in infancy. In C. E. Izard (Ed.), *Measuring emotions in infants and children.* Cambridge: Cambridge University Press.

Kagan, J. (1987). Perspectives on infancy. In J. Osofsky (Ed.), *Handbook of infant development* (3rd ed., pp. 1150–1192). New York: Wiley.

Kagan, J. (1994). On the nature of emotion. In N. Fox (Ed.), *The development of emotion regulation: Monographs of the Society for Research in Child Development, 59* (2–3, Serial No. 240) pp. 7–24.

Kagan, J., Reznick, J. S., & Snidman, N. (1988). Biological bases of childhood shyness. *Science, 240,* 167–171.

Kahneman, D., Slovic, P., & Tversky, A. (1982). *Judgment under uncertainty: Heuristics and biases.* Cambridge: Cambridge University Press.

Kalin, N. H. (1993, May). The neurobiology of fear. *Scientific American, 268,* 54–60.

Kandel, E. R., Schwartz, J. H., & Jessell, T. M. (1991). *Principles of neural science* (3rd ed.). Norwalk, CT: Appleton & Lange.

Kane, F., Coulombe, D., & Miliaressis, E. (1991). Amygdaloid self-stimulation: A movable electrode mapping study. *Behavioral Neuroscience, 105,* 926–932.

Kano, T. (1992). *The last ape: Pygmy chimpanzee behavior and ecology* (E. O. Vineberg, Trans.). Stanford, CA: Stanford University Press.

Kant, I. (1784). What is enlightenment? In E. Behler (Ed.), *The German library, Vol. 13. Immanuel Kant: Philosophical writings.* (pp. 263–269). New York: Continuum.

Kashani, J. H., & Orvaschel, H. (1988). Anxiety disorders in mid-adolescence. *American Journal of Psychiatry, 145*, 960–964.

Kashani, J. H., & Orvaschel, H. (1990). A community study of anxiety in children and adolescents. *American Journal of Psychiatry, 147*, 313–318.

Kashani, J., Orvaschel, H., Rosenberg, T., & Reid, J. C. (1989). Psychopathology in a community sample of children and adolescents: A developmental perspective. *Journal of the American Academy of Child and Adolescent Psychiatry, 28*, 701–706.

Kavanagh, D. J. (1992). Recent developments in Expressed Emotion and schizophrenia. *British Journal of Psychiatry, 160*, 601–620.

Kearney, G. D., & McKenzie, S. (1993). Machine interpretation of emotion: Design of a memory-based expert system for interpreting facial expressions in terms of signalled emotions. *Cognitive Science, 17*, 589–622.

Keegan, J. (1994). *A history of warfare.* New York: Vintage.

Keltner, D. (1995). Signs of appeasement: Evidence for the distinct displays of embarrassment, amusement, and shame. *Journal of Personality and Social Psychology, 68*, 441–454.

Kemper, T. D. (1978). *A social-interactional theory of emotions.* New York: Wiley.

Kemper, T. D. (1990). Social relations and emotions: A structural approach. In T. D. Kemper (Ed.), *Research agendas in the sociology of emotions* (pp. 207–237). Albany, NY: State University of New York University Press.

Kendler, K. S., Heath, A., Martin, A., & Eaves, I. J. (1986). Symptoms of anxiety and depression in a volunteer twin population. *Archives of General Psychiatry, 43*, 213–221.

Kendler, K. S., Neale, M. C., Kessler, R. C., Heath, A. C., & Eaves, L. J. (1993a). A twin study of recent life events. *Archives of General Psychiatry, 50*, 789–796.

Kendler, K. S., Neale, M. C., Kessler, R. C., Heath, A. C., & Eaves, L. J. (1993b). A longitudinal twin study of 1-year prevalence of major depression in women. *Archives of General Psychiatry, 50*, 843–852.

Kennedy, S., Kiecolt-Glaser, J. K., & Glaser, R. (1988). Immunological consequences of acute and chronic stressors: Mediating role of interpersonal relationships. *British Journal of Medical Psychology, 61*(1), 77–85.

Kessler, R. C., McGonagle, K. A., Zhao, S., Nelson, C. P., Hughes, M., Eshleman, S., Wittchen, H.-U., & Kendler, K. S. (1994). Lifetime and 12-month prevalence of DSM-III-R psychiatric disorders in the United States: Results from the National Comorbidity Survey. *Archives of General Psychiatry, 51*, 8–19.

Kiecolt-Glaser, J., Kennedy, S., Malkoff, S., Fisher, L., Speicher, C. E., Garner, W., & Glaser, R. (1988). Marital discord and immunity in males. *Psychosomatic Medicine, 50*, 213–229.

Kimsey, S. L., Johnson, P. C., Ritzman, S. E., & Mengel, C. E. (1986). Hematology and immunology studies: The second manned Skylab mission. *Aviation, Space, and Environmental Medicine, 47*, 383–390.

Kitayama, S., & Markus, H. R. (Eds.). (1994). *Emotion and culture: Empirical studies of mutual influence.* Washington, DC: American Psychological Association.

Klaus, M. H., & Kennell, J. H. (1976). *Maternal–infant bonding.* St Louis: Mosby.

Kleinman, A. (1982). Neurasthenia and depression: A study of somatization and culture in China. *Culture, Medicine and Psychiatry, 6,* 117–189.

Kleinman, A. (1988). *Rethinking psychiatry: From cultural category to personal experience.* New York: Free Press.

Klüver, H., & Bucy, P. C. (1937). "Psychic blindness" and other symptoms following bilateral temporal lobectomy. *American Journal of Physiology, 119,* 352–353.

Kopp, C. B. (1989). Regulation of distress and negative emotions: A developmental view. *Developmental Psychology, 25*(3), 343–354.

Kopp, C. B. (1992). Emotional distress and control in young children. In N. Eisenberg & R. A. Fabes (Eds.), *Emotion and its regulation in early development. (New Directions in Child Development, No. 55)* (pp. 41–56). San Francisco: Jossey Bass.

Kovacs, M., Feinberg, T. L., Crouse-Novak, M. A., Paulauskas, S. L., & Finkelstein, R. (1984). Depressive disorder in childhood: A longitudinal prospective study of characteristics and recovery. *Archives of General Psychiatry, 41,* 229–237, 643–649.

Kraemer, G. W. (1992). A psychobiological theory of attachment. *Behavioral and Brain Sciences, 15,* 493–541.

Kraiger, K., Billings, R. S., & Isen, A. M. (1989). The influence of positive affective states on task perceptions and satisfaction. *Organizational Behavior and Human Decision Processes, 44,* 12–25.

Kramer, P. D. (1993). *Listening to Prozac.* New York: Viking.

Kraut, R. E., & Johnson, R. E. (1979). Social and emotional messages of smiling: An ethological approach. *Journal of Personality and Social Psychology, 37,* 1539–1553.

Krebs, J. R., & Dawkins, R. (1984). Animal signals: Mind reading and manipulation. In J. R. Krebs & N. B. Davies (Eds.), *Behavioral ecology* (2nd ed., pp. 380–402). Oxford: Blackwell.

Kuipers, L., & Bebbington, P. (1988). Expressed emotion research in schizophrenia: Theoretical and clinical implications. *Psychological Medicine, 18,* 893–909.

La Freniere, P. J., & Sroufe, L. A. (1984). Profiles of peer competence in the preschool: Interrelations between measures, influence of social ecology, and relation to attachment history. *Developmental Psychology, 21,* 56–69.

Lakoff, G. (1987). *Women, fire and dangerous things: What categories reveal about the mind.* Chicago: University of Chicago Press.

Lambert, M. J., & Bergin, A. E. (1994). The effectiveness of psychotherapy. In A. E. Bergin & S. L. Garfield (Eds.), *Handbook of psychotherapy and behavior change* (4th ed., pp. 143–189). New York: Wiley.

Lancaster, J. B., & Kaplan, H. (1992). Human mating and family formation strategies: The effects of variability among males in quality and the allocation of mating effort and parental investment. In T. Nishida, W. C. McGrew, P. Marler, M. Pickford, & F. B. M. de Waal (Eds.), *Topics in primatology, Vol. 1. Human origins* (pp. 21–33). Tokyo: University of Tokyo Press.

Landman, J. (1993). *Regret: The persistence of the possible.* New York: Oxford University Press.

Lang, P. J. (1985). The cognitive psychophysiology of emotion? Fear and anxiety. In A. H. Tuma & J. D. Maser (Eds.), *Anxiety and the anxiety disorders* (pp. 131–170). Hillsdale, NJ: Erlbaum.

Lang, P. J. (1988). What are the data of emotion. In V. Hamilton, G. H. Bower, & N.

Frijda (Eds.), *Cognitive perspectives on emotion and motivation* (NATO ASI, Series D Vol 44. pp. 173–191). Dordrecht: Kluwer.

Lange, C. (1885). The emotions. In E. Dunlap (Ed.), *The emotions*. Baltimore, MD: Williams & Wilkins (current edition 1922).

La Rochefoucauld (1665). *Maxims* (L. Tancock, Trans.). Harmondsworth: Penguin (current edition 1959).

Larsen, R. J., Kasimatis, M., & Frey, K. (1992). Facilitating the furrowed brow: An unobtrusive test of the facial feedback hypothesis applied to unpleasant affect. *Cognition and Emotion, 6,* 321–338.

Larson, R., & Lampman-Petraitis, C. (1989). Daily emotional states as reported by children and adolescents. *Child Development, 60,* 1250–1260.

Last, C. G., Perrin, S., Hersen, M., & Kazdin, A. E. (1992). DSM-III-R anxiety disorders in children: Sociodemographic and clinical characteristics. *Journal of the American Academy of Child and Adolescent Psychiatry, 31,* 1070–1076.

Lazarus, R. S. (1966). *Psychological stress and the coping process.* New York: McGraw-Hill.

Lazarus, R. S. (1991). *Emotion and adaptation.* New York: Oxford University Press.

Lazarus, R. S., & Lazarus, B. N. (1994). *Passion and reason: Making sense of our emotions.* New York: Oxford University Press.

Leakey, R. (1994). *The origin of humankind.* New York: Basic Books.

Leakey, R., & Lewin, R. (1991). *Origins.* Harmondsworth: Penguin.

Leary, M. R., Britt, T. W., Cutlip, W. D., & Templeton, J. L. (1992). Social blushing. *Psychological Bulletin, 112,* 446–460.

LeDoux, J. E. (1993). Emotional networks in the brain. In M. Lewis & J. M. Haviland (Eds.), *Handbook of emotions* (pp. 109–118). New York: Guilford Press.

LeDoux, J. E. (1994, June). Emotion, memory and the brain. *Scientific American, 220,* 50–57.

LeDoux, J., Ciccetti, P., Xagoraris, A., & Romanski, L. R. (1990). The lateral amygdaloid nucleus: Sensory interface of the amgydala in fear conditioning. *Journal of Neuroscience, 10,* 1062–1069.

Lee, R. B. (1984). *The Dobe !Kung.* New York: Holt, Rinehart & Winston.

Leff, J. (1989). Controversial issues and growing points in research on relatives' Expressed Emotion. *International Journal of Social Psychiatry, 35,* 133–144.

Leff, J., Sartorius, N., Jablensky, A., Korten, A., & Ernberg, G. (1992). The international pilot study of schizophrenia: Five year follow-up findings. *Psychological Medicine, 22,* 131–145.

Levenson, R. W., Ekman, P., & Friesen, W. V. (1990). Voluntary facial action generates emotion-specific autonomic nervous-system activity. *Psychophysiology, 27,* 363–384.

Leventhal, H. (1991). Emotion: Prospects for conceptual and empirical development. In R. J. Lister & H. J. Weingartner (Eds.), *Perspectives on cognitive neuroscience* (pp. 325–348). New York: Oxford University Press.

Levi, P. (1958). *If this is a man* (S. Woolf, Trans.). London: Sphere (current edition 1987).

Levy, R. J. (1984). Emotion, knowing, and culture. In R. A. Shweder & R. A. Levine (Eds.), *Culture theory: Essays on mind, self, and emotion* (pp. 214–237). Cambridge: Cambridge University Press.

Levy, S. M., Hoberman, R. B., Lippman, M., D'Angelo, T., & Lee, J. (1991).

Immunological and psychosocial predictors of disease recurrence in patients with early stage breast cancer. *Behavioral Medicine, 17,* 67–75.

Lewis, C. S. (1936). *The allegory of love: A study in medieval tradition.* Oxford: Oxford University Press.

Lewis, Marc (1995). Cognition-emotion feedback and the self-organization of developmental paths. *Human Development, 38,* 71–102.

Lewis, Michael (1990). Models of developmental psychopathology. In M. Lewis & S. M. Miller (Eds.), *Handbook of Developmental Psychopathology* (pp. 15–28). New York: Plenum.

Lewis, Michael (1992). *Shame: The exposed self.* New York: Free Press.

Lewis, Michael (1993). Self-conscious emotions: embarrassment, pride, shame, and guilt. In M. Lewis & J. M. Haviland (Eds.), *Handbook of Emotions* (pp. 563–573). New York: Guilford.

Lewis, Michael (1995, Jan–Feb). Self-conscious emotions. *American Scientist, 83,* 68–78.

Lewis, Michael, Alessandri, S. M., & Sullivan, M. W. (1990). Violation of expectancy, loss of control and anger expressions in young infants. *Developmental Psychology, 26*(5), 745–751.

Lewis, Michael, & Feiring, C. (1989). Infant, mother, and mother–infant interaction behavior and subsequent attachment. *Child Development, 60*(4), 831–837.

Lewis, Michael, Feiring, C., McGuffog, C., & Jaskir, J. (1984). Predicting psychopathology in 6-year-olds from early social relationships. *Child Development, 55,* 123–136.

Lewis, Michael, & Haviland, J. M. (Eds.). (1993). *Handbook of emotions.* New York: Guilford.

Lewis, Michael, Sullivan, M. W., Stanger, C., & Weiss, M. (1989). Self-development and self-conscious emotions. *Child Development, 60,* 146–156.

Lichtheim, M. (1973). *Ancient Egyptian literature: Vol. 1. The Old and Middle Kingdoms.* Berkeley: University of California Press.

Liebowitz, M. R. (1983). *The chemistry of love.* Boston: Little, Brown.

Lindsley, D. B. (1951). Emotions. In S. S. Stevens (Ed.), *Handbook of experimental psychology* (pp. 473–516). New York: Wiley.

Linton, M. (1982). Transformations of memory in everyday life. In U. Neisser (Ed.), *Memory observed: Remembering in natural contexts* (pp. 77–91). San Francisco: Freeman.

Lipsey, M. W., & Wilson, D. B. (1993). The efficacy of psychological, educational, and behavioral treatment. *American Psychologist, 48,* 1181–1209.

Littenberg, R., Tulkin, S., & Kagan, J. (1971). Cognitive components of separation anxiety. *Developmental Psychology, 4,* 387–388.

Loftus, E. F., & Doyle, J. M. (1987). *Eyewitness testimony: Civil and criminal.* New York: Kluwer.

Loftus, E., & Ketcham, K. (1994). *The myth of repressed memory: False memories and allegations of sexual abuse.* New York: St. Martin's Press.

Loftus, E. F., & Loftus, G. R. (1980). On the permanence of stored information in the human brain. *American Psychologist, 35,* 409–420.

Londerville, S., & Main, M. (1981). Security of attachment, compliance, and maternal training methods in the second year of life. *Developmental Psychology, 17,* 289–299.

Lorenz, K. (1935). Der Kumpan in der Umwelt des Vogels. *Journal of Ornithology, 83,*

137–213. [Companionship in bird life.] In C. Schiller (Ed. & Trans.), *Instinctive behavior: Development of a modern concept*. London: Methuen, pp. 83–128.

Lorenz, K. (1937). Über die Bildung des Instinktbegriffes. *Die Naturwissenschaften, 25,* 289–331 [The conception of instinctive behavior.] In C. Schiller (Ed. & Trans.) *Instinctive behavior: Development of a modern concept*, London: Methuen, pp. 176–208.

Lorenz, K. (1967). *On aggression* (M. Latzke, Trans.). London: Methuen.

Lorenz, K., & Tinbergen, N. (1938). Taxis und Instinkthandlung in der Eirollbewegung der Graugans. *Zeitschrift für Tierpsychologi, 2,* 1–29 [Taxis and instinctive action in the egg-retrieving behavior of the greylag goose.] In C. Schiller (Ed. & Trans.), *Instinctive behavior: Development of a modern concept*, London: Methuen, pp. 176–208).

Lovejoy, C. O. (1981). The origin of man. *Science, 211,* 341–350.

Luborsky, L., & Crits-Christoph, P. (1990). *Understanding transference*. New York: Basic Books.

Lutkenhaus, P., Grossmann, K. E., & Grossmann, K. (1985). Infant–mother attachment at twelve months and style of interaction with a stranger at the age of three years. *Child Development, 56,* 1538–1542.

Lutz, C. A. (1988). *Unnatural emotions: Everyday sentiments on a Micronesian atoll and their challenge to Western theory*. Chicago: University of Chicago Press.

Lyons-Ruth, K., Alpern, L., & Repacholi, B. (1993). Disorganized infant attachment classification and maternal psychosocial problems as predictors of hostile-aggressive behavior in the preschool classroom. *Child Development, 64,* 572–585.

Lyons-Ruth, K., Connell, D. B., Grunebaum, H. U., & Botein, S. (1990). Infants at social risk: Maternal depression and family support services as mediators of infant development and security of attachment. *Child Development, 61,* 85–98.

Lytton, H. (1990). Child and parent effects in boys' conduct disorder. A reinterpretation. *Developmental Psychology, 26,* 683–704.

Lyubomirsky, S., & Nolen-Hoeksema, S. (1993). Self-perpetuating properties of dysphoric rumination. *Journal of Personality and Social Psychology, 65,* 339–349.

Maccoby, E. E., & Martin, J. (1983). Socialization in the context of the family: Parent-child interaction. In P. H. Mussen (Ed.), *Handbook of child psychology*. New York: Wiley.

MacDonald, K. (1992). Warmth as a developmental construct: An evolutionary analysis. *Child Development, 63,* 753–773.

Macintyre, M. (1986). Female autonomy in a matrilineal society. In N. Grieve & A. Burns (Eds.), *Australian women: New feminist perspectives* (pp. 248–256). Melbourne: Oxford University Press.

Mackie, D. M., & Worth, L. T. (1989). Processing deficits and the mediation of positive affect in persuasion. *Journal of Personality and Social Psychology, 57,* 27–40.

Mackie, D. M., & Worth, L. T. (1991). Feeling good, but not thinking straight: The impact of positive mood on persuasion. In J. P. Forgas (Ed.), *Emotion and social judgments* (pp. 201-219). Oxford: Pergamon.

MacLean, P. D. (1949). Psychosomatic disease and the "visceral brain": recent developments bearing on the Papez theory of emotion. *Psychosomatic Medicine, 11,* 338–353.

MacLean, P. D. (1990). *The triune brain in evolution*. Plenum: New York.

MacLean, P. D. (1993). Cerebral evolution of emotion. In M. Lewis & J. M. Haviland (Eds.), *Handbook of emotions* (pp. 67–83). New York: Guilford.

Maestripieri, D., Schino, G., Aurieli, F., & Troisi, A. (1992). A modest proposal: displacement activities as an indicator of emotions in primates. *Animal Behavior, 44*, 967–979.

Magai, C., & McFadden, S. H. (1995). *The role of emotions in social and personality development.* New York: Plenum.

Magnusson, D. (1988). *Paths through life: A longitudinal research program.* Hillsdale, NJ: Erlbaum.

Maier, S. F., Watkins, L. R., & Fleshner, M. (1994). Psychoneuroimmunology: The interface between behavior, brain, and immunity. *American Psychologist, 49*, 1004–1017.

Main, M., Kaplan, N., & Cassidy, J. (1985). Security in infancy, childhood, and adulthood: A move to the level of representation. In I. Bretherton & E. Waters (Eds.), *Growing points of attachment theory and research. Monographs of the Society for Research in Child Development, 50*, (1–2, Serial No. 209), pp. 65–106.

Main, M., & Solomon, J. (1986). Discovery of a disorganized/disoriented attachment pattern. In M. W. Brazelton (Ed.), *Affective development in infancy* (pp. 95–124). Norwood, NJ: Ablex.

Main, M., & Solomon, J. (1990). Procedures for identifying infants as disorganized/disoriented during the Ainsworth Strange Situation. In M. Greenberg, D. Cicchetti, & E. M. Cummings (Eds.), *Attachment in the preschool years: Theory, research and intervention* (pp. 121–160). Chicago: University of Chicago Press.

Malatesta, C. Z., Culver, C., Tesman, J. R., & Shepard, B. (1989a). *The development of emotion expression during the first two years of life. Monographs of the Society for Research in Child Development, 54* (1–2, Serial No. 219), 1–103.

Malatesta, C. Z., Culver, C., Tesman, J. R., & Shepard, B. (1989b). Engaging the commentaries: When is an infant affective expression an emotion? In C. Z. Malatesta, C. Culver, J. R. Tesman, & B. Shepard (Eds.), *The development of emotion expression during the first two years of life. Monographs of the Society for Research in Child Development. 54*, (1–2, Serial No. 219), 125–136.

Malatesta, C. Z., Grigoryev, P., Lamb, C., Albin, M., & Culver, C. (1986). Emotion socialization and expressive development in preterm and full term infants. *Child Development, 57*, 316–330.

Malatesta, C. Z., & Haviland, J. M. (1982). Learning display rules: the socialization of emotion expression in infancy. *Child Development, 53*, 991–1003.

Mandler, G. (1964). The interruption of behavior. In *Nebraska Symposium on Motivation* (Vol. 12). Lincoln, NA: Nebraska University Press.

Mandler, G. (1984). *Mind and body: Psychology of emotions and stress.* New York: Norton.

Mangelsdorf, S., Gunnar, M., Kestenbaum, R., Lang, S., & Andreas, D. (1990). Infant proness-to-distress temperament, maternal personality and mother–infant attachment: Association and goodness of fit. *Child Developement, 61*, 820–831.

Manstead, A. S. R., & Wagner, H. L. (1981). Arousal, cognition, and emotion: An appraisal of two-factor theory. *Current Psychological Reviews, 1*, 35–54.

Marcus, S. (1984). Freud and Dora: Story, history, case history (Originally published Winter, 1974, in *Partisan Review*). In S. Marcus (Ed.), *Freud and the culture of psychoanalysis* (pp. 42–86). New York: Norton.

Marks, J. (1992). The promises and problems of molecular anthropology in hominid origins. In T. Nishida, W. C. McGrew, P. Marler, M. Pickford, & F. B. M. de Waal (Eds.), *Topics in primatology, Vol. 1. Human origins* (pp. 441–453). Tokyo: University of Tokyo Press.

Markus, H. R., & Kitayama, S. (1991). Culture and the self: Implications for cognition, emotion, and motivation. *Psychological Review, 98,* 224–253.

Markus, H. R., & Kitayama, S. (1994). The cultural construction of self and emotion: Implications for social behavior. In S. Kitayama & H. R. Markus (Eds.). *Emotion and culture: Empirical studies of mutual influence* (pp. 89–130). Washington, DC: American Psychological Association.

Marshall, L. (1976). *The !Kung of Nyae Nyae.* Cambridge, MA: Harvard University Press.

Martinez, P., & Richters, J. E. (1993). The NIMH Community Violence Project: II. Children's distress symptoms associated with violence exposure. *Psychiatry: Interpersonal and Biological Processes, 56,* 22–35.

Mason, W. A., & Mendoza, S. P. (Eds.). (1993). *Primate social conflict.* Albany, NY: State University of New York Press.

Matas, L., Arend, R. A., & Sroufe, L. A. (1978). Continuity of adaptation in the second year: The relationship between quality of attachment and later competence. *Child Development, 49,* 547–556.

Matheny, A. P., & Dolan, A. B. (1975). Persons, situations, and time: A genetic view of behavioral change in children. *Journal of Personality and Social Psychology, 14,* 224–234.

Matheny, A. P., Wilson, R. S., Dolan, A. B., & Krantz, J. Z. (1981). Behavior contrasts in twinships: Stability and patterns of differences in childhood. *Child Development, 52,* 579–588.

Mathews, A. (1993). Biases in emotional processing. *The Psychologist: Bulletin of the British Psychological Society, 6,* 493–499.

Mathews, A., & Klug, F. (1993). Emotionality and interference with color-naming in anxiety. *Behavior Research and Therapy, 29,* 147–160.

Mathews, A. M., Gelder, M. G., & Johnson, D. W. (1981). *Agoraphobia: Nature and treatment.* London: Tavistock.

Matsumoto, D., Kudoh, T., Scherer, K., & Wallbott, H. (1988). Antecedents of and reactions to emotions in the United States and Japan. *Journal of Cross Cultural Psychology, 19,* 267–286.

Maynard-Smith, J. (1984). *Evolution and the theory of games.* Cambridge: Cambridge University Press.

Maziade, M., Cote, R., Thivierge, J., Boutin, P., & Thivierge, J. (1990). Significance of extreme temperament in infancy for clinical status in preschool years. II Patterns of temperament change and implications for the appearance of disorders. *British Journal of Psychiatry, 154,* 544–551.

McCrea, R. R. (1992). The five factor model: issues and applications. *Journal of Personality and Social Psychology (Special issue), 60* (2).

McGee, R., Feehan, M., Williams, S., Partridge, F., Silva, P. A., & Kelly, J. (1990). DSM-III disorders in a large sample of adolescents. *Journal of the American Academy of Child and Adolescent Psychiatry, 29,* 611–619.

McGoldrick, M., Anderson, C. M., & Walsh, F. (1991). *Women in families: A framework for family therapy.* New York: Norton.

McNally, R. J., Kaspi, S. P., Riemann, B. C., & Zeitlin, S. B. (1990). Selective processing of threat cues in posttraumatic stress disorder. *Journal of Abnormal Psychology, 99,* 398–402.

Mechanic, D. (1982). *Symptoms, illness behavior, and help seeking.* New Brunswick, NJ: Rutgers University Press.

Melzoff, A. N. (1993). The centrality of motor coordination and proprioception in social and cognitive development. In G. J. P. Savelsbergh (Ed.), *The development of coordination in infancy* (pp. 463–496). Amsterdam: Elsevier.

Mesquita, B., & Frijda, N. (1992). Cultural variations in emotions: A review. *Psychological Bulletin, 112,* 179–204.

Metalsky, G. L., Joiner, T. E., Hardin, T. S., & Abramson, L. Y. (1993). Depressive reactions for failure in a naturalistic setting: A test of the the hopelessness and self-esteem theories of depression. *Journal of Abnormal Psychology, 102,* 101–109.

Miklowitz, D. J., Goldstein, M. J., Nuechterlein, K. H., Snyder, K. S., & Mintz, J. (1988). Family factors and the course of bipolar affective disorder. *Archives of General Psychiatry, 45,* 225–231.

Miller, G. A., Galanter, E., & Pribram, K. H. (1960). *Plans and the structure of behavior.* New York: Holt, Rinehart and Winston.

Miller, I. W., Keitner, G. I., Whisman, M. A., Ryan, C. E., Epstein, N. B., & Bishop, D. S. (1992). Depressed patients with dysfunctional families: Description and course of illness. *Journal of Abnormal Psychology. 101,* 637–646.

Miller, W. L. (1994). The politics of emotion display in heroic society. In N. Frijda (Ed.), Proceedings of the 8th conference of the International Society for Research on Emotions. Cambridge, 14–17 July. Storrs, CT: ISRE Publications (pp. 43–46).

Minde, K., Goldberg, S., Perrotta, M., Washington, J., Lojkasek, M., Corter, C., & Parker, K. (1989). Continuities and discontinuities in the development of 64 very small premature infants to 4 years of age. *Journal of Child Psychology and Psychiatry, 30,* 391–404.

Mineka, S., & Cook, M. (1993). Mechanisms involved in the observational conditioning of fear. *Journal of Experimental Psychology: General, 122,* 24–38.

Minuchin, S., Rosman, B. L., & Baker, L. (1978). *Psychosomatic families: Anorexia nervosa in context.* Cambridge, MA: Harvard University Press.

Mischel, W. (1968). *Personality and assessment.* New York: Wiley.

Mitchell, S. A. (1988). *Relational concepts in psychoanalysis.* Cambridge, MA: Harvard University Press.

Miyake, K., Campos, J., Kagan, J., & Bradshaw, D. L. (1986). Issues in socioemotional development. In H. Stevenson, H. Azuma, & K. Hakuta (Eds.), *Child development and education in Japan* (pp. 239–261). New York: Freeman.

Miyake, K., Chen, S.-J., & Campos, J. J. (1985). Infant temperament, mother's mode of interaction, and attachment in Japan: An interim report. In I. Bretherton & E. Waters (Eds.), *Growing points of attachment theory and research. Monographs of the Society for Research in Child Development, 50* (1–2, Serial No. 209), pp. 276–297.

Monroe, S. M., & Wade, S. L. (1988). Life events. In C. G. Last & M. Hersen (Eds.), *Handbook of anxiety disorders* (pp. 293–305). New York: Pergamon Press.

Montepare, J. M., Goldstein, S. B., & Clausen, A. (1987). The identification of emotions from gait information. *Journal of Nonverbal Behavior, 11,* 33–42.

Moreno, J. L. (1940). Mental catharsis and the psychodrama. *Sociometry, 1,* 1209–244.

Morris, D., Collett, P., Marsh, P., & O'Shaughnessy, M. (1979). *Gestures: Their origin and distribution.* London: Cape.

Morsbach, H., & Tyler, W. J. (1986). A Japanese emotion: *Amae.* In R. Harré (Ed.), *The social construction of emotions* (pp. 289–307). Oxford: Blackwell.

Murphy, E. (1982). Social origins of depression in old age. *British Journal of Psychiatry, 141,* 135–142.

Nance, J. (1975). *The gentle Tasaday.* New York: Harcourt Brace Jovanovich.

Neisser, U. (1988). Five kinds of self-knowledge. *Philosophical Psychology, 1,* 135–59.

Neisser, U., & Harsch, N. (1992). Phantom flashbulbs: False recollections of hearing the news about Challenger. In E. Winograd & U. Neisser (Eds.), *Affect and accuracy in recall: Studies of "flashbulb memories"* (pp. 9–31). Cambridge: Cambridge University Press.

Nelson, C. A. (1987). The recognition of facial expression in the first two years of life: Mechanisms of development. *Child Development, 58,* 889–909.

Nesse, R. M. (1990). Evolutionary explanations of emotions. *Human Nature, 1,* 261–283.

Nesse, R. M. (1991, November/December). What good is feeling bad? The evolutionary benefits of psychic pain. *The Sciences,* 30–37.

Neu, J. (1977). *Emotion, thought and therapy.* London: Routledge & Kegan Paul.

Neu, J. (1987). "A tear is an intellectual thing." *Representations, 19,* 35–61.

Niedenthal, P. M., & Setterlund, M. B. (1994). Emotion congruence in perception. *Personality and Social Psychology Bulletin, 20,* 401–411.

Nishida, T., Hasegawa, T., Hayaki, H., Takahata, Y., & Uehara, S. (1992). Meat-sharing as a coalition strategy by an alpha male chimpanzee. In T. Nishida, W. C. McGrew, P. Marler, M. Pickford, & F. B. M. de Waal (Eds.), *Topics in primatology, Vol 1. Human origins* (pp. 159–174). Tokyo: University of Tokyo Press.

Nolen-Hoeksema, S., & Morrow, J. (1991). A prospective study of depression and post traumatic stress symptoms after a natural disaster: The 1989 Loma Prieta earthquake. *Journal of Personality and Social Psychology, 61,* 115–121.

Nolen-Hoeksema, S., Morrow, J., & Fredrickson, B. J. (1993). Response styles and the duration of episodes of depressed mood. *Journal of Abnormal Psychology, 102,* 20–28.

Nolen-Hoeksema, S., Parker, L. E., & Larson, J. (1994). Ruminative coping with depressed mood following loss. *Journal of Personality and Social Psychology, 67,* 92–104.

Nowlis, V., & Nowlis, H. H. (1956). The description and analysis of mood. *Annals of the New York Academy of Sciences, 65,* 345–355.

Nussbaum, M. C. (1986). *The fragility of goodness: Luck and ethics in Greek tragedy and philosophy.* Cambridge: Cambridge University Press.

Oatley, K. (1992). *Best laid schemes: The psychology of emotions.* New York: Cambridge University Press.

Oatley, K. (1994). A taxonomy of the emotions of literary response and a theory of identification in fictional narrative. *Poetics, 23,* 53–74.

Oatley, K., & Bolton, W. (1985). A social-cognitive theory of depression in reaction to life events. *Psychological Review, 92,* 372–388.

Oatley, K., & Duncan, E. (1992). Incidents of emotion in daily life. In K. T. Strongman (Ed.), *International review of studies on emotion* (pp. 250–293). Chichester: Wiley.

Oatley, K., & Jenkins, J. M. (1992). Human emotions: Function and dysfunction. *Annual Review of Psychology, 43*, 55–85.

Oatley, K., & Johnson-Laird, P. N. (1987). Towards a cognitive theory of emotions. *Cognition and Emotion, 1*, 29–50.

Oatley, K., & Johnson-Laird, P. N. (1995). The communicative theory of emotions: Empirical tests, mental models, and implications for social interaction. In L. L. Martin & A. Tesser (Eds.), *Goals and affect*. Hillsdale, NJ: Erlbaum.

Oatley, K., & Perring, C. (1991). A longitudinal study of psychological and social factors affecting recovery from psychiatric breakdown. *British Journal of Psychiatry, 158*, 28–32.

Offord, D. R., Boyle, M. H., & Racine, Y. (1989). Ontario child health study: Correlates of disorder. *Journal of the American Academy of Child and Adolescent Psychiatry, 28*, 856–860.

Offord, D. R., Boyle, M. H., Racine, Y. A., Fleming, J. E., Cadman, D. T., Munroe Blum, H., Byrne, C., Links, P. S., Lipman, E. L., MacMillan, H. L., Rae-Grant, N. I., Sanford, M. N., Szatmari, P., Thomas, H., & Woodward, C. A. (1992). Outcome, prognosis and risk in a longitudinal follow-up study. *Journal of the American Academy of Child and Adolescent Psychiatry, 31*, 916–923.

Offord, D. R., Boyle, M. H., Szatmari, P., Rae-Grant, N. I., Links, P. S., Cadman, D. T., Byles, J. A., Crawford, J. W., Munroe Blum, H., Byrne, C., Thomas, H., & Woodward, C. A. (1987). Ontario Child Health Study: II. Six-month prevalence of disorder and rates of service utilization. *Archives of General Psychiatry, 44*, 832–836.

Ofshe, R., & Watters, E. (1994). *Making monsters: False memories, psychotherapy, and sexual hysteria*. New York: Scribners.

Öhman, A. (1986). Face the beast and fear the face: Animal and social fears as prototypes for evolutionary analyses of emotion. *Psychophysiology, 23*, 123–145.

Olds, J. (1955). Physiological mechanisms of reward. In M. R. Jones (Ed.), *Nebraska symposium on motivation* (pp. 73–134). Lincoln, NE: University of Nebraska Press.

Olds, J. (1956, October). Pleasure centers in the brain. *Scientific American*, pp. 105–116.

Olds, J., & Milner, P. (1954). Positive reinforcement produced by electrical stimulation of septal area and other regions of rat brain. *Journal of Comparative and Physiological Psychology, 47*, 419–427.

O'Leary, A. (1990). Stress, emotion, and human immune function. *Psychological Bulletin, 108*, 363–382.

Olson, D. R. (1994). *The world on paper*. New York: Cambridge University Press.

Oltmanns, T. F., & Emery, R. E. (1995). *Abnormal psychology*. Englewood Cliffs, NJ: Prentice-Hall.

Olweus, D. (1979). Stability of aggressive reaction patterns in males: A review. *Psychological Bulletin, 86*, 852–875.

Olweus, D. (1980). Familial and temperamental determinants of aggressive behavior in adolescent boys: A causal analysis. *Developmental Psychology, 16*, 644–660.

Onstad, S., Syre, I., Torgenson, S., & Kringlen, E. (1991). Twin concordance for DSM-III-R schizophrenia. *Acta Psychiatrica Scandinavica, 83*, 395–401.

Oppenheim, D., Sagi, A., & Lamb, M. E. (1988). Infant–adult attachments on the Kibbutz and their relation to socioemotional development 4 years later. *Developmental Psychology, 24*, 427–433.

Orlinsky, D. E., & Howard, K. I. (1980). Gender and psychotherapeutic outcome. In A. M. Brodsky & R. T. Hare-Martin (Eds.), *Women and psychotherapy* (pp. 3–34). New York: Guilford.

Ortony, A., & Turner, T. J. (1990). What's basic about basic emotions? *Psychological Review, 74*, 431–461.

Osgood, C. E., May, W. H., & Miron, M. S. (1975). *Cross-cultural universals of affective meaning*. Urbana, IL: Illinois University Press.

Oster, H., Hegley, D., & Nagel, L. (1992). Adult judgments and fine-grained analysis of infant facial expressions: testing the validity of a priori coding formulas. *Developmental Psychology, 28*, 1115–1131.

Oster, H., & Rosenstein, D. (in press). *Baby FACS: Analyzing facial movements in infants*. Palo Alto, CA: Consulting Psychologists Press.

Ozer, D. J., & Reise, S. P. (1994). Personality assessment. *Annual Review of Psychology, 45* 357–388.

Panksepp, J. (1993). Neurochemical control of moods and emotions: Amino acids to neuropeptides. In M. Lewis & J. M. Haviland (Eds.) *Handbook of emotions* (pp. 87–107). New York: Guilford.

Panksepp, J., Newman, J. D., & Insel, T. R. (1992). Critical conceptual issues in the analysis of separation-distress systems of the brain. In K. T. Strongman (Ed.), *International review of studies on emotion* (Vol. 2, pp. 51–72). Chichester: Wiley.

Papez, J. W. (1937). A proposed mechanism of emotion. *Archives of Neurology and Psychiatry, 38*, 725–743.

Papousek, H., Jürgens, U., & Papousek, M. (Eds.). (1992). *Non-vocal communication: Comparative and developmental approaches*. New York: Cambridge University Press.

Parrott, W. G. (1993). Beyond hedonism: Motives for inhibiting good moods and for maintaining bad moods. In D. M. Wegner & J. W. Pennebaker (Eds.), *Handbook of mental control* (pp. 278–305). Englewood Cliffs, NJ: Prentice-Hall.

Parrott, W. G., & Sabini, J. (1990). Mood and memory under natural conditions: Evidence for mood incongruent recall. *Journal of Personality and Social Psychology, 59*, 321–336.

Parry, G., & Shapiro, D. A. (1986). Social support and life events in working-class women. *Archives of General Psychiatry, 43*, 315–323.

Pascal, B. (1670). *Pensées* (L. Lafuma, Ed., J. Warrington, Trans.). London: Everyman Library (current edition 1960).

Patterson, G. R. (1982). *Coercive family process*. Eugene, OR: Castalia.

Patterson, G. R. (1985). A microsocial analysis of anger and irritable behavior. In M. A. Chesney & R. H. Rosenman (Eds.), *Anger and hostility in cardiovascular and behavioral disorders*. Washington: Hemisphere Publishing Corporation.

Patterson, G. R. (1986). Performance models for antisocial boys. *American Psychologist, 41*, 432–444.

Patterson, G. R., Capaldi, D., & Bank, L. (1991). The early starter model for predicting delinquency. In D. J. Pepler & K. H. Rubin (Eds.), *The development and treatment of childhood aggression*. Hillsdale, NJ: Erlbaum

Paulhan, F. (1887). *The laws of feeling*. London: Kegan-Paul, French, Trubner & Co. (current edition 1930).

Pavlov, I. P. (1927). *Conditioned reflexes* (G.V. Anrep, Trans.). New York: Dover (current edition 1960).

Paykel, E. S., Emms, E. M., Fletcher, J., & Rassaby, E. S. (1980). Life events and social support in puerperal depression. *British Journal of Psychiatry, 136*, 339–346.

Pennebaker, J. W. (1989). Confession, inhibition, and disease. In L. Berkowitz (Ed.), *Advances in experimental social psychology* (Vol. 22, pp. 211–244). San Diego: Academic Press.

Pennebaker, J. W., Kiecolt-Glaser, J. K., & Glaser, R. (1988). Disclosure of traumas and immune function: Health implications of psychotherapy. *Journal of Consulting and Clinical Psychology, 56*, 239–245.

Perls, F., Hefferline, R. F., & Goodman, P. (1951). *Gestalt therapy*. New York: Julian Press.

Perrow, C. (1984). *Normal accidents: Living with high-risk technologies*. New York: Basic Books.

Peters-Martin, P., & Wachs, T. (1984). A longitudinal study of temperament and its correlates in the first 12 months. *Infant behavior and development, 7*, 285–298.

Peterson, G., Mehl, L., & Leiderman, H. (1979). The role of some birth related variables in father attachment. *American Journal of Orthopsychiatry, 40*, 330–338.

Pettit, G. S., & Bates, J. E. (1989). Family interaction patterns and children's behavior problems from infancy to 4 years. *Developmental Psychology, 25*, 413–420.

Petty, R., & Cacioppo, J. (1986). The elaboration likelihood model of persuasion. In L. Berkowitz (Ed.), *Advances in experimental social psychology* (Vol. 19, pp. 124–205). New York: Academic Press.

Pilowsky, I., & Katsikitis, M. (1994). The classification of facial emotions: A computer based taxonomic approach. *Journal of Affective Disorders, 30*, 61–71.

Pinney, T. (Ed.) (1963). *Essays of George Eliot*. New York: Columbia University Press.

Pittam, J., & Scherer, K. R. (1993). Vocal expression and communication of emotion. In M. Lewis & J. M. Haviland (Eds.), *Handbook of emotions* (pp. 185–197). New York: Guilford.

Planalp, S., DeFrancisco, V. L., & Rutherford, D. (in press). Varieties of cues to emotion. *Cognition and Emotion*.

Plato (375 BCE). *The republic*. Harmondsworth, Middlesex: Penguin (current edition 1955).

Plomin, R. (1988). *Development, genetics and psychology*. Hillsdale, NJ: Erlbaum.

Plomin, R., & Bergeman, C. S. (1991). The nature of nurture: Genetic influence on environmental measures. *Behvioral and Brain Sciences, 14*, 373–427.

Plomin, R., Chipuer, H. M., & Loelin, J. C. (1990). Behavioral genetics and personality. In L. A. Pervin (Ed.), *Handbook of personality* (pp. 225–243). New York: Guilford.

Plomin, R., Lichtenstein, P., Pedersen, N., McClearn, G. E., & Nesselroade, J. R. (1990). Genetic influences on life events during the last half of the life span. *Psychology of Aging, 5*, 25–30.

Plutchik, R. (1991). Emotions and evolution. In K. T. Strongman (Ed.), *International review of studies on emotion* (Vol 1, pp. 37–58). Chichester: Wiley.

Polanyi, M. (1966). *The implicit dimension*. Garden City, NJ: Doubleday.

Polya, G. (1957). *How to solve it: A new aspect of mathematical method* (2nd ed.). Garden City: NY Doubleday.

Popper, K. R. (1962a). *Conjectures and refutations*. New York, NY: Basic Books.

Popper, K. R. (1962b). *The open society and its enemies* (Vol. 2, 4th ed.). London: Routledge & Kegan Paul.

Prior, M., Smart, D., Sanson, A., & Oberklaid, F. (1993). Sex differences and psychological adjustment from infancy to eight years. *Journal of the American Academy of Child and Adolescent Psychiatry, 32,* 291–304.

Proust, M. (1913–1927). *A la recherche du temps perdu* [Remembrance of things past] (C. K. Scott-Moncreiff, T. Kilmartin, & A. Mayor, Trans.). London: Chatto & Windus (current edition 1981).

Purkis, J. (1985). *A preface to George Eliot.* London: Longman.

Putnam, H. (1975). The meaning of meaning. In K. Gunderson (Ed.), *Language, mind and knowledge. Minnesota studies in the philosophy of science* (Vol. 7). Minneapolis, MN: University of Minnesota Press.

Pynoos, R. S., & Nader, K. (1989). Children's memory and proximity to violence. *Journal of the American Academy of Child and Adolescent Psychiatry, 28,* 236–241.

Pyszczynski, T., & Greenberg, J. (1987). Self-regulatory perseveration and the depressive self-focusing style: A self-awareness theory of reactive depression. *Psychological Bulletin, 102,* 122–138.

Quiggle, N. L., Garber, J., Panak, W. F., & Dodge, K. A. (1992). Social information processing in aggressive and depressed children. *Child Development, 63,* 1305–1320.

Quintillian (circa 90). *Institutio Oratoria, VI, in* Loeb Classical Library: Quintillian, II. Cambridge, MA: Harvard University Press.

Quinton, D., & Rutter, M. (1988). *Parenting breakdown: The making and breaking of inter-generational links.* Aldershot: Avebury.

Quinton, D., Rutter, M., & Liddle, C. (1984). Institutional rearing, parental difficulties, and marital support. *Psychological Medicine, 14,* 107–124.

Quinton, D., Rutter, M., & Gulliver, L. (1990). Continuities in psychiatric disorders from childhood to adulthood in children of psychiatric patients. In L. Robins & M. Rutter (Eds.), *Straight and devious pathways from childhood to adulthood* (pp. 259–278). Cambridge: Cambridge University Press.

Radke-Yarrow, M., Cummings, E. M., Kuczynski, L., & Chapman, M. (1985). Patterns of attachment in two and three-year-olds in normal families and families with parental depression. *Child Development, 56,* 884–893.

Radke-Yarrow, M., Richters, J., & Wilson, W. E. (1988). Child development in a network of relationships. In R. A. Hinde & J. Stevenson-Hinde (Eds.), *Relationships within families* (pp. 48–67). Oxford: Clarendon Press.

Rahe, R. H. (1972). Subjects' recent life changes and their near-future illness reports. *Annals of Clinical Research, 4,* 250–265.

Raleigh, M. J., McGuire, M. T., Brammer, G. L., Pollack, D. B., & Yuwiler, A. (1991). Serotonergic mechanisms promote dominance acquisition in adult male vervet monkeys. *Brain Research, 559,* 181–190.

Ramirez, A. J. (1988). Life events and cancer: Conceptual and methodological issues. In M. Watson, S. Greer, & C. Thomas (Eds.), *Psychosocial oncology.* Oxford: Pergamon.

Reiman, E. M., Fusselman, M. J., Fox, P. T., & Raichle, M. E. (1989). Neuroanatomical correlates of anticipatory anxiety. *Science, 243,* 1071–1074.

Reisenzein, R. (1983). The Schachter theory of emotion: Two decades later. *Psychological Bulletin, 94,* 239–264.

Reisenzein, R. (1992a). A structuralist reconstruction of Wundt's three-dimensional theory of emotion. In H. Westmeyer (Ed.), *The structuralist program in psychology: foundations and applications* (pp. 141–189). Toronto: Hopgrefe & Huber.

Reisenzein, R. (1992b). Stumpf's cognitive-evaluative theory of emotion. *American Psychologist, 47*, 34–45.

Rende, R. D. (1993). Longitudinal relations between temperament traits and behavioral syndromes in middle childhood. *Journal of the American Academy of Child and Adolesent Psychiatry, 32*, 287–290.

Rheingold, H. R., & Eckerman, C. O. (1970). The infant separates himself from his mother. *Science, 168*, 78–90.

Richards, I. A. (1925). *Principles of literary criticism.* New York: Harcourt Brace Jovanovich.

Richards, M. P. M., & Bernal, J. (1972). An observational study of mother–infant interaction. In N. Blurton-Jones (Ed.), *Ethological studies of child behavior.* New York: Cambridge University Press.

Richman, N., Stevenson, J., & Graham, P. J. (1982). *Preschool to school.* London: Academic Press.

Richters, J. E., & Martinez, P. (1993). The NIMH Community Violence Project: I. Children as victims and witnesses of violence. *Psychiatry: Interpersonal and Biological Processes, 56*, 7–21.

Riley, V. (1981). Psychoneuroendocrine influences on immunocompetence and neoplasia. *Science, 212*, 1100–1109.

Rimé, B., Mesquita, B., Philippot, P., & Boca, S. (1991). Beyond the emotional event: Six studies on the social sharing of emotions. *Cognition and Emotion, 5*, 435–465.

Rimé, B., Philippot, P., & Cisamolo, D. (1990). Social schemata of peripheral changes in emotion. *Journal of Personality and Social Psychology, 59*, 38–49.

Roberts, R. E. (1981). Sex differences in depression reexamined. *Journal of Health and Social Behavior, 22*, 394–400.

Roberts, W., & Strayer, J. (1987). Parent responses to the emotional distress of their children: Relations with children's competence. *Developmental Psychology, 23*, 415–425.

Robertson, D. W. (1972). The concept of courtly love as an impediment to the understanding of medieval texts. In F. X. Newman (Ed.), *The meaning of courtly love* (pp. 1–18). Albany: State University of New York Press.

Robins, L. N. (1978). Sturdy childhood predictors of adult antisocial behavior: Replications from longitudinal studies. *Psychological Medicine, 8*, 611–622.

Robins, L. N. (1986). The consequence of conduct disorder in girls. In D. Olweus, J. Vkicj, & M. Radke–Yarrow (Eds.), *Development of antisocial and prosocial behavior* (pp. 385–414). Orlando, FL: Academic Press.

Robins, L. N., & Regier, D. A. (1991). *Psychiatric disorders in America: The epidemiologic catchment area study.* New York: Free Press.

Robinson, L. A., Berman, J. S., & Neimeyer, R. A. (1990). Psychotherapy for the treatment of depression: A comprehensive review of controlled outcome studies. *Psychological Bulletin, 108*, 30–49.

Rogers, C. R. (1951). *Client-centered therapy.* Boston: Houghton Mifflin.

Roseman, I. J. (1991). Appraisal determinants of discrete emotions. *Cognition and Emotion, 5*, 161–200.

Rosenbaum, J. F., Biederman, J., & Gersten, M., et al. (1988). Behavioral inhibition in children with parents with panic disorder and agoraphobia. *Archives of General Psychiatry, 45*, 463–470.

Rosenberg, D., & Bloom, H. (1990). *The book of J.* New York: Grove Weidenfeld.

Rosenberg, E. L., & Ekman, P. (1994). Coherence between expressive and experiential systems in emotion. *Cognition and Emotion, 8,* 201–229.

Rosenman, R. H., Brand, R. J., Jenkins, C. D., Friedman, M., Straus, R., & Wurm, M. (1975). Coronary heart disease in the Western collaborative group study. *Journal of the American Medical Association, 233,* 872–877.

Ross, E. D. (1984). Right hemisphere's role in language, affective behavior, and emotion. *Trends in Neuroscience, 7,* 342–346.

Rothbart, M. K. (1981). Measurement of temperament in infancy. *Child Development, 52,* 569–578.

Rothbart, M. K. (1986). Longitudinal observation of infant temperament. *Developmental Psychology, 22,* 356–365.

Rothbart, M. K., Ziaie, H., & O'Boyle, C. G. (1992). Self regulation and emotion in infancy. In N. Eisenberg & R. A. Fabes (Eds.), *Emotion and its regulation in early development. (New Directions in Child Development, No. 55)* (pp. 7–24). San Francisco: Jossey-Bass.

Rousseau, J-J. (1755). Discourse on the origin and basis of inequality among men. In *The essential Rousseau* (pp. 125–201). New York: Penguin (current edition 1975).

Rousseau, J.-J. (1762). The social contract, or principles of political right. In *The essential Rousseau* (pp. 1–124). New York: Penguin.

Rozin, P., & Fallon, A. E. (1987). A perspective on disgust. *Psychological Review, 94,* 23–41.

Rozin, P., Haidt, J., & McCauley, C. R. (1993). Disgust. In M. Lewis & J. M. Haviland (Eds.), *Handbook of emotions* (pp. 575–594). New York: Guilford.

Rubin, K. H. (1993). The Waterloo longitudinal project: Correlates and consequences of social withdrawal from childhood to adolescence. In K. H. Rubin & J. Asendorpf (Eds.), *Social withdrawal, inhibition and shyness in childhood* (pp. 291–314). Hillsdale, NJ: Erlbaum.

Ruckmick, C. A. (1936). *The psychology of feeling and emotion.* New York: McGraw-Hill.

Russell, J. A. (1978). Evidence of convergent validity on the dimensions of affect. *Journal of Personality and Social Psychology, 36,* 1152–1168.

Russell, J. A. (1980). A circumplex model of affect. *Journal of Personality and Social Psychology, 39,* 1161–1178.

Russell, J. A. (1991a). Culture and categorization of emotions. *Psychological Bulletin, 110,* 426–450.

Russell, J. A. (1991b). In defense of a prototype approach to emotion concepts. *Journal of Personality and Social Psychology, 60,* 37–47.

Russell, J. A. (1994). Is there universal recognition of emotion from facial expression? A review of methods and studies. *Psychological Bulletin, 115,* 102–141.

Russell, J. A. (in press). What does a facial expression mean? In J. A. Russell & J. M. Fernandez-Dols (Eds.), *The psychology of facial expression.* New York: Cambridge University Press.

Rutter, M. (1979). Protective factors in children's responses to stress and disadvantage. In M. W. Kent & J. E. Rolf (Eds.), *Primary prevention in psychopathology, Vol. 3. Social competence in children* (pp. 49–74). Hanover, NH: University Press of New England.

Rutter, M. (1992). Psychosocial resilience and protective mechanisms. In J. E. Rolf, D. Masten, D. Cicchetti, K. Nuechterlein, & S. Wientraub (Eds.), *Risk and protective factors in the development of psychopathology.* New York: Cambridge University Press.

Rutter, M., & Giller, H. (1983). *Juvenile delinquency: Trends and perspectives.* Harmondsworth: Penguin.

Rutter, M., Graham, P., Chadwick, O., & Yule, W. (1976). Adolescent turmoil: Fact or fiction? *Journal of Child Psychology and Psychiatry, 17,* 35–56.

Rutter, M., Macdonald, H., Le Couteur, A., Harrington, R., Bolton, P., & Bailey, A. (1990). Genetic factors in child psychiatric disorders: II. Empirical findings. *Journal of Child Psychology and Psychiatry, 31,* 39–84.

Rutter, M., Maughan, B., Mortimore, P., & Ouston, J. (1979). *Fifteen thousand hours: Secondary schools and their effects on children.* London: Open Books.

Rutter, M., & Rutter, Marjorie (1992) *Developing minds: Challenge and continuity across the life span.* Harmondsworth: Penguin.

Rutter, M., Taylor, E., & Hersov, L. (Eds.). (1994). *Child and adolescent psychiatry: Modern approaches* (3rd ed.). Oxford: Blackwell.

Rutter, M., Tizard, J., & Whitmore, K. (1970). *Education, health and behavior.* London: Longmans.

Rutter, M., Tuma, A. H., & Lann, I. S. (1988). *Assessment and diagnosis in child psychopathology.* London: David Fulton.

Rutter, M., Yule, B., Quinton, D., Rowlands, O., Yule, W., & Berger, M. (1975). Attainment and adjustment in two geographical areas: III. Some factors accounting for area differences. *British Journal of Psychiatry, 126,* 520–533.

Saarni, C. (1984). An observational study of children's attempts to monitor their expressive behavior. *Child Development, 55, 1504–1513.*

Sacks, O. (1973). *Awakenings.* London: Duckworth.

Sagi, A., Lamb, M. E., Lewkowicz, K. S., Shoham, R., Dvir, R., & Estes, D. (1985). Security of infant–mother, father, and metapelet attachments among kibbutz-reared Israeli children. *Monographs of the Society for Research in Child Development. 50* (1–2, Serial No. 209), 257–276.

Salaman, E. (1982). A collection of moments. In U. Neisser (Ed.), *Memory observed: Remembering in natural contexts* (pp. 49–63). San Francisco: Freeman.

Salovey, P. (1991). *The psychology of jealousy and envy.* New York: Guilford.

Sapolsky, R. M. (1993). The physiology of dominance in stable and unstable social hierarchies. In W. A. Mason & S. P. Mendoza (Eds.), *Primate social conflict* (pp. 171–204). Albany, NY: State University of New York Press.

Sarason, B. R., Shearin, E. N., Pierce, G. R., & Sarason, G. R. (1987). Interrelations of social support measures: Theoretical and practical implications. *Journal of Personality and Social Psychology, 52,* 813–832.

Savage-Rumbaugh, E. S., Murphy, J., Sevcik, R. A., Brakke, K. E., Williams, S. L., & Rumbaugh, D. M. (1993). Language comprehension in ape and child. *Monographs of the Society for Research in Child Development, 58* (3–4, Serial No. 233).

Scarr, S., & Salapatek, P. (1970). Patterns of fear development during infancy. *Merrill-Palmer Quarterly, 16,* 53–90.

Schachter, S., & Singer, J. (1962). Cognitive, social and physiological determinants of emotional state. *Psychological Review, 69,* 379–399.

Schank, R., & Abelson, R. (1977). *Scripts, plans, goals and understanding: An inquiry into human knowledge structures.* Hillsdale, NJ: Erlbaum.

Scheff, T. J. (1979). *Catharsis in healing, ritual, and drama.* Berkeley: University of California Press.

Scheff, T. J. (1990). *Microsociology: Discourse, emotion, and social structure.* Chicago: University of Chicago Press.

Scherer, K. R. (1993). Studying the emotion-antecedent appraisal process: An expert system approach. *Cognition and Emotion, 7,* 325–355.

Schiff, B. B., & Lamon, M. (1989). Inducing emotion by unilateral contraction of facial muscles: A new look at hemispheric specialization and the experience of emotion. *Neuropsychologia, 27,* 923–935.

Schiff, B. B., & Lamon, M. (1994). Inducing emotion by unilateral contraction of hand muscles. *Cortex, 30,* 247–254.

Schwartz, N., & Clore, G. L. (1988). How do I feel about it? The informative function of affective states. In K. Fiedler & J. P. Forgas (Eds.), *Affect, cognition, and social behavior* (pp. 44–62). Toronto: Hogrefe.

Sebeok, T. A., & Umiker–Sebeok, J. (1983). "You know my method": A juxtaposition of Charles S. Peirce and Sherlock Holmes. In U. Eco & T. A. Sebeok (Eds.), *The sign of three: Dupin, Holmes, Peirce* (pp. 11–54). Bloomington: Indiana University Press.

Selye, H. (1936). A syndrome produced by diverse nocuous agents. *Nature, 138,* 32.

Seth, V. (1993). *A suitable boy.* Boston: Little, Brown.

Shaffer, J. B. P., & Galinsky, M. D. (1974). *Models of group therapy and sensitivity training.* Englewood Cliffs, NJ: Prentice Hall.

Shakespeare, W. (1600). *Hamlet.* London: Methuen (current edition 1981).

Shakespeare, W. (1623). As you like it. In A. Harbage (Ed.), *The complete Pelican Shakespeare: Comedies and romances* (pp. 200–229). Harmondsworth: Penguin (current edition 1969).

Shaver, P., Hazan, C., & Bradshaw, D. (1988). Love as attachment: The integration of three behavioral systems. In R. J. Sternberg & M. L. Barnes (Eds.), *The psychology of love* (pp. 68–99). New Haven, CT: Yale University Press.

Shaver, P. R., Wu, S., & Schwartz, J. C. (1992). Cross-cultural similarities and differences in emotion and its representation. In M. S. Clark (Ed.), *Review of Personality and Social Psychology, Vol. 13. Emotion* (pp. 175–212). Newbury Park, CA: Sage.

Shekelle, R. B., Gale, M., & Ostfield, A. (1983). Hostility, risk of coronary heart disease, and mortality. *Psychosomatic Medicine, 45,* 109–114.

Shelley, M. (1818). *Frankenstein, or modern Prometheus.* Harmondsworth: Penguin (current edition 1985).

Sherif, M. (1956, November). Experiments in group conflict. *Scientific American, 195* 54–58.

Sherif, M., & Sherif, C. W. (1953). *Groups in harmony and in tension.* New York: Harper & Row.

Shields, S. A. (1991). Gender in the psychology of emotion: A selective research review. In K. T. Strongman (Ed.), *International Review of Studies in Emotion* (Vol. 1, pp. 227–245). Chichester, Wiley.

Shimanoff, S. B. (1984). Commonly named emotions in everyday conversation. *Perceptual and Motor Skills, 58,* 114.

Shostak, M. (1981). *Nisa.* New York: Vintage.

Shrout, P. E., Link, B. G., Dohrenwend, B. P., Skodal, A. E., Stueve, A., & Mirtznik, J. (1989). Characterizing life events as risk factors for depression: The role of fateful loss events. *Journal of Abnormal Psychology, 98,* 460–467.

Shweder, R. (1990). In defense of moral realism: Reply to Gabannesch. *Child Development, 61,* 2060–2067.

Sibley, C., & Ahlquist, J. E. (1984). The phylogeny of the hominid primates, as indicated by DNA-RNA hybridization. *Journal of Molecular Evolution, 20,* 2–15.

Siegel, A., & Brutus, M. (1990). Neural substrates of aggression and rage in the cat. *Progress in Psychobiology and Physiological Psychology, 14,* 135–233.

Siegel, A., & Pott, C. B. (1988). Neural substrates of aggression and flight in the cat. *Progress in Neurobiology, 31,* 261–283.

Simon, H. A. (1967). Motivational and emotional controls of cognition. *Psychological Review, 74,* 29–39.

Simons, R. L., Whitbeck, L. B., Conger, R. D., & Chyi-In, W. (1991). Intergenerational transmission of harsh parenting. *Developmental Psychology, 27(1),* 159–171.

Singer, J. A., & Salovey, P. (1993). *The remembered self: Emotion and memory in personality.* New York: Free Press.

Singer, J. A., & Singer, J. L. (1992). Transference in psychotherapy and daily life: Implications of current memory and social cognition research. In J. W. Barron, M. N. Eagle, & D. L. Wolinsky (Eds.), *Interface of psychoanalysis and psychology* (pp. 516–538). Washington, DC: American Psychological Association.

Slaby, R. G., & Guerra, N. G. (1988). Cognitive mediators of aggression in adolescent offenders: 1. Assessment. *Developmental Psychology, 24,* 580–588.

Sloane, R. B., Staples, F. R., Cristol, A. H., Yorkston, N. J., & Whipple, K. (1975). *Psychotherapy versus behavior therapy.* Cambridge, MA: Harvard University Press.

Smith, A. (1759). *The theory of moral sentiments.* Oxford: Oxford University Press (1976).

Smith, H. P. R. (1967). Heart rate of pilots flying aircraft on scheduled airline routes. *Aerospace Medicine, 38,* 1117–1119.

Smith, M. L., Glass, G. V., & Miller, T. I. (1980). *The benefits of psychotherapy.* Baltimore, MD: Johns Hopkins University Press.

Smuts, B. B. (1985). *Sex and friendship in baboons.* New York: Aldine.

Snyder, J., & Patterson, G. R. (1986). The effects of consequences on patterns of social interaction: A quasi-experimental approach to reinforcement in natural interaction. *Child Development, 57,* 1257–1268.

Sogon, S., & Masutani, M. (1989). Identification of emotion from body movements. *Psychological Reports, 65,* 35–46.

Solomon, R. C. (1977). *The passions.* New York: Anchor.

Solomon, Z., & Bromet, E. (1982). The role of social factors in affective disorder: An assessment of the vulnerability model of Brown and his colleagues. *Psychological Medicine, 12,* 125–130.

Sorce, J. F., Emde, R. N., Campos, J., & Klinnert, M. D. (1985). Maternal emotional signaling: Its effect on the visual cliff behavior of 1-year-olds. *Developmental Psychiatry, 21,* 195–200.

Sorenson, E. R. (1975). Culture and the expression of emotion. In T. R. Williams (Ed.), *Psychological Anthropology* (pp. 361–372). Chicago: Aldine.

Sorenson, E. R. (1976). *The edge of the forest: Land, childhood and change in a New Guinea protoagricultural society.* Washington, DC: Smithsonian Institution Press.

Spangler, G., & Grossmann, K. E. (1993). Biobehavioral organization in securely and insecurely attached infants. *Child Development, 64,* 1439–1450.

Spiegel, D., Kramer, H. C., Bloom, J. R., & Gottheil, E. (1989). Effect of psychosocial treatment on survival of patients with metastatic breast cancer. *Lancet, 2* (8668) 888–890.

Spielberger, C. D., & Krasner, S. S. (1988). The assessment of state and trait anxiety. In R. Noyes, M. Roth, & G. D. Burrows (Eds.), *Handbook of anxiety, Vol. 2. Classification, etiological factors, and associated disturbances* (pp. 31–51). New York: Elsevier.

Spinoza, B. (1675). *The ethics* (R. H. M. Elwes, Trans.). New York: Dover (current edition 1955).

Spock, B. (1945). *The common sense book of baby and child care.* New York: Dell, Sloan & Pearce.

Sroufe, A. (1978). The ontogenesis of emotion. In J. Osofsky (Ed.), *Handbook of infancy* (pp. 462–516). New York: Wiley.

Sroufe, L., & Waters, E. (1976). The ontogenesis of smiling and laughter: A perspective on the organization of development in infancy. *Psychological Review, 83,* 173–189.

Sroufe, L. A., Schork, E., Motti, E., Lawroski, N., & LaFreniere, P. (1984). The role of affect in emerging social competence. In C. Izard, J. Kagan, & R. Zajonc (Eds.), *Emotion, cognition and behavior* (pp. 289–319). New York: Cambridge University Press.

Stanislavski, C. (1965). *An actor prepares* (E. R. Habgood, Trans.). New York: Theater Arts Books.

Starkstein, S. E., & Robinson, R. G. (1991). The role of the frontal lobes in affective disorder following stroke. In H. S. Levin, H. M. Eisenberg, & A. L. Benton (Eds.), *Frontal lobe function and dysfunction* (pp. 288–303). New York: Oxford University Press.

Stearns, C. Z. (1993). Sadness. In M. Lewis & J. M. Haviland (Eds.), *Handbook of emotions* (pp. 547–561). New York: Guilford.

Stearns, P. N., & Haggarty, T. (1991). The role of fear: Transitions in American emotional standards for children, 1850–1950. *The American Historical Review, 96,* 63–94.

Stein, N. L., Bernas, R. S., Calicchia, D. J., & Wright, A. (in press). Understanding and resolving arguments: The dynamics of negotiation. In B. Britton & A. G. Graesser (Eds.), *Models of understanding.* Hillsdale, NJ: Erlbaum.

Stein, N., Folkman, S., Trabasso, T., & Christopher-Richards, A. (1995). The role of appraisal processes in predicting psychological well-being. In *Roshomon Conference, Center for the Study of AIDS Prevention,* January 3 & 4.

Stein, N. L., & Levine, L. J. (1989). The causal organization of emotional knowledge. *Cognition and Emotion, 3,* 343–378.

Stein, N. L., Liwag, M., & Trabasso, T. (1995). Remembering the distant past: Understanding and remembering emotional events. Paper presented to the Biennial Meeting of the Society for Research In Child Development. Indianapolis, March 30–April 2.

Stein, N. L., & Oatley, K. (Eds.). (1992). *Basic emotions.* Hove: Erlbaum.

Stein, N. L., Trabasso, T., & Liwag, M. (1993). The representation and organization of emotional experience: Unfolding the emotion episode. In M. Lewis & J. M. Haviland (Eds.), *Handbook of emotions* (pp. 279–300). New York: Guilford.

Stein, N. L., Trabasso, T., & Liwag, M. (1994). The Rashomon phenomenon: Personal frames and future-oriented appraisals in memory for emotional events. In M. M.

Haith, J. B. Benson, R. J. Roberts, & B. F. Pennington (Eds.), *Future oriented processes*. Chicago: University of Chicago Press.

Steiner, J. E. (1979). Human facial expressions in response to taste and smell stimulation. In H. Reese & L. P. Lipsitt (Eds.), *Advances in child development and behavior* (pp. 257–293). New York: Academic.

Stemmler, D. G. (1989). The autonomic differentiation of emotions revisited: Convergent and discriminant validation. *Psychophysiology, 26*, 617–632.

Stenberg, C. R., & Campos, J. J. (1990). The development of anger expressions in infancy. In N. Stein, B. Leventhal, & T. Trabasso (Eds.), *Psychological and biological approaches to emotion* (pp. 247–282). Hillsdale, NJ: Lawrence Erlbaum.

Stern, D. (1985). *The interpersonal world of the infant*. New York: Basic Books.

Stern, D. (1994). One way to build a clinically relevant baby. *Infant Mental Health Journal, 15*, 9–25.

Sternberg, K. J., Lamb, M. E., Greenbaum, C., Cicchetti, D., Dawud, S., Cortes, R. M., Krispin, O., & Lorey, F. (1993). Effects of domestic violence on children's behavior problems and depression. *Developmental Psychology*, 44–52.

Sternberg, R. J., & Barnes, M. (1988). *The psychology of love*. New Haven, CT: Yale University Press.

Stevenson, R. L. (1886). *Dr Jekyll and Mr Hyde*. (Current edition 1979, Harmondsworth: Penguin).

Strachey, J. (1934). The nature of the therapeutic action in psychoanalysis. *International Journal of Psychoanalysis, 15*, 127–159.

Strack, F., Martin, L. L., & Stepper, S. (1988). Inhibiting and facilitating conditions of the human smile: A nonobtrusive test of the facial feedback hypothesis. *Journal of Personality and Social Psychology, 54*, 768–777.

Strauss, E., & Moscovitch, M. (1981). Perception of facial expressions. *Brain and Language, 13*, 308–332.

Strayer, F. F. (1980). Social ecology of the preschool peer group. In W. A. Collins (Ed.), *Development of cognition affect and social relations: Minnesota symposia in child development*. Hillsdale, NJ: Erlbaum.

Stringer, C., & Gamble, C. (1993). *In search of the Neanderthals*. New York: Thames and Hudson.

Stroebe, W., Stroebe, M. S., Gergen, K. J., & Gergen, M. (1982). The effects of bereavement on mortality: A social psychological analysis. In J. R. Eiser (Ed.), *Social psychology and behavioral medicine* (pp. 527–560). Chichester: Wiley.

Stroop, J. R. (1935). Studies of interference in serial verbal reactions. *Journal of Experimental Psychology, 18*, 643–662.

Stubbe, D. E., Zahner, G. E. P., Goldstein, M. J., & Leckman, J. F. (1993). Diagnostic specificity of a brief measure of expressed emotion: A community study of children. *Journal of Child Psychology and Psychiatry, 34*, 139–154.

Sturgeon, D., Turpin, D., Kuipers, L., Berkowitz, R., & Leff, J. (1984). Psychophysiological responses of schizophrenic patients to high and low Expressed Emotion relatives: A follow-up study. *British Journal of Psychiatry, 145*, 62–69.

Sullivan, M. W., Lewis, M., & Alessandri, S. M. (1992). Cross-age stability in emotional expressions during learning and extinction. *Developmental Psychology, 28*, 58–63.

Sulloway, F. J. (1979). *Freud, biologist of the mind: Beyond the psychoanalytic legend*. New York: Basic Books.

Suomi, S. J., & Harlow, H. F. (1972). Social rehabilitation of isolate reared monkeys. *Developmental Psychology, 6,* 487–496.

Svejda, M. J., Campos, J. J., & Emde, R. N. (1980). Mother–infant "bonding": Failure to generalize. *Child Development, 56,* 775–779.

Svejda, M. J., Pannabecker, B. J., & Emde, R. N. (1982). Parent-to-infant attachment: A critique of the the early "bonding" model. In R. N. Emde & R. J. Harmon (Eds.), *The development of attachment and affiliative systems* (pp. 83–93). New York: Plenum.

Tajfel, H., & Turner, J. (1979). An integrative theory of intergroup conflict. In W. G. Austin & S. Worchel (Eds.), *The social psychology of intergroup relations.* Monterey, CA: Brooks Cole.

Tannen, D. (1991). *You just don't understand: Women and men in conversation.* New York: Ballantine.

Tarrier, N., Barrowclough, C., Porceddu, K., & Watts, S. (1988). The assessment of psychophysiological reactivity to the Expressed Emotion of the relatives of schizophrenic patients. *British Journal of Psychiatry, 152,* 618–624.

Tasker, P. (1987). *The Japanese.* New York: Dutton.

Tavris, C. (1982). *Anger: The misunderstood emotion.* New York: Simon & Schuster.

Taylor, G. J., Bagby, R. M., & Parker, J. D. A. (1991). The alexithymia construct: A potential program for psychosomatic medicine. *Psychosomatics, 32,* 153–164.

Taylor, J. (Ed.) (1959). *Selected writings of John Hughlings-Jackson.* New York: Basic Books.

Teasdale, J. (1988). Cognitive vulnerability to persistent depression. *Cognition and Emotion, 2,* 247–274.

Terwogt, M. M., Schene, J., & Harris, P. L. (1986). Self-control of emotional reactions by young children. *Journal of Child Psychology and Psychiatry, 27,* 357–366.

Thayer, R. E., Newman, J. R., & McCain, T. M. (1994). Self-regulation of mood: Strategies for changing a bad mood, raising energy, and reducing tension. *Journal of Personality and Social Psychology, 67,* 910–925.

Thoits, P. A. (1986). Social support as coping assistance. *Journal of Consulting and Clinical Psychology, 54,* 416–423.

Thoits, P. A. (in press). Identity-relevant events and psychological symptoms: A cautionary tale. *Journal of Health and Social Behavior.*

Thomas, A., & Chess, S. (1977). *Temperament and development.* New York: Brunner/ Mazel.

Thomas, E. M. (1989). *The harmless people* (revised ed.). New York: Random House.

Thompson, R. A. (1994). Emotion regulation: A theme in search of definition. *Monographs of the Society for Research in Child Development, 59* (2–3, Serial No. 240), 25–52.

Thompson, R. A., Connell, J. P., & Bridges, L. J. (1988). Temperament, emotion, and social interactive behavior in the strange situation: A component process analysis of attachment system functioning. *Child Development, 59,* 1102–1110.

Tillitski, C. J. (1990). A meta-analysis of estimated effect sizes for group versus individual versus control treatments. *International Journal of Group Psychotherapy, 40,* 215–224.

Tinbergen, N. (1951). *The study of instinct.* Oxford: Oxford University Press.

Tizard, B., & Hodges, J. (1978). The effect of early institutional rearing on the development of eight-year-old children. *Journal of Child Psychology and Psychiatry, 19,* 99–118.

Tomkins, S. S. (1962). *Affect, imagery, consciousness, Vol. 1. The positive affects*. New York: Springer.

Tomkins, S. S. (1963). *Affect, imagery, consciousness, Vol. 2. The negative affects*. New York: Springer.

Tomkins, S. S. (1970). Affect as the primary motivational system. In M. B. Arnold (Ed.), *Feelings and emotions: The Loyola symposium* (pp. 101–110). New York: Academic Press.

Tomkins, S. S. (1979). Script theory: Differential magnification of affects. In H. E. Howe & R. A. Dienstbier (Eds.), *Nebraska symposium on motivation, 1978* (pp. 201–236). Lincoln, NA: University of Nebraska Press.

Tomkins, S. S. (1995). *Exploring affect: The selected writings of Sylvan S. Tomkins* (Ed. E.V. Demos). New York: Cambridge University Press.

Tooby, J., & Cosmides, L. (1990). The past explains the present: Emotional adaptations and the structure of ancestral environments. *Ethology and Sociobiology, 11,* 375–424.

Totman, R. (1988). Stress, language, and illness. In S. Fisher & J. Reason (Eds.), *Handbook of life stress, cognition, and health*. Chichester: Wiley.

Tousignant, M., & Maldonado, M. (1989). Sadness, depression, and social reciprocity in highland Equador. *Social Science and Medicine, 28,* 899–904.

Trevarthen, C. (1979). Communication and cooperation in early infancy. In M. Bullowa (Ed.), *Before speech: The beginning of interpersonal communication* (pp. 321–347). Cambridge: Cambridge University Press.

Triandis, H. (1972). *The analysis of subjective culture*. New York: Wiley.

Tronick, E. Z. (1989). Emotions and emotional communications in infants. *American Psychologist, 44,* 112–119.

Tronick, E. Z., Cohn, J., & Shea, E. (1986). The transfer of affect between mothers and infants. In T. B. Brazelton & M. W. Yogman (Eds.), *Affective development in infancy*. Norwood, NJ: Ablex.

Tropp, M. (1976). *Mary Shelley's monster*. Boston: Houghton Mifflin.

Tucker, D. M., & Frederick, S. L. (1989). Emotion and brain lateralization. In H. Wagner & A. Manstead (Eds.), *Handbook of social psychophysiology* (pp. 27–70). Chichester: Wiley.

Ucros, C. G. (1989). Mood-state-dependent memory: A meta-analysis. *Cognition and Emotion, 3,* 139–167.

Vaccarino, F. J., Schiff, B. B., & Glickman, S. E. (1989). A biological view of reinforcement. In S. B. Klein & R. R. Mowrer (Eds.), *Contemporary learning theories*. Hillsdale, NJ: Erlbaum.

Valenstein, E. (1973). *Brain control*. New York: Wiley.

Valenstein, E. S., Cox, V. C., & Kakolewski, J. W. (1970). Reexamination of the role of the hypothalamus in motivation. *Psychological Review, 77,* 16–31.

Valins, S. (1966). Cognitive effects of false heart-rate feedback. *Journal of Personality and Social Psychology, 4,* 400–408.

Van Bezooijen, R., Van Otto, S. A., & Heenan, T. A. (1983). Recognition of vocal dimensions of emotion: a three-nation study to identify universal characteristics. *Journal of Cross-Cultural Psychology, 14,* 387–406.

Van Brakel, J. (1994). Emotions: a cross-cultural perspective on forms of life. In W. M. Wentworth & J. Ryan (Eds.), *Social perspectives on emotion* (Vol. 2). Greenwich, CT: JAI Press.

Van den Berghe, P. L. (1979). *Human family systems: An evolutionary view.* Amsterdam: Elsevier.

Van Eerdewegh, M. M., Bieri, M. D., Parrilla, R. H., & Clayton, P. G. (1982). The bereaved child. *British Journal of Psychiatry, 140,* 23–29.

Van Ijzendoorn, M. H. (1992). Intergenerational transmission of parenting: A review of studies in nonclinical populations. *Developmental Review, 12,* 76–99.

Van Sommers, P. (1988). *Jealousy.* Harmondsworth: Penguin.

Vaughn, B., Egeland, B., Sroufe, L. A., & Waters, E. (1979). Individual differences in infant–mother attachment at twelve and eighteen months. Stability and change in families under stress. *Child Development, 59,* 971–975.

Vaughn, B., Stevenson-Hinde, J., Waters, E., Kotsaftis, A., Lefever, G., Shouldice, A., Trudel, M., & Belsky, J. (1992). Attachment, security, and temperament in infancy and early childhood: Some conceptual clarifications. *Developmental Psychology, 28,* 463–473.

Vaughn, C. E., & Leff, J. P. (1976). The influence of family and social factors on the course of psychiatric illness: A comparison of schizophrenic and depressed patients. *British Journal of Psychiatry, 129,* 125–137.

Veblen, T. (1899). *The theory of the leisure class: An economic study of institutions.* New York: Macmillan.

Velez, C. N., Johnson, J., & Cohen, P. (1989). A longitudinal analysis of selected risk factors for childhood psychopathology. *Journal of the American Academy of Child and Adolescent Psychiatry, 28,* 861–864.

Velten, E. (1968). A laboratory task for induction of mood states. *Behavior Research and Therapy, 6,* 473–482.

Verhulst, F. C., Koot, H. M., & Berden, G. F. M. (1990). Four year follow up of an epidemiological sample. *Journal of the American Academy of Child and Adolescent Psychiatry, 29,* 440–448.

Visalberghi, E., & Sonetti, M. G. (1994). Lorenz's concept of aggression and recent primatological studies on aggressive and reconciliatory behaviors. *La Nuova Critica,* Nuova serie, 23–24, 57–67.

Von Holst, E., & Von Saint Paul, U. (1963). On the functional organization of drives. *Animal Behavior, 11,* 1–20.

Von Uexküll, J. (1934). A stroll through the worlds of animals and men. In C. H. Schiller (Ed.), *Instinctive behavior: Development of a modern concept* (pp. 5–80). London: Methuen (current edition 1957).

Vygotsky, L. S. (1987). Emotions and their development in childhood. In R. W. Rieber & A. S. Carton (Eds.), *Collected works of L. S. Vygotsky* (Vol. 1, pp. 325–337). New York: Plenum.

Waganaar, W. A. (1986). My memory: A study of autobiographical memory over six years. *Cognitive Psychology, 18,* 225–252.

Wagner, H. (1989). The peripheral physiological differentiation of emotions. In H. Wagner & A. Manstead (Eds.), *Handbook of social psychophysiology* (pp. 77–98). Chichester: Wiley.

Wagner, H. L., MacDonald, C. J., & Manstead, A. S. R. (1986). Communication of individual emotions by spontaneous facial expression. *Journal of Personality and Social Psychology, 50,* 737–743.

Walden, T. A., & Ogan, T. A. (1988). The development of social referencing. *Child Development, 59,* 1230–1240.

Walker-Andrews, A. S. (1986). Intermodal perception of expressive behaviors: Relation of eye and voice? *Developmental Psychology, 22,* 373–77.

Wallbott, H. G., & Scherer, K. (1986). How universal and specific is emotional experience? Evidence from 27 countries on five continents. *Social Science Information, 25,* 763–795.

Washburn, S. L. (1991). Biochemical insights into our ancestry. In M. H. Robinson & L. Tiger (Eds.), *Man and beast revisited* (pp. 61–73). Washington, DC: Smithsonian Institute Press.

Waters, E., Merrick, S. K., Albersheim, L. J., & Treboux, D. (1995). Attachment security from infancy to early adulthood: A 20-year longitudinal study of attachment security in infancy and early adulthood. Paper presented to the Biennial Meeting of the Society for Research on Child Development, Indianapolis, March 30 – April 2.

Watson, D., & Tellegen, A. (1985). Towards a consensual structure of mood. *Psychological Bulletin, 98,* 219–235.

Watts, A. W. (1957). *The way of Zen.* New York: Pantheon.

Wegner, D. M., & Pennebaker, J. W. (Eds.). (1993). *Handbook of mental control.* Englewood Cliffs, NJ: Prentice Hall.

Weisfeld, G. E. (1980). Social dominance and human motivation. In D. R. Omark, F. F. Strayer, & D. G. Freedman (Eds.), *Dominance relations: An ethological view of human conflict and social interaction* (pp. 273–286). New York: Garland.

Weisfeld, G. E. (1993). The adaptive value of humor and laughter. *Ethology and Sociobiology, 14,* 141–169.

Weisfeld, G. E., & Beresford, J. M. (1982). Erectness of posture as an indicator of dominance or success in humans. *Motivation and Emotion, 6,* 113–131.

Weiskrantz, L. (1956). Behavioral changes associated with ablation of the amygdaloid complex in monkeys. *Journal of Comparative and Physiological Psychology, 49,* 381–391.

Weissman, M. M. (1987). Advances in psychiatric epidemiology: Rates and risks for depression. *American Journal of Public Health, 77,* 445–451.

Weissman, M. M., & Boyd, J. H. (1983). The epidemiology of affective disorders: Rates and risk factors. In L. Grinspoon (Ed.), *Psychiatry Update.* Washington, DC: American Psychiatric Press.

Weissman, M. M., Gammon, G. D., & John, K. et al. (1987). Children of depressed parents: Increased psychopathology and early onset of major depression. *Archives of General Psychiatry, 44,* 847–853.

Weisz, J. R., Suwanlert, S., Chaiyasit, W., & Walter, B. A. (1987). Over- and undercontrolled clinic referral problems among Thai and American children and adolescents: The wat and wai of cultural differences. *Journal of Consulting and Clinical Psychology, 55,* 719–726.

Wellman, H. M. (1995). Young children's conception of mind and emotion: Evidence from English speakers. In J. Russell, J.-M. Fernandez-Dols, A. S. R. Manstead, & J. Wellenkamp (Eds.), *Everyday concepts of emotion.* (NATO ASI series D, Vol. 81) (pp. 289–313). Dordrecht: Kluwer.

Werner, E. E. (1989, April). Children of the Garden Island. *Scientific American, 260,* 106–111.

Werner, E. E., & Smith, R. S. (1982). *Vulnerable but invincible: A longitudinal study of resilient children and youth.* New York: McGraw-Hill.

Whitbeck, L. B., Hoyt, R. L., Simons, R. L., Conger, R. D., Elder, G. H., Lorenz, F.

O., & Huck, S. (1992). Intergenerational continuity of parental rejection and depressed affect. *Journal of Personality and Social Psychology, 63,* 1036–1045.

Wiener, B., & Graham, S. (1989). Understanding the motivational role of affect: Lifespan research from an attributional perspective. *Cognition and Emotion, 3,* 401–419.

Wierzbicka, A. (1994). Language of emotions. In J. Russell, J.-M. Fernandez-Dols, A. S. R. Manstead, & J. Wellenkamp(Eds), *Everyday concepts of emotion.* (NATO ASI series D, Vol. 81), (pp. 17–47) Dordrecht: Kluwer.

Wig, N. N., Menon, D. K., Bedi, H., Ghosh, A., Kuipers, L., Leff, J. P., Korten, A., Day, R., Sartorius, N., & Ernberg, G. (1987). Expressed Emotion and schizophrenia in North India: Cross-cultural transfer of ratings of relatives' Expressed Emotion. *British Journal of Psychiatry, 151,* 156–165.

Wiggins, J. S., & Pincus, A. L. (1992). Personality structure and assessment. *Annual Review of Psychology, 43,* 473–504.

Williams, J. M. G., Watts, F. N., MacLeod, C., & Mathews, A. (1988). *Cognitive psychology and emotional disorders.* Chichester: Wiley.

Williams, S., Anderson, J., McGee, R., & Silva, P. A. (1990). Risk factors for behavioral and emotional disorder in preadolescent children. *Journal of the American Academy of Child and Adolescent Psychiatry, 29,* 413–419.

Wilson, A. C., & Cann, R. L. (1992, April). The recent African genesis of humans. *Scientific American, 266,* 68–73.

Windle, M., & Lerner, R. M. (1986). The "goodness of fit" model of temperament-context relations: Interaction or correlation. In J. V. Lerner & R. M. Lerner (Eds.), *Temperament and social interaction in infants and children. New directions for child development* (Vol. 31, pp. 109–119). San Francisco: Jossey-Bass.

Winnicott, D. W. (1958). *Through paediatrics to psychoanalysis.* London: Tavistock.

Wolff, P. (1963). Observations on the early development of smiling. In B. Foss (Ed.), *Determinants of infant behavior* (Vol. 2, pp. 81–109). New York: Wiley.

Wolff, P. (1987). *The development of behavioral states and the expression of emotions in early infancy.* Chicago: University of Chicago Press.

Wolpe, J. (1958). *Psychotherapy by reciprocal inhibition.* Stanford, CA: Stanford University Press.

Woolf, V. (1919, November 20). Review of *Middlemarch. Times Literary Supplement.*

Woolf, V. (1965). *Jacob's Room.* Harmondsworth: Penguin.

Wordsworth, W. (1802). Preface to *Lyrical Ballads* of 1802. In S. Gill (Ed.), *William Wordsworth.* Oxford: Oxford University Press (1984).

World Health Organization (1979). *Schizophrenia: An international follow-up study.* Chichester: Wiley.

World Health Organization (1983). *Depressive disorders in different cultures.* Geneva, Switzerland: World Health Organization.

World Health Organization (1992). *The ICD-10 classification of mental and behavioural disorders: Clinical descriptions and diagnostic guidelines.* Geneva: World Health Organization.

Worobey, J., & Blajda, V. M. (1989). Temperament ratings at 2 weeks, 2 months, and 1 year: Differential stability of activity and emotionality. *Developmental Psychology, 25,* 257–263.

Worth, L. T., & Mackie, D. M. (1987). Cognitive mediation of positive affect in persuasion. *Social Cognition, 5,* 76–94.

References

Wright, M. R. (1981). *Empedocles, the extant fragments*. New Haven, CT: Yale University Press.

Wright, R. (1992). *Stolen continents: The "New World" through Indian eyes*. Toronto: Penguin.

Wundt, W. (1897). *Outlines of psychology* (C.H. Judd, Trans.). New York: Stechert.

Yates, F. A. (1964). *Giordano Bruno and the Hermetic tradition*. London: Routledge & Kegan Paul.

Yuille, J. C., & Cutshall, J. L. (1986). A case study of eyewitness testimony to a crime. *Journal of Applied Psychology, 71*, 291–301.

Zahn-Waxler, C., & Kochanska, G. (1990). Origins of guilt. In R. Thompson (Ed.), *Socioemotional development. Nebraska Symposium on Motivation* (pp. 183–258). Lincoln: University of Nebraska Press.

Zahn-Waxler, C., Radke-Yarrow, M., & King, R. A. (1979). Child rearing and children's prosocial initiations towards victims of distress. *Child Development, 50*, 319–330.

Zahn-Waxler, C., Radke-Yarrow, M., Wagner, E., & Chapman, M. (1992). Development of concern for others. *Developmental Psychology, 28*, 126–136.

Zajonc, R. B. (1980). Feeling and thinking: Preferences need no inferences. *American Psychologist, 35*, 151–175.

Zajonc, R. B., Murphy, S. T., & Inglehart, M. (1989). Feeling and facial efference: Implications of the vascular theory of emotion. *Psychological Review, 96*, 395–416.

Zonderman, A. B., Costa, P. T., & McCrae, R. R. (1989). Depression as a risk for cancer: Morbidity and mortality in a nationally representative sample. *Journal of the American Medical Association, 262*, 1191–1195.

Subject index

abduction, 258
acetyl choline, 152, 153
action readiness, 95, 98, 105, 106, 129, 168, 169, 322
adrenaline, 115, 121, 153
adult attachment, 197, 198
infant attachment style and, 355
Adult Attachment Interview, 196, 197
affection, 5, 44, 51, 55, 73, 77, 78, 85, 91, 94, 201, 202, 206, 209, 217, 218, 219, 256–90, 304, 312–14, 338, 373
action readiness and, 124
emotional expressions of, 4
in psychomotor epileptic auras, 143
affective defense reaction, 24
affective styles, 149
AFFEX, 108, 165, 167, 168, 171
aggression, 285, 286
in cats, 141
in children in abusive homes, 243
in children in coercive families, 207
in competition, 121
and conflict, 293
displays and reward, 205
in ex-institutionalized children, 239
and externalizing disorders, 249
and frustration, 114
gender differences in, 227, 230, 231
as innate drive, 294
and internalizing disorders, 224
and mutually coercive patterns, 245
in parents, 236

prompted by induced anger, 260
reduction of, in depression, 334
in reptiles, 158
sequence in primates, 295
stability in, 231–2
suppression of, 238
the Vikings and, 310
the Yanomamö and, 297, 298
agoraphobia, 317, 329, 332, 358
agreeableness, 218, 220
alcohol or drug abuse, 317
alexithymia, 339, 342
symptoms, 339
altruism, 54, 92
amae, 44, 53
ambivalence, 161, 186, 187, 343
amygdala, 133, 140, 141, 151–2, 158
role in appraisal, 152
anger, 5, 68, 87, 112, 113, 156, 285, 292, 314
and action readiness, 124
actions specific to, 114
and approach, 262
Aristotle's definition of, 12
and assertion of power, 287
and babies' unmet goals, 200
as a basic emotion, 102
children's exposure to, 235–6
and competition, 83
and controllability, 45, 185
and depression, 330, 333
depression and expression of, 333
and ego-involvement, 101
emotional expressions of, 4
function of, 256
heart rate and, 116
and independence, 43
and individual rights, 59, 303
in individualistic cultures, 300

infants' communication of, 176
infants with depressed mother and, 236
management of, 296
in the management of action, 260
in marriage, 310, 313
mechanisms eliciting, 295
in men with spinal injuries, 111–13
presence of in early infancy, 165
in psychomotor epileptic auras, 143
relation of nor-adrenaline to, 121
role of in aggressive societies, 300
and separation during Strange Situation, 196
sequence of, 98
and shame or humiliation, 91
and skin temperature, 116
and submission, 285, 294
and thought patterns, 104
and vengeance, 301
and violence, 299
see also anger and aggression
anger and aggression, 114, 207, 226–7, 230, 234, 285, 311
achieving goals through, 227
and Expressed Emotion, 338
and externalizing disorders, 224, 249
rarity of, 299
in relationships, 301, 302
anticipatory eagerness, 156
anti-depressants, 74, 125, 153, 254, 363
antisocial personality, 317
disorder, 233

Author index

Page numbers refer to mentions in the text; mentions in Further Readings, and in the References, are excluded.